T0369955

VW Caddy Diesel
Owners Workshop Manual

Mark Storey

Models covered

(6390 - 10AY1 - 384)

Caddy panel vans with 1.6 litre (1598cc), 1.9 litre (1896cc) & 2.0 litre (1968cc)
turbo-diesel engines

Does NOT cover petrol models or four-wheel-drive '4-Motion' versions
Does NOT cover features specific to Caddy Life, Caddy Maxi or Caddy Maxi Life,
or facelifted range introduced October 2015

© **Haynes Group Limited 2020**

ABCDE
FGHIJ
KLM

Printed in India

A book in the **Haynes Owners Workshop Manual Series**

Haynes Group Limited
Sparkford, Yeovil, Somerset BA22 7JJ, England

Haynes North America, Inc
2801 Townsgate Road, Suite 340, Thousand Oaks, CA 91361

ISBN **978 1 78521 390 8**

British Library Cataloguing in Publication Data
A catalogue record for this book is available from the British Library.

The manufacturer's authorised representative in the EU for product safety is:

HaynesPro BV
Stationsstraat 79 F, 3811MH Amersfoort, The Netherlands
gpsr@haynes.co.uk

Contents

LIVING WITH YOUR VW CADDY

Contents

REPAIRS AND OVERHAUL

Engine and Associated Systems

Transmission

Brakes and suspension

Body equipment

REFERENCE

Index

The Caddy models covered by this manual date from June 2003 to December 2015. Only one body style is a available with either 5 or 7 seats.

Models are available with a range of engines, including 1.6, 1.9 and 2.0 litre versions. Early models use 1.9 or 2.0 litre 'Pumpe Duse' (PD) engines. These are unit injector engines where the injector pressurises and injects the fuel. On later models (around 2010) the PD engines were replaced with CR (Common Rail) engines where the injectors are supplied with high pressure fuel from a reservoir (the 'common rail'). All the engines are of a well-proven design and, provided regular maintenance is carried out, are unlikely to give trouble.

Fully-independent front suspension is fitted, with the components attached to a subframe assembly. The rear suspension uses a traditional rigid axle and leaf spring set up.

A five or six-speed manual gearbox is fitted, with a six or seven-speed DSG semi-automatic transmission also available.

A wide range of standard and optional equipment is available within the model range to suit most tastes, including air conditioning.

For the home mechanic, Caddy models are straightforward vehicles to maintain, and most of the items requiring frequent attention are easily accessible.

Your Caddy Manual

The aim of this manual is to help you get the best value from your vehicle. It can do so in several ways. It can help you decide what work must be done (even should you choose to get it done by a garage). It will also provide information on routine maintenance and servicing, and give a logical course of action and diagnosis when random faults occur. However, it is hoped that you will use the manual by tackling the work yourself. On simpler jobs it may even be quicker than booking the car into a garage and going there twice, to leave and collect it. Perhaps most important, a lot of money can be saved by avoiding the costs a garage must charge to cover its labour and overheads.

The manual has drawings and descriptions to show the function of the various components so that their layout can be understood. Tasks are described and photographed in a clear step-by-step sequence.

References to the 'left' and 'right' of the vehicle are in the sense of a person in the driver's seat facing forward.

Acknowledgements

Thanks are due to Draper Tools Limited, who provided some of the workshop tools, and to all those people at Sparkford who helped in the production of this manual.

This manual is not a direct reproduction the vehicle manufacturer's data, and its publication should not be taken as implying any technical approval by the vehicle manufacturers or importers.

We take great pride in the accuracy of information given in this manual, but vehicle manufacturers make alterations and design changes during the production run of a particular vehicle of which they do not inform us. No liability can be accepted by the authors or publishers for loss, damage or injury caused by any errors in, or omissions from, the information given.

VW Caddy

Working on your car can be dangerous. This page shows just some of the potential risks and hazards, with the aim of creating a safety-conscious attitude.

General hazards

Scalding

• Don't remove the radiator or expansion tank cap while the engine is hot.

• Engine oil, transmission fluid or power steering fluid may also be dangerously hot if the engine has recently been running.

Burning

• Beware of burns from the exhaust system and from any part of the engine. Brake discs and drums can also be extremely hot immediately after use.

Crushing

• When working under or near a raised vehicle, always supplement the jack with axle stands, or use drive-on ramps.

Never venture under a car which is only supported by a jack.

• Take care if loosening or tightening high-torque nuts when the vehicle is on stands. Initial loosening and final tightening should be done with the wheels on the ground.

Fire

• Fuel is highly flammable; fuel vapour is explosive.

• Don't let fuel spill onto a hot engine.

• Do not smoke or allow naked lights (including pilot lights) anywhere near a vehicle being worked on. Also beware of creating sparks (electrically or by use of tools).

• Fuel vapour is heavier than air, so don't work on the fuel system with the vehicle over an inspection pit.

• Another cause of fire is an electrical overload or short-circuit. Take care when repairing or modifying the vehicle wiring.

• Keep a fire extinguisher handy, of a type suitable for use on fuel and electrical fires.

Electric shock

• Ignition HT and Xenon headlight voltages can be dangerous, especially to people with heart problems or a pacemaker. Don't work on or near these systems with the engine running or the ignition switched on.

• Mains voltage is also dangerous. Make sure that any mains-operated equipment is correctly earthed. Mains power points should be protected by a residual current device (RCD) circuit breaker.

Fume or gas intoxication

• Exhaust fumes are poisonous; they can contain carbon monoxide, which is rapidly fatal if inhaled. Never run the engine in a confined space such as a garage with the doors shut.

• Fuel vapour is also poisonous, as are the vapours from some cleaning solvents and paint thinners.

Poisonous or irritant substances

• Avoid skin contact with battery acid and with any fuel, fluid or lubricant, especially antifreeze, brake hydraulic fluid and Diesel fuel. Don't syphon them by mouth. If such a substance is swallowed or gets into the eyes, seek medical advice.

• Prolonged contact with used engine oil can cause skin cancer. Wear gloves or use a barrier cream if necessary. Change out of oil-soaked clothes and do not keep oily rags in your pocket.

• Air conditioning refrigerant forms a poisonous gas if exposed to a naked flame (including a cigarette). It can also cause skin burns on contact.

Asbestos

• Asbestos dust can cause cancer if inhaled or swallowed. Asbestos may be found in gaskets and in brake and clutch linings. When dealing with such components it is safest to assume that they contain asbestos.

Special hazards

Hydrofluoric acid

• This extremely corrosive acid is formed when certain types of synthetic rubber, found in some O-rings, oil seals, fuel hoses etc, are exposed to temperatures above 4000C. The rubber changes into a charred or sticky substance containing the acid. *Once formed, the acid remains dangerous for years. If it gets onto the skin, it may be necessary to amputate the limb concerned.*

• When dealing with a vehicle which has suffered a fire, or with components salvaged from such a vehicle, wear protective gloves and discard them after use.

The battery

• Batteries contain sulphuric acid, which attacks clothing, eyes and skin. Take care when topping-up or carrying the battery.

• The hydrogen gas given off by the battery is highly explosive. Never cause a spark or allow a naked light nearby. Be careful when connecting and disconnecting battery chargers or jump leads.

Air bags

• Air bags can cause injury if they go off accidentally. Take care when removing the steering wheel and trim panels. Special storage instructions may apply.

Diesel injection equipment

• Diesel injection pumps supply fuel at very high pressure. Take care when working on the fuel injectors and fuel pipes.

⚠ *Warning: Never expose the hands, face or any other part of the body to injector spray; the fuel can penetrate the skin with potentially fatal results.*

Remember...

DO

• Do use eye protection when using power tools, and when working under the vehicle.

• Do wear gloves or use barrier cream to protect your hands when necessary.

• Do get someone to check periodically that all is well when working alone on the vehicle.

• Do keep loose clothing and long hair well out of the way of moving mechanical parts.

• Do remove rings, wristwatch etc, before working on the vehicle – especially the electrical system.

• Do ensure that any lifting or jacking equipment has a safe working load rating adequate for the job.

DON'T

• Don't attempt to lift a heavy component which may be beyond your capability – get assistance.

• Don't rush to finish a job, or take unverified short cuts.

• Don't use ill-fitting tools which may slip and cause injury.

• Don't leave tools or parts lying around where someone can trip over them. Mop up oil and fuel spills at once.

• Don't allow children or pets to play in or near a vehicle being worked on.

The following pages are intended to help in dealing with common roadside emergencies and breakdowns. You will find more detailed fault finding information at the back of the manual, and repair information in the main chapters.

If your car won't start and the starter motor doesn't turn

- ☐ If it's a model with automatic transmission, make sure the selector is in the P or N position.
- ☐ Open the bonnet and make sure that the battery terminals are clean and tight.
- ☐ Switch on the headlights and try to start the engine. If the headlights go very dim when you're trying to start, the battery is probably flat. Try jump starting using another car.

If your car won't start even though the starter motor turns as normal

- ☐ Is there fuel in the tank?
- ☐ Is there moisture on electrical components under the bonnet? Switch off the ignition, and then wipe off any obvious dampness with a dry cloth. Spray a water-repellent aerosol product (WD-40 or equivalent) on the fuel system electrical connectors like those shown in the photos. Note that diesel engines do not normally suffer from damp.

A Check the condition and security of the battery connections (under cover).

B Check the fuses in the fusebox located on the left-hand side of the engine compartment.

C Check the security of all the accessible wiring plugs.

Check that electrical connections are secure (with the ignition switched off) and spray them with a water-dispersant spray like WD-40 if you suspect a problem due to damp.

Jump starting

 Jump starting will get you out of trouble, but you must correct whatever made the battery go flat in the first place. There are three possibilities:

1 *The battery has been drained by repeated attempts to start, or by leaving the lights on.*

2 *The charging system is not working properly (alternator drivebelt slack or broken, alternator wiring fault or alternator itself faulty).*

3 *The battery itself is at fault (electrolyte low, or battery worn out).*

When jump-starting a car, observe the following precautions:

Caution: Remove the key in case the central locking engages when the jump leads are connected.

✓ Before connecting the booster battery, make sure that the ignition is switched off.
✓ Ensure that all electrical equipment (lights, heater, wipers, etc) is switched off.
✓ Take note of any special precautions printed on the battery case.
✓ Make sure that the booster battery is the same voltage as the discharged one in the vehicle.

✓ If the battery is being jump-started from the battery in another vehicle, the two vehicles MUST NOT TOUCH each other.
✓ Make sure that the transmission is in neutral (or PARK, in the case of automatic transmission).

 Budget jump leads can be a false economy, as they often do not pass enough current to start large capacity or diesel engines. They can also get hot.

1 Connect one end of the red jump lead to the positive (+) terminal of the flat battery

2 Connect the other end of the red lead to the positive (+) terminal of the booster battery.

3 Connect one end of the black jump lead to the negative (-) terminal of the booster battery

4 Connect the other end of the black jump lead to a suitable metal part of the engine on the vehicle to be started.

5 Make sure that the jump leads will not come into contact with the fan, drive-belts or other moving parts of the engine.

6 Start the engine using the booster battery and run it at idle speed. Switch on the lights, rear window demister and heater blower motor, then disconnect the jump leads in the reverse order of connection. Turn off the lights etc.

Wheel changing

Preparation

- [ ] When a puncture occurs, stop as soon as it is safe to do so.
- [ ] Park on firm level ground, if possible, and well out of the way of other traffic.
- [ ] Use hazard warning lights if necessary.
- [ ] If you have one, use a warning triangle to alert other drivers of your presence.
- [ ] Apply the handbrake and engage first or reverse gear (or Park on models with automatic transmission).
- [ ] Chock the wheel diagonally opposite the one being removed – a couple of large stones will do for this.
- [ ] If the ground is soft, use a flat piece of wood to spread the load under the jack.
- [ ] The spare wheel is located in the floor beneath the load area. Lift up the cover to access the wheel and tool kit.

Warning: Do not change a wheel in a situation where you risk being hit by other traffic. On busy roads, try to stop in a lay-by or a gateway. Be wary of passing traffic while changing the wheel – it is easy to become distracted by the job in hand.

Note: *A full size spare wheel is supplied with most models in the range. Some models may have a compressor and bottle of tyre sealant supplied instead.*

1 Lower both bolts from the cradle…

2 …remove the right-hand bolt

3 Fit the wheel brace and disengage the cradle via the keyhole slot

4 Lower the wheel and cradle. Remove the wheel and place it under the sill

5 The jack is located at the rear right-hand side. Some models may have the jack (and tools) fitted behind the drivers front seat

6 Remove the wheel trim by twisting and pulling.

7 On models with alloy wheels, use the special adapter when slackening the locking wheel bolts.

8 Slacken the wheel nuts a half turn in a diagonal sequence

9 Make sure the jack is located on firm ground. Locate the jacking point (arrow mark in the sill) and then engage the jack head correctly with the sill. Raise the jack until the wheel is raised clear of the ground.

10 Unscrew the wheel bolts and remove the wheel. Place the wheel under the vehicle sill in case the jack fails.

11 Fit the spare wheel and screw in the bolts. Lightly tighten the bolts with the wheel brace then lower the car to the ground.

12 Securely tighten the wheel bolts in a diagonal sequence.

13 On models fitted with a compressor remove the compressor from the vehicle and then remove the valve core with the provided tool

14 Shake the sealant bottle and empty the entire contents into the tyre

15 Fit the compressor and inflate the tyre to a maximum of 2.5 Bar. If the pressure is low, drive the vehicle a metre to distribute the fluid and try again. If the pressure will not hold the tyre is beyond repair. If all is well drive for 10 minutes and check the pressure again. Replace the tyre at the earliest opportunity DO NOT exceed 50 mph.

16 Where provided, fit the warning sticker to the instrument panel

Finally . . .

- ☐ Remove the wheel chock.
- ☐ Check the tyre pressure on the wheel just fitted. If it is low, or if you don't have a pressure gauge with you, drive slowly to the next garage and inflate the tyre to the correct pressure.
- ☐ The wheel bolts should be slackened and retightened to the specified torque at the earliest possible opportunity (see Chapter or 1).
- ☐ Have the damaged tyre or wheel repaired as soon as possible, or another puncture will leave you stranded.

Towing

When all else fails, you may find yourself having to get a tow home – or of course you may be helping somebody else. Long-distance recovery should only be done by a garage or breakdown service. For shorter distances, DIY towing using another car is easy enough, but observe the following points:

☐ Use a proper tow-rope – they are not expensive. The vehicle being towed must display an ON TOW sign in its rear window.

☐ Always turn the ignition key to the 'on' position when the vehicle is being towed, so that the steering lock is released, and the direction indicator and brake lights work.

☐ The towing eye is kept with the jack and other tools (see Wheel changing). To fit the eye, press one side of the cover and it will pivot open. Screw the eye firmly into position **(see illustrations)**.

☐ Before being towed, release the handbrake and select neutral on the transmission.

☐ Note that greater-than-usual pedal pressure will be required to operate the brakes, since the vacuum servo unit is only operational with the engine running.

☐ The driver of the car being towed must keep the tow-rope taut at all times to avoid snatching.

☐ Make sure that both drivers know the route before setting off.

☐ Only drive at moderate speeds and keep the distance towed to a minimum. Drive smoothly and allow plenty of time for slowing down at junctions.

Flip open the cover

Fit the towing eye (left-hand thread)…

…and fully tighten with the wheel brace (or similar)

Identifying leaks

Puddles on the garage floor or drive, or obvious wetness under the bonnet or underneath the car, suggest a leak that needs investigating. It can sometimes be difficult to decide where the leak is coming from, especially if an engine undershield is fitted. Leaking oil or fluid can also be blown rearwards by the passage of air under the car, giving a false impression of where the problem lies.

 Warning: Most automotive oils and fluids are poisonous. Wash them off skin, and change out of contaminated clothing, without delay.

 The smell of a fluid leaking from the car may provide a clue to what's leaking. Some fluids are distinctively coloured. It may help to remove the engine undershield, clean the car carefully and to park it over some clean paper overnight as an aid to locating the source of the leak. Remember that some leaks may only occur while the engine is running.

Sump oil

Engine oil may leak from the drain plug...

Oil from filter

...or from the base of the oil filter.

Gearbox oil

Gearbox oil can leak from the seals at the inboard ends of the driveshafts.

Antifreeze

Leaking antifreeze often leaves a crystalline deposit like this.

Brake fluid

A leak occurring at a wheel is almost certainly brake fluid.

Power steering fluid

Power steering fluid may leak from the pipe connectors on the steering rack.

Introduction

There are some very simple checks which need only take a few minutes to carry out, but which could save you a lot of inconvenience and expense.

☐ These checks require no great skill or special tools, and the small amount of time they take to perform could prove to be very well spent, for example:

☐ Keeping an eye on tyre condition and pressures, will not only help to stop them wearing out prematurely, but could also save your life.

☐ Many breakdowns are caused by electrical problems. Battery-related faults are particularly common, and a quick check on a regular basis will often prevent the majority of these.

☐ If your car develops a brake fluid leak, the first time you might know about it is when your brakes don't work properly. Checking the level regularly will give advance warning of this kind of problem.

☐ If the oil or coolant levels run low, the cost of repairing any engine damage will be far greater than fixing the leak, for example.

Underbonnet check points

▲ **CR engine (PD engines similar)**

A *Engine oil level dipstick*

B *Engine oil filler cap*

C *Coolant expansion tank*

D *Brake (and clutch) fluid reservoir*

E *Screen washer fluid reservoir*

F *Battery*

Engine oil level

HAYNES HiNT *If the oil is checked immediately after driving the vehicle, some of the oil will remain in the upper engine components, resulting in an inaccurate reading on the dipstick.*

Before you start

✔ Make sure that the car is on level ground.
✔ Check the oil level before the car is driven, or at least 5 minutes after the engine has been switched off.

The correct oil

Modern engines place great demands on their oil. It is very important that the correct oil for your car is used (see *Lubricants and fluids*).

Car care

● If you have to add oil frequently, you should check whether you have any oil leaks. Place some clean paper under the car overnight, and check for stains in the morning. If there are no leaks, then the engine may be burning oil.
● Always maintain the level between the upper and lower dipstick marks (see photo 2). If the level is too low, severe engine damage may occur. Oil seal failure may result if the engine is overfilled by adding too much oil.

1 The dipstick is located at the front of the engine (see Underbonnet check points); the dipstick is often brightly coloured or has a picture of an oil-can on the top for identification. Withdraw the dipstick.

2 The oil level on the end of the dipstick, which should be between the upper (MAX) mark and lower (MIN) mark (both types of dipstick shown).

3 Oil is added through the filler cap aperture, unscrew the cap.

4 Top-up the level; a funnel may help to reduce spillage. Add the oil slowly, checking the level on the dipstick often. Don't overfill (see Car care).

Brake (and clutch) fluid level

 Warning: Brake fluid can harm your eyes and damage painted surfaces, so use extreme caution when handling and pouring it.

 Warning: Do not use fluid that has been standing open for some time, as it absorbs moisture from the air, which can cause a dangerous loss of braking effectiveness.

Before you start
✔ Make sure that your car is on level ground.

Safety first!
● If the reservoir requires repeated topping-up this is an indication of a fluid leak somewhere in the system, which should be investigated immediately.

● If a leak is suspected, the car should not be driven until the braking system has been checked. Never take any risks where brakes are concerned.

1 The upper (MAX) fluid level marking is on the side of the reservoir, which is located at the rear of the engine compartment. Remove the air intake pipe to improve access. First wipe clean the area around the filler cap with a clean cloth.

2 If topping-up is necessary, unscrew the cap and remove it along with the rubber seal.

3 Carefully add fluid, avoiding spilling it on the surrounding paintwork. Use only the specified hydraulic fluid. After filling to the correct level, refit the cap and diaphragm and tighten it securely. Wipe off any spilt fluid.

Coolant level

 Warning: Do not attempt to remove the expansion tank pressure cap when the engine is hot, as there is a very great risk of scalding. Do not leave open containers of coolant about, as it is poisonous.

Car care
● With a sealed-type cooling system, adding coolant should not be necessary on a regular basis. If frequent topping-up is required, it is likely there is a leak. Check the radiator, all hoses and joint faces for signs of staining or wetness, and rectify as necessary.

● It is important that antifreeze is used in the cooling system all year round, not just during the winter months. Don't top up with water alone, as the antifreeze will become diluted.

1 The coolant level must be checked with the engine cold; the coolant level should be between the MAX and MIN marks on the expansion tank.

2 If topping-up is necessary, remove the pressure cap (see Warning) from the expansion tank. Slowly unscrew the cap to release any pressure present in the cooling system, and remove the cap.

3 Add a mixture of water and antifreeze to the expansion tank until the coolant level is between the level marks. Once the level is correct, securely refit the cap.

Electrical systems

✔ Check all external lights and the horn. Refer to Chapter 12 Section 12,2 for details if any of the circuits are found to be inoperative.

✔ Visually check all accessible wiring connectors, harnesses and retaining clips for security, and for signs of chafing or damage.

HAYNES HiNT *If you need to check your brake lights and indicators unaided, back up to a wall or garage door and operate the lights. The reflected light should show if they are working properly.*

1 If a single indicator light, brake light, sidelight or headlight has failed, it is likely that a bulb has blown, and will need to be renewed. Refer to Chapter 12, Section 5 for details. If both brake lights have failed, it is possible that the switch has failed (see Chapter 9, Section 18).

2 If more than one indicator or tail light has failed, it is likely that either a fuse has blown or that there is a fault in the circuit. The main fuses are located behind the facia right-hand storage compartment. Additional fuses and relays are located in a fusebox on the left-hand side of the engine compartment.

3 To renew a blown fuse, simply pull it out and fit a new fuse of the correct rating **(see Wiring diagrams)**. If the fuse blows again, it is important that you find out why – a complete checking procedure is given in Chapter 12, Section 2.

Battery

Caution: Before carrying out any work on the vehicle battery, read the precautions given in 'Safety first! 0 ' at the start of this manual.

✔ Make sure that the battery tray is in good condition, and that the clamp is tight. Corrosion on the tray, retaining clamp and the battery itself can be removed with a solution of water and baking soda. Thoroughly rinse all cleaned areas with water. Any metal parts damaged by corrosion should be covered with a zinc-based primer, then painted.

✔ Periodically (approximately every three months), check the charge condition of the battery, as described in Chapter 5A, Section 3.

✔ If the battery is flat, and you need to jump start your vehicle, see *Jump starting*. .

HAYNES HiNT *Battery corrosion can be kept to a minimum by applying a layer of petroleum jelly to the clamps and terminals after they are reconnected.*

1 Lift the plastic cover (or insulation cover) to gain access to the battery positive terminal, which is located on the left-hand side of the engine compartment. The exterior of the battery should be inspected periodically for damage such as a cracked case or cover.

2 Check the battery lead clamps for tightness to ensure good electrical connections, and check the leads for signs of damage.

3 If corrosion (white, fluffy deposits) are evident, remove the cables from the battery terminals, clean them with a small wire brush, then refit them. Automotive stores sell a tool for cleaning the battery post ...

4 ... as well as the battery cable clamps. Note: VW specifically prohibit the use of grease on the battery terminals.

Wiper blades

1 Check the condition of the wiper blades: if they are cracked or show signs of deterioration, or if the glass swept area is smeared, renew them. For maximum clarity of vision, wiper blades should be renewed annually.

2 To remove a windscreen wiper blade, turn the ignition on, then turn the ignition off, and press the wiper switch stalk down once. This places the arms in the 'service' position. Lift the wiper from the screen and press the securing clip …

3 … slide the blade upwards from the end of the wiper arm, taking care not to allow the wiper arm to spring back and damage the windscreen. When completed, return the blades to the park position by pressing the wiper switch stalk again.

4 Some models have a wiper blade that lifts off

5 To remove the rear wiper blade, tilt the wiper blade away from the screen, depress the side tabs…

6 …and unhook the blade

Screen washer fluid level

● Screenwash additives not only keep the windscreen clean during bad weather, they also prevent the washer system freezing in cold weather – which is when you are likely to need it most. Don't top-up using plain water, as the screenwash will become diluted, and will freeze in cold weather.

 Warning: On no account use engine coolant antifreeze in the screen washer system – this may damage the paintwork.

1 The washer fluid reservoir is located in the right-hand side of the engine compartment. To check the fluid level, open the cap and then look down the clear filler neck.

2 If topping-up is necessary, add water and a screenwash additive in the quantities recommended on the bottle.

Tyre condition and pressure

It is very important that tyres are in good condition, and at the correct pressure – having a tyre failure at any speed is highly dangerous.

Tyre wear is influenced by driving style – harsh braking and acceleration, or fast cornering, will all produce more rapid tyre wear. As a general rule, the front tyres wear out faster than the rears. Interchanging the tyres from front to rear ("rotating" the tyres) may result in more even wear. However, if this is completely effective, you may have the expense of replacing all four tyres at once!

Remove any nails or stones embedded in the tread before they penetrate the tyre to cause deflation. If removal of a nail does reveal that the tyre has been punctured, refit the nail so that its point of penetration is marked. Then immediately change the wheel, and have the tyre repaired by a tyre dealer.

Regularly check the tyres for damage in the form of cuts or bulges, especially in the sidewalls. Periodically remove the wheels, and clean any dirt or mud from the inside and outside surfaces. Examine the wheel rims for signs of rusting, corrosion or other damage. Light alloy wheels are easily damaged by "kerbing" whilst parking; steel wheels may also become dented or buckled. A new wheel is very often the only way to overcome severe damage.

New tyres should be balanced when they are fitted, but it may become necessary to re-balance them as they wear, or if the balance weights fitted to the wheel rim should fall off. Unbalanced tyres will wear more quickly, as will the steering and suspension components. Wheel imbalance is normally signified by vibration, particularly at a certain speed (typically around 50 mph). If this vibration is felt only through the steering, then it is likely that just the front wheels need balancing. If, however, the vibration is felt through the whole car, the rear wheels could be out of balance. Wheel balancing should be carried out by a tyre dealer or garage.

1 *Tread Depth - visual check*
The original tyres have tread wear safety bands (B), which will appear when the tread depth reaches approximately 1.6 mm. The band positions are indicated by a triangular mark on the tyre sidewall (A).

2 *Tread Depth - manual check*
Alternatively, tread wear can be monitored with a simple, inexpensive device known as a tread depth indicator gauge.

3 *Tyre Pressure Check*
Check the tyre pressures regularly with the tyres cold. Do not adjust the tyre pressures immediately after the vehicle has been used, or an inaccurate setting will result.

Tyre tread wear patterns

Shoulder Wear

Underinflation (wear on both sides)
Under-inflation will cause overheating of the tyre, because the tyre will flex too much, and the tread will not sit correctly on the road surface. This will cause a loss of grip and excessive wear, not to mention the danger of sudden tyre failure due to heat build-up.
Check and adjust pressures
Incorrect wheel camber (wear on one side)
Repair or renew suspension parts
Hard cornering
Reduce speed!

Centre Wear

Overinflation
Over-inflation will cause rapid wear of the centre part of the tyre tread, coupled with reduced grip, harsher ride, and the danger of shock damage occurring in the tyre casing.
Check and adjust pressures

If you sometimes have to inflate your car's tyres to the higher pressures specified for maximum load or sustained high speed, don't forget to reduce the pressures to normal afterwards.

Uneven Wear

Front tyres may wear unevenly as a result of wheel misalignment. Most tyre dealers and garages can check and adjust the wheel alignment (or "tracking") for a modest charge.
Incorrect camber or castor
Repair or renew suspension parts
Malfunctioning suspension
Repair or renew suspension parts
Unbalanced wheel
Balance tyres
Incorrect toe setting
Adjust front wheel alignment
Note: *The feathered edge of the tread which typifies toe wear is best checked by feel.*

Power steering fluid level

Before you start

✔ Park the vehicle on level ground
✔ Set the steering wheel straight-ahead
✔ The engine should be cold and turned off

Note: *For the check to be accurate, the steering must not be turned once the engine has been stopped.*

1 The reservoir is mounted at the rear, right-hand side of the engine compartment.

2 Wipe clean the area around the filler cap, then unscrew it from the reservoir.

3 The filler cap is also a dipstick. Wipe clean the dipstick, refit it (the cap must be screwed in) and then remove it to check the level. If the engine oil temperature is above 50 degrees use the 'hot' scale to check the level.

4 If topping-up is necessary, use the specified type of fluid – do not overfill the reservoir. Take care not to introduce dirt into the system when topping-up. When the level is correct, securely refit the cap.

Lubricants and fluids

Note: *Using lubricants and fluids that do not meet the VW standard may invalidate the warranty*

Engine

Standard (distance/time) service interval:	Multigrade (high-lubricity) engine oil, viscosity SAE 5W/40 to 20W/50
Engines without particulate filter	VW 505 01, 507 00 or better
Engines with particulate filter	VW 507 00 or better
LongLife (variable) service interval:	VW LongLife engine oil
Engines without particulate filter	VW 506 01, 507 00 or better
Engines with particulate filter	VW 507 00 or better

Cooling system

Cooling system . . . .   VW additive G12 plus-plus (TL-VW 774 G) or G12 plus (TL-VW 774 F) – antifreeze and corrosion protection

Manual transmission

02Q	Synthetic gear oil, viscosity SAE 75W/80 (VW G052 527 A20)
0A4	Synthetic gear oil, viscosity SAE 75W/80 (VW G052 512 A2/A6)

DSG semi-automatic transmissions

DSG semi-automatic transmissions . . . .   ATF (VW G052 182 A2/A6)

Braking system

Braking system . . . .   Hydraulic fluid to SAE J1703F or DOT 4

Tyre pressures

Note: *The recommended tyre pressures for each vehicle are given on a sticker attached to the inside of the fuel filler flap or the drivers side B-pillar. The pressures given are for the original equipment tyres – the recommended pressures may vary if any other make or type of tyre is fitted; check with the tyre manufacturer or supplier for latest recommendations. The following pressures are typical.*

All models	Front	Rear
Normal load	2.0 bars (29 psi)	2.0 bars (29 psi)
Full load	2.3 bars (33 psi)	2.8 bars (41 psi)
Emergency spare wheel	4.2 bars (61 psi)	

Chapter 1
Routine maintenance and servicing

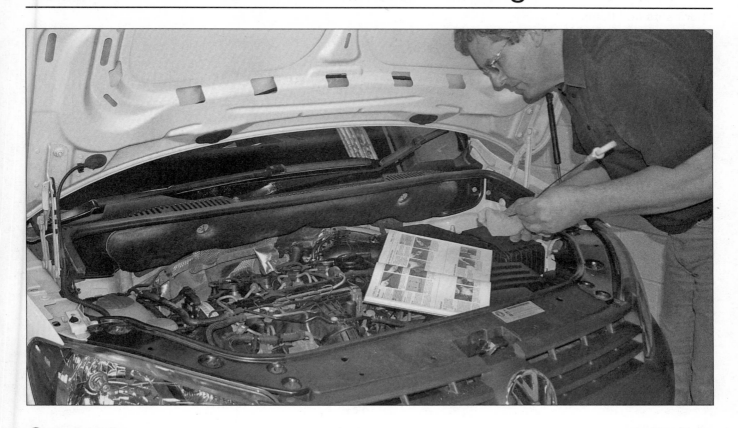

Contents

Degrees of difficulty

Easy, suitable for novice with little experience	**Fairly easy,** suitable for beginner with some experience	**Fairly difficult,** suitable for competent DIY mechanic	**Difficult,** suitable for experienced DIY mechanic	**Very difficult,** suitable for expert DIY or professional

1   Servicing specifications

Lubricants and fluids
Refer to Lubricants, fluids and tyre pressures

Engine codes*
1.9 litre – 'PD' (unit injector)	BKC, BJB, BLS and BSU
2.0 litre – 'PD' (unit injector)	BDJ, BST and BMM
1.6 litre – 'CR' (common rail injection)	CAYE, CAYD
2.0 litre – 'CR' (common rail injection)	CFJA, CFHC, CFHF, CLCA, CFHE, CLCB and CHWA

*See *'Vehicle identification'* at the end of the manual for the location of the engine code markings

Capacities

Engine oil (including filter)
PD 1.9 litre (BJB)	4.6 litres
PD 1.9 litre (BLS and BSU)	4.3 litres
PD 2.0 litre (BDJ)	4.0 litres
PD 2.0 litre (BMM and BST)	4.3 litres
CR engines (all versions)	4.3 litres

Cooling system
All engines	8.0 litres

Transmission*
Manual transmission:
Type 0A4	1.7 litres
Type 0AH	2.1 litres
Type 02Q	2.3 litres

* *See Chapter 7A for application details*
DSG transmission:
Type 02E	5.2 litres (refill capacity)
Type 0AM	1.7 litres (refill capacity)

* *See Chapter 7B for application details*

Fuel tank (approximate)
All models	60 litres

Washer reservoirs
Models with headlight washers	5.5 litres
Models without headlight washers	3.0 litres

Cooling system
Antifreeze mixture:
40% antifreeze	Protection down to -25°C
50% antifreeze	Protection down to -35°C

Note: *Refer to antifreeze manufacturer for latest recommendations.*

Brakes
Brake pad lining minimum thickness:
Front	2.0 mm
Rear	2.0 mm

Torque wrench settings

	Nm	lbf ft
Manual gearbox filler/drain plug:		
Multi-point socket head	30	22
Hexagon socket head	45	31
DSG gearbox drain/filler plug:		
02E transmission	45	31
0AM transmission	30	22
Oil filter cap	25	18
Roadwheel bolts	120	89
Sump drain plug	30	22

2 Maintenance schedule

1 The maintenance intervals in this manual are provided with the assumption that you, not the dealer, will be carrying out the work. These are the minimum intervals recommended by us for vehicles driven daily. If you wish to keep your vehicle in peak condition at all times, you may wish to perform some of these procedures more often. We encourage frequent maintenance, since it enhances the efficiency, performance and resale value of your vehicle.

2 When the vehicle is new, it should be serviced by a dealer service department (or other workshop recognised by the vehicle manufacturer as providing the same standard of service), in order to preserve the warranty.

The vehicle manufacturer may reject warranty claims if you are unable to prove that servicing has been carried out as and when specified, using only original equipment parts or parts certified to be of equivalent quality.

3 All VW Caddy models are equipped with a service interval display indicator in the instrument panel. Every time the engine is started the panel will illuminate for approximately 20 seconds with service information. With the standard non-variable display, the service intervals are in accordance with specific distances and time periods. With the LongLife display, the service interval is variable according to the number of starts, length of journeys, vehicle speeds, brake pad wear, bonnet opening frequency, fuel consumption, oil level and oil temperature, however the vehicle must be serviced at least every two years. The service reminder is displayed 20 days before the service is due.

Once the service interval has been reached, the display will flash 'Spanner' or ' Service Now'. Note that if the variable (LongLife) service interval is being used, the engine must only be filled with the recommended long-life engine oil (see *Lubricants and fluids*).

4 After completing a service, VW technicians use a special instrument to reset the service display to the next service interval, and a print-out is put in the vehicle service record. The display can be reset by the owner as described in Section 8, but note that for models using the 'LongLife' interval, the procedure will automatically reset the display to the 10 000 miles 'distance' interval. To have the display reset to the 'variable' (LongLife) interval, it is necessary to take the vehicle to a VW dealer (or suitably equipped garage) who will use a special instrument to encode the on-board computer.

Every 250 miles

☐ Refer to *Weekly checks*

Every 10 000 miles or 12 months, whichever comes first

☐ Renew the engine oil and filter (Section 6)

Note: *Frequent oil and filter changes are good for the engine. We recommend changing the oil at least once a year.*

☐ Check the front and rear brake pad thickness (Section 7)
☐ Reset the service interval display (Section 8)

Every 20 000 miles or 2 years, whichever comes first

In addition to the items listed above, carry out the following:

☐ Check the condition of the exhaust system and its mountings (Section 9)
☐ Check all underbonnet components and hoses for fluid and oil leaks (Section 10)
☐ Renew the fuel filter* (Section Section)
☐ Check the condition of the auxiliary drivebelt (Section 11)
☐ Check the coolant antifreeze concentration (Section 12)
☐ Check the brake hydraulic circuit for leaks and damage (Section 13)
☐ Check the headlight beam adjustment (Section 14)
☐ Renew the pollen filter element (Section 15)
☐ Check the underbody protection for damage (Section 17)
☐ Check the condition of the driveshaft gaiters (Section 18)
☐ Check the steering and suspension components for condition and security (Section 19)
☐ Check the battery condition, security and electrolyte level (Section 20)
☐ Lubricate all hinges and locks (Section 21)
☐ Check the condition of the airbag unit(s) (Section 22)
☐ Check the operation of the windscreen/tailgate/headlight washer system(s) (as applicable) (Section 23)
☐ Check the engine management self-diagnosis memory for faults (Section 24)
☐ Carry out a road test and check exhaust emissions (Section 25)
* Only when using diesel fuel not conforming to DIN EN 590 or when using RME fuel (diester)

Every 40 000 miles or 4 years, whichever comes first

Note: *Many dealers perform these tasks at every second service.*
☐ Renew DSG transmission oil renewal (Section 26)
☐ Renew the air filter element (Section 27)
☐ Renew the fuel filter* (Section 28)
☐ Check the condition of the auxiliary drivebelt (Section 29)
* Only when using diesel fuel conforming to DIN EN 590

Every 60 000 miles or 4 years

☐ Renew the timing belt and tensioner roller (Section 30)

Note: *VW specify a timing belt renewal interval of 130 000 miles for all common rail engines and 75 000 miles for PD engines up to 2006. After 2006 the interval for PD engines is increased to 93 000 miles. They specify a tensioner roller renewal with the belt change. However, if the vehicle is used mainly for short journeys, we recommend that a shorter renewal interval be adhered to. The belt and tensioner renewal interval is very much up to the individual owner but, bearing in mind that severe engine damage will result if the belt breaks in use, we recommend a shorter interval.*

Note: *Always check with the vehicle manufacturer for the latest belt change intervals – they are often subject to change without notice.*

Note: *It is increasingly considered best practise to always replace the idlers, tensioner and coolant pump whenever the timing belt is replaced. Note also that most manufacturers will not guarantee a belt unless the tensioners and rollers have been replaced at the same time.*

Every 95 000 miles, then every 19 000 miles

☐ Check the particulate filter ash deposit mass (Section 33)

Every 2 years

☐ Renew the brake (and clutch) fluid (Section 31)
☐ Renew the coolant* (Section 32)
* **Note:** *This work is not included in the VW schedule and should not be required if the recommended VW G12 LongLife coolant antifreeze/inhibitor is used.*

Front underbody view (undershield removed)

1 Sump drain plug
2 Manual transmission drain plug
3 Auxiliary belt
4 Radiator and electric cooling fans
5 Air duct/hoses to intercooler
6 Starter motor
7 Engine oil level/temperature sensor
8 Front anti-roll bar drop-links
9 Front brake calipers
10 Front suspension lower arms
11 Steering track rod arms
12 Front suspension subframe
13 Exhaust pipe

Rear underbody view

1 Exhaust rear silencer
2 Leaf spring
3 Rear anti-roll bar
4 Rear anti-roll bar drop link
5 Spare wheel
6 Rear axle
7 Rear shock absorber
8 Fuel tank
9 Handbrake cables

Underbonnet view of a 1.6 litre CR model

1 Engine oil filler cap
2 Engine oil dipstick
3 Coolant expansion reservoir
4 Windscreen/headlight/rear window washer
   fluid reservoir
5 Fuel filter
6 Air filter housing
7 Battery (under cover)
8 Fusebox
9 Common rail
10 High pressure pump
11 Brake fluid reservoir

4 Introduction

1 This Chapter is designed to help the home mechanic maintain his/her vehicle for safety, economy, long life and peak performance.
2 The Chapter contains a master maintenance schedule, followed by Sections dealing specifically with each task in the schedule. Visual checks, adjustments, component renewal and other helpful items are included.

Refer to the accompanying illustrations of the engine compartment and the underside of the vehicle for the locations of the various components.
3 Servicing your vehicle will provide a planned maintenance programme, which should result in a long and reliable service life. This is a comprehensive plan, so maintaining some items but not others, will not produce the same results.
4 As you service your vehicle, you will discover that many of the procedures can – and should – be grouped together, because of the particular procedure being performed, or because of the proximity of two otherwise unrelated components to one another. For example, if the vehicle is raised for any reason, the exhaust can be inspected at the same time as the suspension and steering components.
5 The first step in this maintenance programme is to prepare yourself before the actual work begins. Read through all the Sections relevant to the work to be carried out, then make a list and gather all the parts and tools required. If a problem is encountered, seek advice from a parts specialist, or a dealer service department.

5 Regular maintenance

1 If, from the time the vehicle is new, the routine maintenance schedule is followed closely, and frequent checks are made of fluid levels and high-wear items, as suggested throughout this manual, the engine will be kept in relatively good running condition, and the need for additional work will be minimised.
2 It is possible that there will be times when the engine is running poorly due to the lack of regular maintenance. This is even more likely if a used vehicle, which has not received regular and frequent maintenance checks, is purchased. In such cases, additional work may need to be carried out, outside of the regular maintenance intervals.
3 If engine wear is suspected, a compression test (refer to Chapter 2A Section 2, Chapter 2B Section 2 or Chapter 2C Section 2) will provide valuable information regarding the overall performance of the main internal components. Such a test can be used as a basis to decide on the extent of the work to

6.2a The engine undertray is secured by a number of screws

6.2b Pull up the engine cover upwards to release it

be carried out. If, for example, a compression test indicates serious internal engine wear, conventional maintenance as described in this Chapter will not greatly improve the performance of the engine, and may prove a waste of time and money, unless extensive overhaul work is carried out first.

4 The following series of operations are those most often required to improve the performance of a generally poor-running engine:

Primary operations

a) *Clean, inspect and test the battery (See Weekly checks).*
b) *Check all the engine-related fluids (See Weekly checks).*
c) *Drain the water from the fuel filter (Section Section).*
d) *Check the condition and tension of the auxiliary drivebelt (Section 11).*
e) *Check the condition of the air filter, and renew if necessary (Section 27).*
f) *Check the condition of all hoses, and check for fluid leaks (Section 10).*

5 If the above operations do not prove fully effective, carry out the following secondary operations:

Secondary operations

6 All items listed under Primary operations, plus the following:

6.3 Undo the sump drain plug

a) *Check the charging system (see Chapter 5A).*
b) *Check the preheating system (see Chapter 5B).*
c) *Renew the fuel filter (Section 28) and check the fuel system (see Chapter 4A).*

6 Engine oil and filter renewal

1 Frequent oil and filter changes are the most important preventative maintenance procedures, which can be undertaken by the DIY owner. As engine oil ages, it becomes diluted and contaminated, which leads to premature engine wear.

2 Before starting this procedure, gather all the necessary tools and materials. Also make sure that you have plenty of clean rags and newspapers handy, to mop-up any spills. Ideally, the engine oil should be warm, as it will drain better, and more built-up sludge will be removed with it. Take care, however, not to touch the exhaust or any other hot parts of the engine when working under the vehicle. To avoid any possibility of scalding, and to protect yourself from possible skin irritants and other harmful contaminants in used engine oils, it is advisable to wear gloves when carrying out this work. Access

6.6 Remove the solenoid valve

to the underside of the vehicle will be greatly improved if it can be raised on a lift, driven onto ramps, or jacked up and supported on axle stands (see *Jacking and vehicle support*). Whichever method is chosen, make sure that the vehicle remains level, or if it is at an angle, that the drain plug is at the lowest point. Undo the retaining screws and (where fitted) remove the engine undertray, then also remove the engine top cover – again where fitted **(see illustrations)**.

3 Slacken the sump drain plug about half a turn. Position the draining container under the drain plug, and then remove the plug completely **(see illustration and Haynes Hint)**. To drain all oil from the engine, loosen the cap from the top of the oil filter housing using a socket or spanner – this will allow the oil to drain from the filter housing into the sump.

> **HAYNES HiNT** *Keep the drain plug pressed into the sump while unscrewing it by hand the last couple of turns. As the plug releases, move it away sharply so the stream of oil issuing from the sump runs into the container, not up your sleeve.*

4 Allow some time for the old oil to drain, noting that it may be necessary to reposition the container as the oil flow slows to a trickle.

5 After all the oil has drained, wipe off the drain plug with a clean rag, and fit a new sealing washer. Clean the area around the drain plug opening, and refit the plug. Tighten the drain plug to the specified torque. Note: On some engines, the sealing washer is integral with the drain plug. On these engines, the drain plug must be renewed.

6 Place absorbent cloths around the oil filter housing to catch any spilt oil. Where necessary, unbolt the bracket and unclip the solenoid valve from above the oil filter **(see illustration)**.

6.7a Use a 32 mm socket to unscrew the filter cap ...

6.7b ... and withdraw the filter and cap

6.8 Remove the O-ring

7 Fully unscrew the cap from the top of the oil filter and remove it together with the filter element. Unclip the filter element from the cap and dispose of it **(see illustrations)**.

8 Remove the O-ring seal from the cap **(see illustration)** and then using a clean rag, wipe all oil and sludge from the inside of the filter housing and cap.

9 The new filter will be supplied with a large sealing O-ring and a small O-ring (already fitted in most cases). Some makes of filter may require the fitting of the small O-ring. Fit the new sealing ring(s) and then refit the assembly and tighten the cap to the specified torque. (The correct torque is shown on the cap) Make sure the filter element is engaged with the cap and the correct way up **(see illustrations)**. Wipe up any spilt oil before refitting the engine top cover.

10 Remove the old oil and all tools from under the car and then lower the car to the ground.

11 Remove the dipstick, and then unscrew the oil filler cap from the cylinder head cover. Fill the engine, using the correct grade and type of oil (see *Lubricants and fluids*). A funnel may help to reduce spillage. Pour in half the specified quantity of oil first **(see illustration)**, then wait a few minutes for the oil to run to the sump (see *Weekly checks*). Continue adding oil a small quantity at a time until the level is up to the maximum mark on the dipstick. Refit the filler cap.

6.9a The new oil filter comes with two O-ring seals. Check that the smaller O-ring is already fitted or supplied with the filter

6.9b Fit the main seal to the oil filter cap in the position shown ...

6.9c ... and then snap the new filter into the cap

6.9d Lubricate the O-ring seals with clean engine ...

6.9e ...then refit to the oil filter housing

6.9f Tighten to the specified torque

6.11 Pour in half the specified quantity of oil first, wait, then add the rest

7.1 The outer brake pads can be observed through the holes in the wheels

7.3 The thickness (a) of the brake pad linings must not be less than the specified amount

12 Start the engine and run it for a few minutes; check for leaks around the oil filter cap. Note that there may be a few seconds delay before the oil pressure warning light goes out when the engine is started, as the oil circulates through the engine oil galleries and the new oil filter before the pressure builds-up.

⚠ **Warning: Do not increase the engine speed above idling while the oil pressure light is illuminated, as considerable damage can be caused to the turbocharger.**

13 Switch off the engine, and wait a few minutes for the oil to settle in the sump once more. With the new oil circulated and the filter completely full, recheck the level on the dipstick, and add more oil as necessary.

14 Raise the front of the vehicle again and check around the sump drain plug for oil leaks. If all is well, refit the engine undershield. Lower the vehicle to the ground and fit the engine top cover.

15 Dispose of the used engine oil safely, with reference to General repair procedures in the Reference section of this manual.

7 Brake pad check

1 The outer brake pads can be checked without removing the wheels, by observing the brake pads through the holes in the wheels **(see illustration)**. If necessary, remove the wheel trim. The thickness of the pad lining must not be less than the dimension given in the Specifications.

2 If the outer pads are worn near their limits, it is worthwhile checking the inner pads as well. Apply the handbrake then jack up vehicle and support it on axle stands (see *Jacking and vehicle support*). Remove the roadwheels.

3 Use a steel rule to check the thickness of the brake pads, and compare with the minimum thickness given in the Specifications **(see illustration)**.

4 For a comprehensive check, the brake pads should be removed and cleaned. The operation of the caliper can then also be checked, and the condition of the brake disc itself can be fully examined on both sides. Refer to Chapter 9 Section 4 (front) or Chapter 9 Section 8 (rear).

5 If any pad's friction material is worn to the specified minimum thickness or less, all four pads at the front or rear, as applicable, must be renewed as a set.

6 On completion of the check, refit the roadwheels and lower the vehicle to the ground.

8 Resetting the service interval display

1 After all necessary maintenance work has been completed; the service interval display must be reset. VW technicians use a special dedicated instrument to do this, and a print-out is then put in the vehicle service record. It is possible for the owner to reset

8.3 The reset switch

the display as described in the following paragraphs, but note that the procedure will automatically reset the display to a 10 000 mile interval. Note: Some models will need to be changed to 'fixed service intervals' using diagnostic equipment before the reset procedure will work.

2 To continue with the 'variable' intervals which take into consideration the number of starts, length of journeys, vehicle speeds, brake pad wear, bonnet opening frequency, fuel consumption, oil level and oil temperature, the display must be reset by a VW dealership using the special dedicated instrument.

3 The Service Interval Display (SID) is reset using the '00/SET' switch in the centre of the instrument panel **(see illustration)**.

4 To reset the SID:

a) Switch off the ignition.

b) Press and hold down the trip reset swicth '0.0' at the base of the instrument panel.

c) Switch the ignition on.

d) Wait until 'Reset oil change service? or 'Reset inspection service ?' is displayed.

e) Release the reset switch.

f) Then briefly press the switch once (within 20 seconds).

g) After a short time the display returns to the normal display. The SID in now reset.

h) Turn the ignition off.

9 Exhaust system check

1 With the engine cold (at least an hour after the vehicle has been driven), check the complete exhaust system from the engine to the end of the tailpipe. The exhaust system is most easily checked with the vehicle raised on a hoist, or suitably supported on axle stands, so that the exhaust components are readily visible and accessible (see *Jacking and vehicle support*).

2 Check the exhaust pipes and connections for evidence of leaks, severe corrosion and damage. Make sure that all brackets and mountings are in good condition, and that all relevant nuts and bolts are tight. Leakage at any of the joints or in other parts of the system will usually show up as a black sooty stain in the vicinity of the leak.

3 Rattles and other noises can often be traced to the exhaust system, especially the brackets and mountings. Try to move the pipes and silencers. If the components are able to come into contact with the body or suspension parts, secure the system with new mountings. Otherwise separate the joints (if possible) and twist the pipes as necessary to provide additional clearance.

10 Hose and fluid leak check

1 Visually inspect the engine joint faces, gaskets and seals for any signs of water or oil leaks. Pay particular attention to the areas around the camshaft cover, cylinder head, oil filter and sump joint faces. Bear in mind that, over a period of time, some very slight seepage from these areas is to be expected – what you are really looking for is any indication of a serious leak. Should a leak be found, renew the offending gasket or oil seal by referring to the appropriate Chapters in this manual.

2 Also check the security and condition of all the engine-related pipes and hoses. Ensure that all cable-ties or securing clips are in place and in good condition. Clips, which are broken or missing, can lead to chafing of the hoses, pipes or wiring, which could cause more serious problems in the future.

3 Carefully check the radiator hoses and heater hoses along their entire length. Renew any hose that is cracked, swollen or deteriorated. Cracks will show up better if the hose is squeezed. Pay close attention to the hose clips that secure the hoses to the cooling system components. Hose clips can pinch and puncture hoses, resulting in cooling system leaks.

4 Inspect all the cooling system components (hoses, joint faces, etc) for leaks **(see Haynes Hint)**. Where any problems of this nature are found on system components, renew the component or gasket with reference to Chapter 3.

5 Where applicable, inspect the automatic transmission fluid cooler hoses for leaks or deterioration.

6 With the vehicle raised, inspect the fuel tank and filler neck for punctures, cracks and other damage. The connection between the filler neck and tank is especially critical. Sometimes a rubber filler neck or connecting hose will leak due to loose retaining clamps or deteriorated rubber.

A leak in the cooling system will usually show up as white- or antifreezecoloured deposits on the area adjoining the leak.

7 Carefully check all rubber hoses and metal fuel lines leading away from the tank. Check for loose connections, deteriorated hoses, crimped lines, and other damage. Pay particular attention to the vent pipes and hoses, which often loop up around the filler neck and can become blocked or crimped. Follow the lines to the front of the vehicle, carefully inspecting them all the way. Renew damaged sections as necessary.

8 From within the engine compartment, check the security of all fuel hose attachments and pipe unions, and inspect the fuel hoses and vacuum hoses for kinks, chafing and deterioration.

11 Auxiliary drivebelt check

1 Apply the handbrake, then jack up the front of the vehicle and support it on axle stands (see *Jacking and vehicle support*).

2 Using a socket on the crankshaft pulley bolt, turn the engine slowly clockwise so that the full length of the auxiliary drivebelt can be examined. Look for cracks, splitting and fraying on the surface of the belt; check also for signs of glazing (shiny patches) and separation of the belt plies. If damage or wear is visible, or if there are traces of oil or grease on it, the belt should be renewed (see Section 29).

12 Antifreeze check

1 The cooling system should be filled with the recommended G12 antifreeze and corrosion protection fluid – do not mix this antifreeze with any other type. Over a period of time, the concentration of fluid may be reduced due to topping-up (this can be avoided by topping-up with the correct antifreeze mixture – see Specifications) or fluid loss. If loss of coolant has been evident, it is important to

make the necessary repair before adding fresh fluid.

2 With the engine cold, carefully remove the cap from the expansion tank. If the engine is not completely cold, place a cloth rag over the cap before removing it, and remove it slowly to allow any pressure to escape.

3 Antifreeze checkers are available from car accessory shops. Draw some coolant from the expansion tank and observe how many plastic balls are floating in the checker. Usually, 2 or 3 balls must be floating for the correct concentration of antifreeze, but follow the manufacturer's instructions.

4 If the concentration is incorrect, it will be necessary to either withdraw some coolant and add antifreeze, or alternatively drain the old coolant and add fresh coolant of the correct concentration (see Section 32).

13 Brake hydraulic circuit check

1 Check the entire brake hydraulic circuit for leaks and damage. Start by checking the master cylinder in the engine compartment. At the same time, check the vacuum servo unit and ABS units for signs of fluid leakage.

2 Raise the front and rear of the vehicle and support it on axle stands (see *Jacking and vehicle support*). Check the rigid hydraulic brake lines for corrosion and damage.

3 At the front of the vehicle, check that the flexible hydraulic hoses to the calipers are not twisted or chafing on any of the surrounding suspension components. Turn the steering on full lock to make this check. Also check that the hoses are not brittle or cracked.

4 Lower the vehicle to the ground after making the checks.

14 Headlight beam adjustment

1 Accurate adjustment of the headlight beam is only possible using optical beam-setting equipment, and this work should therefore be carried out by a VW dealer or service station with the necessary facilities. MOT test centres have this equipment.

2 Basic adjustments can be carried out in an emergency, and further details are given in Chapter 12, Section 9.

15 Pollen filter element renewal

1 The pollen filter is located in the heater unit and is accessed from inside the car, on the passenger's side.

2 Remove the clips and withdraw the facia lower trim from beneath the glovebox **(see illustration)**.

3 Slide the cover to the left to remove the access cover **(see illustration)**. On some models there maybe a screw securing the cover in place.

4 Slide out the pollen filter element downwards from the heater unit **(see illustration)**.

5 Fit the new element then **(see illustration)** refit the access cover, making sure that the locating lugs are fitted correctly in the housing. If any of the lugs have been broken off, fit a screw into the cover to make sure it is secure.

6 Refit the trim beneath the facia/glovebox.

16 Manual transmission oil level check

1 There is no requirement to check the manual transmission fluid level – the transmission is effectively sealed for life. However the transmission should be checked for leaks. Full details of refilling and checking the transmission oil level are given in Chapter 7A Section 4.

17 Underbody protection check

1 Raise and support the vehicle on axle stands (see *Jacking and vehicle support*). Using an electric torch or lead light, inspect the entire underside of the vehicle, paying particular attention to the wheel arches. Look for any damage to the flexible underbody coating, which may crack or flake off with age, leading to corrosion. Also check that the wheel arch liners are securely attached with any clips provided – if they come loose, dirt may get in behind the liners and defeat their purpose. If there is any damage to the under seal, or any corrosion, it should be repaired before the damage gets too serious.

18 Driveshaft gaiter check

1 With the vehicle raised and securely supported on stands, slowly rotate the roadwheel. Inspect the condition of the outer constant velocity (CV) joint rubber gaiters, squeezing the gaiters to open out the folds. Check for signs of cracking, splits or deterioration of the rubber, which may allow the grease to escape, and lead to water and grit entry into the joint. Also check the security and condition of the retaining clips. Repeat these checks on the inner joints **(see illustration)**. If any damage or deterioration

15.2 Remove the facia lower trim from beneath the glovebox

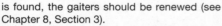

15.4 … then slide out the pollen filter element

15.3 Remove the access cover…

15.5 Observe the air flow direction marked on the filter

is found, the gaiters should be renewed (see Chapter 8, Section 3).

2 At the same time, check the general condition of the CV joints themselves by first holding the driveshaft and attempting to rotate the wheel. Repeat this check by holding the inner joint and attempting to rotate the driveshaft. Any appreciable movement indicates wear in the joints, wear in the driveshaft splines, or a loose driveshaft retaining nut.

19 Steering and suspension check

1 Raise the front and rear of the vehicle, and securely support it on axle stands (see *Jacking and vehicle support*).

18.1 Check the condition of the driveshaft gaiters

2 Visually inspect the track rod end balljoint dust cover, the lower front suspension balljoint dust cover, and the steering rack-and-pinion gaiters for splits **(see illustration)** chafing or deterioration. Any wear of these components will cause loss of lubricant, together with dirt and water entry, resulting in rapid deterioration of the balljoints or steering gear.

3 Check the power steering fluid hoses for chafing or deterioration, and the pipe and hose unions for fluid leaks. Also check for signs of fluid leakage under pressure from the steering gear rubber gaiters, which would indicate failed fluid seals within the steering gear.

4 Grasp the roadwheel at the 12 o'clock and 6 o'clock positions, and try to rock it **(see illustration)**. Very slight free play may be felt,

19.2 Check the rack gaiters for spilts

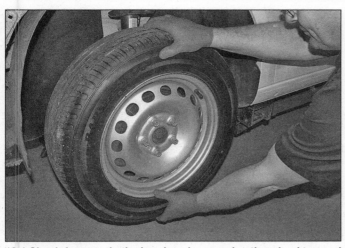

19.4 Check for wear in the bearings by grasping the wheel top and bottom and trying to rock it

19.5 Check for wear in the bearings and ball joints by grasping the wheel at the sides and trying to rock it

but if the movement is appreciable, further investigation is necessary to determine the source. Continue rocking the wheel while an assistant depresses the footbrake. If the movement is now eliminated or significantly reduced, it is likely that the hub bearings are at fault. If the free play is still evident with the footbrake depressed, then there is wear in the suspension joints or mountings.

5 Now grasp the wheel at the 9 o'clock and 3 o'clock positions, and try to rock it as before **(see illustration)**. Any movement felt now may again be caused by wear in the hub bearings or the steering track rod balljoints. If the inner or outer balljoint is worn, the visual movement will be obvious.

6 Using a large screwdriver or flat bar, check for wear in the suspension mounting bushes by levering between the relevant suspension component and its attachment point. Some movement is to be expected as the mountings are made of rubber, but excessive wear should be obvious. Also check the condition of any visible rubber bushes, looking for splits, cracks or contamination of the rubber.

7 With the car standing on its wheels, have an assistant turn the steering wheel back-and-forth about an eighth of a turn each way. There should be very little, if any, lost movement between the steering wheel and roadwheels. If this is not the case, closely observe the joints and mountings previously described, but in addition, check the steering column universal joints for wear, and the rack-and-pinion steering gear itself.

8 Check for any signs of fluid leakage around the front suspension struts and rear shock absorber. Should any fluid be noticed, the suspension strut or shock absorber is defective internally, and should be renewed. Note: Suspension struts/shock absorbers should always be renewed in pairs on the same axle to ensure correct vehicle handling.

9 The efficiency of the suspension strut/shock absorber may be checked by bouncing the vehicle at each corner. Generally speaking, the body will return to its normal position and stop after being depressed. If it rises and returns on a rebound, the suspension strut/shock absorber is probably suspect. Examine also the suspension strut/shock absorber upper and lower mountings for any signs of wear.

20 Battery check

1 The battery is located on the left-hand side of the engine compartment. Remove the cover **(see illustrations)** to gain access to the battery.

2 Check that both battery terminals and all the fuse holder connections are securely attached **(see illustration)** and are free from corrosion. Note: Before disconnecting the terminals from the battery, refer to Chapter 5A Section 3.

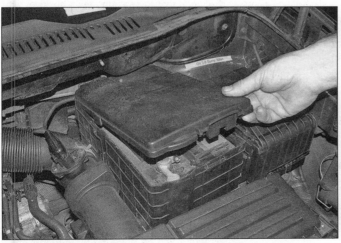

20.1a Unclip the cover – models with a hard cover

20.1b Open the cover – models with an insulated cover

20.2 Check that the terminals are secure

20.3 Check that the battery clamp is secure

3 Check the battery casing for signs of damage or cracking and check the battery retaining clamp bolt is securely tightened **(see illustration)**. If the battery casing is damaged in any way the battery must be renewed (see Chapter 5A, Section 3).
4 On completion refit the battery cover.

21 Hinge and lock lubrication

1 Lubricate the hinges of the bonnet, doors and tailgate with light general-purpose oil. Similarly, lubricate all latches, locks and lock strikers. At the same time, check the security and operation of all the locks, adjusting them if necessary (see Chapter 11, Section 11).
2 Lightly lubricate the bonnet release mechanism and cable with suitable grease.

22 Airbag unit check

1 Inspect the exterior condition of the airbag(s) for signs of damage or deterioration. If an airbag shows signs of damage, it must be renewed (Chapter 12, Section 27). Note that it is not permissible to attach any stickers to the surface of the airbag, as this may affect the deployment of the unit.

23 Windscreen/tailgate/ headlight washer system check

1 Check that each of the washer jet nozzles are clear and that each nozzle provides a strong jet of washer fluid.
2 The tailgate/rear door jet (where fitted) should be aimed to spray at the centre of the screen, using a pin.

3 The windscreen washer nozzles should be aimed slightly above the centre of the screen using a small screwdriver to turn the jet eccentric (see Chapter 12, Section 21).
4 The headlight inner jet should be aimed slightly above the horizontal centreline of the headlight, and the outer jet should be aimed slightly below the centreline. VW technicians use a special tool to adjust the headlight jet after pulling the jet out onto its stop.
5 Especially during the winter months, make sure that the washer fluid frost concentration is sufficient.

24 Engine management self- diagnosis memory fault check

1 This work should be carried out by a VW dealer or a diagnostic specialist using suitable equipment. Note however that simple diagnostic tools are now widely available. Most of the lower priced tools will only access the mandatory OBD (On Board Diagnostics) emissions related fault codes. The diagnostic socket is located below the facia, next tot eh fuse box **(see illustration)**.

24.1 Diagnostic socket

25 Road test and exhaust emissions check

Instruments and electrical equipment

1 Check the operation of all instruments and electrical equipment including the air conditioning system.
2 Make sure that all instruments read correctly, and switch on all electrical equipment in turn, to check that it functions properly.

Steering and suspension

3 Check for any abnormalities in the steering, suspension, handling or road 'feel'.
4 Drive the vehicle, and check that there are no unusual vibrations or noises, which may indicate wear in the driveshafts, wheel bearings, etc.
5 Check that the steering feels positive, with no excessive 'sloppiness', or roughness, and check for any suspension noises when cornering and driving over bumps.

Drivetrain

6 Check the performance of the engine, clutch (where applicable), gearbox/transmission and driveshafts.
7 Listen for any unusual noises from the engine, clutch and gearbox/transmission.
8 Make sure the engine runs smoothly at idle, and there is no hesitation on accelerating.
9 Check that, where applicable, the clutch action is smooth and progressive, that the drive is taken up smoothly, and that the pedal travel is not excessive. Also listen for any noises when the clutch pedal is depressed.
10 On manual gearbox models check that all gears can be engaged smoothly without noise, and that the gear lever action is smooth and not abnormally vague or 'notchy'.

27.2 Undo the retaining screws ...

27.3 ... and lift off the upper cover

11 On automatic transmission models, make sure that all gearchanges occur smoothly, without snatching, and without an increase in engine speed between changes. Check that all the gear positions can be selected with the vehicle at rest. If any problems are found, they should be referred to a VW dealer.

12 Listen for a metallic clicking sound from the front of the vehicle, as the vehicle is driven slowly in a circle with the steering on full-lock. Carry out this check in both directions. If a clicking noise is heard, this indicates wear in a driveshaft joint, in which case renew the joint if necessary.

Braking system

13 Make sure that the vehicle does not pull to one side when braking, and that the wheels do not lock when braking hard.

14 Check that there is no vibration through the steering when braking.

15 Check that the handbrake operates correctly without excessive movement of the lever, and that it holds the vehicle stationary on a slope.

16 Test the operation of the brake servo unit as follows. With the engine off, depress the footbrake four or five times to exhaust the vacuum. Hold the brake pedal depressed, and then start the engine. As the engine starts, there should be a noticeable 'give' in the brake pedal as vacuum builds-up. Allow the engine to run for at least two minutes, and then switch it off. If the brake pedal is depressed now, it should be possible to detect a hiss from the servo as the pedal is depressed. After about four or five applications, no further hissing should be heard, and the pedal should feel considerably harder.

17 Under controlled emergency braking, the pulsing of the ABS unit must be felt at the footbrake pedal.

Exhaust emissions check

18 Although not part of the manufacturer's maintenance schedule, this check will normally be carried out on a regular basis according to the country the vehicle is operated in. Currently in the UK, exhaust emissions testing is included as part of the annual MOT test after the vehicle is 3 years old. In Germany the test is made when the vehicle is 3 years old, then repeated every 2 years.

26 DSG transmission oil renewal

1 Renew the transmission oil as described in Chapter 7B Section 6.

27 Air filter element renewal

Note: *There are two versions of the air filter fitted. Models with engine code BST and BDJ have a cylindrical filter fitted.*

1 The air cleaner is located in front of the battery in the left-hand front corner of the engine compartment.

2 Undo the cover retaining screws and lift the air cleaner cover, taking care not to put any strain on the intake ducting and air mass meter **(see illustration)**.

3 With the cover raised, withdraw the air filter element, noting how it is fitted **(see illustration)**.

4 The removal procedure is slightly different on engine codes BST and BDJ **(see illustrations)**.

27.4a Remove the screws and lift off the cover

27.4b Unscrew and remove the collar

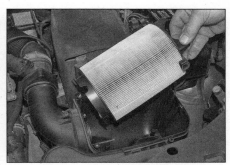

27.4c Lift out the air filter

5 Remove any debris that may have collected inside the air cleaner.

6 Fit a new air filter element in position, ensuring that the edges are securely seated.

7 Refit the lid and tighten the screws, then refit the engine top cover.

28 Fuel filter renewal

Note: *Carry out this procedure at this interval only when using diesel fuel conforming to DIN EN 590 (standard fuel in the UK).*

1 The fuel filter is mounted in the right-hand front corner of the engine compartment. Place rags around the filter to absorb any fuel that may be spilt.

2 Before removing the fuel filter, clean around the fuel pipes on the top of the filter housing to prevent any dirt entering the fuel system **(see illustrations)**.

3 Undo the screws and lift the cover complete with fuel hoses from the top of the filter housing and move it to one side **(see illustrations)**. Remove the seal and discard, as a new one must be used on refitting.

4 Withdraw the old filter element out from the housing and discard **(see illustration)**.

5 Use a pipette/syringe to draw out the dirty fuel and water residue from inside the fuel filter lower housing. Then insert the new filter element **(see illustrations)**.

6 To help the engine start easier (to prevent having to bleed the system), top up the lower filter housing to within 15 ml of the top with clean diesel, making sure that no dirt or water enters the system.

7 Fit a new seal to the cover, then refit the cover back on the lower filter housing, making sure the top is located in the filter correctly **(see illustrations)**. Press down firmly and evenly, then insert the screws and tighten them in a diagonal sequence.

8 Start and run the engine at idle, then check around the fuel filter for fuel leaks. Note: It may take a few seconds of cranking before the engine starts. If the engine does not start the

28.2a Clean around the top of the fuel filter …

28.2b … and place some cloth to catch spilt fuel

28.3a Carefully prise up the top …

28.3b … and remove it from the filter housing

28.4 Remove the old filter element …

28.5a …then use a pipette to draw out the old fuel …

28.5b … and insert the new filter element

28.7a Fit new seal …

28.7b … then refit the upper cover

28.8 Bleeding the fuel system with a vacuum pump

29.6a Turn the tensioner clockwise...

29.6b ...or use an adjustable spanner (alternative type of tensioner)

system must be bleed using a vacuum tool or hand primer **(see illustration)**. Identify the fuel return line from the injectors and remove it from the filter. Connect the vacuum pump or hand primer and draw fuel up to the filter. Reconnect the filter fuel line and start the vehicle.

29 Auxiliary drivebelt check and renewal

Check

1 See Section 11, for information on checking the condition of the drivebelt.
2 There are two different types of tensioning system fitted to diesel engines as well as a stretch belt that has no tensioner. The routing of the belt is the same (except for models with no AC) although the procedure for belt renewal is different.
3 When the belt is removed, check all pulleys are free from any damage and are secure. Also check that the alternator and air-conditioning compressor (where fitted) are mounted securely.

Renewal

4 For improved access, apply the handbrake,

29.6c ... and lock the tensioner in position

and then jack up the front of the vehicle and support it on axle stands (see *Jacking and vehicle support*).
5 Remove the right-hand front roadwheel, and then where required remove the wing liner from the inner wheel arch.

With tensioner spring element

6 Use a spanner on the centre bolt and turn the tensioner clockwise. Lock the tensioner in its released position by inserting a locking pin (Allen key or similar) through the lug into the tensioner body. An alternative tensioner

29.7a If the belt is to be refitted, mark the direction of rotation

maybe fitted, but the principle is identical **(see illustrations)**.
7 Note how the drivebelt is routed, then remove it from the crankshaft pulley **(see illustrations)**, alternator pulley, and air conditioning compressor pulley (as applicable).
8 Locate the new drivebelt on the pulleys, then by holding the pressure of the tensioner with a spanner, remove the locking pin. Slowly release the pressure on the spanner **(see illustration)**, so that the tensioner takes up the slack in the belt. Check that the belt is located correctly in the multi-grooves in the pulleys.

29.7b Note the fitted position of the belt before removal

29.8 With the locking pin removed, slowly take up the slack in the belt

29.11 Auxiliary drivebelt with tensioning roller

29.18a Aftermarket tool (A) and the tool supplied with the belt (B)

9 Start the engine and check that the drivebelt runs, as it should over the pulleys. Make sure that all tools and hands are kept clear of the drivebelt with the engine running.

10 With the engine stopped, refit the access panel and roadwheel, and then lower the vehicle to the ground. Refit the engine top cover if removed.

With tensioner roller

11 Undo the tensioner roller retaining bolt, and remove the tensioner roller from the engine. Note the retaining bolt is below the tensioner roller, and goes up through the mounting bracket in a vertical direction **(see illustration)**. Discard the retaining bolt, as a new one will be required for refitting.

12 Note how the drivebelt is routed, then remove it from the crankshaft pulley, alternator pulley, and air-conditioning compressor pulley (as applicable).

13 Locate the new drivebelt on the pulleys,

then fit the tensioner roller, making sure its guide pin is located correctly in the mounting bracket.

14 Fit the new retaining bolt, and then tighten to the following five stages:
a) *Tighten bolt by hand at this point.*
b) *Tighten bolt until it reaches stop.*
c) *Turn the bolt back through 90°*
d) *Tighten bolt to 30Nm.*
e) *Tighten a further 90°*

15 When tensioner roller is fitted and the belt is tensioned, check the tensioner retaining bolt. The part of the bolt that has protruded out through the upper end of the mounting bracket (behind the tensioner roller) must not protrude more than 2.5mm higher than the outer surface of the tensioner roller. This ensures that the bolt has been tightened to its end stop.

16 Start the engine and check that the drivebelt runs, as it should over the pulleys. Make sure that all tools and hands are kept clear of the drivebelt with the engine running.

17 With the engine stopped, refit the access panel and roadwheel, and then lower the vehicle to the ground. Refit the engine top cover if removed.

Stretch belt models

Note: *A special tool will be required to fit the replacement belt. This tool is supplied with a genuine replacement belt, but the tools are also widely available in the aftermarket* **(see illustration)**.

18 On these models the belt must be cut to remove it, using either a sharp knife or pliers. Cut and remove the belt **(see illustration)**.

19 Place the new belt over the alternator pulley, locating it correctly in the pulley grooves.

20 Locate the special tool at the bottom of the crankshaft pulley and then push the belt onto the tool and partially over the crankshaft pulley **(see illustration)**.

21 Whilst holding the belt and tool in position fit a socket and ratchet to the crankshaft pulley. Slowly rotate the crankshaft pulley whilst applying pressure to the tool and belt. Continue to rotate the pulley whilst guiding the belt (and tool) onto the crankshaft pulley **(see illustration)**. As the crankshaft rotates check that the belt is still located correctly in the grooves of the alternator pulley.

22 Continue rotating the crankshaft pulley until the special tool can be removed and the belt is seated correctly in the grooves of both the crankshaft pulley and the alternator pulley. Rotate the belt a complete revolution after the tool has been removed to check and settle the belt in position.

29.18b Cut the old belt off

29.20 Fit the special tool to the crankshaft pulley

29.21 Turn the crankshaft to lift the new belt over and onto the pulley

23 With the engine stopped, refit the wing liner and roadwheel, and then lower the vehicle to the ground. Refit the engine top cover if removed.

30 Timing belt and tensioner roller renewal

1 Refer to Chapter 2A, Section 7 (1.6 litre common rail engines), Chapter 2B, Section 7 (2.0 litre common rail engines) or Chapter 2C Section 7 (PD engines) for details of renewing the timing belt and tensioner roller.

31 Brake (and clutch) fluid renewal

⚠️ **Warning: Brake hydraulic fluid can harm your eyes and damage painted surfaces, so use extreme caution when handling and pouring it. Do not use fluid that has been standing open for some time, as it absorbs moisture from the air. Excess moisture can cause a dangerous loss of braking effectiveness.**

1 The procedure is similar to that for the bleeding of the hydraulic system as described in Chapter 9, Section 2, except that the brake fluid reservoir should be emptied by siphoning, using an old, clean antifreeze tester or similar before starting, and allowance should be made for the old fluid to be expelled when bleeding a section of the circuit. Since the clutch hydraulic system also uses fluid from the brake system reservoir, it should also be bled at the same time by referring to Chapter 6, Section 2.

2 Working as described in Chapter 9, Section 2, open the first bleed screw in the sequence, and pump the brake pedal gently until nearly all the old fluid has been emptied from the master cylinder reservoir.

3 Top-up to the MAX level with new fluid, and continue pumping until only the new fluid remains in the reservoir, and new fluid can be seen emerging from the bleed screw. Tighten the screw, and top the reservoir level up to the MAX level line.

4 Work through all the remaining bleed screws in the sequence until new fluid can be seen at all of them. Be careful to keep the master cylinder reservoir topped-up to above the MIN level at all times, or air may enter the system and greatly increase the length of the task.

5 When the operation is complete, check that all bleed screws are securely tightened, and that their dust caps are refitted. Wash off all traces of spilt fluid, and recheck the master cylinder reservoir fluid level.

6 On models with manual transmission, once the brake fluid has been changed the clutch fluid should also be renewed. Referring to Chapter 6, Section 2, bleed the clutch until new fluid is seen to be emerging from the slave cylinder bleed screw, keeping the master cylinder fluid level above the MIN level line at all times to prevent air entering the system. Once the new fluid emerges, securely tighten the bleed screw then disconnect and remove the bleeding equipment. Securely refit the dust cap then wash off all traces of spilt fluid.

7 On all models, ensure the master cylinder fluid level is correct (see *Weekly checks*) and thoroughly check the operation of the brakes and (where necessary) clutch before taking the car on the road.

32 Coolant renewal

Note: *This work is not included in the VW schedule and should not be required if the recommended VW G12 LongLife coolant antifreeze/inhibitor is used. However, if standard antifreeze/inhibitor is used, the work should be carried out at the recommended interval.*

⚠️ **Warning: Wait until the engine is cold before starting this procedure. Do not allow antifreeze to come in contact with your skin, or with the painted surfaces of the vehicle. Rinse off spills immediately with plenty of water. Never leave antifreeze lying around in an open container, or in a puddle in the driveway or on the garage floor. Children and pets are attracted by its sweet smell, but antifreeze can be fatal if ingested.**

Cooling system draining

Note: *All PD engines (except those with engine code BMM) have a drain plug fitted. CR engines do not have a drain plug.*

1 With the engine completely cold, unscrew the expansion tank cap.

2 Firmly apply the handbrake then jack up the front of the vehicle and support it on axle stands (see *Jacking and vehicle support*). Undo the retaining screws and remove the engine undertray(s) to gain access to the base of the radiator.

3 Position a suitable container beneath the coolant drain outlet, which is fitted to the coolant bottom hose end fitting. Loosen the drain plug (there is no need to remove it completely) and allow the coolant to drain into the container. If desired, a length of tubing can be fitted to the drain outlet to direct the flow of coolant during draining. Where no drain outlet is fitted to the hose end fitting, remove the retaining clip and disconnect the bottom hose from the radiator to drain the coolant **(see illustration)**. Also see Chapter 3 Section 2.

4 Where fitted, release the clamps and disconnect the hoses from the electric coolant circulation pump (see Chapter 3 Section 7), located at the front side of the cylinder block, below the oil cooler **(see illustration)**.

5 To fully drain the system also disconnect

32.3 Draining the coolant

32.4 Disconnect the hose from the circulation pump

one of the coolant hoses from the oil cooler, which is located at the front of the cylinder block.

6 If the coolant has been drained for a reason other than renewal, then provided it is clean, it can be re-used, though this is not recommended.

7 Once all the coolant has drained, securely tighten the radiator drain plug or reconnect the bottom hose to the radiator (as applicable). Also reconnect the coolant hose to the oil cooler and secure it in position with the retaining clip. Refit the undertray(s), tighten the retaining screws securely.

Cooling system flushing

8 If the recommended VW coolant has not been used and coolant renewal has been neglected, or if the antifreeze mixture has become diluted, the cooling system may gradually lose efficiency, as the coolant passages become restricted due to rust, scale deposits, and other sediment. The cooling system efficiency can be restored by flushing the system clean.

9 The radiator should be flushed separately from the engine, to avoid excess contamination.

Radiator flushing

10 To flush the radiator, first tighten the radiator drain plug.

11 Disconnect top and bottom hoses and any other relevant hoses from the radiator (see Chapter 3 Section 2).

12 Insert a garden hose into the radiator top inlet. Direct a flow of clean water through the radiator, and continue flushing until clean water emerges from the radiator bottom outlet.

13 If after a reasonable period, the water still does not run clear, the radiator can be flushed with a good proprietary cleaning agent. It is important that their manufacturer's instructions are followed carefully. If the contamination is particularly bad, insert the hose in the radiator bottom outlet, and reverse-flush the radiator.

Engine flushing

14 To flush the engine, remove the thermostat (see Chapter 3 Section 4).

15 With the bottom hose disconnected from the radiator, insert a garden hose into the coolant housing. Direct a clean flow of water through the engine, and continue flushing until clean water emerges from the radiator bottom hose.

16 When flushing is complete, refit the thermostat and reconnect the hoses.

Cooling system filling

17 Before attempting to fill the cooling system, ensure the drain plug (where fitted) is securely closed and make sure that all hoses are connected and are securely retained by their clips. If the recommended VW coolant is not being used, ensure that a suitable antifreeze mixture is used all year round, to prevent corrosion of the engine components (see following sub-Section). Note: VW recommend that only distilled water should be used.

18 Remove the expansion tank filler cap and slowly fill the system with the coolant. Continue to fill the cooling system until bubbles stop appearing in the expansion tank. Help to bleed the air from the system by repeatedly squeezing the radiator bottom hose.

19 When no more bubbles appear, top the coolant level up to the MAX level mark then securely refit the cap to the expansion tank.

20 Run the engine at a fast idle speed until the cooling fan cuts in. Wait for the fan to stop then switch the engine off and allow the engine to cool.

21 When the engine has cooled, check the coolant level with reference to *Weekly checks*. Top-up the level if necessary, and refit the expansion tank cap.

Antifreeze mixture

22 If the recommended VW coolant is not being used, the antifreeze should always be renewed at the specified intervals. This is necessary not only to maintain the antifreeze properties, but also to prevent corrosion, which would otherwise occur as the corrosion inhibitors become progressively less effective.

23 Always use an ethylene-glycol based antifreeze which is suitable for use in mixed-metal cooling systems. The quantity of antifreeze and levels of protection are indicated in the Specifications.

24 Before adding antifreeze, the cooling system should be completely drained, preferably flushed, and all hoses checked for condition and security.

25 After filling with antifreeze, a label should be attached to the expansion tank, stating the type and concentration of antifreeze used, and the date installed. Any subsequent topping-up should be made with the same type and concentration of antifreeze.

Caution: Do not use engine antifreeze in the windscreen/tailgate washer system, as it will damage the vehicle paintwork. A screenwash additive should be added to the washer system in the quantities stated on the bottle.

33 Particulate filter ash deposit mass check

1 Eventually, the amount of ash deposited in the particle filter by the filtration process will cause a blockage, and engine running problems. VW state that the maximum amount of ash is 60g. At this point, the particle filter must be renewed. Unfortunately, the mass of the ash can only be established using dedicated VW diagnostic equipment, connected to the vehicle through the diagnostic plug under the drivers side of the facia. Consequently, we recommend this task is entrusted to a VW dealer or suitably equipped specialist.

Chapter 2 Part A
1.6 litre common rail (CR) diesel engine in-car repair procedures

Contents

Degrees of difficulty

Easy, suitable for novice with little experience	**Fairly easy,** suitable for beginner with some experience	**Fairly difficult,** suitable for competent DIY mechanic	**Difficult,** suitable for experienced DIY mechanic	**Very difficult,** suitable for expert DIY or professional

Specifications

General

	Power	Torque
Manufacturer's engine codes*:		
1599 cc (1.6 litre), 16-valve, DOHC . . . . CAYD and CAYE		
Maximum outputs:		
Engine code:		
CAYE.	55 kW @ 4200 rpm	230 Nm @ 1500 to 2500 rpm
CAYD	75 kW @ 4400 rpm	250 Nm @ 1500 to 2500 rpm
Bore	79.5 mm	
Stroke	80.5 mm	
Compression ratio	16.5 : 1	
Firing order	1 – 3 – 4 – 2	
No.1 cylinder location.	Timing belt end	

* Note: *See 'Vehicle identification' at the end of this manual for the location of engine code markings.*

Lubrication system

Oil pump type.	Gear type, belt-driven from crankshaft
Oil pressure switch (green).	0.5 bar
Oil pressure (oil temperature 80°C):	
Minimum @ idling	0.6 bar
Minimum @ 2000 rpm.	1.0 bar
Maximum @ high rpm.	5.0 bar

Torque wrench settings

	Nm	lbf ft
Ancillary (alternator, etc) bracket mounting bolts*:		
Stage 1 (all six bolts)...	40	30
Stage 2 (for two lower bolts)..	Angle-tighten a further 45°	
Stage 2 (for four upper bolts)	Angle-tighten a further 90°	
Auxiliary drivebelt tensioner securing bolt:		
Stage 1	20	15
Stage 2	Angle-tighten a further 180°	
Big-end bearing caps bolts*:		
Stage 1	30	22
Stage 2	Angle-tighten a further 90°	
Camshaft retaining frame bolts	10	7
Camshaft cover bolts...	10	7
Camshaft sprocket hub centre bolt	100	74
Camshaft sprocket-to-hub bolts*:		
Stage 1	20	15
Stage 2	Angle-tighten a further 45°	
Common rail bolts	22	16
Coolant pump bolts	15	11
Crankshaft oil seal housing bolts....................................	15	11
Crankshaft pulley-to-sprocket bolts*:		
Stage 1	10	7
Stage 2	Angle-tighten a further 90°	
Crankshaft sprocket bolt*:		
Stage 1	120	89
Stage 2	Angle-tighten a further 90°	
Cylinder head bolts*:		
Stage 1	35	26
Stage 2	60	44
Stage 3	Angle-tighten a further 90°	
Stage 4	Angle-tighten a further 90°	
Engine mountings:		
RH engine mounting*:		
Mounting bracket to engine:		
Stage 1	40	30
Stage 2	Angle-tighten a further 180°	
Mounting to body:		
Stage 1	40	30
Stage 2	Angle-tighten a further 90°	
Mounting to bracket:		
Stage 1	60	44
Stage 2	Angle-tighten a further 90°	
LH engine/transmission mounting*:		
Mounting to body:		
Stage 1	40	30
Stage 2	Angle-tighten a further 90°	
Mounting to bracket on transmission:		
Stage 1	60	44
Stage 2	Angle-tighten a further 90°	
Rear mounting link*:		
Link-to-transmission:		
Short (front) bolt:		
Stage 1	40	30
Stage 2	Angle-tighten a further 90°	
Long (rear) bolt:		
Stage 1	60	44
Stage 2	Angle-tighten a further 90°	
Link-to-subframe:		
Stage 1	100	74
Stage 2	Angle-tighten a further 90°	
Flywheel*:		
Stage 1	60	44
Stage 2	Angle-tighten a further 90°	
Fuel pump hub nut..	95	70
Fuel pump sprocket bolts*..	20	15
Main bearing cap bolts*:		
Stage 1	65	48
Stage 2	Angle-tighten a further 90°	

Torque wrench settings (continued)

	Nm	lbf ft
Oil cooler screws	11	7
Oil drain plug*	30	22
Oil filter housing-to-cylinder block bolts*:		
Stage 1	14	10
Stage 2	Angle-tighten a further 180°	
Oil filter cover	25	18
Oil level/temperature sensor-to-sump bolts	9	7
Oil pick-up pipe securing bolts	9	7
Oil pressure warning light switch	22	16
Oil pump securing bolts	16	11
Piston oil spray jet bolt	27	19
Sump:		
Sump-to-cylinder block bolts	13	9
Sump-to-transmission bolts	40	30
Thermostat housing	15	11
Timing belt outer cover bolts	10	7
Timing belt tensioner roller securing nut:		
Stage 1	20	15
Stage 2	Angle-tighten a further 45°	
Timing belt idler pulleys:		
Lower idler roller nut	20	15
Upper idler roller (small) bolt	15	11
Upper idler roller (large) bolt*:		
Stage 1	50	37
Stage 2	Angle-tighten a further 90°	

*Do not re-use fasteners

1 General Information

How to use this Chapter

1 This Part of Chapter 2 describes those repair procedures that can reasonably be carried out on the engine while it remains in the vehicle. If the engine has been removed from the vehicle and is being dismantled as described in Part D, any preliminary dismantling procedures can be ignored.

2 Note that while it may be possible physically to overhaul certain items while the engine is in the vehicle, such tasks are not usually carried out as separate operations, and usually require the execution of several additional procedures (not to mention the cleaning of components and of oilways); for this reason, all such tasks are classed as major overhaul procedures, and are described in Part D of this Chapter.

Engine description

3 Throughout this Chapter, engines are referred to by type, and are identified and referred to by the manufacturer's code letters. A listing of all engines covered, together with their code letters, is given in the Specifications at the start of this Chapter.

4 The engines are water-cooled, double overhead camshafts (DOHC), in-line four-cylinder units, with cast-iron cylinder blocks and aluminium-silicone alloy cylinder heads. All are mounted transversely at the front of the vehicle, with the transmission bolted to the left-hand end of the engine.

5 The crankshaft is of five-bearing type, and thrustwashers are fitted to the centre main bearing (No.3) to control crankshaft endfloat.

6 Drive for the exhaust camshaft is by a toothed timing belt from the crankshaft, with the intake camshaft driven by interlocking gears at the left-hand end of both camshafts. The gears incorporate a toothed backlash compensator element. Each camshaft is mounted at the top of the cylinder head, and is secured by a bearing frame/ladder.

7 The valves are closed by coil springs, and run in guides pressed into the cylinder head. The valves are operated by roller rocker arms incorporating hydraulic tappets.

8 The gear-type oil pump is driven by a belt from the right-hand (timing belt) end of the crankshaft. Oil is drawn from the sump through a strainer, and then forced through an externally mounted, renewable filter. From there, it is distributed to the cylinder head, where it lubricates the camshaft journals and hydraulic tappets, and also to the crankcase, where it lubricates the main bearings, connecting rod big-ends, gudgeon pins and cylinder bores. A coolant-fed oil cooler is fitted to the oil filter housing on all engines. Oil jets are fitted to the base of each cylinder – these spray oil onto the underside of the pistons, to improve cooling.

9 All engines are fitted with a combined brake servo vacuum pump, driven by the camshaft on the transmission end of the cylinder head.

10 On all engines, engine coolant is circulated by a pump, driven by the timing belt. For details of the cooling system, refer to Chapter 3.

Operations with engine in car

11 The following operations can be performed without removing the engine:
a) Compression pressure – testing.
b) Camshaft cover – removal and refitting.
c) Crankshaft pulley – removal and refitting.
d) Timing belt covers – removal and refitting.
e) Timing belt – removal, refitting and adjustment.
f) Timing belt tensioner and sprockets – removal and refitting.
g) Camshaft oil seals – renewal.
h) Camshafts and hydraulic tappets – removal, inspection and refitting.
i) Cylinder head – removal and refitting.
j) Cylinder head and pistons – decarbonising.
k) Sump – removal and refitting.
l) Oil pump – removal, overhaul and refitting.
m) Crankshaft oil seals – renewal.
n) Engine/transmission mountings – inspection and renewal.
o) Flywheel/driveplate – removal, inspection and refitting.

Note: *It is possible to remove the pistons and connecting rods (after removing the cylinder head and sump) without removing the engine. However, this is not recommended. Work of this nature is more easily and thoroughly completed with the engine on the bench, as described in Chapter 2D.*

2 Compression and leakdown tests – description and interpretation

Compression test

Note: *A compression tester suitable for use with diesel engines will be required for this test.*

1 When engine performance is down, or if misfiring occurs which cannot be attributed to the ignition or fuel systems, a compression test can provide diagnostic clues as to the engine's condition. If the test is performed regularly, it can give warning of trouble before any other symptoms become apparent.

2 The engine must be fully warmed-up to normal operating temperature, the battery must be fully charged, and you will require the aid of an assistant.

3 Remove the glow plugs as described in Chapter 5B, Section 2, and then fit a compression tester to the No.1 cylinder glow plug hole. The type of tester that screws into the plug thread is preferred. Note: Part of the glow plug removal procedure is to disconnect the fuel injector wiring plugs. As a result of the plugs being disconnected and the engine cranked, faults may be stored in the ECU memory. These must be erased after the compression test.

4 Have your assistant crank the engine for several seconds on the starter motor. After one or two revolutions, the compression pressure should build-up to a maximum figure and then stabilise. Record the highest reading obtained.

5 Repeat the test on the remaining cylinders, recording the pressure in each.

6 The cause of poor compression is less easy to establish on a diesel engine than on a petrol engine. The effect of introducing oil into the cylinders (wet testing) is not conclusive, because there is a risk that the oil will sit in the recess on the piston crown, instead of passing to the rings. However, the following can be used as a rough guide to diagnosis.

7 All cylinders should produce very similar pressures. Any difference greater than that specified indicates the existence of a fault. Note that the compression should build-up quickly in a healthy engine. Low compression on the first stroke, followed by gradually increasing pressure on successive strokes, indicates worn piston rings. A low compression reading on the first stroke, which does not build-up during successive strokes, indicates leaking valves or a blown head gasket (a cracked head could also be the cause).

8 A low reading from two adjacent cylinders is almost certainly due to the head gasket having blown between them and the presence of coolant in the engine oil will confirm this.

9 On completion, remove the compression tester, and refit the glow plugs, with reference to Chapter 5B, Section 2.

10 Reconnect the wiring to the injector solenoids. Finally, have a VW dealer or suitably equipped specialist erase any fault codes from the ECU memory.

Leakdown test

11 A leakdown test measures the rate at which compressed air fed into the cylinder is lost. It is an alternative to a compression test, and in many ways it is better, since the escaping air provides easy identification of where pressure loss is occurring (piston rings, valves or head gasket).

12 The equipment required for leakdown testing is unlikely to be available to the home mechanic. If poor compression is suspected, have the test performed by a suitably equipped garage.

3 Engine assembly and valve timing marks – general information and usage

General information

1 TDC is the highest point in the cylinder that each piston reaches as it travels up-and-down when the crankshaft turns. Each piston reaches TDC at the end of the compression stroke and again at the end of the exhaust stroke, but TDC generally refers to piston position on the compression stroke. No 1 piston is at the timing belt end of the engine.

2 Positioning No 1 piston at TDC is an essential part of many procedures, such as timing belt removal and camshaft removal.

3 The design of the engines covered in this Chapter is such that piston-to-valve contact may occur if the camshaft or crankshaft is turned with the timing belt removed. For this reason, it is important to ensure that the camshaft and crankshaft do not move in relation to each other once the timing belt has been removed from the engine.

Setting TDC on No 1 cylinder

Note: *VAG special tool T10050 is required to lock the crankshaft sprocket in the TDC position. Alternatively obtain a tool from automotive tool specialists. Try asttools.co.uk.*

4 Raise the front of the vehicle and support it securely on axle stands (see *Jacking and vehicle support*). Remove the front right-hand road wheel, then release the fasteners and remove the lower section of the wheelarch liner.

5 Remove the auxiliary drivebelt as described in Chapter 1, Section 29

6 Remove the crankshaft pulley/vibration damper as described in Section 5.

7 Remove the timing belt outer covers as described in Section 6.

8 Using a spanner or socket on the crankshaft sprocket bolt, turn the crankshaft in the normal direction of rotation (clockwise) until the alignment mark on the face of the sprocket is almost vertical, and the hole in the camshaft sprocket hub aligns with the hole in the cylinder head **(see illustration)**.

9 While in this position it should be possible to insert the VAG tool T10050 to lock the crankshaft, and a 6 mm diameter rod/drill bit to lock the camshafts **(see illustrations)**. Note: The mark on the crankshaft sprocket and the mark on the VAG tool must align, whilst at the same time the shaft of tool must engage in the drilling in the crankshaft oil seal housing.

10 The engine is now set to TDC on No.1 cylinder.

3.8 The alignment mark on the crankshaft sprocket should be almost vertical

3.9a Fit the tool to the hole in the oil seal housing...

3.9b ...so the marks on the tool and sprocket align

3.9c Insert a 6 mm locking tool into the camshaft hub ...

3.9d ...with the arrow almost at the 12 o'clock position

4 Camshaft cover – removal and refitting

Removal

1 Remove the fuel injectors (Chapter 4A Section 5) and fuel rail (Chapter 4A Section 12).
2 Remove the timing belt upper cover as described in Section 6.
3 Note their fitted positions, then disconnect the vacuum hoses from the camshaft cover, and release them, and the wiring loom from the retaining clips at the rear of the cover (**see illustration**).
4 Squeeze together the sides of the collar, and disconnect the breather hose from the camshaft cover (**see illustration**).
5 Release the wiring from the clips at the rear of the cover, then unscrew the camshaft cover

retaining bolts and lift the cover away. If the cover sticks, do not attempt to lever it off – instead free it by working around the cover and tapping it lightly with a soft-faced mallet (**see illustration**).
6 Recover the camshaft cover gasket. Inspect the gasket carefully, and renew it if damage or deterioration is evident – note that the retaining bolts and seals must be pushed fully through the cover (**see illustrations**).
7 Clean the mating surfaces of the cylinder head and camshaft cover thoroughly, removing all traces of oil – take care to avoid damaging the surfaces as you do this.

Refitting

8 Refit the camshaft cover by following the removal procedure in reverse, tightening the cover retaining bolts to the specified torque, starting with the centre bolts and working outwards.

5 Crankshaft pulley – removal and refitting

Removal

1 Switch off the ignition and all electrical consumers and remove the ignition key.
2 Raise the front right-hand side of the vehicle, and support securely on axle stands (see *Jacking and vehicle support*). Remove the roadwheel.
3 Remove the securing fasteners and withdraw the lower section of the front wheel arch liner.
4 Slacken the bolts securing the crankshaft pulley to the sprocket (**see illustration**). If necessary, the pulley can be prevented from turning by counterholding with a spanner or socket on the crankshaft sprocket bolt.

4.3 Unclip the wiring from the retaining clips

4.4 Squeeze together the sides of the collar to disconnect the breather hose

4.5 Undo the bolts and lift away the camshaft cover

4.6a Renew the cover seal if necessary

4.6b Bolts and seals must be pushed fully through the cover before fitting the gasket

5.4 Undo the pulley bolts, counterholding it with a socket on the centre sprocket bolt

6.1 Pull the engine cover upwards from the mountings

6.2 Unclip the hoses from the retaining clips

6.3a Disconnect the wiring connector ...

6.3b ...undo the two retaining bolts ...

6.3c ... and withdraw the mounting bracket

6.4 Remove the washer reservoir filler neck

5 Remove the auxiliary drivebelt, as described in Chapter 1, Section 29.

6 Unscrew the bolts securing the pulley to the sprocket, and remove the pulley. Discard the bolts – new ones must be fitted.

Refitting

7 Refit the pulley over the locating peg on the crankshaft sprocket, then fit the new pulley securing bolts.

8 Refit and tension the auxiliary drivebelt as described in Chapter 1, Section 29.

9 Prevent the crankshaft from turning as during removal, then fit the pulley securing bolts, and tighten to the specified torque.

10 Refit the wheel arch liner.

11 Refit the roadwheel and lower the vehicle to the ground.

6 Timing belt covers – removal and refitting

Upper outer cover

1 Where fitted, pull the engine top cover upwards to release the mountings (see illustration).

2 Release the hoses from the retaining clips on the right-hand side of the cylinder head and move them to one side (see illustration).

3 Disconnect the wiring plug, undo the retaining bolts, and remove the pressure differential sender (for particulate filter) including bracket from the top of the engine mounting and move it to one side (see illustrations).

4 Undo the retaining bolt, then twist the washer reservoir filler neck to remove it from engine compartment (see illustration).

5 Undo the retaining bolts and nut, then remove the fuel filter from the engine mounting and move it to one side (see illustrations). The fuel hoses do not need to be disconnected from the filter.

6 To make access easier, undo the retaining bolt, disconnect the wiring connector and move the coolant reservoir to one side (see illustration).

6.5a Undo the filter retaining bolts/nut...

6.5b ... and release the fuel pipe retaining clip

6.6 Move the coolant reservoir to one side

6.7 Disconnect the temperature sensor wiring connector

6.8a Release the rear lower clip...

6.8b ... the two upper front clips...

6.8c ...and manoeuvre the upper cover from place

6.12a Undo the lower cover retaining bolts

6.12b ...and manoeuvre the lower cover from place

7 Disconnect the radiator outlet temperature sensor wiring plug **(see illustration)**.

8 Release the 3 clips and remove the timing belt upper cover **(see illustrations)**.

9 Refitting is a reversal of removal, noting that the lower edge of the upper cover engages with the lower cover.

Lower outer cover

10 Remove the upper cover as described previously.

11 If not already done, remove the crankshaft pulley as described in Section 5.

12 Unscrew the five bolts securing the lower cover, and remove it **(see illustrations)**.

13 Refitting is a reversal of removal; noting that the upper edge of the lower cover engages with the upper cover.

Rear cover

14 Remove the timing belt, tensioner and sprockets as described in Section 7 and Section 8.

15 Undo the retaining bolt and remove the rear hub cover from the end of the camshaft.

16 Slacken and withdraw the retaining bolts and lift the timing belt inner cover from the studs on the end of the engine, and remove it from the engine compartment **(see illustrations)**. It may be required to remove the coolant pump (Chapter 3 Section 7), before the rear cover can be removed.

17 Refitting is a reversal of removal.

6.16a Remove the retaining bolts...

6.16b ...and remove the rear cover

7.0 Two types of tensioner type (A) and (B)

A Roller tensions clockwise
B Roller tensions anti-clockwise

7.4 Slacken the sprocket-to-hub bolts

7.6 Insert an Allen key, slacken the nut, and rotate the hub anti-clockwise until a 2 mm rod/drill bit can be inserted to lock the hub to the pulley

7 Timing belt – removal, inspection and refitting

Note: It is consider best practise to always replace the tensioner, idler and coolant pump whenever the timing belt is replaced. Any mounting studs should also be replaced at the same time. Most of the components (apart from the coolant pump) will be supplied with a timing belt kit. Note also that most manufactures will not guarantee a belt against premature failure if the idler(s) and tensioner are not replaced with the belt.

Note: There are two types of tensioner fitted to this engine (see illustration). Check to see which type is fitted before removing the timing belt. Type A tensioner requires a locking pin for installation and it tensions the belt by rotating clockwise. Type B tensioner does not require a locking pin for installation and it tensions the belt by rotating anti-clockwise. See text.

Removal

1 The primary function of the toothed timing belt is to drive the camshaft, but it also drives the coolant pump and high-pressure fuel pump. Should the belt slip or break in service, the valve timing will be disturbed and piston-to-valve contact may occur, resulting in serious engine damage. For this reason, it is important that the timing belt is tensioned

correctly, and inspected regularly for signs of wear or deterioration.
2 Switch off the ignition and all electrical consumers and remove the ignition key.
3 Set the engine to TDC on No. 1 cylinder as described in Section 3.
4 Slacken the three bolts securing the sprocket to the camshaft hub by 90° **(see illustration)**.
5 Slacken the three bolts securing the sprocket to the high-pressure fuel pump by 90° **(see illustration)**.

Type A tensioner

6 Insert a suitable Allen key into the tensioner hub, then slacken the retaining nut and rotate the tensioner hub anti-clockwise until it can be locked in place using a 2.0 mm pin/drill bit **(see illustration)**.
7 Leaving the pin in place, now rotate the tensioner hub clockwise to the stop, and hand-tighten the retaining nut **(see illustration)**.

Type B tensioner

8 Insert a suitable Allen key into the tensioner hub, then slacken the retaining nut and rotate the tensioner hub clockwise, until the tensioner hub is loosened. When in position hand-tighten the retaining nut.

All engines

9 If the original timing belt is to be refitted, mark the running direction of the belt, to ensure correct refitting.
Caution: If the belt appears to be in good condition and can be re-used, it is essential that it is refitted the same way around, otherwise accelerated wear will result, leading to premature failure.
10 Slide the belt from the sprockets, taking care not to twist or kink the belt excessively if it is to be re-used.

Inspection

11 Examine the belt for evidence of contamination by coolant or lubricant. If this is the case, find the source of the contamination before progressing any further. Check the belt for signs of wear or damage, particularly around the leading edges of the belt teeth. Renew the belt if its condition is in doubt; the cost of belt renewal is negligible compared with potential cost of the engine repairs, should the belt fail in service. The belt must be renewed if it has covered the mileage given in Chapter 1, however, if it has covered less, it is prudent to renew it regardless of condition, as a precautionary measure.
12 If the timing belt is not going to be refitted for some time, it is a wise precaution to hang a warning label on the steering wheel, to remind yourself (and others) not to attempt to start the engine. Have the battery disconnected to prevent any engine damage.
13 If the tensioner roller is to be renewed, the engine mounting will also need to be removed, as described in Section 16. Then the tensioner removed as described in Section 8.

7.5 Slacken the high-pressure fuel pump sprocket bolts

7.7 Rotate the tensioner hub clockwise until it hits the stop

7.16 Rotate the high-pressure fuel pump clockwise until a 6 mm drill bit/rod can be inserted into the housing and hub

7.17a Rotate the sprockets fully clockwise until the fuel pump sprocket...

7.17b ...and camshaft sprocket bolts are at the end of the elongated holes

Refitting

14 Ensure that the crankshaft and camshaft are still set to TDC on No 1 cylinder, as described in Section 3. The camshaft sprocket bolts should be renewed, and slackened at this point.

15 Renew the high-pressure fuel pump sprocket bolts one at a time. They should also be slackened.

16 Using a screwdriver on the bolts heads, rotate the high-pressure fuel pump clockwise until a 6.0 mm locking pin/drill bit can be inserted into the housing adjacent to the sprocket, locking the pump in place **(see illustration)**.

17 Rotate the camshaft sprocket and high-pressure fuel pump sprocket fully clockwise so that the securing bolts are at the end of the elongated holes **(see illustrations)**.

18 Loop the timing belt loosely under the crankshaft sprocket. **Note:** *Observe any direction of rotation markings on the belt.*

19 Fit the belt around the tensioner pulley, engage the timing belt teeth with the camshaft sprockets, then manoeuvre it into position around the coolant pump sprocket and the fuel pump sprocket. Make sure that the belt teeth seat correctly on the sprockets. **Note:** *Slight adjustment to the position of the camshaft sprocket may be necessary to achieve this. Avoid bending the belt back on itself or twisting it excessively as you do this.*

20 Finally, fit the belt around the idler roller **(see illustration)**. Ensure that any slack in the belt is in the section of belt that passes over the tensioner roller.

Type A tensioner

21 Loosen the timing belt tensioner securing nut, and pull out the tensioner locking pin. Turn

the tensioner clockwise with an Allen key until the pointer is just past the middle of the gap in the tensioner base plate **(see illustrations)**. With the tensioner held in this position, tighten the securing nut to the specified torque and angle.

Type B tensioner

22 Loosen the timing belt tensioner securing nut, and turn the tensioner anti-clockwise with an Allen key until the pointer is just past the middle of the gap in the tensioner base plate **(see illustration)**. With the tensioner held in this position, tighten the securing nut to the specified torque and angle.

All engines

23 Counterhold the camshaft sprocket and fuel pump sprocket with a home made tool to prevent any rotation, and then tighten the camshaft sprocket and fuel pump sprocket bolts to 20 Nm **(see illustrations)**.

7.20 Timing belt routing

7.21a Rotate the tensioner clockwise ...

7.21b ...until the pointer is just past the gap in the base plate

7.22 Turn the tensioner anti-clockwise and secure the retaining nut (1)

7.23a Counterhold the camshaft sprocket ...

7.23b ... and the pump sprocket, while the bolts are tightened

7.24a Remove the upper locking pins ...

7.24b ... and crankshaft locking tool

7.26 Check the pointer (arrowed) is centred or within 5mm to the right of the gap in the base plate

7.27 Slight misalignment of the pump sprocket timing hole is acceptable

24 Remove the sprockets' locking tools and the crankshaft locking tool **(see illustrations)**.
25 Using a spanner or wrench and socket on the crankshaft pulley centre bolt, rotate the crankshaft clockwise through two complete revolutions. Reset the engine to TDC on No.1 cylinder, with reference to Section 3 and refit the crankshaft locking tool.
26 Check that the tensioner roller indicator arm is centred, or within a maximum of 5 mm to the right of the notch in the base plate **(see illustration)**. If not, hold the tensioner hub stationary with an Allen key, slacken the retaining nut and position the arm in the centre of the notch. Tighten the retaining nut to the specified torque. Remove the Allen key.
27 Check that the camshaft sprocket locking pin can still be inserted. **Note:** *It's very difficult*

to align the locking point of the fuel pump hub again **(see illustration)**. However, a slight misalignment of holes will not affect engine performance.
28 If the camshaft sprocket locking pin cannot be inserted, pull the crankshaft locking tool slight away from the engine, and rotate the crankshaft anti-clockwise slightly past TDC. Now slowly rotate the crankshaft clockwise until the camshaft sprocket locking tool can be inserted.
29 If the locating pin of the crankshaft locking tool is to the left of the corresponding hole, slacken the camshaft sprocket bolts, slowly rotate the crankshaft clockwise until the locking tool can be fully inserted. Tighten the camshaft sprocket bolts to 20 Nm.
30 If the locating pin of the crankshaft locking

tool is to the right of the corresponding hole, slacken the camshaft sprocket bolts, rotate the crankshaft anti-clockwise slightly until the pin is to the left of the hole, then slowly rotate it clockwise until the lock tool can be fully inserted. Tighten the camshaft sprocket bolts to 20 Nm.
31 Remove the crankshaft and camshaft locking tools, then rotate the crankshaft 2 complete revolutions clockwise and check the locking tools can be reinserted. If necessary, repeat the adjustment procedure described previously.
32 Tighten the camshaft and fuel pump sprocket bolts to the specified torque and angles.
33 The remainder of refitting is a reversal of removal.

8 Timing belt tensioner and sprockets – removal and refitting

Timing belt tensioner

Removal

1 In order to remove the timing belt tensioner, the engine mounting bracket must first be removed. Either support the engine from above using a crossbeam or an engine hoist or support if from underneath with a trolley jack and block of wood.
2 Remove the timing belt as described in Section 7.
3 Undo the bolts and remove the right-hand engine mounting.
4 Undo the bolt securing the coolant pipe to the mounting bracket **(see illustration)**.
5 Working in the wheelarch area, undo the nut securing the lower end of the coolant pipe.
6 Undo the 3 retaining bolts and remove the engine mounting bracket **(see illustration)**.
7 Unscrew the timing belt tensioner nut, and remove the tensioner from the engine.

Refitting

8 When refitting the tensioner to the engine, ensure that the lug on the tensioner backplate engages with the corresponding cut-out in the rear timing belt cover, then refit the tensioner nut **(see illustration)**.

8.4 Coolant pipe upper mounting bolt and lower mounting nut

8.6 Engine mounting bracket bolts

8.8 Ensure the lug on the backplate engages with the cut-out in the timing belt cover

8.11 Timing belt idler pulleys

8.17 Using a puller to remove the crankshaft sprocket

8.27 Fabricate a home made tool to counterhold the hub. Undo the bolt...

9 The remainder of refitting is a reversal of removal.

Idler pulleys

Removal

10 Remove the timing belt as described in Section 7.
11 Unscrew the relevant idler pulley/roller securing bolt/nut, and then withdraw the pulley **(see illustration)**.

Refitting

12 Refit the pulley and tighten the securing bolt or nut to the specified torque. Note: Renew the large roller/pulley retaining bolt (where applicable).
13 Refit and tension the timing belt as described in Section 7.

Crankshaft sprocket

Note: *A new crankshaft sprocket securing bolt must be used on refitting.*

Removal

14 Remove the timing belt as described in Section 7.
15 The sprocket securing bolt must now be slackened, and the crankshaft must be prevented from turning as the sprocket bolt is unscrewed. To hold the sprocket, make up a suitable tool, and screw it to the sprocket using a two bolts screwed into two of the crankshaft pulley bolt holes.
16 Hold the sprocket using the tool, then slacken the sprocket securing bolt. Take care, as the bolt is very tight. Do not allow the crankshaft to turn as the bolt is slackened.
17 Unscrew the bolt, and slide the sprocket from the end of the crankshaft, noting which way round the sprocket's raised boss is fitted. If required, use a puller to withdraw the sprocket from the end of the crankshaft **(see illustration)**.

Refitting

18 Commence refitting by positioning the sprocket on the end of the crankshaft.
19 Fit a new sprocket securing bolt, then counterhold the sprocket using the method employed on removal, and tighten the bolt to the specified torque in the two stages given in the Specifications.

20 Refit the timing belt as described in Section 7.

Camshaft sprocket

Removal

21 Remove the timing belt as described in Section 7, then rotate the crankshaft 90° anti-clockwise to prevent any accidental piston-to-valve contact.
22 Unscrew and remove the three retaining bolts and remove the camshaft sprocket from the camshaft hub.

Refitting

23 Refit the sprocket ensuring that it is fitted the correct way round, as noted before removal, then insert the new sprocket bolts, and tighten by hand only at this stage.
24 If the crankshaft has been turned, turn the crankshaft clockwise 90° back to TDC.
25 Refit and tension the timing belt as described in Section 7.

Camshaft hub

Note: *VAG technicians use special tool T10051 to counterhold the hub, however it is possible to fabricate a suitable alternative.*

Removal

26 Remove the camshaft sprocket as described previously in this Section.
27 Engage special tool T10051 with the three locating holes in the face of the hub to prevent the hub from turning. If this tool is not available, fabricate a suitable alternative.

Whilst holding the tool, undo the central hub retaining bolt about two turns **(see illustration)**.
28 Slide the hub from the camshaft. If necessary, attach VW tool T10052 (or a similar three-legged puller) to the hub, and evenly tighten the puller until the hub is free of the camshaft taper **(see illustration)**.

Refitting

29 Ensure that the camshaft taper and the hub centre is clean and dry, locate the hub on the taper, noting that the built-in key in the hub taper must align with the keyway in the camshaft taper **(see illustration)**.
30 Hold the hub in this position with tool T10051 (or similar home-made tool), and tighten the central bolt to the specified torque.
31 Refit the camshaft sprocket as described previously in this Section.

Coolant pump sprocket

32 The coolant pump sprocket is integral with the coolant pump. Refer to Chapter 3 for details of coolant pump removal.

9   Camshaft and hydraulic tappets – removal, inspection and refitting

Note: *A new camshaft oil seal(s) will be required on refitting. VW removal tool T40094 (or similar tool) will be required to refit the camshafts – this is necessary to prevent*

8.28 ...and slide the hub from the camshaft

8.29 Ensure the integral key aligns with the keyway in the camshaft

9.4a Using flat metal bar and cable ties to secure the camshafts ...

9.4b ... to the upper ladder frame for removal

9.7 Make alignment marks for the position of the sprockets

damage to the retaining frame and cylinder head as the camshafts are refitted.

Removal

1 With the timing set at TDC, remove the camshaft hub (see Section 8).

2 Remove the camshaft cover (see Section 4).

3 Remove the brake vacuum pump as described in Chapter 9, Section 21.

4 If the camshafts are not going to be renewed, use two flat pieces of metal flat bar and cable ties and secure the two camshafts to the retaining frame **(see illustrations)**. Progressively unscrew the camshaft retaining frame bolts in the reverse of the sequence shown in illustration 9.27, and carefully remove the retaining frame, complete with camshafts. Remove the oil seal from the end of the camshaft and discard it – a new one will be required for refitting.

5 If the camshafts are going to be renewed, progressively unscrew the camshaft retaining frame bolts in the reverse of the sequence shown in illustration 9.27, and carefully remove the retaining frame. Then carefully lift the camshafts from the cylinder head, keeping them identified for location. Remove the oil seal from the end of the camshaft and discard it – a new one will be required for refitting.

6 Lift the rocker arms and hydraulic tappets from place. Store the rockers and tappets in a container with numbered compartments to ensure they are refitted to their correct locations. It is recommended that the tappets are kept immersed in oil for the period they are removed from the cylinder head.

Inspection

7 If the camshafts are still secured to the retaining frame, mark the two sprockets in relation with each other, then cut the cable ties to remove them from the frame **(see illustration)**. With the camshafts removed, examine the retaining frame and the bearing locations in the cylinder head for signs of obvious wear or pitting. If evident, a new cylinder head will probably be required. Also check that the oil supply holes in the cylinder head are free from obstructions.

8 Visually inspect the camshafts for evidence of wear on the surfaces of the lobes and journals. Normally their surfaces should be smooth and have a dull shine; look for scoring, erosion or pitting and areas that appear highly polished, indicating excessive wear. Accelerated wear will occur once the hardened exterior of the camshaft has been damaged, so always renew worn items. Note: If these symptoms are visible on the tips of the camshaft lobes, check the corresponding rocker arm, as it will probably be worn as well.

9 If the machined surfaces of the camshaft appear discoloured or blued, it is likely that it has been overheated at some point, probably due to inadequate lubrication. This may have distorted the shaft, so have the camshaft runout and endfloat checked by an automotive engine reconditioning specialist.

10 Inspect the hydraulic tappets for obvious signs of wear or damage **(see illustration)**, and renew if necessary. Check that the oil holes in the tappets are free from obstructions.

9.10 Check the tappets for wear

9.12 VW special tool no. T40094 shown

Refitting

11 Oil the rocker arms and hydraulic tappets, and then refit them to their original positions.

 Warning: After fitting hydraulic tappets, wait a minimum of 30 minutes (or preferably, leave overnight) before starting the engine; to allow the tappets time to settle, otherwise the valve heads will strike the pistons.

Using VW special tool No.T40094

12 If the camshafts were removed from the retaining frame, use the VW special tool No.T40094, as shown in the following procedures **(see illustration)**.

13 Position the inlet camshaft as shown with the cylinder head bolt indents facing outwards, then slide the end support into the slot in the end of the camshaft **(see illustrations)**.

9.13a Position the inlet camshaft on the tool with the head bolt indent facing outwards ...

9.13b ...then slide the end of the special tool, in to the slot in the end of the camshaft

9.14a Position the exhaust camshaft on the tool with the head bolt indent facing outwards …

9.14b … then fit special tool clamp into the slot in the end of the exhaust camshaft

9.15 Tighten the thumbwheel to align the gear teeth. Ensure the clamping jaw with the arrow is seated on the wider gear

9.16 Slide the exhaust camshaft to the inlet camshaft until the teeth are in mesh

9.17a Lubricate the bearing mountings …

9.17b …and fit the upper ladder frame to the camshafts

14 Position the exhaust camshaft on the supports, again with the cylinder head bolt indents facing outwards, and then fit the locating clamp into the slot in the end of the camshaft **(see illustrations)**.

15 Fit the VW clamping tool No.T40096 to the double gear on the exhaust camshaft, tightening the knurled thumb wheel until the faces of the gear teeth are in alignment **(see illustration)**. Note some camshafts only have a single sprocket, so will not require this procedure.

16 Slide the exhaust camshaft towards the inlet camshaft until the gear teeth engage **(see illustration)**.

17 Ensure the gasket faces of the retaining frame are clean, then apply a smear of clean engine oil to the bearing surfaces and lower the frame into position over the camshafts **(see illustrations)**. Ensure the bearing surfaces locate correctly on the camshafts.

18 Fit the clamping tool No.T40095 over the camshafts and frame, and tighten the thumbwheels to hold the camshafts in position in the frame **(see illustration)**.

19 Slide out locking clamps from each end of the camshafts **(see illustrations)**, and then lift the camshafts, retaining frame and clamping tool from the VW special tool no. 40094.

Without VW special tool

20 Ensure the gasket faces of the retaining frame are clean, then apply a smear of clean engine oil to the bearing surfaces and turn it upside down on a clean surface.

21 Position the camshafts on the retaining frame with the cylinder head bolt indents facing outwards. Align the marks made on the camshaft sprockets on removal **(see illustration 9.7)**.

22 If a double gear is fitted to the exhaust camshaft, fit the VW clamping tool No.T40096 (or similar) to align the faces of the teeth. If the VW clamping tool is not available use two flat bladed screwdrivers and a pair of pliers, this

9.18 Secure the camshafts in place in the frame using tool No. T40095

9.19a Slide the locking tool out from the end of the inlet camshaft …

9.19b … and remove the locking clamp from the end of the exhaust camshaft

9.22a VW special tool for aligning teeth on sprocket

9.22b Using two flat bladed screwdrivers and a pair of pliers to align teeth

9.23a Inlet camshaft slot needs to be horizontal

9.23b Slot in end of exhaust camshaft should be at the 12 o'clock position

9.24 Camshafts are secured to the ladder frame with two pieces of flat bar and cable ties

9.25a Apply a 2.0 mm thick bead of sealant …

will need an assistant to keep firm pressure on the camshafts to make sure they locate in the retaining frame correctly **(see illustrations)**. Note some camshafts only have a single sprocket, so will not require this procedure.

23 With the marks on the sprockets aligned and the cylinder head bolt indents facing outwards, the slot in the end of the inlet camshaft (that drives the vacuum pump) should be horizontal and the slot in the end of the exhaust camshaft (that locates the timing belt sprocket) should be at the top when fitted **(see illustrations)**.

24 With the camshafts correctly in position, ensuring the camshafts locate correctly in the bearing surfaces on the retaining frame, use two flat pieces of metal flat bar and cable ties to secure them in position **(see illustration)**.

Caution: Make sure the camshafts are located correctly in the bearing surfaces on the retaining frame, otherwise damage can occur, and this could damage the retaining frame when tightening down onto the cylinder head. The retaining frame is matched to the cylinder head and can only be purchased with a new cylinder head. If there is any doubt, then the VW special tool should be used – see previous refitting procedure.

All

25 Ensure the sealing surfaces of the cylinder head are clean, and then apply a 2.0 mm wide bead of sealant (D 176 501 A1 or equivalent) as shown. Take care not to apply too much

9.25b … to the area shown by the grey line, taking care not to block the oil holes

sealant, ensuring the oil holes supply holes are not blocked **(see illustrations)**.

26 Fit a new sealing cap to the timing belt end of the cylinder head and make sure the

locating dowels are fitted to the cylinder head **(see illustrations)**.

27 Apply a smear of clean engine oil to the bearing surfaces and place the camshafts,

9.26a Fit a new seal/end cap to the cylinder head

9.26b Check that the locating dowels are in place

9.27 Camshaft retaining frame bolt tightening sequence

9.28 Remove the cable ties and flat bar from the top of the ladder frame

frame and clamping tool in place on the cylinder head. Progressively, carefully, hand tighten the frame retaining bolts in the sequence shown **(see illustration)**, until the retaining frame makes contact with the cylinder head over the complete surface, then tighten the bolts to the specified torque, again in the correct sequence.

28 Remove the gear aligning tool (T40096) and the clamping tool (T40095), or the metal flat bars and cable ties from the top of the camshaft retaining frame **(see illustration)**.

29 Renew the camshaft oil seal as described in Section 10.

30 The remainder of refitting is a reversal of removal.

10 Camshaft oil seals – renewal

Right-hand oil seal

1 Remove the camshaft sprocket and hub, as described in Section 8.

2 Drill two small holes into the existing oil seal, diagonally opposite each other. Take great care to avoid drilling through into the seal housing or camshaft sealing surface. Thread two self-tapping screws into the holes, and using a pair of pliers, pull on the heads of the screws to extract the oil seal **(see illustration)**.

3 Clean out the seal housing and the sealing surface of the camshaft by wiping it with a lint-free cloth. Remove any swarf or burrs that may cause the seal to leak.

4 Do not lubricate the lip and outer edge of the new oil seal, push it over the camshaft until it is positioned in place above its housing. To prevent damage to the sealing lips, wrap some adhesive tape around the end of the camshaft **(see illustration)**.

5 Using a hammer and a socket of suitable diameter, drive the seal squarely into its housing. Make sure the seal is fitted the correct way around, some have 'OUTSIDE' stamped on the seal **(see illustration)**. Note: Select a socket that bears only on the hard outer surface of the seal, not the inner lip that can easily be damaged.

6 Refit the camshaft sprocket and its hub, as described in Section 8.

Left-hand oil seal

7 The left-hand camshaft oil seal is formed by the brake vacuum pump seal. Refer to Chapter 9, Section 21, for details of brake vacuum pump removal and refitting.

11 Cylinder head – removal, inspection and refitting

Note: The cylinder head must be removed with the engine cold. New cylinder head bolts and a new cylinder head gasket will be required on refitting, and suitable studs will be required to guide the cylinder head into position – see text.

10.2 Screw in a self-tapping screw, then pull the screw and seal from place

10.5 Note some seals have 'OUTSIDE' to show fitted position

Removal

1 Remove the battery as described in Chapter 5A Section 3.

2 Drain the cooling system (Chapter 1 Section 32) and engine oil (Chapter 1 Section 6).

3 Pull the plastic cover on the top of the engine upwards to release it from its mountings.

4 Remove the air filter housing as described in Chapter Section.

5 Undo the bolts and remove the battery tray **(see illustration)**.

6 Remove the radiator cooling fan(s) and shroud as described in Chapter 3 Section 5.

7 Undo the bolts and remove the air hose/duct from the intercooler to the turbocharger. Release the wiring looms from the clips as necessary to enable the duct to be manoeuvred from place.

10.4 Using a plastic sleeve to slide seal over end of camshaft

11.5 Battery tray securing bolts

11.11 Remove the charge air pipe from the turbocharger

11.14 Disconnect the vacuum pipe

11.19a Disconnect the oil pressure switch wiring connector

11.19b Undo the retaining bolt/screw and remove the lifting bracket

8 Remove the camshaft cover as described in Section 4.

9 Remove the camshaft sprocket and hub as described in Section 8.

10 Remove the inlet manifold as described in Chapter Section.

11 Undo the retaining bolts, and remove the charge air pipe from the turbocharger **(see illustration)**.

12 Remove the EGR pipes from the cylinder head as described in Chapter 4B Section 3.

13 Remove the exhaust manifold as described in Chapter 4B Section 5. There is no need to completely remove the particulate filter from the vehicle. Slacken the Allen bolt and release the clamp securing the diesel particulate filter/catalytic converter to the turbocharger, then undo the bolts/nuts securing the brackets to the cylinder block/head and lay the filter/converter to one side.

14 Apply a little lubrication spray to the rubber sleeve, pull up the pipe from the vacuum pump, then undo the 4 retaining bolts and remove the vacuum pump from the left-hand end of the cylinder head **(see illustration)**. Renew the pump-to-cylinder head seal/gasket (Chapter 9 Section 21).

15 Disconnect the coolant temperature sensor wiring plug at the left-hand end of the cylinder head, and release the wiring loom from any retaining clips.

16 Disconnect the gearchange cables from the levers on the transmission as described in Chapter 7A Section 2 7A,2 (manual transmission) or (DSG transmission).

17 Undo the bolts/nut, securing the gearchange bracket to the top of the transmission. Move the bracket and cables to one side.

18 Note their fitted locations, then release the clamps and disconnect the various coolant hoses from the cylinder head.

19 Disconnect the wiring connector from the oil pressure switch, undo the bolt securing the pipe bracket at the left-hand end of the cylinder head **(see illustrations)**, and the bolt securing the lifting bracket on the rear of the head.

20 Undo the bolt securing the timing belt guard adjacent to the timing belt tensioner, and the bolt securing the camshaft position sensor, then remove the tensioner retaining nut **(see illustration)**.

21 Using an M12 multi-splined tool (12 pointed star), undo the cylinder head bolts, working from the outside-in, evenly and gradually **(see illustration)**. Remove the bolts and recover the washers. Check that nothing remains connected, and starting at the gearbox side, lift the cylinder head from the engine block, sliding the belt tensioner from the mounting stud as the cylinder head is removed. Seek assistance if possible, as it is a heavy assembly, especially as it is being removed complete with the manifolds.

22 Remove the gasket from the top of the block, noting the locating dowels. If the dowels are a loose fit, remove them and store them with the head for safekeeping. Do not discard the gasket yet – it will be needed for identification purposes.

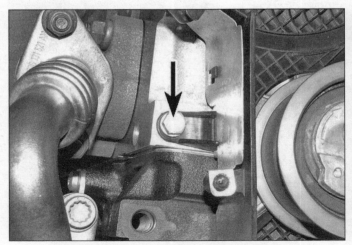

11.20 Undo the bolt securing the timing belt guard

11.21 Undo the cylinder head bolts using a M12 multi-splined (12 pointed star) tool

11.24 The holes identify the thickness of the cylinder head gasket

11.27 Measure the piston protrusion using a DTI gauge

11.39 Ensure the dowels are in place, then fit the new gasket with the part number uppermost

Inspection

23 Dismantling and inspection of the cylinder head is covered in Chapter 2D.

Cylinder head gasket selection

Note: *A dial test indicator (DTI) will be required for this operation.*

24 Examine the old cylinder head gasket for manufacturer's identification markings **(see illustration)**. These will be in the form of holes, and a part number on the edge of the gasket. Unless new pistons have been fitted, the new cylinder head gasket must be of the same size as the old one.

25 If new piston assemblies have been fitted as part of an engine overhaul, or if a new short engine is to be fitted, the projection of the piston crowns above the cylinder head mating face of the cylinder block at TDC must be measured. This measurement is used to determine the thickness of the new cylinder head gasket required.

26 Anchor a dial test indicator (DTI) to the top face (cylinder head gasket mating face) of the cylinder block, and zero the gauge on the gasket mating face.

27 Rest the gauge probe on No 1 piston crown, and turn the crankshaft slowly by hand until the piston reaches TDC. Measure and record the maximum piston projection at TDC **(see illustration)**.

28 Repeat the measurement for the remaining pistons, and record the results.

29 If the measurements differ from piston-to-piston, take the highest figure, and use this to determine the thickness of the head gasket required as follows.

Piston projection	Gasket identification (number of holes)
0.91 to 1.00 mm	1
1.01 to 1.10 mm	2
1.11 to 1.20 mm	3

30 Purchase a new gasket according to the results of the measurements.

Refitting

31 The mating faces of the cylinder head and block must be perfectly clean before refitting the head. Use a scraper to remove all traces of gasket and carbon, also clean the tops of the pistons. Take particular care with the aluminium surfaces, as the soft metal is easily damaged.

32 Make sure that debris is not allowed to enter the oil and water passages – this is particularly important for the oil circuit, as carbon could block the oil supply to the camshaft and crankshaft bearings. Using adhesive tape and paper, seal the water, oil and bolt holes in the cylinder block.

33 To prevent carbon entering the gap between the pistons and bores, smear a little grease in the gap. After cleaning a piston, rotate the crankshaft to that the piston moves down the bore, and then wipe out the grease and carbon with a cloth rag. Clean the other piston crowns in the same way.

34 Check the head and block for nicks, deep scratches and other damage. If slight, they may be removed carefully with a file. More serious damage may be repaired by machining, but this is a specialist job.

35 If warpage of the cylinder head is suspected, use a straight-edge to check it for distortion, as described in Chapter 2D Section 7.

36 Ensure that the cylinder head bolt holes in the crankcase are clean and free of oil. Syringe or soak up any oil left in the bolt holes. This is most important in order that the correct bolt tightening torque can be applied,

and to prevent the possibility of the block being cracked by hydraulic pressure when the bolts are tightened.

37 Turn the crankshaft anti-clockwise all the pistons at an equal height, approximately half-way down their bores from the TDC position (see Section 3). This will eliminate any risk of piston-to-valve contact as the cylinder head is refitted.

38 Where applicable, refit the manifolds with reference to Chapter 4A Section 6 and Chapter 4B Section 5.

39 Ensure that the cylinder head locating dowels are in place in the cylinder block, and then fit the new cylinder head gasket over the dowels, ensuring that the part number is uppermost **(see illustration)**. Note that VW recommend that the gasket is only removed from its packaging immediately prior to fitting.

40 Lower the cylinder head into position on the gasket, ensuring that it engages correctly over the dowels. Refit the timing belt tensioner as the cylinder head is refitted.

41 Fit the washers in place then fit the new cylinder head bolts to the locations, and screw them in as far as possible by hand. Do not oil the bolt threads.

42 Working progressively, in sequence, tighten all the cylinder head bolts to the specified Stage 1 torque **(see illustrations)**.

43 Again working progressively, in sequence, tighten all the cylinder head bolts to the specified Stage 2 torque.

44 Tighten all the cylinder head bolts, in

11.42a Cylinder head bolt tightening sequence

11.42b Tighten the cylinder head bolts to the Stage 1 torque

11.44 Use an angle-tightening gauge

12.4 Slacken the two retaining clips

sequence, through the specified Stage 3 angle **(see illustration)**.

45 Finally, tighten all the cylinder head bolts, in sequence, through the specified Stage 4 angle.

46 The remainder of the refitting procedure is a reversal of the removal procedure, noting the following points:

a) *Tighten all fasteners to their specified torque where given.*

b) *Renew all seals and gaskets.*

c) *Refill the cooling system as described, in Chapter 1, Section 32.*

d) *Refill the engine oil, as described in Chapter 1, Section 6.*

e) *Ensure all wiring is correctly routed.*

f) *Run the vehicle and make sure the cooling fans operate when the engine gets up to temperature.*

12 Sump – removal and refitting

Removal

1 Apply the handbrake, then jack up the front of the vehicle and support securely on axle stands (see *Jacking and vehicle support*).

2 Remove the securing screws and withdraw the engine undershield(s).

3 Drain the engine oil as described in Chapter 1, Section 6.

4 Release the retaining clips and remove the air hose from the intercooler outlet to the charge air pipe **(see illustration)**.

5 Undo the retaining bolts, release the clamp and move the charger air pipe from the front of the cylinder block **(see illustrations)**. Disconnect the charger air pressure sensor wiring plug.

6 Disconnect the wiring connector from the oil level/temperature sender in the sump.

7 Release the retaining clips and (where fitted) remove the sump insulation cover from the sump **(see illustrations)**.

8 Unscrew and remove the bolts securing

12.5a Undo the retaining bolt on the end of the sump…

12.5b …and the bolt on the front of the cylinder block …

12.5c …then disconnect the pressure switch wiring connector

12.7a Release the two clips at the rear of the sump

12.7b At the front, prise down the centre pin and pull the clip downwards

12.7c Remove the insulation cover from the around the sump

12.8a Undo the three transmission to sump bolts…

12.8b … and also the four bolts at the transmission end of the sump

12.8c Lower the sump from the cylinder block

the sump to the cylinder block, and the bolts securing the sump to the transmission casing, then withdraw the sump (see illustrations). If necessary, release the sump by tapping with a soft-faced hammer.

Refitting

9 Begin refitting by thoroughly cleaning the mating faces of the sump and cylinder block. Ensure that all traces of old sealant are removed.
10 Ensure that the cylinder block mating face of the sump is free from all traces of old sealant, oil and grease, and then apply a 2.0 to 3.0 mm thick bead of silicone sealant (VW D 176 404 A2 or equivalent) to the sump (see illustration). Note that the sealant should be run around the inside of the bolt holes in the sump. The sump must be fitted within 5 minutes of applying the sealant.
11 Offer the sump up to the cylinder block, then refit the sump-to-cylinder block bolts, and lightly tighten them by hand, working progressively in a diagonal sequence. Note: If the sump is being refitted with the engine and transmission separated, make sure that the sump is flush with the flywheel end of the cylinder block.
12 Refit the sump-to-transmission casing bolts, and tighten them lightly, using a socket.
13 Again working in a diagonal sequence, lightly tighten the sump-to-cylinder block bolts, using a socket.
14 Tighten the sump-to-transmission casing bolts to the specified torque.

15 Working in a diagonal sequence, progressively tighten the sump-to-cylinder block bolts to the specified torque.
16 The remainder of refitting is a reversal of removal, noting to allow at least 30 minutes from the time of refitting the sump for the sealant to dry, then refill the engine with oil, with reference to Chapter 1, Section 6.

13 Oil pump and drive belt
– removal, inspection and refitting

Oil pump removal

1 Remove the sump as described in Section 12.
2 Unscrew the flange bolts and remove the oil pick-up pipe/filter from the oil pump (see illustration). Recover the O-ring seal and discard, as a new one will be required for refitting.
3 Unscrew the securing bolt, and remove the oil baffle from the cylinder block (see illustration).
4 Unscrew and remove the mounting bolts, and release the oil pump from the dowels in the crankcase (see illustration). Unhook the oil pump drive sprocket from the belt and withdraw the oil pump and oil pick-up pipe from the engine. Note, the bolt holding the baffle plate is also one of the pump mounting bolts.

12.10 Apply a bead of sealant around the inside of the bolt holes

Oil pump inspection

5 Clean the pump thoroughly, and inspect for signs of damage or wear. If evident, renew the oil pump.

13.2 Remove the oil pick-up pipe/filter

13.3 Remove the oil baffle plate bolt (which is also one of the oil pump mounting bolts)

13.4 Oil pump mounting bolts

13.11 Fit a new seal to the end of the oil pick-up pipe

14.3 Flywheel bolts are offset and can only be fitted in one position – DSG transmission shown

14.5 Use a locking tool to counterhold the flywheel

Oil pump refitting

6 Prime the pump with oil by pouring oil into the pick-up pipe aperture while turning the driveshaft.

7 If the drive belt and crankshaft sprocket have been removed, delay refitting them until after the oil pump has been mounted on the cylinder block.

8 Engage the oil pump sprocket with the drive belt, and then locate the oil pump on the dowels. Refit and tighten the mounting bolts to the specified torque.

9 Where applicable, refit the drive belt and crankshaft sprocket using a reversal of the removal procedure.

10 Refit the oil baffle plate, and tighten the securing bolt.

11 Refit the pick-up pipe to the oil pump, using a new O-ring seal, and tighten the securing bolts **(see illustration)**.

12 Refit the sump as described in Section 12.

Oil pump drive belt and sprockets

Note: *VW sealant (D 176 404 A2 or equivalent) will be required to seal the crankshaft oil seal housing on refitting, and it is advisable to fit a new crankshaft oil seal.*

Removal

13 Proceed as described in paragraphs 1 and 2.

14 To remove the belt, remove the timing belt as described in Section 7, then unbolt the crankshaft oil seal housing from the cylinder block, as described in Section 15. Unhook the belt from the sprocket on the end of the crankshaft.

15 The oil pump drive sprocket is a press-fit on the crankshaft, and cannot easily be removed. Consult a VW dealer for advice if the sprocket is worn or damaged.

Inspection

16 It is wise to renew the belt in any case if the engine is to be overhauled, If there is any doubt as to the condition of the belt, renew it.

Refitting

17 If the oil pump has been removed, refit the oil pump as described previously in this Section before refitting the belt and sprocket.

18 Engage the oil pump sprocket with the belt, then engage the belt with the crankshaft sprocket.

19 Fit a new crankshaft oil seal to the housing, and refit the housing as described in Section 15.

20 Where applicable, refit the oil baffle and pick-up pipe, and tighten the securing bolts.

21 Refit the sump as described in Section 12.

14 Flywheel – removal, inspection and refitting

Removal

1 On manual gearbox models, remove the gearbox (see Chapter 7A, Section 3) and clutch (see Chapter 6, Section 6).

2 On semi-automatic (DSG) transmission models, remove the transmission as described in.

3 The flywheel can only be fitted in one position due to the offset of the flywheel mounting holes in the end of the crankshaft **(see illustration)**. **Note:** *manual models are fitted with a dual-mass flywheel.*

4 Rotate the outside of the dual-mass flywheel so that the bolts align with the holes (if necessary).

5 Unscrew the bolts and remove the flywheel. Using a locking tool, counter-hold the flywheel to prevent it from turning **(see illustration)**. Discard the bolts, as new ones must be fitted. Note: In order not to damage the flywheel, do

not allow the bolt heads to make contact with the flywheel during the unscrewing procedure.

Inspection

6 Check the dual-mass flywheel for wear and damage. Examine the starter ring gear for excessive wear to the teeth. If the driveplate or its ring gear are damaged, the complete driveplate must be renewed. The flywheel ring gear, however, may be renewed separately from the flywheel, but the work should be entrusted to a VW dealer. If the clutch friction face is discoloured or scored excessively, it may be possible to regrind it, but this work should also be entrusted to a VW dealer.

7 The following are guidelines only, but should indicate whether professional inspection is necessary. The dual-mass flywheel should be checked as follows:

8 Warpage: Place a straight edge across the face of the drive surface, and check by trying to insert a feeler gauge between the straight edge and the drive surface **(see illustration)**. The flywheel will normally warp like a bowl – ie. Higher on the outer edge. If the warpage is more than 0.40 mm, the flywheel may need replacing.

9 Free rotational movement: This is the distance the drive surface of the flywheel can be turned independently of the flywheel primary element, using finger effort alone. Move the drive surface in one direction and make a mark where the locating pin aligns with the flywheel edge. Move the drive surface in the other direction (finger pressure only) and make another mark **(see illustration)**. The

14.8 Flywheel warpage check – see text

14.9 Flywheel free rotational movement check alignment marks – see text

14.11 Flywheel lateral movement check marks – see text

14.13 Use new bolts when refitting

15.2 Pull the screw and seal from place using pliers

total of free movement should not exceed 20.0 mm. If it's more, the flywheel may need replacing.

10 Total rotational movement: This is the total distance the drive surface can be turned independently of the flywheel primary element. Insert two bolts into the clutch pressure plate/damper unit mounting holes, and with the crankshaft/flywheel held stationary, use a lever/pry bar between the bolts and use some effort to move the drive surface fully in one direction – make a mark where the locating pin aligns with the flywheel edge. Now force the drive surface fully in the opposite direction, and make another mark. The total rotational movement should not exceed 44.00 mm. If it does, have the flywheel professionally inspected.

11 Lateral movement: The lateral movement (up and down) of the drive surface in relation to the primary element of the flywheel, should not exceed 2.0 mm. If it does, the flywheel may need replacing. This can be checked by pressing the drive surface down on one side into the flywheel (flywheel horizontal) and making an alignment mark between the drive surface and the inner edge of the primary element. Now press down on the opposite side of the drive surface, and make another mark above the original one. The difference

between the two marks is the lateral movement **(see illustration)**.

12 There should be no cracks in the drive surface of the flywheel. If cracks are evident, the flywheel may need replacing.

Refitting

13 Refitting is a reversal of removal. Use new bolts when refitting the flywheel or driveplate **(see illustration)**, and coat the threads of the bolts (if not already coated with locking compound) with locking fluid before inserting them. Tighten them to the specified torque.

15 Crankshaft oil seals – renewal

Note: *The oil seals are a PTFE (Teflon) type and are fitted dry, without using any grease or oil. These have a wider sealing lip and have been introduced instead of the coil spring type oil seal.*

Timing belt end oil seal

1 Remove the timing belt as described in Section 7, and the crankshaft sprocket with reference to Section 8.

2 To remove the seal without removing the

housing, drill two small holes diagonally opposite each other, insert self-tapping screws, and pull on the heads of the screws with pliers **(see illustration)**.

3 Alternatively, to remove the oil seal complete with its housing, proceed as follows.

a) *Remove the sump as described in Section 12. This is necessary to ensure a satisfactory seal between the sump and oil seal housing on refitting.*

b) *Unbolt and remove the oil seal housing.*

c) *Working on the bench, lever the oil seal from the housing using a suitable screwdriver. Take care not to damage the seal seating in the housing.*

4 Thoroughly clean the oil seal seating in the housing.

5 Wind a length of tape around the end of the crankshaft (or a plastic sleeve) to protect the oil seal lips as the seal (and housing, where applicable) is fitted **(see illustration)**.

6 Fit a new oil seal to the housing, pressing or driving it into position using a socket or tube of suitable diameter. Ensure that the socket or tube bears only on the hard outer ring of the seal, and take care not to damage the seal lips. Press or drive the seal into position until it is seated on the shoulder in the housing **(see illustration)**. Make sure that the closed end of the seal is facing outwards.

15.5 Using a plastic sleeve to slide the seal over the end of the crankshaft

15.6 Carefully tap the seal into position

15.12a Remove the intermediate plate from the dowels ...

15.12b ... and from behind the top of the crankshaft seal housing

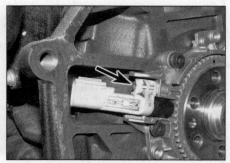

15.13a Undo the crankshaft speed sensor retaining bolt

15.13b Sealing flange bolts

15.14a Screw in three 6 x 35 mm bolts ...

15.14b ...and draw the sealing flange and sender wheel from place

7 If the oil seal housing has been removed, proceed as follows, otherwise proceed to paragraph 11.

8 Clean all traces of old sealant from the crankshaft oil seal housing and the cylinder block, then coat the cylinder block mating faces of the oil seal housing with a 2.0 to 3.0 mm thick bead of silicone sealant (VW D 176 404 A2, or equivalent). Note that the seal housing must be refitted within 5 minutes of applying the sealant.

Caution: DO NOT put excessive amounts of sealant onto the housing as it may get into the sump and block the oil pick-up pipe.

9 Refit the oil seal housing, and tighten the bolts progressively to the specified torque.

10 Refit the sump as described in Section 12.

11 Refit the crankshaft sprocket with reference to Section 8, and the timing belt as described in Section 7.

Flywheel end oil seal

Note: *In these engines, the seal, sealing flange and sender wheel are a complete unit. Special tools are required to refit the sealing flange, and press the sender wheel onto the end of the crankshaft. It is not possible to accurately fit these parts without the tools, which may be available from VW (part no. T10134) and are available from aftermarket automotive tool specialists. E.g. Laser tools).*

12 Remove the flywheel as described in Section 14, then prise the intermediate plate from the locating dowels on the cylinder block and unhook it from behind the top of the seal housing **(see illustrations)**.

13 Undo the bolt securing the crankshaft speed sensor and remove it from the seal housing, then undo the bolts securing the sealing flange to the cylinder block **(see illustrations)**.

14 Insert three 6 x 35 mm bolts into the threaded holes in the sealing flange. Tighten the bolts gradually and evenly, and press the sealing flange, and sender wheel from the crankshaft/cylinder block **(see illustrations)**. The seal, sender wheel and sealing flange are supplied as a complete unit.

15 Ensure the mating face of the cylinder block is clean and free from debris. The new sealing flange/seal/sender wheel assembly is supplied with a sealing lip support ring, which serves as a fitting sleeve, and must not be removed prior to installation. Equally, the sender wheel must not be separated from the assembly.

16 If using the VW tool, proceed as follows. If using an aftermarket tool specialist's product, follow the instructions supplied with the tool. Rotate the large spindle nut until it's level with the end of the clamping surface of the spindle, then clamp the spindle in a vice **(see illustrations)**.

17 Press the tool housing downwards until it rests on the nut and washer. Rotate

15.16a Rotate the nut until its level with the end of the flat clamping surface...

15.16b ...then clamp it in a vice

15.17a Rotate the nut until the inner part of the tool ...

15.17b ...is flush with the flat surface of the housing

15.18a Remove the securing clip ...

15.18b ...the hole in the sender wheel should align with the marking on the flange

15.19a Press the assembly downwards on a clean, flat surface...

15.19b ...so the upper edge of the sender wheel is level with the edge of the flange

the nut until the inner part of the tool is at the same height as the housing (see illustrations).

18 Remove the seal securing clip. The hole on the sender wheel must align with the marking on the sealing flange (see illustrations).

19 Place the flange outer side down on a clean, flat surface, then press the seal guide fitting sleeve (supplied ready fitted), housing, and sender wheel downwards until all the components are flat on the surface. In this position the upper edge of the sender wheel should be level with the edge of the sealing flange (see illustrations).

20 Place the sealing flange on the assembly tool, so the pin locates in the hole in the sender wheel (see illustration).

21 Push the sealing flange and guide fitting sleeve against the tool whilst tightening the 3 knurled screws. Ensure the pin is still located in the sender wheel (see illustration).

22 Ensure the end of the crankshaft is clean, and is locked at TDC on No. 1 cylinder as described in Section 3.

23 Unscrew the large nut to the end of the spindle threads, then press the spindle inwards as far as possible (see illustrations).

24 Align the flat side of the assembly with the sump flange, then secure the tool to the crankshaft using the integral Allen bolts

15.20 Fit the flange to the tool, ensuring the pin locates in the hole

15.21 With the pin engaged in the hole, tighten the 3 knurled screws to secure the flange to the tool

15.23a Unscrew the nut to the end of the thread ...

15.23b ...and push the spindle in as far as possible

15.24 Hand-tighten the hex bolts to secure the tool to the crankshaft

15.25 Use two M7 x 35 mm bolts to guide the sealing flange

15.26 Push the black knob into the hole in the crankshaft

(see illustration). Only hand tighten the bolts.

25 Insert two M7x 35 mm bolts to guide the sealing flange to the cylinder block (see illustration).

26 Using hand pressure alone, push the tool assembly onto the crankshaft until the seal guide fitting sleeve contacts the crankshaft flange, then push the guide pin (black knob) into the hole in the crankshaft. This is to ensure the sender wheel reaches its correct installation position (see illustration).

27 Rotate the large nut until it makes contact with the tool housing, then tighten it to 35 Nm. After tightening this nut, a small air gap must still be present between the sealing flange and cylinder block (see illustrations).

28 Unscrew the large nut; the two M7 x 35 Nm screws, the three knurled screws and the Allen bolts securing the tool to the crankshaft. Remove the tool, and pull the seal guide fitting sleeve from place (if it didn't come out with the tool) (see illustration).

29 Use a vernier caliper or feeler gauge to measure the fitted depth of the sender wheel in relation to the crankshaft flange (see illustration). The correct depth is 0.5 mm.

30 If the gap is correct, fit the sealing flange bolts and tighten them to the specified torque.

31 If the gap is too small, re-attach the tool to the sealing flange and crankshaft, then refit the two M7 x 35 mm guide bolts to the flange. Tighten the large spindle nut to 40 Nm, remove the tool and re-measure the air gap. If

the gap is still too small, re-attach the tool and tighten the spindle nut to 45 Nm. Re-measure the gap. When the gap is correct, refit the flange retaining bolts, and tighten them to the specified torque.

32 The remainder of refitting is a reversal of removal.

16 Engine/transmission mountings – inspection and renewal

Inspection

1 If improved access is required, jack up the front of the vehicle, and support it securely on axle stands (see Jacking and vehicle support). Where fitted, remove the engine cover the engine undershield.

2 Check the mounting rubbers to see if they are cracked, hardened or separated from the metal at any point; renew the mounting if any such damage or deterioration is evident.

3 Check that all the mountings are securely tightened; use a torque wrench to check if possible.

4 Using a large screwdriver or a crowbar, check for wear in the mounting by carefully levering against it to check for free play. Where this is not possible, enlist the aid of an assistant to move the engine/transmission back-and-forth, or from side-to-side, whilst you observe the mounting. While some free play is to be expected, even from new components, excessive wear should be obvious. If excessive free play is found, check first that the fasteners are correctly secured, and then renew any worn components as described in the following paragraphs.

Renewal

Right-hand mounting

Note: New mounting securing bolts will be required on refitting.

5 Attach a hoist and lifting tackle to the engine lifting brackets on the cylinder head, and raise the hoist to just take the weight of the engine. Alternatively the engine can be supported on a trolley jack under the engine. Use a block of wood between the sump and

15.27a After tightening the spindle nut to 35 Nm …

15.27b …there should be an air gap between the sealing flange and the cylinder block

15.28 Remove the tool and seal fitting guide sleeve

15.29 Measure the fitted depth of the sender wheel in relation to the end of the crankshaft

16.6a Disconnect the level sensor wiring plug

16.6b Unclip the wiring loom, unbolt the reservoir and move it to the side

16.6c Unbolt and remove the filler neck

the head of the jack, to prevent any damage to the sump.

6 For improved access, unscrew the coolant reservoir and move it to one side, leaving the coolant hoses connected. Also remove the filler neck from the screen washer bottle **(see illustrations)**.

7 Where fitted, disconnect the wiring plug, undo the retaining bolts, and remove the pressure sensor (including the bracket) from the top of the engine mounting and move it to one side **(see illustrations 6.3a & 6.3b)**.

8 Undo the retaining bolts and move the fuel filter to one side **(see illustration)**. Where applicable, move any wiring harnesses, pipes or hoses to one side to enable removal of the engine mounting.

9 Unscrew the bolts securing the mounting to the engine bracket, and then unscrew the bolts securing it to the body **(see illustrations)**. Withdraw the mounting from the engine compartment.

10 Refitting is a reversal of removal, bearing in mind the following points.

a) *Use new securing bolts.*

b) *There must be at least 10 mm between the engine mounting bracket and the right-hand side chassis member* **(see illustration)**.

c) *The side of the mounting support arm must be parallel to the side of the engine mounting bracket.*

d) *Tighten all fixings to the specified torque.*

Left-hand mounting

Note: *New mounting bolts will be required on refitting.*

11 Where fitted, remove the engine top cover. If the transmission is to be supported from below remove the engine undershield – again where fitted.

12 Attach a hoist and lifting tackle to the engine lifting brackets on the cylinder head, and raise the hoist to just take the weight of the engine and transmission. Alternatively the engine can be supported on a trolley jack under the transmission. Use a block of wood between the transmission and the head of the jack, to prevent any damage to the transmission.

16.8 The fuel filter can be placed on top of the engine

16.9a Remove the small bracket…

16.9b …the mounting to body bolts…

16.9c …and the mounting to engine bracket bolts

16.9d Remove the mounting

16.10 There must be at least 10 mm between the bracket and the chassis member

16.13 Move the loom to the side

16.14a Remove the bolts and…

16.14b …lift out the mounting

16.19 Rear mounting arm-to-transmission bolts

13 Remove the battery and battery tray, as described in (Chapter 5A Section 3). Unclip the wiring loom and move it to the side **(see illustration)**.
14 Unscrew the bolts securing the mounting to the transmission, and the remaining bolts

securing the mounting to the body **(see illustrations)**, then lift the mounting from the engine compartment.
15 Refitting is a reversal of removal, bearing in mind the following points:
a) *Use new mounting bolts.*

b) *The edges of the mounting support arm must be parallel to the edge of the mounting.*
c) *Tighten all fixings to the specified torque.*

Rear mounting (torque arm)

Note: *New mounting bolts will be required on refitting.*
16 Apply the handbrake, then jack up the front of the vehicle and support securely on axle stands (see *Jacking and vehicle support*). Where fitted, remove the engine undershield for access to the rear mounting (torque arm).
17 Support the rear of the transmission beneath the final drive housing. To do this, use a trolley jack and block of wood, or alternatively wedge a block of wood between the transmission and the subframe.
18 Working under the vehicle, unscrew and remove the bolt securing the mounting to the subframe.
19 Unscrew the two bolts securing the mounting to the transmission, then withdraw the mounting from under the vehicle **(see illustration)**.
20 Refitting is a reversal of removal, but use new mounting securing bolts, and tighten all fixings to the specified torque.

---

17 Engine oil cooler/filter housing – removal and refitting

Removal

1 The oil cooler is mounted on the lower part of the oil filter housing on the front of the cylinder block.
2 Position a container beneath the oil filter housing to catch escaping oil and coolant.
3 Clamp the oil cooler coolant hoses to minimise coolant spillage, or drain the cooling system as described in Chapter 1 Section 32.
4 Unscrew the oil cooler retaining screws and remove the oil cooler from the front of the oil filter housing **(see illustrations)**. Recover the O-rings from between the cooler and the oil filter housing, new ones will be required for refitting.
5 If required, disconnect the coolant hose, unclip the dipstick from the side of the housing, then undo the retaining bolts and remove the oil filter housing from the cylinder block **(see illustrations)**.

17.4a Undo the engine oil cooler retaining screws

17.4b Renew the seals/gaskets

17.5a Disconnect the coolant hoses …

17.5b …release the oil dipstick guide tube retaining clip…

17.5c … and undo the filter housing retaining bolts

17.6 Renew the seals/gaskets

18.1 Oil pressure warning light switch
location

18.2 Remove the air intake hose

Refitting

6 Refitting is a reversal of removal, bearing in mind the following points:
a) *Use new oil cooler and housing O-rings* **(see illustration)**.
b) *Tighten the oil cooler and filter housing bolts to the correct torque.*
c) *On completion, check and if necessary top-up the oil and coolant levels.*

18 Oil pressure warning light switch – removal and refitting

Removal

1 The oil pressure warning light switch is fitted to the left-hand rear of the cylinder head **(see illustration)**. Remove the engine top cover to gain access to the switch.
2 Slacken the retraining clips and remove the air intake hose from the turbocharger **(see illustration)**.
3 Disconnect the wiring connector and wipe clean the area around the switch.
4 Unscrew the switch and remove it, along with its sealing washer (where fitted). If the switch is to be left removed from the engine for any length of time, plug the aperture in the cylinder head.

Refitting

5 Examine the sealing washer for signs of damage or deterioration and if necessary renew.

6 Refit the switch, complete with washer (where fitted), and tighten it to the specified torque.
7 Securely reconnect the wiring connector, refit the air intake hose and then, if necessary, top-up the engine oil as described in *Weekly checks*. On completion, refit the engine top cover.

19 Oil level/temperature sender – removal and refitting

Removal

1 The oil level/temperature sender is fitted to bottom of the sump **(see illustration)**.
2 Drain the engine oil as described in Chapter 1B Section 1,6.

19.1 Oil level/temperature sensor location

3 Disconnect the wiring connector from the sender.
4 Release the retaining clips and remove the insulation cover from the sump **(see illustration)**.
5 Wipe clean the area around the sender, then undo the three retaining bolts and remove the sender.

Refitting

6 Examine the sealing washer for signs of damage or deterioration and if necessary renew.
7 Refit the switch and tighten the retaining bolts to the specified torque.
8 Refit the insulation cover, then reconnect the wiring connector and refill the engine with oil (refer to Chapter 1, Section 6).
9 On completion, check and, if necessary, top-up the engine oil as described in *Weekly checks*.

19.4 Remove the insulation cover to
access the bolts

Chapter 2 Part B
2.0 litre common rail (CR) diesel engine in-car repair procedures

Contents

Degrees of difficulty

Easy, suitable for novice with little experience	**Fairly easy,** suitable for beginner with some experience	**Fairly difficult,** suitable for competent DIY mechanic	**Difficult,** suitable for experienced DIY mechanic	**Very difficult,** suitable for expert DIY or professional

Specifications

General

Manufacturer's engine codes: * . . . .
   1968 cc (2.0 litre), 16-valve, DOHC . . . .   CFHC, CFJA, CFHE, CFHF, CLCA and CLCB

Maximum outputs:

	Power	Torque
Engine code CFHC	103 kW @ 4200 rpm	320 Nm @ 1750 to 2500 rpm
Engine code CFJA	125 kW @ 4200 rpm	320 Nm @ 1750 to 2500 rpm
Engine code CFHE	62 kW @ 4600 rpm	2000 Nm @ 1750 to 2750 rpm
Engine code CFHF	81 kW @ 4200 rpm	280Nm @ 1750 to 2750 rpm
Engine code CLCA	81 kW @ 4200 rpm	250Nm @ 1500 to 2500 rpm
Engine code CLCB	103 kW @ 4200 rpm	320Nm @ 1750 to 2500 rpm

Bore . . . .   81.0 mm
Stroke . . . .   95.5 mm
Compression ratio . . . .   16.5 : 1

Compression pressures:
   Minimum compression pressure . . . .   Approximately 19.0 bar
   Maximum difference between cylinders. . . . .   Approximately 5.0 bar
Firing order . . . .   1 – 3 – 4 – 2
No 1 cylinder location. . . . .   Timing belt end

* Note: *See 'Vehicle identification' at the end of this manual for the location of engine code markings.*

Lubrication system

Oil pump type. . . . .   Gear type, chain-driven from crankshaft
Oil pressure switch. . . . .   0.3 to 0.6 bar
Oil pressure (oil temperature 80°C):
   Minimum @ idling . . . .   0.8 bar
   Minimum @ 2000 rpm: . . . .   2.0 bar

Torque wrench settings

	Nm	lbf ft
Ancillary (alternator, etc) bracket mounting bolts: *		
Stage 1	40	30
Stage 2	Angle-tighten a further 45°	
Auxiliary drivebelt tensioner securing bolt:		
Stage 1	20	15
Stage 2	Angle-tighten a further 180°	
Big-end bearing caps bolts: *		
Stage 1	30	22
Stage 2	Angle-tighten a further 90°	
Camshaft bearing frame bolts/nut	10	7
Camshaft cover bolts.	10	7
Camshaft sprocket hub centre bolt	100	74
Camshaft sprocket-to-hub bolts: *		
Stage 1	20	15
Stage 2	Angle-tighten a further 45°	
Common rail bolts	22	16
Coolant pump bolts	15	11
Crankshaft oil seal housing bolts	15	11
Crankshaft pulley-to-sprocket bolts: *		
Stage 1	10	7
Stage 2	Angle-tighten a further 90°	
Crankshaft sprocket bolt: *		
Stage 1	120	89
Stage 2	Angle-tighten a further 90°	
Cylinder head bolts: *		
Stage 1	30	22
Stage 2	50	37
Stage 3	Angle-tighten a further 90°	
Stage 4	Angle-tighten a further 90°	
Engine mountings: *		
RH engine mounting:		
Mounting bracket to engine:		
Stage 1	40	30
Stage 2	Angle-tighten a further 180°	
Mounting to body:		
Stage 1	40	30
Stage 2	Angle-tighten a further 90°	
Mounting to bracket:		
Stage 1	60	44
Stage 2	Angle-tighten a further 90°	
LH engine/transmission mounting:		
Mounting to body:		
Stage 1	40	30
Stage 2	Angle-tighten a further 90°	
Mounting to bracket on transmission:		
Stage 1	60	44
Stage 2	Angle-tighten a further 90°	
Rear mounting link:		
M10 strength class 8.8:		
Stage 1	40	30
Stage 2	Angle-tighten a further 90°	
M10 strength class 10.9:		
Stage 1	50	37
Stage 2	Angle-tighten a further 90°	
M12:		
Stage 1	60	44
Stage 2	Angle-tighten a further 90°	
Flywheel: *		
Stage 1	60	44
Stage 2	Angle-tighten a further 90°	
Fuel injector:		
Retaining nuts.	22	16
Cover bolts	5	4
Fuel pump hub nut	95	70
Fuel pump sprocket bolts: *		
Stage 1	20	15
Stage 2	Angle-tighten a further 90°	

Torque wrench settings (continued)

	Nm	lbf ft
Intermediate gear bolt: *		
Stage 1	90	66
Stage 2	Angle-tighten a further 90°	
Main bearing cap bolts: *		
Stage 1	65	48
Stage 2	Angle-tighten a further 90°	
Oil cooler screws (CFFA, CFFB & CFGB)	11	7
Oil cooler centre bolt (CBAA, CBAB & CBBB)	25	18
Oil drain plug*	30	22
Oil filter housing-to-cylinder block bolts: *		
Stage 1	15	11
Stage 2	Angle-tighten a further 90°	
Oil filter cover	25	18
Oil level/temperature sensor-to-sump bolts	10	7
Oil pick-up pipe securing bolts	10	7
Oil pressure warning light switch	20	15
Oil pump securing bolts:		
M6	10	7
M7: *		
Stage 1	13	10
Stage 2	Angle-tighten a further 90°	
Piston oil spray jet bolt	25	18
Sump:		
Sump-to-cylinder block bolts	15	11
Sump-to-transmission bolts	45	33
Thermostat housing	15	11
Timing belt outer cover bolts	10	7
Timing belt tensioner roller securing nut:		
Stage 1	20	15
Stage 2	Angle-tighten a further 45°	
Timing belt idler pulleys:		
Lower idler roller nut	20	15
Upper idler roller (small) bolt	20	15
Upper idler roller (large) bolt: *		
Stage 1	50	37
Stage 2	Angle-tighten a further 90°	

* Do not re-use fasteners

1 General Information

How to use this Chapter

1 This Part of Chapter 2 describes those repair procedures that can reasonably be carried out on the engine while it remains in the vehicle. If the engine has been removed from the vehicle and is being dismantled as described in Part D, any preliminary dismantling procedures can be ignored.

2 Note that while it may be possible physically to overhaul certain items while the engine is in the vehicle, such tasks are not usually carried out as separate operations, and usually require the execution of several additional procedures (not to mention the cleaning of components and of oilways); for this reason, all such tasks are classed as major overhaul procedures, and are described in Part D of this Chapter.

Engine description

3 Throughout this Chapter, engines are referred to by type, and are identified and referred to by the manufacturer's code letters. A listing of all engines covered, together with their code letters, is given in the Specifications at the start of this Chapter.

4 The engines are water-cooled, double overhead camshafts (DOHC), in-line four-cylinder units, with cast-iron cylinder blocks and aluminium-silicon alloy cylinder heads. All are mounted transversely at the front of the vehicle, with the transmission bolted to the left-hand end of the engine.

5 The crankshaft is of five-bearing type, and thrustwashers are fitted to the centre main bearing to control crankshaft endfloat.

6 Drive for the exhaust camshaft is by a toothed timing belt from the crankshaft, with the intake camshaft driven by interlocking gears at the left-hand end of both camshafts. The gears incorporate a toothed backlash compensator element. Each camshaft is mounted at the top of the cylinder head, and is secured by a bearing frame/ladder.

7 The valves are closed by coil springs, and run in guides pressed into the cylinder head. The valves are operated by roller rocker arms incorporating hydraulic tappets.

8 A twin, counter-rotating balance shaft assembly is fitted to the base of the cylinder block. The rearmost balance shaft is driven by a gear on the crankshaft, via an intermediate gear bolted to the balance shaft housing. The two balance shafts are geared together.

9 The gear-type oil pump is driven by the front balance shaft. Oil is drawn from the sump through a strainer, and then forced through

an externally-mounted, renewable filter. From there, it is distributed to the cylinder head, where it lubricates the camshaft journals and hydraulic tappets, and also to the crankcase, where it lubricates the main bearings, connecting rod big-ends, gudgeon pins and cylinder bores. A coolant-fed oil cooler is fitted to the oil filter housing on all engines. Oil jets are fitted to the base of each cylinder – these spray oil onto the underside of the pistons, to improve cooling.

10 All engines are fitted with a brake servo vacuum pump driven by the camshaft on the transmission end of the cylinder head.

11 On all engines, engine coolant is circulated by a pump, driven by the timing belt. For details of the cooling system, refer to Chapter 3.

Operations with engine in car

12 The following operations can be performed without removing the engine:

a) *Compression pressure – testing.*
b) *Camshaft cover – removal and refitting.*
c) *Crankshaft pulley – removal and refitting.*
d) *Timing belt covers – removal and refitting.*
e) *Timing belt – removal, refitting and adjustment.*
f) *Timing belt tensioner and sprockets – removal and refitting.*
g) *Camshaft oil seals – renewal.*
h) *Camshafts and hydraulic tappets – removal, inspection and refitting.*
i) *Cylinder head – removal and refitting.*
j) *Cylinder head and pistons – decarbonising.*
k) *Sump – removal and refitting.*
l) *Oil pump – removal, overhaul and refitting.*
m) *Crankshaft oil seals – renewal.*
n) *Engine/transmission mountings – inspection and renewal.*
o) *Flywheel – removal, inspection and refitting.*

Note: *It is possible to remove the pistons and connecting rods (after removing the cylinder head and sump) without removing the engine. However, this is not recommended. Work of this nature is more easily and thoroughly completed with the engine on the bench, as described in Chapter 2D.*

2 Compression and leakdown tests – description and interpretation

Compression test

Note: *A compression tester suitable for use with diesel engines will be required for this test.*

1 When engine performance is down, or if misfiring occurs which cannot be attributed to the ignition or fuel systems, a compression test can provide diagnostic clues as to the engine's condition. If the test is performed regularly, it can give warning of trouble before any other symptoms become apparent.

2 The engine must be fully warmed-up to normal operating temperature, the battery must be fully charged, and you will require the aid of an assistant.

3 Remove the glow plugs as described in Chapter 5B, Section 2, and then fit a compression tester to the No 1 cylinder glow plug hole. The type of tester that bolts into the plug thread is preferred. Note: Part of the glow plug removal procedure is to disconnect the fuel injector wiring plugs. As a result of the plugs being disconnected and the engine cranked, faults will be stored in the ECM memory. These must be erased after the compression test.

4 Have your assistant crank the engine for several seconds on the starter motor. After one or two revolutions, the compression pressure should build-up to a maximum figure and then stabilise. Record the highest reading obtained.

5 Repeat the test on the remaining cylinders, recording the pressure in each.

6 The cause of poor compression is less easy to establish on a diesel engine than on a petrol engine. The effect of introducing oil into the cylinders (wet testing) is not conclusive, because there is a risk that the oil will sit in the recess on the piston crown, instead of passing to the rings. However, the following can be used as a rough guide to diagnosis.

7 All cylinders should produce very similar pressures. Any difference greater than that specified indicates the existence of a fault. Note that the compression should build-up quickly in a healthy engine. Low compression on the first stroke, followed by gradually increasing pressure on successive strokes, indicates worn piston rings. A low compression reading on the first stroke, which does not build-up during successive strokes, indicates leaking valves or a blown head gasket (a cracked head could also be the cause).

8 A low reading from two adjacent cylinders is almost certainly due to the head gasket having blown between them and the presence of coolant in the engine oil will confirm this.

9 On completion, remove the compression tester, and refit the glow plugs, with reference to Chapter 5B, Section 2.

10 Reconnect the wiring to the injector solenoids. Finally, have a VW dealer or suitably equipped specialist erase the fault codes from the ECM memory.

Leakdown test

11 A leakdown test measures the rate at which compressed air fed into the cylinder is lost. It is an alternative to a compression test, and in many ways it is better, since the escaping air provides easy identification of where pressure loss is occurring (piston rings, valves or head gasket).

12 The equipment required for leakdown testing is unlikely to be available to the home mechanic. If poor compression is suspected, have the test performed by a suitably equipped garage.

3 Engine assembly and valve timing marks – general information and usage

General information

1 TDC is the highest point in the cylinder that each piston reaches as it travels up-and-down when the crankshaft turns. Each piston reaches TDC at the end of the compression stroke and again at the end of the exhaust stroke, but TDC generally refers to piston position on the compression stroke. No 1 piston is at the timing belt end of the engine.

2 Positioning No 1 piston at TDC is an essential part of many procedures, such as timing belt removal and camshaft removal.

3 The design of the engines covered in this Chapter is such that piston-to-valve contact may occur if the camshaft or crankshaft is turned with the timing belt removed. For this reason, it is important to ensure that the camshaft and crankshaft do not move in relation to each other once the timing belt has been removed from the engine.

Setting TDC on No 1 cylinder

Note: *VAG special tool T10050 is required to lock the crankshaft sprocket in the TDC position. Alternatively obtain a tool from automotive tool specialists.*

4 Raise the front of the vehicle and support it securely on axle stands (see *Jacking and vehicle support*). Remove the front right-hand roadwheel, then release the fasteners and remove the lower section of the wheel arch liner.

5 Remove the auxiliary drivebelt as described in Chapter 1, Section 29.

6 Remove the crankshaft pulley/vibration damper as described in Section 5.

7 Remove the timing belt outer covers as described in Section 6.

8 Using a spanner or socket on the crankshaft sprocket bolt, turn the crankshaft in the normal direction of rotation (clockwise) until the alignment mark on the face of the sprocket is almost vertical, and the hole in the camshaft sprocket hub aligns with the hole in the cylinder head (**see illustration**).

9 While in this position it should be possible

3.8 The alignment mark on the crankshaft sprocket should be almost vertical

3.9a Fit the tool to the hole in the oil seal housing…

3.9b … so the marks on the tool and sprocket align

3.9c Insert a 6 mm drill bit/rod to lock the camshaft hub

to insert the VAG tool T10050 to lock the crankshaft, and a 6 mm diameter rod/drill bit to lock the camshafts **(see illustrations)**. Note: The mark on the crankshaft sprocket and the mark on the VAG tool must align, whilst at the same time the shaft of tool must engage in the drilling in the crankshaft oil seal housing.
10 The engine is now set to TDC on No 1 cylinder.

4 Camshaft cover – removal and refitting

4.3 Disconnect the vacuum hoses from the camshaft cover

4.4 Squeeze together the sides of the collar and disconnect the breather hose

Removal

1 Remove the fuel injectors (Chapter 4A Section 5) and fuel rail (Chapter 4A Section 12).
2 Remove the timing belt upper cover as described in Section 6.
3 Note their fitted positions, then disconnect the vacuum hoses from the camshaft cover, and release them and the wiring loom from the retaining clips at the left-hand end of the cover **(see illustration)**.
4 Squeeze together the sides of the collar, and disconnect the breather hose from the camshaft cover **(see illustration)**.
5 Release the wiring from the clips at the rear of the cover, then unscrew the camshaft cover retaining bolts and lift the cover away. If the cover sticks, do not attempt to lever it off – instead free it by working around the cover and tapping it lightly with a soft-faced mallet **(see illustration)**.
6 Recover the camshaft cover gasket. Inspect the gasket carefully, and renew it if damage or deterioration is evident – note that the retaining bolts and seals must be pushed fully through the cover **(see illustrations)**.
7 Clean the mating surfaces of the cylinder head and camshaft cover thoroughly, removing all traces of oil – take care to avoid damaging the surfaces as you do this.

Refitting

8 Refit the camshaft cover by following the removal procedure in reverse, tightening the cover retaining bolts to the specified torque in the sequence shown **(see illustration)**.

4.5 Undo the bolts and lift away the camshaft cover

4.6a Renew the cover seal if necessary

4.6b Bolts and seals must be pushed fully through the cover before fitting the gasket

4.8 Cylinder head cover bolt tightening sequence

5.4 Undo the pulley bolts, counterholding it with a socket on the centre sprocket bolt

6.1 Pull the engine cover upwards from the mountings

6 Timing belt covers –
removal and refitting

Upper outer cover

1 Pull the engine top cover upwards to release the mountings **(see illustration)**.
2 Disconnect the wiring plug, undo the retaining bolt, and remove the exhaust gas pressure sensor bracket by pushing it forwards **(see illustration)**.
3 Disconnect the wiring plug, unclip the fuel hoses, then release the clamps and disconnect the hoses from the filter **(see illustrations)**. Note the fitted locations of the hoses to aid refitting. Plug the openings to prevent contamination.
4 Undo the bolts/nut and remove the fuel filter assembly **(see illustration)**. Release the hose clamp, as the filter assembly is withdrawn.
5 Disconnect the fuel temperature sensor wiring plug, then release the clamp and disconnect the fuel supply pipe from the high-pressure fuel pump **(see illustration)**. Plug the openings to prevent contamination, and place a rag above the alternator to prevent fuel ingress.
6 Slide up the hose retaining clips, then undo the two retaining bolts and remove the supplementary fuel pump **(see illustration)**.
7 Disconnect the radiator outlet temperature sensor wiring plug, then release the three clips

5 Crankshaft pulley –
removal and refitting

Removal

1 Switch off the ignition and all electrical consumers and remove the ignition key.
2 Raise the front right-hand side of the vehicle, and support securely on axle stands (see *Jacking and vehicle support*). Remove the roadwheel.
3 Remove the securing fasteners and withdraw the lower section of the front wheel arch liner.
4 Slacken the bolts securing the crankshaft pulley to the sprocket **(see illustration)**. If necessary, the pulley can be prevented from

turning by counterholding with a spanner or socket on the crankshaft sprocket bolt.
5 Remove the auxiliary drivebelt, as described in Chapter 1, Section 29.
6 Unscrew the bolts securing the pulley to the sprocket, and remove the pulley. Discard the bolts – new ones must be fitted.

Refitting

7 Refit the pulley over the locating peg on the crankshaft sprocket, then fit the new pulley securing bolts.
8 Refit and tension the auxiliary drivebelt as described in Chapter 1, Section 29.
9 Prevent the crankshaft from turning as during removal, then fit the pulley securing bolts, and tighten to the specified torque.
10 Refit the wheel arch liner.
11 Refit the roadwheel and lower the vehicle to the ground.

6.2 Disconnect the wiring plug and undo the retaining bolt

6.3a Note their positions, then disconnect the hoses from the fuel filter

6.3b Plug the openings to prevent contamination

6.4 Undo the nut/bolts and remove the fuel filter

6.5 Disconnect the fuel supply hose and temperature sensor

6.6 Supplementary fuel pump retaining bolts

6.7a Disconnect the temperature sensor wiring plug

6.7b Release the clips…

6.7c … and manoeuvre the timing belt upper cover from place

and remove the timing belt upper cover **(see illustrations)**.

8 Refitting is a reversal of removal, noting that the lower edge of the upper cover engages with the centre cover.

Centre outer cover

9 Remove the crankshaft pulley as described in Section 5. It is assumed that, if the centre cover is being removed, the lower cover will be also – if not, simply remove the components described in Section 5 for access to the crankshaft pulley, and leave the pulley in position.
10 Undo the retaining nuts/bolts and move the coolant pipe that lies across the centre cover, away towards the inner wing.
11 With the upper cover removed (paragraphs 1 to 6), unscrew and remove the three retaining bolts from the centre cover. Withdraw the centre cover from the engine, noting how it fits over the lower cover **(see illustration)**. Note if the auxiliary belt tensioner is in the 'locked' position as described in the belt removal procedure, the locking drill bit/rod must be removed for access to the cover retaining bolt.
12 Refitting is a reversal of the removal procedure, using a little thread-locking compound on the retaining bolts.

Lower outer cover

13 Remove the upper and centre covers as described previously.
14 If not already done, remove the crankshaft pulley as described in Section 5.
15 Unscrew the remaining bolts securing the lower cover, and remove it **(see illustration)**.
16 Refitting is a reversal of removal; locate the centre cover in place before fitting the top two bolts.

Rear cover

17 Remove the timing belt, tensioner and sprockets as described in Section 7 and Section 8.
18 Slacken and withdraw the retaining bolts and lift the timing belt inner cover from the studs on the end of the engine, and remove it from the engine compartment.
19 Refitting is a reversal of removal.

6.11 Centre timing belt cover bolts

6.15 Lower cover retaining bolts

7 Timing belt – removal, inspection and refitting

Note: *It is considered best practise to always replace the tensioner, idler and coolant pump whenever the timing belt is replaced. Any mounting studs should also be replaced at the same time. Most of the components (apart from the coolant pump) will be supplied with a timing belt kit. Note also that most manufactures will not guarantee a belt against premature failure if the idler(s) and tensioner are not replaced with the belt.*

Removal

1 The primary function of the toothed timing belt is to drive the camshaft, but it also drives the coolant pump and high-pressure

fuel pump. Should the belt slip or break in service, the valve timing will be disturbed and piston-to-valve contact may occur, resulting in serious engine damage. For this reason, it is important that the timing belt is tensioned correctly, and inspected regularly for signs of wear or deterioration.
2 Switch off the ignition and all electrical consumers and remove the ignition key.
3 Set the engine to TDC on No1 cylinder as described in Section 3.
4 Slacken the three bolts securing the sprocket to the camshaft hub **(see illustration)**.
5 Slacken the three bolts securing the sprocket to the high-pressure fuel pump **(see illustration)**.
6 Insert a suitable Allen key into the tensioner hub, then slacken the retaining nut and rotate the tensioner hub anti-clockwise until it can

7.4 Slacken the sprocket-to-hub bolts

7.5 Slacken the high-pressure fuel pump sprocket bolts

be locked in place using a 2.0 mm pin/drill bit (see illustration).

7 Now rotate the tensioner hub clockwise to the stop, and hand-tighten the retaining nut.

8 If the original timing belt is to be refitted, mark the running direction of the belt, to ensure correct refitting.

Caution: If the belt appears to be in good condition and can be re-used, it is essential that it is refitted the same way around, otherwise accelerated wear will result, leading to premature failure.

9 Slide the belt from the sprockets, taking care not to twist or kink the belt excessively if it is to be re-used.

Inspection

10 Examine the belt for evidence of contamination by coolant or lubricant. If this is the case, find the source of the contamination before progressing any further. Check the belt for signs of wear or damage, particularly around the leading edges of the belt teeth. Renew the belt if its condition is in doubt; the cost of belt renewal is negligible compared with potential cost of the engine repairs, should the belt fail in service. The belt must be renewed if it has covered the mileage given in Chapter Section, however, if it has covered less, it is prudent to renew it regardless of condition, as a precautionary measure.

11 If the timing belt is not going to be refitted for some time, it is a wise precaution to hang a warning label on the steering wheel, to remind your self (and others) not to attempt to start the engine.

Refitting

12 Ensure that the crankshaft and camshaft are still set to TDC on No 1 cylinder, as described in Section 3. The camshaft sprocket bolts should be renewed, and slackened at this point.

13 Renew the high-pressure fuel pump sprocket bolts one at a time. They should be kept loose.

14 Using a screwdriver on the bolts heads, rotate the high-pressure fuel pump clockwise until a 6.0 mm locking pin/drill bit can be inserted into the housing adjacent to the sprocket, locking the pump in place (see illustration).

15 Rotate the camshaft sprocket and high-pressure fuel pump sprocket fully clockwise so that the securing bolts are at the end of the elongated holes (see illustrations).

16 Loop the timing belt loosely under the crankshaft sprocket. **Note:** *Observe any direction of rotation markings on the belt.*

17 Fit the belt around the tensioner pulley, engage the timing belt teeth with the camshaft sprockets, then manoeuvre it into position around the coolant pump sprocket and the fuel pump sprocket. Make sure that the belt teeth seat correctly on the sprockets. **Note:** *Slight adjustment to the position of the camshaft sprocket may be necessary to achieve this. Avoid bending the belt back on itself or twisting it excessively as you do this.*

18 Finally, fit the belt around the idler roller (see illustration). Ensure that any slack in the belt is in the section of belt that passes over the tensioner roller.

19 Loosen the timing belt tensioner securing nut, and pull out the tensioner locking pin. Turn the tensioner clockwise with an Allen key until the pointer is just past the middle of the gap in the tensioner backplate (see illustration). With the tensioner held in this position, tighten

7.6 Using an Allen key, slacken the nut, and rotate the hub anti-clockwise until a 2 mm rod/drill bit can be inserted to lock the hub to the pulley

7.14 Rotate the high-pressure fuel pump clockwise until a 6 mm drill bit/rod can be inserted into the housing and hub

7.15a Rotate the sprockets fully clockwise until the fuel pump sprocket ...

7.15b ... and camshaft sprocket bolts are at the end of the elongated holes

7.18 Timing belt routing

the securing nut to the specified torque and angle.

20 Counterhold the camshaft sprocket with a homemade tool to prevent any rotation, and then tighten the camshaft sprocket and fuel pump sprocket bolts to 20 Nm (15 lbf ft). Remove the sprockets locking tools and the crankshaft locking tool.

21 Using a spanner or wrench and socket on the crankshaft pulley centre bolt, rotate the crankshaft clockwise through two complete revolutions. Reset the engine to TDC on No1 cylinder, with reference to Section 3 and refit the crankshaft locking tool.

22 Check that the tensioner roller indicator arm is centred, or within a maximum of 5 mm to the right of the notch in the backplate **(see illustration)**. If not, hold the tensioner hub stationary with an Allen key, slacken the retaining nut and position the arm in the centre of the notch. Tighten the retaining nut to the specified torque. Remove the Allen key.

23 Check that the camshaft sprocket locking pin can still be inserted. Note: It's very difficult to align the locking point of the fuel pump hub again. However, a misalignment of holes will not affect engine performance.

24 If the camshaft sprocket locking pin cannot be inserted, pull the crankshaft locking tool slight away from the engine, and rotate the crankshaft anti-clockwise slightly past TDC. Now slowly rotate the crankshaft clockwise until the camshaft sprocket locking tool can be inserted.

25 If the locating pin of the crankshaft locking tool is to the left of the corresponding hole, slacken the camshaft sprocket bolts, slowly rotate the crankshaft clockwise until the locking tool can be fully inserted. Tighten the camshaft sprocket bolts to 20 Nm (15 lbf ft).

26 If the locating pin of the crankshaft locking tool is to the right of the corresponding hole, slacken the camshaft sprocket bolts, rotate the crankshaft anti-clockwise slightly until the pin is to the left of the hole, then slowly rotate it clockwise until the lock tool can be fully inserted. Tighten the camshaft sprocket bolts to 20 Nm (15 lbf ft).

27 Remove the crankshaft and camshaft locking tools, then rotate the crankshaft two complete revolutions clockwise and check the

7.19 Rotate the tensioner clockwise until the pointer is just past the gap in the backplate

locking tools can be reinserted. If necessary, repeat the adjustment procedure described previously.

28 Tighten the camshaft and fuel pump sprocket bolts to the specified torque and angles.

29 The remainder of refitting is a reversal of removal.

8 Timing belt tensioner and sprockets – removal and refitting

Timing belt tensioner

Removal

1 In order to remove the timing belt tensioner, the engine mounting bracket must first be removed. Either support the engine from above using a crossbeam or an engine hoist, or support if from underneath with a trolley jack and block of wood.

2 Remove the timing belt as described in Section 7.

3 Undo the bolts and remove the right-hand engine mounting.

4 Undo the bolt securing the coolant pipe to the mounting bracket **(see illustration)**.

5 Working in the wheel arch area, undo the nut securing the lower end of the coolant pipe.

6 Undo the 3 retaining bolts and remove the engine mounting bracket **(see illustration)**.

7.22 The pointer should be centred in, or within 5 mm to the right of, the gap in the backplate

7 Unscrew the timing belt tensioner nut, and remove the tensioner from the engine.

Refitting

8 When refitting the tensioner to the engine, ensure that the lug on the tensioner backplate engages with the corresponding cut-out in the rear timing belt cover, then refit the tensioner nut **(see illustration)**.

9 The remainder of refitting is a reversal of removal.

Idler pulleys

Removal

10 Remove the timing belt as described in Section 7.

11 Unscrew the relevant idler pulley/roller securing bolt/nut, and then withdraw the pulley.

Refitting

12 Refit the pulley and tighten the securing bolt or nut to the specified torque. Note: Renew the large roller/pulley retaining bolt (where applicable).

13 Refit and tension the timing belt as described in Section 7.

Crankshaft sprocket

Note: A new crankshaft sprocket securing bolt must be used on refitting.

Removal

14 Remove the timing belt as described in Section 7.

8.4 Coolant pipe upper mounting bolt and lower mounting nut

8.6 Engine mounting bracket bolts

8.8 Ensure the lug on the backplate engages with the cut-out in the timing belt cover

8.27 Fabricate a home-made tool to counterhold the hub. Undo the bolt …

8.28 … and slide the hub from the camshaft

8.29 Ensure the integral key aligns with the keyway in the camshaft

15 The sprocket securing bolt must now be slackened, and the crankshaft must be prevented from turning as the sprocket bolt is unscrewed. To hold the sprocket, make up a suitable tool, and bolt it to the sprocket using two bolts bolted into two of the crankshaft pulley bolt holes.

16 Hold the sprocket using the tool, then slacken the sprocket securing bolt. Take care, as the bolt is very tight. Do not allow the crankshaft to turn as the bolt is slackened.

17 Unscrew the bolt, and slide the sprocket from the end of the crankshaft, noting which way round the sprocket's raised boss is fitted.

Refitting

18 Commence refitting by positioning the sprocket on the end of the crankshaft.

19 Fit a new sprocket securing bolt, then counter hold the sprocket using the method employed on removal, and tighten the bolt to the specified torque in the two stages given in the Specifications.

20 Refit the timing belt as described in Section 7.

Camshaft sprocket

Removal

21 Remove the timing belt as described in Section 7, then rotate the crankshaft 90° anti-clockwise to prevent any accidental piston-to-valve contact.

22 Unscrew and remove the three retaining bolts and remove the camshaft sprocket from the camshaft hub.

Refitting

23 Refit the sprocket ensuring that it is fitted the correct way round, as noted before removal, then insert the new sprocket bolts, and tighten by hand only at this stage.

24 If the crankshaft has been turned, turn the crankshaft clockwise 90° back to TDC.

25 Refit and tension the timing belt as described in Section 7.

Camshaft hub

Note: *VAG technicians use special tool T10051 to counter hold the hub, however it is possible to fabricate a suitable alternative.*

Removal

26 Remove the camshaft sprocket as described previously in this Section.

27 Engage special tool T10051 with the three locating holes in the face of the hub to prevent the hub from turning. If this tool is not available, fabricate a suitable alternative. Whilst holding the tool, undo the central hub retaining bolt about two turns **(see illustration)**.

28 Remove the central hub retaining bolt, and slide the hub from the camshaft. If necessary, attach VW tool T10052 (or a similar three-legged puller) to the hub, and evenly tighten the puller until the hub is free of the camshaft taper **(see illustration)**.

Refitting

29 Ensure that the camshaft taper and the hub centre are clean and dry, locate the hub on the taper, noting that the built-in key in the hub taper must align with the keyway in the camshaft taper **(see illustration)**.

30 Hold the hub in this position with tool T10051 (or similar home-made tool), and tighten the central bolt to the specified torque.

31 Refit the camshaft sprocket as described previously in this Section.

Coolant pump sprocket

32 The coolant pump sprocket is integral with the coolant pump. Refer to Chapter 3 for details of coolant pump removal.

---

9 Camshaft and hydraulic tappets – removal, inspection and refitting

Note: *A new camshaft oil seal(s) will be required on refitting. VW removal tool T40094 (or similar tool) will be required to refit the camshafts – this is necessary to prevent damage to the retaining frame and cylinder head as the camshafts are refitted.*

Removal

1 Remove the camshaft hub as described in Section 8.

2 Remove the camshaft cover as described in Section 4.

3 Remove the brake vacuum pump as described in Chapter 9, Section 21.

4 Progressively unscrew the camshaft retaining frame bolts in the reverse of the sequence shown in illustration 9.20, and carefully remove the retaining frame.

5 Carefully lift the camshafts from the cylinder head, keeping them identified for location. Remove the oil seal from the end of the camshaft and discard it – a new one will be required for refitting.

6 Lift the rocker arms and hydraulic tappets from place. Store the rockers and tappets in a container with numbered compartments to ensure they are refitted to their correct locations. It is recommended that the tappets are kept immersed in oil for the period they are removed from the cylinder head.

Inspection

7 With the camshafts removed, examine the retaining frame and the bearing locations in the cylinder head for signs of obvious wear or pitting. If evident, a new cylinder head will probably be required. Also check that the oil supply holes in the cylinder head are free from obstructions.

8 Visually inspect the camshafts for evidence of wear on the surfaces of the lobes and journals. Normally their surfaces should be smooth and have a dull shine; look for scoring, erosion or pitting and areas that appear highly polished, indicating excessive wear. Accelerated wear will occur once the hardened exterior of the camshaft has been damaged, so always renew worn items. Note: If these symptoms are visible on the tips of the camshaft lobes, check the corresponding rocker arm, as it will probably be worn as well.

9 If the machined surfaces of the camshaft appear discoloured or blued, it is likely that it has been overheated at some point, probably due to inadequate lubrication. This may have distorted the shaft, so have the camshaft runout and endfloat checked by an automotive engine reconditioning specialist.

10 Inspect the hydraulic tappets for obvious signs of wear or damage, and renew if necessary. Check that the oil holes in the tappets are free from obstructions.

Refitting

11 Oil the rocker arms and hydraulic tappets, and then refit them to their original positions.

12 Warning: After fitting hydraulic tappets, wait a minimum of 30 minutes (or preferably, leave overnight) before starting the engine, to allow the tappets time to settle, otherwise the valve heads will strike the pistons.

9.13a The different elements of tool No T40094

9.13b Position tools No 1, 2, 9 and 10 as shown

9.14 Position the inlet camshaft on the tool with the bolt indent facing outwards, then slide tool No 8 in to the slot in the end of the camshaft and use a 0.50 mm feeler gauge to remove any free play

9.15 Fit tool No 11 into the slot in the end of the exhaust camshaft

9.16 Tighten the thumbwheel to align the gear teeth. Ensure the clamping jaw with the arrow in seated on the wider gear

13 To set up the tool, remove the supports number 3, 4 and 5, then install the supports number 1, 2, 9 and 10 as shown (see illustrations).
14 Position the inlet camshaft as shown with the cylinder head bolt indent facing outwards, then slide the support number 8 into the slot in the end of the camshaft and remove any free play with a 0.50 mm feeler gauge (see illustration).
15 Position the exhaust camshaft on supports numbers 9 and 10, and fit the tool No 11 into the slot in the end of the camshaft (see illustration).

16 Fit the clamping tool No T40096 to the gear on the exhaust camshaft, tightening the knurled thumb wheel until the faces of the gear teeth are in alignment. If necessary, use a 13 mm spanner (see illustration).
17 Slide the exhaust camshaft towards the inlet camshaft until the gear teeth engage.
18 Ensure the gasket faces of the retaining frame are clean, then apply a smear of clean engine oil to the bearing surfaces and lower the frame into position over the camshafts. Ensure the bearing surfaces locate correctly on the camshafts.

19 Fit the clamping tool No T40095 over the camshafts and frame, and tighten the thumbwheels to hold the camshafts in position in the frame (see illustration).
20 Ensure the sealing surfaces of the cylinder head are clean, and then apply a 2.0 mm wide bead of sealant (D 176 501 A1 or equivalent) as shown. Take care not to apply too much sealant, ensuring the oil holes supply holes are not blocked (see illustration).
21 Slide out tool No's 8 and 11, then lift the camshafts, retaining frame and clamping tool from the tool No T40094. Place the camshafts,

9.19 Secure the camshafts in place in the frame using tool No T40095

9.20 Apply a 2.0 mm thick bead of sealant to the area shown by the grey line. Take care not to block the oil holes

9.21 Camshaft retaining frame bolt tightening sequence

10.2 Bolt in a self-tapping screw, then pull the bolt and seal from place

frame and tool in place on the cylinder head. Progressively and carefully, hand-tighten the frame retaining bolts in the sequence shown, until the retaining frame makes contact with the cylinder head over the complete surface, then tighten the bolts to the specified torque, again in the correct sequence **(see illustration)**.

22 Remove the gear aligning tool (T40096) and the clamping tool (T40095).

23 Renew the camshaft oil seal (Section 10), then drive in a new sealing cap.

24 The remainder of refitting is a reversal of removal.

10 Camshaft oil seals – renewal

Right-hand oil seal

1 Remove the camshaft sprocket and hub, as described in Section 8.

2 Drill two small holes into the existing oil seal, diagonally opposite each other. Take great care to avoid drilling through into the seal housing or camshaft sealing surface. Thread two self-tapping screws into the holes, and using a pair of pliers, pull on the heads of the screws to extract the oil seal **(see illustration)**.

3 Clean out the seal housing and the sealing

surface of the camshaft by wiping it with a lint-free cloth. Remove any swarf or burrs that may cause the seal to leak.

4 Do not lubricate the lip and outer edge of the new oil seal, push it over the camshaft until it is positioned in place above its housing. To prevent damage to the sealing lips, wrap some adhesive tape around the end of the camshaft.

5 Using a hammer and a socket of suitable diameter, drive the seal squarely into its housing. Note: Select a socket that bears only on the hard outer surface of the seal, not the inner lip that can easily be damaged.

6 Refit the camshaft sprocket and its hub, as described in Section 8.

Left-hand oil seal

7 The left-hand camshaft oil seal is formed, by the brake vacuum pump seal, which is fitted to the cylinder head. Refer to Chapter 9, Section 21 for details of brake vacuum pump removal and refitting.

11 Cylinder head – removal, inspection and refitting

Note: *The cylinder head must be removed with the engine cold. New cylinder head bolts and a new cylinder head gasket will be required on refitting, and suitable studs will*

be required to guide the cylinder head into position – see text.

Removal

1 Remove the battery as described in Chapter 5A, Section 3.

2 Drain the cooling system (Chapter 1, Section 32) and engine oil (Chapter 1, Section 6).

3 Pull the plastic cover on the top of the engine upwards from its mountings.

4 Remove the air filter housing as described in Chapter Section.

5 Undo the 3 bolts and remove the battery tray **(see illustration)**.

6 Remove the radiator cooling fan(s) and shroud as described in Chapter 3, Section 5.

7 Undo the bolts and remove the air hose/duct from the intercooler to the turbocharger. Release the wiring looms from the clips as necessary to enable the duct to be manoeuvred from place.

8 Remove the camshaft cover as described in Section 4.

9 Remove the camshaft sprocket and hub as described in Section 8.

10 Disconnect the wiring plugs from the EGR valve and throttle body/intake manifold flap.

11 Disconnect the charge air pressure sensor wiring plug, then undo the 2 retaining bolts, release the clamps, and remove the charge air pipe and hose from the front of the engine **(see illustrations)**.

11.5 Battery tray bolts

11.11a Disconnect the pressure sensor wiring plug...

11.11b ... then remove the charge air pipe and hose

11.12 Oil level dipstick guide tube bolt

11.13 EGR pipe-to-valve bolts

11.14 Charge air pipe retaining bolt. Note the position of the vacuum hoses

11.15 With some lubrication, the hose connection pulls up from the vacuum pump

11.19 EGR pipe-to-cooler bolts

11.21 Remove the EGR pipe between the manifold and cooler

12 Undo the bolt securing the oil level dipstick guide tube to the throttle body/intake manifold flap **(see illustration)**.

13 Undo the 2 bolts securing the connecting pipe to the EGR valve **(see illustration)**.

14 Undo the front retaining bolt, twist the charge air pipe clockwise and disconnect it from the turbocharger. Note their fitted positions, and unclip the vacuum hoses from the charge air pipe **(see illustration)**.

15 Apply a little lubrication spray to the rubber sleeve, pull up the pipe from the vacuum pump, then undo the 4 retaining bolts and remove the vacuum pump from the left-hand end of the cylinder head **(see illustration)**. Renew the pump-to-cylinder head seal.

16 Disconnect the coolant temperature sensor wiring plug at the left-hand end of the cylinder head, and release the wiring loom from any retaining clips.

17 Disconnect the gear change cables from the levers on the transmission, as described in Chapter 7A, Section 2 (manual transmission), or (DSG transmission).

18 Undo the bolts/nut, securing the gear-change bracket to the top of the transmission. Move the bracket and cables to one side.

19 Undo the bolts securing the EGR pipe to the cooler at the left-hand end of the engine, and the nut securing the bracket to the cylinder head, then remove the pipe **(see illustration)**. Recover the gasket at each end.

20 Working underneath the vehicle, slacken the Allen bolt and release the clamp securing

the diesel particulate filter/catalytic converter to the turbocharger, then undo the bolts/nuts securing the brackets to the cylinder block/head and lay the filter/converter to one side.

21 Undo the nuts and multi-spline bolts securing the EGR pipe to the right-hand end of the exhaust manifold and EGR cooler **(see illustration)**. Remove the pipe and recover the gaskets.

22 Trace the exhaust manifold gas temperature sensor wiring back, releasing it from any retaining clips, disconnect its wiring plug at the bulkhead, and slide it from the retaining bracket. Unclip the wiring loom from the top of the turbocharger heat shield.

23 Undo the bolt securing the support bracket/oil return pipe to the underside of

the turbocharger, and then undo the bolt securing the top of the support bracket to the underside of the turbocharger. Now pull and twist the support bracket to disconnect it from the oil return pipe at the top. Remove the pipe/bracket **(see illustrations)**. Note the O-ring and copper sealing washer on the lower banjo bolt, and the two O-rings fitted to the base of the oil return pipe still fitted to the turbocharger.

24 Note their fitted locations, then release the clamps and disconnect the various coolant hoses from the cylinder head.

25 Undo the bolt securing the turbocharger oil supply pipe bracket at the left-hand end of the cylinder head, the nut securing the bracket on the rear of the head, then undo the

11.23a Undo the banjo bolt at the base of the turbocharger support bracket/oil return pipe and the bolt at the top

11.23b Note the 2 O-ring seals at the base of the oil return pipe

11.26 Undo the bolt securing the timing belt guard

11.27 Undo the boost pressure solenoid valve nuts

11.28 Undo the cylinder head bolts using a M12 multi-splined (12-pointed star) tool

union bolts and remove the pipe. Renew any seals.

26 Undo the bolt securing the timing belt guard adjacent to the timing belt tensioner, and the bolt securing the camshaft position sensor, then remove the tensioner retaining nut **(see illustration)**.

27 Disconnect the turbocharger wastegate position sensor wiring plug, and the intake manifold changeover valve wiring plug. Note their fitted positions and disconnect the vacuum hoses from the EGR cooler (where the plastic pipe joins the metal pipe at the back of the cylinder head) and the turbocharger wastegate actuator. Undo the nuts securing the boost pressure solenoid valve to the bulkhead. Release the loom wiring plug, lay the wiring loom and vacuum hoses over the front of the engine, clear of the cylinder head **(see illustration)**. Make a final check to ensure all relevant wiring and vacuum hoses have been disconnected. Note the loom/hose routing to aid refitting.

28 Using an M12 multi-splined tool (12-pointed star), undo the cylinder head bolts, working from the outside-in, evenly and gradually **(see illustration)**. Remove the bolts and recover the washers. Check that nothing remains connected, and starting at the gearbox side, lift the cylinder head from the engine block, sliding the belt tensioner from the mounting stud as the cylinder head is removed. Seek assistance if possible, as it

is a heavy assembly, especially as it is being removed complete with the manifolds.

29 Remove the gasket from the top of the block, noting the locating dowels. If the dowels are a loose fit, remove them and store them with the head for safekeeping. Do not discard the gasket yet – it will be needed for identification purposes. If desired, the manifolds can be removed from the cylinder head with reference to Chapter 4A Section 6 (inlet manifold) or Chapter 4B, Section 5 (turbocharger/exhaust manifold).

Inspection

30 Dismantling and inspection of the cylinder head is covered in Chapter 2D, Section 6.

Cylinder head gasket selection

Note: *A dial test indicator (DTI) will be required for this operation.*

31 Examine the old cylinder head gasket for manufacturer's identification markings **(see illustration)**. These will be in the form of holes, and a part number on the edge of the gasket. Unless new pistons have been fitted, the new cylinder head gasket must be of the same type as the old one.

32 If new piston assemblies have been fitted as part of an engine overhaul, or if a new short engine is to be fitted, the projection of the piston crowns above the cylinder head mating face of the cylinder block at TDC must be measured. This measurement is used to

determine the thickness of the new cylinder head gasket required.

33 Anchor a dial test indicator (DTI) to the top face (cylinder head gasket mating face) of the cylinder block, and zero the gauge on the gasket mating face.

34 Rest the gauge probe on No 1 piston crown, and turn the crankshaft slowly by hand until the piston reaches TDC. Measure and record the maximum piston projection at TDC **(see illustration)**.

35 Repeat the measurement for the remaining pistons, and record the results.

36 If the measurements differ from piston-to-piston, take the highest figure, and use this to determine the thickness of the head gasket required as follows.

Piston projection	Gasket identification (number of holes)
0.91 to 1.00 mm	1
1.01 to 1.10 mm	2
1.11 to 1.20 mm	3

37 Purchase a new gasket according to the results of the measurements.

Refitting

38 The mating faces of the cylinder head and block must be perfectly clean before refitting the head. Use a scraper to remove all traces of gasket and carbon, also clean the tops of the pistons. Take particular care with the aluminium surfaces, as the soft metal is easily damaged.

39 Make sure that debris is not allowed to enter the oil and water passages – this is particularly important for the oil circuit, as carbon could block the oil supply to the camshaft and crankshaft bearings. Using adhesive tape and paper, seal the water, oil and bolt holes in the cylinder block.

40 To prevent carbon entering the gap between the pistons and bores, smear a little grease in the gap. After cleaning a piston, rotate the crankshaft to that the piston moves down the bore, and then wipe out the grease and carbon with a cloth rag. Clean the other piston crowns in the same way.

41 Check the head and block for nicks,

11.31 The holes identify the thickness of the cylinder head gasket

11.34 Measure the piston protrusion using a DTI guage

11.46 Ensure the dowels are in place, then fit the new gasket with the part number uppermost

11.49a Cylinder head bolt tightening sequence

11.49b Tighten the cylinder head bolts to the Stage 1 torque

deep scratches and other damage. If slight, they may be removed carefully with a file. More serious damage may be repaired by machining, but this is a specialist job.

42 If warpage of the cylinder head is suspected, use a straight-edge to check it for distortion, as described in Chapter 2D, Section 7.

43 Ensure that the cylinder head bolt holes in the crankcase are clean and free of oil. Syringe or soak up any oil left in the bolt holes. This is most important in order that the correct bolt tightening torque can be applied, and to prevent the possibility of the block being cracked by hydraulic pressure when the bolts are tightened.

44 Turn the crankshaft anti-clockwise all the pistons at an equal height, approximately halfway down their bores from the TDC position (see Section 3). This will eliminate any risk of piston-to-valve contact as the cylinder head is refitted.

45 Where applicable, refit the manifolds with reference to Chapter 4A Section 6 (inlet manifold) or Chapter 4B, Section 5 (turbocharger/exhaust manifold).

46 Ensure that the cylinder head locating dowels are in place in the cylinder block, and

then fit the new cylinder head gasket over the dowels, ensuring that the part number is uppermost **(see illustration)**. Note that VW recommend that the gasket is only removed from its packaging immediately prior to fitting.

47 Lower the cylinder head into position on the gasket, ensuring that it engages correctly over the dowels. Refit the timing belt tensioner as the cylinder head is refitted.

48 Fit the washers in place then fit the new cylinder head bolts to the locations, and bolt them in as far as possible by hand. Do not oil the bolt threads.

49 Working progressively, in sequence, tighten all the cylinder head bolts to the specified Stage 1 torque **(see illustrations)**.

50 Again working progressively, in sequence, tighten all the cylinder head bolts to the specified Stage 2 torque.

51 Tighten all the cylinder head bolts, in sequence, through the specified Stage 3 angle **(see illustration)**.

52 Finally, tighten all the cylinder head bolts, in sequence, through the specified Stage 4 angle.

53 The remainder of the refitting procedure is a reversal of the removal procedure, noting the following points:

a) *Tighten all fasteners to their specified torque where given.*

b) *Renew all seals and gaskets.*

c) *Refill the cooling system, as described in Chapter 1, Section 32.*

d) *Refill the engine oil, as described in Chapter 1, Section 6.*

e) *Ensure all wiring is correctly routed.*

12 Sump – removal and refitting

Removal

1 Apply the handbrake, then jack up the front of the vehicle and support securely on axle stands (see *Jacking and vehicle support*).

2 Remove the securing bolts and withdraw the engine undershield(s).

3 Drain the engine oil as described in Chapter 1, Section 6.

4 Raise the retaining clip and remove the air duct from the intercooler outlet **(see illustration)**.

5 Undo the retaining bolts, release the clamp and remove the charge air pipe from the

11.51 Use an angle-tightening gauge

12.4 Raise the clip and disconnect the air duct from the intercooler

12.6 Electric coolant circulation pump
retaining bolt

12.9a Pull the insulation down at the rear
to release the clips

12.9b At the front, prise down the centre
pin and pull the clip downwards

front of the cylinder block (see illustration 11.11a and 11.11b). Disconnect the charge air pressure sensor wiring plug as the pipe is withdrawn.

6 Undo the retaining bolt and move the electric coolant circulation pump to one side (see illustration).

7 Undo the bolt securing the turbo-to-intercooler air pipe to the sump.

8 Disconnect the wiring connector from the oil level/temperature sender in the sump.

9 Pull the sump insulation cover downwards at the rear to release the retaining clips, then prise down the centre clip and pull the clip on the front side of the cover downwards (where fitted) (see illustrations).

10 Unscrew and remove the bolts securing the sump to the cylinder block, and the bolts securing the sump to the transmission casing, then withdraw the sump. If necessary,

12.12 Apply a bead of sealant around the
inside of the bolt holes

release the sump by tapping with a soft-faced hammer.

Refitting

11 Begin refitting by thoroughly cleaning the mating faces of the sump and cylinder block. Ensure that all traces of old sealant are removed.

12 Ensure that the cylinder block mating face of the sump is free from all traces of old sealant, oil and grease, and then apply a 2.0 to 3.0 mm thick bead of silicone sealant (VW D 176 404 A2 or equivalent) to the sump (see illustration). Note that the sealant should be run around the inside of the bolt holes in the sump. The sump must be fitted within 5 minutes of applying the sealant.

13 Offer the sump up to the cylinder block, then refit the sump-to-cylinder block bolts, and lightly tighten them by hand, working progressively in a diagonal sequence. Note: If the sump is being refitted with the engine and transmission separated, make sure that the sump is flush with the flywheel end of the cylinder block.

14 Refit the sump-to-transmission casing bolts, and tighten them lightly, using a socket.

15 Again working in a diagonal sequence, lightly tighten the sump-to-cylinder block bolts, using a socket.

16 Tighten the sump-to-transmission casing bolts to the specified torque.

17 Working in a diagonal sequence, progressively tighten the sump-to-cylinder block bolts to the specified torque.

18 The remainder of refitting is a reversal of removal, noting to allow at least 30 minutes from the time of refitting the sump for the sealant to dry, then refill the engine with oil, with reference to Chapter 1, Section 6.

13 Oil pump – removal, inspection and refitting

Removal

1 Remove the sump as described in Section 12.

2 Unbolt and remove the pick up pipe.

3 Unbolt and remove the baffle plate and then unbolt the oil pump. Unhook the pump from the drive belt as the pump is removed.

Inspection

4 Inspect the drive belt teeth for damage and replace the belt if necessary. A high mileage belt may sag, but this should not be a cause for concern. If in doubt always replace the belt.

5 No parts are available for the oil pump. If defective the oil pump must be renewed. Consult a VW dealer or parts specialist.

Refitting

6 Refitting is a reversal of removal, noting the following:
a) Replace the O-ring seal.
b) Prime the oil pump with clean oil.
c) Tighten the bolts to the specified torque.
d) Refit the sump.
e) Refill the engine with fresh oil and check the level.
f) Check the oil warning light is working.
g) Disable the injectors (or use a remote starter) and crank the engine until the oil warning light extinguishes.

14 Flywheel – removal, inspection and refitting

Removal

1 On manual transmission models, remove the transmission (see Chapter 7A, Section 3) and clutch (see Chapter 6, Section 6).

2 On automatic transmission models, remove the semi-automatic (DSG) transmission as described in.

3 Manual models are fitted with a dual-mass flywheel, which can only be fitted in one position due to the offset of the mounting bolt holes in the end of the crankshaft.

4 Rotate the outside of the dual-mass flywheel so that the bolts align with the holes (if necessary).

14.5 Use a locking tool to counterhold the flywheel

14.9 Flywheel warpage check – see text

5 Unscrew the bolts and remove the flywheel. Use a locking tool to counterhold the flywheel **(see illustration)**. Discard the bolts, as new ones must be fitted. Note: In order not to damage the flywheel, do not allow the bolt heads to make contact with the flywheel during the unscrewing procedure.

Inspection

6 Check the flywheel for wear and damage. Examine the starter ring gear for excessive wear to the teeth. If the driveplate or its ring gear is damaged, the complete driveplate must be renewed. The flywheel ring gear, however, may be renewed separately from the flywheel, but the work should be entrusted to a VW dealer. If the clutch friction face is discoloured or scored excessively, it may be possible to regrind it, but this work should also be entrusted to a VW dealer.

7 The following are guidelines only, but should indicate whether professional inspection is necessary. The dual-mass flywheel should be checked as follows:

8 There should be no cracks in the drive surface of the flywheel. If cracks are evident, the flywheel may need renewing.

Warpage

9 Place a straightedge across the face of the drive surface, and check by trying to insert a feeler gauge between the straightedge and the drive surface **(see illustration)**. The flywheel will normally warp like a bowl – i.e. higher on the outer edge. If the warpage is more than 0.40 mm, the flywheel may need renewing.

Free rotational movement

10 This is the distance the drive surface of the flywheel can be turned independently of the flywheel primary element, using finger effort alone. Move the drive surface in one direction and make a mark where the locating pin aligns with the flywheel edge. Move the drive surface in the other direction (finger pressure only) and make another mark **(see illustration)**. The total of free movement should not exceed 20.0 mm. If it's more, the flywheel may need renewing.

Total rotational movement

11 This is the total distance the drive surface can be turned independently of the flywheel primary element. Insert two bolts into the clutch pressure plate/damper unit mounting holes, and with the crankshaft/flywheel held stationary, use a lever/pry bar between the bolts and use some effort to move the drive surface fully in one direction – make a mark where the locating pin aligns with the flywheel edge. Now force the drive surface fully in the opposite direction, and make another mark. The total rotational movement should not exceed 44.0 mm. If it does, have the flywheel professionally inspected.

Lateral movement

12 The lateral movement (up and down) of the drive surface in relation to the primary element of the flywheel should not exceed 2.0 mm. If it does, the flywheel may need renewing. This can be checked by pressing the drive surface down on one side into the flywheel (flywheel horizontal) and making an alignment mark between the drive surface and the inner edge of the primary element. Now press down on the opposite side of the drive surface, and make another mark above the original one. The difference between the two marks is the lateral movement **(see illustration)**.

Refitting

13 Refitting is a reversal of removal. Use new bolts when refitting the flywheel or driveplate, and coat the threads of the bolts with locking fluid before inserting them. Tighten them to the specified torque.

15 Crankshaft oil seals – renewal

Note: *The oil seals are a PTFE (Teflon) type and are fitted dry, without using any grease or oil. These have a wider sealing lip and have been introduced instead of the coil spring type oil seal.*

Timing belt end oil seal

1 Remove the timing belt as described in Section 7, and the crankshaft sprocket with reference to Section 8.

2 To remove the seal without removing the housing, drill two small holes diagonally

14.10 Flywheel free rotational movement check alignment marks – see text

14.12 Flywheel lateral movement check marks – see text

15.2 Pull the screw and seal from place using pliers

15.3 Prise the oil seal from the crankshaft oil seal housing

15.9 Slide the oil seal housing over the end of the crankshaft

opposite each other, insert self-tapping screws, and pull on the heads of the screws with pliers **(see illustration)**.

3 Alternatively, to remove the oil seal complete with its housing, proceed as follows.

a) *Remove the sump as described in Section 12. This is necessary to ensure a satisfactory seal between the sump and oil seal housing on refitting.*

b) *Unscrew and remove the oil seal housing.*

c) *Working on the bench, lever the oil seal from the housing using a suitable screwdriver. Take care not to damage the seal seating in the housing* **(see illustration)**.

4 Thoroughly clean the oil seal seating in the housing.

5 Wind a length of tape around the end of the crankshaft to protect the oil seal lips as the seal (and housing, where applicable) is fitted.

6 Fit a new oil seal to the housing, pressing or driving it into position using a socket or tube of suitable diameter. Ensure that the socket or tube bears only on the hard outer ring of the seal, and take care not to damage the seal lips. Press or drive the seal into position until it is seated on the shoulder in the housing. Make sure that the closed end of the seal is facing outwards.

7 If the oil seal housing has been removed, proceed as follows, otherwise proceed to paragraph 11.

8 Clean all traces of old sealant from the crankshaft oil seal housing and the cylinder block, then coat the cylinder block mating faces of the oil seal housing with a 2.0 to 3.0 mm thick bead of silicone sealant (VW D 176 404 A2, or equivalent). Note that the seal

housing must be refitted within 5 minutes of applying the sealant.

Caution: DO NOT put excessive amounts of sealant onto the housing as it may get into the sump and block the oil pick-up pipe.

9 Refit the oil seal housing, and tighten the bolts progressively to the specified torque **(see illustration)**.

10 Refit the sump as described in Section 12.

11 Refit the crankshaft sprocket with reference to Section 8, and the timing belt as described in Section 7.

Flywheel end oil seal

Note: *In these engines, the seal, sealing flange and sender wheel are a complete unit. Special tools are required to refit the sealing flange, and press the sender wheel onto the end of the crankshaft. It is not possible to accurately fit these parts without the tools, which may be available from VW (part No T10134) and are available from aftermarket automotive tool specialists.*

12 Remove the flywheel as described in Section 14, then prise the intermediate plate from the locating dowels on the cylinder block.

13 Undo the bolts securing the sealing flange to the cylinder block **(see illustration)**.

14 Insert three 6 x 35 mm bolts into the threaded holes in the sealing flange. Tighten the bolts gradually and evenly, and press the sealing flange and sender wheel from the crankshaft/cylinder block **(see illustration)**. The seal, sender wheel and sealing flange are supplied as a complete unit.

15 Ensure the mating face of the cylinder block is clean and free from debris. The new sealing flange/seal/sender wheel assembly is supplied with a sealing lip support ring, which serves as a fitting sleeve, and must not be removed prior to installation. Equally, the sender wheel must not be separated from the assembly.

16 If using the VW tool, proceed as follows. If using an aftermarket tool specialist's product, follow the instructions supplied with the tool. Rotate the large spindle nut until it's level with the end of the clamping surface of the spindle, then clamp the spindle in a vice **(see illustrations)**.

17 Press the tool housing downwards until it

15.13 Sealing flange bolts

15.14 Bolt in three 6 x 35 mm bolts and draw the sealing flange and sender wheel from place

15.16a Rotate the nut until it is level with the end of the clamping surface...

15.16b ... then clamp it in a vice

15.17 Rotate the nut until the inner part of the tool is flush with the housing

15.18a Remove the securing clip …

15.18b … the hole in the sender wheel should align with the marking on the flange

rests on the nut and washer. Rotate the nut until the inner part of the tool is at the same height as the housing (**see illustration**).

18 Remove the seal securing clip. The hole on the sender wheel must align with the marking on the sealing flange (**see illustrations**).

19 Place the flange outer side down on a clean, flat surface, then press the seal guide fitting sleeve (supplied ready fitted), housing, and sender wheel downwards until all the components are flat on the surface. In this position the upper edge of the sender wheel should be level with the edge of the sealing flange (**see illustrations**).

20 Place the sealing flange on the assembly tool, so the pin locates in the hole in the sender wheel (**see illustration**).

21 Push the sealing flange and guide fitting sleeve against the tool whilst tightening the 3 knurled bolts. Ensure the pin is still located in the sender wheel (**see illustration**).

22 Ensure the end of the crankshaft is clean, and is locked at TDC on No 1 cylinder as described in Section 3.

23 Unscrew the large nut to the end of the spindle threads, then press the spindle inwards as far as possible (**see illustration**).

24 Align the flat side of the assembly with the sump flange, then secure the tool to the crankshaft using the integral Allen bolts (**see illustration**). Only hand-tighten the bolts.

25 Insert two M7 x 35 mm bolts to guide the sealing flange to the cylinder block (**see illustration**).

15.19a Press the assembly downwards on a clean, flat surface …

15.19b … so the upper edge of the sender wheel is level with the edge of the flange

15.20 Fit the flange to the tool, ensuring the pin locates in the hole

15.21 With the pin engaged in the hole, tighten the 3 knurled bolts to secure the flange to the tool

15.23 Unscrew the nut to the end of the thread, and push the spindle in as far as possible

15.24 Hand-tighten the Allen bolts to secure the tool to the crankshaft

15.25 Use 2 M7 x 35 mm bolts to guide the sealing flange

15.26 Push the black knob into the hole in the crankshaft

15.27 After tightening the spindle nut there should be an air gap between the sealing flange and the cylinder block

15.29 Measure the fitted depth of the sender wheel in relation to the end of the crankshaft

26 Using hand-pressure alone, push the tool assembly onto the crankshaft until the seal guide fitting sleeve contacts the crankshaft flange, then push the guide pin (black knob) into the hole in the crankshaft. This is to ensure the sender wheel reaches its correct installation position (see illustration).

27 Rotate the large nut until it makes contact with the tool housing, then tighten it to 35 Nm (26 lbf ft). After tightening this nut, a small air gap must still be present between the sealing flange and cylinder block (see illustration).

28 Unscrew the large nut; the two M7 x 35 mm bolts, the three knurled bolts and the Allen bolts securing the tool to the crankshaft. Remove the tool, and pull the seal guide fitting sleeve from place (if it didn't come out with the tool).

29 Use a vernier caliper or feeler gauge to measure the fitted depth of the sender wheel in relation to the crankshaft flange (see illustration). The correct depth is 0.5 mm.

30 If the gap is correct, fit the sealing flange bolts and tighten them to the specified torque.

31 If the gap is too small, re-attach the tool to the sealing flange and crankshaft, then refit the two M7 x 35 mm guide bolts to the flange. Tighten the large spindle nut to 40 Nm (30 lbf ft), remove the tool and measure the air gap. If the gap is still too small, re-attach the tool and tighten the spindle nut to 45 Nm (33 lbf

ft). Measure the gap again. When the gap is correct, refit the flange retaining bolts, and tighten them to the specified torque.

32 The remainder of refitting is a reversal of removal.

16 Engine/transmission mountings – inspection and renewal

Inspection

1 If improved access is required, jack up the front of the vehicle, and support it securely on axle stands (see Jacking and vehicle support). Where fitted, remove the engine cover the engine undershield.

2 Check the mounting rubbers to see if they are cracked, hardened or separated from the metal at any point; renew the mounting if any such damage or deterioration is evident.

3 Check that all the mountings are securely tightened; use a torque wrench to check if possible.

4 Using a large screwdriver or a crowbar, check for wear in the mounting by carefully levering against it to check for free play. Where this is not possible, enlist the aid of an assistant to move the engine/transmission back-and-forth, or from side-to-side, whilst you observe the mounting. While some free play is to be expected, even

from new components, excessive wear should be obvious. If excessive free play is found, check first that the fasteners are correctly secured, and then renew any worn components as described in the following paragraphs.

Renewal

Right-hand mounting

Note: New mounting securing bolts will be required on refitting.

5 Attach a hoist and lifting tackle to the engine lifting brackets on the cylinder head, and raise the hoist to just take the weight of the engine. Alternatively the engine can be supported on a trolley jack under the engine. Use a block of wood between the sump and the head of the jack, to prevent any damage to the sump.

6 For improved access, unscrew the coolant reservoir and move it to one side, leaving the coolant hoses connected. Also remove the filler neck from the screen washer bottle (see illustrations).

7 Where fitted, disconnect the wiring plug, undo the retaining bolts, and remove the pressure sensor (including the bracket) from the top of the engine mounting and move it to one side (see illustrations 6.3a & 6.3b).

8 Undo the retaining bolts and move the fuel filter to one side (see illustration). Where applicable, move any wiring harnesses, pipes

16.6a Disconnect the level sensor wiring plug

16.6b Unclip the wiring loom, unbolt the reservoir and move it to the side

16.6c Unbolt and remove the filler neck

16.8 The fuel filter can be placed on top of the engine

16.9a Remove the small bracket...

16.9b ...the mounting to body bolts...

16.9c ...and the mounting to engine bracket bolts

16.9d Remove the mounting

16.10 There must be at least 10 mm between the bracket and the chassis member

or hoses to one side to enable removal of the engine mounting.

9 Unscrew the bolts securing the mounting to the engine bracket, and then unscrew the bolts securing it to the body **(see illustrations)**. Withdraw the mounting from the engine compartment.

10 Refitting is a reversal of removal, bearing in mind the following points.

a) *Use new securing bolts.*

b) *There must be at least 10 mm between the engine mounting bracket and the right-hand side chassis member* **(see illustration)**.

c) *The side of the mounting support arm must be parallel to the side of the engine mounting bracket.*

d) *Tighten all fixings to the specified torque.*

Left-hand mounting

Note: *New mounting bolts will be required on refitting.*

11 Where fitted, remove the engine top cover. If the transmission is to be supported from below remove the engine undershield – again where fitted.

12 Attach a hoist and lifting tackle to the engine lifting brackets on the cylinder head, and raise the hoist to just take the weight of the engine and transmission. Alternatively the engine can be supported on a trolley jack under the transmission. Use a block of wood between the transmission and the head of the jack, to prevent any damage to the transmission.

13 Remove the battery and battery tray, as described in (Chapter 5A Section 3). Unclip the wiring loom and move it to the side **(see illustration)**.

14 Unscrew the bolts securing the mounting to the transmission, and the remaining bolts securing the mounting to the body **(see illustrations)**, then lift the mounting from the engine compartment.

15 Refitting is a reversal of removal, bearing in mind the following points:

a) *Use new mounting bolts.*

b) *The edges of the mounting support arm must be parallel to the edge of the mounting.*

c) *Tighten all fixings to the specified torque.*

16.13 Move the loom to the side

16.14a Remove the bolts and...

16.14b ...lift out the mounting

16.19 Rear mounting arm-to-transmission bolts

Rear mounting (torque arm)

Note: *New mounting bolts will be required on refitting.*

16 Apply the handbrake, then jack up the front of the vehicle and support securely on axle stands (see *Jacking and vehicle support*). Where fitted, remove the engine undershield for access to the rear mounting (torque arm).

17 Support the rear of the transmission beneath the final drive housing. To do this, use a trolley jack and block of wood, or alternatively wedge a block of wood between the transmission and the subframe.

18 Working under the vehicle, unscrew and remove the bolt securing the mounting to the subframe.

19 Unscrew the two bolts securing the mounting to the transmission, then withdraw the mounting from under the vehicle **(see illustration)**.

20 Refitting is a reversal of removal, but use new mounting securing bolts, and tighten all fixings to the specified torque.

17 Engine oil cooler/filter housing – removal and refitting

Removal

1 The oil cooler is mounted on the lower part of the oil filter housing on the front of the cylinder block, which is the same as the 1.6 litre diesel engine. Refer to Chapter 2A, Section 17, for the removal and refitting procedure

18 Oil pressure warning light switch – removal and refitting

1 The oil pressure warning light switch is fitted to the left-hand rear of the cylinder head, which is the same as the 1.6 litre diesel engine. Refer to Chapter 2A, Section 18, for the removal refitting procedure.

19 Oil level/temperature sender – removal and refitting

1 The oil level/temperature sender is fitted to bottom of the sump, which is the same as the 1.6 litre diesel engine. Refer to Chapter 2A, Section 19, for the removal refitting procedure

Chapter 2 Part C
1.9 and 2.0 litre unit injector (PD) diesel engine in-car repair procedures

Contents

Degrees of difficulty

Easy, suitable for novice with little experience	Fairly easy, suitable for beginner with some experience	Fairly difficult, suitable for competent DIY mechanic	Difficult, suitable for experienced DIY mechanic	Very difficult, suitable for expert DIY or professional

Specifications

General

Manufacturer's engine codes*:
1896 cc (1.9 litre), 8-valve, turbo, SOHC	BKC, BJB, BLS, BSU, BDJ and BST
1968 cc (2.0 litre), 8-valve, turbo, SOHC	BMM
1968 cc (2.0 litre), 8-valve SOHC (no turbocharger).	BDJ and BST

Maximum outputs:

	Power	Torque
Engine code BKC	77 kW at 4000 rpm	250 Nm at 1900 rpm
Engine code BJB	77 kW @ 4000 rpm	250 Nm at 1900 rpm
Engine code BLS	77 kW at 4000 rpm	250 Nm at 1900 rpm
Engine code BSU	55 kW @ 4000 rpm	210 Nm at 1900 rpm
Engine code BDJ	51 kW @ 4200 rpm	140 Nm at 2200 to 2400 rpm
Engine code BST	51 kW @ 4200 rpm	140 Nm at 2200 to 2400 rpm
Engine code BMM	103 kW at 4000 rpm	320 Nm at 1750 to 2500 rpm

Bore:
1896 cc engines	79.5 mm
1968 cc engines	81.0 mm
Stroke	95.5 mm

Compression ratio:
Engine code BKC, BJB, BLS, BSU, BDJ and BST	19.0 : 1
Engine code BMM	18.5 : 1

Compression pressures:
Minimum compression pressure	Approximately 19.0 bar
Maximum difference between cylinders.	Approximately 5.0 bar
Firing order	1 – 3 – 4 – 2
No 1 cylinder location.	Timing belt end

* **Note:** *See 'Vehicle identification' at the end of this manual for the location of engine code markings.*

Camshaft

Camshaft endfloat (maximum)	0.15 mm
Camshaft bearing running clearance (maximum).	0.11 mm
Camshaft run-out (maximum).	0.01 mm

Lubrication system

Oil pump type. . . . . Gear type, chain-driven from crankshaft
Oil pressure (oil temperature 80°C, at 2000 rpm). . . . . 2.0 bar

Torque wrench settings

	Nm	lbf ft
Ancillary (alternator, etc) bracket mounting bolts.	45	33
Air conditioning compressor	45	33
Alternator and tensioner.	25	18
Auxiliary drivebelt tensioner securing bolt	25	18
Big-end bearing caps bolts*:		
Stage 1	30	22
Stage 2	Angle-tighten a further 90°	
Camshaft bearing cap bolts*:		
SOHC engines:		
Stage 1	8	6
Stage 2	Angle-tighten a further 90°	
Camshaft bearing frame bolts*:		
DOHC engines	20	15
Camshaft cover nuts/bolts.	10	7
Camshaft sprocket hub centre bolt	100	74
Camshaft sprocket-to-hub bolts	25	18
Coolant pump bolts	15	11
Crankshaft oil seal housing bolts	15	11
Crankshaft pulley-to-sprocket bolts:		
Stage 1	10	7
Stage 2	Angle-tighten a further 90°	
Crankshaft sprocket bolt*:		
Stage 1	120	89
Stage 2	Angle-tighten a further 90°	
Cylinder head bolts*:		
Stage 1	35	26
Stage 2	60	44
Stage 3	Angle-tighten a further 90°	
Stage 4	Angle-tighten a further 90°	
Driveplate:		
Stage 1	60	44
Stage 2	Angle-tighten a further 90°	
Engine mountings:		
RH engine mounting:		
Mounting to engine:		
Stage 1	60	44
Stage 2	Angle-tighten a further 90°	
Mounting to body:		
Stage 1	40	30
Stage 2	Angle-tighten a further 90°	
LH engine mounting:		
Mounting to body:		
Stage 1	60	44
Stage 2	Angle-tighten a further 90°	
Mounting to transmission:		
Stage 1	40	30
Stage 2	Angle-tighten a further 90°	
Rear mounting link:		
To transmission:		
Stage 1	40	30
Stage 2	Angle-tighten a further 90°	
To subframe:		
Stage 1	100	74
Stage 2	Angle-tighten a further 90°	
Flywheel:		
Stage 1	60	44
Stage 2	Angle-tighten a further 90°	
Glow plugs:		
SOHC engines	15	11
DOHC engines	10	7
Injector rocker arm shafts*:		
Stage 1	20	15
Stage 2	Angle-tighten a further 90°	

Torque wrench settings

	Nm	lbf ft
Main bearing cap bolts*:		
Stage 1	65	48
Stage 2	Angle-tighten a further 90°	
Oil drain plug	30	22
Oil filter housing-to-cylinder block bolts*:		
Stage 1	15	11
Stage 2	Angle-tighten a further 90°	
Oil filter cover	25	18
Oil level/temperature sensor-to-sump bolts	10	7
Oil pick-up pipe securing bolts	15	11
Oil pressure relief valve plug	40	30
Oil pressure warning light switch	20	15
Oil pump chain tensioner bolt	15	11
Oil pump securing bolts	15	11
Oil pump sprocket securing bolt:		
Stage 1	20	15
Stage 2	Angle-tighten a further 90°	
Piston oil spray jet bolt	25	18
Sump:		
Sump-to-cylinder block bolts	15	11
Sump-to-transmission bolts	45	33
Tandem pump	20	15
Thermostat housing	15	11
Timing belt idler pulley bolt	20	15
Timing belt outer cover bolts	10	7
Timing belt rear cover-to-cylinder head bolt	10	7
Timing belt tensioner roller securing nut:		
Stage 1	20	15
Stage 2	Angle-tighten a further 45°	
Timing belt idler pulleys:		
Lower right-hand idler roller (below coolant pump sprocket) bolt*:		
Stage 1	40	30
Stage 2	Angle-tighten a further 90°	
Upper idler roller bolt	20	15
Turbocharger/exhaust manifold	20	15
Turbocharger oil supply line union nut	22	16

Use new fixings

1 General Information

How to use this Chapter

1 This Part of Chapter 2 describes those repair procedures that can reasonably be carried out on the engine while it remains in the vehicle. If the engine has been removed from the vehicle and is being dismantled as described in Part D, any preliminary dismantling procedures can be ignored.

2 Note that while it may be possible physically to overhaul certain items while the engine is in the vehicle, such tasks are not usually carried out as separate operations, and usually require the execution of several additional procedures (not to mention the cleaning of components and of oilways); for this reason, all such tasks are classed as major overhaul procedures, and are described in Part D of this Chapter.

Engine description

3 Throughout this Chapter, engines are referred to by type, and are identified and referred to by the manufacturer's code letters. A listing of all engines covered, together with their code letters, is given in the Specifications at the start of this Chapter.

4 The engines are water-cooled, single overhead camshaft, in-line four-cylinder units, with cast-iron cylinder blocks and aluminium-alloy cylinder heads. All are mounted transversely at the front of the vehicle, with the transmission bolted to the left-hand end of the engine.

5 The crankshaft is of five-bearing type, and thrustwashers are fitted to the centre main bearing to control crankshaft endfloat.

6 Drive for the camshaft is by a toothed timing belt from the crankshaft. Each camshaft is mounted at the top of the cylinder head, and is secured by bearing caps.

7 The valves are closed by coil springs, and run in guides pressed into the cylinder head. The camshaft actuates the valves directly, through hydraulic tappets.

8 The gear-type oil pump is driven by a chain from a sprocket on the crankshaft. Oil is drawn from the sump through a strainer, and then forced through an externally-mounted, renewable filter. From there, it is distributed to the cylinder head, where it lubricates the camshaft journals and hydraulic tappets, and also to the crankcase, where it lubricates the main bearings, connecting rod big-ends, gudgeon pins and cylinder bores. A coolant-fed oil cooler is fitted to the oil filter housing on all engines. Oil jets are fitted to the base of each cylinder – these spray oil onto the underside of the pistons, to improve cooling.

9 All engines are fitted with a combined brake servo vacuum pump and fuel lift pump (tandem pump), driven by the camshaft on the transmission end of the cylinder head.

10 On all engines, engine coolant is circulated by a pump, driven by the timing belt. For details of the cooling system, refer to Chapter.

Operations with engine in car

11 The following operations can be performed without removing the engine:

a) Compression pressure – testing.
b) Camshaft cover – removal and refitting.
c) Crankshaft pulley – removal and refitting.
d) Timing belt covers – removal and refitting.
e) Timing belt – removal, refitting and adjustment.
f) Timing belt tensioner and sprockets – removal and refitting.

g) *Camshaft oil seals – renewal.*
h) *Camshaft(s) and hydraulic tappets – removal, inspection and refitting.*
i) *Cylinder head – removal and refitting.*
j) *Cylinder head and pistons – decarbonising.*
k) *Sump – removal and refitting.*
l) *Oil pump – removal, overhaul and refitting.*
m) *Crankshaft oil seals – renewal.*
n) *Engine/transmission mountings – inspection and renewal.*
o) *Flywheel/driveplate – removal, inspection and refitting.*

Note: *It is possible to remove the pistons and connecting rods (after removing the cylinder head and sump) without removing the engine. However, this is not recommended. Work of this nature is more easily and thoroughly completed with the engine on the bench, as described in Chapter Section.*

2 Compression and leakdown tests – description and interpretation

Compression test

Note: *A compression tester suitable for use with diesel engines will be required for this test.*

1 When engine performance is down, or if misfiring occurs which cannot be attributed to the ignition or fuel systems, a compression test can provide diagnostic clues as to the engine's condition. If the test is performed regularly, it can give warning of trouble before any other symptoms become apparent.

2 The engine must be fully warmed-up to normal operating temperature, the battery must be fully-charged, and you will require the aid of an assistant.

3 Disconnect the injector solenoids by disconnecting the connector at the end of the cylinder head **(see illustration)**. Note: As a result of the wiring being disconnected, faults will be stored in the ECU memory. These must be erased after the compression test.

4 Remove the glow plugs as described in Chapter Section, then fit a compression tester to the No 1 cylinder glow plug hole. The type of tester which screws into the plug thread is preferred.

5 Have your assistant crank the engine for several seconds on the starter motor. After one or two revolutions, the compression pressure should build-up to a maximum figure and then stabilise. Record the highest reading obtained.

6 Repeat the test on the remaining cylinders, recording the pressure in each.

7 The cause of poor compression is less easy to establish on a diesel engine than on a petrol engine. The effect of introducing oil into the cylinders (wet testing) is not conclusive, because there is a risk that the oil will sit in the recess on the piston crown, instead of passing to the rings. However, the following can be used as a rough guide to diagnosis.

8 All cylinders should produce very similar pressures. Any difference greater than that specified indicates the existence of a fault. Note that the compression should build-up quickly in a healthy engine. Low compression on the first stroke, followed by gradually increasing pressure on successive strokes, indicates worn piston rings. A low compression reading on the first stroke, which does not build-up during successive strokes, indicates leaking valves or a blown head gasket (a cracked head could also be the cause).

9 A low reading from two adjacent cylinders is almost certainly due to the head gasket having blown between them and the presence of coolant in the engine oil will confirm this.

10 On completion, remove the compression tester, and refit the glow plugs, with reference to Chapter Section.

11 Reconnect the wiring to the injector solenoids. Finally, have a VW dealer or suitably equipped garage erase the fault codes from the ECU memory.

Leakdown test

12 A leakdown test measures the rate at which compressed air fed into the cylinder is lost. It is an alternative to a compression test, and in many ways it is better, since the escaping air provides easy identification of where pressure loss is occurring (piston rings, valves or head gasket).

13 The equipment required for leakdown testing is unlikely to be available to the home mechanic. If poor compression is suspected, have the test performed by a suitably-equipped garage.

3 Engine assembly and valve timing marks – general information and usage

General information

1 TDC is the highest point in the cylinder that each piston reaches as it travels up-and-down when the crankshaft turns. Each piston reaches TDC at the end of the compression stroke and again at the end of the exhaust stroke, but TDC generally refers to piston

2.3 Disconnect the injector solenoids wiring plug connector

position on the compression stroke. No 1 piston is at the timing belt end of the engine.

2 Positioning No 1 piston at TDC is an essential part of many procedures, such as timing belt removal and camshaft removal.

3 The design of the engines covered in this Chapter is such that piston-to-valve contact may occur if the camshaft or crankshaft is turned with the timing belt removed. For this reason, it is important to ensure that the camshaft and crankshaft do not move in relation to each other once the timing belt has been removed from the engine.

Setting TDC on No 1 cylinder

Note: *VAG special tool T10050 (early) or T10100 (late) is required to lock the crankshaft sprocket in the TDC position. The early type tool locates directly onto the sprocket teeth, but, the contour of the teeth on the later type means that the tool must be pushed onto the sprocket teeth from the right-hand end of the engine.*

4 Remove the auxiliary drivebelt(s) as described in Chapter Section.

5 Remove the crankshaft pulley/vibration damper as described in Section 5.

6 Remove the timing belt covers as described in Section 6.

7 Remove the glow plugs, as described in Chapter Section, to allow the engine to turn more easily.

8 Using a spanner or socket on the crankshaft sprocket bolt, turn the crankshaft in the normal direction of rotation (clockwise) until the alignment mark on the face of the sprocket is almost vertical for tool T10050, or at 2 o'clock for tool T10100 **(see illustrations)**.

3.8a TDC setting tools

3.8b Position the crankshaft so that the mark on the sprocket is almost vertical…

3.8c … then insert the VW tool T10050 …

3.8d … and align the marks on the tool and sprocket

9 On some engine codes, the arrow (marked 4Z) on the rear section of the upper timing belt upper cover aligns between the two lugs on the rear of the camshaft hub sender wheel **(see illustration)**.

10 While in this position it should be possible to insert the VAG tool to lock the crankshaft, and a 6 mm diameter rod to lock the camshaft(s) **(see illustrations)**. **Note:** *The mark on the crankshaft sprocket and the mark on the VAG tool must align, whilst at the same time the shaft of tool must engage in the drilling in the crankshaft oil seal housing.*

11 The engine is now set to TDC on No 1 cylinder.

3.9 Align the arrow on the rear of the cover between the lugs on the rear of the camshaft hub sender wheel

3.10a Using the VAG tool to lock the crankshaft at TDC

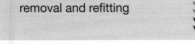

4 Camshaft cover – removal and refitting

Removal

1 Remove the dipstick and (where fitted) prise off and remove the engine top cover, then disconnect the breather hose from the camshaft cover **(see illustrations)**.

2 On models with engine codes BKC, BLS and BSU remove the charge air pipe and disconnect the inlet manifold flap motor **(see illustrations)**. Where required disconnect the vacuum hose.

3 Unclip, unbolt and move to the side the fuel

3.10b Insert a 6 mm drill bit through the camshaft hub into the cylinder head to lock the camshaft

4.1a Remove the engine cover

4.1b Unclip the breather hose

4.2a Disconnect the wiring plug, unclip the loom…

4.2b …and unbolt the support bracket

4.3 Unbolt the fuel lines

4.5 Remove the cover

4.6 Ensure the retaining bolts are pushed fully through the gasket before refitting the camshaft cover

4.8a Apply sealant to the base of the camshaft bearing caps – at both ends

4.8b Camshaft cover tightening sequence

5.3 Removing the intercooler air duct for access to the crankshaft pulley

5.4 Prising out the crankshaft pulley centre cap

5.5 Showing the four crankshaft pulley bolts

lines from the front of the cylinder head (see illustration).

4 Remove the timing belt upper cover as described in Section 6.

5 Unscrew the camshaft cover retaining bolts and lift the cover away (see illustration). Note that the rear right-hand bolt is difficult to access on some models. If it sticks, do not attempt to lever it off – instead free it by working around the cover and tapping it lightly with a soft-faced mallet.

Note: *Some early models feature a cover for which no replacement gasket is available. If the gasket is damaged these models must have the camshaft cover (and gasket) replaced.*

6 Recover the camshaft cover gasket. Inspect the gasket carefully, and renew it if damage or deterioration is evident – note that the retaining bolts must be pushed fully through the gasket before refitting the cover (see illustration).

7 Clean the mating surfaces of the cylinder head and camshaft cover thoroughly, removing all traces of oil and old gasket – take care to avoid damaging the surfaces as you do this.

Refitting

8 Refit the camshaft cover by following the removal procedure in reverse, noting the following points:
a) *Apply suitable sealant to the points where the camshaft bearing cap contacts the cylinder head (see illustration).*
b) *Tighten the camshaft cover retaining nuts/ bolts progressively to the specified torque in the sequence shown (see illustration).*

5 Crankshaft pulley – removal and refitting

Removal

1 Switch off the ignition and all electrical consumers and remove the ignition key.

2 For improved access, raise the front right-hand side of the vehicle, and support securely on axle stands (see Jacking and vehicle support). Remove the roadwheel.

3 Remove the securing screws and (where fitted) withdraw the engine undertray(s) and/ or wheel arch liner panels. Unscrew the nut at the rear, and the washer-type fasteners further forward, then where necessary release the air hose clip and manipulate out the plastic air duct for the intercooler (see illustration).

4 On models fitted with a fuel fired auxiliary heater unbolt the coolant pipes and move them to the side. Where applicable, prise the cover from the centre of the pulley to expose the securing bolts (see illustration).

5 Slacken the bolts securing the crankshaft pulley to the sprocket (see illustration). If necessary, the pulley can be prevented from turning by counterholding with a spanner or socket on the crankshaft sprocket bolt.

5.7 Removing the crankshaft pulley

6.1 Removing the air intake hose from across the top of the timing belt cover

6 Remove the auxiliary drivebelt, as described in Chapter Section.

7 Unscrew the bolts securing the pulley to the sprocket, and remove the pulley (see illustration).

Refitting

8 Refit the pulley over the locating peg on the crankshaft sprocket, then refit the pulley securing bolts.

9 Refit and tension the auxiliary drivebelt as described in Chapter Section.

10 Prevent the crankshaft from turning as during removal, then fit the pulley securing bolts, and tighten to the specified torque.

11 Refit the engine undertray(s), wheel arch liners and the intercooler air duct, as applicable.

12 Refit the roadwheel and lower the vehicle to the ground.

6 Timing belt covers –
removal and refitting

Upper outer cover

1 Where applicable, release the retaining clips and remove the air intake hose from across the top of the timing belt cover (see illustration).

2 Release the uppermost part of the timing belt outer cover by prising open the metal spring clips, then withdraw the cover away from the engine. (see illustrations).

3 Refitting is a reversal of removal, noting that the lower edge of the upper cover engages with the centre cover.

Centre outer cover

4 Remove the auxiliary drivebelt as described in Chapter Section.

5 Remove the crankshaft pulley as described in Section 5. It is assumed that, if the centre cover is being removed, the lower cover will be also – if not, simply remove the components described in Section 5 for access to the crankshaft pulley, and leave the pulley in position.

6 With the upper cover removed (paragraphs 1 to 3), unscrew and remove the retaining bolts from the centre cover. Withdraw the

centre cover from the engine, noting how it fits over the lower cover.

7 Refitting is a reversal of the removal procedure.

Lower outer cover

8 Remove the upper and centre covers as described previously.

9 If not already done, remove the crankshaft pulley as described in Section 5.

10 Unscrew the remaining bolt(s) securing the lower cover, and lift it out.

11 Refitting is a reversal of removal; locate the centre cover in place before fitting the top two bolts.

Rear cover

12 Remove the upper, centre and lower covers as described previously.

6.2a Release the retaining clips...

7.0a Engine mounting support close to the engine (V1)

13 Remove the timing belt, tensioner and sprockets as described in Section 7 and Section 8.

14 Slacken and withdraw the retaining bolts and lift the timing belt inner cover from the studs on the end of the engine, and remove it from the engine compartment.

15 Refitting is a reversal of removal.

7 Timing belt – removal,
inspection and refitting

Note: *On all engines except those with the engine code BMM there are two versions of the right-hand engine mounting. Version one covers the timing belt and must be removed. Models fitted with version two allow the belt to be removed without the need to remove the mounting for belt removal (see illustrations). However in practise removal of the mounting makes access considerable easier.*

Note: *It is consider best practise to always replace the tensioner, idler and coolant pump whenever the timing belt is replaced. Any mounting studs should also be replaced at the same time. Most of the components (apart from the coolant pump) will be supplied with a timing belt kit. Note also that most manufactures will not guarantee a belt against premature failure if the idler(s) and tensioner are not replaced with the belt.*

6.2b ... and withdraw the upper cover

7.0b ...and further from the engine (V2)

7.5a Use a spanner to turn the tensioner clockwise…

7.5b …then lock with a suitable metal rod…

7.5c …remove the auxiliary drivebelt…

Removal

1 The primary function of the toothed timing belt is to drive the camshaft, but it also drives the coolant pump. Should the belt slip or break in service, the valve timing will be disturbed and piston-to-valve contact may occur, resulting in serious engine damage. For this reason, it is important that the timing belt is tensioned correctly, and inspected regularly for signs of wear or deterioration.

2 Switch off the ignition and all electrical consumers and remove the ignition key.

3 Apply the handbrake, then jack up the front of the vehicle and support securely on axle stands (see Jacking and vehicle support).

4 Remove the securing screws and withdraw the engine undertray. Remove the wheel arch liner. Where fitted, remove the engine cover.

5 Remove the auxiliary drivebelt as described in Chapter Section, then unbolt and remove the drivebelt tensioner **(see illustrations)**.

6 Remove the crankshaft pulley/vibration damper as described in Section 5.

7 Where fitted remove the intercooler charge air pipe.

8 Remove the timing belt covers as described in Section 6.

9 Support the engine and remove the right-hand engine mounting as described in Section Section.

10 Remove the fuel filter from its bracket and place to one side.

11 Unbolt the filler neck from the screen washer reservoir.

12 Where applicable, unbolt the fuel filter bracket from the engine mounting.

13 Unbolt the coolant expansion tank and position it to one side. Note: Do not disconnect the hoses.

14 Set the engine to TDC on No 1 cylinder as described in Section 3.

15 If the original timing belt is to be refitted, mark the running direction of the belt, to ensure correct refitting.

Caution: If the belt appears to be in good condition and can be re-used, it is essential that it is refitted the same way around, otherwise accelerated wear will result, leading to premature failure.

16 Loosen the bolts securing the sprocket(s) to the camshaft(s) while holding the sprockets with a suitable tool **(see illustration)**.

17 Loosen the timing belt tensioner securing nut, then use circlip pliers or an Allen key (as applicable) to turn the tensioner anti-clockwise until a suitable pin or drill bit can be inserted through the locking holes. Now, turn the tensioner clockwise to the stop and tighten the securing nut.

18 Slide the belt from the sprockets, taking care not to twist or kink the belt excessively if it is to be re-used. If the belt is to be replaced remove the tensioner and idler. Also consider replacing the coolant pump – see the note at the beginning of this Section.

Inspection

19 Examine the belt for evidence of contamination by coolant or lubricant. If this is the case, find the source of the contamination before progressing any further. Check the belt for signs of wear or damage, particularly around the leading edges of the belt teeth. Renew the belt if its condition is in doubt; the cost of belt renewal is negligible compared with potential cost of the engine repairs, should the belt fail in service. The belt must be renewed if it has covered the mileage given in Chapter Section, however, if it has covered less, it is prudent to renew it regardless of condition, as a precautionary measure.

20 If the timing belt is not going to be refitted for some time, it is a wise precaution to hang a warning label on the steering wheel, to remind yourself (and others) not to attempt to start the engine.

Refitting

21 Ensure that the crankshaft and camshaft are still set to TDC on No 1 cylinder, as described in Section 3. Fit the new tensioner and idler as described in Section 8.

22 Position the camshaft sprocket(s) so that the securing bolts are in the centre part of the elongated holes **(see illustration)**.

23 Loop the timing belt loosely under the crankshaft sprocket. **Note:** *Observe any direction of rotation markings on the belt.*

7.5d …and unbolt the tensioner

7.16 Using a home-made tool to hold the camshaft sprocket while loosening the bolts

7.22 Position the camshaft sprocket so that the securing bolts are in the centre part of the elongated holes

24 Engage the timing belt teeth with the camshaft sprocket(s) **(see illustration)**, then manoeuvre it into position around the tensioning roller, crankshaft sprocket, and finally around the coolant pump sprocket. Make sure that the belt teeth seat correctly on the sprockets. **Note:** *Slight adjustment to the position of the camshaft sprocket may be necessary to achieve this.* Avoid bending the belt back on itself or twisting it excessively as you do this. Ensure that any slack in the belt is in the section of belt that passes over the tensioner roller.

25 Loosen the timing belt tensioner securing nut, and turn the tensioner anti-clockwise with the circlip pliers or an Allen key (as applicable) until the locking pin can be removed. Now, turn the tensioner clockwise until the pointer is in the middle of the gap in the tensioner base plate **(see illustration)**. With the tensioner held in this position, tighten the securing nut to the specified torque and angle.

26 Tighten the camshaft sprocket bolts to the specified torque, remove the sprocket locking pin(s) and the crankshaft locking tool.

27 Using a spanner or wrench and socket on the crankshaft pulley centre bolt, rotate the crankshaft through two complete revolutions. Reset the engine to TDC on No 1 cylinder, with reference to Section 3 and check that the crankshaft and camshaft sprocket locking pins can still be inserted. If the camshaft sprocket locking pin(s) cannot be inserted, slacken the retaining bolts, turn the hub(s) until the pin(s) fit, and tighten the sprocket retaining bolts to the specified torque.

28 Refit the coolant expansion tank.

29 Where applicable, refit the fuel filter bracket to the engine mounting.

30 Refit the screen washer reservoir filler neck.

31 Refit the fuel filter to its bracket, and where necessary reconnect the fuel lines and intercooler charge air pipe.

32 Where applicable, refit the right-hand engine mounting as described in Section Section.

33 Refit the timing belt covers as described in Section 6.

34 Refit the crankshaft pulley/vibration damper as described in Section 5.

35 Refit the auxiliary drivebelt and tensioner with reference to Chapter Section.

36 Refit the engine undertray(s), right-hand wheel arch liner and engine top cover, and lower the vehicle to the ground.

---

8 Timing belt tensioner and sprockets – removal and refitting

Timing belt tensioner

Note: *Early versions of the tensioner only had holes for a pin type spanner. Later tensioners have provision for the use of a hex key.*

Removal

1 Remove the timing belt as described in Section 7.

7.24 Fitting the timing belt

2 Unscrew the timing belt tensioner nut, and remove the tensioner from the engine **(see illustration)**.

3 When refitting the tensioner to the engine, ensure that the lug on the tensioner backplate engages with the corresponding cut-out in the rear timing belt cover, then refit the tensioner nut **(see illustration)**.

Refitting

4 Fitting new studs to the tensioner and idler is recommended **(see illustration)**. Refit and tension the timing belt as described in Section 7, making sure that the tensioner backplate is correctly engaged with the hole in the cylinder head.

Idler pulleys
Removal

5 Remove the timing belt as described in Section 7.

8.2 Timing belt tensioner nut

8.4 Lock two nuts together and replace the tensioner and idler mounting studs

7.25 The tensioner correctly tensioned

6 Unscrew the relevant idler pulley securing bolt/nut, then withdraw the pulley **(see illustration)**.

Refitting

7 Refit the pulley and tighten the securing bolt or nut to the specified torque. Note: Renew the bolt (where applicable).

8 Refit and tension the timing belt as described in Section 7.

Crankshaft sprocket

Note: *A new crankshaft sprocket securing bolt must be used on refitting.*

Removal

9 Remove the timing belt as described in Section 7.

10 The sprocket securing bolt must now be slackened, and the crankshaft must be prevented from turning as the sprocket bolt

8.3 Ensure that the lug on the tensioner backplate engages with the cut-out in the rear timing belt cover

8.6 Remove the idler

8.14 Fitting a new crankshaft sprocket securing bolt

8.22 Using a fabricated tool to counterhold the camshaft hub

8.23 Attach a three-legged puller to the hub, and evenly tighten the puller until the hub is free of the camshaft taper

is unscrewed. To hold the sprocket, make up a suitable tool, and screw it to the sprocket using a two bolts screwed into two of the crankshaft pulley bolt holes.

11 Hold the sprocket using the tool, then slacken the sprocket securing bolt. Take care, as the bolt is very tight. Do not allow the crankshaft to turn as the bolt is slackened.

12 Unscrew the bolt, and slide the sprocket from the end of the crankshaft, noting which way round the sprocket's raised boss is fitted.

Refitting

13 Commence refitting by positioning the sprocket on the end of the crankshaft, with the raised boss fitted as noted on removal.

14 Fit a new sprocket securing bolt, then counterhold the sprocket using the method employed on removal, and tighten the bolt to the specified torque in the two stages given **(see illustration)**.

15 Refit the timing belt as described in Section 7.

Camshaft sprocket

Removal

16 Remove the timing belt as described in Section 7.

17 Unscrew and remove the three retaining bolts and remove the camshaft sprocket from the camshaft hub.

Refitting

18 Refit the sprocket ensuring that it is fitted the correct way round, as noted before removal, then insert the sprocket bolts, and tighten by hand only at this stage.

19 If the crankshaft has been turned, turn the crankshaft clockwise 90° back to TDC.

20 Refit and tension the timing belt as described in Section 7.

Camshaft hub

Note: *VAG technicians use special tool T10051 to counterhold the hub, however it is possible to fabricate a suitable alternative – see below.*

Removal

21 Remove the camshaft sprocket as described previously in this Section.

22 Engage special tool T10051 with the three locating holes in the face of the hub to prevent the hub from turning. If this tool is not available, fabricate a suitable alternative. Whilst holding the tool, undo the central hub retaining bolt about two turns **(see illustration)**.

23 Leaving the central hub retaining bolt in place, attach VW tool T10052 (or a similar three-legged puller) to the hub, and evenly tighten the puller until the hub is free of the camshaft taper **(see illustration)**. Remove the central hub retaining bolt once the taper is released.

Refitting

24 Ensure that the camshaft taper and the hub centre is clean and dry, locate the hub on the taper, noting that the built-in key in the hub taper must align with the keyway in the camshaft taper **(see illustration)**.

25 Hold the hub in this position with tool T10051 (or similar home-made tool), and

tighten the central bolt to the specified torque.

26 Refit the camshaft sprocket as described previously in this Section.

Coolant pump sprocket

27 The coolant pump sprocket is integral with the coolant pump. Refer to Chapter Section for details of coolant pump removal.

---

9 Pump injector rocker shaft assembly – removal and refitting

Removal

1 Remove the camshaft cover as described in Section 4. In order to ensure that the rocker arms are refitted to their original locations, use a marker pen or paint and number the arms 1 to 4, with No 1 nearest the timing belt end of the engine. If the arms are not fitted to their original locations the injector basic clearance setting procedure must be carried out as described in Chapter 4A Section 5.

2 Slacken the locknut of the adjustment screw on the end of the rocker arm above the respective injector, and undo the adjustment screw until the rocker arm lies against the plunger pin of the injector. Starting at the outside and working in, gradually and evenly slacken and remove the rocker shaft retaining bolts. Lift off the rocker shaft. Discard the rocker shaft bolts, new ones must be fitted **(see illustrations)**.

8.24 The built in key in the hub taper must align with the keyway in the camshaft taper

9.2a Slackening the rocker shaft adjustment screws

9.2b Starting with the outer bolts first, carefully and evenly slacken the rocker shaft retaining bolts

Refitting

3 Thoroughly check the rocker shaft, rocker arms and camshaft bearing cap seating surface for any signs of excessive wear or damage.

4 Smear some grease (VW No G000 100) onto the contact face of each rocker arm adjustment screw, and refit the rocker shaft assembly, tightening the new retaining bolts as follows. Starting from the inside out, hand-tighten the bolts. Again, from the inside out, tighten the bolts to the Stage one torque setting. Finally, from the inside out, tighten the bolts to the Stage two angle tightening setting.

5 Attach a DTI (Dial Test Indicator) gauge to the cylinder head upper surface, and position the DTI probe against the top of the adjustment screw. Turn the crankshaft until the rocker arm roller is on the highest point of its corresponding camshaft lobe, and the adjustment screw is at its lowest. Once this position has been established, remove the DTI gauge, screw the adjustment screw in until firm resistance is felt, and the injector spring cannot be compressed further. Turn the adjustment screw anti-clockwise 180°, and tighten the locknut to the specified torque. Repeat this procedure for any other injectors that have been refitted.

6 Refit the camshaft cover and upper timing belt cover, as described in Section 4.

7 Start the engine and check that it runs correctly.

10 Camshaft and hydraulic tappets – removal, inspection and refitting

Note: *New camshaft oil seal(s) will be required on refitting.*

Removal

1 Turn the crankshaft to position No 1 piston at TDC on the firing stroke, and lock the camshaft and the fuel injection sprocket in position, as described in Section 3.

2 Remove the timing belt as described in Section 7.

3 Remove the camshaft sprocket(s) and hubs as described in Section 8.

4 Remove the tandem fuel/brake vacuum pump as described in Chapter Section **(see illustration)**.

5 Remove the injector rocker arms and shaft as described in Section 9.

6 Check the camshaft bearing caps for identification markings **(see illustration)**. The bearing caps are normally stamped with their respective cylinder numbers. If no marks are present, make suitable marks using a scriber or punch. The caps should be numbered from 1 to 5, with No 1 at the timing belt end of the engine. Note on which side of the bearing caps the marks are made to ensure that they are refitted the correct way round.

7 The camshaft rotates in shell bearings. As the camshaft bearing caps are removed, recover the shell bearing halves from the camshaft. Number the back of the bearings with a felt pen to ensure that, if re-used, the bearings are fitted to their original locations. Note: Fitted into the cylinder head, under each camshaft bearing cap, is a washer for each cylinder head bolt.

8 Unscrew the securing nuts, and remove Nos 1, 3 and 5 bearing caps.

9 Working progressively, in a diagonal sequence, slacken the nuts securing Nos 2 and 4 bearing caps. Note that as the nuts are slackened, the valve springs will push the camshaft up.

10 Once the nuts securing Nos 2 and 4 bearing caps have been fully slackened, lift off the bearing caps.

11 Carefully lift the camshaft from the cylinder head, keeping it level and supported at both ends as it is removed so that the journals and lobes are not damaged. Remove the oil seal from the end of the camshaft and discard it – a new one will be required for refitting **(see illustration)**.

12 Lift the hydraulic tappets from their bores in the cylinder head, and store them with the valve contact surfaces facing downwards, to prevent the oil from draining

out. It is recommended that the tappets are kept immersed in oil for the period they are removed from the cylinder head. Make a note of the position of each tappet, as they must be refitted in their original locations on reassembly – accelerated wear leading to early failure will result if the tappets are interchanged.

13 Recover the lower shell bearing halves from the cylinder head; number the back of the shells with a felt pen to ensure that, if re-used, the bearings are fitted to their original locations.

Inspection

14 With the camshaft(s) removed, examine the bearing caps/frame and the bearing locations in the cylinder head for signs of obvious wear or pitting. If evident, a new cylinder head will probably be required. Also check that the oil supply holes in the cylinder head are free from obstructions.

15 Visually inspect the camshaft for evidence of wear on the surfaces of the lobes and journals. Normally their surfaces should be smooth and have a dull shine; look for scoring, erosion or pitting and areas that appear highly polished, indicating excessive wear. Accelerated wear will occur once the hardened exterior of the camshaft has been damaged, so always renew worn items. Note: If these symptoms are visible on the tips of the camshaft lobes, check the corresponding tappet, as it will probably be worn as well.

16 If the machined surfaces of the camshaft appear discoloured or blued, it is likely that it has been overheated at some point, probably due to inadequate lubrication. This may have distorted the shaft, so check the run-out as follows: place the camshaft between two V-blocks and using a DTI gauge, measure the run-out at the centre journal. If it exceeds the figure quoted in the Specifications at the start of this Chapter, renew the camshaft.

17 To measure the camshaft endfloat, temporarily refit the camshaft to the cylinder head, then fit Nos 1 and 5 bearing caps and tighten the retaining nuts to the specified torque setting. Anchor a DTI gauge to the

10.4 Tandem fuel/brake vacuum pump

10.6 Check the camshaft bearing caps for markings

10.11 Remove the camshaft oil seal

10.17 Checking camshaft endfloat using a DTI gauge

timing belt end of the cylinder head (see illustration). Push the camshaft to one end of the cylinder head as far as it will travel, then rest the DTI gauge probe on the end face of the camshaft, and zero the gauge. Push the camshaft as far as it will go to the other end of the cylinder head, and record the gauge reading. Verify the reading by pushing the camshaft back to its original position and checking that the gauge indicates zero again. Note: The hydraulic tappets must not be fitted whilst this measurement is being taken.

18 Check that the camshaft endfloat measurement is within the limit listed in the Specifications Section. If the measurement is outside the specified limit, wear is unlikely to be confined to any one component, so renewal of the camshaft, cylinder head and bearing caps must be considered.

19 The camshaft bearing running clearance should now be measured. This will be difficult to achieve without a range of micrometers or internal/external expanding calipers, measure the outside diameters of the camshaft bearing surfaces and the internal diameters formed by the bearing caps/frame (and shell bearings where applicable) and the bearing locations in the cylinder head. The difference between these two measurements is the running clearance.

20 Compare the camshaft running clearance measurements with the figure given in the Specifications; if any are outside the specified tolerance, the camshaft, cylinder head and bearing caps/frame (and shell bearings where applicable) should be renewed.

21 Inspect the hydraulic tappets for obvious signs of wear or damage, and renew if necessary. Check that the oil holes in the tappets are free from obstructions.

Refitting

22 Smear some clean engine oil onto the sides of the hydraulic tappets, and offer them into position in their original bores in the cylinder head. Push them down until they contact the valves, then lubricate the camshaft lobe contact surfaces.

23 Lubricate the camshaft and cylinder head bearing journals and shell bearings with clean engine oil.

24 Carefully lower the camshaft into position in the cylinder head making sure that the cam lobes for No 1 cylinder are pointing upwards.

25 Refit a new camshaft oil seal on the end of the camshaft. Make sure that the closed end of the seal faces the camshaft sprocket end of the camshaft, and take care not to damage the seal lip. Locate the seal against the seat in the cylinder head.

26 Oil the upper surfaces of the camshaft bearing journals and shell bearings, then fit Nos 2 and 4 bearing caps. Ensure that they are fitted the right way round and in the correct locations, then progressively tighten the retaining nuts in a diagonal sequence to the specified torque. Note that as the nuts are tightened, the camshaft will be forced down against the pressure of the valve springs.

27 Fit bearing caps 1, 3 and 5 over the camshaft and progressively tighten the nuts to the specified torque. Note that it may be necessary to locate No 5 bearing cap by tapping lightly on the end of the camshaft.

28 Refit the injector rocker arms as described in Section 9.

29 Renew the camshaft oil seal(s) as applicable with reference to Section 12.

30 Refit the tandem fuel/brake vacuum pump (where fitted) as described in Chapter Section.

31 Refit the camshaft sprocket(s) and hubs as described in Section 8.

32 Refit the timing belt as described in Section 7.

11 Hydraulic tappets – testing

Warning: After fitting hydraulic tappets, wait a minimum of 30 minutes (or preferably, leave overnight) before starting the engine, to allow the tappets time to settle, otherwise the valve heads will strike the pistons.

1 The hydraulic tappets are self-adjusting, and require no attention whilst in service.

2 If the hydraulic tappets become excessively noisy, their operation can be checked as described below.

3 Start the engine, and run it until it reaches normal operating temperature, increase the

11.8 Press down on the tappet using a wooden or plastic instrument

engine speed to approximately 2500 rpm for 2 minutes.

4 If any hydraulic tappets are heard to be noisy, carry out the following checks.

5 Remove the camshaft cover as described in Section 4.

6 Using a socket or spanner on the crankshaft sprocket bolt, turn the crankshaft until the tip of the camshaft lobe above the tappet to be checked is pointing vertically upwards.

7 Using feeler blades, check the clearance between the top of the tappet, and the cam lobe. If the play is in excess of 0.1 mm, renew the relevant tappet. If the play is less than 0.1 mm, or there is no play, proceed as follows.

8 Press down on the tappet using a wooden or plastic instrument (see illustration). If free play in excess of 1.0 mm is present before the tappet contacts the valve stem, renew the relevant tappet.

9 On completion, refit the camshaft cover as described in Section 4.

12 Camshaft oil seals – renewal

Right-hand oil seal(s)

1 Remove the timing belt as described in Section 7.

2 Remove the camshaft sprocket and hub, as described in Section 8.

3 Drill two small holes into the existing oil seal, diagonally opposite each other. Take great care to avoid drilling through into the seal housing or camshaft sealing surface. Thread two self-tapping screws into the holes, and using a pair of pliers, pull on the heads of the screws to extract the oil seal.

4 Clean out the seal housing and the sealing surface of the camshaft by wiping it with a lint-free cloth. Remove any swarf or burrs that may cause the seal to leak.

5 Do not lubricate the lip and outer edge of the new oil seal, push it over the camshaft until it is positioned in place above its housing. To prevent damage to the sealing lips, wrap some adhesive tape around the end of the camshaft.

6 Using a hammer and a socket of suitable diameter, drive the seal squarely into its housing. Note: Select a socket that bears only on the hard outer surface of the seal, not the inner lip which can easily be damaged.

7 Refit the camshaft sprocket and its hub, as described in Section 8.

8 Refit and tension the timing belt as described in Section 7.

Left-hand oil seal

9 The left-hand camshaft oil seal is formed by the brake vacuum pump seal. Refer to Chapter Section for details of brake vacuum pump removal and refitting.

13.3 Removing the panel from the rear of the engine compartment

13.4a Disconnect the wiring…

13.4b …and vacuum hose…

13 Cylinder head – removal, inspection and refitting

Note: *The cylinder head must be removed with the engine cold. New cylinder head bolts and a new cylinder head gasket will be required on refitting, and suitable studs will be required to guide the cylinder head into position – see text.*

Removal

1 Switch off the ignition and all electrical consumers, and remove the ignition key.
2 Drain the cooling system and engine oil as described in Chapter.
3 Remove the front section of the plenum chamber as described in Chapter Section **(see illustration)**.
4 Remove the air filter complete with the air mass meter and air ducts. Also, where applicable, unbolt and remove the duct from the turbocharger **(see illustrations)**.
5 Disconnect the fuel supply and return lines, and also the coolant hoses from the cylinder head. In the interests of safety, it is recommended that the fuel is syphoned from the tandem pump on the left-hand end of the cylinder head. If necessary, the pump may be unbolted and removed **(see illustration)**.
6 Remove the fuel filter from its mounting bracket and position to one side.

13.4c …then release the clip…

13.4d …undo the screw…

13.4e …remove the upper…

13.4f …and lower covers…

13.4g …and remove the air cleaner and ducting

13.4h Removing the duct from the turbocharger

13.5 Undo the four tandem pump retaining bolts

13.12a Where applicable, undo the bolt from the inner cover...

13.12b ...and the one on the side of the cover

13.13 Unscrew the bolt and remove the camshaft position sensor

7 Remove the front exhaust pipe as described in Chapter Section.

8 Where fitted, remove the turbocharger support and oil return line from the turbocharger. Also, remove the oil supply pipe and place to one side.

9 Remove the camshaft cover as described in Section 4.

10 Remove the timing belt as described in Section 7. Where the right-hand engine mounting has been removed, ensure the engine is supported adequately on a trolley jack and block of wood.

11 Remove the camshaft sprocket and timing belt tensioner as described in Section 8.

12 Where applicable, unscrew the bolt(s) securing the rear timing belt cover to the cylinder head **(see illustrations)**.

13 Remove the camshaft position sensor from the right-hand end of the cylinder head **(see illustration)**.

14 Remove the exhaust gas recirculation connecting pipe **(see illustration)**.

15 Note the locations of all the electrical wiring, then disconnect them methodically **(see illustration)**.

16 Disconnect all vacuum and coolant hoses **(see illustrations)**.

17 Using a multi-splined tool, undo the cylinder head bolts, working from the outside-in, evenly and gradually **(see illustration)**. Check that nothing remains connected, and lift the cylinder head from the engine block. Seek assistance if possible, as it is a heavy assembly, especially as it is being removed complete with the manifolds.

18 Remove the gasket from the top of the block, noting the locating dowels. If the dowels are a loose fit, remove them and store them with the head for safe-keeping. Do not discard the gasket yet – it will be needed

for identification purposes. If desired, the manifolds can be removed from the cylinder head with reference to Chapter Section (inlet manifold) or Chapter Section (exhaust manifold).

Inspection

19 Dismantling and inspection of the cylinder head is covered in Chapter Section.

Cylinder head gasket selection

Note: *A dial test indicator (DTI) will be required for this operation.*

20 Examine the old cylinder head gasket for manufacturer's identification markings **(see illustration)**. These will be in the form of holes or notches, and a part number on the edge of the gasket. Unless new pistons have been fitted, the new cylinder head gasket must be of the same type as the old one.

13.14 EGR connecting pipe at the flap housing

13.15 Disconnect the central connector for the injectors

13.16a Disconnect the coolant hose from the end of the cylinder head

13.16b Disconnect the vacuum pipes

13.17 Cylinder head bolt slackening sequence

13.20 The thickness of the cylinder head gasket can be identified by notches or holes

21 If new piston assemblies have been fitted as part of an engine overhaul, or if a new short engine is to be fitted, the projection of the piston crowns above the cylinder head mating face of the cylinder block at TDC must be measured. This measurement is used to determine the thickness of the new cylinder head gasket required.

22 Anchor a dial test indicator (DTI) to the top face (cylinder head gasket mating face) of the cylinder block, and zero the gauge on the gasket mating face.

23 Rest the gauge probe on No 1 piston crown, and turn the crankshaft slowly by hand until the piston reaches TDC. Measure and record the maximum piston projection at TDC **(see illustration)**.

24 Repeat the measurement for the remaining pistons, and record the results.

25 If the measurements differ from piston-to-piston, take the highest figure, and use this to determine the thickness of the head gasket required as follows.

Piston projection	Gasket identification (number of holes/ notches)
0.91 to 1.00 mm	1
0.01 to 1.10 mm	2
1.11 to 1.20 mm	3

26 Purchase a new gasket according to the results of the measurements.

Refitting

Note: *If a VW exchange cylinder head, complete with camshaft(s), is to be fitted, the manufacturers recommend the following:*
a) *Lubricate the contact surfaces between the tappets and the cam lobes before fitting the camshaft cover.*
b) *Do not remove the plastic protectors from the open valves until immediately before fitting the cylinder head.*
c) *Additionally, if a new cylinder head is fitted, VW recommend that the coolant is renewed.*

27 The mating faces of the cylinder head and block must be perfectly clean before refitting the head. Use a scraper to remove all traces of gasket and carbon, also clean the tops of the pistons. Take particular care with the aluminium surfaces, as the soft metal is easily damaged.

13.23 Measuring the piston projection at TDC using a dial gauge

28 Make sure that debris is not allowed to enter the oil and water passages – this is particularly important for the oil circuit, as carbon could block the oil supply to the camshaft and crankshaft bearings. Using adhesive tape and paper, seal the water, oil and bolt holes in the cylinder block.

29 To prevent carbon entering the gap between the pistons and bores, smear a little grease in the gap. After cleaning a piston, rotate the crankshaft to that the piston moves down the bore, then wipe out the grease and carbon with a cloth rag. Clean the other piston crowns in the same way.

30 Check the head and block for nicks, deep scratches and other damage. If slight, they may be removed carefully with a file. More serious damage may be repaired by machining, but this is a specialist job.

31 If warpage of the cylinder head is suspected, use a straight-edge to check it for distortion, as described in Chapter Section.

32 Ensure that the cylinder head bolt holes in the crankcase are clean and free of oil. Syringe or soak up any oil left in the bolt holes. This is most important in order that the correct bolt tightening torque can be applied, and to prevent the possibility of the block being cracked by hydraulic pressure when the bolts are tightened.

33 Turn the crankshaft anti-clockwise all the pistons at an equal height, approximately half-way down their bores from the TDC position (see Section 3). This will eliminate any risk of piston-to-valve contact as the cylinder head is refitted.

13.35 Two of the old head bolts can be used as cylinder head alignment guides

34 Where applicable, refit the manifolds with reference to Chapter Section and Chapter Section.

35 To guide the cylinder head into position, screw two long studs (or old cylinder head bolts with the heads cut off, and slots cut in the ends to enable the bolts to be unscrewed) into the cylinder block **(see illustration)**.

36 Ensure that the cylinder head locating dowels are in place in the cylinder block, then fit the new cylinder head gasket over the dowels, ensuring that the part number is uppermost. Where applicable, the OBEN/ TOP marking should also be uppermost. Note that VW recommend that the gasket is only removed from its packaging immediately prior to fitting.

37 Lower the cylinder head into position on the gasket, ensuring that it engages correctly over the guide studs and dowels.

38 Fit the new cylinder head bolts to the eight remaining bolt locations, and screw them in as far as possible by hand.

39 Unscrew the two guide studs from the exhaust side of the cylinder block, then screw in the two remaining new cylinder head bolts as far as possible by hand.

40 Working progressively, in sequence, tighten all the cylinder head bolts to the specified Stage 1 torque **(see illustrations)**.

41 Again working progressively, in sequence, tighten all the cylinder head bolts to the specified Stage 2 torque.

42 Tighten all the cylinder head bolts, in sequence, through the specified Stage 3 angle **(see illustration)**.

13.40a Cylinder head bolt tightening sequence

13.40b Using a torque wrench to tighten the cylinder head bolts

13.42 Angle-tighten the cylinder head bolts

43 Finally, tighten all the cylinder head bolts, in sequence, through the specified Stage 4 angle.

44 After finally tightening the cylinder head bolts, turn the camshaft so that the cam lobes for No 1 cylinder are pointing upwards.

45 Where applicable, reconnect the lifting tackle to the engine lifting brackets on the cylinder head, then adjust the lifting tackle to support the engine. Once the engine is adequately supported using the cylinder head brackets, disconnect the lifting tackle from the bracket bolted to the cylinder block, and unbolt the improvised engine lifting bracket from the cylinder block. Alternatively, remove the trolley jack and block of wood from under the sump.

46 The remainder of the refitting procedure is a reversal of the removal procedure, bearing in mind the following points.

a) *Refit the injector rocker shaft.*

b) *Refit the camshaft cover with reference to Section 4.*

c) *On turbo models, use new sealing rings when reconnecting the turbocharger oil return pipe to the cylinder block.*

d) *Reconnect the exhaust front section to the exhaust manifold or turbocharger, as applicable, with reference to Chapter Section.*

e) *Refit the timing belt tensioner with reference to Section 8.*

f) *Refit the camshaft sprocket as described in Section 8, and refit the timing belt as described in Section 7.*

g) *Refill the cooling system and engine oil as described in Chapter.*

14 Sump – removal and refitting

Note: *VW sealant (D 176 404 A2 or equivalent) will be required to seal the sump on refitting.*

Removal

1 Apply the handbrake, then jack up the front of the vehicle and support securely on axle stands (see Jacking and vehicle support).

2 Remove the securing screws and withdraw the engine undertray and where fitted remove the sump insulation.

3 Drain the engine oil as described in Chapter Section.

4 Where fitted, disconnect the wiring connector from the oil level/temperature sender in the sump **(see illustration)**.

5 Unscrew and remove the bolts securing the sump to the cylinder block, and the bolts securing the sump to the transmission casing, then withdraw the sump. If necessary, release the sump by tapping with a soft-faced hammer.

6 If desired, unbolt the oil baffle plate from the cylinder block.

Refitting

7 Begin refitting by thoroughly cleaning the mating faces of the sump and cylinder block. Ensure that all traces of old sealant are removed.

8 Where applicable, refit the oil baffle plate, and tighten the securing bolts.

9 Ensure that the cylinder block mating face of the sump is free from all traces of old sealant, oil and grease, and then apply a 2.0 to 3.0 mm thick bead of silicone sealant (VW D 176 404 A2 or equivalent) to the sump **(see illustration)**. Note that the sealant should be run around the inside of the bolt holes in the sump. The sump must be fitted within 5 minutes of applying the sealant.

10 Offer the sump up to the cylinder block, then refit the sump-to-cylinder block bolts, and lightly tighten them by hand, working progressively in a diagonal sequence. Note: If the sump is being refitted with the engine and transmission separated, make sure that the sump is flush with the flywheel/driveplate end of the cylinder block.

11 Refit the sump-to-transmission casing bolts, and tighten them lightly, using a socket.

12 Again working in a diagonal sequence, lightly tighten the sump-to-cylinder block bolts, using a socket.

13 Tighten the sump-to-transmission casing bolts to the specified torque.

14 Working in a diagonal sequence, progressively tighten the sump-to-cylinder block bolts to the specified torque.

15 Refit the wiring connector to the oil level/temperature sender (where fitted), then refit the engine undertray(s), and lower the vehicle to the ground.

16 Allow at least 30 minutes from the time of refitting the sump for the sealant to dry, then refill the engine with oil, with reference to Chapter Section.

15 Oil pump, drive chain and sprockets – removal, inspection and refitting

Oil pump removal

1 Remove the sump as described in Section.

2 Unscrew the securing bolts, and remove the oil baffle from the cylinder block.

3 Unscrew and remove the three mounting bolts, and release the oil pump from the dowels in the crankcase **(see illustration)**. Unhook the oil pump drive sprocket from the chain and withdraw the oil pump and oil pick-up pipe from the engine. Note that the tensioner will attempt to tighten the chain, and it may be necessary to use a screwdriver to hold it in its released position before releasing the oil pump sprocket from the chain.

4 If desired, unscrew the flange bolts and remove the suction pipe from the oil pump. Recover the O-ring seal. Unscrew the bolts and remove the cover from the oil pump. Note: If the oil pick-up pipe is removed from the oil pump, a new O-ring will be required on refitting.

14.4 Disconnect the wiring connector from the oil level/temperature sender

14.9 Apply the sealant around the inside of the bolt holes

Oil pump inspection

5 Clean the pump thoroughly, and inspect the gear teeth/rotors for signs of damage or wear. If evident, renew the oil pump.

6 To remove the sprocket from the oil pump, unscrew the retaining bolt and slide off the sprocket (note that the sprocket can only be fitted in one position).

Oil pump refitting

7 Prime the pump with oil by pouring oil into the pick-up pipe aperture while turning the driveshaft.

8 Refit the cover to the oil pump and tighten the bolts securely. Where applicable, refit the pick-up pipe to the oil pump, using a new O-ring seal, and tighten the securing bolts.

9 If the drive chain, crankshaft sprocket and tensioner have been removed, delay refitting them until after the oil pump has been mounted on the cylinder block. If they have not been removed, use a screwdriver to press the tensioner against its spring to provide sufficient slack in the chain to refit the oil pump.

10 Engage the oil pump sprocket with the drive chain, then locate the oil pump on the dowels. Refit and tighten the three mounting bolts to the specified torque.

11 Where applicable, refit the drive chain, tensioner and crankshaft sprocket using a reversal of the removal procedure.

12 Refit the oil baffle, and tighten the securing bolts.

13 Refit the sump as described in Section.

Oil pump drive chain and sprockets

Note: *VW sealant (D 176 404 A2 or equivalent) will be required to seal the crankshaft oil seal housing on refitting, and it is advisable to fit a new crankshaft oil seal.*

Removal

14 Proceed as described in paragraphs 1 and 2.

15 To remove the oil pump sprocket, unscrew the securing bolt, then pull the sprocket from the pump shaft, and unhook it from the drive chain.

16 To remove the chain, remove the timing belt as described in Section, then unbolt the crankshaft oil seal housing from the cylinder block. Unbolt the chain tensioner from the cylinder block, then unhook the chain from the sprocket on the end of the crankshaft.

17 The oil pump drive sprocket is a press-fit on the crankshaft, and cannot easily be removed. Consult a VW dealer for advice if the sprocket is worn or damaged.

Inspection

18 Examine the chain for wear and damage. Wear is usually indicated by excessive lateral play between the links, and excessive noise in operation. It is wise to renew the chain in any case if the engine is to be overhauled. Note that the rollers on a very badly worn chain

1 Oil pump
2 Oil pump sprocket
3 Bolt
4 Oil pump drive chain
5 Crankshaft oil seal housing
6 Bolt
7 Drive chain tensioner
8 Sump
9 Seal
10 Sump drain plug
11 Dowels
12 O-ring
13 Oil pick-up pipe
14 Oil baffle
15 Seal
16 Oil level/temperature sender
17 Bolt
18 Oil spray jet
19 bolt

15.3 Sump and oil pump components

16.5 Use a locking tool to counterhold the flywheel

16.9 Flywheel warpage check – see text

16.10 Flywheel free rotational movement check alignment marks – see text

16.12 Flywheel lateral movement check marks – see text

may be slightly grooved. If there is any doubt as to the condition of the chain, renew it.

19 Examine the teeth on the sprockets for wear. Each tooth forms an inverted V. If worn, the side of each tooth under tension will be slightly concave in shape when compared with the other side of the tooth (ie, the teeth will have a hooked appearance). If the teeth appear worn, the sprocket should be renewed (consult a VW dealer for advice if the crankshaft sprocket is worn or damaged).

Refitting

20 If the oil pump has been removed, refit the oil pump as described previously in this Section before refitting the chain and sprocket.
21 Refit the chain tensioner to the cylinder block, and tighten the securing bolt to the specified torque. Make sure that the tensioner spring is correctly positioned to pretension the tensioner arm.
22 Engage the oil pump sprocket with the chain, then engage the chain with the crankshaft sprocket. Use a screwdriver to press the tensioner against its spring to provide sufficient slack in the chain to engage the sprocket with the oil pump. Note that the sprocket will only fit in one position.
23 Refit the oil pump sprocket bolt, and tighten to the specified torque.
24 Fit a new crankshaft oil seal to the housing, and refit the housing as described in Section.
25 Where applicable, refit the oil baffle, and tighten the securing bolts.
26 Refit the sump as described in Section.

16 Flywheel – removal, inspection and refitting

Removal

1 On manual transmission models, remove the transmission (see Chapter 7A, Section 3) and clutch (see Chapter 6, Section 6).
2 On automatic transmission models, remove the semi-automatic (DSG) transmission as described in.
3 Manual models are fitted with a dual-mass flywheel, which can only be fitted in one position due to the offset of the mounting bolt holes in the end of the crankshaft.
4 Rotate the outside of the dual-mass flywheel so that the bolts align with the holes (if necessary).
5 Unscrew the bolts and remove the flywheel. Use a locking tool to counterhold the flywheel **(see illustration)**. Discard the bolts, as new ones must be fitted. Note: In order not to damage the flywheel, do not allow the bolt heads to make contact with the flywheel during the unscrewing procedure.

Inspection

6 Check the flywheel for wear and damage. Examine the starter ring gear for excessive wear to the teeth. If the driveplate or its ring gear is damaged, the complete driveplate must be renewed. The flywheel ring gear,

however, may be renewed separately from the flywheel, but the work should be entrusted to a VW dealer. If the clutch friction face is discoloured or scored excessively, it may be possible to regrind it, but this work should also be entrusted to a VW dealer.
7 The following are guidelines only, but should indicate whether professional inspection is necessary. The dual-mass flywheel should be checked as follows:
8 There should be no cracks in the drive surface of the flywheel. If cracks are evident, the flywheel may need renewing.

Warpage

9 Place a straightedge across the face of the drive surface, and check by trying to insert a feeler gauge between the straightedge and the drive surface **(see illustration)**. The flywheel will normally warp like a bowl – i.e. higher on the outer edge. If the warpage is more than 0.40 mm, the flywheel may need renewing.

Free rotational movement

10 This is the distance the drive surface of the flywheel can be turned independently of the flywheel primary element, using finger effort alone. Move the drive surface in one direction and make a mark where the locating pin aligns with the flywheel edge. Move the drive surface in the other direction (finger pressure only) and make another mark **(see illustration)**. The total of free movement should not exceed 20.0 mm. If it's more, the flywheel may need renewing.

Total rotational movement

11 This is the total distance the drive surface can be turned independently of the flywheel primary element. Insert two bolts into the clutch pressure plate/damper unit mounting holes, and with the crankshaft/flywheel held stationary, use a lever/pry bar between the bolts and use some effort to move the drive surface fully in one direction – make a mark where the locating pin aligns with the flywheel edge. Now force the drive surface fully in the opposite direction, and make another mark. The total rotational movement should not exceed 44.0 mm. If it does, have the flywheel professionally inspected.

Lateral movement

12 The lateral movement (up and down) of the

drive surface in relation to the primary element of the flywheel should not exceed 2.0 mm. If it does, the flywheel may need renewing. This can be checked by pressing the drive surface down on one side into the flywheel (flywheel horizontal) and making an alignment mark between the drive surface and the inner edge of the primary element. Now press down on the opposite side of the drive surface, and make another mark above the original one. The difference between the two marks is the lateral movement **(see illustration)**.

Refitting

13 Refitting is a reversal of removal. Use new bolts when refitting the flywheel or driveplate, and coat the threads of the bolts with locking fluid before inserting them. Tighten them to the specified torque.

17 Crankshaft oil seals – renewal

Note: *The oil seals are a PTFE (Teflon) type and are fitted dry, without using any grease or oil. These have a wider sealing lip and have been introduced instead of the coil spring type oil seal.*
Note: *If the oil seal housing is removed, suitable sealant (VW D 176 404 A2, or equivalent) will be required to seal the housing on refitting.*

Timing belt end oil seal

1 Remove the timing belt as described in Section 7, and the crankshaft sprocket with reference to Section 8.
2 To remove the seal without removing the housing, drill two small holes diagonally opposite each other, insert self-tapping screws, and pull on the heads of the screws with pliers **(see illustration)**.
3 Alternatively, to remove the oil seal complete with its housing, proceed as follows.
a) *Remove the sump as described in Section. This is necessary to ensure a satisfactory seal between the sump and oil seal housing on refitting.*
b) *Unbolt and remove the oil seal housing.*
c) *Working on the bench, lever the oil seal from the housing using a suitable screwdriver. Take care not to damage the seal seating in the housing* **(see illustration)**.

17.2 Removing the crankshaft oil seal using self-tapping screws

17.3 Prising the oil seal from the crankshaft oil seal housing

17.9 Slide the oil seal housing over the end of the crankshaft

17.17 Locate the crankshaft oil seal fitting tool over the end of the crankshaft

4 Thoroughly clean the oil seal seating in the housing.

5 Wind a length of tape around the end of the crankshaft to protect the oil seal lips as the seal (and housing, where applicable) is fitted.

6 Fit a new oil seal to the housing, pressing or driving it into position using a socket or tube of suitable diameter. Ensure that the socket or tube bears only on the hard outer ring of the seal, and take care not to damage the seal lips. Press or drive the seal into position until it is seated on the shoulder in the housing. Make sure that the closed end of the seal is facing outwards.

7 If the oil seal housing has been removed, proceed as follows, otherwise proceed to paragraph 11.

8 Clean all traces of old sealant from the crankshaft oil seal housing and the cylinder block, then coat the cylinder block mating faces of the oil seal housing with a 2.0 to 3.0 mm thick bead of sealant (VW D 176 404 A2, or equivalent). Note that the seal housing must be refitted within 5 minutes of applying the sealant.

Caution: DO NOT put excessive amounts of sealant onto the housing as it may get into the sump and block the oil pick-up pipe.

9 Refit the oil seal housing, and tighten the bolts progressively to the specified torque **(see illustration)**.

10 Refit the sump as described in Section Section.

11 Refit the crankshaft sprocket with reference to Section 8, and the timing belt as described in Section 7.

Flywheel/driveplate end oil seal

Note: *The seal housing and crank sensor must be correctly positioned, and this requires a special tool.*

12 Remove the flywheel as described in Section Section.

13 Remove the sump as described in Section Section. This is necessary to ensure a satisfactory seal between the sump and oil seal housing on refitting.

14 Unbolt and remove the oil seal housing, complete with the oil seal.

15 The new oil seal will be supplied ready-fitted to a new oil seal housing.

16 Thoroughly clean the oil seal housing mating face on the cylinder block.

17 New oil seal/housing assemblies are supplied with a fitting tool to prevent damage to the oil seal as it is being fitted. Locate the tool over the end of the crankshaft **(see illustration).**

18 If the original oil seal housing was fitted using sealant, apply a thin bead of suitable sealant (VW D 176 404 A2, or equivalent) to the cylinder block mating face of the oil seal housing. Note that the seal housing must be refitted within 5 minutes of applying the sealant.

Caution: DO NOT put excessive amounts of sealant onto the housing as it may get into the sump and block the oil pick-up pipe.

19 Carefully fit the oil seal/housing assembly over the end of the crankshaft, then refit the securing bolts and tighten the bolts progressively, in a diagonal sequence, to the specified torque **(see illustrations)**.

20 Remove the oil seal protector tool from the end of the crankshaft.

21 Refit the sump as described in Section Section.

22 Refit the flywheel as described in Section Section.

18 Engine/transmission mountings – inspection and renewal

Inspection

1 If improved access is required, jack up the front of the vehicle, and support it securely on axle stands (see *Jacking and vehicle support*). Remove the engine top cover, which also incorporates the air filter, and then remove the engine undershield(s).

2 Check the mounting rubbers to see if they are cracked, hardened or separated from the metal at any point; renew the mounting if any such damage or deterioration is evident.

3 Check that all the mountings are securely tightened; use a torque wrench to check if possible.

4 Using a large screwdriver or a crowbar, check for wear in the mounting by carefully levering against it to check for free play. Where this is not possible, enlist the aid of

17.19a Fit the oil seal/housing assembly over the end of the crankshaft…

17.19b …then tighten the securing bolts to the specified torque

18.7 Remove the air duct

18.8 Undo the filter retaining bolts/nut

18.9a Remove the bracket

18.9b With the engine supported remove the mounting

18.10 There must be at least 10 mm between the bracket and the chassis member

an assistant to move the engine/transmission back-and-forth, or from side-to-side, whilst you observe the mounting. While some free play is to be expected, even from new components, excessive wear should be obvious. If excessive free play is found, check first that the fasteners are correctly secured, and then renew any worn components as described in the following paragraphs.

Renewal

Note: *New mounting securing bolts will be required on refitting.*

Right-hand mounting

5 Attach a hoist and lifting tackle to the engine lifting brackets on the cylinder head, and raise the hoist to just take the weight of the engine. Alternatively the engine can be supported on a trolley jack under the engine. Use a block of wood between the sump and

the head of the jack, to prevent any damage to the sump.
6 For improved access, unscrew the coolant reservoir and move it to one side, leaving the coolant hoses connected.
7 Remove the air intake pipe **(see illustration)**.
8 Undo the retaining bolts and move the fuel filter to one side **(see illustration)**. Where applicable, move any wiring harnesses, pipes or hoses to one side to enable removal of the engine mounting.
9 Unscrew the bolts securing the mounting to the engine bracket, and then unscrew the bolts securing it to the body. Withdraw the mounting from the engine compartment **(see illustrations)**.
10 Refitting is a reversal of removal, bearing in mind the following points.
a) *Use new securing bolts.*
b) *There must be at least 10 mm between*

the engine mounting bracket and the right-hand side chassis member **(see illustration)**.
c) *The side of the mounting support arm must be parallel to the side of the engine mounting bracket.*
d) *Tighten all fixings to the specified torque.*

Left-hand mounting

11 Remove the engine top cover.
12 Attach a hoist and lifting tackle to the engine lifting brackets on the cylinder head, and raise the hoist to just take the weight of the engine and transmission. Alternatively the engine can be supported on a trolley jack under the transmission. Use a block of wood between the transmission and the head of the jack, to prevent any damage to the transmission.
13 Remove the battery and battery tray, as described in Chapter 5A Section 3.
14 Unscrew the bolts securing the mounting to the transmission, and the remaining bolts securing the mounting to the body, then lift the mounting from the engine compartment **(see illustration)**.
15 Refitting is a reversal of removal, bearing in mind the following points:
a) *Use new mounting bolts.*
b) *The edges of the mounting support arm must be parallel to the edge of the mounting.*
c) *Tighten all fixings to the specified torque.*

Rear mounting (torque arm)

16 Apply the handbrake, then jack up the front of the vehicle and support securely on axle stands (see *Jacking and vehicle support*). Remove the engine undershield(s) for access to the rear mounting (torque arm).
17 Support the rear of the transmission beneath the final drive housing. To do this, use a trolley jack and block of wood, or alternatively wedge a block of wood between the transmission and the subframe.
18 Working under the vehicle, unscrew and remove the bolt securing the mounting to the subframe.
19 Unscrew the two bolts securing the mounting to the transmission, then withdraw the mounting from under the vehicle **(see illustration)**.
20 Refitting is a reversal of removal, but use new mounting securing bolts, and tighten all fixings to the specified torque.

18.14 Remove the transmission to mounting bracket

18.19 Rear torque arm

19 Engine oil cooler – removal and refitting

Note: *New sealing rings will be required on refitting.*

Removal

1 The oil cooler is mounted under the oil filter housing on the front of the cylinder block **(see illustration)**. Note that the oil cooler fitted to 2.0 litre models is slightly different.
2 Position a container beneath the oil filter to catch escaping oil and coolant.
3 Clamp the oil cooler coolant hoses to minimise coolant spillage, then remove the clips, and disconnect the hoses from the oil cooler. Be prepared for coolant spillage.
4 Unscrew the oil cooler securing plate from the bottom of the oil filter housing, then slide off the oil cooler. Recover the O-rings from the top and bottom of the oil cooler.

Refitting

5 Refitting is a reversal of removal, bearing in mind the following points:
a) Use new oil cooler O-rings.
b) Tighten the oil cooler securing plate securely.
c) On completion, check and if necessary top-up the oil and coolant levels.

20 Oil pressure warning light switch – removal and refitting

Removal

1 The oil pressure warning light switch is fitted to the oil filter housing **(see illustration 19.1)**. Remove the engine top cover to gain access to the switch (see Section 4).
2 Disconnect the wiring connector and wipe clean the area around the switch.
3 Unscrew the switch from the filter housing and remove it, along with its sealing washer. If the switch is to be left removed from the engine for any length of time, plug the oil filter housing aperture.

Refitting

4 Examine the sealing washer for signs of damage or deterioration and if necessary renew.
5 Refit the switch, complete with washer, and tighten it to the specified torque.
6 Securely reconnect the wiring connector then check and, if necessary, top-up the engine oil as described in Weekly checks. On completion, refit the engine top cover.

1 Oil filter housing
2 Gasket
3 Seal
4 Union
5 Oil line
6 Oil pressure switch
7 Sealing plug
8 Oil filter top cover
9 O-ring seal
10 Oil filter
11 O-ring seal (part of filter)
12 Oil cooler lower cap
13 Seal
14 Oil cooler
15 Seal

6367 Fig.02c-19.01 HAYNES

19.1 Oil filter and oil cooler mounting details (1.9 litre engine)

Notes

Chapter 2 Part D
Engine removal and overhaul procedures

Contents

Degrees of difficulty

Easy, suitable for novice with little experience	**Fairly easy,** suitable for beginner with some experience	**Fairly difficult,** suitable for competent DIY mechanic	**Difficult,** suitable for experienced DIY mechanic	**Very difficult,** suitable for expert DIY or professional

Specifications

Engine codes*

1.9 litre – 'PD' (unit injector) . . . . BKC, BJB, BLS and BSU
2.0 litre – 'PD' (unit injector) . . . . BDJ, BST and BMM
1.6 litre – common rail injection . . . . CAYE, CAYD
2.0 litre – common rail injection . . . . CFJA, CFHC, CFHF, CLCA, CFHE, CLCB and CHWA
*See 'Vehicle identification' at the end of the manual for the location of the engine code markings

Crankshaft

	New	Wear limit
Endfloat		
1.6 litre engines	0.07 to 0.17 mm	0.37 mm
1.9 and 2.0 litre engines	0.07 to 0.23 mm	0.30 mm

Spigot bearing

Fitted depth in end of crankshaft:
  1.6 litre engines . . . .   1.5 to 1.8 mm
  2.0 litre engines . . . .   2.0 mm

Cylinder head

Minimum permissible dimension between top of valve stem
  and top surface of cylinder head: . . . .   No reworking permitted
Minimum cylinder head height: . . . .   No reworking permitted
Maximum cylinder head gasket face distortion: . . . .   0.1 mm

Valves

	Inlet valves	Exhaust valves
Valve stem diameter:		
1.6 litre CR engines	5.968 to 5.982 mm	5.958 to 5.972 mm
1.9 litre PD engines.	6.980 mm	6.956 mm
2.0 litre PD engines.	6.980 mm	6.956 mm
2.0 litre CR engines	5.975 mm	5.965 mm
Valve seat angle (all engines)	45°	45°

Torque wrench settings

Refer to Chapter 2A Specifications, Chapter 2B Specifications or Chapter 2C Specifications as applicable.

1 General Information

How to use this Chapter

1 Included in this Part of Chapter 2 are details of removing the engine from the car and general overhaul procedures for the cylinder head, cylinder block and all other engine internal components.

2 The information given ranges from advice concerning preparation for an overhaul and the purchase of new parts, to detailed step-by-step procedures covering removal, inspection, renovation and refitting of engine internal components.

3 After Section 8, all instructions are based on the assumption that the engine has been removed from the car. For information concerning in-car engine repair, as well as the removal and refitting of those external components necessary for full overhaul, refer to the relevant in-car repair procedure section (Chapter 2A, Chapter 2B and Chapter 2C) and to Section 5 of this Chapter. Ignore any preliminary dismantling operations described in the relevant in-car repair sections that are no longer relevant once the engine has been removed from the car.

4 Apart from torque wrench settings, which are given at the beginning of the relevant in-car repair procedure in Chapter 2A 2A Section 0, 2B 2B Section 0 or 2C 2C Section 0 all specifications relating to engine overhaul are given at the beginning of this Part of Chapter 2.

2 Engine overhaul –
general information

1 It is not always easy to determine when, or if, an engine should be completely overhauled, as a number of factors must be considered.

2 High mileage is not necessarily an indication that an overhaul is needed, while low mileage does not preclude the need for an overhaul. Frequency of servicing is probably the most important consideration. An engine, which has had regular and frequent oil and filter changes, as well as other required maintenance, should give many thousands of miles of reliable service. Conversely, a neglected engine may require an overhaul very early in its life.

3 Excessive oil consumption is an indication that piston rings, valve seals and/or valve guides are in need of attention. Make sure that oil leaks are not responsible before deciding that the rings and/or guides are worn. Perform a compression (or leakdown) test, as described in Part A, B or C of this Chapter (as applicable), to determine the likely cause of the problem.

4 Check the oil pressure with a gauge fitted in place of the oil pressure switch,

and then compare it with that specified (see Specifications in Part A, B or C of this Chapter). If it is extremely low, the main and big-end bearings, and/or the oil pump, are probably worn.

5 Loss of power, rough running, knocking or metallic engine noises, excessive valve gear noise, and high fuel consumption may also point to the need for an overhaul, especially if they are all present at the same time. If a complete service does not remedy the situation, major mechanical work is the only solution.

6 An engine overhaul involves restoring all internal parts to the specification of a new engine. During an overhaul, the pistons and the piston rings are renewed. New main and big-end bearings are generally fitted (where possible); if necessary, the crankshaft may be renewed to restore the journals. The valves are also serviced as well, since they are usually in less-than-perfect condition at this point. While the engine is being overhauled, other components, such as the starter and alternator, can be overhauled as well. The end result should be an as-new engine that will give many trouble-free miles. Note: Critical cooling system components such as the hoses, thermostat and coolant pump should be renewed when an engine is overhauled. The radiator should be checked carefully, to ensure that it is not clogged or leaking. Also, it is a good idea to renew the oil pump whenever the engine is overhauled.

7 Before beginning the engine overhaul, read through the entire procedure, to familiarise yourself with the scope and requirements of the job. Overhauling an engine is not difficult if you follow carefully all of the instructions, have the necessary tools and equipment, and pay close attention to all specifications. It can, however, be time-consuming. Plan on the car being off the road for a minimum of two weeks, especially if parts must be taken to an engineering works for repair or reconditioning. Check on the availability of parts and make sure that any necessary special tools and equipment are obtained in advance. Most work can be done with typical hand tools, although a number of precision measuring tools are required for inspecting parts to determine if they must be renewed. Often the engineering works will handle the inspection of parts and offer advice concerning reconditioning and renewal. Note: Always wait until the engine has been completely dismantled, and until all components (especially the cylinder block and the crankshaft) have been inspected, before deciding what service and repair operations must be performed by an engineering works. The condition of these components will be the major factor to consider when determining whether to overhaul the original engine, or to buy a reconditioned unit. Do not, therefore, purchase parts or have overhaul work done on other components until they have been thoroughly inspected. As a general rule, time is the primary cost of an overhaul, so it does not pay to fit worn or sub-standard parts.

8 As a final note, to ensure maximum life and minimum trouble from a reconditioned engine, everything must be assembled with care, in a spotlessly clean environment.

3 Engine/transmission removal
– preparation and precautions

1 If you have decided that the engine must be removed for overhaul or major repair work, several preliminary steps should be taken.

2 Locating a suitable place to work is extremely important. Adequate workspace, along with storage space for the vehicle, will be needed. If a workshop or garage is not available, at the very least a solid, level, clean work surface is required.

3 If possible, clear some shelving close to the work area and use it to store the engine components and ancillaries as they are removed and dismantled. In this manner, the components stand a better chance of staying clean and undamaged during the overhaul. Laying out components in groups together with their fixings bolts, screws, etc, will save time and avoid confusion when the engine is refitted.

4 Clean the engine compartment and engine before beginning the removal procedure; this will help visibility and help to keep tools clean.

5 The help of an assistant is essential; there are certain instances when one person cannot safely perform all of the operations required to remove the engine from the vehicle. Safety is of primary importance, considering the potential hazards involved in this kind of operation. A second person should always be in attendance to offer help in an emergency. If this is the first time you have removed an engine, advice and aid from someone more experienced would also be beneficial.

6 Plan the operation ahead of time. Before starting work, obtain (or arrange for the hire of) all of the tools and equipment you will need. Access to the following items will allow the task of removing and refitting the engine to be completed safely and with relative ease: a hoist and lifting tackle – rated in excess of the weight of the engine, complete sets of spanners and sockets as described at the rear of this manual, wooden blocks, and plenty of rags and cleaning solvent for mopping-up spilled oil, coolant and fuel. A selection of different-sized plastic storage bins will also prove useful for keeping dismantled components grouped together. If any of the equipment must be hired, make sure that you arrange for it in advance, and perform all of the operations possible without it beforehand; this may save you time and money.

7 Plan on the vehicle being out of use for quite a while, especially if you intend to carry out an engine overhaul. Read through the whole of this Section and work out a strategy based on your own experience, and the tools, time and workspace available to you. Some

4.4 Remove the battery and tray

4.6a Disconnect the bonnet open warning light switch

4.6b Unscrew the crossmember mounting bolts...

4.6c ...and fit threaded rods...

4.6d ...or the correct factory tool

4.6e Pull the lock carrier forward a maximum of 100 mm

of the overhaul processes may have to be carried out by a VW dealer or an engineering works – these establishments often have busy schedules, so it would be prudent to consult them before removing or dismantling the engine, to get an idea of the amount of time required to carry out the work.

8 When removing the engine from the vehicle, be methodical about the disconnection of external components. Labelling cables and hoses as they are removed will greatly assist the refitting process.

9 Always be extremely careful when lifting the engine from the engine compartment. Serious injury can result from careless actions. If help is required, it is better to wait until it is available rather than risk personal injury and/or damage components by continuing alone. By planning ahead and taking your time, a job of this nature, although major, can be accomplished successfully and without incident.

4 Engine and transmission – removal and refitting

Removal

1 The easiest method of engine and transmission removal for the home mechanic is to remove the lock carrier and remove the engine from the front of the vehicle On models with air conditioning the the system must

be evacuated using specialist equipment. This service is available from the the dealers and most garages will also have the correct equipment. Mobile AC specialists may also operate in your area. Note: It is a criminal offence to knowingly discharge the refrigerant gas to the atmosphere.

2 Switch off the ignition and all electrical consumers, and remove the ignition key.

3 Remove the engine top cover (where fitted) and air filter housing complete with all the associated air ducting (as described in Chapter 4A Section 3).

4 Remove the battery and battery tray as described in Chapter 5A Section 3 **(see illustration)**.

5 Apply the handbrake, then jack up the front of the vehicle and support it on axle stands (see *Jacking and vehicle support*). Remove both front roadwheels.

6 Move the lock carrier, located at the front of the engine compartment, to its Service position as follows.

a) *Remove the front bumper (Chapter 11, Section 6).*

b) *Disconnect the bonnet release cable and warning light switch plug* **(see illustration)**.

c) *Remove the charge air ducts from the turbocharger/intercooler (see Chapter 4B).*

d) *Support the lock carrier, then unscrew the mounting bolts and substitute them with a threaded rod on each side of the car* **(see illustration)**.

e) *Carefully pull the lock carrier forwards approximately 10 cm to provide access to the front of the engine* **(see illustration)**.

7 At this point, the lock carrier is in the service position. This allows access (or at least improves access) to the radiator, starter motor, coolant hoses, alternator, condenser and compressor. If the lock carrier is to be removed completely the AC system must be evacuated, before proceeding further.

⚠ *Warning: Have the air conditioning system discharged by a suitably qualified specialist before attempting to remove the lock carrier.*

8 Drain the cooling system as described in Chapter 1 Section 32 **(see illustration)** and disconnect the coolant hoses. Unplug

4.8a Remove the bottom hose to drain the cooling system

4.8b Disconnect the wiring plug and unclip the loom

4.9a Remove the wiring loom from the front of the engine

4.9b Disconnect the main supply cables at the fusebox

the wiring loom from the cooling fans and headlights **(see illustration)**. Check that all connections between the lock carrier and the engine/body have been disconnected or removed and then with the aid of an assistant remove the complete lock carrier from the vehicle.

9 Noting their locations, disconnect all wiring, coolant hoses, vacuum hoses and fuel lines from the engine/transmission, with reference to the relevant Chapters of this Manual. Alternatively, the engine wiring loom may remain on the engine by disconnecting it from the left-hand side of the engine compartment, and removing the engine management ECU as described in Chapter 4A Section 4 **(see illustrations)**. Tape over or plug fuel lines to prevent entry of dust and dirt.

10 Remove the front exhaust pipe with reference to Chapter 4B Section 10.

11 Unbolt the rear engine support/torque arm from the transmission **(see illustration)**.

12 Disconnect the gearchange mechanism with reference to Chapter 7A Section 2 or **(see illustration)**.

13 On manual transmission models, remove the clutch slave cylinder (02S transmissions) or disconnect the clutch supply hose (02Q transmissions). Note: Do not depress the clutch pedal once the slave cylinder has been removed.

14 Refer to Chapter 3 Section 10 and unbolt the air conditioning compressor from the front of the engine, without disconnecting the refrigerant lines. Suspend the compressor to one side of the engine compartment.

15 Refer to Chapter 8 Section 2, and disconnect the driveshafts from the transmission drive flanges. Suspend them from the underbody **(see illustration)**.

16 Unbolt the coolant expansion reservoir for access to the right-engine mounting.

17 Connect a engine crane/hoist and lifting tackle to the engine lifting brackets on the cylinder head. We used a third strap to balance the engine. Raise the hoist to just take the weight of the engine/transmission **(see illustration)**.

18 Unbolt the right- and left-hand engine mountings with reference to Chapter 2A Section 16, Chapter 2B Section 16 or Chapter 2C Section 18.

19 Make a final check to ensure that all relevant wiring, hoses and pipes have been disconnected, then carefully swivel the engine/transmission assembly away from the sides of the engine compartment, lift it upwards or lower it (see paragraph 1) and withdraw forwards from the front of the car.

Separation
Engine and manual transmission

20 Remove the starter motor as described in Chapter 5A Section 8.

21 Where applicable, unscrew the bolt securing the small engine-to-transmission plate to the transmission.

22 Ensure that both engine and transmission are adequately supported, and then unscrew the remaining engine-to-transmission bolts, noting the location of each bolt, and the locations of any brackets secured by the bolts.

23 Carefully withdraw the transmission from the engine, ensuring that the weight of the transmission is not allowed to hang on the input shaft while it is engaged with the clutch friction disc. Recover the engine-to-transmission plate.

Engine and DSG (dual clutch) transmission

24 Remove the starter motor (Chapter 5A Section 8).

25 Disconnect the coolant hoses from the gearbox oil cooler. Plug the openings to prevent contamination.

26 Disconnect the wiring harness between the engine and gearbox, and move to one side.

27 Ensure that both engine and transmission are adequately supported, and then unscrew the engine-to-transmission bolts, noting the location of each bolt, and the locations of any brackets secured by the bolts.

4.11 Remove the rear engine support/ torque arm

4.12 Disconnect the gearchange cables

4.15 Suspend the driveshafts clear of the transmission

4.17 Lift the engine/transmission with a hoist

28 Carefully withdraw the transmission from the engine (take care – the transmission is heavy).

Reconnection and refitting

Engine and manual transmission

29 Reconnection and refitting are a reversal of removal, bearing in mind the following points:
a) Smear the splines of the transmission input shaft with a little high melting-point grease.
b) Ensure that any brackets noted before removal are in place on the engine-to-transmission bolts.
c) Tighten all fixings to the specified torque, where given.
d) Where applicable, have the air conditioning system recharged with refrigerant by a suitably qualified professional.
e) Ensure that all wiring, hoses and pipes are correctly reconnected and routed as noted before removal.
f) Ensure that the fuel lines are correctly reconnected.
g) On completion, refill the cooling system as described in or Chapter 1, Section 32.

Engine and DSG (dual clutch) transmission

30 Reconnection and refitting are a reversal of removal, bearing in mind the following points:
a) When fitting the torque converter (where applicable), make sure that both the drive pins engage with the transmission fluid pump.
b) On completion, check and if necessary top-up the transmission fluid level as described in or Chapter 1, Section 26.

5 Engine overhaul – preliminary information

1 It is much easier to dismantle and work on the engine if it is mounted on a portable engine stand. These stands can often be hired from a tool hire shop. Before the engine is mounted on a stand, the flywheel should be removed, so that the stand bolts can be tightened into the end of the cylinder block/crankcase. Note: Do not measure cylinder bore dimensions with the engine mounted on this type of stand.

2 If a stand is not available, it is possible to dismantle the engine with it blocked up on a sturdy workbench, or on the floor. Be very careful not to tip or drop the engine when working without a stand.
3 If you intend to obtain a reconditioned engine, all ancillaries must be removed first, to be transferred to the new engine (just as they will if you are doing a complete engine overhaul yourself). These components include the following (it may be necessary to transfer additional components, such as the oil level dipstick/tube assembly, oil filter housing, etc, depending on which components are supplied with the reconditioned engine:
a) Alternator (including mounting brackets) and starter motor (Chapter 5A).
b) The glow plug/preheating system components (Chapter 5B).
c) All fuel system components, including fuel injectors, all sensors and actuators (Chapter).
d) The brake vacuum pump (Chapter Section).
e) All electrical switches, actuators and sensors, and the engine wiring harness (Chapter 12).
f) Inlet and exhaust manifolds/turbocharger.
g) Engine mountings (see Chapter 2A Section 16, Chapter 2B Section 16 or Chapter 2C Section 18).
h) Clutch components (Chapter Section).

All engines

Note: When removing the external components from the engine, pay close attention to details that may be helpful or important during refitting. Note the fitted position of gaskets, seals, spacers, pins, washers, bolts, and other small components.
4 If you are obtaining a short engine (the engine cylinder block/crankcase, crankshaft, pistons and connecting rods, all fully assembled), then the cylinder head, sump, oil pump, timing belt(s) and chain (as applicable – together with tensioner(s) and covers), auxiliary drivebelt (together with its tensioner), coolant pump, thermostat housing, coolant outlet elbows, oil filter housing and where applicable oil cooler will also have to be removed.
5 If you are planning a full overhaul, the engine can be dismantled in the order given below:

a) Inlet and exhaust manifolds.
b) Timing belt or timing chain (as applicable), sprockets and tensioner (see the relevant part of Chapter 2).
c) Cylinder head (see the relevant part of Chapter 2).
d) Flywheel/driveplate (see the relevant part of Chapter 2).
e) Sump (see the relevant part of Chapter 2).
f) Oil pump (see the relevant part of Chapter 2).
g) Piston/connecting rod assemblies (see Section 9).
h) Crankshaft (see Section 10).

6 Cylinder head – dismantling

Note: A valve spring compressor tool will be required for this operation.
1 With the cylinder head removed, proceed as follows.
2 Remove the inlet and exhaust manifolds (and turbocharger, where applicable).
3 Remove the camshaft and hydraulic tappets, as described in Chapter 2A, Section 9, Chapter 2B, Section 9 or Chapter 2C Section 10.
4 Remove the glow plugs, with reference to Chapter 5B, Section 2.
5 Remove the fuel injectors, with reference to Chapter Section.
6 Unscrew the nut and remove the timing belt tensioner pulley from the stud on the timing belt end of the cylinder head.
7 Unbolt any remaining auxiliary brackets and/or engine lifting brackets from the cylinder head as necessary, noting their locations to aid refitting.
8 Turn the cylinder head over, and rest it on one side.
9 Using a valve spring compressor, compress each valve spring in turn until the split collets can be removed. Release the compressor, and lift off the spring cap and spring. If, when the valve spring compressor is screwed down, the spring cap refuses to free and expose the split collets, DO NOT tap the top of the tool to release the collets, instead use a small screwdriver to split the collets away from the stem **(see illustrations)**.

6.9a Use a valve spring compressor to compress the valve spring

6.9b Remove the spring cap...

6.9c ...and valve spring

6.10a Use a removal tool...

6.10b ...to remove the valve stem oil seals

6.11 Remove the valve

10 Using a pair of pliers, or a removal tool, carefully extract the valve stem oil seal from the top of the valve guide **(see illustrations)**.
11 Withdraw the valve from the gasket side of the cylinder head **(see illustration)**.
12 It is essential that each valve is stored together with its collets, cap, spring and spring seat. The valves should be kept in their correct sequences, unless they are so badly worn that they are to be renewed.

7 Cylinder head and valves – cleaning and inspection

1 Thorough cleaning of the cylinder head and valve components, followed by a detailed inspection, will enable you to decide how much valve service work must be carried out during engine overhaul. Note: If the engine has been severely overheated, it is best to assume that the cylinder head is warped, so check carefully for signs of this.

Cleaning

2 Using a suitable degreasing agent, remove all traces of oil deposits from the cylinder head, paying particular attention to the camshaft bearing surfaces, hydraulic tappet bores, valve guides and oil ways. Scrape off any traces of old gasket from the mating surfaces, taking care not to score or gouge them. If using emery paper, do not use a grade of less than 100. Turn the head over and, using a blunt blade, scrape any carbon deposits from the combustion chambers and ports. Finally, wash the entire head casting with a suitable solvent to remove the remaining debris.
3 Clean the valve heads and stems using a fine wire brush (or a power-operated wire brush). If the valve is covered with heavy carbon deposits, scrape off the majority of the deposits with a blunt blade first, then use the wire brush.
4 Thoroughly clean the remainder of the components using solvent and allow them to dry completely. Discard the oil seals, as new ones must be fitted when the cylinder head is reassembled.

Inspection

Cylinder head

5 Examine the head casting closely to identify any damage or cracks that may have developed. Cracks can often be identified from evidence of coolant or oil leakage. Pay particular attention to the areas around the valve seats and spark plug/fuel injector holes. If cracking is discovered in this area, VW state that on diesel engines, the cylinder head may be re-used, provided the cracks are no larger than 0.5 mm wide. More serious damage will mean the renewal of the cylinder head casting.
6 Moderately pitted and scorched valve seats can be repaired by lapping the valves in during reassembly, as described later in this Chapter. Badly worn or damaged valve seats may be restored by re-cutting where permitted, however, the maximum permissible reworking dimension must not be exceeded, only minimal reworking being possible (see note at beginning of paragraph 5). To calculate the maximum permissible reworking dimension, proceed as follows **(see illustration)** :
a) *If a new valve is to be fitted, use the new valve for the following calculation.*
b) *Insert the valve into its guide in the cylinder head, and push the valve firmly on to its seat.*
c) *Using a flat edge placed across the top surface of the cylinder head, measure the distance between the top face of the valve stem, and the top surface of the cylinder head. Record the measurement obtained.*

d) *Consult the Specifications, and look up the value for the minimum permissible dimension between the top face of the valve stem and the top surface of the cylinder head.*
e) *Now take the measured distance and subtract the minimum permissible dimension, to give the maximum permissible reworking dimension; e.g.*
f) *Measured distance (34.4 mm)*
g) *Minus Minimum permissible dimension (34.0 mm) = Maximum permissible reworking dimension (0.4 mm).*
7 Measure any distortion of the gasket surfaces using a straight-edge and a set of feeler blades. Take one measurement longitudinally on the manifold mating surface(s). Take several measurements across the head gasket surface, to assess the level of distortion in all planes **(see illustration)**. Compare the measurements with the figures in the Specifications.
8 If the head is distorted beyond the specified limit, the head must be renewed.

Camshaft

9 Inspection of the camshaft is covered in Chapter 2A 2A Section 9, 2B 2B Section 9 or 2C 2C Section 10.

Valves and associated components

10 Examine each valve closely for signs of wear. Inspect the valve stems for wear ridges, scoring or variations in diameter; measure their diameters at several points along their lengths with a micrometer, and compare with

7.6 Measure the distance (A) between the top face of the valve stem and the top surface of the cylinder head

7.7 Measure the distortion of the cylinder head gasket surface

7.10 Measure the diameter of the valve stems using a micrometer

7.13 Measure the free length of each valve spring

7.14 Check the squareness of a valve spring

the figures given in the Specifications **(see illustration)**.

11 The valve heads should not be cracked, badly pitted or charred. Note that light pitting of the valve head can be rectified by lapping-in the valves during reassembly, as described in Section 8.

12 Check that the valve stem end face is free from excessive pitting or indentation; this could be caused by defective hydraulic tappets.

13 Using vernier calipers, measure the free length of each of the valve springs. As a manufacturer's figure is not quoted, the only way to check the length of the springs is by comparison with a new component. Note that valve springs are usually renewed during a major engine overhaul **(see illustration)**.

14 Stand each spring on its end on a flat surface, against an engineer's square **(see illustration)**. Check the squareness of the spring visually, and renew it if it appears distorted.

15 Renew the valve stem oil seals regardless of their apparent condition.

8 Cylinder head – reassembly

Note: *A valve spring compressor tool will be required for this operation.*

1 To achieve a gas-tight seal between the valves and their seats, it will be necessary to lap-in (or grind-in) the valves. To complete this process you will need a quantity of fine/coarse grinding paste and a grinding tool – this can either be of the rubber sucker type, or the automatic type which is driven by a rotary power tool.

2 Smear a small quantity of fine grinding paste on the sealing face of the valve head. Turn the cylinder head over so that the combustion chambers are facing upwards and insert the valve into the correct guide. Attach the grinding tool to the valve head and using a backward/forward rotary action, grind the valve head into its seat. Periodically lift the valve and rotate it to redistribute the grinding paste **(see illustration)**.

3 Continue this process until the contact between valve and seat produces an unbroken, matt grey ring of uniform width, on both faces. Repeat the operation on the remaining valves.

4 If the valves and seats are so badly pitted that coarse grinding paste must be used, bear in that there is a maximum permissible reworking dimension for the valves and seats. Refer to the Section at the beginning of this Chapter for the minimum dimension from the end of the valve stem to the top face of the cylinder head. If this minimum dimension is exceeded due to excessive lapping-in, the hydraulic tappets may not operate correctly, and the cylinder head must be renewed.

5 Assuming the repair is feasible, work as described previously, but use coarse grinding paste initially, to achieve a dull finish on the valve face and seat. Wash off the coarse paste with solvent and repeat the process using fine grinding paste to obtain the correct finish.

6 When all the valves have been ground in, remove all traces of grinding paste from the cylinder head and valves using solvent, and allow the head and valves to dry completely.

7 Turn the cylinder head on its side.

8 Working on one valve at a time, lubricate the valve stem with clean engine oil, and insert the valve into its guide. Fit one of the protective plastic sleeves (where supplied) to fit over the end of the valve stem – this will protect the oil seal as it is being fitted **(see illustrations)**.

9 Dip a new valve stem seal in clean engine oil, and carefully push it over the valve stem and onto the top of the valve guide – take care not to damage the stem seal as it is fitted. Use a suitable long-reach socket or a valve stem seal fitting tool to press the seal firmly into position**(see illustration)**. Remove the protective sleeve from the valve stem.

8.2 Grinding in a valve

8.8a Lubricate the valve stem with clean engine oil

8.8b Fit a protective sleeve over the valve stem before fitting the stem seal

8.9 Use a long-reach socket to fit a valve stem oil seal

8.10 Fit a valve spring...

8.11a ...and upper spring seat ...

8.11b ... then compress a valve spring using a compressor tool

8.11c Use grease to hold the split collets in the groove

10 Locate the valve spring over the valve stem, ensuring that the lower end of the spring seats correctly on the cylinder head **(see illustration)**.

11 Fit the upper spring seat over the top of the spring, then using a valve spring compressor, compress the spring until the upper seat is pushed beyond the collet grooves in the valve stem. Refit the split collets. Gradually release the spring compressor, checking that the collets remain correctly seated as the spring extends. When correctly seated, the upper spring seat should force the collets securely into the grooves in the end of the valve stem **(see illustrations)**.

12 Repeat this process for the remaining sets of valve components, ensuring that all components are refitted to their original locations. To settle the components after installation, strike the end of each valve

stem with a mallet, using a block of wood to protect the stem from damage. Check before progressing any further that the split collets remain firmly seated in the grooves in the end of the valve stem.

13 Refit any auxiliary brackets and/or engine lifting brackets to their original locations, as noted before removal.

14 Refit the timing belt tensioner pulley to the stud on the cylinder head, and refit the securing nut.

15 Refit the fuel injectors, with reference to Chapter Section.

16 Refit the glow plugs, with reference to Chapter 5B, Section 2.

17 Refit the hydraulic tappets and camshaft, as described in Chapter 2A, Section 9, Chapter 2B, Section 9 or Chapter 2C Section 10.

18 Refit the inlet and exhaust manifolds (and turbocharger, where applicable).

9 Piston/connecting rod assemblies – removal

1 Remove the cylinder head, sump, baffle plate, oil pump and pick-up pipe as described in Chapter 2A (1.6 CR engines), Chapter 2B (2.0 CR engines) or Chapter 2C (PD engines).

2 Inspect the tops of the cylinder bores for ridges at the point where the pistons reach top dead centre. These must be removed otherwise the pistons may be damaged when they are pushed out of their bores. Use a scraper or ridge reamer to remove the ridges. Such a ridge indicates excessive wear of the cylinder bore.

3 Check the connecting rods and big-end caps for identification markings. Both connecting rods and caps should be marked with the cylinder number on one side of each assembly. Note that No 1 cylinder is at the timing belt end of the engine. If no marks are present, using a hammer and centre-punch, paint or similar, mark each connecting rod and big-end bearing cap with its respective cylinder number – note on which side of the connecting rods and caps the marks are made **(see illustration)**.

4 Similarly, check the piston crowns for direction markings. An arrow on each piston crown should point towards the timing belt end of the engine. On some engines, this mark may be obscured by carbon build-up, in which case the piston crown should be cleaned to check for a mark. In some cases, the direction arrow may have worn off, in which case a suitable mark should be made on the piston crown using a scriber – do not deeply score the piston crown, but ensure that the mark is easily visible.

5 Turn the crankshaft to bring No's 1 and 4 pistons to bottom dead centre.

6 Unscrew the bolts or nuts, as applicable, from No 1 piston big-end bearing cap. Lift off the cap, and recover the bottom half bearing shell. If the bearing shells are to be re-used, tape the cap and bearing shell together. Note that if the bearing shells are to be re-used, they must be fitted to the original connecting rod and cap **(see illustrations)**.

9.3 Mark the big-end caps and connecting rods with their cylinder numbers

9.6a Unscrew the big-end bearing cap bolts...

9.6b ...and remove the cap

9.7 Wrap the threaded ends of the bolts with tape

9.12a Remove the securing bolts...

9.12b ...and withdraw the piston cooling oil spray jets

9.12c Piston cooling spray jet and retainer

10.5 Slacken and remove the main bearing cap bolts

11.1 EGR cooler located on the rear of the engine

7 Where the bearing caps are secured with nuts, wrap the threaded ends of the bolts with insulating tape to prevent them scratching the crankpins and bores when the pistons are removed **(see illustration)**.

8 Using a hammer handle, push the piston up through the bore, and remove it from the top of the cylinder block. Where applicable, take care not to damage the piston cooling oil spray jets in the cylinder block as the piston/connecting rod assembly is removed. Recover the upper bearing shell, and tape it to the connecting rod for safe-keeping.

9 Loosely refit the big-end cap to the connecting rod, and secure with the bolts or nuts, as applicable – this will help to keep the components in their correct order.

10 Remove No.4 piston assembly in the same way.

11 Turn the crankshaft as necessary to bring No's 2 and 3 pistons to bottom dead centre, and remove them in the same way.

12 Where applicable, remove the securing bolts, and withdraw the piston cooling oil spray jets from the bottom of the cylinder block **(see illustrations)**.

10 Crankshaft – removal

Note: *If no work is to be done on the pistons and connecting rods, there is no need to push the pistons out of the cylinder bores. The pistons should just be pushed far enough up*

the bores so that they are positioned clear of the crankshaft journals.

1 Remove the timing belt and crankshaft sprocket, sump and oil baffle plate, oil pump and pick-up pipe, flywheel/driveplate, and the crankshaft oil seal housings, as described in Chapter 2A, Chapter 2B or Chapter 2C.

2 Remove the pistons and connecting rods, or disconnect them from the crankshaft, as described in Section 9 (see Note at the beginning of this Section).

3 Check the crankshaft endfloat as described in Section 13, then proceed as follows.

4 The main bearing caps should be numbered 1 to 5 from the timing belt end of the engine. If the bearing caps are not marked, mark them accordingly using a centre-punch. Note the orientation of the markings to ensure correct refitting.

5 Slacken and remove the main bearing cap bolts, and lift off each cap. If the caps appear to be stuck, tap them with a soft-faced mallet to free them from the cylinder block **(see illustration)**. Recover the lower bearing shells, and tape them to their caps for safekeeping.

6 Recover the lower crankshaft endfloat control thrustwasher halves from either side of the No 3 main bearing cap, noting their orientation.

7 Lift the crankshaft from the cylinder block. Take care, as the crankshaft is heavy. On engines with a crankshaft speed/position sensor fitted, lay the crankshaft on wooden blocks – do not rest the crankshaft on the sensor wheel.

8 Recover the upper bearing shells from

the cylinder block, and tape them to their respective caps for safekeeping. Similarly, recover the upper crankshaft endfloat control thrustwasher halves, noting their orientation.

9 On engines with a crankshaft speed/position sensor wheel, unscrew the securing bolts, and remove the sensor wheel, noting which way round it is fitted.

11 Cylinder block/crankcase – cleaning and inspection

Cleaning

1 Remove all external components and electrical switches/sensors from the block, including mounting brackets, coolant pump, oil filter housing, oil cooler and EGR cooler **(see illustration)**, etc. For complete cleaning, the core plugs should ideally be removed. Drill a small hole in the plugs, and then insert a self-tapping screw into the hole. Extract the plugs by pulling on the screw with a pair of grips, or by using a slide hammer.

2 Scrape all traces of gasket and sealant from the cylinder block/crankcase, taking care not to damage the sealing surfaces.

3 Remove all oil gallery plugs (where fitted). The plugs are usually very tight – they may have to be drilled out, and the holes re-tapped. Use new plugs when the engine is reassembled.

4 If the casting is extremely dirty, it should be steam-cleaned. After this, clean all oil holes and galleries one more time. Flush all internal passages with warm water until the water runs clear. Dry thoroughly, and apply a light film of oil to all mating surfaces and cylinder bores, to prevent rusting. If you have access to compressed air, use it to speed up the drying process, and to blow out all the oil holes and galleries.

Warning: Wear eye protection when using compressed air.

5 If the castings are not very dirty, you can do an adequate cleaning job with hot, soapy water and a stiff brush. Take plenty of time, and do a thorough job. Regardless of the cleaning method used, be sure to clean all oil holes and galleries very thoroughly, and to dry all components well. Protect the cylinder bores as described above, to prevent rusting.

6 Where applicable, check the piston cooling oil spray jets for damage, and renew if necessary. Check the oil spray hole and the oil passages for blockage.

7 All threaded holes must be clean, to ensure accurate torque readings during reassembly. To clean the threads, run the correct-size tap into each of the holes to remove rust, corrosion, thread sealant or sludge, and to restore damaged threads **(see illustration)**. If possible, use compressed air to clear the holes free of debris produced by this operation. Note: Take extra care to exclude all cleaning liquid from blind tapped holes, as the casting may be cracked by hydraulic action if a bolt is threaded into a hole containing liquid.

8 After coating the mating surfaces of the new core plugs with suitable sealant, fit them to the cylinder block. Make sure that they are driven in straight and seated correctly, or leakage could result.

9 Apply suitable sealant to the new oil gallery plugs, and insert them into the holes in the block. Tighten them securely.

10 If the engine is not going to be reassembled immediately, cover it with a large plastic bag to keep it clean; protect all mating surfaces and the cylinder bores, to prevent rusting.

Inspection

11 Visually check the castings for cracks and corrosion. Look for stripped threads in the threaded holes. If there has been any

history of internal coolant leakage, it may be worthwhile having an engine overhaul specialist check the cylinder block/crankcase for cracks with special equipment. If defects are found, have them repaired, if possible, or renew the assembly.

12 Check each cylinder bore for scuffing and scoring.

13 If in any doubt as the condition of the cylinder block have the block/bores inspected and measured by an engine reconditioning specialist. They will be able to advise on whether the block is serviceable, whether a re-bore is necessary, and supply the appropriate pistons and rings.

14 If the bores are in reasonably good condition and not excessively worn, then it may only be necessary to renew the piston rings.

15 If this is the case, the bores should be honed, to allow the new rings to bed-in correctly and provide the best possible seal. Consult an engine reconditioning specialist

16 If the oil/water pump housing was removed, it can be refitted at this stage if wished. Use a new gasket, and before fully tightening the bolts, align the housing faces with those of the engine block.

17 The cylinder block/crankcase should now be completely clean and dry, with all components checked for wear or damage, and repaired or overhauled as necessary.

18 Apply a light coating of engine oil to the mating surfaces and cylinder bores to prevent rust forming.

19 Refit as many ancillary components as possible, for safekeeping. If reassembly is not to start immediately, cover the block with a large plastic bag to keep it clean, and protect the machined surfaces as described above to prevent rusting.

12 Piston/connecting rod assemblies – cleaning and inspection

Cleaning

1 Before the inspection process can begin, the piston/connecting rod assemblies must be cleaned, and the original piston rings removed from the pistons.

2 The rings should have smooth, polished working surfaces, with no dull or carbon-coated sections (showing that the ring is not sealing correctly against the bore wall, so allowing combustion gases to blow by) and no traces of wear on their top and bottom surfaces. The end gaps should be clear of carbon, but not polished (indicating a too-small end gap), and all the rings (including the elements of the oil control ring) should be free to rotate in their grooves, but without excessive up-and-down movement. If the rings appear to be in good condition, they are probably fit for further use; check the end gaps (in an unworn part of the bore) as described in Section 16.

3 If any of the rings appears to be worn or damaged, or has an end gap significantly different from the specified value, the usual course of action is to renew all of them as a set. Note: While it is usual to renew piston rings when an engine is overhauled, they may be re-used if in acceptable condition. If re-using the rings, make sure that each ring is marked during removal to ensure that it is refitted correctly.

4 Carefully expand the old rings over the top of the pistons. The use of two or three old feeler blades will be helpful in preventing the rings dropping into empty grooves **(see illustration)**. Be careful not to scratch the piston with the ends of the ring. The rings are brittle, and will snap if they are spread too far. They are also very sharp – protect your hands and fingers. Note that the third ring incorporates an expander. Keep each set of rings with its piston if the old rings are to be re-used. Note which way up each ring is fitted to ensure correct refitting.

5 Scrape away all traces of carbon from the top of the piston. A hand-held wire brush (or a piece of fine emery cloth) can be used, once the majority of the deposits have been scraped away.

6 Remove the carbon from the ring grooves in the piston, using an old ring. Break the ring in half to do this (be careful not to cut your fingers – piston rings are sharp). Be careful to remove only the carbon deposits – do not remove any metal, and do not nick or scratch the sides of the ring grooves.

7 Once the deposits have been removed, clean the piston/connecting rod assembly with paraffin or a suitable solvent, and dry thoroughly. Make sure that the oil return holes in the ring grooves are clear.

Inspection

8 If the pistons and cylinder bores are not damaged or worn excessively, and if the cylinder block does not need to be re-bored, the original pistons can be refitted.

9 Have the pistons and cylinder bore measure by an engine reconditioning specialist. They will be able to advise on possible repairs, and supply the correct replacement parts. Note: If the cylinder block was re-bored during a previous overhaul, oversize pistons may already have been fitted.

11.7 To clean the cylinder block threads, run a correct-size tap into the holes

12.4 Old feeler blades can be used to prevent piston rings from dropping into empty grooves

12.17 Measure the piston ring-to-groove clearance using a feeler blade

12.20a Use a small flat-bladed screwdriver to prise out the circlip...

12.20b ...then push out the gudgeon pin and separate the piston and connecting rod

10 Normal piston wear shows up as even vertical wear on the piston thrust surfaces, and slight looseness of the top ring in its groove. New piston rings should always be used when the engine is reassembled.

11 Carefully inspect each piston for cracks around the skirt, around the gudgeon pin holes, and at the piston ring 'lands' (between the ring grooves).

12 Look for scoring and scuffing on the piston skirt, holes in the piston crown, and burned areas at the edge of the crown. If the skirt is scored or scuffed, the engine may have been suffering from overheating, and/or abnormal combustion, which caused excessively high operating temperatures. The cooling and lubrication systems should be checked thoroughly.

13 Scorch marks on the sides of the pistons show that blow-by has occurred.

14 A hole in the piston crown, or burned areas at the edge of the piston crown, indicates that abnormal combustion (pre-ignition, knocking, or detonation) has been occurring.

15 If any of the above problems exist, the causes must be investigated and corrected, or the damage will occur again. The causes may include incorrect ignition/injection pump timing, inlet air leaks or incorrect air/fuel mixture (petrol engines), or a faulty fuel injector (diesel engines).

16 Corrosion of the piston, in the form of pitting, indicates that coolant has been leaking into the combustion chamber and/or the crankcase. Again, the cause must be corrected, or the problem may persist in the rebuilt engine.

17 Locate a new piston ring in the appropriate groove and measure the ring-to-groove clearance using a feeler blade **(see illustration)**. Note that the rings are of different widths, so use the correct ring for the groove. Compare the measurements with those listed; if the clearances are outside of the tolerance band, then the piston must be renewed. Confirm this by checking the width of the piston ring with a micrometer.

18 Examine each connecting rod carefully for signs of damage, such as cracks around the big-end and small-end bearings. Check that the rod is not bent or distorted. Damage is highly unlikely, unless the engine has been seized or badly overheated. Detailed checking of the connecting rod assembly can only be carried out by a VW dealer or engine repair specialist with the necessary equipment.

19 The gudgeon pins are of the floating type, secured in position by two circlips. The pistons and connecting rods can be separated as follows.

20 Using a small flat-bladed screwdriver, prise out the circlips, and push out the gudgeon pin **(see illustrations)**. Hand pressure should be sufficient to remove the pin. Identify the piston and rod to ensure correct reassembly. Discard the circlips – new ones must be used on refitting. If the gudgeon pin proves difficult to remove, heat the piston to 60°C with hot water – the resulting expansion will then allow the two components to be separated.

21 Examine the gudgeon pin and connecting rod small-end bearing for signs of wear or

damage. It should be possible to push the gudgeon pin through the connecting rod bush by hand, without noticeable play. Wear can be cured by renewing both the pin and bush. Bush renewal, however, is a specialist job – press facilities are required, and the new bush must be reamed accurately.

22 Examine all components, and obtain any new parts from your VW dealer or engine reconditioning specialist. If new pistons are purchased, they will be supplied complete with gudgeon pins and circlips. Circlips can also be purchased individually.

23 The orientation of the piston with respect to the connecting rod must be correct when the two are reassembled. The piston crown is marked with an arrow (which may be obscured by carbon deposits); this must point towards the timing belt/chain end of the engine when the piston is installed. The connecting rod and its bearing cap both have recesses machined into them on one side, close to their mating surfaces – these recesses must both face the same way as the arrow on the piston crown (ie, towards the timing belt/chain end of the engine) when correctly installed. Reassemble the two components to satisfy this requirement **(see illustrations)**.

24 Apply a smear of clean engine oil to the gudgeon pin. Slide it into the piston and through the connecting rod small-end. Check that the piston pivots freely on the rod, then secure the gudgeon pin in position with two new circlips. Ensure that each circlip is correctly located in its groove in the piston.

25 Repeat the cleaning and inspection process for the remaining pistons and connecting rods.

13 Crankshaft – checking endfloat, spigot bearing, and inspection	

Checking endfloat

1 If the crankshaft endfloat is to be checked, this must be done when the crankshaft is still installed in the cylinder block/crankcase, but is free to move (see Section 10).

2 Check the endfloat using a dial gauge in contact with the end of the crankshaft.

12.23a The piston crown is marked with an arrow which must point towards the timing belt/chain end of the engine

12.23b The recesses in the connecting rod and bearing cap must face the timing belt/chain end of the engine

13.2 Measure crankshaft endfloat using a dial gauge

13.3 Measure crankshaft endfloat using feeler blades

13.7 Check the depth of the bearing using a vernier gauge

Push the crankshaft fully one way, and then zero the gauge. Push the crankshaft fully the other way, and check the endfloat. The result can be compared with the specified amount, and will give an indication as to whether new thrustwasher halves are required **(see illustration)**. Note that all thrustwashers must be of the same thickness.

3 If a dial gauge is not available, feeler blades can be used. First push the crankshaft fully towards the flywheel end of the engine, and then use feeler blades to measure the gap between the web of No 3 crankpin and the thrustwasher halves **(see illustration)**.

Spigot bearing

Note: *On DSG semi-automatic transmissions, the spigot needle roller bearing needs to be renewed; every time the transmission is removed from the engine.*

4 On some models, there is a bearing positioned in the end of the crankshaft, which supports the transmission shaft.

5 Remove the transmission as described in Chapter 7A, Section 3 (manual transmission) or (DSG transmissions)

6 On manual models, remove the clutch assembly as described in Chapter 6, Section 6.

7 Before removing the bearing, check the fitted depth of the bearing inside the end of the crankshaft **(see illustration)**. See specifications at the beginning of this Chapter to find the relevant depth for each engine.

8 Using an internal puller, slide the bearing out from the centre of the crankshaft **(see illustrations)**.

9 Using a drift, drive the bearing into the end of the crankshaft **(see illustration)**, taking care not to drive it in to far, as noted on removal. Also see specifications at the beginning of Chapter for depth of bearing.

 Warning: If the new bearing is driven into the end of the crankshaft to far, then it will need to be completely removed and another new one fitted.

Inspection

10 Clean the crankshaft using paraffin or a suitable solvent, and dry it, preferably with compressed air if available. Be sure to clean the oil holes with a pipe cleaner or similar probe, to ensure that they are not obstructed.

Warning: Wear eye protection when using compressed air.

11 Check the main and big-end bearing journals for uneven wear, scoring, pitting and cracking.

12 Big-end bearing wear is accompanied by distinct metallic knocking when the engine is running (particularly noticeable when the engine is pulling from low speed) and some loss of oil pressure.

13 Main bearing wear is accompanied by severe engine vibration and rumble – getting progressively worse as engine speed increases – and again by loss of oil pressure.

14 Check the bearing journal for roughness by running a finger lightly over the bearing surface. Any roughness (which will be accompanied by obvious bearing wear) indicates that the crankshaft requires regrinding (where possible) or renewal.

15 If the crankshaft has been reground, check for burrs around the crankshaft oil holes (the holes are usually chamfered, so burrs should not be a problem unless regrinding has been carried out carelessly). Remove any burrs with a fine file or scraper, and thoroughly clean the oil holes as described previously.

16 Have the crankshaft measured and inspected by an engine reconditioning specialist. They will be able to advise any possible repairs and supply the correct parts.

17 Check the oil seal contact surfaces at each end of the crankshaft for wear and damage. If the seal has worn a deep groove in the surface of the crankshaft, consult an engine overhaul specialist; repair may be possible, but otherwise a new crankshaft will be required.

18 If the crankshaft journals have not already been reground, it may be possible to have the crankshaft reconditioned, and to fit undersize shells (see Section 17). If no undersize shells are available and the crankshaft has worn beyond the specified limits, it will have to be renewed. Consult your VW dealer or engine specialist for further information on parts availability.

13.8a Using an internal bearing puller ...

13.8b ... to withdraw the bearing

13.9 Using a drift to carefully tap the bearing back into position

14 Main and big-end bearings
– inspection and selection

Inspection

1 Even though the main and big-end bearings should be renewed during the engine overhaul, the old bearings should be retained for close examination, as they may reveal valuable information about the condition of the engine **(see illustration)**.

2 Bearing failure can occur due to lack of lubrication, the presence of dirt or other foreign particles, overloading the engine, or corrosion. Regardless of the cause of bearing failure, the cause must be corrected before the engine is reassembled, to prevent it from happening again.

3 When examining the bearing shells, remove them from the cylinder block/crankcase, the main bearing caps, the connecting rods and the connecting rod big-end bearing caps. Lay them out on a clean surface in the same general position as their location in the engine. This will enable you to match any bearing problems with the corresponding crankshaft journal. Do not touch any shell's internal bearing surface with your fingers while checking it, or the delicate surface may be scratched.

4 Dirt and other foreign matter get into the engine in a variety of ways. It may be left in the engine during assembly, or it may pass through filters or the crankcase ventilation system. It may get into the oil, and from there into the bearings. Metal chips from machining operations and normal engine wear are often present. Abrasives are sometimes left in engine components after reconditioning, especially when parts are not thoroughly cleaned using the proper cleaning methods. Whatever the source, these foreign objects often end up embedded in the soft bearing material, and are easily recognised. Large particles will not embed in the bearing, but will score or gouge the bearing and journal. The best prevention for this cause of bearing failure is to clean all parts thoroughly, and keep everything spotlessly clean during engine assembly. Frequent and regular engine oil and filter changes are also recommended.

5 Lack of lubrication (or lubrication breakdown) has a number of interrelated causes. Excessive heat (which thins the oil), overloading (which squeezes the oil from the bearing face) and oil leakage (from excessive bearing clearances, worn oil pump or high engine speeds) all contribute to lubrication breakdown. Blocked oil passages, which usually are the result of misaligned oil holes in a bearing shell, will also oil-starve a bearing, and destroy it. When lack of lubrication is the cause of bearing failure, the bearing material is wiped or extruded from the steel backing of the bearing. Temperatures may increase to the point where the steel backing turns blue from overheating.

6 Driving habits can have a definite effect on bearing life. Full-throttle, low-speed operation (labouring the engine) puts very high loads on bearings, tending to squeeze out the oil film. These loads cause the bearings to flex, which produces fine cracks in the bearing face (fatigue failure). Eventually, the bearing material will loosen in pieces, and tear away from the steel backing.

7 Short-distance driving leads to corrosion of bearings, because insufficient engine heat is produced to drive off the condensed water and corrosive gases. These products collect in the engine oil, forming acid and sludge. As the oil is carried to the engine bearings, the acid attacks and corrodes the bearing material.

8 Incorrect bearing installation during engine assembly will lead to bearing failure as well. Tight-fitting bearings leave insufficient bearing running clearance, and will result in oil starvation. Dirt or foreign particles trapped behind a bearing shell result in high spots on the bearing, which lead to failure.

9 Do not touch any shell's internal bearing surface with your fingers during re-assembly, as there is a risk of scratching the delicate surface, or of depositing particles of dirt on it.

10 As mentioned at the beginning of this Section, the bearing shells should be renewed as a matter of course during engine overhaul. To do otherwise is false economy.

Selection

11 Main and big-end bearings for the engines described in this Chapter are available in standard sizes and a range of undersizes to suit reground crankshafts.

12 Have the crankshaft measured by an engine reconditioning specialist. They will be able to supply the correctly sized bearings.

15 Engine overhaul –
reassembly sequence

1 Before reassembly begins, ensure that all new parts have been obtained, and that all necessary tools are available. Read through the entire procedure to familiarise yourself with the work involved, and to ensure that all items necessary for reassembly of the engine are at hand. In addition to all normal tools and materials, thread-locking compound will be needed. A suitable tube of liquid sealant will also be required for the joint faces that are fitted without gaskets.

2 In order to save time and avoid problems, engine reassembly can be carried out in the following order, referring to Part A, B, C or D of this Chapter unless otherwise stated. Where applicable, use new gaskets and seals when refitting the various components.
a) *Crankshaft (Section 17).*
b) *Piston/connecting rod assemblies (Section 18).*
c) *Oil pump.*
d) *Sump.*
e) *Flywheel/driveplate.*
f) *Cylinder head.*
g) *Timing belt/chain, tensioner and sprockets.*
h) *Engine external components.*

3 At this stage, all engine components should be absolutely clean and dry, with all faults repaired. The components should be laid out (or in individual containers) on a completely clean work surface.

16 Piston rings – refitting

1 Before fitting new piston rings, the ring end gaps must be checked as follows.

2 Lay out the piston/connecting rod assemblies and the new piston ring sets, so that the ring sets will be matched with the same piston and cylinder during the end gap measurement and subsequent engine reassembly.

3 Insert the top ring into the first cylinder, and push it down the bore using the top of the piston. This will ensure that the ring remains square with the cylinder walls. Position the ring approximately 15.0 mm the bottom of the cylinder bore, at the lower limit of ring travel. Note that the top and second compression rings are different.

4 Measure the end gap using feeler blades, and compare the measurements with the

Typical bearing failures

FATIGUE FAILURE — CRATERS OR POCKETS

IMPROPER SEATING — BRIGHT (POLISHED) SECTIONS

SCRATCHED BY DIRT — DIRT EMBEDDED INTO BEARING MATERIAL

LACK OF OIL — OVERLAY WIPED OUT

EXCESSIVE WEAR — OVERLAY WIPED OUT

TAPERED JOURNAL — RADIUS RIDE

H 28395

14.1 Typical bearing failures

16.4 Check a piston ring end gap using a feeler blade

16.9 Piston ring TOP marking

17.2 Bearing shell correctly refitted

A Recess in cylinder block
B Lug on bearing shell
C Oil hole

figures given in the Specifications **(see illustration)**.

5 If the gap is too small (unlikely if genuine VW parts are used), it must be enlarged, or the ring ends may contact each other during engine operation, causing serious damage. Ideally, new piston rings providing the correct end gap should be fitted. As a last resort, the end gap can be increased by filing the ring ends very carefully with a fine file. Mount the file in a vice equipped with soft jaws, slip the ring over the file with the ends contacting the file face, and slowly move the ring to remove material from the ends. Take care, as piston rings are sharp, and are easily broken.

6 With new piston rings, it is unlikely that the end gap will be too large. If the gaps are too large, check that you have the correct rings for your engine and for the particular cylinder bore size.

7 Repeat the checking procedure for each ring in the first cylinder, and then for the rings in the remaining cylinders. Remember to keep rings, pistons and cylinders matched up.

8 Once the ring end gaps have been checked and if necessary corrected, the rings can be fitted to the pistons.

9 Fit the piston rings using the same technique as for removal. Fit the bottom (oil control) ring first, and work up. Note that a two- or three-section oil control ring may be fitted; where a two-section ring is fitted, first insert the wire expander, then fit the ring. Ensure that the rings are fitted the correct way up – the top surface of the rings is normally marked TOP **(see illustration)**. Offset the piston ring gaps by 120° from each other. Note: Always follow any instructions supplied with the new piston ring sets – different manufacturers may specify different procedures. Do not mix up the top and second compression rings, as they have different cross-sections.

17 Crankshaft – refitting

1 Wipe off the surfaces of the bearing shells in the crankcase and bearing caps.

2 Press the bearing shells into their locations, ensuring that the tab on each shell engages in the notch in the cylinder block or bearing cap, and that the oil holes In the cylinder block and bearing shell are aligned **(see illustration)**.

Take care not to touch any shells bearing surface with your fingers.

3 Where applicable, refit the crankshaft speed/position sensor wheel, and tighten the securing bolts to the specified torque. Make sure that the sensor wheel is correctly orientated as noted before removal.

4 Liberally coat the bearing shells in the crankcase with clean engine oil of the appropriate grade **(see illustration)**. Make sure that the bearing shells are still correctly seated in their locations.

5 Lower the crankshaft into position so that No 1 cylinder crankpin is at BDC, ready for fitting No 1 piston. Ensure that the crankshaft endfloat control thrustwasher halves, either side of the No 3 main bearing location, remain in position. Where applicable, take care not to damage the crankshaft speed/position sensor wheel as the crankshaft is lowered into position.

6 Lubricate the lower bearing shells in the main bearing caps with clean engine oil. Make sure that the crankshaft endfloat control thrustwasher halves are still correctly seated either side of No 3 bearing cap **(see illustrations)**.

7 Fit the main bearing caps in the correct order and orientation – No 1 bearing cap must be at the timing belt end of the engine and the bearing shell tab locating recesses in the crankcase and bearing caps must be adjacent to each other **(see illustration)**. Insert the

17.4 Lubricate the upper bearing shells

17.6a Lubricate the lower bearing shells...

17.6b ...and make sure that the thrustwashers are correctly seated

17.7 Fitting No 1 main bearing cap

bearing cap bolts (using new bolts where necessary), and hand-tighten them only.

8 Working from the centre bearing cap outwards, tighten the bearing cap bolts to their specified torque. On engines where two Stages are given for the torque, tighten all bolts to the Stage 1 torque, then go round again, and tighten all bolts through the Stage 2 angle **(see illustrations)**.

9 Check that the crankshaft rotates freely by turning it by hand. If resistance is felt, recheck the bearing running clearances, as described previously.

10 Check the crankshaft endfloat as described at the beginning of Section 13. If the thrust surfaces of the crankshaft have been checked and new thrustwashers have been fitted, then the endfloat should be within specification.

11 Refit the pistons and connecting rods or reconnect them to the crankshaft as described in Section Section.

12 Refit the timing belt and crankshaft sprocket, sump and oil baffle plate, oil pump and pick-up pipe, flywheel/driveplate, and the crankshaft oil seal housings, as described in Chapter 2A, Chapter 2B or Chapter 2C.

18 Piston/connecting rod assemblies – refitting

Note: *A piston ring compressor tool will be required for this operation.*

1 Note that the following procedure assumes that the crankshaft main bearing caps are in place.

2 Where applicable, refit the piston cooling oil spray jets to the bottom of the cylinder block, and tighten the securing bolts to the specified torque.

3 On engines where the big-end bearing caps are secured by nuts, fit new bolts to the connecting rods. Tap the old bolts out of the connecting rods using a soft-faced mallet, and tap the new bolts into position.

4 Ensure that the bearing shells are correctly fitted, as described at the beginning of this Section. If new shells are being fitted, ensure that all traces of the protective grease are cleaned off using paraffin. Wipe dry the shells and connecting rods with a lint-free cloth.

5 Lubricate the cylinder bores, the pistons, piston rings and upper bearing shells with clean engine oil **(see illustrations)**. Lay out each piston/connecting rod assembly in order on a clean work surface. Where the bearing caps are secured with nuts, pad the threaded ends of the bolts with insulating tape to prevent them scratching the crankpins and bores when the pistons are refitted.

6 Start with piston/connecting rod assembly No 1. Make sure that the piston rings are still spaced as described in Section 16, then clamp them in position with a piston ring compressor tool.

7 Insert the piston/connecting rod assembly

17.8a Tighten the main bearing cap bolts to the specified torque...

17.8b ...then through the specified angle

into the top of cylinder No 1. Lower the big-end in first, guiding it to protect the cylinder bores. Where oil jets are located at the bottoms of the bores, take particular care not to damage them when guiding the connecting rods onto the crankpins.

8 Ensure that the orientation of the piston in its cylinder is correct – the piston crown, connecting rod and big-end bearing cap have markings, which must point towards the timing belt end of the engine when the piston is installed in the bore **(see illustration)** – refer to Section 12 for details.

9 Using a block of wood or hammer handle against the piston crown, tap the assembly into the cylinder until the piston crown is flush with the top of the cylinder **(see illustration)**.

10 Ensure that the bearing shell is still correctly installed in the connecting rod, and

then liberally lubricate the crankpin and both bearing shells with clean engine oil.

11 Taking care not to mark the cylinder bores; tap the piston/connecting rod assembly down the bore and onto the crankpin. On engines where the big-end caps are secured by nuts, remove the insulating tape from the threaded ends of the connecting rod bolts. Oil the bolt threads, and on engines where the big-end caps are secured by bolts, oil the undersides of the bolt heads.

12 Fit the big-end bearing cap, tightening its retaining nuts or bolts (as applicable) finger-tight at first. The connecting rod and its bearing cap both have recesses machined into them on one side, close to their mating surfaces – these recesses must both face the same way as the arrow on the piston crown (i.e. towards the timing end of the engine)

18.5a Lubricate the pistons...

18.5b ...and big-end upper bearing shells with clean engine oil

18.8 Piston orientation and coding

18.9 Using a hammer handle to tap the piston into its bore

18.13a Tighten the big-end bearing cap bolts/nuts to the specified torque...

18.13b ...then through the specified angle

when correctly installed. Reassemble the two components to satisfy this requirement.

13 Tighten the retaining bolts or nuts (as applicable) to the specified torque and angle, in the two stages given in the Specifications **(see illustrations)**.

14 Refit the other three remaining piston/ connecting rod assemblies in the same way.

15 Rotate the crankshaft by hand. Check that it turns freely; some stiffness is to be expected if new parts have been fitted, but there should be no binding or tight spots.

16 If new pistons have been fitted, or if a new short engine has been fitted, the projection of the piston crowns above the cylinder head mating face of the cylinder block at TDC must be measured. This measurement is used to determine the thickness of the new cylinder head gasket required. This procedure is described as part of the Cylinder head – removal, inspection and refitting procedure in Chapter 2A 2A Section 11, 2B 2B Section 11 or 2C 2C Section 13 as applicable.

17 Proceed as follows according to engine type:

a) *On 1.6 litre diesel engines, refit the oil pump and pick-up pipe, sump and oil baffle plate, cylinder head, as described in Chapter 2A.*

b) *On all other diesel engines, refit the oil pump and pick-up pipe, sump and oil baffle plate and cylinder head, as described in Chapter 2B or Chapter 2C.*

19 Engine – initial start-up after overhaul and reassembly

1 Refit the remainder of the engine components in the order listed in Section 5 of this Chapter. Refit the engine to the vehicle as described in the relevant Section of this Chapter. Double-check the engine oil and coolant levels, and make a final check that everything has been reconnected. Make sure that there are no tools or rags left in the engine compartment.

2 Where necessary, reconnect the battery leads with reference to Chapter 5A Section 3.

3 Disconnect the injector harness wiring plug at the end of the cylinder head – refer to Chapter Section, for details.

4 Turn the engine using the starter motor until the oil pressure warning lamp goes out.

5 If the lamp fails to extinguish after several seconds of cranking, check the engine oil level and oil filter security. Assuming these are correct, check the security of the oil pressure

switch cabling – do not progress any further until you are satisfied that oil is being pumped around the engine at sufficient pressure.

6 Reconnect the injector wiring plug.

7 Start the engine, but be aware that as fuel system components have been disturbed, the cranking time may be a little longer than usual.

8 While the engine is idling, check for fuel, water and oil leaks. Don't be alarmed if there are some odd smells and the occasional plume of smoke as components heat up and burn off oil deposits.

9 Assuming all is well; keep the engine idling until hot water is felt circulating through the top hose.

10 After a few minutes, recheck the oil and coolant levels, and top-up as necessary.

11 There is no need to retighten the cylinder head bolts once the engine has been run following reassembly.

12 If new pistons, rings or crankshaft bearings have been fitted, the engine must be treated as new, and run-in for the first 600 miles. Do not operate the engine at full-throttle, or allow it to labour at low engine speeds in any gear. It is recommended that the engine oil and filter be changed at the end of this period.

Chapter 3
Cooling, heating and air conditioning systems

Contents

Degrees of difficulty

| **Easy,** suitable for novice with little experience | | **Fairly easy,** suitable for beginner with some experience | | **Fairly difficult,** suitable for competent DIY mechanic | | **Difficult,** suitable for experienced DIY mechanic | | **Very difficult,** suitable for expert DIY or professional | |

Specifications

Cooling system pressure cap
Opening pressure... 1.4 to 1.6 bar

Thermostat

Thermostat	Begins to open	Fully open
1.6 litre engine	92°C	107°C
1.9 and 2.0 litre engines	85°C	105°C

Capacity
All models... 8.0 litres (approximately)

Air-conditioning
Refrigerant:
  Capacity .... 525 ± 25g
  Type R134a
Compressor make/type:
  Denso 7SEU17C
  Zexel.. DSC17E
  Sanden .... 11PXE14, 6PXE14 or PXE16
Refrigerant oil type:
  Zexel.. G 052 200 A2
  Sanden .... G 052 154 A2

Torque wrench settings	Nm	lbf ft
Coolant pump...	9	6
Compressor bolts...	25	18
Radiator	5	4
Radiator cooling fan shroud bolts	5	4
Thermostat cover bolts	15	11

1 General information and precautions

1 A pressurised cooling system is used, with a pump, an aluminium crossflow radiator, one or two electric cooling fans, a thermostat, a heater matrix and the interconnecting hoses. On automatic (DSG) transmission models, there is also a separate transmission oil cooler. On all diesel engines, the thermostat is located in the front, right-hand side of the cylinder block, in the coolant return from the radiator.

2 The system functions as follows. Coolant is circulated through the cylinder block and head passages by the coolant pump which is driven by the auxiliary drivebelt by the timing belt on all engines. On common rail diesel engines, an electrically operated coolant pump is also fitted. The coolant cools the cylinder bores, combustion surfaces, valve seats, exhaust gas (via the EGR cooler) and the engine oil.

3 When the engine is cold, the thermostat is closed and the coolant only circulates around the engine and the heater matrix in the passenger compartment, however, when the engine reaches a predetermined temperature, the thermostat opens and the coolant passes through the radiator for additional cooling. The coolant enters the top of the radiator and is cooled, as it circulates down through the cooling tubes, by the inrush of air when the car is in forward motion. Airflow is supplemented by the action of the electric cooling fans when necessary. Upon leaving the bottom of the radiator, the coolant returns to the engine and the cycle is repeated.

4 Refer to Section 11 for information on the air conditioning system.

Precautions

 Warning: Do not attempt to remove the expansion tank filler cap or disturb any part of the cooling system while the engine is hot, as there is a high risk of scalding. If the expansion tank filler cap must be removed before the engine and radiator have fully cooled (even though this is not recommended) the pressure in the cooling system must first be relieved. Cover the cap with a thick layer of cloth, to avoid scalding, and slowly unscrew the filler cap until a hissing sound can be heard. When the hissing has stopped, indicating that the pressure has reduced, slowly unscrew the filler cap until it can be removed; if more hissing sounds are heard, wait until they have stopped before unscrewing the cap completely. At all times keep well away from the filler cap opening.

 Warning: Do not allow antifreeze to come into contact with skin or painted surfaces of the vehicle. Rinse off spills immediately with plenty of water. Never leave antifreeze lying around in an open container or in a puddle in the driveway or on the garage floor. Children and pets are attracted by its sweet smell. Antifreeze can be fatal if ingested.

Warning: If the engine is hot, the electric cooling fan may start rotating even if the engine is not running, so be careful to keep hands, hair and loose clothing well clear when working in the engine compartment.

Warning: Refer to Section 11 for additional precautions to be observed when working on models with air conditioning.

2 Cooling system hoses – disconnection and renewal

Note: Refer to the warnings given in Section 1 of this Chapter before proceeding.

1 If the checks described in the relevant part of Chapter 1 reveal a faulty hose, it must be renewed as follows.

2 First drain the cooling system as described in Chapter 1 Section 32. If the coolant is not due for renewal, it may be re-used if it is collected in a clean container.

3 To disconnect a hose, release its retaining clips **(see illustration)**, then move them along the hose, clear of the relevant inlet/outlet union. Carefully work the hose free.

4 In order to disconnect the radiator inlet and outlet hoses (or heater hoses), apply pressure to hold the hose on to the relevant union, pull out the spring clip and pull the hose from the union **(see illustrations)**. Note that the radiator inlet and outlet unions are fragile; do not use excessive force when attempting to remove the hoses. If a hose proves to be difficult to remove, try to release it by rotating the hose ends before attempting to free it.

5 When fitting a hose, first slide the clips onto the hose, and then work the hose into position. If clamp type clips were originally fitted, it is a good idea to use screw type clips when refitting the hose. If the hose is stiff, use a little soapy water as a lubricant, or soften the hose by soaking it in hot water.

6 Work the hose into position, checking that it is correctly routed, and then slide each clip along the hose until it passes over the flared end of the relevant union, before securing it in position with the retaining clip.

7 Prior to refitting a radiator inlet or outlet hose, renew the connection O-ring regardless of condition. The connections are a push-fit over the radiator unions.

8 Refill the cooling system as described in Chapter 1 Section 32.

9 Check thoroughly for leaks as soon as possible after disturbing any part of the cooling system.

3 Radiator – removal, inspection and refitting

Removal

1 Switch off the ignition and all electrical consumers.

2 Remove the air filter housing and associated pipework as described in Chapter 4A Section 3.

3 Jack up and support the front of the vehicle – see 'Jacking and support 13 ' in the reference section.

4 Remove the engine undershield (where fitted) and then drain the cooling system as described Chapter 1 Section 32. If the coolant is not due for renewal, it may be re-used if it is collected in a clean container.

5 Move the lock carrier into the service position as described in Chapter 2D

2.3 Using grips to release the hose clip

2.4a Pull out the retaining clip to release the radiator hoses ...

2.4b ... and the heater hoses

3.6 Release the intercooler hoses

3.7 Disconnect the cooling fan wiring connector

Section 4. On common rail engines and non-turbocharged engines remove the radiator fan(s) as described in Section 5 There is no need to move the lock carrier into the service position, unless the radiator and cooling fans are to be removed together.

6 Release the spring clips and on turbocharged models, disconnect the intercooler hoses **(see illustration)**.

7 Release the locking clip and disconnect the cooling fan wiring block connector from the lower left-hand side of the radiator cowling **(see illustration)**.

8 At this point the cooling fan assembly can be removed as described in Section 5. Alternatively they can be left in place and lowered with the radiator.

9 Release the spring clip and pull off the upper coolant hose **(see illustrations)**.

10 If not already done so, remove the lower coolant hose.

11 On models fitted with AC, remove the bumper cover and unbolt the condenser from the radiator – see Section 10. Undo the two retaining bolts and (if the cooling fans have been removed) withdraw the radiator out through the top of the engine compartment **(see illustrations)**. If the fans are still in position lower the radiator from the vehicle.

3.9a Release the spring clip and...

Inspection

12 If the radiator has been removed due to suspected blockage, reverse flush it as described in the relevant part of Chapter 1.

13 Clean dirt and debris from the radiator fins, using an airline (in which case, wear eye protection) or a soft brush. Be careful, as the fins are sharp and easily damaged.

14 If necessary, a radiator specialist can perform a 'flow test' on the radiator, to establish whether an internal blockage exists.

3.9b ...pull off the radiator coolant hose

15 A leaking radiator must be replaced. Do not attempt to weld or solder a leaking radiator, as damage may result.

16 On models fitted with a flexible mounting, check the condition of the mountings and replace if necessary **(see illustration)**.

Refitting

17 Refitting is a reversal of removal. On completion, refill the cooling system using the correct type of antifreeze as described in Chapter 1 Section 32

3.11a Undo the radiator securing nuts (1.6 CR engine model shown) ...

3.11b ... and lift out the radiator

3.16 Check the mountings

4 Thermostat – removal, testing and refitting

Removal

1 The thermostat is located behind the alternator at the front right-hand side of the engine cylinder block **(see illustration)**. There are two types of thermostat fitted to diesel models:
a) *Single hose to the thermostat cover – the thermostat can be renewed separately.*
b) *Three hoses to the thermostat housing – the thermostat is part of the housing and can only be renewed as a complete assembly.*
2 Remove the engine cover and then drain the cooling system as described in Chapter 1 Section 32. If the coolant is not due for renewal, it may be re-used if it is collected in a clean container.

PD engines

3 Remove the alternator as described in Chapter 5A Section 5.
4 On 2.0 litre engines, disconnect the coolant temperatures sensor wiring plug and then remove the outlet hose from the thermostat.
5 Remove the housing bolts and then remove the cover. Rotate the thermostat to remove it from the housing and then recover the seal **(see illustration)**.

Common rail engines with three outlets

Note: *All 2.0 litre engines have the three outlet type thermostat housing fitted, as do some 1.6 litre engines. Note also that some common rail engines have a thermostat housing that*

4.1 Location of thermostat

appears to have a removable thermostat (secured by screws at the base of the housing) but this is not (at the time of writing) available as a separate part.
6 Remove the air filter housing as described in Chapter Section.
7 Remove the battery and then remove the battery support tray as described in Chapter 5A Section 3.
8 Remove the alternator **(see illustration)** as described in Chapter 5A Section 5.
9 Disconnect the crankcase breather hose and the remove the air intake pipe from the turbocharger. Unclip the vacuum hoses as required.
10 Unclip the wiring loom from the front of the engine and then slacken the hose clips from the air intake duct. Unbolt the duct and remove it.
11 Release the spring clips (or worm drive clips) and then unbolt and remove the intercooler lower duct **(see illustration)**.

4.5 The thermostat housing (PD engines)

12 Unbolt and then remove the dipstick guide tube.
13 Slacken the hose clips and then remove the hoses from the thermostat housing. Unbolt the coolant pipe from the top of the transmission to remove it. Release main hose at the radiator outlet and remove it.
14 Remove the mounting bolts, pull off the housing and recover the seal **(see illustrations)**.

Common rail engines with a single outlet

15 Remove the mounting bolts, slacken the clamps and remove the intercooler outlet hose.
16 Unclip the coolant hose. Release the spring clip from the thermostat housing and remove the hose **(see illustration)**.

4.8 The thermostat housing bolts are behind the alternator (1.6 engine shown)

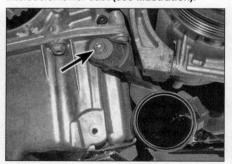
4.11 Remove the retaining bolt

4.14a Remove the bolts

4.14b Remove the thermostat

4.14c Check the condition of the seal

4.16 Release the retaining clip

4.17a Remove the thermostat housing ...

4.17b ... and renew the seal

17 Unscrew the two securing bolts, and remove the thermostat cover/housing complete with the thermostat. Note the locations of any brackets secured by the bolts. Recover the O-ring if it is loose **(see illustrations)**.

18 Remove the thermostat by twisting the thermostat 90° clockwise, and then pull it from the cover.

Testing

19 If there is any question about the operation of the thermostat, it's best to renew it – they are not usually expensive items. Testing involves heating in, or over, an open pan of boiling water, which carries with it the risk of scalding. A thermostat that has seen more than five years' service may well be past its best already.

20 A rough test of the thermostat, may be made by suspending it with a piece of string in a container full of water, but not touching the container. Heat the water to bring it to the boil – the thermostat must open by the time the water boils. If not, renew it.

21 If a thermometer is available, the precise opening temperature of the thermostat may be determined, and compared with the figures given in the Specifications. The opening temperature is also marked on the thermostat.

22 A thermostat which fails to close as the water cools must also be renewed.

Refitting

23 Refitting is a reversal of removal, bearing in mind the following points.
a) *Refit the thermostat using a new O-ring.*
b) *Insert the thermostat into the cover and twist 90° anti-clockwise (where applicable). The thermostat should be fitted with the brace almost vertical.*
c) *Ensure that any brackets are in place on the thermostat cover bolts as noted before removal.*
d) *Refit the alternator (where applicable) with reference to Chapter 5A, Section 5.*
e) *Refill the cooling system with the correct type and quantity of coolant as described in Chapter 1, Section 32.*

---

5 Electric cooling fans – testing, removal and refitting

Testing

1 Depending on the model, there may be one or two electric cooling fans fitted. The cooling fans are supplied with current through the ignition switch, cooling fan control unit (located on the motor), temperature sensor(s), the relays and fuses/fusible link (see Chapter 12). The engine management ECU activates the fan(s) according to the engine coolant temperature sensor(s). Testing of the cooling fan circuit is as follows:

2 If a fan does not appear to work, first check the fuses and fusible links. If they are good, run the engine until normal operating temperature is reached, then allow it to idle. If the fan does not cut-in within a few minutes, the cause may be the temperature sender (where applicable), which can be checked by a VW dealer (or suitably equipped garage) using specialist diagnostic equipment.

3 The motors can be checked, by disconnecting the motor wiring connector and connecting a 12-volt supply directly to the motor terminals. If the motor is faulty, it must be renewed, as no spares are available.

4 If the fan still fails to operate, check the cooling fan circuit wiring (Chapter 12). Check each wire for continuity and ensure that all connections are clean and free of corrosion.

5 On models with a cooling fan control unit, if no fault can be found, then it is likely that the cooling fan control unit is faulty. Testing of the unit should be entrusted to a VW dealer or specialist; if the unit is faulty it must be renewed.

Removal

6 Jack up and support the front of the vehicle (see 'Jacking and support 13 '). Remove the engine undershield. Note that it is also just about possible to remove the fan assembly with the vehicle on the ground, but much easier with access to the fixings from below.

7 On models fitted with 1.9 litre and 2.0 litre PD engines move the lock carrier into the service position as described in Chapter 2D Section 4.

8 Remove the air filter intake housing **(see illustrations)**.

5.8a Unbolt and then...

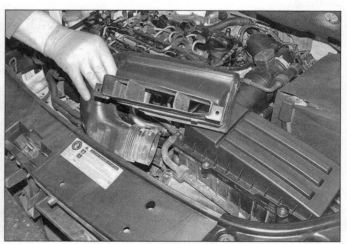

5.8b ...remove the intake housing

5.9a Disconnect the wiring plug

5.9b Remove the lower (one side shown)…

5.9c …and then the upper fixings

5.9d Lift out the fans…

5.9e …or single fan

5.9f Undo the fixings and remove the fan(s) from the shroud

9 Disconnect the wiring plug, unscrew the fixings and then lift the fans and shrouds up and out of the engine bay (see illustrations).

Refitting

10 Refitting is a reversal of removal.

6 Cooling system electrical sensors – testing, removal and refitting

Testing

1 The switch/sensor contains a thermistor, which consists of an electronic component whose electrical resistance decreases at a predetermined rate as its temperature rises. When the coolant is cold, the switch/sensor resistance is high, current flow through the gauge is reduced, and the gauge needle points towards the 'cold' end of the scale. No resistance-to-temperature values are available. Therefore the only method of accurately checking the switch/sensor is with dedicated diagnostic equipment. Basic testing is possible using a multimeter in much the same way as testing a thermostat (see illustration). The resistance of the sensor will change with a change in temperature and a sensor that is open circuit is faulty. If the switch/sensor is faulty, it must be renewed.

Coolant temperature sensors

2 All models (except 2.0 litre PD engines) have two coolant temperature sensors fitted. The sensors are fitted to the radiator outlet hose (close to the radiator) and in the coolant distribution housing on the left-hand side of the cylinder head.

Sensors fitted to coolant housing

3 Remove the engine cover from the top of the engine.
4 To access the temperature sensor fitted at the left-hand end of the cylinder head, remove the air cleaner assembly as described in Chapter Section.
5 Slacken the retaining clip, undo the two retaining bolts and move the charge air ducting away from the coolant housing (see illustrations).
6 Either drain the cooling system, as described in Chapter 1, Section 32, or have

6.1 Checking the resistance

6.5a Slacken the retaining clip…

6.5b … and undo the two retaining bolts

6.7 Disconnect the wiring plug

6.8a Pull out the clip and remove the sensor...

6.8b ... and recover the O-ring from the housing

6.10a Coolant hose sensor (common rail engine)

6.10b Coolant hose sensor (1.9 PD engine)

ready a suitable plug that can be used to plug the switch aperture whilst it is removed.

7 Disconnect the wiring plug from the sensor **(see illustration)**.

8 Pull out the retaining clip and withdraw the sensor from the housing. Recover the O-ring **(see illustrations)**.

9 Refitting is a reversal of removal. Bearing in mind the following points.
a) *Refit the sensor with a new O-ring.*
b) *Refill the cooling system as described in Chapter 1, Section 32. Otherwise top-up as described in 'Weekly checks'.*

Sensors fitted to coolant hoses

10 The sensor is located in the hose positioned to the right-hand side of the engine on 1.6 and 2.0 litre common rail engines. On

1.9 PD engines the sensor is fitted to the left-hand side **(see illustrations)**. Remove the sensor from the hose as described in paragraphs 6 to 8.

11 Refitting is a reversal of removal. Bearing in mind the following points:
a) *Refit the sensor with a new O-ring.*
b) *Refill the cooling system as described in Chapter 1 Section 32.*

7 Coolant pump – removal and refitting

Note: *Best practise is to always replace the coolant pump when the timing belt is*

replaced. *If replacing the coolant pump because it is faulty (leaking) always replace the timing belt and tensioners.*

Timing belt driven coolant pump

1 Drain the cooling system as described in Chapter 1 Section 32.

2 Remove the camshaft timing belt as described in Chapter 2A Section 7 (1.6 litre common rail engines) Chapter 2B Section 7 (2.0 litre common rail engines) or Chapter 2C Section 7 (1.9 and 2.0 litre 'PD' engines)

3 Unscrew the coolant pump retaining bolts, and remove the pump from the engine block. Recover the O-ring seal from the groove in the pump. If the pump is faulty, it must be renewed **(see illustrations)**.

7.3a Undo the coolant pump bolts ...

7.3b ... remove it from the cylinder block ...

7.3c ... and renew the O-ring seal

7.7 Disconnect the wiring plug

7.8 Disconnect the coolant hoses

7.9 Undo the pump bracket retaining bolt

4 Refitting is a reversal of removal, bearing in mind the following points.
a) Fit the coolant pump with a new O-ring.
b) Lubricate the O-ring with coolant.
c) Refill the cooling system as described in Chapter 1, Section 32.

Electric circulation pump (1.6 litre common rail engines)

5 Raise the front of the vehicle and support is securely on axle stands (see Jacking and vehicle support).
6 Undo the fasteners and remove the engine undertray.
7 Disconnect the wiring plug connector to the pump (see illustration).
8 Fit hose clamps to the coolant hoses connected to the pump, and release the clips

and disconnect the hoses from the pump (see illustration). Be prepared for some loss of coolant.
9 Undo the retaining bolt and remove the pump (see illustration).
10 Refitting is a reversal of removal. Top up the coolant, as described in Weekly checks 0 Section 5.

8 Heating and ventilation system – general information

1 The heating/ventilation system consists of a four-speed blower motor (housed in the passenger compartment), face-level vents in

the centre and at each end of the facia, and air ducts to the front and rear footwells.
2 The control unit is located in the facia, and the controls operate flap valves to deflect and mix the air flowing through the various parts of the heating/ventilation system. The flap valves are contained in the air distribution housing, which acts as a central distribution unit, passing air to the various ducts and vents.
3 Cold air enters the system through the grille at the rear of the engine compartment. A pollen filter is fitted to filter out dust, soot, pollen and spores from the air entering the vehicle.
4 The airflow, which can be boosted by the blower, flows through the various ducts, according to the settings of the controls. Stale air is expelled through ducts beneath the rear bumper. If warm air is required, the cold air is passed through the heater matrix, which is heated by the engine coolant.
5 If necessary, the outside air supply can be closed off, allowing the air inside the vehicle to be re-circulated. This can be useful to prevent unpleasant odours entering from outside the vehicle, but should only be used briefly, as the recirculated air quality inside the vehicle will soon deteriorate.

9.2a Working from the base, carefully release the trim …

9.2b …from each side and remove it

9 Heating and ventilation system components – removal and refitting

Heater/ventilation control unit

1 Switch off the ignition and all electrical consumers.
2 Carefully lever the trim panel from around the heater control panel, releasing the securing clips (see illustrations).
3 Set the heat control to cold, the the distribution to 'footwell' and turn off the blower. Undo the retaining screws and manoeuvre the control panel out from the facia (see illustration).
4 As the panel is withdrawn, release the locking clips and disconnect the wiring connectors from the rear of the unit (see illustration. Where fitted unclip the bowden

9.3 Undo the heater control retaining screws

9.4a Release the locking clips and disconnect the wiring connectors

9.4b The bowden cable location (shown with the audio unit removed for clarity)

9.7 Disconnect the heater hoses from the bulkhead

9.9 Slacken the securing bolt

cable or cables **(see illustration)**. Not that access to the cables is greatly improved if the audio unit is removed first as described in Chapter 12 Section 22.

5 Refitting is a reversal of removal, but when reconnecting the bowden cable and before fitting the trim panel turn the air distribution control knob to 'screen', turn the blower motor to full speed and check that air is blown on the windscreen. If the air comes from the footwells the cable must be repositioned.

Heater matrix

6 At the rear of the engine compartment, remove the front section of the plenum chamber, as described in Chapter 12, Section 19. This will make access to the coolant hoses on the bulkhead easier.

7 Using hose clamps, clamp the heater matrix inlet and return hoses located on the bulkhead at the rear of the engine compartment. Place a container beneath the hoses, then release the retaining clips and disconnect them **(see illustration)**. Note the location of the hoses for correct refitting.

8 With the hoses disconnected, remove the coolant from the matrix by blowing air into the upper tube, preferably using an airline, then

the coolant can be caught coming out of the lower tube using a container.

Caution: Always use eye protection when using an airline.

9 Loosen (but do not remove) the bolt located between the matrix upper and lower tubes **(see illustration)**. This allows the coolant supply pipes to move slightly which makes removal of the matrix easier.

10 Working in the passenger side foot well, undo the retaining screw and unclip the panel from the front of the centre console **(see illustration)**.

9.10 Remove the console side trim panel

11 Remove the passenger side storage compartment or glovebox from the facia, as described in Chapter 11, Section 24 and then remove the footwell air distribution duct.

12 If not already done so release the two retaining clips and remove the insulation trim from under the left-hand side of the facia **(see illustrations)**.

13 Undo the retaining screw and remove the passenger side footwell vent **(see illustration)**.

14 Disconnect the wiring connector, then (on models with AC) undo the retaining bolt and

9.12a Undo the two fasteners…

9.12b … and remove the trim panel

9.13 Undo the retaining screw and remove the heater ducting

9.14a Disconnect the wiring connector ...

9.14b ... undo the retaining bolt...

9.14c ... and release the operating lever

remove the flap motor from the side of the heater unit. As the motor is withdrawn, unclip the operating arm from the flap lever **(see illustrations)**.

15 Release the wiring loom from the lower part of the cover, then undo the retaining screws and remove the cover from the heater matrix **(see illustrations)**.

16 Place cloth rags or similar on the floor beneath the heater matrix, then release the pipe clamps and pull the coolant pipes from the matrix **(see illustrations)**. Take care not to damage the pipes as they are removed.

17 Withdraw the heater matrix out from the heater unit **(see illustration)**.

18 Refitting is a reversal of removal, noting the following.

a) Fit the coolant pipe new seals to the heater matrix.

b) Make sure the foam seal is fitted correctly around the perimeter of the matrix.

c) When reconnecting the coolant pipes to the heater matrix, moisten the seals with coolant.

d) Make sure the conical ends of the pipes, locate in the matrix and the clamps must turn easily before tightening them securely.

e) Check that the rubber grommet in the bulkhead is correctly located in its hole.

f) Refill the cooling system and top-up the coolant level with reference to ' Weekly checks ' at the beginning of this Manual.

Heater housing

⚠ *Warning: Refer to the precautions given in Section 11.*

19 On models fitted with AC, it is not possible to remove the housing without opening the refrigerant circuit to the air-conditioning evaporator. The system must be de-gassed – the VW dealer will have suitable equipment as will many local garages and mobile AC specialists.

20 Remove the facia panel, as described in Chapter 11, Section 26 and then remove the crossmember as described in Chapter 11 Section 27.

21 At the rear of the engine compartment, remove the front section of the plenum chamber, as described in Chapter 12, Section 19. Undo the heater housing securing bolt, behind the wiper motor at the rear of the bulkhead **(see illustration)**.

22 Using hose clamps, clamp the heater matrix inlet and return hoses located on the bulkhead at the rear of the engine

9.15a Unclip the wiring loom ...

9.15b ...then undo the bolts and remove the plastic cover

9.16a Release the pipe clamps...

9.16b ...and pull the coolant pipes from the matrix

9.17 Withdraw the matrix from the heater unit

9.21 Heater housing unit retaining bolt

9.22a Release the retaining clips...

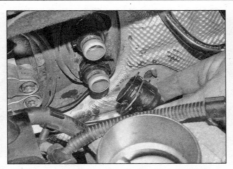

9.22b ... and disconnect the heater hoses from the bulkhead

9.25a Unscrew the bolts and remove the refrigerant lines from the evaporator

9.25b Plug the lines and evaporator while they are disconnected

9.28 Unclip the wiring loom retaining clips

9.29 Remove the central support legs

compartment. Place a container beneath the hoses, then pull out the clips and disconnect them **(see illustrations)**. Note the location of the hoses for correct refitting.

23 With the hoses disconnected, remove the coolant from the matrix by blowing air into the upper tube; preferably using an airline, then the coolant can be caught coming out of the lower tube using a container.

 Warning: Always use eye protection when using an airline.

24 Where fitted, remove the cover from over the expansion valve on the bulkhead, by unscrewing the nut and releasing the retaining clips.

25 With the refrigerant evacuated, unscrew the bolts securing the refrigerant lines to the evaporator on the bulkhead at the rear

of the engine compartment, and detach them. Recover the seals and plug the lines and evaporator openings to prevent entry of foreign matter and water vapour. Discard the seals, as new ones must be used on refitting **(see illustrations)**.

26 Remove the right- and left-hand rear footwell ducts from the heater unit. Also remove the centre console air duct.

27 Inside the car, place cloth rags or similar on the floor beneath the heater unit.

28 Note the location and routing of all wiring then disconnect it from the heater unit and metal support frame **(see illustration)**. Also note the location of plastic cable ties to ensure correct refitting.

29 Unbolt and remove the two central support legs located over the heater unit **(see illustration)**.

30 Remove the two air inlet ducts from the top of the heater **(see illustrations)**.

31 Undo the two retaining bolts from the mounting bracket on the right-hand side of the heater housing **(see illustration)**.

32 Carefully pull the heater unit from the bulkhead, taking care not to damage or bend the matrix tubes on the bulkhead. The help of an assistant may be required. Be prepared for coolant spillage as the assembly is removed from inside the car. As the heater unit assembly is removed, undo the fastener and release the wiring loom from the left-hand rear of the heater blower unit.

33 If necessary, the heater may be further dismantled on the bench.

34 Refitting is a reversal of removal, but refill the cooling system and top-up the coolant with reference to *Weekly checks* at

9.30a Remove the upper air inlet duct...

9.30b ... and lower air inlet duct

9.31 Undo the side support mounting bracket bolts

9.35 Heater control flap servo-motors

9.40 Remove the retaining screw – where fitted

9.41a Release the locking peg …

9.41b … and remove the heater blower

9.45a Disconnect the wiring connector …

9.45b … and unclip the heater blower resistor

the beginning of this Manual. Have the air-conditioning system refilled by a VW dealer or an air conditioning specialist, when finished.

Fresh air/recirculating/ temperature/ flap positioning servomotors

Note: *Depending on model (No AC, manual AC or climate control), there may be up to five air flap servomotors fitted. When there are five motors fitted, there are usually two each side of the heater housing and one by the blower motor housing.*

35 On the vehicle shown there are three air flap motors to the left-hand side of the heater housing **(see illustration)**, depending on which one is going to be worked on, remove the passenger side glovebox and relevant facia trim panels, with reference to Chapter 11, Section 24.

36 Disconnect the wiring, undo the motor

retaining bolt(s), then remove it from its mountings and separate it from the air flap lever **(see illustrations 9.14a, 9.14b & 9.14c)**.

37 Refitting is a reversal of removal. Note that if the motor is renewed, its basic settings must be reprogrammed by a VW dealer or suitably equipped garage using specialist equipment.

Heater blower motor

38 Switch off the ignition and all electrical consumers.

39 Undo the screws and remove the cover from under the heater blower motor **(see illustrations 9.12a & 9.12b)**.

40 Disconnect the wiring connector from the blower motor, and where fitted undo the single securing screw **(see illustration)**.

41 Release the catch and turn the blower motor clockwise to remove it from the heater housing **(see illustrations)**.

42 Refitting is a reversal of removal. Turn the blower motor anti-clockwise, in the direction of the arrow on the housing to lock the catch in position, if required fit screw to housing to secure the motor.

Heater blower motor series resistor

43 Switch off the ignition and all electrical consumers.

44 Undo the screws and remove the cover from under the heater blower motor **(see illustrations 9.11a & 9.11b)**.

45 Disconnect the wiring from the blower series resistor, then remove the resistor by pressing the catch upwards **(see illustrations)**.

Caution: The resistor may be very hot if the heater has recently been in use.

46 Refitting is the reverse of removal.

Footwell air temperature sensor

Note: *Not all sensor are fitted to all models.*

47 There are two sensors, one fitted to each side of the heater housing in the front footwell air ducting.

48 Remove the passenger side glovebox from the facia, to access the left-hand sensor. Remove the driver's side lower facia trim panels to access the right-hand sensor. Refer to Chapter 11, Section 24, for further information.

49 Reaching up behind the facia, disconnect the wiring plug connector, then turn the sensor 90° and pull it from the heater ducting **(see illustrations)**.

9.49a Disconnect the wiring connector …

9.49b … and remove the air temperature sensor

9.53 Right-hand side air vent temperature sensor

9.57a Disconnect the wiring connector …

9.57b … and release the securing clip

50 Refitting is a reversal of the removal procedure.

Side vent temperature sender

51 Switch off the ignition and all electrical consumers.
52 Unclip the trim panel from the relevant end of the facia.
53 Disconnect the wiring plug from the sender **(see illustration)**.
54 Turn the sender through 90°, and withdraw it from the housing.
55 Refitting is a reversal of removal.

Ambient temperature sender

56 Reach up behind the bumper, at the front, left-hand side of the radiator to locate the sensor. If required, remove the front bumper as described in Chapter 11, Section 6.
57 Disconnect the wiring connector, and then unclip the sender from its mounting bracket **(see illustrations)**.
58 Refitting is a reversal of removal. Make sure the wiring is fully connected to prevent entry of water.

Sunlight sensor

59 The sensor is fitted to the front centre of the facia close to the windscreen.
60 Remove the central storage compartment and push the sensor up from below. Alternatively, protect the facia and prise the sensor from the facia using a trim tool. Disconnect the wiring plug and remove the sensor.
61 Refitting is a reversal of removal.

Fuel fired auxiliary heater

62 Disconnect the battery as described in Chapter 5A Section 3.
63 The heater (where fitted) is located behind the front bumper next to the screen washer fluid reservoir on the right-hand side of the vehicle.
64 Remove the front bumper cover as described in Chapter 11 Section 6.
65 Remove the right-hand wing liner and then remove the screen washer reservoir as described in Chapter 12 Section 21.
66 Anticipating some coolant spillage, clamp

the coolant hoses and then remove the spring type hose clips.
67 Unbolt and then move to the side the heater exhaust pipes.
68 Disconnect the wiring plug **(see illustration)** and then (anticipating some fuel spillage) disconnect the fuel lines. Seal the fuel lines with suitable plugs.
69 Unbolt and remove the heater.
70 Refitting is a reversal of removal, noting the following points:
a) *Check the coolant level and top up as required (see Chapter 0 Section 5).*
b) *Check the fuel lines for leaks before refitting the bumper cover and the wing liner.*

---

10 Air conditioning system components – removal and refitting

⚠️ *Warning: Refer to the precautions given in Section 11, before working on the air-conditioning system.*

1 Before working on any components in the air-conditioning system, have the refrigerant evacuated from the air conditioning system by a VW dealer or refrigeration specialist.
Caution: The air conditioning compressor is driven permanently by the auxiliary drivebelt, and is not fitted with a magnetic clutch. It is not recommended that the

9.68 Disconnect the wiring plug

engine be started without refrigerant being present in the system, as the compressor may overheat causing internal damage. Note also that if the refrigerant circuit is not opened within 10 minutes of evacuation, slight pressure may develop due to re-evaporation.

Evaporator

2 Remove the heater matrix and heater housing, as described earlier in Section 9.
3 Remove the rubber gaiter and foam cushion from around the coolant and refrigerant pipes **(see illustration)**.
4 Release any retaining clips and remove the coolant pipes from the housing **(see illustration)**.
5 Noting the routing and their fitted

10.3 Remove the rubber grommet from the pipes

10.4 Remove the heater pipes from the housing

10.5a Release the wiring loom from the retaining clips …

10.5b … and locating pegs on the heater housing

10.6 Unscrew the bolts securing the two sections of the heater housing

10.7a Unscrew the bolts and separate the evaporator housing …

10.7b …then withdraw the evaporator

connections remove the wiring loom from around the heater housing **(see illustrations)**.

6 Working your way around the housing, undo the retaining bolts and split the housing into two parts **(see illustration)**.

7 To remove the evaporator, undo the retaining bolts and split the upper and lower halves of the housing, then withdraw the evaporator from the housing together with the refrigerant lines and rubber grommet **(see illustrations)**.

8 Refitting is a reversal of removal, fit new seals and have the system recharged by a VW dealer or refrigeration specialist.

Condenser

Note: *It is possible to remove the cooling fans,*

radiator, intercooler and condenser as a single unit complete with the headlights and lock panel. If this approach is adopted the aid of an assistant is essential.

9 Have the refrigerant evacuated from the air conditioning system by a VW dealer or refrigeration specialist and then drain the cooling system as described in Chapter 1 Section 32.

10 Remove the bumper cover as described in Chapter 11 Section 6.

11 Move the lock carrier to the service position (as described in Chapter 2D Section 4).

12 Undo the screws and disconnect the refrigerant lines from the condenser **(see illustration)**. Recover the seals and plug the

lines and condenser openings to prevent entry of foreign matter and water vapour.

13 Remove the protective cover from the condenser. Unbolt the condenser from the radiator and then remove the condenser upwards. Where fitted recover the spacer from the refrigerant pipes.

14 Refitting is a reversal of removal, but fit new seals, and have the system recharged by a VW dealer or refrigeration specialist.

Compressor

15 Have the refrigerant evacuated from the air conditioning system by a VW dealer or refrigeration specialist.

16 Chock the rear roadwheels, then jack up the front of the vehicle and support on axle stands (see *Jacking and vehicle support*). Remove the left-hand roadwheel.

17 Remove the left-hand wing liner and the the auxiliary drivebelt as described in Chapter 1, Section 29. On models fitted with hydraulic power steering remove the power steering pump as described in Chapter 10 Section 24. Where required disconnect the battery and remove the alternator (Chapter 5A Section 5)

18 Unscrew the retaining bolts and disconnect the refrigeant lines from the compressor **(see illustration)**. Remove the O-ring seals and renew them if necessary. Plug the open pipes and ports to prevent the ingress of moisture.

19 Disconnect the wiring plug connector from the rear of the compressor **(see illustration)**.

10.12 Disconnect the refrigerant lines from the condenser

10.18 Undo the refrigerant line securing bolts on the compressor (Denso/Zexel compressor shown)

10.19 Disconnect the wiring connector

10.20 Air conditioning compressor securing bolts

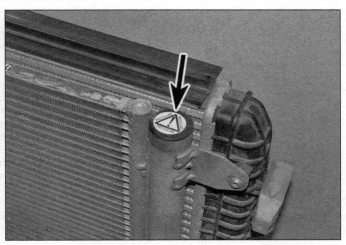

10.24 Unscrew cap to access receiver/drier

20 Undo the retaining bolts **(see illustration)** and withdraw the compressor from the mounting bracket.

21 Refitting is a reversal of the removal procedure, ensure that all the fixings are tightened to the specified torque settings, where given. On completion, have new O-rings fitted to the refrigerant lines, and then have the system recharged by a VW dealer or refrigeration specialist. On models fitted with hydraulic power steering refit the pump and bleed the system as described in Chapter 10 Section 24.

Receiver/drier

Note: *Check for the availability of parts before removal, there are different makes of receiver/drier and some cannot be renewed separately from the condenser.*

22 The receiver/drier is attached to the left-hand side of the condenser. On some models the receiver drier can be removed after the air filter inlet has been removed, on most models complete (or partial) removal of the condenser will be required.

23 Remove the condenser, as described in paragraphs 9 to 14.

Modine type

24 Unscrew the cap (with a T50 torx socket)

from the top of the receiver/drier **(see illustration)**. Peel back the warning label, where fitted.

Caution: DO NOT remove this cap if the system has not been evacuated, as it will be under high pressure.

25 Insert a bolt into the receiver/drier sealing cover, push downwards slightly and extract the retaining circlip. Using a hooked length of welding rod, pull the receiver/drier element from place.

Showa type

26 The receiver/drier is bolted to the side of the condenser, undo the retaining bolt(s) and withdraw it from the condenser.

27 Refitting is a reversal of the removal procedure, ensure that all the fixings are tightened to the specified torque settings, where given. On completion, fit new O-rings and then have the system recharged by a VW dealer or refrigeration specialist.

Evaporator temperature sensor

28 The sensor is located to the right-hand side of the heater housing, behind the evaporator **(see illustration)**, to the left of the clutch pedal.

29 Working in the driver's side foot well, undo

the retaining screw and unclip the panel from the front of the centre console.

30 Disconnect the wiring plug connector, then rotate the sensor 90° and pull it from the housing **(see illustration)**.

31 Refitting is a reversal of the removal procedure.

> **11 Air conditioning system**
> – general information and
> precautions

General information

1 Air conditioning is fitted as standard to most models, and is available as manually operated (Climatic) or automatically-operated (Climatronic). The Climatronic system works in conjunction with the heating and air conditioning systems to maintain a selected vehicle interior temperature fully automatically.

2 The air conditioning system enables the temperature of incoming air to be lowered, and dehumidifies the air, which makes for rapid demisting and increased comfort. The cooling side of the system works in the same way as a domestic refrigerator. Refrigerant gas is drawn into a belt-driven compressor and passes into a condenser mounted in front of the radiator, where it loses heat and becomes liquid. The liquid passes through an expansion valve to an evaporator, where it changes from liquid under high pressure to gas under low pressure. This change is accompanied by a drop in temperature, which in turn cools the evaporator. The refrigerant returns to the compressor and the cycle begins again.

3 Air blown through the evaporator passes to the air distribution unit, where it is mixed with hot air blown through the heater matrix to achieve the desired temperature in the passenger compartment.

4 The operation of the system is controlled electronically by coolant temperature switches, and pressure switches which are

10.28 Evaporator temperature sensor

10.30 Disconnect the wiring connector from the sensor

screwed into the compressor high-pressure line. Any problems with the system should be referred to a VW dealer or an air conditioning specialist.

5 The only operation that can be carried out easily without discharging the refrigerant is the renewal of the compressor drivebelt, which is covered in the relevant part of Chapter 1. Removal of the evaporator and condenser requires the evacuation of the refrigerant. If necessary the compressor can be unbolted and moved aside, without disconnecting its flexible hoses, after removing the drivebelt **(see illustration)**.

Precautions

• *When an air conditioning system is fitted, it is necessary to observe special precautions whenever dealing with any part of the system, its associated components and any items which require disconnection of the system. If for any reason the system must be disconnected, entrust this task to your VW dealer or an air conditioning specialist.*

 Warning: The refrigeration circuit contains a refrigerant and it is therefore dangerous to disconnect any part of the system without specialised knowledge and equipment. The refrigerant is potentially dangerous and should only be handled by qualified persons. If it is splashed onto the skin it can cause frostbite. It is not itself poisonous, but in the presence of a naked flame (including a cigarette) it forms a poisonous gas. Uncontrolled discharging of the refrigerant is dangerous and potentially damaging to the environment.

• *Do not operate the air conditioning system if it is known to be short of refrigerant, as this may damage the compressor.*

Chapter 4 Part A
Diesel engine fuel systems

Contents

Degrees of difficulty

Easy, suitable for novice with little experience	**Fairly easy,** suitable for beginner with some experience	**Fairly difficult,** suitable for competent DIY mechanic	**Difficult,** suitable for experienced DIY mechanic	**Very difficult,** suitable for expert DIY or professional

Specifications

Engine codes*

1.9 litre – 'PD' (unit injector)	BKC, BJB, BLS and BSU
2.0 litre – 'PD' (unit injector)	BDJ, BST and BMM
1.6 litre – common rail injection	CAYE, CAYD
2.0 litre – common rail injection	CFJA, CFHC, CFHF, CLCA, CFHE, CLCB and CHWA

*See 'Vehicle identification' at the end of the manual for the location of the engine code markings

General

Fuel injection system	Electronic, direct, unit injectors or common rail injection
Firing order	1-3-4-2
Maximum engine speed	N/A (ECU controlled)
Engine fast idle speed	N/A (ECU controlled)

Tandem pump (PD Unit injector engines only)

Fuel pressure at 1500 rpm	3.5 bar

Turbocharger

Type	Garrett or KKK

Torque wrench settings

	Nm	lbf ft
Camshaft position sensor	10	7
Common fuel rail	15	11
EGR pipe flange bolts	25	18
EGR valve mounting bolt:		
CR engines	20	15
PD engines except BDJ and BST engine codes	22	16
PD engines BDJ and BST	20	15
Engine speed/TDC sender	5	4
Flap motor housing	10	7
Injector clamp/mounting:		
1.9 litre PD unit injector engines*:		
Stage 1	12	9
Stage 2	Angle-tighten a further 270°	
2.0 litre PD unit injector engines*:		
Stage 1	3	2
Stage 2	Angle-tighten a further 90°	
Stage 3	Angle-tighten a further 180°	
Common rail injector engines*:		
Stage 1	2	1
Stage 2	8	6
Stage 3	Angle-tighten a further 270°	

Torque wrench settings (continued)

	Nm	lbf ft
Inlet manifold to cylinder head:		
PD engines*	22	16
CR engines	8	6
Pump injector rocker shaft bolts*:		
Stage 1	20	15
Stage 2	Angle-tighten a further 90°	
Tandem pump bolts:		
Upper	20	15
Lower	10	7

* Use new fixings

---

1 General information and precautions

General information

1 All engines covered by this Manual are fitted with a direct-injection fuelling system, incorporating a fuel tank, an engine-bay mounted fuel filter with an integral water separator, fuel supply and return lines and four fuel injectors. Models with the 1.9 or 2.0 litre PD Unit injector engines, also have a fuel cooler mounted beneath the right-hand side of the car, on the underbody.

2 However, two different types of fuel injection system are fitted. The first is first is known as the 'PD' (Pumpe Duse) or Unit injector system, where fuel is delivered by a camshaft driven 'tandem pump' at low pressure to the injectors (known as 'Unit injectors'). A 'roller rocker' assembly, mounted above the camshaft bearing caps, uses an extra set of camshaft lobes to compress the top of each injector once per firing cycle. This arrangement creates high injection pressures. The precise timing of the pre-injection and main injection is controlled by the engine management ECM and a solenoid on each injector.

3 The second type is the familiar Common Rail system, where fuel is supplied from a timing belt-driven high-pressure pump to a common fuel rail (or reservoir). The four injectors are fitted into the cylinder head and are connected to the fuel rail by rigid metal pipes. The precise timing of the pre-, main, and post-injections are controlled by the engine management ECM and an electrically operated Piezo crystal incorporated into the injector design. All engines are fitted with a turbocharger.

1.7 The EOBD diagnostic connector is located under the drivers side of the facia

4 The direct-injection fuelling system is controlled electronically by a diesel engine management system, comprising an Electronic Control Module (ECM) and its associated sensors, actuators and wiring. In addition, the ECM manages the operation of the Exhaust Gas Recirculation (EGR) emission control system (Chapter Section), the turbocharger boost pressure control system (on models fitted with a turbocharger) and the glow plug control system (Chapter Section).

5 A flap valve/throttle valve module fitted to the intake manifold is closed by the ECM for 3 seconds as the engine is switched off, to minimise the air intake as the engine shuts down. This minimises the vibration felt as the pistons come up against the volume of highly compressed air present in the combustion chambers.

6 It should be noted that fault diagnosis of the diesel engine management system is only possible with dedicated electronic test equipment. Problems with the system's operation should therefore be referred to a VW dealer or suitably-equipped specialist for assessment. Once the fault has been identified, the removal/refitting sequences detailed in the following Sections will then allow the appropriate component(s) to be renewed as required.

7 The EOBD diagnostic connector is located under the drivers side of the facia **(see illustration)**.

Precautions

8 Many of the operations described in this Chapter involve the disconnection of fuel lines, which may cause an amount of fuel spillage. Before commencing work, refer to the warnings below and the information in *Safety first!* at the beginning of this manual.

⚠ *Warning: When working on any part of the fuel system, avoid direct contact skin contact with diesel fuel – wear protective clothing and gloves when handling fuel system components. Ensure that the work area is well-ventilated to prevent the build-up of diesel fuel vapour.*

• *Fuel injectors operate at extremely high pressures and the jet of fuel produced at the nozzle is capable of piercing skin, with potentially fatal results. When working with pressurised injectors, take care to avoid exposing any part of the body to the fuel spray. It is recommended that a diesel fuel systems specialist should carry out any pressure testing of the fuel system components.*

• *Under no circumstances should diesel fuel be allowed to come into contact with coolant hoses – wipe off accidental spillage immediately. Hoses that have been contaminated with fuel for an extended period should be renewed.*

• *Diesel fuel systems are particularly sensitive to contamination from dirt, air and water. Pay particular attention to cleanliness when working on any part of the fuel system, to prevent the ingress of dirt. Thoroughly clean the area around fuel unions before disconnecting them. Only use lint-free cloths and clean fuel for component cleansing.*

• *Store dismantled components in sealed containers to prevent contamination and the formation of condensation.*

2 Fuel pipe and connectors

1 Disconnect the cable from the negative battery terminal (see Chapter 5A Section 3) before proceeding.

2 The fuel supply pipe connects the fuel pump in the fuel tank to the fuel filter on the engine.

3 Whenever you're working under the vehicle, be sure to inspect all fuel and evaporative emission pipes for leaks, kinks, dents and other damage. Always replace a damaged fuel pipe immediately.

4 If you find signs of dirt in the pipes during disassembly, disconnect all pipes and blow them out with compressed air. Inspect the fuel strainer on the fuel pump pick-up unit for damage and deterioration.

Steel tubing

5 It is critical that the fuel pipes be replaced with pipes of equivalent type and specification.

6 Some steel fuel pipes have threaded fittings. When loosening these fittings, hold the stationary fitting with a spanner while turning the union nut.

Plastic tubing

 Warning: When removing or installing plastic fuel tubing, be careful not to bend or twist it too much, which can damage it. Also, plastic fuel tubing is NOT heat resistant, so keep it away from excessive heat.

7 When replacing fuel system plastic tubing, use only original equipment replacement plastic tubing.

Flexible hoses

8 When replacing fuel system flexible hoses, use original equipment replacements, or hose to the same specification.

9 Don't route fuel hoses (or metal pipes) within 100 mm of the exhaust system or within 280 mm of the catalytic converter. Make sure that no rubber hoses are installed directly against the vehicle, particularly in places where there is any vibration. If allowed to touch some vibrating part of the vehicle, a hose can easily become chafed and it might start leaking. A good rule of thumb is to maintain a minimum of 8.0 mm clearance around a hose (or metal pipe) to prevent contact with the vehicle underbody.

Disconnecting Fuel pipe Fittings

10 Typical fuel pipe fittings:

2.10a Two-tab type fitting; depress both tabs with your fingers, then pull the fuel pipe and the fitting apart

2.10b On this type of fitting, depress the two buttons on opposite sides of the fitting, then pull it off the fuel pipe

2.10c Threaded fuel pipe fitting; hold the stationary portion of the pipe or component (A) while loosening the union nut (B) with a flare-nut spanner

2.10d Plastic collar-type fitting; rotate the outer part of the fitting

2.10e Metal collar quick-connect fitting; pull the end of the retainer off the fuel pipe and disengage the other end from the female side of the fitting…

2.10f …insert a fuel pipe separator tool into the female side of the fitting, push it into the fitting and pull the fuel pipe off the pipe

2.10g Some fittings are secured by lock tabs. Release the lock tab (A) and rotate it to the fully-opened position, squeeze the two smaller lock tabs (B)…

2.10h …then push the retainer out and pull the fuel pipe off the pipe

2.10i Spring-lock coupling; remove the safety cover, install a coupling release tool and close the tool around the coupling…

2.10j …push the tool into the fitting, then pull the two pipes apart

2.10k Hairpin clip type fitting: push the legs of the retainer clip together, then push the clip down all the way until it stops and pull the fuel pipe off the pipe

3.1a Unclip the cover from the air intake

3.1b Release the securing clips ...

3.1c ...and remove the air ducting

3.2 Disconnect the air mass meter wiring plug (common rail shown)

3.3a Disconnecting the vacuum pipe on common rail engines

3.3b The vacuum pipe on PD engines

3.4 Disconnect the air intake hose

3 Air filter assembly – removal and refitting

Note: *There are variations in the procedure for removing the air filter assembly, however the removal procedure is essentially the same for all models.*

Removal

1 Unclip the plastic cover from the air intake ducting, then release the two securing clips (one at each side) and remove the ducting from the front crossmember **(see illustrations)**. Note, on some models there may be a retaining screw securing the inner part of the lower ducting to the crossmember.

2 Disconnect the wiring plug from the air mass meter **(see illustration)**.

3 Disconnect the vacuum pipe from the air intake hose **(see illustrations)**.

4 Loosen the clip and disconnect the air duct from the air mass meter **(see illustration)**.

5 Undo the retaining bolt and lift the air cleaner assembly upwards to release it from the locating pegs **(see illustrations)**. As the air cleaner is removed, withdraw the water drain hose, under the air filter assembly out from the inner wing panel.

3.5a Undo the retaining screw ...

3.5b ... and remove the air filter assembly out of the engine compartment

3.5c Release the drain tube as it is removed

3.6 Make sure the assembly is located correctly on the mounting pegs

4.1 Release the wiring connector locking clip

4.2 Undo the pedal retaining bolt

Refitting

6 Refit the air filter assembly by following the removal procedure in reverse. Make sure the assembly is located correctly on the lower mounting pegs **(see illustration)**.

4 Diesel engine management system – component removal and refitting

Throttle pedal/position sensor

1 Release the securing clip and disconnect the wiring connector from the top of the accelerator pedal **(see illustration)**.
2 Prise off the cap, and undo the screw securing the throttle pedal to the bulkhead **(see illustration)**.
3 The throttle pedal is clipped to two metal pegs in the floor panel, using a lever and thin screwdriver, release the securing clips **(see illustration)**.
4 The outer clip can be released by pressing the screwdriver inwards to release the securing clip, whilst levering the pedal upwards. Then insert the screwdriver into the inner slot and push it to the left to release the securing clip **(see illustrations)**. Withdraw

the throttle pedal from the floor panel and out from the vehicle.
5 Refitting is a reversal of removal.

Throttle valve housing/module (Common rail engines)

6 Where fitted, remove the engine cover **(see illustration)**.
7 Slacken the retaining clips and remove the air intake rubber hose from the throttle housing **(see illustration)**. If required, undo the bolts securing the air intake plastic hose from the intercooler to the throttle housing, this will allow easier removal of the intake rubber hose.

4.3 Throttle pedal securing pegs in the floor panel

4.4a Release the outer clip by pressing the screwdriver forwards

4.4b Release the inner clip by pushing the screwdriver inwards, and then to the left to release the clip

4.4c Direction to release the two securing clips

4.6 Remove the engine cover

4.7 Slacken the two retaining clips

4.8 Disconnect the wiring plug

4.9 Undo the dipstick tube retaining bolt

4.10a Undo the three retaining bolts ...

4.10b ... and remove the throttle housing module

4.11 Fit a new seal to the housing on refitting

14 Where fitted disconnect the flap control motor wiring plug from the housing.
15 Disconnect the EGR vacuum hose from the top of the housing and where required unbolt the EGR valve pipe and recover the gasket.
16 Unscrew the bolts **(see illustration)** securing the flap housing to the EGR valve/housing/manifold, remove the flap housing and recover the O-ring seal.

Refitting

17 Refitting is a reversal of removal. Renew the O-ring seal if it appears damaged.

Coolant temperature sensors

18 Refer to Chapter Section.

Fuel temperature sensor

Removal

19 The fuel temperature sensor is located in the fuel return line to the fuel filter in the engine compartment on PD unit injection engines or in the fuel supply line at the top of the high-pressure fuel pump on common rail injection engines. First, disconnect the wiring.
20 On PD unit injection engines, remove the securing clip, then extract the sensor from the fuel line housing and recover the O-ring seal.

8 Disconnect the wiring plug connector, from the throttle housing/module **(see illustration)**.
9 Undo the retaining bolt and disconnect the dipstick guide tube from the throttle housing **(see illustration)**.
10 Unscrew and remove the retaining bolts, then lift the throttle housing/module away from the inlet manifold **(see illustrations)**. Recover the O-ring seal; a new one will be required for refitting.
11 Refitting is a reversal of removal, noting the following:
a) *Use a new throttle housing-to-inlet manifold seal* **(see illustration)**.
b) *Tighten the throttle housing bolts evenly to the specified torque.*

c) *Ensure that all hoses and electrical connectors are refitted securely.*

Inlet manifold flap motor/ housing (PD engines)

Note: *On some models the inlet manifold flap housing is vacuum-operated and is incorporated into the EGR valve, whereas other engine codes have a separate electrically-operated flap motor.*

Removal

12 Remove the engine cover.
13 Loosen the clip (or release the spring clip) and disconnect the air trunking from the flap housing **(see illustrations)**.

4.13a Release the spring clip and...

4.13b ...remove the ducting

4.16 Remove the bolts

4.21 Fuel temperature sensor – common rail engines

4.25 The charge air pressure sensor (common rail engine shown)

21 On common rail injection engines, release the clamps and disconnect the hoses from the sensor assembly **(see illustration)**.

Refitting

22 Refit the fuel temperature sensor by reversing the removal procedure, using a new O-ring seal (where applicable).

Inlet air temperature sensor
PD unit injection engines only

23 All models have an air temperature sensor built into the air mass meter – this sensor is an integral part of the air mass meter, and cannot be renewed separately.

Charge air pressure/ temperature sensor

Removal

24 The charge air pressure and temperature sensor is fitted either on the intercooler inlet elbow (engine codes BMM, BLS and BSU), or on the air hose from the intercooler to the inlet manifold (engine codes BKC and BJB). On these engines access to the sensor is from above. On all common rail engines the sensor is fitted to the lower hose. On these engines, jack up the front of the vehicle and support it on axle stands (see Jacking and vehicle support), then remove the engine undertray.
25 Disconnect the wiring then undo the screw and remove the sensor from its location **(see illustration)**.

Refitting

26 Refit the sensor by reversing the removal procedure, using a new O-ring seal.

Engine speed/TDC sensor

Note: *Access to the sensor is limited. Removing the oil cooler hoses and coolant hoses along with placing the lock carrier in the service position (Chapter Section) improves access. Note that the illustrations show the sensor position with the transmission removed for clarity.*

27 The engine speed/TDC sensor is mounted on the front cylinder block, adjacent to the mating surface of the block and transmission bellhousing **(see illustration)**.
28 Access is from beneath the engine compartment. Apply the handbrake, and then jack up the front of the vehicle and support it on axle stands (see Jacking and vehicle support). Remove the engine undertray.
29 Remove the retaining screw and withdraw

4.27 Crankshaft position speed sensor

4.29b … and withdraw the sensor

the sensor from the cylinder block **(see illustrations)**.
30 Refit the sensor by reversing the removal procedure.

Air mass meter

Removal

31 On all models the air mass meter is located in the outlet from the air cleaner assembly on the left-hand side of the engine compartment **(see illustration)**.

4.29a Undo the retaining bolt …

4.31 Air mass meter location on engine code BKC

4.32a Disconnecting the wiring plug on PD engines and..

4.32b ...on common rail engines

4.32c Release the spring clip

4.40 Sometimes it is possible to remove the shear bolts with pliers

4.41 Remove the bolts

4.42 Disconnect the wiring plugs by levering up the catch

32 Disconnect the wiring plug, loosen the clips and disconnect the air ducting from the air mass meter **(see illustrations)**.

33 On common rail engines remove the screws and remove the meter and housing from the air filter housing. On PD engines remove the screws and lift the meter from the housing. Note however that replacement air mass meters are often supplied complete with the housing to avoid damage in transit.

Caution: Handle the air mass meter carefully – its internal components are easily damaged.

Refitting

34 Refitting is a reversal of removal. Renew the O-ring seal if it appears damaged.

Absolute pressure (altitude) sensor

35 The absolute pressure sensor is an integral part of the ECU, and hence cannot be renewed separately.

Clutch pedal switch

Removal

36 The clutch pedal switch is clipped to the clutch master cylinder on the pedal bracket. Remove the master cylinder as described in Chapter Section.

37 Unclip the pedal switch from the bottom of the master cylinder.

Refitting

38 Refitting is a reversal of removal.

Electronic control unit (ECU)

Caution: Always wait at least 30 seconds after switching off the ignition before disconnecting the wiring from the ECU. When the wiring is disconnected, all the learned values are erased, however any Specifications of the fault memory are retained. Note that if the ECU is renewed, the identification of the new ECU must be transferred to the immobiliser control

unit by a VW dealer or suitably equipped garage.

Removal

39 The ECU is located centrally behind the engine compartment bulkhead, in the plenum chamber. Remove the wiper arms and cowl panel and front section of the plenum chamber as for windscreen wiper motor removal and refitting (as described in Chapter Section).

40 Where the cover is secured with pop-rivets or shear bolts, drill them out **(see illustration)**. Where it is secured with bolts, unscrew and remove them.

41 Remove the security cover then unbolt the ECU **(see illustration)**.

42 Pull the ECU forward, rotate it slightly and disconnect the wiring plugs **(see illustration)**.

43 Remove the ECU.

Refitting

44 Refitting is a reversal of removal. Make sure that the locating tab is correctly engaged **(see illustration)** before refitting the mounting bolts. Fit new shear bolts

Fuel pressure regulating valve (common rail engines)

45 The fuel pressure regulating valve is fitted to the left-hand end of the fuel rail **(see illustration)**. If the valve is removed from the fuel rail, then it will need to be renewed, as it has a deformable sealing lip as part of the valve.

46 To check the operation of the regulating valve, first disconnect the fuel return hose from the fuel rail and plug the end **(see**

4.44 The rear locating tab

4.45 Fuel pressure regulator valve

4.46 Disconnect the fuel hose

4.49 Pressure regulator valve fitted to the left-hand end of the fuel rail

4.52 Disconnect the wiring connector from the fuel pressure sender

illustration). Then fit a piece of hose to the fuel rail and the other end into a container. There are three checks that can be made, the first two with the engine running and the third if the vehicle will not start:

a) *Start the engine and run at idle for 30 seconds, there should be approx. 75ml of fuel (1.6 litre engines) or 100ml of fuel (2.0 litre engines) in the container.*

b) *Start engine and increase engine speed to 2000rpm, there should be 0ml of fuel in the container (allow for a few droplets of fuel).*

c) *On vehicles that will not run, turn the ignition key and crank the engine, there should be 0ml of fuel in the container (allow for a few droplets of fuel).*

47 If any of these readings are not attained, renew the regulating valve.

48 To renew the valve, remove the fuel rail as described in Section Section.

49 Clean around the valve, then slacken the valve from the end of the fuel rail **(see illustration)** ; counterhold the fuel rail using the flats on the housing. Plug the end of the rail to prevent dirt from entering.

50 Fit the new valve by reversing the removal procedure, making sure that the threads are all clean before fitting. Check the deformable seal on the new valve, before fitting, to check it is not damaged. Apply a small amount of Molybdenum grease to seal and threads.

Fuel pressure sender (common rail engines)

51 The fuel pressure sender is fitted to the

4.53 The fuel pressure sender is fitted to the right-hand end of the fuel rail

right-hand end of the fuel rail. If the engine will not start, disconnect the fuel pressure sender wiring connector and see if the engine will start. If the engine starts, the fuel pressure sender is faulty. With the connector removed a value is taken from the control unit, so that the engine will start, in this mode the maximum engine speed is limited to 3000rpm.

52 To renew the sender, first disconnect the wiring plug connector **(see illustration)**.

53 Clean around the sender, then slacken it from the end of the fuel rail **(see illustration)** ; plug the end of the rail to prevent dirt from entering.

54 Refit the pressure sender by reversing the removal procedure, making sure that the threads are all clean before refitting. The sender has a deformable seal, check for damage. Keep the threads free of oil and grease.

4.55 Camshaft position sensor

Camshaft position sensor

55 The camshaft position sensor (Hall sender) is located behind the timing belt cover, below the camshaft sprocket **(see illustration)**.

56 Remove the timing belt, as described in Chapter Section (1.6 litre common rail engine) Chapter Section (2.0 litre common rail engine) or Chapter Section (1.9 and 2.0 litre PD engines).

57 Disconnect the sensor wiring plug connector, located at the rear of the oil filter housing against the cylinder block **(see illustration)**.

58 To make access easier undo the retaining bolt and remove the timing belt idler pulley **(see illustration)**.

59 Using a screwdriver prise out the aperture cover in the rear plastic cover, then withdraw the wiring plug through the cover, unhooking it from the rear cover **(see illustration)**.

4.57 Disconnect the sensor wiring connector

4.58 Unbolt the Idler pulley

4.59 Prise up the aperture cover

5.1 A storage rack is simple to construct

5.4 Undo the adjustment screw until the rocker arm lies against the plunger pin of the injector

5.6 Remove the clamping block securing bolt

60 Undo the retaining bolt and remove the camshaft sensor from the cylinder head.
61 Refitting is a reversal of removal, but tighten the bolt to the specified torque setting and fit rubber plugs to the aperture for the wiring in the rear plastic cover.

5 Injectors – general information, removal and refitting

⚠️ **Warning: Exercise extreme caution when working on the fuel injectors. Never expose the hands or any part of the body to injector spray, as the high pressure can cause the fuel to penetrate the skin, with possibly fatal results. You are strongly advised to have any work which involves testing the injectors under pressure carried out by a dealer or fuel injection specialist. Refer to the precautions given in Section of this Chapter before proceeding.**

General information

1 Injectors do deteriorate with prolonged use, and it is reasonable to expect them to need reconditioning or renewal after 60 000 miles (100 000 km) or so. Accurate testing, overhaul

and calibration of the injectors must be left to a specialist.
Note: *Take care not to allow dirt into the injectors or fuel pipes during this procedure. Do not drop the injectors or allow the needles at their tips to become damaged. The injectors are precision-made to fine limits, and must not be handled roughly. Keep the injectors identified for position to ensure correct refitting. Always keep the injectors upright at all times where possible. Store them securely* **(see illustration)**

PD Engines

Removal

2 With reference to Chapter Section and Chapter Section, remove the upper timing belt cover and camshaft cover.
3 Using a spanner or socket, turn the crankshaft pulley until the rocker arm for the injector which is to be removed, is at its highest, ie, the injector plunger spring is under the least amount of tension.
4 Slacken the locknut of the adjustment screw on the end of the rocker arm above the injector, and undo the adjustment screw until the rocker arm lies against the plunger pin of the injector **(see illustration)**.
5 Starting at the outside and working in, gradually and evenly slacken and remove the rocker shaft retaining bolts. Lift off the

rocker shaft. Check the contact face of each adjustment screw, and renew any that show signs of wear.
6 Undo the clamping block securing bolt and remove the block from the side of the injector **(see illustration)**.
7 Using a small screwdriver, carefully prise the wiring connector from the injector.
8 VW technicians use a slide hammer (tool T10055) to pull the injector from the cylinder head. This is a slide hammer which engages in the side of the injector. If this tool is not available, it is possible to fabricate an equivalent using a short section of angle-iron, a length of threaded rod, a cylindrical weight, and two locknuts. Weld/braze the rod to the angle-iron, slide the weight over the rod, and lock the two nuts together at the end of the rod to provide the stop for the weight **(see illustration)**. Seat the slide hammer/tool in the slot on the side on the injector, and pull the injector out using a few gently taps. Recover circlip, the heat shield and O-rings and discard. New ones must be used for refitting **(see illustration)**.
9 If required, the injector wiring loom/rail can be removed from the cylinder head by undoing the two retaining nuts/bolts at the back of the head. To prevent the wiring connectors fouling the cylinder head casting as the assembly is withdrawn, insert the connectors into the storage slots in the plastic wiring rail. Carefully

a 5 mm
b 15 mm
c 25 mm
d Weld/braze the rod to the angle-iron
e Threaded rod
f Cylindrical weight
g Locknut

H32626

5.8a Unit injector removal tool

5.8b Seat the slide hammer/tool in the slot on the side on the injector, and pull the injector out

5.9a Undo the two nuts at the back of the head and slide the injector loom/rail out

5.9b The injector connectors will slide into the loom/rail to prevent them from being damaged as the assembly iswithdrawn/ inserted into the cylinder head

5.10 Care must be used to ensure that the injector O-rings are fitted without being twisted

push the assembly to the rear, and out of the casting (see illustrations).

Refitting

10 Prior to refitting the injectors, the three O-rings, heat insulation washer and clip must be renewed. Due to the high injection pressures, it is essential that the O-rings are fitted without being twisted. VW recommend the use of three special assembly sleeves to install the O-rings squarely. It may be prudent to entrust O-ring renewal to a VW dealer or suitably-equipped injection specialist, rather than risk subsequent leaks (see illustration).

11 After renewing the O-rings, fit the heat shield and secure it in place with the circlip (see illustration).

12 Smear clean engine oil onto the O-rings, and push the injector evenly down into the cylinder head onto its stop.

13 Fit the clamping block alongside the injector, but only hand-tighten the new retaining bolt at this stage.

14 It is essential that the injectors are fitted at right-angles to the clamping block. In order to achieve this, measure the distance from the rear face of the cylinder head to the rounded section of the injector (see illustrations). The dimensions (a) are as follows:

    Cylinder 1 = 333.0 ± 0.8 mm
    Cylinder 2 = 245.0 ± 0.8 mm
    Cylinder 3 = 153.6 ± 0.8 mm
    Cylinder 4 = 65.6 ± 0.8 mm

15 Once the injector(s) are aligned correctly,

1 Bolt
2 Clamping block
3 Cylinder head
4 Bolt
5 Rocker arm
6 Nut
7 Adjuster
8 Unit injector
9 O-ring
10 O-ring
11 O-ring
12 Heat shield
13 Circlip

5.11 Unit injector

5.14a Measure the distance (a) from the rear of the cylinder head to the rounded section of the injector (see text)

5.14b Use a set square against the edge of the injector...

5.14c ...and measure the distance to the rear of the cylinder head

5.17 Attach a DTI (Dial Test Indicator) gauge to the cylinder head upper surface, and position the DTI probe againstthe top of the adjustment screw

tighten the clamping bolt to the specified Stage 1 torque setting, and the Stage 2 angle tightening setting. Note: If an injector has been renewed, it is essential that the adjustment screw, locknut of the corresponding rocker and ball-pin are renewed at the same time. The ball-pins simply pull out of the injector spring cap. There is an O-ring in each spring cap to stop the ball-pins from falling out.

16 Smear some grease (VW No G000 100) onto the contact face of each rocker arm adjustment screw, and refit the rocker shaft assembly to the camshaft bearing caps, tightening the retaining bolts as follows. Starting from the inside out, hand-tighten the bolts. Again, from the inside out, tighten the bolts to the Stage 1 torque setting. Finally, from the inside out, tighten the bolts to the Stage 2 angle tightening setting.

17 The following procedure is only necessary

5.22 Fit sealing caps to prevent dirt ingress

if an injector has been removed and refitted/renewed. Attach a DTI (Dial Test Indicator) gauge to the cylinder head upper surface, and position the DTI probe against the top of the adjustment screw **(see illustration)**. Turn the crankshaft until the rocker arm roller is on the highest point of its corresponding camshaft lobe, and the adjustment screw is at its lowest. Once this position has been established, remove the DTI gauge, screw the adjustment screw in until firm resistance is felt, and the injector spring cannot be compressed further. Turn the adjustment screw anti-clockwise 180°, and tighten the locknut to the specified torque. Repeat this procedure for any other injectors that have been refitted.

18 Reconnect the wiring plug to the injector.

19 Refit the camshaft cover and upper timing belt cover, as described in Chapter Section and Chapter Section.

20 Bleed the fuel system as described in Section Section.

Common rail engines

Removal

Note: *Take care not to allow dirt into the injectors or fuel pipes during this procedure. Do not drop the injectors or allow the needles at their tips to become damaged. The injectors are precision-made to fine limits, and must not be handled roughly. Keep the injectors identified for position to ensure correct refitting.*

21 Pull the plastic cover over the engine upwards from its mountings. Where fitted, remove the foam insulation over the injectors.

22 Ensure the area around the injectors and the pipes/return hoses is clean and free from debris. The use of a vacuum cleaner is recommended. Plug all fuel lines when they have been disconnected to prevent any dirt ingress **(see illustration)**.

1.6 litre engine

23 Disconnect the injector wiring plug connectors **(see illustration)**.

24 Using a pair of long-nose pliers, withdraw the retaining clip from the side of the injector and remove the fuel return hose **(see illustrations)**. Discard the o-ring seals, as new ones will be required for refitting.

25 Counterhold the injector with an open-ended spanner when releasing the pipe union. Undo the unions and remove the high-pressure pipes from between the fuel rail and the injectors **(see illustrations)**. Plug the openings to prevent contamination.

26 Undo the bolt securing the injector clamp **(see illustration)**, note that one clamp secures two injectors in place.

5.23 Disconnect the wiring plugs from the injectors

5.24a Remove the retaining clips …

5.24b … and disconnect the fuel return pipes

5.25a Use two spanners to counterhold the fuel pipe to the injector …

5.25b …and remove the high pressure fuel pipes

5.26 Remove the injector clamp retaining bolts

5.28 Remove two injectors at a time with retaining clamp

5.30a Hold down the outer tabs, and prise up the centre piece…

5.30b …then pull the return hose connector upwards from the injector

27 VW technicians use a slide hammer (tool T10055) and adapter (T10402) to pull the injector from the cylinder head. If this tool is not available, it may be possible to fabricate an equivalent tool to pull the injector out of the cylinder head.

28 Two injectors will need to be removed together, as the clamping piece is slotted into both injectors. Recover the copper seal and O-rings and discard. New ones must be used for refitting **(see illustration)**. Note: The injectors can only be refitted to their original positions. Mark the injectors to avoid confusion if refitting the original injectors.

2.0 litre engines

29 Disconnect the injector wiring plug connectors.

30 Push the return hose connector downwards at its outer tabs, then pull up the centre piece and disconnect them from the top of the injectors **(see illustrations)**. Plug the openings to prevent contamination.

31 Undo the unions and remove the high-pressure pipes from between the fuel rail and the injectors. Counterhold the injector with an open-ended spanner when releasing the pipe union **(see illustrations 4.43a & 4.43b)**.

32 Undo the bolt securing the injector clamp between the two injectors, note that one clamp secures two injectors in place.

33 VW technicians use a slide hammer (tool T10055) and adapter (T10415) to pull the injector from the cylinder head. If this tool is not available, it may be possible to fabricate

5.35a Carefully prise out the seal …

an equivalent tool to pull the injector out of the cylinder head.

34 Two injectors will need to be removed together, as the clamping piece is slotted into both injectors. Recover the copper seal and O-rings and discard. New ones must be used for refitting. Note: The injectors can only be refitted to their original positions. Mark the injectors to avoid confusion if refitting the original injectors.

Refitting

35 If required, renew the injector seals in the top of the camshaft cover. Using a screwdriver, prise the seal out from the cover; the new seal can then be pressed firmly into the cover **(see illustrations)**. There are different size seals depending on engine code, make sure the correct seals are supplied. Also make sure the

5.35b …making sure the spring does not fall into the cover

spring on the inside lip of the seal does not drop into the camshaft cover.

36 Ensure the area around the injector locations in the cylinder head are clean and free from debris. Use a vacuum cleaner if available. Clean any carbon deposits from the injector and sealing surfaces with a cloth soaked in clean engine oil or rust-releasing spray.

37 To remove the copper sealing washer, spray rust-releasing spray around the injector nozzle, then clamp the seal in a vice, and use a twisting motion to pull the injector from the seal. Push the new copper seal into place **(see illustrations)**. Do not touch the very end of the injector, or you could block up the nozzle.

38 On 1.6 litre engines, apply a little clean engine oil to the return pipe connection, and fit the new O-ring **(see illustration)**.

5.37a Clean off the carbon around the end of the injector …

5.37b … and fit a new sealing washer

5.38 Fit new O-ring seals to the fuel return lines

5.39 Fit the new return pipe O-ring to the top of the injector

5.40 Fit a new main O-ring seal without twisting it

5.41a Lubricate the seal with some clean oil …

39 On 2.0 litre engines, apply a little clean engine oil to the return pipe connection on the injector, and fit the new O-ring (see illustration).

40 To renew the main injector O-ring seal, VW specify the use of tool no. T10377. This tool allows the O-ring to slide over the end of the injector without twisting. With care, the seals can be fitted without the tool (see illustrations).

41 Apply a smear of clean engine oil to the main O-ring seal, and insert the injector into place in the cylinder head (see illustrations). Note that if the original injectors are being refitted, they must go into their original positions. Tighten the injector clamping bolt/ nut to the specified torque.

42 Refit the high-pressure fuel pipes and tighten the unions to the specified torque. Note that the pipes may be re-used providing the tapered seats are undamaged and the pipes are not deformed, constricted or corroded. Counterhold the injector with an open-ended spanner when tightening the pipe union.

43 On 1.6 litre engines, when fitting the return hoses to the sides of the injector, use new securing clips (see illustration).

44 The remainder of refitting is a reversal of removal, noting the following:

a) If one or more injectors have been renewed, the 'injector delivery calibration values' and 'injector voltage calibration values' must be entered into the ECM using VW diagnostic equipment. Entrust this task to a VW dealer or suitably equipped specialist.

b) After completion of the work, the fuel system must be bled as described in Chapter Section.

6 Inlet manifold –
    removal and refitting

PD Engines

Removal

1 All PD engines have a conventional inlet manifold. 1.9 litre engines have a simple manifold fitted with an EGR control and

5.41b …then slide the injectors down into the cylinder head

throttle valve/shut down valve mounted at one end. 2.0 litre engines have an inlet manifold with a centrally mounted EGR control and throttle valve/shut down valve (see illustrations). Note the illustrations show typical manifolds – there are variations, but all are similar.

2 Where fitted, remove the engine cover by pulling it up.

3 Remove the flap motor and EGR valve with reference to Section of this Chapter, and to Chapter Section.

4 Access can be improved where required

5.43 Fit new clips to secure the fuel return lines

if the front section of the plenum chamber is removed as described in Chapter Section.

5 Where applicable, remove the heat shield from the manifold, then unscrew the mounting bolts and remove the inlet manifold from the cylinder head. Recover the gasket and discard, as a new one must be used on refitting.

Refitting

6 Refitting is a reversal of removal, using new manifold, EGR pipe and manifold flap assembly gaskets/O-rings. Tighten the mounting bolts to the specified torque.

1 Inlet manifold
2 O-ring seal
3 Combined EGR valve and flap housing
4 Screw
5 Gasket
6 EGR pipe
7 Screw
8 Bracket
9 Vacuum actuator (electric on some engines)
10 Vacuum hose to solenoid

H46298

6.1a Typical inlet manifold details (1.9 litre PD engines)

6.1b Inlet manifold 2.0 litre PD engine (BMM)

1 Gasket	5 Inlet flap (anti-shudder control)
2 Manifold	6 EGR valve
3 Seal	7 Gasket
4 EGR housing	8 Pipe (to EGR cooler)

6.1c Inlet manifold 2.0 litre PD engine (BDJ and BST)

1 Inlet flap (anti-shudder control)	6 Seal
2 Seal	7 Gasket
3 Inlet manifold	8 Gasket
4 Breather hose (from crankcase)	9 EGR valve
5 Air temperature sensor	10 Vacuum control for EGR

Common rail engines

Removal

Plastic manifold

7 Remove the throttle housing, as described in Section of this Chapter.
8 Remove the fuel rail from the top of the inlet manifold, as described in Section Section.
9 Undo the two retaining screws and move the coolant return pipe to one side **(see illustration)**.
10 Undo the two retaining screws and move the fuel return pipe to one side **(see illustration)**.
11 Where fitted, disconnect the wiring plug connector from the manifold flap motor **(see illustration)**.

12 Undo the retaining screw and remove the EGR cooler changeover valve from the manifold **(see illustration)**.

13 Slacken the retaining clamp and disconnect the EGR pipe **(see illustration)**.
14 Undo the manifold retaining bolts, starting

6.9 Undo the coolant pipe retaining screws

6.10 Undo the fuel line retaining screws

6.11 Disconnect the wiring connector

6.12 Undo the solenoid valve mounting bracket securing bolt

6.13 Slacken the EGR pipe retaining clamp

6.14a Undo the retaining bolts...

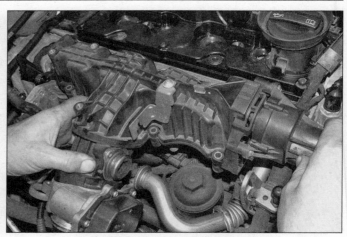

6.14b ...and remove the inlet manifold

6.14c Cover the inlet manifold recess with tape

6.15 Renew the inlet manifold seals

from the outside and working inwards in a diagonal sequence **(see illustrations)**. Lift the manifold from the cylinder head and retrieve the gasket seals; discard, as new ones will be required for refitting.

Refitting

15 Refitting is a reversal of removal, using new seals and gaskets **(see illustration)**. Remember to renew any self-locking nuts. Tighten the manifold retaining bolts to the specified torque setting, starting from the inside and working outwards in a diagonal sequence.

7 Fuel filter – renewal

1 Refer to Chapter Section.

8 Fuel lift pump and gauge sender unit – removal and refitting

Note: Observe the precautions in Section before working on any component in the fuel system.

> ⚠ **Warning:** Avoid direct skin contact with fuel – wear protective clothing and gloves when handling fuel system components. Ensure that the work area is well ventilated to prevent the build-up of fuel vapour.

General information

1 The fuel lift pump and gauge sender unit are combined in one assembly, which is mounted in the top of the fuel tank. The fuel tank must be removed to access the assembly (Section 9). The unit protrudes into the fuel tank, and its removal involves exposing the contents of the tank to the atmosphere.

Removal

2 Ensure that the vehicle is parked on a level surface, then disconnect the battery negative lead and position it away from the terminal. Note: Refer to Chapter Section.

3 Remove the fuel tank as described in Section 9.

4 Note the position of the alignment marks, then unscrew and remove the securing ring. Use a pair of water pump pliers (or home-made tool) to grip and rotate the securing ring **(see illustrations)**.

5 Lift out the lift pump/gauge sender unit, holding it above the level of the fuel in the tank

8.4a Note the alignment marks...

8.4b ...then use a suitable tool to unscrew...

8.4c ...and remove the securing ring

8.5 Removing the lift pump/gauge sender unit from the fuel tank

8.6 Lift pump/gauge sender unit removed from the car

8.8 If not removed with the unit, recover the rubber seal and check its condition

until the excess fuel has drained out. Recover the flange and seal **(see illustration)**.

6 With the pump/sender unit removed from the car, lay it on an absorbent card or rag **(see illustration)**. Inspect the float at the end of the sender unit swinging arm for punctures and fuel ingress – renew the unit if it appears damaged.

7 The fuel pick-up incorporated in the assembly is spring-loaded to ensure that it always draws fuel from the lowest part of the tank. Check that the pick-up is free to move under spring tension with respect to the sender unit body.

8 Inspect the rubber seal from the fuel tank aperture for signs of fatigue – renew it if necessary **(see illustration)**.

9 Inspect the sender unit wiper and track; clean off any dirt and debris that may have accumulated, and look for breaks in the track.

10 If required, the sender unit can be separated from the assembly. Two versions are fitted.

Version One

11 Disconnect the two small wires (note their positions), then remove the four screws and slide the unit downwards to remove **(see illustrations)**.

12 The unit top plate can be removed by releasing the plastic tags at either side; recover the large spring that fits onto a peg on the plate underside **(see illustrations)**.

Version Two

13 Gently pull the sender unit to the side and upwards at the same time. If the sender unit is reluctant to release, gently push the retaining

tabs outwards at the same time as pull the sender unit upwards **(see illustrations)**.

14 Note their fitted positions, release the clips and disconnect the sender unit wiring

8.11a Disconnect the small wires…

8.12a Prise up the retaining tags …

plugs **(see illustration)**. Note: On later sender units, the plugs are released by depressing the clips on the frontandrear of the plastic housing.

8.11b …then undo the screws and slide out the sender unit

8.12b …and recover the spring fitted under the top plate

8.13a Press the clips to the outside…

8.13b …and slide the sender unit upwards

8.14 Depress the clips and pull the wiring plugs from the sender

Refitting

15 Refit the lift pump/sender unit by following the removal procedure in reverse, noting the following points:

a) *Take care not to bend the float arm as the unit is refitted.*

b) *Smear the outside of tank aperture rubber seal with clean fuel or lubricating spray, to ease fitting. Locate the seal in the tank aperture before fitting the lift pump/sender unit* **(see illustrations)**.

c) *Tighten the securing ring to the specified torque setting.*

d) *Reconnect the fuel hoses to the correct ports – observe the direction-of-flow arrow markings, and refer to paragraph 6. Ensure that the fuel hose fittings click fully into place.*

e) *On completion, check that all associated pipes are securely clipped to the tank, then run the engine and check for fuel leaks.*

8.15a Locate the seal in the tank aperture...

8.15b ...then fit the lift pump/sender unit

9 Fuel tank – removal and refitting

Note: *Observe the precautions in Section before working on any component in the fuel system.*

Removal

1 Before the tank can be removed, it must be drained of as much fuel as possible. As no drain plug is provided, it is preferable to carry out this operation with the tank almost empty.

2 Open the fuel filler flap, and unscrew the fuel filler cap – leave the cap loosely in place.

3 Disconnect the battery negative lead and position it away from the terminal (Chapter Section), then using a hand pump or syphon, remove any remaining fuel from the tank.

4 Loosen the left-hand rear wheel bolts, then jack up the rear of the car (see Chock the front roadwheels, then jack up the rear of the vehicle and support on axle stands (see 'Jacking and vehicle support'). Remove the relevant rear roadwheel. and remove the left-hand rear wheel.

5 Undo the retaining screws, release the retaining clips and remove the left-hand rear wheel arch liner.

6 Open the fuel filler flap, and unscrew the fuel cap from the top of the filler neck.

7 Unscrew the bolts at the filler neck.

Caution: Residual fuel pressure always remains in the fuel system long after the engine has been switched off.

8 Disconnect the fuel lines from the connections at the front of the fuel tank **(see illustration)**.

9 Position a trolley jack under the centre of the tank. Insert a block of wood between the jack head and the tank to prevent damage to the tank surface. Raise the jack until it just takes the weight of the tank.

10 Unscrew the mounting bolts and detach the tank straps **(see illustration)**.

11 Lower the jack and tank away from the underside of the vehicle until it is possible to reach up and disconnect the fuel gauge sender/pump wiring plug.

12 Continue to lower the tank, whilst guiding the filler neck through the leaf spring. Remove the tank from the vehicle.

13 If the tank is contaminated with sediment or water, remove the fuel pump/sender unit (see Section) and swill the tank out with clean fuel. The tank is injection-moulded from a synthetic material, and if damaged, it should be renewed. However, in certain cases it may be possible to have small leaks or minor damage repaired. Seek the advice of a suitable specialist before attempting to repair the fuel tank.

Refitting

14 Refitting is the reverse of the removal procedure, noting the following points:

a) *When lifting the tank back into position, make sure the mounting rubbers are correctly positioned, and take care to ensure none of the hoses get trapped between the tank and vehicle body.*

b) *Ensure that all pipes and hoses are correctly routed, are not kinked, and are securely held in position with their retaining clips.*

c) *Tighten the tank strap retaining bolts to the specified torque.*

d) *On completion, refill the tank with fuel, and exhaustively check for signs of leakage prior to taking the vehicle out on the road.*

9.8 Disconnect the fuel lines

9.10 Remove the tank straps

10.4 Fuel tandem pump securing bolts

1 Brake servo hose   *3 Fuel return hose*
2 Fuel supply hose   *4 Tandem pump*

10 Fuel pump –
removal and refitting

Tandem fuel pump (PD unit injection engines only)

Note: *Disconnecting the central connector for the unit injectors may cause a fault code to be logged by the engine management ECU. This code can only be erased by a VW dealer or suitably-equipped specialist.*

Removal

1 The tandem fuel pump is located on the left-hand end of the cylinder head. It is effectively a vacuum pump (for the braking system) and a fuel lift pump (for the fuel injection system). First, remove the engine top cover.
2 Disconnect the fuel supply hose (marked white) and the return hose (marked blue) from the fuel filter and drain all fuel from the hoses into a suitable container.
3 Remove the air cleaner assembly together with the air mass meter and air ducting, with reference to Section.
4 Release the retaining clip (where fitted) and disconnect the brake servo pipe from the tandem pump **(see illustration)**.
5 Disconnect the fuel supply hose (marked white) and the return hose (marked blue) from the tandem pump.
6 Unscrew the four retaining bolts and remove the tandem pump from the cylinder head. Recover the gasket and discard, as a new one must be used on refitting. There are no serviceable parts within the tandem pump. If the pump is faulty, it must be renewed.

Refitting

7 Refitting is a reversal of removal, but use a new gasket and tighten the mounting bolts to the specified torque. Ensure the pump pinion engages correctly with the drive slot in the camshaft **(see illustration)**. It is recommended that the tandem pump is primed with fuel as follows. Disconnect the fuel filter return hose (marked blue), and connect the hose to a hand vacuum pump.

10.7 Ensure that the tandem pump pinion engages correctly with the drive slot in the camshaft

10.13 Remove the lifting bracket from above the fuel pump

Operate the vacuum pump until fuel comes out of the return hose. Take care not to suck any fuel into the vacuum pump. Reconnect the return hose to the fuel filter.
8 Have the engine management ECU's fault memory interrogated and erased by a VW dealer or suitably-equipped specialist.

High pressure fuel pump (common rail engines)

Removal

1.6 litre engines

9 Remove the timing belt and pump sprocket as described in Chapter Section and Chapter Section.
10 Disconnect the wiring connector from the fuel metering valve on top of the fuel pump **(see illustration)**.
11 Undo the two retaining screws and move

10.15 Disconnect the fuel hoses from the pump

10.10 Disconnect the pump wiring connector

10.14 Remove the high pressure fuel line from the pump

the coolant return pipe to one side **(see illustration 6.10)**.
12 Undo the two retaining screws and move the fuel return pipe to one side **(see illustration 6.11)**.
13 Undo the pipe retaining bracket screw and the two retaining bolts, then remove the lifting eye from the front of the engine **(see illustration)**.
14 Slacken the fuel pipe unions and remove the high-pressure pipe from the pump to the fuel rail **(see illustration)**.
15 Release the retaining clips and disconnect the two fuel hoses from the top of the fuel pump **(see illustration)**.
16 Counterhold the pump hub using VW tool No. T10051, and undo the pump hub nut. In the absence of this special tool, counterhold the hub using something to lock the sprocket, whilst the centre nut is slackened **(see illustration)**.

10.16 Remove the fuel pump centre hub nut

10.18 Fuel pump mounting bolts

10.20 Release the clip and disconnect the fuel supply hose

10.25 Fuel pump return hose

17 Using a suitable two-legged puller (VW tool No. T40064) and two bolts, remove the hub complete with sprocket from the pump shaft.

18 Undo the 3 retaining bolts and remove the pump **(see illustration)**.

2.0 litre engines

19 Remove the timing belt and pump sprocket as described in Chapter Section and Chapter Section.

20 Disconnect the fuel supply hose from the pump **(see illustration)**. Plug all openings to prevent contamination.

21 Disconnect the wiring plug from the sensor on the pump.

22 Slacken the unions and disconnect the high-pressure fuel pipe between the pump and common fuel rail. Undo the retaining screws to release the fuel pipe from the support brackets.

23 On some models it may be necessary to disconnect he wiring connectors from the glow plugs. Pulling only under the ridge at the top of the connectors, disconnect the wiring connectors. Note: Take care not to damage the connectors or wiring, as the glow plug wiring loom/connectors are only available as a complete assembly.

24 Undo the bolts securing the coolant pipe to the intake manifold, and position the pipe to one side.

25 Disconnect the fuel return pipes from the pump and the common fuel rail **(see illustration)**.

26 Counterhold the pump hub using VW tool

No. T10051, and undo the pump hub nut. In the absence of this special tool, counterhold the hub using a suitable C-spanner **(see illustration)**.

27 Using a suitable two-legged puller and two 8 mm bolts, remove the hub from the pump shaft **(see illustrations)**.

28 Undo the 3 retaining bolts and remove the pump.

Refitting

29 Refitting is a reversal of removal, noting the following points:

a) *Ensure all fuel pipes/hose connections are clean and free from debris.*

b) *The high-pressure fuel pipe from the pump to the common rail maybe re-used providing it's not been damaged.*

c) *Tighten all fasteners to their specified torque where given.*

d) *Fill the pump with clean fuel through the fuel supply pipe aperture prior to starting* **(see illustration)**.

e) *Bleed the fuel system as described in Section.*

Supplementary fuel pump (common rail engines only)

Removal

30 The supplementary fuel pump is not fitted to all models, where fitted, it is located on a bracket bolted to the top of the right-hand engine mounting **(see illustration)**.

31 Disconnect the wiring plug from the

10.26 Counterhold the pump hub with a C-spanner, and undo the nut

10.27a Use a two-legged puller and 8 mm bolts to pull the hub from the pump shaft

10.27b Note the locating peg in the pump shaft

10.29 The triangles adjacent to the pump apertures indicate fuel flow

10.30 Supplementary fuel pump location

exhaust gas pressure sensor, then undo the retaining bolt and move the sensor and bracket to one side **(see illustration)**.

32 Undo the retaining bolts and lift the supplementary fuel pump upwards to access the fuel pipes and wiring plug **(see illustration)**.

33 Release the fuel hoses from the retaining clips, and disconnect the fuel pump wiring plug.

34 Release the clamps and disconnect the fuel supply pipe from the fuel filter. Plug/cover the openings to prevent contamination.

35 Disconnect the fuel temperature sensor wiring plug, release the clamp and disconnect the fuel supply pipe from the high-pressure fuel pump. Plug/cover the openings to prevent contamination.

Refitting

36 Refitting is a reversal of removal, noting the following points:
a) *Ensure the hoses are not kinked.*
b) *Ensure all connections are clean and free from debris.*
c) *Note the hose connections: The return hose is blue (or blue markings), and the supply hose is white.*
d) *Bleed the system as described in Section.*

11 Fuel system bleeding

PD engines

1 Attach a hand-held vacuum pump to the return outlet (coloured blue) from the tandem fuel pump, and operate the pump until a steady stream of fuel appears from the outlet. Start the engine and check for leaks. See also Chapter Section (Fuel filter)

Common rail engines

2 Prime the high pressure fuel pump by filling it with clean diesel through the fuel supply aperture **(see illustration 10.29a)**, then operate the starter for shorts bursts (no more than 10 seconds at a time) until the engine starts. Operate the engine at a fast idle (approx 2000 rpm) for several minutes before allowing it to return to its normal idle speed.

3 If the engine fails to start, it must be filled/bled using VW diagnostic equipment (VAS5051 etc.). Using this equipment operates the electric fuel pumps for 3 minutes. Alternatively remove the access cover from the in tank fuel pump, identify the pump supply wiring and supply the pump directly with 12 volts (see the wiring diagrams at the end of this manual for details).

4 Once the engine has been started, test drive the vehicle over a distance of at least 15 miles with at least one period of full acceleration. If there is any air left in the fuel system, the engine management ECM may switch to 'limp home' mode, and store a fault code. Have the

10.31 Undo the retaining screw

fault code cleared and road test the vehicle again.

12 Fuel rail –
removal and refitting

Note: *Observe the precautions in Section before working on any component in the fuel system.*

Removal

1 Remove the engine cover by pulling it upwards and then remove the foam insulation (where fitted) **(see illustrations 3.6a and 3.6b)**. Ensure the area around the fuel rail and pipes is clean and free from debris. If available, use a vacuum cleaner.

12.3a Remove the high pressure pipes from the rail and injectors ...

12.4a Disconnect the hose from the return pipe ...

10.32 Undo the bolts and remove the pump bracket

2 Disconnect the wiring connectors from the fuel injectors.

3 Counterhold the injector with an open-ended spanner when releasing the pipe union. Undo the unions and remove the high-pressure pipes from between the fuel rail and the injectors **(see illustrations)**. Plug the openings to prevent contamination.

4 Release the retaining clips and disconnect the fuel return hose from the fuel rail **(see illustrations)**

5 Undo the retaining bolts, disconnect the coolant return hose from the expansion tank, and move the coolant pipe/hose to one side **(see illustration 5.10)**.

6 Slacken the fuel pipe unions and remove the high-pressure pipe from the pump to the fuel rail **(see illustration 9.14)**.

12.3b ...and fit sealing caps to prevent dirt ingress

12.4b ...and the return pipe from the fuel rail

12.7 Lift the wiring loom over and place to one side

12.8a Undo the fuel rail mounting bolts – 1.6 litre engines

12.8b Undo the fuel rail mounting bolts – 2.0 litre engines

7 Disconnect the wiring plugs from the glow plugs, fuel pressure regulating valve, and the fuel pressure sensor at each end of the fuel rail. Unclip the wiring loom retaining bracket from the top of the fuel rail and move it to one side **(see illustration)**.

8 Undo the multi-spline retaining bolts and remove the fuel rail **(see illustrations)**.

9 If required, note their fitted positions, then unscrew the fuel pressure sensor and

pressure regulating valve from the fuel rail, as described in Section. Note: VW insist that once removed, the pressure regulating valve cannot be re-used.

Refitting

10 Where applicable, refit the fuel pressure sensor and the new regulating valve to the fuel rail, and tighten them to the specified torque. Note that the threads of the sensors must be clean and free from oil and grease.

11 The remainder of refitting is a reversal of removal, noting the following points:

a) *Refit the high-pressure fuel pipes and tighten the unions to the specified torque. Note that the high-pressure fuel pipes may be re-used providing the tapered seats are undamaged and the pipes are not deformed, constricted or corroded.*

b) *After completion of the work, the fuel system must be bled as described in Section.*

Chapter 4 Part B
Emission control and exhaust systems

Contents

Degrees of difficulty

Easy, suitable for novice with little experience	Fairly easy, suitable for beginner with some experience	Fairly difficult, suitable for competent DIY mechanic	Difficult, suitable for experienced DIY mechanic	Very difficult, suitable for expert DIY or professional

Specifications

Engine codes*
1.9 litre – 'PD' (unit injector) . . . . BKC, BJB, BLS and BSU
2.0 litre – 'PD' (unit injector) . . . . BDJ, BST and BMM
1.6 litre – common rail injection . . . . CAYE, CAYD
2.0 litre – common rail injection . . . . CFJA, CFHC, CFHF, CLCA, CFHE, CLCB and CHWA
*See 'Vehicle identification' at the end of the manual for the location of the engine code markings

Emission control applications
1.6 litre CR . . . . EGR and combined catalytic converter and particulate filter. EU5 emissions standard.
1.9 litre PD . . . . EGR and combined catalytic converter. No particulate filter fitted to BJB models and optional on BLS and BSU. BJB meets EU3 emissions standards. BLS and BSU engines meet EU4 standards.
2.0 litre PD . . . . EGR and combined catalytic converter. BST complies with EU4 emissions standard and BDJ engine complies with EU3 standards BMM has particulate filter and meets EU4 emissions standards.
2.0 litre CR . . . . EGR and combined catalytic converter and particulate filter. EU5 emissions standard.

Torque wrench settings

	Nm	lbf ft
1.9/2.0 litre PD engines		
EGR cooler/valve to bracket/cylinder head	10	7
EGR coolant outlet pipe	22	16
EGR recirculation pipe (to manifold)	25	18
EGR recirculation pipe (to valve)	22	16
EGR valve to cooler	10	7

Torque wrench settings (continued)

	Nm	lbf ft
EGR valve to inlet manifold (BMM engine)	10	7
Exhaust gas temperature sensor	45	33
Exhaust system clamp:		
Sleeve with individual clamps	25	18
Sleeve with single clamp	35	26
Catalytic converter support bracket	40	30
Lambda (O2) sensor	50	37
Particulate filter/catalytic converter clamp (to turbocharger)	7	5
Particulate filter support bracket (on subframe)	25	18
Particulate filter pressure sensor line (at filter)	45	33
Turbocharger/manifold heat shield nuts*	25	18
Turbocharger/manifold to cylinder head nuts/bolts*	25	18
Turbocharger oil drain bolts	20	15
Turbocharger oil drain connector (to block)	40	30
Turbocharger oil drain pipe union nut	22	16
Turbocharger oil feed supply connector	30	22
Turbocharger oil feed pipe union nut	22	16
1.6/2.0 litre common rail engines		
Catalytic converter/particulate filter mounting bracket nuts/bolts	25	18
Particulate filter/catalytic converter clamp (to turbocharger)	7	5
EGR mounting bolts	9	6
EGR recirculation pipe bolts	9	6
EGR recirculation pipe nuts	24	18
Exhaust gas temperature probe	60	44
Exhaust system clamp:		
Sleeve with individual clamps	25	18
Sleeve with single clamp	35	26
Lambda (O2) sensor	50	37
Particulate filter pressure sensor line (at filter)	45	33
Particulate filter support bracket (on subframe)	25	18
Turbocharger/manifold to cylinder head nuts*	24	18
Turbocharger oil drain banjo bolt*	30	22
Turbocharger oil feed pipe	22	16
Turbocharger oil drain (at turbocharger) bolts*	17	13

*Use new fixings

1 General Information

Emission control systems

1 All diesel-engined models have a crankcase emission control system, and in addition, are fitted with a catalytic converter. All diesel engines are fitted with an Exhaust Gas Recirculation (EGR) system to reduce exhaust emissions.

Crankcase emission control

2 To reduce the emission of unburned hydrocarbons from the crankcase into the atmosphere, the engine is sealed and the blow-by gases and oil vapour are drawn from inside the crankcase, through a wire mesh oil separator, into the inlet tract to be burned by the engine during normal combustion.

3 Under conditions of high manifold depression, the gases will be sucked positively out of the crankcase. Under conditions of low manifold depression, the gases are forced out of the crankcase by the (relatively) higher crankcase pressure. If the engine is worn, the raised crankcase pressure (due to increased blow-by) will cause some of the flow to return under all manifold conditions.

Exhaust emission control

4 An oxidation catalyst is fitted in the exhaust system of all diesel-engined models. This has the effect of removing a large proportion of the gaseous hydrocarbons, carbon monoxide and particulates present in the exhaust gas. Some models covered in this manual, have a particulate filter, which is fitted behind the catalytic converter in order to filter out soot particles.

5 An Exhaust Gas Recirculation (EGR) system is fitted to all diesel-engined models. This reduces the level of nitrogen oxides produced during combustion by introducing a proportion of the exhaust gas back into the inlet manifold under certain engine operating conditions. The system is controlled electronically by the diesel engine management ECU.

Exhaust systems

6 The exhaust system consists of the exhaust manifold, front flexible pipe with catalytic converter/particulate filter and rear pipe section including silencer. The turbocharger is integral with the exhaust manifold, and is driven by the exhaust gases.

7 The system is supported by various metal brackets screwed to the vehicle floor, with rubber vibration dampers fitted to suppress noise.

2 Crankcase emission system – general information

1 The crankcase emission control system consists of hoses connecting the crankcase to the air cleaner, cylinder head cover and/or inlet manifold (see illustration).

2 The system requires no attention other than to check at regular intervals that the hoses and pressure-regulating valve are free of blockages and in good condition.

2.1 Disconnecting the breather hose

3 Exhaust Gas Recirculation (EGR) system – component removal

1 The EGR system consists of the EGR valve, which directs exhaust gas from the exhaust manifold to the inlet manifold, and a control (changeover) valve that actuates the system according to engine load and speed **(see illustration)**. There is a vacuum-operated changeover unit, which is fitted on the EGR cooler for recirculating the exhaust gas. All this is connected by a series of vacuum hoses, and metal corrugated cooler pipes. There is also a recirculation potentiometer fitted to the EGR valve, this is controlled directly from the engine management ECU, which then activates the control motor.

2 A wide range of EGR control valves, coolers, sensors and actuators are fitted to the Caddy range. The exact detail of removal (and refitting) varies between models, but the principle of removal is the same for all models **(see illustrations)**.

3 The EGR valve and cooler are either integrated as a single assembly or fitted as separate assemblies. The gas cooler uses coolant from the engine cooling system to

3.1 Typical vacuum hose layout

1 EGR cooler changeover vacuum unit
2 Cylinder head cover
3 EGR cooler changeover valve
4 Non-return valve
5 Vacuum pump connection
6 To brake servo
7 Air filter
8 Silencer
9 Charge pressure control solenoid valve
10 EGR valve

3.2a Typical EGR and cooler fitted to most 1.9 litre PD engines

1 EGR cooler
2 Inlet manifold with control valve
3 By-pass (change-over) valve
4 Connector pipes
5 Gaskets

1 EGR cooler
2 Connecting pipes
3 Vacuum unit
4 Vacuum pipe
5 Gaskets
6 Heat shield

H48709

3.2b EGR cooler system – 2.0 litre PD engines (8 valve)

cool the exhaust gases before passing them to the inlet manifold. The system is activated by a solenoid valve mounted at the front of the inlet manifold, which is controlled by the ECU.

4 Where an integrated cooler/EGR valve is fitted, it is joined to the exhaust manifold and cylinder head by flanged corrugated metal pipes. The system is activated by a solenoid valve mounted at the front of the inlet manifold, which is controlled by the ECU.

EGR cooler 'change-over' solenoid valve

5 The EGR vacuum-solenoid valve is either mounted on the front of the inlet manifold or integrated into the vacuum solenoid valve block **(see illustrations)**. Do not confuse the EGR solenoid with the turbo charge pressure control solenoid, which is mounted on the bulkhead.

6 Disconnect the wiring plug from the solenoid valve **(see illustration)**.

7 Unclip the valve from the mounting bracket **(see illustration)**, then identify the vacuum hoses for refitting and disconnect them from the valve.

8 Refitting is a reversal of removal. Ensure that the hoses and wiring plug are reconnected securely and correctly.

1 EGR cooler and EGR valve
2 Recirculation pipe
3 Vacuum line
4 Gasket
5 Clamp

6367 Fig. 04b-03.02c HAYNES

3.2c EGR cooler and valve fitted to common rail engines

3.5a The six pin solenoid valve block

1 Vaccum supply
2 EGR valve
3 By-pass (change-over) flap of EGR cooling
4 Air filter
5 Vacuum reservoir
6 Turbocharger vacuum control

3.5b The seven pin valve block

1 Vacant
2 Vacuum supply
3 EGR valve
4 By-pass (change-over) flap of EGR cooling
5 Air filter
6 Vacuum reservoir
7 Turbocharger vacuum control

3.5c EGR cooler solenoid valve

EGR valve

Engine code BMM

9 Remove the throttle valve housing from the inlet manifold, as described in Chapter 4A Section 6.
10 Undo the bolts securing the pipe to the left-hand side of the EGR valve **(see illustration)**.
11 Disconnect the wiring plug connector from the right-hand side of the EGR valve.

12 Undo the bolts and detach the valve from the inlet manifold. Discard the O-ring seal – a new one must be fitted.
13 Refitting is a reversal of removal, using a new EGR valve O-ring seal, and tightening the retaining bolts to the specified torque.

All other engine codes

14 The EGR valve is incorporated into the EGR cooler, remove the cooler as described in paragraphs 20 to 26. At the time of writing,

it was not possible to separate the EGR valve from the cooler.

EGR cooler

15 Remove the exhaust front pipe/catalytic converter/ particulate filter as described in Section 10.
16 Drain the cooling system as described in Chapter 1, Section 32. If required the coolant hoses can be clamped before removal, to save draining the complete system.

Engine codes BMM

17 Release the retaining clips and disconnect the coolant hoses from the EGR cooler. Be prepared for coolant spillage.
18 Undo the retaining bolts and disconnect the EGR metal connecting pipes from each end of the cooler.
19 Undo the upper bolts and lower banjo bolt and remove the turbocharger oil return pipe/ support from the rear of the engine.
20 Disconnect the vacuum hose from vacuum unit on the lower part of the cooler, then undo the retaining bolts, and remove the cooler from the rear of the engine.

All other engine codes

21 Release the retaining clips and disconnect the coolant hoses from each end of the EGR cooler **(see illustrations)**. Be prepared for coolant spillage.
22 Undo the two retaining screws from

3.6 Disconnect the wiring connector ...

3.7 ...then unclip the valve from the bracket

3.10 EGR pipe-to-valve bolts

3.21a Disconnect the coolant hose from the cooler

3.21b Release the retaining clips and remove hose

3.22 Remove the EGR pipe from the cooler to the manifold

3.23a Undo the EGR pipe bolts to the cooler

3.23b Undo the EGR pipe bolts to the cylinder head

3.24a Undo the upper bolts…

3.24b …and lower banjo bolts …

3.24c …then remove the pipes and support bracket

the cooler, the two retaining nuts from the exhaust manifold and remove the EGR metal connecting pipe **(see illustration)**.
23 Undo the two retaining screws from the cooler, the two retaining screws from the cylinder head and remove the EGR metal connecting pipe **(see illustrations)**.
24 Undo the upper bolts and lower banjo bolt and remove the turbocharger oil return pipe/support from the rear of the engine **(see illustrations)**.
25 Disconnect the wiring plug connector from the EGR valve **(see illustration)**.
26 Disconnect the vacuum hose from vacuum unit on the lower part of the cooler **(see illustration)**, then undo the four retaining bolts, and remove the cooler from the rear of the engine.
27 Refitting is a reversal of removal, using

new gaskets **(see illustration)**, and tightening the retaining bolts to the specified torque.

4 Turbocharger – general information and precautions

General information

1 A turbocharger is fitted to all engines, except 2.0 litre engines with codes BDJ and BST. The turbocharger is integral with the exhaust manifold.
2 The turbocharger increases engine efficiency by raising the pressure in the inlet manifold above atmospheric pressure. Instead of the air simply being sucked into the cylinders, it is forced in.

3 Energy for the operation of the turbocharger comes from the exhaust gas. The gas flows through a specially shaped housing (the turbine housing) and in so doing, spins the turbine wheel. The turbine wheel is attached to a shaft, at the end of which is another vaned wheel, known as the compressor wheel. The compressor wheel spins in its own housing, and compresses the inducted air on the way to the inlet manifold.
4 Between the turbocharger and the inlet manifold, the compressed air passes through an intercooler (see Section 8 for details). The purpose of the intercooler is to remove from the inducted air some of the heat gained in being compressed. Because cooler air is denser, removal of this heat further increases engine efficiency.
5 Boost pressure (the pressure in the inlet

3.25 Disconnect the wiring connector from the EGR valve

3.26 EGR cooler securing bolts

3.27 Fit new gaskets to the EGR pipes

5.6a Disconnecting the breather hose...

5.6b ...undo the retaining screw...

5.6c ...and disconnect the air intake hose

manifold) is limited by a wastegate, which diverts the exhaust gas away from the turbine wheel in response to a pressure-sensitive actuator.

6 The turbo shaft is pressure-lubricated by an oil feed pipe from the engine oil filter mounting. The shaft 'floats' on a cushion of oil. Oil is returned to the sump through a return pipe that connects to the rear of the cylinder block.

Precautions

7 The turbocharger operates at extremely high speeds and temperatures. Certain precautions must be observed to avoid premature failure of the turbo, or injury to the operator.

8 • Do not operate the turbo with any parts exposed – foreign objects falling onto the rotating vanes could cause excessive damage and (if ejected) personal injury.

9 • Cover the turbocharger air inlet ducts to prevent debris entering, and clean using lint-free cloths only.

10 • Do not race the engine immediately after start-up, especially if it is cold. Give the oil a few seconds to circulate.

11 • Observe the recommended intervals for oil and filter changing, and use a reputable oil of the specified quality. Neglect of oil changing, or use of inferior oil, can cause carbon formation on the turbo shaft and subsequent failure. Thoroughly clean the area around all oil pipe unions before disconnecting them, to prevent the ingress of dirt. Store dismantled components in a sealed container to prevent contamination.

5.7a Disconnect the wiring connector...

5.7b ...and the vacuum hose from the vacuum pump

5 Turbocharger and exhaust manifold – removal and refitting

Note: *This Section describes removal of the turbocharger together with the exhaust manifold. On all diesel engines covered in this manual, the turbocharger cannot be removed from the exhaust manifold.*

Removal

1 Apply the handbrake, then jack up the front of the vehicle and support it on axle stands (see *Jacking and vehicle support*). Remove the engine compartment undertray and the engine top cover.

2 Remove the plenum chamber front panel as described in Chapter 12 Section 19.

3 Remove the air filter assembly and ducting as described in Chapter Section.

4 On 1.9 and 2.0 litre PD engines, remove the subframe (Chapter 10 Section 21) and the right-hand driveshaft (Chapter 8 Section 2).

5 Remove the exhaust front pipe/catalytic converter/ particulate filter as described in Section 10.

6 Undo the retaining bolt, unclip the breather pipe and disconnect the air intake hose from the turbocharger **(see illustrations)**.

7 Disconnect the wiring connector and vacuum pipe from the vacuum unit on top of the turbocharger **(see illustrations)**.

8 Trace the wiring from the exhaust gas temperature sensor and then disconnect the sensor wiring plug. Detach the connector from the bracket **(see illustrations)**.

9 Slacken the retaining clips, undo the two retaining bolts and withdraw the pulsation damper from the charge air ducting to the turbo **(see illustration)**.

10 Undo the retaining screws and remove the

5.8a Locate the exhaust gas temperature sensor...

5.8b ...and disconnect the wiring connector on the bulkhead

5.9 Disconnect the charge air pipe/ pulsation damper from the turbo

5.12 Undo the two retaining screws from the heat shield

5.14 Remove the turbocharger/manifold from the engine compartment

5.15a Fit new exhaust manifold gasket...

5.15b ...oil return/supply pipe gasket...

5.15c ...oil return banjo bolt...

5.15d ...and oil supply sealing washers

EGR metal connecting pipes, with reference to Section 3.

11 Undo the two upper securing bolts and the lower banjo bolts for the oil supply and return for the turbocharger. Then remove the oil return pipe/support from the rear of the engine (**see illustrations 3.24a, 3.24b & 3.24c**).

12 Undo the two retaining screws and remove the heat shield from the manifold (**see illustration**).

13 Check around the turbocharger/exhaust manifold and unclip any wiring or hoses still connected, noting their fitted position and the routing of all cables.

14 Undo the retaining nuts and manoeuvre the exhaust manifold/turbocharger assembly out from the engine compartment (**see illustration**).

Refitting

15 Refit the turbocharger by following the removal procedure in reverse, noting the following points:

a) Renew exhaust manifold gaskets, sealing washers and O-rings (**see illustration**).

b) Fit a new gasket to the oil return pipe upper flange (**see illustration**).

c) Fit a new banjo bolt to the oil return pipe (**see illustration**).

d) Fit new sealing washers to the oil supply pipe (**see illustration**).

e) Before reconnecting the oil supply pipe, fill the turbocharger with fresh oil using an oil can.

f) Tighten all nuts and bolts to the specified torque, where given.

g) Ensure that the air hose clips are securely tightened, to prevent air leaks.

h) When the engine is started after refitting, allow it to idle for approximately one minute to give the oil time to circulate around the turbine shaft bearings. Check for signs of oil or coolant leakage from the relevant unions.

6 Turbocharger charge control system components – description, removal and refitting

Description

1 The turbocharger pressure valve is operated by vacuum supplied by the brake vacuum pump mounted on the left-hand end of the cylinder head. The vacuum supply is controlled by an electrically operated solenoid valve activated by the engine management ECU. The solenoid valve is mounted on the bulkhead at the rear of the engine compartment. The valve has three hoses connecting it to the air cleaner, turbocharger and vacuum pump. It is important that the hoses are connected correctly to the solenoid valve (**see illustration 3.1**).

Charge pressure control solenoid valve

2 The charge pressure solenoid valve is mounted at the rear of the engine compartment (**see illustration**) on the bulkhead.

3 Disconnect the wiring from the valve (**see illustration**).

6.2 Charge pressure solenoid valve

6.3 Disconnect the wiring connector ...

6.4 ... unclip the vacuum pipes ...

6.5 ... and disconnect them from the solenoid valve

4 Undo the two retaining nuts and withdraw the solenoid valve away from the bulkhead, unclipping the vacuum hoses from their retaining clips (see illustration).

5 Remove the vacuum hoses from the ports on the control solenoid valve (see illustration), noting their order of connection carefully to aid correct refitting.

6 Refitting is a reversal of removal.

Charge pressure valve (wastegate)

7 The charge pressure valve is an integral part of the turbocharger, and cannot be renewed separately.

7 Exhaust manifold and catalytic converter – removal and refitting

Note: This Section describes removal of the exhaust manifold on non-turbo models fitted with engine code BDJ and BST. On turbo models, the exhaust manifold and turbocharger are integral, and removal and refitting procedures are described in Section 5.

Removal

1 Apply the handbrake, then jack up the front of the vehicle and support it on axle stands (see Jacking and vehicle support). Remove the engine compartment undertray and the engine top cover.

2 Remove the right-hand driveshaft as described in Chapter 8 Section 2.

3 Remove the front suspension subframe as follows as described in Chapter 10 Section 21.

4 Where fitted, unscrew the bolts from the auxiliary heater coolant pipes.

5 Remove the EGR connecting pipe from the exhaust manifold and from the inlet manifold.

6 Unscrew the retaining nuts, and separate the exhaust downpipe from the manifold. Also, unbolt the support bracket.

7 Unscrew the exhaust manifold mounting bolts.

8 Push the engine forwards as far as possible, then slide the exhaust manifold off its studs and lower it from the engine. Recover the

gasket from the cylinder head and discard it as a new one must be used on refitting.

Refitting

9 Refit the exhaust manifold by following the removal procedure in reverse, but renew all gaskets and tighten all nuts and bolts to the specified torque, where given.

8 Intercooler – general information, removal and refitting

General information

1 The intercooler is effectively an 'air radiator', used to cool the pressurised inlet air before it enters the engine.

2 When the turbocharger compresses the

inlet air, one side-effect is that the air is heated, causing it to expand. If the inlet air can be cooled, a greater effective volume of air will be inducted, and the engine will produce more power.

3 The compressed air from the turbocharger, which would normally be fed straight into the inlet manifold, is instead ducted around the engine to the base of the intercooler. The intercooler is mounted at the front of the car, in the airflow. The heated air entering the base of the unit rises upwards, and is cooled by the airflow over the intercooler fins, much as with the radiator. When it reaches the top of the intercooler, the cooled air is then ducted into the throttle housing.

4 There is a charge air pressure/temperature sensor fitted to the air inlet ducting from the intercooler to the inlet manifold. See Chapter 4A Section 4, for removal and refitting procedure.

Removal

5 The intercooler is located in front of the radiator on the lock carrier (the crossmember incorporating the headlights and radiator grille). Remove the radiator as described in Chapter 3 Section 3, for access to the intercooler. This procedure may include moving the lock carrier to its Service position (Chapter 2D Section 4).

6 Slacken the retaining clips (or release the spring type clips on some models) and release the air ducts from the inlet and outlet elbows at the bottom of the intercooler (see illustrations).

8.6a Remove the charge air hoses ...

8.6b ...from both sides of the intercooler

8.6c Where fitted release the spring clips...

8.6d ...and remove the hoses

8.7a Undo the retaining screws ...

8.7b ...to release the intercooler mountings

8.9 Undo the retaining screw

7 Working from the front of the vehicle, undo the two retaining screws (one at each side) to release the intercooler side mountings **(see illustrations)**.

8 Tilt the intercooler and air-conditioning condenser backwards slightly On models fitted with AC take care not to damage the refrigerant pipes.

Warning: Refer to the precautions given in Chapter 3 Section 11, before working on the air-conditioning system.

9 On models fitted with AC, undo the screw at the right-hand lower side of the intercooler to release the refrigerant pipe mounting bracket **(see illustration)**.

10 Working at the front of the vehicle, undo the four retaining screws (two at each side) and pull the intercooler upwards to release it from the lower crossmember, then withdraw

it from out of the engine compartment **(see illustrations)**. On models fitted with AC, make sure the condenser is secured safely to the front crossmember, to prevent any damage to the fins or the refrigerant pipes.

Refitting

11 Refitting is a reversal of removal, noting the following points:

a) *Make sure the mountings on the side of the intercooler are not damaged* **(see illustration)**.

b) *Check the rubber grommets are still located in the lower crossmember* **(see illustration)**.

c) *Refer to Chapter 3, Section 3, when refitting the radiator.*

d) *Ensure that the air hose clips are securely refitted, to prevent air leaks.*

8.10a Undo the two retaining screws...

8.10b ...and the two from the other side of the condenser

9 Catalytic converter/ particulate filter – removal and refitting

⚠️ *Warning: Allow ample time for the exhaust system to cool before starting work. In particular, note that the catalytic converter runs at very high temperatures. If there is any chance that the system may still be hot, wear suitable gloves.*

Note: *This Section describes removal of the exhaust front flexible pipe complete with the catalytic converter or the combined catalytic and particulate filter (depending on the model). On 1.9 and 2.0 litre PD engines the subframe will need to be removed, to allow enough room for the assembly to be lowered out from under the rear of the engine. On Common rail (CR) engines removal (whilst awkward) is possible with the subframe in position.*

1 Disconnect the battery negative lead and position it away from the terminal – see 'disconnecting the battery' in Chapter 5A Section 3.

2 Working at the engine compartment bulkhead, disconnect the wiring plugs for the oxygen sensor and exhaust gas temperature sensors **(see illustration 6.2)**.

3 Trace the wiring back from the sensors, noting their routing and release the wiring harness from the retaining clips **(see**

8.10c Remove the intercooler

8.11a Check the condition of the mounting...

8.11b ...and the rubber grommets in the crossmember

9.3 Unclip the wiring loom

9.4 Undo the exhaust/turbo securing clamp

9.5 Unclip the hoses from the retaining clips on the timing cover

illustration). Note the sensors can stay fitted to the exhaust at this point, if a new catalytic converter/particulate is fitted, then the sensors can be swapped over with the system of the vehicle.

4 Slacken the retaining bolt to release the clamp between the turbocharger and the catalytic converter/particulate filter **(see illustration).**

5 Release the hoses from the timing cover **(see illustration)**, release the retaining clip and disconnect the pressure hose from the exhaust to the differential pressure sender.

6 Working at the right-hand rear corner of the cylinder head, slacken and remove the upper mounting bolt **(see illustration).**

7 Apply the handbrake, then jack up the front

of the vehicle and support it on axle stands (see *Jacking and vehicle support*). Remove the engine compartment undertray.

8 On PD engines, remove the front subframe, as described in Chapter 10, Section 21. On common rail engines remove the engine pendulum mount as described in Chapter 2A Section 16 or Section.

9 Where fitted, undo the two retaining bolts and remove the heat shield from above the right-hand drive shaft.

10 To prevent any damage to the front flexible pipe use a couple of pieces of metal bar and some retaining clips to prevent the flexible pipe from bending to far and getting damaged **(see illustration).**

Caution: Handle the flexible, braided

section of the front pipe carefully, and do not bend it excessively, if it is bent more than 10° it could get damaged.

11 Slacken the retaining bolts and slide the exhaust clamp to the rear of the vehicle, to disengage the exhaust front pipe from the rear section. Where required remove the transmission tunnel support struts **(see illustration).**

12 Undo the nuts securing the catalytic converter/particulate filter lower support bracket to the cylinder block **(see illustrations).**

13 Carefully manoeuvre the catalytic converter/particulate filter downwards from place. On common rail engines the assembly must be rotated as it is removed. Take care

9.6 Undo the retaining bolt

9.10 Support the flexible pipe with flat metal bar and securing clips

9.11 Slide the exhaust clamp along the exhaust

9.12a Undo the upper securing nuts ...

9.12b ...and lower securing nuts ...

9.12c ...then remove the lower mounting bracket

not to damage any wiring, making sure that all wiring has been disconnected and release from their retaining clips. Also take care not to bend the flexible section of the exhaust pipe at an angle of more than 10°.

Refitting

14 Refit the exhaust catalytic converter/particulate filter assembly by following the removal procedure in reverse, but renew all gaskets **(see illustration)** and tighten all nuts and bolts to the specified torque, where given.

9.14 Renew the gasket between the particulate filter and the turbo

10.4 Slacken the bolts on the exhaust pipe clamp

10 Exhaust system – component renewal

⚠ **Warning: Allow ample time for the exhaust system to cool before starting work. In particular, note that the catalytic converter runs at very high temperatures. If there is any chance that the system may still be hot, wear suitable gloves.**

Removal

1 All models have simple exhaust system fitted. The original VW system fitted in the factory is in two sections. The front section includes the catalytic converter (or 'catalyst'), and (on certain models) the particulate filter. The rear section, which connects to the front section under the centre of the vehicle has a single silencer fitted. A cutting point is marked on the original factory exhaust just in front of the rear silencer. This allows replacement of the rear silencer without the need to replace the complete system.

2 To remove part of the system, first jack up the rear of the car and support it on axle stands (see *Jacking and vehicle support*). Alternatively, position the car over an inspection pit or on car ramps.

Front pipe (catalytic converter/particulate filter)

Caution: Handle the flexible, braided section of the front pipe carefully, and do not bend it excessively, if it is bent more than 10° it could get damaged.

3 The front flexible pipe section is part of the catalytic converter/particulate filter, remove

the front pipe assembly as described in Section 9.

Rear pipe and silencer

4 Unscrew the clamp bolt securing the rear section of exhaust to the front section **(see illustration)**.

5 Release the silencer from the rubber mountings, then twist it from the centre section and withdraw it from under the car **(see illustrations)**.

6 If required, undo the retaining bolts and remove the mounting brackets from across the exhaust tunnel, to make removal easier **(see illustration)**.

Refitting

7 Each section is refitted by a reversal of the removal sequence, noting the following points:

a) Ensure that all traces of corrosion have been removed from the flanges or pipe ends, and renew all necessary gaskets.

b) The design of the clamps used between the exhaust sections means that they play a greater role in ensuring a gas-tight seal – fit new clamps if they are in less than perfect condition.

c) When fitting the clamps, use the markings on the pipes as a guide to the clamp's correct fitted position.

d) Inspect the mountings for signs of damage or deterioration, and renew as necessary.

e) If using exhaust assembly paste, make sure this is only applied to joints downstream of the catalyst.

f) Prior to tightening the exhaust system mountings and clamps, ensure that all rubber mountings are correctly located and that there is adequate clearance between the exhaust system and vehicle underbody.

11 Catalytic converter – general information and precautions

1 The catalytic converter fitted to diesel models is simpler than that fitted to petrol models, but it still needs to be treated with respect to avoid problems. The converter is a reliable and simple device which needs no maintenance in itself, but there are some facts of which an owner should be aware if the converter is to function properly for its full service life:

a) DO NOT use fuel or engine oil additives – these may contain substances harmful to the catalytic converter.

b) DO NOT continue to use the car if the engine burns (engine) oil to the extent of leaving a visible trail of blue smoke.

c) Remember that the catalytic converter is FRAGILE – do not strike it with tools during servicing work, and take care handling it when removing it from the car for any reason.

d) The catalytic converter, used on a well-maintained and well-driven car, should last for between 50,000 and 100,000 miles – if the converter is no longer effective, it must be renewed.

10.5a Rear silencer exhaust rubber mounting

10.5b Rubber mounting on centre section of exhaust

10.6 Mounting bracket across exhaust tunnel

Chapter 5 Part A
Starting and charging systems

Contents

Degrees of difficulty

Easy, suitable for novice with little experience		**Fairly easy,** suitable for beginner with some experience		**Fairly difficult,** suitable for competent DIY mechanic		**Difficult,** suitable for experienced DIY mechanic		**Very difficult,** suitable for expert DIY or professional	

Specifications

General
System type .... 12 volt, negative earth

Starter motor
Rating .... 12V, 2.0 kW

Battery
Ratings .... 36 to 72 Ah (depending on model and market)

Alternator
Rating .... 55, 60, 70 or 90 amp
Minimum brush length .... 5.0 mm

Torque wrench settings

	Nm	lbf ft
Alternator lead (B+) nut	15	11
Alternator mounting bolts		
All engines except 2.0 litre common rail	20	15
2.0 litre common rail engines	25	18
Battery lead clamp (positive and negative)	6	4
Battery clamping plate bolt	35	26
Battery-to-starter positive cable retaining nut	20	15
Starter wiring bracket retaining nut	23	16
Starter mounting bolts:		
M10	40	30
M12	75	55

1 General information and precautions

General information

1 The engine electrical system consists of the charging and starting systems. Because of their engine-related functions, these are covered separately from the body electrical devices such as the lights, instruments, etc (which are covered in Chapter 12).

2 The electrical system is of the 12-volt negative earth type.

3 The battery is of the maintenance-free (sealed for life) type and is charged by the alternator, which is belt-driven from the crankshaft pulley.

4 The starter motor is of the pre-engaged type, with an integral solenoid. On starting, the solenoid moves the drive pinion into engagement with the flywheel ring gear before the starter motor is energised. Once the engine has started, a one-way clutch prevents the motor armature being driven by the engine until the pinion disengages from the flywheel.

5 Further details of the various systems are given in the relevant Sections of this Chapter. While some repair procedures are given, the usual course of action is to renew the component concerned. The owner whose interest extends beyond mere component renewal should obtain a copy of the Automotive Electrical & Electronic Systems Manual

Precautions

 Warning: It is necessary to take extra care when working on the electrical system to avoid damage to semi-conductor devices (diodes and transistors), and to avoid the risk of personal injury. In addition to the precautions given in 'Safety First! 0 ' observe the following when working on the system:

Warning: Always remove rings, watches, etc, before working on the electrical system. Even with the battery disconnected, capacitive discharge could occur if a component's live terminal is earthed through a metal object. This could cause a shock or nasty burn.

Warning: Do not reverse the battery connections. Components such as the alternator, electronic control units, or any other components having semi-conductor circuitry could be irreparably damaged.

Warning: Never disconnect the battery terminals, the alternator, any electrical wiring or any test instruments when the engine is running.

 Warning: Do not allow the engine to turn the alternator when the alternator is not connected.

 Warning: Never test for alternator output by flashing the output lead to earth.

Warning: Always ensure that the battery negative lead is disconnected when working on the electrical system.

 Warning: If the engine is being started using jump leads and a slave battery, connect the batteries positive-to-positive and negative-to-negative (see Jump starting at the beginning of the manual). This also applies when connecting a battery charger.

Warning: Before using electric-arc welding equipment on the car, disconnect the battery, alternator and components such as the electronic control units (where applicable) to protect them from the risk of damage.

Caution: Certain audio units fitted as standard equipment by VW have a built-in security code to deter thieves. The unit is linked to the instrument panel and after disconnecting the battery the audio unit will be recognised and there will be no need to enter the code. However if the unit is not recognised it will be necessary to enter the security code. Refer to 'Disconnecting the battery' in this Section 3.

2 Battery – testing and charging

Testing

1 All original equipment batteries are sealed for life maintenance-free batteries. These may be one of three types:

a) Standard lead acid. Sealed for life with a visual charge indicator fitted.

b) Absorbent Glass Mat (AGM) Lead acid battery with the electrolyte absorbed in a glass matrix. No visual indicator fitted.

c) Enhanced Flooded Battery (EFB). Visual indicator fitted. Used on some stop-start models.

2 Topping-up and testing of the electrolyte in each cell is not possible. The condition of the battery can therefore only be tested using a battery condition indicator or a voltmeter.

3 All models (except those with AGM batteries) are fitted with a maintenance-free battery with a built-in charge condition indicator. The indicator is located in the top of the battery casing, and indicates the condition of the battery from its colour. If the indicator shows green, then the battery is in a good state of charge. If the indicator turns darker, eventually to black, then the battery requires

charging, as described later in this Section. If the indicator shows clear/yellow, then the electrolyte level in the battery is too low to allow further use, and the battery should be renewed. Do not attempt to charge, load or jump-start a battery when the indicator shows clear/yellow.

Note: *From 2009 VW introduced batteries that only have a two colour visual indicator. If the indicator shows black there is sufficient electrolyte in the cell, if the indicator shows light yellow the electrolyte level is low and the battery must be replaced. Note that the indicator is only a guide to the electrolyte level on one cell and is not a guide to the state of charge.*

4 If testing the battery using a voltmeter, connect the voltmeter across the battery and note the voltage **(see illustration)**. The test is only accurate if the battery has not been subjected to any kind of charge for the previous six hours. If this is not the case, switch on the headlights for 30 seconds, then wait four to five minutes before testing the battery after switching off the headlights. All other electrical circuits must be switched off, so check that the doors and tailgate are fully shut when making the test.

5 If the voltage reading is less than 12.2 volts, then the battery is discharged, whilst a reading of 12.2 to 12.4 volts indicates a partially discharged condition. The battery should be recharged as described later in this Section.

6 The preferable method of testing the battery is to use a digital battery analyser. Most garages (and battery supply specialists) will have one. These machines are capable of assessing the condition and performance of the battery without removing it from the vehicle or disconnecting the battery terminals.

Charging

Note: *The following is intended as a guide only. Always refer to the manufacturer's recommendations (often printed on a label attached to the battery) before charging a battery.*

7 If the battery is to be recharged, we recommend that you use an 'intelligent'

2.4 Checking the battery voltage

2.7a Battery charging using a modern battery charger

2.7b Some types of 'intelligent' charger may also have a battery testing capability

3.2 Open the cover

charger **(see illustrations)**. Where an AGM or EFB battery is fitted it is essential that the charger is specifically capable of charging these types of battery. Whilst some chargers are capable of safely charging the battery with the battery connected to the vehicle, if you are unsure, always disconnect the battery. If the battery is disconnected (e.g. if it is to be removed and recharged on the bench), note that certain 'learned' values will be lost from the engine management ECU memory, requiring the car to be driven over a short distance after refitting the battery. Also, when the battery is reconnected, the warning lights for the ESP and electro-mechanical steering will light up and stay on. They will extinguish if you drive briefly in a straight line at a speed of 9 to 13 mph.

3 Battery – disconnecting, reconnecting, removal and refitting

Disconnecting the battery

Note: *If the vehicle has a security-coded audio unit, make sure that you have the code*

number before disconnecting the battery; refer to cautions in Section 1.

1 Lower the drivers window and remove the key from the ignition.

2 The battery is located on the left-hand side of the engine compartment. Open the cover to gain access to the battery **(see illustration)**. A rigid cover and housing is fitted to some models, other models have an insulated cover.

3 Loosen the clamp nut and disconnect the battery negative lead (-) **(see illustration)**.

4 Move the negative (earth) lead away from the terminal. Cover the lead (or battery terminal) with a suitable insulator (a plastic bag is ideal) or simply secure it to the side with a cable tie.

Reconnecting the battery

5 Reconnect the negative lead. Push it down until it is flush with the battery terminal post and then tighten the nut to the specified torque.

6 Refit the battery cover and close the bonnet.

7 Reach through the open drivers window and turn on the ignition. Wait a minute or so to allow the on board computer systems to boot up and for the battery voltage to stabilise.

8 Start the vehicle (from outside where possible) and then open and close all the power windows. Hold the window switch in the fully down position for two seconds and then in the fully closed position for two seconds. Repeat the procedure for the other switch. Adjust the clock time and if necessary re-activate the audio unit by inserting the security code (where applicable).

9 To restore the electric window automatic opening/closing function (on models with global closing) ensure all windows and doors are closed, and then lock the vehicle via the driver's door. Now unlock the driver's door, and then lock it again – hold the key in the locking position for at least one second.

10 After reconnecting the battery and starting the vehicle the ESP (Electronic Stability Programme) the TCS (Traction Control System) and the power steering warning light will remain on until the vehicle is driven in a straight line at a speed of 10 mph or more.

Removal

11 Disconnect the battery negative cable as described above and then disconnect the battery positive cable **(see illustration)**.

3.3 Disconnect the battery negative terminal

3.11 Disconnect the positive lead

12 Unclip the front cover and then unscrew the retaining clamp bolt. Lift the battery from the engine compartment. **(see illustrations).**
13 If necessary the battery tray can now be removed. Remove the air filter housing as described in Chapter 4A Section 3. Remove the rear section of the battery surround (where fitted) and then unbolt and remove the battery tray **(see illustrations).**

Refitting

14 Refit the battery by following the removal procedure in reverse.

3.12a Remove the surround (hard plastic type shown)

3.12b Remove the retaining clamp bolt...

4 Alternator/charging system – testing in vehicle

Note: *Refer to Section 1 of this Chapter before starting work.*

1 If the charge warning light fails to illuminate when the ignition is switched on, first check the alternator wiring connections for security. If the light still fails to illuminate, check the continuity of the warning light feed wire from the alternator to the bulbholder. If all is satisfactory, the alternator is at fault and should be renewed or taken to an auto-electrician for testing and repair.
2 Similarly, if the charge warning light comes on with the ignition, but is then slow to go out when the engine is started, this may indicate an impending alternator problem. Check all the items listed in the preceding paragraph, and refer to an auto-electrical specialist if no obvious faults are found.
3 If the charge warning light illuminates when the engine is running, stop the engine and check that the auxiliary drivebelt is not broken (see Chapter 1 Section 11) and that the alternator connections are secure. If all is so far satisfactory, check the alternator brushes and slip-rings as described in Section 6. If the fault persists, the alternator should be renewed, or taken to an auto-electrician for testing and repair.
4 If the alternator output is suspect even though the warning light functions correctly, the regulated voltage may be checked as follows.

3.12c ...and remove the clamp

3.12d Lift out the battery

5 Connect a voltmeter across the battery terminals, and start the engine.
6 Increase the engine speed until the voltmeter reading remains steady; the reading should be approximately 12 to 13 volts, and no more than 14 volts.
7 Switch on as many electrical accessories (e.g. the headlights, heated rear window and heater blower) as possible, and check that the alternator maintains the regulated voltage at around 13 to 14 volts.
8 If the regulated voltage is not as stated, this may be due to worn brushes, weak brush springs, a faulty voltage regulator, a faulty diode, a severed phase winding or worn or damaged slip-rings. The brushes and slip

rings may be checked (see Section 6), but if the fault persists, the alternator should be renewed or taken to an auto-electrician.

5 Alternator – removal and refitting

Removal

1 Disconnect the battery negative lead and position it away from the terminal, refer to Section 3.
2 Remove the dipstick (PD engines) and then (where fitted) pull the engine cover upward

3.13a Remove the rear section...

3.13b ...remove the bolts...

3.13c ...and lift out the support tray

5.2 Unclip and remove the engine cover

5.8 Move the filter to one side

5.9 Disconnecting the alternator wiring plug connector

to release it from the top of the engine **(see illustration)**.

3 Remove the auxiliary drivebelt as described in Chapter 1 Section 29.

4 On all models except 1.9 PD engines, move the lock carrier into the service position as described in Chapter 2D Section 4.

Common rail engines

5 On 1.6 litre engines with AC, disconnect the wiring plug from the rear of the AC compressor and then unbolt the AC compressor. DO NOT disconnect the refrigerant hoses.

6 Secure the AC compressor by suspending it from the bonnet slam panel with stout cord or cable ties. Do not strain or kink the refrigerant hoses.

7 On 2.0 litre models remove the charge air pipe from the top of the alternator.

8 Remove the bolts from the fuel filter housing and secure it to the side – there is no need to disconnect the fuel lines **(see illustration)**.

9 Remove the alternator upper mounting bolt and slacken the lower bolt. Rotate the alternator away from the engine. Disconnect the upper wiring plug and then remove the cap from the main output terminal (B+) **(see illustration)**. Disconnect the wiring plug and then unbolt the loom retaining clip from the bottom of the alternator.

10 Remove the alternator lower bolt **(see illustration)** and then lift the alternator up and out of the engine bay.

PD engines

11 If not already done so, unclip the fuel/coolant lines from the charge air pipe. Release the spring clip and then unbolt and remove the charge air pipe **(see illustration)**. On 2.0 litre engines note the positions of the vacuum pipes and then remove the vacuum reservoir.

12 On 1.9 litre engines, remove the engine undershield and then disconnect the MAP sensor wiring plug from the lowers section of

the charge air to intercooler pipe. Release the lower spring clip **(see illustration)** unbolt and then remove the pipe.

13 At the rear of the alternator, disconnect the wiring plug, remove the blanking cap and then unbolt the main output lead (B+) from the alternator **(see illustration)**. Remove the cable clamp from the alternator.

14 Remove the mounting bolts **(see illustration)** and lift out the alternator.

Refitting

15 Refitting is a reversal of removal. Refer to or Chapter 1, Section 29, as applicable for details of refitting and tensioning the auxiliary drivebelt. Tighten the alternator mounting bolts to the specified torque. Before fitting the alternator, it may be necessary to tap the sliding sleeve in the alternator housing back a couple of millimeters **(see illustration)**, so that it can be easily refitted to the mounting bracket.

5.10 Alternator mounting bolts

5.11 Remove the pipe

5.12 Release the spring clip

5.13 The wiring plugs at the rear of the alternator

5.14 Remove the bolts

5.15 Tap the spacer down slightly to aid refitting

6.3 On the Bosch type, remove the outer cover...

6.4a ...undo the screws...

6.4b ...and remove the brush holder/ regulator

6 Alternator – brush holder/ regulator module renewal

Removal

1 Remove the alternator, as described in Section 5.

2 Place the alternator on a clean work surface, with the pulley facing down.

Bosch

3 Undo the screw and the two retaining nuts, and lift away the outer plastic cover **(see illustration)**.

4 Unscrew the three securing screws, and remove the voltage regulator **(see illustrations)**.

Valeo

5 Prise off the spring clips, and remove the outer plastic cover **(see illustration)**.

6 Undo the two screws and single nut, and remove the voltage regulator **(see illustrations)**.

7 Slide off the brush cover by depressing the lugs on each side.

Inspection

8 Measure the free length of the brush contacts **(see illustration)**. Check the measurement with the Specifications; renew the module if the brushes are worn below the minimum limit.

9 Clean and inspect the surfaces of the slip-rings **(see illustration)**, at the end of the alternator shaft. If they are excessively worn, or damaged, the alternator must be renewed.

Refitting

Bosch

10 Refit the voltage regulator using a reversal of the removal procedure, tightening the screws securely. On completion, refer to Section 5 and refit the alternator.

Valeo

11 Depress the carbon brushes into the housing, then refit the voltage regulator and tighten the screws and nut securely. Slide on the brush cover until it is heard to engage. On completion, refer to Section 5 and refit the alternator.

7 Starting system – testing

Note: *Refer to Section 1 of this Chapter before starting work.*

1 If the starter motor fails to operate when the ignition key is turned to the appropriate position, the following possible causes may be to blame:

b) *The battery is faulty.*

c) *The electrical connections between the switch, solenoid, battery and starter motor are somewhere failing to pass the necessary current from the battery through the starter to earth.*

d) *The solenoid is faulty.*

e) *The starter motor is mechanically or electrically defective.*

6.5 On the Valeo type, remove the outer plastic cover...

6.6a ...undo the two bolts and single nut...

6.6b ...and remove the voltage regulator

6.8 Measure the brush length

6.9 Clean and inspect the surfaces of the slip-rings

8.5 Disconnecting the starter wiring plug connector

8.6 Unbolt the main cable from the starter motor

8.7 Disconnect the earth cable – where fitted

2 To check the battery, switch on the headlights. If they dim after a few seconds, this indicates that the battery is discharged – recharge (see Section 2) or renew the battery. If the headlights glow brightly, operate the ignition switch and observe the lights. If they dim, then this indicates that current is reaching the starter motor; therefore the fault must lie in the starter motor. If the lights continue to glow brightly (and no clicking sound can be heard from the starter motor solenoid), this indicates that there is a fault in the circuit or solenoid – see following paragraphs. If the starter motor turns slowly when operated, but the battery is in good condition, then this indicates that either the starter motor is faulty, or there is considerable resistance somewhere in the circuit.

3 If a fault in the circuit is suspected, disconnect the battery leads (including the earth connection to the body), the starter/solenoid wiring and the engine/transmission earth strap – see disconnecting the battery in Section 3. Thoroughly clean the connections, and reconnect the leads and wiring, then use a voltmeter or test light to check that full battery voltage is available at the battery positive lead connection to the solenoid, and that the earth is sound.

4 If the battery and all connections are in good condition, check the circuit by disconnecting the wire from the solenoid blade terminal. Connect a voltmeter or test light between the wire end and a good earth (such as the battery negative terminal), and check that the wire is live when the ignition switch is turned to the start position. If it is, then the circuit is sound

– if not the circuit wiring can be checked as described in Chapter 12.

5 The solenoid contacts can be checked by connecting a voltmeter or test light between the battery positive feed connection on the starter side of the solenoid, and earth. When the ignition switch is turned to the start position, there should be a reading or lighted bulb, as applicable. If there is no reading or lighted bulb, the solenoid is faulty and should be renewed.

6 If the circuit and solenoid are proved sound, the fault must lie in the starter motor. It may be possible to have the starter motor overhauled by a specialist, but check on the availability and cost of spares before proceeding, as it may prove more economical to obtain a new or exchange motor.

---

8 Starter motor –
removal and refitting

Removal

1 Disconnect the battery negative lead – see disconnecting the battery in Section 3.

2 Where fitted, pull the engine cover upward to release it from the top of the engine **(see illustration 5.2)**.

3 Remove the air filter housing as described in Chapter Section.

4 Slide the protective cover from the rear of the starter motor. Note: On some models disconnect the solenoid wiring connector first.

5 Release the securing clip and disconnect

the wiring connector from the solenoid **(see illustration)**.

6 Unscrew the nut to disconnect the battery positive lead from the starter motor **(see illustration)**.

7 Where applicable, unscrew the nut from the upper starter bolt and disconnect the earth cable **(see illustration)**.

8 Unscrew the nut from the lower starter mounting bolt, and then remove the wiring loom support bracket **(see illustration)**.

9 Unscrew the mounting bolts noting their fitted position, then guide the starter motor out of the bellhousing aperture and out of the engine compartment **(see illustrations)**. Note: On vehicle with DSG transmissions, the starter motor upper bolt is also one of the transmission securing bolts.

Refitting

10 Refit the starter motor by following the removal procedure in reverse. Tighten the mounting bolts to the specified torque.

---

9 Starter motor –
testing and overhaul

1 If the starter motor is thought to be defective, it should be removed from the vehicle and taken to an auto-electrician for assessment. In the majority of cases, new starter motor brushes can be fitted at a reasonable cost. However, check the cost of repairs first as it may prove more economical to purchase a new or exchange motor.

8.8 Removing the wiring loom support bracket

8.9a Starter motor mounting bolts

8.9b Remove the starter motor

Chapter 5 Part B
Preheating system

Contents

Degrees of difficulty

Easy, suitable for novice with little experience | **Fairly easy,** suitable for beginner with some experience | **Fairly difficult,** suitable for competent DIY mechanic | **Difficult,** suitable for experienced DIY mechanic | **Very difficult,** suitable for expert DIY or professional

Specifications

Glow plugs

Electrical resistance	1.0 ohm
Current consumption (typical – no value quoted by VW).	8 amps (per plug)

Torque wrench setting	Nm	lbf ft
Glow plug to cylinder head:		
PD engines.	15	11
Common rail engines	18	13

1 General Information

1 To assist cold starting and to control emissions during the warm up phase, diesel engine models are fitted with a preheating system, which consists of four glow plugs, a glow plug control unit, a facia-mounted warning light and the associated electrical wiring. The glow plug control unit on some models, is incorporated in the ECU, other models have a control unit/relay located under the fusebox in the engine compartment (see Section 3).

2 The glow plugs are miniature electric heating elements, encapsulated in a metal case with a probe at one end and electrical connection at the other. Each inlet tract has a glow plug threaded into it, which is positioned directly in line with the incoming spray of fuel. When the glow plug is energised, the fuel passing over it is heated, allowing its optimum combustion temperature to be achieved more readily in the combustion chamber.

3 The duration of the preheating period is governed by the ECU, which monitors the temperature of the engine through the coolant temperature sensor and alters the preheating time to suit the conditions. Pre-heating only takes place at coolant temperature below 9°C.

4 A facia-mounted warning light informs the driver that preheating is taking place. The light extinguishes when sufficient preheating has taken place to allow the engine to be started, but power will still be supplied to the glow plugs for a further period until the engine is started. If no attempt is made to start the engine, the power supply to the glow plugs is switched off to prevent battery drain and glow plug burn-out. If the warning light flashes, or comes on during normal driving, this indicates a fault with the diesel engine management system, which should be investigated by a VW dealer or suitably equipped garage as soon as possible.

5 After the engine has been started, the glow plugs continue to operate for a further period of time. This helps to improve fuel combustion whilst the engine is warming-up, resulting in quieter, smoother running and reduced exhaust emissions. On models fitted with a DPF (Diesel Particulate Filter) the glow plugs are used to assist with filter cleaning when regeneration of the filter takes place.

2.4 Testing the glow plugs using a multimeter

2.11a Glow plug wiring connector for No 1 injector

2.11b Removing the wiring loom/rail from the glow plugs

2 Glow plugs –
testing, removal and refitting

⚠️ *Warning: A correctly functioning glow plug will become red-hot in a very short time. This should be in mind when removing the glow plugs, if they have recently been in use. If a glow plug is dropped, it may be damaged internally, which could result in ceramic fragments entering the engine causing extensive damage. Do not fit a glow plug that has been dropped.*

Testing

Caution: Do not apply battery voltage directly to the glow plugs. All engines covered by this manual uses either a 7 volt or 5 volt system. Applying 12 volts to the glow plugs for any length of time will destroy the glow plugs.

1 If the system malfunctions, testing is ultimately by substitution of known good units, but some preliminary checks may be made as described in the following paragraphs.

2 Where fitted, remove the engine top cover.

3 Disconnect the wiring plugs from the glow plugs (as described for glow plug removal below) and connect a multimeter between the glow plug and a good earth – the battery negative terminal is ideal.

4 Select the ohms range on the meter and check the resistance of each glow plug in turn. Expect a reading of 5 ohms or less for a glow plug in good working order. Any reading over 5 ohms and the glow plug is faulty and should be replaced **(see illustration)**. Note that most faulty glow plugs will be open circuit.

5 Next check the supply voltage to the glow plugs. With the meter set to the volts range, connect the positive probe to the wiring loom. To fool the engine management system into thinking that the engine is cold, disconnect the coolant temperature sensor. Note that this is not a foolproof method of guaranteeing the operation of the glow plugs, as the engine management system may consider the open circuit voltage from the coolant temperature sensor as implausible when checked against the ambient air or oil temperature sensor for example.

6 With the meter connected, turn on the ignition. The meter should briefly show battery voltage, before dropping to either 4.4 or 7 volts and then dropping to zero as the preheating ends.

7 If no supply voltage can be detected at the glow plug, then either the glow plug relay (where applicable) or the supply wiring must be faulty. Also check that the glow plug fuse or fusible link has not blown – if it has, this may indicate a serious wiring fault. Investigate the cause or consult a VW

dealer (or suitably equipped garage) for advice.

8 As a final check, remove the glow plugs and inspect them visually, as described in the next sub-Section. A badly burned or charred stem may be an indication of a faulty fuel injector.

Removal

Note: *Refer to the Warning at the start of this Section before proceeding.*
Removal of the glow plugs is often considerably easier if the engine is warm.

PD unit injection engines

9 Disconnect the battery as described in Chapter 5A Section 3.

10 Pull the plastic cover on the top of the engine upwards from its mountings. Where fitted, remove the noise insulation from above the injectors.

11 Disconnect the wiring connectors from the glow plugs. Label the connectors where necessary to make refitting easier **(see illustrations)**. On some models the glow plug wiring is clipped to the injector leak-off hoses – make sure that the clips are not lost as the wiring is removed.

12 Unscrew and remove the glow plug(s).

13 Inspect the glow plug stems for signs of damage. A badly burned or charred stem may be an indication of a faulty fuel injector.

Common rail injection engines

14 Remove the engine cover and (where fitted) remove the noise insulation.

15 Disconnect the wiring plugs from the injectors, exhaust gas pressure sensor and fuel rail pressure sensor **(see illustration)**.

16 To make access easier, disconnect the wiring plugs from the injectors, exhaust gas pressure sensor, and fuel rail pressure sensor.

17 Undo the retaining bolts and detach the coolant pipe from the intake manifold. Move the pipe to the front of the manifold.

18 Release the retaining clip and disconnect the fuel return hose from the fuel rail **(see illustration)**. Be prepared for fuel spillage.

19 Pull the connectors from the top of the glow plugs and move the wiring loom to one

2.15 Disconnect the wiring plugs from the injectors

2.18 Disconnect the return hose from the fuel rail

2.19a Release the wiring loom clips at each plug

2.19b Using long nose pliers …

2.19c … pull the connectors from the top of the glow plugs

side. Be sure to only pull on the underside of the ridge at the top of the connectors **(see illustrations)**.

20 Clean the area around the glow plugs; use a vacuum cleaner if possible. Spray brake cleaner (or similar) around the glow plug opening, letting it penetrate briefly, and then blow out with compressed air.

Caution: Always wear protective goggles to protect your eyes, when using compressed air.

21 Using an extension and a deep 10 mm socket, unscrew and remove the glow plug(s) from the cylinder head **(see illustration)**. Note that the plug must be kept 'straight' when being removed, as it can be easily damaged.

Refitting

22 Refitting is a reversal of removal, but tighten the glow plugs to the specified torque.

3 Glow plug control unit – removal and refitting

Note: *The glow plug control unit may be incorporated inside the engine management ECU. Follow the procedure below for models with separate glow plug control unit.*

Removal

1 The glow plug control unit (where applicable) is located under the fuse box in the engine compartment **(see illustration)**.

2 To gain access to the control unit, remove the battery and battery tray, as described in Chapter 5A, Section 3.

3 Release the retaining clip and slide the control unit mounting bracket from the underside of the fusebox housing **(see illustration)**.

4 Disconnect the wiring connector and remove the control unit

Refitting

5 Refitting is a reversal of removal.

2.21 Remove the glow plugs

3.1 Glow plug control unit location

3.3 Slide the control unit out and disconnect the wiring connector

Notes

Chapter 6
Clutch

Contents

Degrees of difficulty

Easy, suitable for novice with little experience	Fairly easy, suitable for beginner with some experience	Fairly difficult, suitable for competent DIY mechanic	Difficult, suitable for experienced DIY mechanic	Very difficult, suitable for expert DIY or professional

Specifications

General
Type:
  Luk clutch . . . . Single dry friction disc, diaphragm spring with spring-loaded hub, self-adjusting pressure plate (SAC)
  Sachs clutch. . . . . Single dry friction disc, diaphragm spring with spring-loaded hub
Clutch operation. . . . . Hydraulic with master and slave cylinders

Torque wrench settings

	Nm	lbf ft
Clutch pedal crash bar bolts*:		
1 bolt fitment	20	15
2 bolt fitment	10	7
Clutch pedal mounting bracket nuts*	25	18
Clutch pedal pivot nut*	25	18
Clutch pressure plate-to-flywheel bolts*:		
M7 bolt	20	15
M6 bolt	13	10
Concentric clutch slave cylinder bolts (6-speed only): *		
Metal version	12	9
Plastic version (use thread lock)	15	11
Clutch slave cylinder bolts	20	15

*Use new bolts/nuts

2.2 Preparing to bleed the clutch on models fitted with a conventional slave cylinder

2.3a Clutch slave cylinder bleed screw on 5-speed models

2.3b Clutch bleed screw – 02Q transmissions

1 General Information

1 The clutch is of single dry plate type, incorporating a diaphragm spring pressure plate, and is hydraulically operated.
2 The pressure plate is bolted to the rear face of the flywheel, and the friction disc is located between the pressure plate and the flywheel friction surface. The friction disc hub is splined to the transmission input shaft and is free to slide along the splines. Friction lining material is riveted to each side of the disc, and the disc hub incorporates cushioning springs to absorb transmission shocks and ensure a smooth take-up of drive.
3 On all transmissions except 02Q, when the clutch pedal is depressed, the slave cylinder pushrod moves the release lever forwards. On 02Q transmissions, the slave cylinder is fitted concentrically around the transmission input shaft within the bellhousing. The release bearing is forced onto the pressure plate diaphragm spring fingers. As the centre of the diaphragm spring is pushed in, the outer part of the spring moves out and releases the pressure plate from the friction disc. Drive then ceases to be transmitted to the transmission.
4 When the clutch pedal is released, the diaphragm spring forces the pressure plate into contact with the linings on the friction disc, and at the same time pushes the disc

slightly forward along the input shaft splines into engagement with the flywheel. The friction disc is now firmly sandwiched between the pressure plate and flywheel. This causes drive to be taken up.
5 As the linings wear on the friction disc, the pressure plate rest position moves closer to the flywheel resulting in the 'rest' position of the diaphragm spring fingers being raised. The hydraulic system requires no adjustment since the quantity of hydraulic fluid in the circuit automatically compensates for wear every time the clutch pedal is operated.

2 Hydraulic system – bleeding

⚠️ *Warning: Hydraulic fluid is poisonous, thoroughly wash off spills from bare skin without delay. Seek immediate medical advice if any fluid is swallowed or gets into the eyes. Certain types of hydraulic fluid are inflammable and may ignite when brought into contact with hot components. Hydraulic fluid is also an effective paint stripper. If spillage occurs onto painted bodywork or fittings, it should be washed off immediately, using copious quantities of cold water. It is also hygroscopic (i.e. it can absorb moisture from the air) which then renders it useless. Old fluid may have suffered contamination, and should never be re-used.*

1 If any part of the hydraulic system is dismantled, or if air has accidentally entered the system, the system will need to be bled. The presence of air is characterised by the pedal having a spongy feel and it results in difficulty in changing gear.
2 On 02Q transmissions (fitted with a concentric clutch slave cylinder) the design of the clutch hydraulic system makes bleeding using the conventional method of pumping the clutch pedal hard to achieve. In order to remove all air present in the system, the best approach is to use pressure bleeding equipment. This is available from auto accessory shops at relatively low cost. An alternative method is to reverse bleed the

clutch by pushing fluid back towards the master cylinder using a large syringe filled with brake/clutch fluid. Conventional bleeding is possible on models fitted with an external slave cylinder **(see illustration)**.
3 When pressure bleeding equipment is used, should be connected to the brake/clutch hydraulic fluid reservoir in accordance with the manufacturer's instructions. The system is bled through the bleed screw of the clutch slave cylinder (all transmissions except 02Q), which is located on the top of the transmission housing. On 02Q transmissions, the slave cylinder bleed screw is located at the front of the transmission, above the starter motor **(see illustrations)**.
4 Bleed the system until the fluid being ejected is free from air bubbles. Close the bleed screw, then disconnect and remove the bleeding equipment.
5 Check the operation of the clutch to see that it is satisfactory. If air still remains in the system, repeat the bleeding operation.
6 Discard any fluid that is bled from the system, even if it looks clean. Hydraulic fluid absorbs water and its re-use can cause internal corrosion of the master and slave cylinders, leading to excessive wear and failure of the seals.

3 Clutch pedal – removal and refitting

Removal

1 Move the driver's seat fully to the rear, and adjust the steering column to its highest position.
2 Disconnect the battery negative lead and position it away from the terminal – see Chapter 5A Section 3.
3 Remove the driver's side lower facia trim panel, with reference to Chapter 11, Section 26.
4 Release the retaining clip and unclip the wiring loom guide from under the steering column **(see illustration)**.
5 Undo the retaining bolt(s) and remove the crash bar from above the clutch pedal. There are two types of crash bar fitted; depending

3.4 Unclip the wiring bracket from the steering column

1 Clutch pedal
2 Pivot pin
3 Bearing bushes
4 Over centre spring
5 Mounting bracket
6 Seal
7 Master cylinder
8 Seal
9 Pivot bolt
10 Pedal securing clip

H48710

3.8 Clutch pedal assembly

H48707

3.9 Master cylinder pushrod to pedal securing clip

1 Master cylinder pushrod
2 Securing clip
3 Clutch pedal

4 Master cylinder – removal, overhaul and refitting

Note: *Refer to the warning at the beginning of Section 2 regarding the hazards of working with hydraulic fluid.*

Removal

Note: *Access can be improved if the windscreen cowl panel and plenum chamber front panel are removed first, as described in Chapter 12 Section 19.*

1 The clutch master cylinder is located through the bulkhead and is attached to the clutch pedal mounting bracket **(see illustration)**. Hydraulic fluid for the unit is supplied from the brake master cylinder reservoir.

2 Before proceeding, place cloth rags on the carpet inside the car to prevent damage from spilt hydraulic fluid.

3 Remove the engine top cover/air filter assembly.

4 Working down the back of the engine compartment, clamp the hydraulic fluid hose (if it's rubber) leading from the brake fluid reservoir to the clutch master cylinder using a brake hose clamp. If the hose is plastic, then the end will need to be plugged to prevent fluid loss.

5 Similarly (where possible), clamp the rubber section of the hydraulic hose leading from the master cylinder to the slave cylinder using a brake hose clamp, to prevent loss of hydraulic fluid. The rubber section of pipe may be further down towards the slave cylinder.

6 Position a suitable container, or a wad of clean cloth, beneath the master cylinder to catch escaping hydraulic fluid. Release the clip and disconnect the fluid supply hose from the master cylinder – be prepared for fluid spillage **(see illustration)**.

7 Pull the fluid outlet hose retaining clip from the union on the master cylinder, then pull the

on vehicle, there could be either one or two bolts securing the crash bar.

6 Where fitted, release the securing clips and remove the insulation padding from around the clutch pedal mounting bracket.

7 Where fitted disconnect the wiring plug and then rotate the clutch pedal position switch through 45 degrees anti-clockwise to remove it. Note: On later models this switch is fitted to the master cylinder.

8 Undo the retaining nut and remove the pedal pivot bolt, move the pedal downwards and withdraw the over-centre spring from inside the top of the mounting bracket **(see illustration)**. Note: The clutch pedal will still be attached to the master cylinder pushrod.

9 Working at each side of the clutch pedal, release the retaining clip to disengage the master cylinder pushrod from the pedal **(see illustration)**. The pedal can now be removed from the mounting bracket.

10 If required, undo the three mounting nuts and remove the mounting bracket from the bulkhead. Discard the self-locking nuts, as new ones will be required for refitting

Refitting

11 Refitting is a reversal of removal, bearing in mind the following points:

a) *Press the pushrod retaining clip firmly into the pedal until it is heard to engage.*

b) *Two types of clutch pedal switch are fitted to early models. One has a coloured plunger tip – on these the tip must NOT be extended before installation. The other version has a plain coloured plunger – on these the plunger must be fully extended before installation.*

c) *Tighten all fixings to the specified torque, where given.*

d) *On completion, check the brake/clutch fluid level, and top-up if necessary.*

4.1 Location of master cylinder on bulkhead

4.6 Disconnect the fluid supply hose

4.7 Master cylinder hose connection

1 Fluid pipe connection
2 Seal
3 Securing clip
4 Master cylinder

pipe from the union **(see illustration)**. Again, be prepared for fluid spillage.
8 Disconnect the wiring from the clutch position sender on the side of the master cylinder – later models only.
9 Working inside the vehicle, remove the clutch pedal and mounting bracket as described in Section 3.
10 Release the clip and withdraw the master cylinder from the mounting bracket by twisting it anti-clockwise.

Overhaul

11 No spare parts are available from VW for the master cylinder. If the master cylinder is faulty or worn, the complete assembly must be renewed.

Refitting

12 Refitting is a reversal of removal, but bleed the clutch hydraulic system as described in Section 2.

---

5   Slave cylinder – removal, overhaul and refitting

Removal

0A4 and 0AH transmissions

1 The slave cylinder is located on the top of the transmission casing **(see illustration)**.
2 Remove the battery and battery tray with reference to Chapter 5A, Section 3.
3 Remove the air cleaner housing, as described in Chapter.
4 Disconnect the gear selector cables from the gear selector levers, as described in Chapter 7A, Section 2. Withdraw the retaining clips and remove the outer cables from the mounting bracket, then unbolt the mounting bracket from the top of the transmission.
5 Undo the bolts and (where fitted) remove the gearbox support bracket from above the slave cylinder **(see illustration)**.
Caution: Refer to the warning at the

beginning of Section 2 regarding the hazards of working with hydraulic fluid.
6 Place a wad of clean rag beneath the fluid line connection on the slave cylinder to catch escaping fluid.
7 Release the fluid pipe retaining clip from the union on the slave cylinder, then pull the pipe from the union. Position the fluid pipe clear of the slave cylinder, and plug the end. Be prepared for some fluid spillage.
8 Unscrew the two bolts securing the slave cylinder to the transmission casing, and withdraw the slave cylinder from the transmission **(see illustration)**.

02Q transmission

9 Remove the transmission as described in Chapter 7A.
10 Release the retaining clip and pull the fluid bleeder connection from the outside of the transmission casing **(see illustration)**.
11 Undo the bolts and remove the slave cylinder/release bearing assembly **(see illustration)**.

Overhaul

12 No spare parts are available from VW for the slave cylinder. If the slave cylinder is faulty or worn, the complete assembly must be renewed.

Refitting

13 Refitting is a reversal of removal, bearing in mind the following points:
Tighten all fixings to the specified torque where given.
On completion, bleed the clutch hydraulic system as described in Section 2.

---

6   Clutch friction disc and pressure plate – removal, inspection and refitting

---

Warning: Dust created by clutch wear and deposited on the clutch components may contain asbestos, which is a health hazard. DO NOT blow it out with compressed air or inhale any of it. DO NOT use petrol or petroleum-based solvents to clean off the dust. Brake system cleaner or methylated spirit should be used to flush the dust into a suitable receptacle. After the clutch

5.1 Clutch slave cylinder

5.5 Remove the support bracket

5.8 Removing the clutch slave cylinder from the transmission

5.10 Prise up the clip and pull the connection from place- 02Q transmissions

5.11 Slave cylinder/release bearing retaining bolts – 02Q transmissions

6.3a Undo the pressure plate retaining screws

6.3b Ensure the stop pin is free to move

6.11 The friction disc should be marked 'Getriebeseite' or 'Gearbox side'

components are wiped clean with clean rags, dispose of the contaminated rags and cleaner in a sealed container.

Note: *New clutch pressure plate securing bolts will be required on refitting. It is recommended that a friction disc centralising tool be used when refitting the clutch.*

Note: *Always inspect the dual mass flywheel (as described in the relevant engine Chapter) and replace it if necessary.*

Removal

1 Access to the clutch is obtained by removing the transmission as described in Chapter 7A Section 3.

2 Mark the clutch pressure plate and flywheel in relation to each other.

3 Hold the flywheel stationary, and then unscrew the clutch pressure plate bolts ¼ of a turn at a time **(see illustration)**. With the bolts unscrewed two or three turns, check that the pressure plate is not binding on the dowel pins. If necessary, use a screwdriver to release the pressure plate. On models with the Sachs clutch, as the bolts are removed the stop pin must slacken. If it doesn't, press the pin towards the flywheel **(see illustration)**.

4 Remove all the bolts, then lift the clutch pressure plate and friction disc from the flywheel.

Inspection

Note: *Due to the amount of work necessary to remove and refit clutch components, it is usually considered good practice to renew the clutch friction disc, pressure plate assembly and release bearing as a matched set, even if only*

one of these is actually worn enough to require renewal. It is also worth considering the renewal of the clutch components on a preventative basis if the engine and/or transmission have been removed for some other reason.

5 Clean the pressure plate friction surface, clutch friction disc and flywheel. Do not inhale the dust, as it may contain asbestos which is dangerous to health.

6 Examine the fingers of the diaphragm spring for wear or scoring. If the depth of wear exceeds half the thickness of the fingers, a new pressure plate assembly must be fitted.

7 Examine the pressure plate for scoring, cracking, distortion and discoloration. Light scoring is acceptable, but if excessive, a new pressure plate assembly must be fitted. If the distortion of the friction surface exceeds 1.0 mm, renew it.

8 Examine the friction disc linings for wear and cracking, and for contamination with oil or grease. The linings are worn excessively if they are worn down to, or near, the rivets. Check the disc hub and splines for wear by temporarily fitting it on the transmission input shaft. Renew the friction disc as necessary.

9 Examine the flywheel friction surface for scoring, cracking and discoloration (caused by overheating). If excessive, it may be possible to have the flywheel machined by an engineering works, otherwise it should be renewed.

10 Ensure that all parts are clean, and free of oil or grease, before reassembling. Apply just a small amount of lithium-based grease (VW No. G000100) to the splines of the friction disc hub. Do not use copper-based grease. Note

that new pressure plates and clutch covers may be coated with protective grease. It is only permissible to clean the grease away from the friction disc lining contact area. Removal of the grease from other areas will shorten the service life of the clutch.

Refitting

11 Commence reassembly by locating the friction disc on the flywheel, with the raised side of the hub facing outwards (normally marked 'Getriebeseite' or 'Gearbox side'). If possible, the centralising tool (see paragraph 20) should be used to hold the disc on the flywheel at this stage **(see illustration)**.

Models with self-adjusting clutch (SAC)

12 On models with a Self-adjusting clutch (SAC), where a new friction disc is fitted, but the pressure plate is to be re-used, it is necessary to reset the pressure plate adjusting ring prior to assembly as follows.

13 Insert three 8 mm bolts into the pressure plate mounting holes at intervals of 120°. The bolts should be inserted from the flywheel side, and retained by nuts **(see illustration)**.

14 Place the pressure plate face down on the bed of an hydraulic press so that only the heads of the bolts make contact with the press bed, then place a circular spacer over the ends of the diaphragm springs fingers.

15 Use 2 screwdrivers to attempt to rotate the adjuster ring anti-clockwise. Apply just enough pressure with the hydraulic press until it's just possible to move the adjuster ring **(see illustration)**.

6.13 Insert three 8 mm bolts from the flywheel side, and secure with nuts

6.15 The edges of the adjuster ring (B) must be between the notches (A)

6.17 Fit the pressure plate over the locating dowel pins

6.20 With the pressure plate screws tightened, remove the centralising tool

16 Once the adjuster ring edges are between the notches, relieve the pressure. The ring is now reset. Note: New pressure plates are supplied in this reset position.

All models

17 Locate the clutch pressure plate on the disc, and fit it onto the location dowels (see illustration). If refitting the original pressure plate, make sure that the previously-made marks are aligned.

18 Insert the bolts finger-tight to hold the pressure plate in position.

19 The friction disc must now be centralised, to ensure correct alignment of the transmission input shaft with the disc centre. To do this, a proprietary tool may be used, or alternatively, use a wooden mandrel made to fit inside the friction disc and the hole in the centre of the crankshaft. Insert the tool through the friction disc into the crankshaft, and make sure that it is central.

20 Tighten the pressure plate bolts progressively and in diagonal sequence, until the specified torque setting is achieved, then remove the centralising tool (see illustration).

21 Check the release bearing in the transmission bellhousing for smooth operation – if the clutch is to be replaced always renew the release bearing (the bearing is normally part of the clutch kit). Renew it with reference to Section 7.

22 Refit the transmission with reference to Chapter 7A, Section 3.

7 Release bearing and lever – removal, inspection and refitting

Removal

Note: On 02Q transmissions, the release bearing is part of the clutch slave cylinder (see Section 5).

1 Remove the transmission as described in Chapter 7A, Section 3.

2 Using a screwdriver, prise the release lever from the ball-stud on the transmission housing. If this proves difficult, push the retaining spring from the release lever first (see illustration). Where applicable, remove the plastic pad from the stud.

3 Slide the release bearing, together with the lever, from the guide sleeve, and withdraw it over the transmission input shaft.

4 Separate the release bearing from the lever (see illustrations).

5 If the guide sleeve is worn excessively, unbolt it and remove the O-ring seal (see illustration).

Inspection

6 Spin the release bearing by hand, and check it for smooth running. Any tendency to seize or run rough will necessitate renewal of the bearing. If the bearing is to be re-used, wipe it clean with a dry cloth; the bearing should not be washed in a liquid solvent, as this will remove the internal grease.

7 Clean the release lever, ball-stud and guide sleeve.

7.2 Push the spring clip to release the arm from the ball-stud

7.4a Use a screwdriver to depress the retaining tags…

7.4b …then remove the release bearing from the arm

7.5 Guide sleeve on the transmission

7.8 Fitting the guide sleeve with assembled release bearing and lever

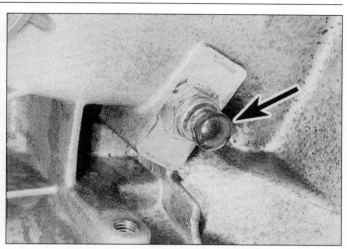

7.9 Lubricate the ball-stud with a little grease

7.11a Locate the spring over the end of the release lever...

7.11b ...and press the spring into the hole...

7.11c ...then press the release lever onto the ball-stud until the spring clip holds it in position

Refitting

8 If the guide sleeve was removed, locate a new O-ring seal over the input shaft, then fit the guide sleeve and tighten the bolts to the specified torque. If preferred, the guide sleeve may be assembled to the release bearing and lever, and the components fitted over the input shaft as one unit (see illustration).

9 Lubricate the ball-stud in the transmission bellhousing with molybdenum sulphide-based grease (see illustration). Also smear a little grease on the release bearing surface which contacts the diaphragm spring fingers in the clutch cover.

10 Push the release bearing into position on the release lever.

11 Fit the retaining spring onto the release lever, then press the release lever onto the ball-stud until the retaining spring holds it in position (see illustrations).

12 Refit the transmission as described in Chapter 7A, Section 3.

Chapter 7 Part A
Manual transmission

Contents

Degrees of difficulty

Easy, suitable for novice with little experience	**Fairly easy,** suitable for beginner with some experience	**Fairly difficult,** suitable for competent DIY mechanic	**Difficult,** suitable for experienced DIY mechanic	**Very difficult,** suitable for expert DIY or professional

Specifications

General

Type . . . . Five or six speed, transversely-mounted, front-wheel-drive layout with integral transaxle differential/final drive and 1 reverse gear

Code:
5-speed 0A4/0AH
6-speed 02Q

Oil capacities

0A4 transmission* . . . . 1.7 litres
0AH transmission* . . . . 2.1 litres
02Q transmission* . . . . 2.3 litres
* Capacities are the refill amounts for a previously fitted transmission

Torque wrench settings

	Nm	lbf ft
Driveshaft flange bolt	30	22
Flywheel cover plate (where fitted)	10	7
Gearchange cable support bracket	20	15
Gear lever housing to body:		
M6 nuts	8	6
M8 nuts	25	18
Left-hand mounting bracket bolts:		
To transmission: *		
Stage 1	40	30
Stage 2	Angle-tighten a further 90°	
Transmission bracket to wing bracket: *		
Stage 1	60	45
Stage 2	Angle-tighten a further 90°	
Bracket to body:		
Stage 1	60	45
Stage 2	Angle-tighten a further 90°	
Transmission minor support bracket bolts: *		
Stage 1	20	15
Stage 2	Angle-tighten a further 90°	
Pendulum mount: *		
M10 X 30 mm bolt		
Stage 1	40	30
Stage 2	Angle-tighten a further 90°	
M10 X 35 mm bolt		
Stage 1	50	37
Stage 2	Angle-tighten a further 90°	
M14 X 70 mm bolt		
Stage 1	100	74
Stage 2	Angle-tighten a further 90°	
Reversing light switch	20	15

Torque wrench settings (continued)

	Nm	lbf ft
Transmission to engine:		
M12 bolts	80	59
M10 bolt	40	30
Oil filler/level plug		
Plug with 12 point socket	45	33
Plug with hex head	30	22

*Do not re-use

1 General Information

1 The manual transmission is bolted directly to the left-hand end of the engine. This layout has the advantage of providing the shortest possible drive path to the front wheels, as well as locating the transmission in the airflow through engine bay, optimising cooling. The unit is cased in aluminium alloy.

2 Drive from the crankshaft is transmitted through the clutch to the gearbox input shaft, which is splined to accept the clutch friction disc.

3 All forward gears are fitted with synchromesh. The floor-mounted gear lever is connected to the gearbox by shift cables.

4 Levers on the transmission actuate internal selector forks, which are connected to the synchromesh sleeves. The sleeves are locked to the gearbox shafts but can slide axially by means of splined hubs, and they press baulk rings into contact with the respective gear/pinion. The coned surfaces between the baulk rings and the pinion/gear act as a friction clutch, that progressively matches the speed of the synchromesh sleeve (and hence the gearbox shaft) with that of the gear/pinion. This allows gearchanges to be carried out smoothly.

5 Drive is transmitted to the differential crownwheel, which rotates the differential case and planetary gears, thus driving the sun gears and driveshafts. The rotation of the differential planetary gears on their shaft allows the inner roadwheel to rotate at a slower speed than the outer roadwheel during cornering.

Note: *There is no recommendation from Volkswagen with regards to changing or checking the transmission oil level. The transmission should be checked for leaks at service time and the conscientious owner might consider changing the oil on a high mileage vehicle.*

2 Gear change housing and cable – removal, refitting and adjustment

Note: *The selector cable end fittings changed diameter from mid 2006. If replacing an early transmission with a later one, the selector levers (on the transmission) will need to be swapped over to the newer transmission.*

Removal

1 Remove the battery and battery tray as described Chapter 5A Section 3.

2 Remove the air filter housing as described in Chapter Section.

3 Prise out the clips securing the inner cable to the lever on the transmission, and the outer cable to the support bracket **(see illustrations)**. Withdraw the cable from the support bracket and discard the clips – new ones must be fitted.

4 Working inside the vehicle, remove the front section of the centre console, as described in Chapter 11 Section 25.

5 Remove the insulation around the base of the gear change housing to access the mounting nuts **(see illustration)**.

6 Raise the front of the vehicle and support it securely on axle stands (see *Jacking and vehicle support*).

7 Remove the centre tunnel front heat shield from the underside of the vehicle to gain access to the base of the selector lever housing and cables **(see illustration)**. It may be necessary to separate the exhaust downpipe from the intermediate pipe with reference Chapter 4B.

8 Working back inside the vehicle, undo the retaining nuts, then remove the bracket and lower the gear change housing downwards. Withdraw it complete with selector cables out from under the vehicle. It may be useful having the aid of an assistant at this point, to be under the vehicle when lowering the gear change housing.

9 To remove the cables from the gear change housing, prise out the clips securing the inner cable to the lower part of the gear lever, and then withdraw the securing clips from the outer cable to the gear change housing. Withdraw the cables and discard the clips – new ones must be fitted.

Refitting

10 Refitting is the reversal of the removal procedure, noting the following points:

a) *Ensure that the cables are correctly routed and secured, as noted on removal.*

b) *Take care not to bend or kink the cables.*

c) *Carry out the cable adjustment procedure described below before reconnecting the cable at the transmission end.*

d) *When refitting the cables, use new clips.*

2.3a Release the gearchange inner cable retaining clips ...

2.3b ...and slide out the outer cable securing clips

2.5 Remove the insulation from around the gearchange

2.7 Lower section of gearchange assembly under vehicle

2.12 Push the collar down and lock in position

2.13 Press down on (A), then push in locking pin (B)

2.14a Unclip the gaiter

2.14b Locking the gear lever in position using a drill bit

2.15 Release the two locking collars back into position

Adjustment

11 Remove the engine top cover, air cleaner housing, and air ducting for access to the top of the transmission. If required remove the battery and battery tray, as described in Chapter 5A Section 3.

12 With the gearchange set in the neutral position, push the two locking collars (one on each cable) forwards to compress the springs, turn them clockwise (looking from the driver's seat) to lock into position **(see illustration)**.

13 Press down on the selector shaft on the top of the transmission, and push the locking pin into the transmission while turning it clockwise, until it engages and the selector shaft cannot move **(see illustration)**.

14 Working inside the vehicle, unclip the gear lever gaiter from the centre console. Still in the neutral position, move the gear lever as far to the left as possible and insert the locking pin (or drill bit) through the hole in the base of the gear lever and into the hole in the housing **(see illustrations)**.

15 Working back in the engine bay, turn the two locking collars on the cables anti-clockwise so that the springs will release them

back into position and lock the cables **(see illustration)**.

16 With the cable adjustment set, the locking pin in the transmission housing, can now be turned anti-clockwise to its original position pointing upwards.

17 Inside the vehicle, remove the locking pin from the gear lever, and then check the operation of the selector mechanism. When the gear lever is at rest in neutral, it should be central, ready to select 3rd or 4th. The gear lever gaiter can now be refitted to the centre console.

18 Refit the air ducting, engine top cover/air filter and battery/tray.

3 Transmission – removal and refitting

Note: *A safe method of supporting the engine while the transmission is removed will be required.The recommended method of removing the transmission is to support the both the engine and transmission with a support bar that fits across the engine bay. Support bars are readily available in the aftermarket, however the special extensions and fittings specified by Volkswagon are not available* **(see illustration)**. *Where the correct support bar is not available the best alternative for the home mechanic is to support the engine with an engine crane (installed from the side) and then support the transmission with a trolley jack or ideally a transmission jack* **(see illustration)**. *Whichever method is used the aid of an assistant is essential.*

6367 Fig. 07a-03.0a HAYNES

3.0a Engine support bar and extensions

3.0b Transmission support jack

3.5 Mounting bracket securing bolts

3.6 Remove the support bracket

3.7a Unbolt and then...

3.7b ...remove the slave cylinder

3.8 Prise up the clip a little and pull the hose from the connection – 02Q transmissions

3.13a Reversing light switch...

Removal

1 Select a solid, level surface to park the vehicle upon. Give yourself enough space to move around it easily. Apply the handbrake and chock the rear wheels.

2 Raise the front of the vehicle and support it securely on axle stands (see *Jacking and vehicle support*). Remove the engine/transmission undertray sections. Position a suitable container beneath the transmission, then unscrew the drain plug and drain the transmission oil.

3 Remove the engine top cover/air filter. Remove the air cleaner housing as described in Chapter Section and where fitted remove the charge air pipe from the turbocharger.

4 Remove the battery and battery tray with reference to Chapter 5A Section 3.

5 Release the retaining clips and disconnect the gear selector cables from the gear selector levers, as described in Section 2. Unbolt and remove the cable mounting bracket from the top of the transmission (see illustration) and on 0AH transmissions remove the operating lever.

6 Undo the retaining bolts, and then remove the support bracket (see illustration), from the top of the transmission.

7 On models with the clutch slave cylinder on the top of the transmission, undo the retaining bolts, remove the cylinder and secure it out of harms way (see illustrations).

8 On 02Q transmissions, seal the slave cylinder flexible hose using a hose clamp, then prise out the clip and pull the fluid pipe from the bleeder connection on the slave cylinder supply pipe (see illustration).

9 Unbolt the earth cable from the engine/transmission or subframe.

10 Remove the upper bolts securing the transmission to the engine.

11 With reference to Chapter 5A Section 8, remove the starter motor.

12 Remove the left-hand wheel arch liner.

13 Disconnect the wiring from the reversing light switch (see illustrations), and where fitted, the neutral position switch on vehicles with a start/stop system.

14 Where fitted unbolt the metal shield from around the right-hand driveshaft. On models with gas discharge headlights (Xenon) disconnect the ride height sensor and secure it to the side.

15 Slacken the clamp securing the exhaust intermediate pipe to the rear section and undo the front mounting bracket bolts (see illustrations). This will allow the engine to be moved forwards and backwards during

3.13b ...or neutral switch – depending on transmission

3.15a Slacken the exhaust clamp ...

3.15b ...and undo the exhaust mounting bracket bolts

3.16 Support the driveshafts

3.18 Unbolt the engine rear mounting torque arm

3.20a Transmission end mounting bracket

the transmission removal and alignment procedures. Consequently, there is no need to completely separate the exhaust pipe sections.

16 With reference to Chapter 8 Section 2, unscrew and remove the bolts securing the driveshafts to the transmission output flanges. On models with an intermediate shaft, remove the shaft as described in Section. Tie the right-hand driveshaft to one side, and then tie the left-hand driveshaft to the suspension strut, so that the shaft is as high as possible **(see illustration)**. Alternatively, completely remove the driveshaft as described in Chapter 8 Section 2.

17 Access can be improved if the radiator cooling fans are removed (Chapter 3 Section 5). Cover the rear of the radiator/cooling fans to prevent it from getting damaged as the engine/transmission is moved forward.

18 Unbolt the engine rear mounting torque arm from the bottom of the transmission **(see illustration)**.

19 Where applicable, unbolt the flywheel cover plate from the transmission bellhousing. On models fitted with the 02Q transmission remove the charge air pipe from the intercooler.

20 Using a suitable hoist (see the note at the beginning of this Section) support the weight of the engine and then unscrew the bolts securing the transmission mounting to the body. Also, unbolt the mounting bracket from the transmission **(see illustrations)**.

21 Lower the engine/transmission assembly slightly and, using a trolley jack/transmission

3.20b Remove the bracket from the transmission

jack, support the transmission. Position the jack so that it can be withdrawn from the left-hand side of the car. As the engine/transmission is moved, make sure any wiring or hoses are not damaged.

22 Unscrew and remove the remaining lower transmission-to-engine mounting bolts, including the bolt located on the left-hand rear of the engine **(see illustration)**.

23 Carefully pull the transmission directly away from the engine, taking care not to allow its weight to rest on the clutch friction disc hub. A second person is helpful to pull the engine as far forwards as possible.

24 On models with driveshafts that have a bolted flange, it will be necessary to manouvre the right-hand driveshaft flange, from around the flywheel on removal. If required, hold the drive flange in position and undo the centre securing bolt, then the drive flange can be

3.22 Undo the rear mounting bolt

removed **(see illustrations)**, make removal of the transmission easier.

Warning: Support the transmission to ensure that it remains steady on the jack head. Keep the transmission level until the input shaft is fully withdrawn from the clutch friction disc.

25 When the transmission is clear of the locating dowels and clutch components, lower the transmission to the ground and withdraw from under the car.

Refitting

26 Refitting the transmission is essentially a reversal of the removal procedure, but note the following points:

a) *Apply a smear of high melting-point grease to the clutch friction disc hub splines; take care to avoid contaminating the friction surfaces.*

3.24a Hold the drive flange in position ...

3.24b ...whilst removing the centre bolt ...

3.24c ...then slide the drive flange from the transmission

b) *In order to align the transmission with the flywheel, gently pull the engine forward as the transmission is manoeuvred into place.*

c) *Tighten the transmission-to-engine bolts to the specified torque.*

d) *Refer to the relevant part of Chapter 2 and tighten the engine mounting bolts to the correct torque.*

e) *Refer to Chapter 8, Section 2, and then tighten the driveshaft bolts to the specified torque.*

f) *On completion, refer to Section 2 and check the gearchange linkage/cable adjustment.*

g) *Refill the transmission with the correct grade and quantity of oil. Refer to 'Lubricants and fluids' and Section 4.*

4 Transmission oil – removal refilling and level checking

Oil level checking

02Q and 0AH Transmissions

1 The vehicle must be on level ground to check the transmission oil level. This can be accomplished by using wheel ramps to raise the front of the vehicle and then raising the rear of the vehicle using a jack and axle stands (see *Jacking and support*). The alternative method is to remove the Air filter housing and check the level from above. Access is restricted, but possible.

2 Where the vehicle has been jacked up to access the filler plug, remove the engine undershield.

3 The oil level should reach the lower edge of the filler/level hole. A certain amount of oil will have gathered behind the filler/level plug, and will trickle out when it is removed **(see illustrations)**. This does not necessarily indicate that the level is correct. To ensure that a true level is established, wait until the initial trickle has stopped, then add oil as necessary until a trickle of new oil can be seen emerging. The level will be correct when the flow ceases; use only good-quality oil of the specified type.

4 If the transmission has been overfilled so

4.8 The oil drain plug (A) and filler level plug (B) on 02Q transmissions

that oil flows out when the filler/level plug is removed, check that the car is completely level (front-to-rear and side-to-side), and allow the surplus to drain off into a suitable container.

5 When the oil level is correct, refit the filler/level plug and tighten it to the specified torque. Note that two versions of the oil filler plug are fitted and they have different torque settings.

6 Wipe off any spilt oil then refit the engine undertray (if removed), tighten the retaining screws securely. Lower the car to the ground. If access has been gained from above, refit the air filter housing.

0A4 Transmissions

7 On these transmissions, it is impossible to check the level of the oil through the 'filler' plug, due to the engine/transmission installation angle; the level of the fluid is above the lower edge of the filler hole. The only method of ensuring the correct fluid level is to completely drain and refill the transmission – as described below.

Draining and refilling

02Q and 0AH Transmissions

8 Raise the front of the vehicle and support it securely on axle stands (see '*Jacking*

4.17 Press down the selector shaft (2), and rotate the locking rod (1) upwards

4.3a Removing the oil level/filler plug on 02Q transmissions

4.3b The plug location on 0AH transmissions

and vehicle support '). Remove the engine/transmission undershield. Position a suitable container beneath the transmission, then unscrew the drain plug and drain the transmission oil **(see illustration)**. On 0AH transmissions the drain plug is below the filler/level plug on the differential housing.

9 Remove the filler/level plug from the transmission **(see illustrations 4.3a and 4.3b)**.

10 Refit the drain plug and tighten it to the specified torque. Note that two versions of the oil filler plug are fitted and they have different torque settings.

11 Fill the transmission with oil until it is just below the level of the filler plug. Allow time for the oil to drain down into the transmission and then re-check the level.

12 Fit the engine undershield and lower the vehicle to the ground (if only the front was raised). Remove the air filter housing and (with the vehicle on level ground) check the oil level from above. Add oil as required and then refit the filler/level plug. Again note that two versions of the filler/level plug are fitted.

13 Refit the air filter housing as described in Chapter Section.

0A4 Transmission

14 The vehicle must be on level ground to check/fill the transmission. This can be accomplished by using wheel ramps to raise the front of the vehicle and then raising the rear of the vehicle using a jack and axle stands (see *Jacking and support*).

15 Undo the fasteners and remove the engine undertray.

16 Remove the air cleaner housing as described in Chapter Section.

17 In order to drain the transmission, the pivot pin must be removed from the underside of the transmission casing. However, to prevent the position of the selector forks being altered, press the selector shaft down, then turn the angled locking rod upwards, and lock the shaft in position **(see illustration)**.

18 Place a container under the transmission casing.

19 Unscrew the drain plug from the base of

the differential housing and allow the oil to drain **(see illustration)**.

20 Then undo the retaining bolt, pull out the pivot pin nearest the passenger's roadwheel and allow the oil to drain **(see illustration 4.19)**. The pivot pin O-ring seal must be renewed.

21 When the oil has finished draining, clean the surrounding area, refit the drain plug and tighten it to the specified torque.

22 Rotate the selector-shaft locking rod to its original position.

23 Unscrew the reversing light switch from the top of the transmission casing.

24 Using a 600 mm length of 10 mm (external) diameter hose, and funnel, add 1.7 litres of new oil to the transmission.

25 Refit the reversing light switch, and tighten it to the specified torque.

5 Transmission overhaul – general information

1 The overhaul of a manual transmission is a complex (and often expensive) task for the DIY home mechanic to undertake, which requires access to specialist equipment. It involves dismantling and reassembly of many small components, measuring clearances precisely and if necessary, adjusting them by selecting shims and spacers. Internal transmission components are also often difficult to obtain and in many instances, extremely expensive.

6.2a The reverse light switch on 0A4 transmissions (02Q transmissions are similar)...

4.19 Oil drain plug (A) and pivot pin (B)

Because of this, if the transmission develops a fault or becomes noisy, the best course of action is to have the unit overhauled by a specialist repairer or to obtain an exchange reconditioned unit.

2 Nevertheless, it is not impossible for the more experienced mechanic to overhaul the transmission if the special tools are available and the job is carried out in a deliberate step-by-step manner, to ensure nothing is overlooked.

3 The tools necessary for an overhaul include internal and external circlip pliers, bearing pullers, a slide hammer, a set of pin punches, a dial test indicator and possibly a hydraulic press. In addition, a large, sturdy workbench and a vice will be required.

6.2b ...on 0AH transmissions

4 During dismantling of the transmission, make careful notes of how each component is fitted to make reassembly easier and accurate.

5 Before dismantling the transmission, it will help if you have some idea of where the problem lies. Certain problems can be closely related to specific areas in the transmission, which can make component examination and renewal easier. Refer to the Fault finding Section in this manual for more information.

6 Reversing light switch – testing, removal and refitting

Testing

1 Ensure that the ignition switch is turned to the OFF position.

2 Unplug the wiring harness from the reversing light switch at the connector. The switch is located on the front or top of the casing **(see illustrations)**

3 Connect the probes of a continuity tester, or multimeter set to the resistance measurement function, across the terminals of the reversing light switch.

4 The switch contacts are normally open, so with any gear other than reverse selected, the tester/meter should indicate an open circuit or infinite resistance. When reverse gear is selected, the switch contacts should close, causing the tester/meter to indicate continuity or zero resistance.

5 If the switch does not operate correctly, it should be renewed.

Removal

6 Ensure that the ignition switch is turned to the OFF position.

7 Unplug the wiring harness from the reversing light switch at the connector.

8 Unscrew the switch from the transmission casing, and recover the sealing ring.

Refitting

9 Refitting is a reversal of removal.

Notes

Chapter 7 Part B
DSG semi-automatic transmission

Contents

Degrees of difficulty

Easy, suitable for novice with little experience	Fairly easy, suitable for beginner with some experience	Fairly difficult, suitable for competent DIY mechanic	Difficult, suitable for experienced DIY mechanic	Very difficult, suitable for expert DIY or professional

Specifications

General

Description .... DSG (Direct Shift Gearbox) semi-automatic 6- or 7-forward speeds and 1 reverse. Integral transaxle differential/final drive transmission with multi-plate clutch or dual-clutch.

Application:
   02E (6 speed) .... 1.9 litre PD and 2.0 litre CR engines
   0AM (7 speed) .... 1.6 litre CR engine
Transmission capacity:
   02E (6 speed) .... 5.2 litres
   0AM (7 speed) .... 1.7 litres
Clutch type:
   02E (6-speed) .... Multi-plate (wet clutch), 4 outer plates, 4 inner plates & 1 drive plate.
   0AM (7-speed) .... Two (Dual-clutch) dry friction discs, with spring loaded centre hub.
Clutch operation .... Mechatronic unit (mechanical and electronic).

Torque wrench settings	Nm	lbf ft
Driveshaft flange bolt	30	22
Transmission-to-engine bolts:		
M10 bolts	40	30
M12 bolts	80	59
Transmission mounting bracket-to-casing bolts*:		
Stage 1	40	30
Stage 2	Angle-tighten a further 90°	
Transmission mounting-to-bracket bolts*:		
Stage 1	60	44
Stage 2	Angle-tighten a further 90°	
Drain plug (0AM transmission)	30	22
Drain/level plug (02E transmission)	45	31
Oil level tube (02E transmission)	3	2

*Do not reuse

1.1a Schematic view of the six speed transmission (02E)

A Engine
B Clutch 1
C Clutch 2

D Sub transmission 1 (gears 1, 3, 5 and reverse)
E Sub transmission 2 (Gears 2, 4 and 7)
F Final drive

1.1b Schematic view of the seven speed transmission (0AM)

A Engine
B Dual clutch
C Final drive

D Sub transmission 1 (gears 2, 4, 6 and reverse)
E Sub transmission 2 (gears 1, 3, 5 and 7)

1 General Information

1 The VW semi-automatic Direct Shift Gearbox (DSG) has six- or seven-forward speeds (and one reverse). In contrast to traditional automatic transmissions where a fluid flywheel (torque converter) transmits the power from the engine to the gearbox, the DSG has a multi-plate clutch in the six-speed transmission and a twin-clutch in the seven-speed transmission (see illustrations). The main advantages of the DSG transmission, is near-instant gear changes, with seamless, highly efficient drive, resulting in less exhaust emissions and improved fuel consumption.

2 On the front of the transmission housing is a mechatronic unit, this is made up of mechanical and electronic components. The electronic part of the unit uses information from sensors (e.g. engine speed, road speed, driving mode etc.) to determine the optimum gear and shift commands, the mechanical part then selects the correct gear required. On 6-speed (02E) transmissions, the unit is inside the transmission housing with a pressed steel cover, bolted to the front of the transmission casing. On 7-speed (0AM) transmissions, it is a sealed unit, and is bolted to the front of the transmission (see illustration)

3 On 6-speed (02E) transmissions, the clutch is of a multi-plate type, which runs in the transmission oil. It is made up of four outer plates, which have teeth on the outer edge to locate in the clutch housing, four inner plates with teeth on the inner edge that locate on the clutch inner hub, and one drive plate that is located on the outside of the clutch plate assembly. The four larger outer plates (C1) operate 1st, 3rd, 5th and reverse gears, and then the four smaller inner plates (C2) operate 2nd, 4th and 6th gears. With this system whilst 'C1' has a gear engaged, then 'C2' will pre-select the next gear ready to change gear. The assembly requires special care, as all the components in the assembly are balanced together, during manufacture. The clutch assembly is sealed inside the bell housing by a clutch end cover, which also forms a seal, to prevent loss of oil. If the end cover is removed

for any reason, it will need to be renewed.

4 On 7-speed (0AM) transmissions, the clutch is of a dual-clutch dry plate type, which has two friction discs and a spring loaded centre hub (see illustration). The clutch friction disc nearest the engine is operated by the larger outer release lever (K1) and operates 1st, 3rd, 5th & 7th gears. The clutch friction disc nearest the transmission is operated by the smaller inner release lever (K2) and operates 2nd, 4th, 6th & Reverse gears. With this system whilst 'K1' has a gear engaged, then 'K2' will pre-select the next gear ready to change gear. The clutch assembly can only be purchased as a complete unit, and if renewed, new release levers will also need to be renewed.

5 A fault diagnosis system is integrated into the control unit, but analysis can only be undertaken with specialised equipment. It is important that any transmission fault be identified and rectified at the earliest possible opportunity. A VW dealer or suitable equipped specialist can 'interrogate' the ECM fault memory for stored fault codes, enabling him to pinpoint the fault quickly. Once the fault has been corrected and any fault codes have been cleared, normal transmission operation is restored.

6 Because of the need for special test equipment, the complexity of some of the parts, and the need for scrupulous cleanliness when these transmissions, the work which the owner can do is limited. Most major repairs and overhaul operations should be left to a VW dealer or specialist, who will be equipped with the necessary equipment for fault diagnosis and repair. The information in this Chapter is therefore limited to a description of the removal and refitting of the transmission as a complete unit. The removal, refitting and adjustment of the selector cable is also described.

1.2 Mechatronic unit – 0AM transmissions

1.4 Clutch assembly – 0AM transmissions

**2.0 Breather cap on mechatronic unit –
0AM transmissions**

**2.9 Clamp the transmission cooler hoses –
02E transmissions**

2.11 Undo the earth cable securing nut

7 In the event of a transmission problem occurring, consult a VW dealer or transmission specialist before removing the transmission from the vehicle, since the majority of fault diagnosis is best carried out with the transmission still in the vehicle.

2 Transmission –
removal and refitting

Note: *The mechatronic unit on the front of the 7-speed (0AM) transmission is a sealed unit. If any oil is lost from this mechatronic unit, it will need to be renewed, as it cannot be refilled. Remove the breather cap from the top of the unit and cover with blanking plug, to prevent any loss of oil* **(see illustration)**.

Removal
1 The transmission is removed downwards from the engine compartment. First, select a solid, level surface to park the vehicle upon. Give yourself enough space to move around it easily. Select P, apply the handbrake, and chock the rear wheels.
2 Loosen the front wheel bolts, and the driveshaft hub bolts. Do not undo the hub bolt more than 90° at this point; otherwise the wheel bearing could be damaged, whilst the weight is still on the wheels.
3 Raise the front of the vehicle and rest it securely on axle stands (see *Jacking and vehicle support*). Remove the front wheels. Allow a suitable working clearance

underneath for the eventual withdrawal of the transmission. Undo the fasteners and remove the engine/transmission undershield.
4 Remove the engine cover and then drain the transmission oil, as described in Section 6.
Warning: The mechatronic unit on the front of the 7-speed (0AM) transmission is a sealed unit. If any oil is lost from this unit, it will need to be renewed, as it cannot be refilled. Remove the breather cap from the top of the unit and cover with blanking plug, to prevent any loss of oil.
5 Remove the air filter housing as described in Chapter 4A Section 3 and then remove the battery, complete with the shrouds and support tray (Chapter) 5A Section 3. On 7-speed models unclip the breather hose.
6 Undo the retaining clips and remove the turbocharger intake hose and charge air pipe to the intercooler (Chapter 4B Section 5).
7 Remove the starter motor as described in Chapter 5A Section 8.
8 Disconnect the selector cable from the selector shaft lever on the top of the transmission, as described in Section 4. Position the cable to one side, noting that the retaining clip/circlip must be renewed.
9 On 6-speed (02E) transmissions there is a fluid cooler located on top of the transmission. Clamp off the cooler hoses with brake hose type clamps. Release the retaining clips and detach the hoses from the cooler **(see illustration)**. Take great care not to spill any coolant into the transmission unit, as this will cause damage.

10 Disconnect the wiring plug connectors from the front of the transmission. If required, undo the nuts and detach the wiring loom retainer from the gearbox cover.
11 Disconnect the main and secondary earth cable (where fitted) from either the transmission or the vehicle body **(see illustration)**.
12 Remove the upper engine-to-transmission mounting bolts.
13 Remove the radiator cooling fan assembly as described in Chapter 3 Section 5.
14 Undo the bolts and slide rearwards the exhaust pipe connecting piece between the front and rear sections of the exhaust system. Also undo the retaining bolts and remove the exhaust front mounting bracket **(see illustration)**.
15 Disconnect the wiring plug from the engine oil level/temperature sensor on the sump **(see illustration)** ; this is to prevent it getting damaged when the engine moves forward. Where fitted remove the ride height sensor (HID/Zenon headlight models only).
16 With reference to Chapter 8 Section 2, unscrew and remove the bolts securing the driveshafts to the transmission output flanges. Tie the right-hand driveshaft to one side, and then tie the left-hand driveshaft to the suspension strut, so that the shaft is as high as possible **(see illustration)**. Alternatively, completely remove the driveshaft.
17 Support the engine with a hoist or support bar located on the front wing inner channels. Depending on the engine, temporarily remove components as necessary to attach the hoist.

2.14 Undo the exhaust mounting retaining bolts

2.15 Disconnect the oil level/temperature sensor wiring connector

2.16 Fasten the driveshaft to one side

2.23a Hold the drive flange in position ...

2.23b ...whilst removing the centre bolt ...

2.23c ...then slide the drive flange from the transmission

18 Position a trolley jack underneath the transmission, and raise it to just take the weight of the unit.

19 Undo and remove the bolts securing the left-hand gearbox mounting. By controlling both the engine hoist/support bar and the trolley jack, lower the transmission slightly. To make removal easier undo the retaining bolts and remove the mounting bracket from the top of the transmission casing.

20 On 6-speed (02E) transmissions, undo the retaining bolt and remove the small cover plate located above the right-hand driveshaft flange. On 7-speed transmissions remove the heat shield from above the driveshaft – where fitted.

21 Lower the engine/transmission until there is sufficient clearance between the upper edge of the transmission and the left-hand chassis member.

22 Unscrew and remove the lower bolts securing the transmission to the engine, noting the bolt locations, as they are of different sizes and lengths.

23 On models with driveshafts that have a bolted flange, hold the flange in position and undo the flange securing bolt, then the flange can be removed (see illustrations).

24 Check that all the fixings and attachments are clear of the transmission. Enlist the aid of an assistant to help in guiding and supporting the transmission during its removal.

25 The transmission is located on engine alignment dowels, and if stuck on them, it may be necessary to carefully tap and prise the transmission free of the dowels to allow separation. Once the transmission is disconnected from the location dowels, swivel the unit out and lower it out of the vehicle.

 Warning: Support the transmission to ensure that it remains steady on the jack head.

26 When the transmission is clear of the locating dowels and clutch components, lower the transmission to the ground and withdraw from under the car. Make sure that the transmission does not fall and lose any transmission oil. Also make sure that the clutch assembly comes away with the transmission, and stays inside the bell-housing.

Refitting

27 Refitting the transmission is essentially a reversal of the removal procedure, but note the following points:

a) On 7-speed (0AM) transmissions, renew the needle bearing in the end of the crankshaft (see Chapter 2A Section 14).

b) When reconnecting the transmission to the engine, ensure that the location dowels are in position, and that the transmission is correctly aligned with them before pushing it fully into engagement with the engine.

c) Tighten all retaining bolts to their specified torque wrench settings.

d) Be sure to guide the selector cable into the support bracket as the transmission is refitted – renew the retaining clips.

e) Adjust the selector cable, as described in Section 4.

f) Refer to Chapter 8 Section 2, and then tighten the driveshaft bolts to the specified torque.

g) On completion, check the coolant level.

h) If a new transmission unit has been fitted, it may be necessary to have the transmission ECM 'matched' to the engine management ECM electronically, to ensure correct operation – seek the advice of your VW dealer or suitably equipped specialist.

i) Refill the transmission with the correct grade and quantity of oil, as described in Section 6.

3 Transmission overhaul – general information

1 In the event of a fault occurring, it will be necessary to establish whether the fault is electrical, mechanical or hydraulic in nature, before repair work can be contemplated. Diagnosis requires detailed knowledge of the transmission's operation and construction, as well as access to specialised test equipment, and so is deemed to be beyond the scope of this manual. It is therefore essential that problems with the automatic transmission be referred to a VW dealer or specialist for assessment.

2 Although it is possible to remove the clutch assembly from out of the bell housing, it is not possible to fit a new assembly without the use of special tools. When a new clutch is purchased, there are a number of shims and retaining clips of different thickness in the kit, therefore without the correct tools, it is not possible to correctly install the assembly back in place.

3 Note that a faulty transmission should not be removed before the vehicle has been assessed by a dealer or specialist, as fault diagnosis is best carried out with the transmission still in the vehicle.

4 Selector lever housing and cable – removal, refitting and adjustment

Note: *The selector lever housing and cable should not be separated, remove the housing and cable as a complete unit.*

Removal

1 Move the selector lever to the P position, and remove the battery and battery tray as described in Chapter 5A Section 3.

2 Remove the air cleaner housing as described in Chapter 4A Section 3.

3 Working inside the vehicle, remove the centre console and gear selector knob, as described in Chapter 11 Section 25.

4 Disconnect the wiring connector from the front of the gear selector housing (see illustration).

4.4 Disconnect the wiring connector (7-speed shown)

4.6 Selector cable clip and outer cable circlip

4.7 Prise the inner cable from the ball joint

4.8 Release the outer cable securing clip

6-speed (02E) transmission

5 Working inside the engine compartment, slacken the adjustment screw on the cable end fitting at the transmission end **(see illustration 4.16)**.

6 Prise out the clips securing the cable to the lever on the transmission, and the outer cable to the support bracket **(see illustration)**. Withdraw the cable from the support bracket and discard the clips – new ones must be fitted.

7-speed (0AM) transmission

7 Working inside the engine compartment, use a pair of long-nose pliers to release the cable end fitting from the ball head on the selector lever **(see illustration)**.

8 Prise out the clip securing the outer cable and withdraw the cable from the support bracket on the transmission **(see illustration)**. Discard the retaining clip – as a new one must be fitted.

All transmissions

9 Raise the front of the vehicle and support it securely on axle stands (see *Jacking and vehicle support*).

10 Remove the centre tunnel front heat shield from the underside of the vehicle to gain access to the base of the selector lever housing and cable. It may be necessary to separate the exhaust downpipe from the intermediate pipe with reference to Chapter 4B Section 10.

11 Working inside the vehicle, undo the retaining nuts **(see illustration)**, then remove the bracket and lower the gear selector housing downwards. Withdraw it complete with selector cable out from under the vehicle. It may be useful having the aid of an assistant at this point, to be under the vehicle when lowering the selector housing.

Refitting

12 Refitting is the reversal of the removal procedure, noting the following points:
a) *DO NOT grease the cable end fittings.*
b) *Ensure that the cable is correctly routed and secured, as noted on removal.*
c) *Take care not to bend or kink the cable.*
d) *Carry out the cable adjustment procedure*

described below before reconnecting the cable at the transmission end.
e) *When refitting the outer cable to the support bracket, use new clips.*

Adjustment

13 Inside the car, move the selector lever to the P position.

14 If not already done, disconnect the cable from the selector lever on the transmission.

15 Move the selector lever inside the vehicle from 'P' to 'S' and back, repeatedly, to check that everything moves easily. VW recommend that you do not grease the cable.

16 Reconnect the cable to the lever at the transmission, and then slacken the cable adjusting bolt **(see illustrations)**.

17 Check that both the selector lever inside

the car and the lever on the transmission are in their P positions. Gently rock the levers backwards and forwards to make sure the cable is settled. Do not move either lever out of the P position.

18 The transmission lever is in the P position when:
a) *6-speed 02E transmissions – it's pushed all the way back towards the bulkhead*
b) *7-speed 0AM transmissions – it's pushed back towards the selector cable mounting bracket* **(see illustration)**.

19 When in position, tighten the cable adjusting bolt.

20 Verify the operation of the selector lever by shifting through all gear positions and checking that every gear can be selected smoothly and without delay.

4.11 Gearchange housing mounting nuts

4.16a Secure the outer cable in the bracket ...

4.16b ...and slacken the cable adjustment screw

4.18 Push the lever in the direction show

5 Emergency release of selector lever

1 If the vehicles battery is disconnected or discharged, it is possible to release the selector lever from its locked position. First, ensure the handbrake is fully applied.

2 Carefully prise up the selector lever gaiter surround trim from the console and move it to one side (see illustration).

3 On early models (un to 2010) push the wedge across and into position. On later models (2011 on) press the yellow plastic wedge downwards (see illustration). It should now be possible to move the selector lever to the desired position.

6 Transmission oil renewal

7-speed dual clutch 0AM transmission

Note: *The transmission does not have an oil level checking procedure. If there has been an oil leak from the transmission, after the leak has been rectified, renew the transmission oil as described in the following paragraphs.*

1 Take the vehicle on a short journey to warm the transmission oil, and then park the car on a level surface. For improved access to the drain plug, apply the handbrake, then jack up the front of the vehicle and support it on axle stands (see *Jacking and vehicle support*), but note that the rear of the vehicle should also be raised to ensure all oil is drained.

2 Undo the retaining screws and remove the engine undertray. Wipe clean the area around the transmission drain plug, which is situated on the lower rear of the transmission (see illustration).

3 Place a container under the transmission casing, then unscrew the drain plug from the base of the differential housing, and allow the oil to drain.

4 Remove the battery and battery tray as described in Chapter 5A Section 3.

5 Remove the air filter housing as described in Chapter 4A Section 3.

5.2 Prise up the selector lever gaiter surround trim

5.3 Press down the yellow plastic peg

6 When the oil has finished draining, clean the surrounding area, refit the drain plug and tighten it to the specified torque.

7 Unclip the breather cap from the selector cover plate on the top of the transmission casing (see illustration).

8 Using a length of hose, and funnel, add 1.7 litres of new oil to the transmission. Only use VW recommended oil, for 7-speed dual clutch 0AM transmission.

9 Refit the breather cap, making sure that it is secure. Renew if damaged.

10 The remainder of refitting is a reversal of removal.

6-speed dual clutch 02E transmission

Note: *An accurate fluid level check can only be made with the transmission fluid at a temperature of between 35°C and 45°C, and if it is not possible to ascertain this temperature, it is strongly recommended that the check be made by a VW dealer who will have the instrumentation to check the temperature and to check the transmission electronics for fault codes. Over-filling or under-filling adversely affects the function of the transmission.*

11 Take the vehicle on a short journey to warm the transmission oil. And then park the vehicle on level ground and engage P with the selector lever. Raise the front and rear of the vehicle and support it on axle stands (see *Jacking and vehicle support*), ensuring the vehicle is kept level. Undo the retaining screws and remove the engine undertray to gain access to the base of the transmission unit.

12 Start the engine and run it at idle speed until the transmission fluid temperature reaches 35°C.

13 Unscrew the fluid level plug from the bottom of the transmission sump (see illustration).

14 If fluid continually drips from the level tube as the fluid temperature increases, the fluid level is correct and does not need to be topped-up. Note that there will be some fluid already present in the level tube, and it will be necessary to observe when this amount has drained before making the level check. Make sure that the check is made before the fluid temperature reaches 45°C.

15 If no fluid drips from the level tube, even when the fluid temperature has reached 45°C, it will be necessary to add fluid. VW technicians use an adapter which screws into the bottom of the transmission sump, however, a tube inserted up through the drain plug (into the space above the fluid); will allow fluid to be added. Ideally, the fluid should be allowed to cool before adding the fluid.

16 Check the condition of the seal on the level plug and renew it if necessary by cutting off the old seal and fitting a new one. Refit the plug and tighten to the specified torque.

17 Refit the engine undertray, tighten the retaining screws securely, and lower the vehicle to the ground.

18 Frequent need for topping-up indicates that there is a leak, which should be corrected as soon as possible.

6.2 Transmission oil drain plug – 0AM transmissions

6.7 Breather cap on selector cover – 0AM transmissions

H46291

6.13 Transmission fluid level check - 02E transmissions

1 Level plug   2 Level tube

Chapter 8
Driveshafts

Contents

Degrees of difficulty

Easy, suitable for novice with little experience	Fairly easy, suitable for beginner with some experience	Fairly difficult, suitable for competent DIY mechanic	Difficult, suitable for experienced DIY mechanic	Very difficult, suitable for expert DIY or professional

Specifications

General

Driveshaft type . . . . Steel shafts with outer constant velocity joints and inner tripod or constant velocity joints (according to type).

Type code differences:
VL 100 . . . . CV joints each end, inner joint diameter of 100 mm bolted to transmission drive flanges on each side
VL 107 . . . . CV joints each end, inner joint diameter 107 mm bolted to transmission drive flanges on each side
AAR 3300i . . . . CV outer joint, tripod inner joint body bolted to transmission drive flanges on each side

Lubrication

Overhaul and repair . . . . Use only special grease supplied in sachets with gaiter/overhaul kits
Joint grease type . . . . Refer to VW dealer
Joint grease quantity:
Outer joint . . . . 80 g
Inner joint . . . . 130 g

Torque wrench settings

	Nm	lbf ft
Driveshaft-to-transmission flange bolts:		
Stage 1	10	7
Stage 2:		
M8 x 48 bolts* – (VL100 type joint)	40	30
M10 x 52 bolts* – (VL107 type joint)	70	52
M10 x 23 bolts – (AAR 3300i type joint)	70	52
Hub bolt: *		
Hex head bolt		
Stage 1	200	148
Stage 2	Angle-tighten a further 180°	
12 point bolt with NO ribbing under head		
Stage 1	200	148
Stage 2	Angle-tighten a further 180°	
12 point bolt with ribbing under head		
Stage 1	70	52
Stage 2	Angle-tighten a further 90°	
Intermediate driveshaft bearing bracket	20	15
Lower arm-to-balljoint nuts: *		
Cast steel lower arm	60	44
Forged aluminium lower arm	100	74
Lower rear mounting-to-transmission bolts: *		
Stage 1	50	37
Stage 2	Angle-tighten a further 90°	
Wheel bolts	120	89

*Use new bolts/nuts

1 General Information

1 Drive is transmitted from the differential to the front wheels by means of two steel driveshafts of either solid or hollow construction (depending on model, and which side of the vehicle). Both driveshafts are splined at their outer ends, to accept the wheel hubs, and are secured to the hub by a large bolt. The inner end of each driveshaft is either bolted to a transmission drive flange or splined directly onto the differential splined shaft.

2 The outer ends of each driveshaft are fitted with ball-bearing type constant velocity (CV) joints, to ensure the smooth and efficient transmission of drive at all the angles possible, as the roadwheels move up-and-down with the suspension, and as they turn from side to side under steering.

3 The inner ends of each driveshaft (except for the AAR 3300i type joints) are fitted with ball and cage type constant velocity (CV) joint. The AAR 3300i driveshaft has a triple roller type (tripod) joint fitted to the inner end of the driveshaft.

4 Hytrel (thermoplastic elastomer) gaiters are fitted over the CV joints with steel clips. These gaiters combine the flexibility of rubber with the strength and durability of thermoplastics. The gaiters contain the grease that lubricates the joints, and also protect the joints from the entry of dirt and debris.

2 Driveshafts – removal and refitting

Note: *A new hub bolt will be required on refitting. There are three different types of bolts fitted – two types of 12 point spline headed bolt and a standard hex bolt. One of the 12 point spline bolts has ribs* **(see illustration)** *under the face of the bolt head and one is smooth. The torque setting is different for each type of bolt (see Section), so it is important to make sure you check which is fitted.*

Removal

1 Remove the wheel trim/centre cap (as applicable) then apply the handbrake, and partially unscrew the relevant hub bolt with the vehicle resting on its wheels, by a maximum of 90° – note that the bolt is very tight, and a suitable extension bar will probably be required to aid unscrewing. Also slacken the road wheel securing bolts by half a turn. Note: Do not loosen the bolt more than 90° with the vehicle standing on the ground, as the wheel bearings may be damaged.

2 Apply the handbrake, then jack up the front of the vehicle and support it on axle stands (see *Jacking and vehicle support*). Remove the appropriate front roadwheel.

3 Remove the retaining screws and/or clips, and remove the undershields from beneath the engine/transmission unit to gain access to the driveshafts. Where necessary, also unbolt the heat shield from the transmission housing to improve access to the driveshaft inner joint **(see illustration)**.

4 Unscrew and remove the hub bolt **(see illustration)**. Note: Discard the bolt and obtain a new one, there are three types of bolt fitted, see note at the beginning of this Section.

5 Unscrew the three nuts securing the front suspension lower arm balljoint to the lower arm **(see illustration)**. Discard the nuts, as new ones must be used on refitting.

6 Lever the lower arm downwards to release it from the balljoint studs, then pull the hub carrier outwards, and at the same time withdraw the driveshaft outer constant velocity joint from the hub **(see illustration)**. If the joint splines are a tight fit in the hub, tap the joint out of the hub using a soft-faced mallet and drift. If this fails to free the driveshaft from the hub, the joint will have to be pressed out using a suitable tool bolted to the hub.

7 On some models, in order to gain the necessary clearance required to withdraw the left-hand driveshaft, it may be necessary to unbolt the rear engine transmission mounting from the subframe **(see illustration)**, and move the engine slightly.

8 Proceed as follows according to driveshaft type.

Caution: Support the driveshaft by suspending it with wire or string – do not allow it to hang under its own weight, or the joint may be damaged.

2.0 Flange of bolt is ribbed

2.3 Remove the heat shield

2.4 Remove the driveshaft/hub bolt

2.5 Undo the lower ball joint retaining nuts

2.6 Slide the driveshaft out from the hub assembly

2.7 Unbolt the lower rear mounting bracket

2.9a Make alignment marks...

2.9b ...and remove the drive flange bolts and plates

Inner joint with drive flange – VL100 and VL107

9 Mark the inner joint in relation to the drive flange for refitting. Using a multi-splined tool, unscrew and remove the six bolts securing the inner driveshaft joint to the transmission flange, and recover the retaining plates from underneath the bolts **(see illustrations)**.

Inner joint splined to differential drive shaft – VL107

10 Position a container beneath the transmission to catch spilt oil, and then pull out the driveshaft. The internal driveshaft circlip may be tight in the transmission side gear, in which case careful use of a lever against the transmission casing will be required. Lever against a block of wood to prevent damage to the casing, and take care not to damage the oil seal as the driveshaft is being removed. Note: Pull only on the inner joint body, not the driveshaft itself; otherwise the gaiter may be damaged.

Inner joint triple roller (tripod) located in joint body – AAR 3300i

11 Mark the inner joint body and driveshaft in relation to each other, as the tripod joint will need to be refitted in the joint body in the same position. Loosen the larger retaining clip, ease off the rubber gaiter, and pull the triple roller out of the joint body.

All types

12 Manoeuvre the driveshaft out from underneath the vehicle and (where fitted) recover the gasket from the end of the inner constant velocity joint. Note: Discard the gasket and obtain a new one.
Caution: Do not allow the vehicle to rest on its wheels with one or both driveshaft(s) removed, as damage to the wheel bearings may result.
13 If moving the vehicle is unavoidable, temporarily insert the outer end of the driveshaft(s) in the hub(s), and tighten the driveshaft retaining bolt(s); in this case, the

inner end(s) of the driveshaft(s) must be supported, for example by suspending with string from the vehicle underbody.

Refitting

14 Where applicable, check the condition of the circlip on the inner end of the driveshaft, and if necessary, renew it.
15 As applicable, clean the splines on each end of the driveshaft and in the hub and apply a little oil, and where applicable wipe clean the oil seal in the transmission casing. Check the oil seal and if necessary renew it as described in Chapter 7A or. Smear a little oil on the lips of the oil seal before fitting the driveshaft.

Inner joint with bolted drive flange – VL100 and VL107

16 Ensure that the transmission flange and inner joint mating surfaces are clean and dry. Where necessary, fit a new gasket to the joint by peeling off its backing foil and sticking it in position **(see illustration)**.
17 Manoeuvre the driveshaft into position, aligning the previously made marks **(see illustration)**, and then align the inner joint holes with those on the transmission flange. Refit the new retaining bolts and locking plates, and then tighten the retaining bolts to the specified torque.

2.16 Locate a new gasket on the inner joint

Inner joint splined to differential drive shaft – VL107

18 Locate the inner end of the driveshaft into the transmission – turn the driveshaft as necessary to engage the splines. Press in the driveshaft until the internal circlip engages the groove. Check that the circlip is engaged by attempting to pull out the driveshaft with only moderate force.

Inner joint triple roller (tripod) located in joint body – AAR 3300i

19 Fill the inner joint with the specified quantity of grease, and then locate the driveshaft tripod into the joint body, aligning the previously made marks. Ease the gaiter onto the joint body, and secure the gaiter with a new retaining clip.

All types

20 With the lower arm levered downwards, engage the outer joint with the hub. Fit the new hub bolt and use it to draw the joint fully into position.
21 Align the balljoint studs with the holes in the lower arm, then release the arm and fit the three new nuts. Tighten the nuts to the specified torque.
22 Where applicable, refit the lower rear mounting-to-transmission bolts, and then

2.17 Align the markings made on removal when refitting

1 Hub bolt
2 Outer joint gaiter
3 Gaiter securing clip
4 Driveshaft
5 Inner joint
6 Flange bolts
7 Bolt retaining plate
8 Thrust washer
9 Circlip
10 Washer
11 Gasket
12 Inner joint gaiter
13 Outer joint

3.1a Driveshaft components – models with VL100 CV joint

1 Hub bolt
2 Outer joint
3 Gaiter securing clip
4 Outer joint gaiter
5 Gaiter securing clip
6 Dished spring
7 Thrust washer
8 Circlip
9 Driveshaft
10 Gaiter securing clip
11 Dished washer
12 Inner joint gaiter
13 Gaiter securing clip
14 Bolt
15 Locking plate
16 Metal end cover
17 Inner joint
18 Gasket
19 Circlip
20 Inner cover
21 Intermediate shaft
    (right-hand side only)
22 Bolt
23 Bolt
24 Mounting bracket
25 Bearing support plate

6367 08-03-01B HAYNES

3.1b Driveshaft joint components – models with VL107 CV joint (bolt-on)

3.1c Driveshaft joint components – models with AAR3300i triple roller joints

1 Hub bolt
2 Outer joint
3 Gaiter securing clip
4 Outer joint gaiter
5 Gaiter securing clip
6 Dished spring washer
7 Thrust washer
8 Circlip
9 Driveshaft
10 Gaiter securing clip
11 Inner joint gaiter
12 Gaiter securing clip
13 Triple roller joint
14 Circlip
15 Bolt
16 Bolt
17 Intermediate shaft support
18 Bearing support plate
19 Inner joint (right-hand)
20 Inner joint (right-hand)
21 Bolt

tighten the new bolts to the specified torque.
23 Tighten the driveshaft bolt to the Stage 1 torque setting. **Note:** *The bolt must be tightened with the wheel clear of the ground.* There are three different types of bolts fitted, one is ribbed **(see illustration 2.0)** under the face of the bolt head and one is smooth. See note at the beginning of this Section.
24 Refit the roadwheel and lower the vehicle to the ground, then angle-tighten the driveshaft bolt through the Stage 2 angle (see Section).
25 Once the driveshaft bolt is correctly tightened, tighten the wheel bolts to the specified torque and refit the wheel trim/centre cap.

3 Driveshaft gaiters – renewal

1 Remove the driveshaft from the car, as described in Section 2. Continue as described under the relevant sub-heading. Driveshafts with a tripod type inner joint can be identified by the shape of the inner CV joint; the driveshaft retaining bolt holes are in extensions from the joint, giving it a six-pointed star-shaped exterior, in contrast to the smooth, circular shape

of the ball-and-cage joint **(see illustrations)**.

Outer CV joint gaiter – All types of driveshafts

2 Secure the driveshaft in a vice equipped with soft jaws, and release the two outer joint gaiter retaining clips **(see illustration)**. If necessary, the retaining clips can be cut to release them.
3 Slide the rubber gaiter down the shaft to expose the constant velocity joint, and scoop out excess grease **(see illustration)**.
4 Using a soft-faced mallet, tap the joint off the end of the driveshaft **(see illustration)**.

3.2 Release the outer joint gaiter clips…

3.3 …and slide the gaiter away from the joint

3.4 Use a mallet to drive the outer joint from the driveshaft

3.5 Removing the circlip, thrustwasher and dished washer

3.6 Removing the outer gaiter

3.11 Temporarily tape over the splines to protect the new gaiter

5 Remove the circlip from the driveshaft groove, and slide off the thrustwasher and dished washer, noting which way around it is fitted **(see illustration)**.

6 Slide the rubber gaiter off the driveshaft and discard it **(see illustration)**.

7 Thoroughly clean the constant velocity joint(s) using paraffin, or a suitable solvent, and dry thoroughly. Carry out a visual inspection as follows.

8 Move the inner splined driving member from side-to-side to expose each ball in turn at the top of its track. Examine the balls for cracks, flat spots or signs of surface pitting.

9 Inspect the ball tracks on the inner and outer members. If the tracks have widened, the balls will no longer be a tight fit. At the same time, check the ball cage windows for wear or cracking between the windows.

10 If on inspection any of the constant velocity joint components are found to be worn or damaged, it will be necessary to renew the complete joint assembly. If the joint is in satisfactory condition, obtain a new gaiter and retaining clips, a constant velocity joint circlip and the correct type of grease. Grease is often supplied with the joint repair kit – if not, use good-quality molybdenum disulphide grease.

11 Tape over the splines on the end of the driveshaft, to protect the new gaiter as it is slid into place **(see illustration)**.

12 Slide the new gaiter onto the end of the driveshaft, then remove the protective tape from the driveshaft splines.

13 Slide on the dished washer, making sure its convex side is innermost, followed by the thrustwasher.

14 Pack the joint with half the quantity of the specified type of grease. Work the grease well into the bearing tracks whilst twisting the joint, and fill the rubber gaiter with the remaining half **(see illustrations)**.

15 Fit a new circlip to the driveshaft, then tap the joint onto the driveshaft until the circlip engages in its groove **(see illustrations)**. Make sure that the joint is securely retained by the circlip.

16 Ease the gaiter over the joint, and ensure that the gaiter lips are correctly located on both the driveshaft and constant velocity joint. Lift the outer sealing lip of the gaiter to equalise air pressure within the gaiter **(see illustration)**.

17 Fit the large metal retaining clip to the gaiter. Pull the clip as tight as possible, and

3.14a Pack half of the grease in the joint…

3.14b …and the remaining half in the gaiter

3.15a Fit a new circlip…

3.15b …then refit the outer joint

3.16 Seat the gaiter on the outer joint and driveshaft, then lift its inner lip to equalise the air pressure

3.17a Fit the large metal retaining clip...

3.17b ...and use a suitable tool to tighten it

3.19 Release the gaiter small securing clip...

3.20 ...drive the metal ring from the joint outer member

3.22 Remove the circlip...

3.23a ...followed by the joint...

locate the hooks on the clip in their slots. Remove any slack in the gaiter retaining clip by carefully compressing the raised section of the clip. In the absence of the special tool, a pair of side-cutters may be used, taking care not to cut the clip **(see illustrations)**. Secure the small retaining clip using the same procedure.

18 Check the constant velocity joint moves freely in all directions, then refit the driveshaft to the vehicle, as described in Section 2.

Inner gaiter with bolted drive flange – VL100 and VL107

19 Secure the driveshaft in a vice equipped with soft jaws, then release the gaiter small securing clip, securing the gaiter to the driveshaft **(see illustration)**.

20 Using a hammer and a small drift, carefully drive the gaiter metal ring from the joint outer member **(see illustration)**.

21 Slide the gaiter down the driveshaft to

3.23b ...dished washer...

3.24 ...and gaiter

expose the constant velocity joint, and scoop out excess grease.

22 Remove the circlip from the end of the driveshaft using circlip pliers **(see illustration)**.

23 Press or drive the driveshaft from the joint, taking great care not to damage the joint. Recover

the dished washer fitted between the constant velocity joint and the gaiter **(see illustrations)**.

24 Slide the gaiter from the end of the driveshaft **(see illustration)**.

25 Proceed as described previously in paragraphs 7 to 12 **(see illustrations)**.

3.25a Tilt the splined hub and cage to remove the ball-bearings...

3.25b ...then separate the hub from the cage

3.25c Inner CV joint gaiter repair kit

3.29 Installation position of inner joint gaiter on left-hand driveshaft

A = 17.0 mm

3.30a Pack the inner joint with half of the grease…

3.30b …then pack the gaiter with the remaining half

26 Slide the dished washer onto the driveshaft, making sure its convex side is innermost.

27 Fit the joint to the end of the driveshaft, noting that the chamfered edge of the internal splines on the joint should face towards the driveshaft. Drive or press the joint into position until it contacts the shoulder on the driveshaft.

28 Fit a new circlip to retain the joint on the end of the driveshaft.

29 If the left-hand driveshaft is being worked on, mark the final installation position of the gaiter outboard end on the driveshaft using tape or paint – do not scratch the surface of the driveshaft (see illustration).

30 Pack the joint with the half the recommended quantity of grease (see Specifications), and then pack the gaiter with the remaining half (see illustrations).

31 Slide the gaiter up the driveshaft, and press or drive the gaiter metal ring onto the joint outer member. To ensure the bolt holes are correctly positioned, temporarily fit a couple of flange bolts (see illustrations).

32 If the left-hand driveshaft is being worked on, slide the outboard end of the gaiter into position using the mark made previously (see paragraph 29), then secure the outer gaiter securing clip in position as described in paragraph 17.

33 If the right-hand driveshaft is being worked on, slide the outboard end of the gaiter into position on the driveshaft, then secure the outer gaiter securing clip in position as described in paragraph 17 (see illustration).

34 Check the driveshaft joint moves freely in all directions, then refit the driveshaft to the vehicle, as described in Section 2.

Inner gaiter with splined joint to transmission – VL107

35 Secure the driveshaft in a vice equipped with soft jaws, and release the two inner joint gaiter retaining clips. If necessary, the retaining clips can be cut to release them.

36 Slide the rubber gaiter down the shaft to expose the constant velocity joint, and scoop out excess grease.

37 Using a soft-faced mallet, tap the joint off the end of the driveshaft.

38 Remove the circlip from the end of the driveshaft groove, and then slide the rubber gaiter off the driveshaft and discard it.

39 Proceed as described previously in paragraphs 7 to 12.

40 Pack the joint with half the quantity of specified type of grease. Work the grease well into the bearing tracks whilst twisting the joint, and fill the rubber gaiter with the remaining half.

41 Fit a new circlip to the driveshaft, then tap the joint onto the driveshaft until the circlip engages in its groove. Make sure that the joint is securely retained by the circlip.

42 Ease the gaiter over the joint, and ensure that the gaiter lips are correctly located on both the driveshaft and constant velocity joint. Lift the outer sealing lip of the gaiter to equalise air pressure within the gaiter.

43 Fit the large metal retaining clip to the gaiter, as described in paragraph 17. Secure the small retaining clip using the same procedure.

44 Check the constant velocity joint moves freely in all directions, then refit the driveshaft to the vehicle, as described in Section 2.

Inner gaiter with triple roller (tripod) joint – AAR 3300i

45 Secure the driveshaft in a vice equipped with soft jaws, and clean out the old grease from around the triple roller joint and inside the gaiter.

46 Remove the circlip from the end of the driveshaft.

47 Press or drive the driveshaft from the tripod, taking great care not to damage the surfaces of the roller locating arms.

48 Slide the outer member and the rubber gaiter from the end of the driveshaft.

49 Thoroughly clean the joint components using paraffin, or a suitable solvent, and dry thoroughly. Carry out a visual inspection as follows.

50 Inspect the tripod rollers and the joint outer member for signs of wear, pitting or scuffing on their mating surfaces. Check that

3.31a Temporarily fit one of the flange bolts to ensure the bolt holes are correctly aligned…

3.31b …then drive the metal ring onto the joint outer member

3.33 Installation position of inner joint gaiter on right-hand driveshaft

A Vent chamber in gaiter   B Vent hole

the joint rollers rotate smoothly, with no traces of roughness.

51 If the rollers or outer member shown signs of wear or damage, it will be necessary to renew the complete driveshaft, since the joint is not available separately. If the joint is in satisfactory condition, obtain a repair kit, consisting of a new gaiter, retaining clips, circlip, and the correct type and quantity of grease.

52 Tape over the splines on the end of the driveshaft, to protect the new gaiter as it is slid into place, and then slide the new gaiter over the end of the driveshaft and secure the smaller end in place with a new retaining clip. Remove the protective tape from the driveshaft splines.

53 Press or drive the tripod onto the end of the driveshaft until it contacts the stop, ensuring that the marks made on the end of the driveshaft and the tripod

before dismantling are aligned. Note that the chamfered edge of the internal splines on the tripod should face towards the driveshaft.

54 Fit the new circlip to retain the tripod on the end of the driveshaft.

55 Check the triple roller joint moves freely, then refit the driveshaft to the vehicle, as described in Section 2.

4 Driveshaft overhaul – general information

1 If any of the checks described in Chapter 1 Section 18 reveal wear in any driveshaft joint, first remove the roadwheel trim or centre cap (as applicable) and check that the hub bolt is tight. If the bolt is loose, obtain a new one,

and tighten it to the specified torque (see Section 2). If the bolt is tight, refit the centre cap/trim, and repeat the check on the other hub bolt.

2 Road test the vehicle, and listen for a metallic clicking from the front of the vehicle as the vehicle is driven slowly in a circle on full-lock. If a clicking noise is heard, this indicates wear in the outer constant velocity joint; this means that the joint must be renewed.

3 If vibration consistent with roadspeed is felt through the car when accelerating, there is a possibility of wear in the inner constant velocity joints.

4 To check the joints for wear, remove the driveshafts, then dismantle them as described in Section 3. If any wear or free play is found, the affected joint must be renewed. Refer to a VW dealer for information on the availability of driveshaft components.

Notes

Chapter 9
Braking system

Contents

Degrees of difficulty

Easy, suitable for novice with little experience	**Fairly easy,** suitable for beginner with some experience	**Fairly difficult,** suitable for competent DIY mechanic	**Difficult,** suitable for experienced DIY mechanic	**Very difficult,** suitable for expert DIY or professional 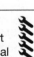

Specifications

Front brakes

Caliper type	FN3 or FS III
Disc diameter:	
FSIII	280 mm
FN3:	
15" wheels	288 mm
Disc thickness.	
New:	
FSIII	22.0 mm
FN3	25.0 mm
Minimum permissible thickness:	
FSIII	19.0 mm
FN3	22.0 mm
Maximum disc run-out	0.1 mm
Brake pad lining thickness (all models):	
New	14.0 mm
Minimum.	2.0 mm

Rear disc brakes

Caliper type:
CII 41	15" wheels
CI 38	15" wheels
Bosch (2011 on)	1ZF/1ZE/1ZA

Disc diameter:
CII 41	256 mm
CI 38	255 mm
Bosch	272 mm

Disc thickness:

New:
CII 41	12.0 mm
CI 38	10.0 mm
Bosch	10.0 mm

Minimum thickness:
CII 41	8.0 mm
CI 38	8.0 mm
Bosch	8.0 mm

Maximum disc run-out	0.1 mm

Brake pad lining thickness:

New
CII 41	11.0 mm
CI 38	11.0 mm
Bosch	11.0 mm
Minimum (friction material)	2.0 mm

Torque wrench settings

	Nm	lbf ft
ABS control unit retaining bolts	8	6
ABS control unit mounting bracket nuts	20	15
ABS wheel sensor retaining bolts	8	6
Brake pedal pivot shaft nut*	25	18
Brake light switch	5	4
Brake pedal mounting bracket*	25	18
Brake disc shield bolts	12	9
Front brake caliper:		
Guide pins	30	22
Mounting bracket bolts (FN3 calipers)	190	141
Hydraulic brake line to caliper banjo bolt	35	26
Hydraulic brake line union nuts	14	10
Master cylinder mounting nuts*	25	18
Rear brake caliper:		
Guide pin bolts*	35	26
Mounting bracket bolts (multi-point socket head): *		
Stage 1	90	66
Stage 2	Angle-tighten a further 90°	
Roadwheel bolts	120	89
Servo unit mechanical vacuum pump	10	8
Servo unit mounting bolts*	25	18

*Use new fasteners

1 General information and precautions

General information

1 The braking system is of servo-assisted, diagonal dual-circuit hydraulic type. The arrangement of the hydraulic system is such that each circuit operates one front and one rear brake from a tandem master cylinder. Under normal circumstances, both circuits operate in unison, but, if there is hydraulic failure in one circuit, full braking force will still be available at two wheels. On petrol engines, vacuum for the servo unit is supplied from the inlet manifold, however, on diesel engines a combined fuel lift pump and vacuum pump is driven off the end of the camshaft.

2 All models covered by this manual are equipped with disc brakes at the front and rear. ABS is fitted as standard to all models (refer to Section 19 for further information on ABS operation).

3 The front disc brakes are actuated by single-piston sliding type calipers, which ensure that equal pressure is applied to each disc pad.

4 The rear brakes are also actuated by single-piston sliding calipers, which incorporate independent mechanical handbrake mechanisms as well.

Precautions

When servicing any part of the system, work carefully and methodically; also observe scrupulous cleanliness when overhauling any part of the hydraulic system. Always renew components in axle sets (where applicable) if in doubt about their condition, and use only genuine VW parts, or at least those of known good quality. Note the warnings given in Safety First! and at relevant points in this Chapter concerning the dangers of asbestos dust and hydraulic fluid.

2 Hydraulic system – bleeding

Warning: Hydraulic fluid is poisonous; wash off immediately and thoroughly in the case of skin contact, and seek immediate medical advice if any fluid is swallowed or gets into the eyes. Certain types of hydraulic fluid are flammable, and may ignite when allowed into contact with hot components; when servicing any hydraulic system, it is safest to assume that the fluid is flammable, and to take precautions against the risk of fire as though it is petrol that is being handled. Hydraulic fluid is also an effective paint stripper, and will attack plastics; if any is spilt, it should be washed off immediately, using copious quantities of fresh water. Finally, it is hygroscopic (it absorbs moisture from the air) – old fluid may be contaminated and unfit for further use. When topping-up or renewing the fluid, always use the recommended type, and ensure that it comes from a freshly opened sealed container.

Note: *VW specify that at least 0.25 litre of brake fluid should be expelled from each caliper.*

General

1 The correct operation of any hydraulic system is only possible after removing all air from the components and circuit; this is achieved by bleeding the system. Since the clutch hydraulic system also uses fluid from the brake system reservoir, it should also be bled at the same time by referring to Chapter 6, Section 2.

2 During the bleeding procedure, add only clean, unused hydraulic fluid of the recommended type; never re-use fluid that has already been bled from the system. Ensure that sufficient fluid is available before starting work.

3 If there is any possibility of incorrect fluid being already in the system, the brake components and circuit must be flushed completely with uncontaminated, correct fluid, and new seals should be fitted to the various components.

4 If hydraulic fluid has been lost from the system, or air has entered because of a leak, ensure that the fault is cured before continuing further.

5 Park the vehicle on level ground, then chock the wheels and release the handbrake.

6 Check that all pipes and hoses are secure, unions tight and bleed screws closed. Clean any dirt from around the bleed screws.

7 Unscrew the master cylinder reservoir cap, and top the reservoir up to the MAX level line; refit the cap loosely, and remember to maintain the fluid level at least above the MIN level line throughout the procedure, or there is a risk of further air entering the system.

8 There is a number of one-man, do-it-yourself brake bleeding kits currently available from motor accessory shops. It is recommended that one of these kits is used whenever possible, as they greatly simplify the bleeding operation, and reduce the risk of expelled air and fluid being drawn back into the system. If such a kit is not available, the basic (two-man) method must be used, which is described in detail below.

9 If a kit is to be used, prepare the vehicle as described previously, and follow the kit manufacturer's instructions, as the procedure may vary slightly according to the type being used; generally, they are as outlined below in the relevant sub-section.

10 Whichever method is used, the same sequence must be followed (paragraph 12) to ensure the removal of all air from the system.

Bleeding sequence

11 If the system has been only partially disconnected, and suitable precautions were taken to minimise fluid loss, it should be necessary only to bleed that part of the system.

12 If the complete system is to be bled, then it should be done working in the following sequence:
a) *Left-hand front brake.*
b) *Right-hand front brake.*
c) *Left-hand rear brake.*
d) *Right-hand rear brake.*

13 If the system is completely empty of fluid, repeat the sequence up to five times, or until the brake pedal feels firm and has an acceptable amount of travel.

Bleeding

Basic (two-man) method

14 Collect together a clean glass jar of reasonable size, a suitable length of plastic or rubber tubing which is a tight fit over the bleed screw, and a ring spanner to fit the screw. The help of an assistant will also be required.

15 Remove the dust cap from the first screw in the sequence **(see illustration)**. Fit the spanner and tube to the screw, place the other end of the tube in the jar, and pour in sufficient fluid to cover the end of the tube.

16 Ensure that the master cylinder reservoir fluid level is maintained at least above the MIN level line throughout the procedure.

17 Have the assistant fully depress the brake pedal several times to build-up pressure, and then maintain it on the final downstroke.

18 While pedal pressure is maintained, unscrew the bleed screw (approximately one turn) and allow the compressed fluid and air to flow into the jar. The assistant should maintain pedal pressure, following it down to the floor if necessary, and should not release it until instructed to do so. When the flow stops, tighten the bleed screw again, have the assistant release the pedal slowly, and recheck the reservoir fluid level.

19 Repeat the steps given in paragraphs 16 and 17 until the fluid emerging from the bleed screw is free from air bubbles. If the master cylinder has been drained and refilled, and air is being bled from the first screw in the sequence, allow approximately five seconds between cycles for the master cylinder passages to refill.

20 When no more air bubbles appear, tighten the bleed screw securely, remove the tube and spanner, and refit the dust cap. Do not overtighten the bleed screw.

21 Repeat the procedure on the remaining screws in the sequence, until all air is removed from the system and the brake pedal feels firm again.

Using a one-way valve kit

22 As their name implies, these kits consist of a length of tubing with a one-way valve fitted, to prevent expelled air and fluid being drawn back into the system; some kits include a translucent container, which can be positioned so that the air bubbles can be more easily seen flowing from the end of the tube.

23 The kit is connected to the bleed screw, which is then opened. The user returns to the driver's seat, depresses the brake pedal with a smooth, steady stroke, and slowly releases it; this is repeated until the expelled fluid is clear of air bubbles **(see illustration)**.

24 Note that these kits simplify work so much that it is easy to forget the master cylinder reservoir fluid level; ensure that this is maintained at least above the MIN level line at all times.

Using a pressure-bleeding kit

25 These kits are usually operated by the

2.15 Remove the dust cap from the first bleed screw in the sequence

2.23 Bleeding a brake using a one-way valve kit

3.3 Using a flare nut spanner

reservoir of pressurised air contained in the spare tyre. However, note that it will be probably necessary to reduce the pressure to less than 1.0 bar (14.5 psi); refer to the instructions supplied with the kit.

26 By connecting a pressurised, fluid-filled container to the master cylinder reservoir, bleeding can be carried out simply by opening each screw in turn (in the specified sequence), and allowing the fluid to flow out until no more air bubbles can be seen in the expelled fluid.

27 This method has the advantage that the large reservoir of fluid provides an additional safeguard against air being drawn into the system during bleeding.

28 Pressure-bleeding is particularly effective when bleeding 'difficult' systems, or when bleeding the complete system at the time of routine fluid renewal.

All methods

29 When bleeding is complete, and firm pedal feel is restored, wash off any spilt fluid, tighten the bleed screws securely, and refit their dust caps.

30 Check the hydraulic fluid level in the master cylinder reservoir, and top-up if necessary (see *Weekly checks*).

31 Discard any hydraulic fluid that has been bled from the system; it will not be fit for re-use.

32 Check the feel of the brake pedal. If it feels at all spongy, air must still be present in the system, and further bleeding is required. Failure to bleed satisfactorily after a reasonable repetition of the bleeding procedure may be due to worn master cylinder seals.

3.6a Brake hose retaining clip

3 Hydraulic pipes and hoses – renewal

Note: *Refer to the note in Section 2 concerning the dangers of hydraulic fluid.*

1 If any pipe or hose is to be renewed, minimise fluid loss by first removing the master cylinder reservoir cap, then tightening it down onto a piece of polythene to obtain an airtight seal. Alternatively, flexible hoses can be sealed, if required, using a proprietary brake hose clamp; metal brake pipe unions can be plugged (if care is taken not to allow dirt into the system) or capped immediately they are disconnected. Place a wad of rag under any union that is to be disconnected, to catch any spilt fluid.

2 If a flexible hose is to be disconnected, where applicable unscrew the brake pipe union nut before removing the spring clip which secures the hose to its mounting bracket.

3 To unscrew the union nuts, it is preferable to obtain a brake pipe spanner (often called a 'flare nut' spanner) of the correct size **(see illustration)** these are available from most large motor accessory shops. Failing this, a close-fitting open-ended spanner will be required, though if the nuts are tight or corroded, their flats may be rounded-off if the spanner slips. In such a case, a self-locking wrench is often the only way to unscrew a stubborn union, but it follows that the pipe and the damaged nuts must be renewed on reassembly. Always clean a union and surrounding area before disconnecting it. If disconnecting a component with more than one union, make a careful note of the connections before disturbing any of them.

4 If a brake pipe is to be renewed, it can be obtained, cut to length and with the union nuts and end flares in place, from VW dealers. All that is then necessary is to bend it to shape, following the line of the original, before fitting it to the car. Alternatively, most motor accessory shops can make up brake pipes from kits, but this requires very careful measurement of the original, to ensure that the new pipe is of the correct length. The safest answer is usually to take the original to the shop as a pattern.

3.6b Locating peg for brake hose end fitting

5 On refitting, do not overtighten the union nuts. It is not necessary to exercise brute force to obtain a sound joint.

6 Ensure that the pipes and hoses are correctly routed, with no kinks, and that they are secured in the clips or brackets provided **(see illustrations)**. After fitting, remove the polythene from the reservoir, and bleed the hydraulic system as described in Section 2. Wash off any spilt fluid, and check carefully for fluid leaks.

4 Front brake pads – renewal

Warning: Renew both sets of front brake pads at the same time – never renew the pads on only one wheel, as uneven braking may result. Note that the dust created by wear of the pads may contain asbestos, which is a health hazard. Never blow it out with compressed air, and don't inhale any of it. An approved filtering mask should be worn when working on the brakes. DO NOT use petrol or petroleum-based solvents to clean brake parts; use brake cleaner or methylated spirit only.

1 One of two types of front caliper may be fitted. The only difference between them is that the FS III caliper does not have an external retaining spring, instead the outer brake pads have a spring fitted to the back of the pad – similar to the inboard spring. Removal and refitting of the brake pads is essentially the same for both types of caliper.

2 Apply the handbrake, then slacken the front roadwheel nuts. Jack up the front of the vehicle and support it on axle stands. Remove both front roadwheels.

3 Follow the accompanying photos **(illustrations 4.3a to 4.3s)** for the actual pad renewal procedure. Be sure to stay in order and read the caption under each illustration, and note the following points:

a) *New pads may have an adhesive foil on the backplates. Remove this foil prior to installation.*

b) *Thoroughly clean the caliper guide surfaces, and apply a little brake assembly (polycarbamide) grease. DO NOT use a copper based grease.*

c) *When pushing the caliper piston back to accommodate new pads, keep a close eye on the fluid lever in the reservoir.*

d) *If there is any doubt as to the condition of the brake pads, always replace them.*

4 Depress the brake pedal repeatedly, until the pads are pressed into firm contact with the brake disc, and normal (non-assisted) pedal pressure is restored.

5 Repeat the above procedure on the remaining front brake caliper.

6 Refit the roadwheels, then lower the vehicle to the ground and tighten the roadwheel nuts to the specified torque.

4.3a Use a screwdriver to carefully prise off the caliper retaining spring

4.3b Where fitted, disconnect the wiring plug from the brake pad warning light

4.3c Prise out the rubber caps…

4.3d …and use a hex key to undo the caliper guide bolts

4.3e Lift the caliper and inner pad from the disc

4.3f Pull the inner brake pad from the caliper piston…

4.3g …and lift the outer pad from the caliper bracket

4.3h Push the piston back into the caliper using a piston retraction tool or G-clamp…

4.3i …however, best practise is to clamp the hose, release the nipple and push the fluid into a brake bleeding bottle

4.3j Clean the pad mounting surfaces with a wire brush and brake cleaner

4.3k Apply a little brake lubricant ('cera-tec') grease to the pad mounting surfaces. DO NOT use a copper based grease

4.3l Fit the outer pad...

4.3m ...and then fit the inner pad to the caliper piston

4.3n Where fitted peel off the protective cover from the adhesive surface of the outer pad

4.3o Slide the caliper with the inner pad fitted over the disc and outer pad

4.3p Refit the caliper guide bolts and tighten them to the specified torque...

4.3q ...and then refit the rubber caps

4.3r Refit the caliper retaining spring...

4.3s ...ensuring that it is located correctly on the caliper mounting bracket

5.8 Use a small screwdriver to extract the caliper piston hydraulic seal

7 Check the hydraulic fluid level as described in *Weekly checks*.
Caution: New pads will not give full braking efficiency until they have bedded-in. Be prepared for this, and avoid hard braking as far as possible for the first hundred miles or so after pad renewal.

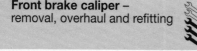

5 Front brake caliper –
removal, overhaul and refitting

Note: Before starting work, refer to the note at the beginning of Section 2 concerning the dangers of hydraulic fluid, and to the warning at the beginning of Section concerning the dangers of asbestos dust.

Removal

1 Apply the handbrake, then jack up the front of the vehicle and support it on axle stands (see *Jacking and vehicle support*). Remove the appropriate roadwheel.
2 Minimise fluid loss by first removing the master cylinder reservoir cap, and then tightening it down onto a piece of polythene, to obtain an airtight seal. Alternatively, use a brake hose clamp, a G-clamp or a similar tool to clamp the flexible hose.
3 Clean the area around the union, and then loosen the brake hose union nut.
4 Remove the brake pads as described in Section 4.
5 Unscrew the caliper from the end of the brake hose and remove it from the vehicle.

Overhaul

6 With the caliper on the bench, wipe away all traces of dust and dirt, but avoid inhaling the dust, as it is injurious to health.
7 Withdraw the partially ejected piston from the caliper body, and remove the dust seal.
8 Using a small screwdriver, extract the piston hydraulic seal, taking great care not to damage the caliper bore **(see illustration)**.
9 Thoroughly clean all components, using only methylated spirit, isopropyl alcohol or clean hydraulic fluid as a cleaning medium. Never use mineral-based solvents such as petrol or paraffin, as they will attack the hydraulic system rubber components. Dry the components immediately, using compressed

air or a clean, lint-free cloth. Use compressed air to blow clear the fluid passages.

10 Check all components, and renew any that are worn or damaged. Check particularly the cylinder bore and piston; these should be renewed if they are scratched, worn or corroded in any way (note that this means the renewal of the complete caliper body assembly). Similarly check the condition of the spacers/guide pins and their bushes/bores (as applicable); both spacers/pins should be undamaged and (when cleaned) a reasonably tight sliding fit in their bores. If there is any doubt about the condition of any component, renew it.

11 If the assembly is fit for further use, obtain the appropriate repair kit; the components are available from VW dealers in various combinations.

12 Renew all rubber seals, dust covers and caps disturbed on dismantling as a matter of course; these should never be re-used.

13 On reassembly, ensure that all components are clean and dry.

14 Thinly coat the piston and piston seal with brake fitting paste (VW part no G 052 150 A2). This should be included in the VW caliper overhaul/repair kit.

15 Fit the new piston (fluid) seal, using only your fingers (no tools) to manipulate it into the cylinder bore groove. Fit the new dust seal to the piston, and refit the piston to the cylinder bore using a twisting motion; ensure that the piston enters squarely into the bore. Press the piston fully into the bore, then press the dust seal into the caliper body.

Refitting

16 Screw the caliper fully onto the flexible hose union.

17 Refit the brake pads as described in Section 4.

18 Securely tighten the brake pipe union nut.

19 Remove the brake hose clamp or polythene, as applicable, and bleed the hydraulic system as described in Section 2. Note that, providing the precautions described were taken to minimise brake fluid loss, it should only be necessary to bleed the relevant front brake.

20 Refit the roadwheel, then lower the vehicle to the ground and tighten the roadwheel bolts to the specified torque.

---

6 Brake disc – inspection, removal and refitting

Note: *Before starting work, refer to the note at the beginning of Section concerning the dangers of asbestos dust.*
Note: *If either disc requires renewal, BOTH should be renewed at the same time, to ensure even and consistent braking. New brake pads should also be fitted.*

6.4 Using a DTI gauge to measure disc run-out

6.8b …and remove the front brake disc

Front brake disc

Inspection

1 Apply the handbrake, then jack up the front of the car and support it on axle stands (see *Jacking and vehicle support*). Remove the appropriate front roadwheel.

2 Slowly rotate the brake disc so that the full area of both sides can be checked; remove the brake pads if better access is required to the inboard surface. Light scoring is normal in the area swept by the brake pads, but if heavy scoring or cracks are found, the disc must be renewed.

3 It is normal to find a lip of rust and brake dust around the perimeter of the disc; this can be scraped off if required. If, however, a lip has formed due to excessive wear of the brake pad swept area, then the disc thickness must be measured using a micrometer. Take measurements at several places around the disc, at the inside and outside of the pad swept area; if the disc has worn at any point to the specified minimum thickness or less, the disc must be renewed.

4 If the disc is thought to be warped, it can be checked for run-out. Either use a dial gauge mounted on any convenient fixed point, while the disc is slowly rotated, or use feeler blades to measure (at several points all around the disc) the clearance between the disc and a fixed point, such as the caliper mounting bracket. If the measurements obtained are at the specified maximum or beyond, the disc is excessively warped, and must be renewed; however, it is worth checking first that the hub

6.8a Undo the retaining screw...

6.13 Remove the rear brake disc

bearings are in good condition. If the run-out is excessive, the disc must be renewed **(see illustration)**.

5 Check the disc for cracks, especially around the wheel bolt holes, and any other wear or damage, and renew if necessary.

Removal

6 Remove the brake pads as described in Section 4.

7 Unscrew the two bolts securing the brake caliper mounting bracket to the hub carrier, then slide the caliper assembly off the disc. Using a piece of wire or string, tie the caliper to the front suspension coil spring, to avoid placing any strain on the brake hose.

8 Use chalk or paint to mark the relationship of the disc to the hub, then remove the screw securing the brake disc to the hub, and remove the disc **(see illustrations)**. If it is tight, apply penetrating fluid, and tap its rear face gently with a hide or plastic mallet. The use of excessive force could cause the disc to be damaged.

Refitting

9 Refitting is the reverse of the removal procedure, noting the following points:
a) *Ensure that the mating surfaces of the disc and hub are clean and flat.*
b) *Align (if applicable) the marks made on removal, and securely tighten the disc retaining screw.*
c) *If a new disc has been fitted, use a suitable solvent to wipe any preservative coating from the disc, before refitting the caliper.*
d) *Slide the caliper into position over the*

7.2a Remove the bolts (rear shown)…

7.2b …and lift of the shield

disc, making sure the pads pass either side of the disc. Tighten the caliper bracket mounting bolts to the specified torque.
e) Fit the pads as described in Section.
f) Refit the roadwheel, then lower the vehicle to the ground and tighten the roadwheel bolts to the specified torque. On completion, repeatedly depress the brake pedal until normal (non-assisted) pedal pressure returns.

Rear brake disc

Inspection

10 Firmly chock the front wheels, then jack up the rear of the car and support it on axle stands. Remove the appropriate rear road-wheel.
11 Inspect the disc as described in paragraphs 1 to 5.

Removal

12 Unscrew the two bolts securing the brake caliper mounting bracket in position, then slide the caliper assembly off the disc. Using a piece of wire or string, tie the caliper to the rear suspension coil spring, to avoid placing any strain on the hydraulic brake hose.
13 Use chalk or paint to mark the relationship of the disc to the hub, then remove the screw securing the brake disc to the hub, and remove the disc **(see illustration)**. If it is tight, apply penetrating fluid, and tap its rear face gently with a hide or plastic mallet. The use of excessive force could cause the disc to be damaged.

Refitting

14 Refitting is a reversal of the removal procedure, noting the following points:
a) Ensure that the mating surfaces of the disc and hub are clean and flat.
b) Align (if applicable) the marks made on removal, and securely tighten the disc retaining screw.
c) If a new disc has been fitted, use a suitable solvent to wipe any preservative coating

from the disc, before refitting the caliper.
d) Slide the caliper into position over the disc, making sure the pads pass either side of the disc. Tighten the caliper bracket mounting bolts to the specified torque. If new discs have been fitted and there is insufficient clearance between the pads to accommodate the new, thicker disc, it may be necessary to push the piston back into the caliper body as described in Section Section.
e) Refit the roadwheel, then lower the vehicle to the ground and tighten the roadwheel bolts to the specified torque. On completion, repeatedly depress the brake pedal until normal (non-assisted) pedal pressure returns.

7 Brake disc shield – removal and refitting

Removal

1 Remove the front or rear brake disc as described in Section 6.
2 Unscrew the securing bolts, and remove the brake disc shield **(see illustrations)**.

Refitting

3 Refitting is a reversal of removal. Tighten the shield retaining bolts to the specified torque. Refit the brake disc with reference to Section 6.

8 Rear brake pads – renewal

 Warning: Renew both sets of rear brake pads at the same time – never renew the pads on only one wheel, as uneven braking may result. Note that the dust created by wear

of the pads may contain asbestos, which is a health hazard. Never blow it out with compressed air, and don't inhale any of it. An approved filtering mask should be worn when working on the brakes. DO NOT use petrol or petroleum-based solvents to clean brake parts; use brake cleaner or methylated spirit only.

1 There are two types of rear brake caliper fitted. Removal and refitting of the brake pads is essentially the same, regardless of the type of caliper fitted.
2 Chock the front wheels, slacken the rear road wheel nuts, then jack up the rear of the vehicle and support it on axle stands (see *Jacking and vehicle support*). Remove the rear wheels.
3 With the handbrake lever fully released, follow the accompanying photos **(see illustrations 8.3a to 8.3q)** for the actual pad renewal procedure. Be sure to stay in order and read the caption under each illustration, and note the following points:
a) If re-installing the original pads, ensure they are fitted to their original position.
b) Thoroughly clean the caliper guide surfaces and guide bolts. Note that the shorter guide bolt is fitted to the top position.
c) If new pads are to be fitted, use a piston retraction tool to push the piston back and twist it clockwise at the same time – keep an eye on the fluid level in the reservoir whilst retracting the piston. Note however that best practise is to clamp the brake flexible hose, open the bleed nipple and push the fluid out, into a brake bleeding bottle.
Caution: Pushing back the piston causes a reverse-flow of brake fluid, which has been known to 'flip' the master cylinder rubber seals, resulting in a total loss of braking. To avoid this, clamp the caliper flexible hose and open the bleed screw – as the piston is pushed back, the fluid can be directed into

8.3a Disconnect the ABS sensor connector. Counterhold the guides…

8.3b …and remove the bolts

8.3c Lift off the caliper

8.3d Remove the brake pads…

8.3e …and then the recover the shims

8.3f Retract the piston using a piston wind back tool

8.3g Select the correct end fitting for the brake tool

8.3h Best practise is always to clamp the hose, open the nipple and push the fluid into a bottle

8.3i Use a wire brush and brake cleaner to thoroughly clean the caliper and the brake pad mounting points

8.3j Check that the guide pins slide freely – clean and lubricate as required

8.3k Fit the new shims and then…

8.3l …apply a little brake grease ('cera-tec' or similar) to the mounting points. DO NOT use a copper based grease.

8.3m Fit the new inner brake pad...

8.3n ...followed by the outer brake pad

8.3o Refit the caliper and then...

a suitable container using a hose attached to the bleed screw. Close the screw just before the piston is pushed fully back, to ensure no air enters the system.

4 Depress the brake pedal repeatedly, until the pads are pressed into firm contact with the brake disc, and normal (non-assisted) pedal pressure is restored.

5 Repeat the above procedure on the remaining brake caliper.

6 If necessary, adjust the handbrake as described in Section 14.

7 Refit the roadwheels, then lower the vehicle to the ground and tighten the roadwheel nuts to the specified torque.

8 Check the hydraulic fluid level as described in *Weekly checks*.

Caution: New pads will not give full braking efficiency until they have bedded-in. Be prepared for this, and avoid hard braking as far as possible for the first hundred miles or so after pad renewal.

8.3p ...fit the new caliper guide bolts

8.3q Tighten the bolts to the specified torque

9 Rear brake caliper – removal, overhaul and refitting

Note: *Before starting work, refer to the note at the beginning of Section 2 concerning the dangers of hydraulic fluid, and to the warning at the beginning of Section concerning the dangers of asbestos dust.*

Removal

1 Chock the front wheels, then jack up the rear of the vehicle and support on axle stands (see *Jacking and vehicle support*). Remove the relevant rear wheel.

2 Minimise fluid loss by first removing the master cylinder reservoir cap, and then tightening it down onto a piece of polythene, to obtain an airtight seal. Alternatively, use a brake hose clamp, a G-clamp or a similar tool to clamp the flexible hose.

3 Clean the area around the union on the caliper, and then loosen the brake hose union nut.

4 Lift the caliper from the brake pads as described in Section Section.

5 Unscrew the caliper from the end of the flexible hose and remove it from the vehicle.

Overhaul

Note: *It is not possible to overhaul the brake caliper handbrake mechanism. If the mechanism is faulty, or fluid is leaking from the handbrake lever seal the caliper assembly must be renewed.*

6 With the caliper on the bench, wipe away all traces of dust and dirt, but avoid inhaling the dust, as it is injurious to health.

7 Using a small screwdriver, carefully prise out the dust seal from the caliper, taking care not to damage the piston.

8 Remove the piston from the caliper bore by rotating it in an anti-clockwise direction. This can be achieved using a suitable pair of circlip pliers engaged in the caliper piston slots. Once the piston turns freely but does not come out any further, the piston can be withdrawn by hand.

9 Using a small screwdriver, extract the piston hydraulic seal(s), taking care not to damage the caliper bore.

10 Withdraw the guide pins from the caliper, and remove the guide sleeve gaiters.

11 Thoroughly clean all components, using only methylated spirit, isopropyl alcohol or clean hydraulic fluid as a cleaning medium. Never use mineral-based solvents such as petrol or paraffin, as they will attack the hydraulic system rubber components. Dry the components immediately, using compressed air or a clean, lint-free cloth. Use compressed air to blow clear the fluid passages.

12 Check all components, and renew any that are worn or damaged. Check particularly the cylinder bore and piston; these should be renewed (note that this means the renewal of the complete caliper body assembly) if they are scratched, worn or corroded in any way. Similarly check the condition of the spacers/guide pins and their bushes/bores (as applicable); both spacers/pins should be undamaged and (when cleaned) a reasonably tight sliding fit in their bores. If there is any doubt about the condition of any component, renew it.

13 If the assembly is fit for further uses obtain the appropriate repair kit; the components are available from VW dealers in various combinations.

14 Renew all rubber seals, dust covers and caps disturbed on dismantling as a matter of course; these should never be re-used.

15 On reassembly, ensure that all components are clean and dry.

16 Smear a thin coat of brake fitting paste (VW part no G 052 150 A2) on the piston, seal and caliper bore. This should be included in the overhaul/repair kit. Fit the new piston (fluid) seal, using only the fingers (no tools) to manipulate into the cylinder bore groove.

17 Fit the new dust seal to the piston groove, then refit the piston assembly. Turn the piston in a clockwise direction, using the method employed on dismantling, until it is fully retracted into the caliper bore.

18 Press the dust seal into position in the caliper housing.

19 Apply the grease supplied in the repair kit, or a copper-based brake grease or anti-seize compound, to the guide pins. Fit the new

gaiters to the guide pins and fit the pins to the caliper ensuring that the gaiters are correctly located in the grooves on both the pins and caliper.

20 Prior to refitting, fill the caliper with fresh hydraulic fluid by slackening the bleed screw and pumping the fluid through the caliper until bubble-free fluid is expelled from the union hole.

Refitting

21 Screw the caliper fully onto the flexible hose union.

22 Refit the caliper over the brake pads as described in paragraphs 10 to 12 of Section Section.

23 Securely tighten the brake pipe union nut.

24 Remove the brake hose clamp or remove the polythene from the fluid reservoir, as applicable, and bleed the hydraulic system as described in Section 2. Note that, providing the precautions described were taken to minimise brake fluid loss, it should only be necessary to bleed the relevant rear brake.

25 Connect the handbrake cable to the caliper, and adjust the handbrake as described in Section 14.

26 Refit the roadwheel, then lower the vehicle to the ground and tighten the roadwheel bolts to the specified torque. On completion, check the hydraulic fluid level as described in *Weekly checks*.

10 Brake pedal – removal and refitting

Removal

1 Disconnect the battery negative lead as described in Chapter 5A Section 3.

2 Remove the driver's side storage/fuse box cover compartment as described in Chapter 11 Section 26.

3 Undo the retaining screw and remove the footwell air vent from above the pedal assembly **(see illustrations)**.

4 Where fitted, remove the crash protection bar **(see illustration)** and then on models with a pedal mounted brake switch, disconnect

10.3 Remove the footwell air ducting

the wiring plug and remove the switch as described in Section 18.

5 It is now necessary to release the brake pedal from the ball on the vacuum servo pushrod. To do this, a VW special tool is available, but a suitable alternative can be improvised **(see illustration)**. Note that the plastic lugs in the pedal are very stiff, and it will not be possible to release them by hand. Depress and hold down the pedal, then, using the tool, release the securing lugs, and pull the pedal from the servo pushrod **(see illustrations)**.

6 Release the retaining clip, then undo and remove the pivot shaft nut **(see illustration)**.

7 Slide the pivot shaft bolt out, until the pedal is free, and then remove the pedal **(see illustration)**.

10.5a Improvised special tool constructed from a modified exhaust clamp, used to release the brake pedal from the servo pushrod

10.4 Remove the crash protection

8 Carefully clean all components, and renew any that are worn or damaged.

Refitting

9 Prior to refitting, apply a smear of multi-purpose grease to the pivot shaft and pedal bearing surfaces.

10 Pull the servo unit pushrod down, and at the same time manoeuvre the pedal into position, ensuring that the pivot bush is correctly located.

11 Hold the servo unit pushrod, and push the pedal back onto the pushrod ball. Make sure the pedal is securely fastened to the pushrod.

12 Insert the pedal pivot bolt and tighten the retaining nut to the specified torque.

13 The remainder of the refitting procedure is the opposite of the removal; refer to the relevant Chapters where applicable.

10.5b Using the tool to release the brake pedal from the servo pushrod

10.5c Rear view of the brake pedal showing plastic lugs securing pedal to servo pushrod

10.6 Remove the securing clip/washer

10.7 Undo the upper pivot bolt

11 Servo unit – testing, removal and refitting

Testing

1 To test the operation of the servo unit, depress the footbrake several times to exhaust the vacuum, then start the engine whilst keeping the pedal firmly depressed. As the engine starts, there should be a noticeable 'give' in the brake pedal as the vacuum builds-up. Allow the engine to run for at least two minutes, and then switch it off. If the brake pedal is now depressed, it should feel normal, but further applications should result in the pedal feeling firmer, with the pedal stroke decreasing with each application.
2 If the servo does not operate as described, first inspect the servo unit non-return valve as described in Section 12. Check the operation of the vacuum pump as described in Section 21.
3 If the servo unit still fails to operate satisfactorily, the fault lies within the unit itself. Repairs to the unit are not possible – if faulty, the servo unit must be renewed.

Removal

4 Remove the master cylinder as described in Section 13.
5 Where applicable remove the heat shield from the servo, then carefully ease the vacuum hose out from the sealing grommet in the front of the servo. Where applicable, also disconnect the wiring from the servo vacuum sensor, then extract the retaining circlip with a screwdriver, and withdraw the sensor from the servo.
6 With reference to Chapter 11, remove the driver's side lower facia trim panels, and the trim panel below the dash.
7 Where fitted, unscrew the two retaining screws and remove the connecting plate between the clutch and brake pedals (manual transmission models only). Also, where fitted, remove the air duct and cover for access to the servo mounting nuts.
8 It is now necessary to release the brake pedal from the ball on the vacuum servo pushrod. To do this, a VW special tool is

available, but a suitable alternative can be improvised (see Section 10). Note that the plastic lugs in the pedal are very stiff, and it will not be possible to release them by hand. Using the tool, release the securing lugs, and pull the pedal from the servo pushrod.
9 To improve access, remove the plenum chamber front panel as described in Chapter 12 Section 19.
10 To gain enough room to remove the brake servo the engine must be moved forward.
11 Jack up and support the front of the vehicle (see 'Jacking and support 13 '), remove the engine undershield and then remove the engine pendulum mounting.
12 Install an engine crane and support the engine. Remove the right-hand engine mounting and then lower the engine slightly (110mm maximum).
13 Working in the footwell, undo the nuts securing the servo unit to the bulkhead, then return to the engine compartment and manoeuvre the servo unit out of position, and recover the gasket where fitted.

Refitting

14 Check the servo unit vacuum hose sealing grommet for signs of damage or deterioration, and renew if necessary.
15 Where applicable, fit a new gasket to the rear of the servo unit, and then reposition the unit in the engine compartment.
16 From inside the vehicle, ensure that the servo unit pushrod is correctly engaged with the brake pedal, and push the pedal onto the pushrod ball. Check the pushrod ball is securely engaged, then refit the servo unit mounting nuts and tighten them to the specified torque.
17 As applicable, refit the connecting plate, air duct and cover.
18 Refit the facia trim panels.
19 Carefully ease the vacuum hose back into position in the servo, taking great care not to displace the sealing grommet. Refit the heat shield to the servo and, where applicable, refit the vacuum sensor and wiring.
20 Refit the master cylinder as described in Section 13 of this Chapter.
21 On completion, start the engine and check for air leaks at the vacuum hose-to-servo unit connection.

12 Servo non-return valve – testing, removal and refitting

1 The non-return valve is located in the vacuum hose leading from the vacuum pump to the brake servo **(see illustration)**.

Removal

2 Ease the vacuum hose out of the servo unit, taking care not to displace the grommet.
3 Note the routing of the hose, then slacken the retaining clip(s) and disconnect the opposite end of the hose assembly from the manifold/vacuum pump **(see illustration)**, and remove it from the car.

Testing

4 Examine the check valve and vacuum hose for signs of damage, and renew if necessary.
5 The valve may be tested by blowing through it in both directions; air should flow through the valve in one direction only; when blown through from the servo unit end of the valve. Renew the valve if this is not the case.
6 Examine the servo unit rubber sealing grommet for signs of damage or deterioration, and renew as necessary.

Refitting

7 Ensure that the sealing grommet is correctly fitted to the servo unit.
8 Ease the hose union into position in the servo, taking great care not to displace or damage the grommet.
9 Ensure that the hose is correctly routed, and connect it to the inlet manifold/vacuum pump, ensuring the hose is secured in the retaining clips.
10 On completion, start the engine and check the valve-to-servo unit connection for signs of air leaks.

13 Master cylinder – removal, overhaul and refitting

Note: *Before starting work, refer to the warning at the beginning of Section 2 concerning the dangers of hydraulic fluid. A new master cylinder O-ring will be required on refitting.*

Removal

1 Disconnect the battery negative lead as described in Chapter 5A Section 3.
2 Where fitted, remove the engine top cover and air inlet trunking. On models fitted with a diesel particulate filter (DPF) remove the heat shield.
3 Remove the timing belt upper cover by unclipping it.
4 On models fitted with a DPF disconnect the wiring plug and remove the pressures sensor complete with the mounting bracket.

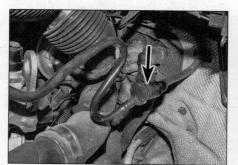

12.1 Non-return valve in vacuum pipe

12.3 Disconnect the hose from the vacuum pump

13.6 Filler cap incorporating brake fluid level warning switch

13.7 Clutch fluid supply hose and union

13.10 Master cylinder securing nuts

5 Where fitted remove the heat shield from the front of the plenum chamber.

6 Remove the master cylinder reservoir cap, disconnecting the wiring plug from the brake fluid level warning switch **(see illustration)**, and then syphon the hydraulic fluid from the reservoir. Note: Do not syphon the fluid by mouth, as it is poisonous; use a syringe or an old antifreeze tester. Also, disconnect the wiring connector from the brake light switch, at the lower part of the master cylinder.

7 On manual transmission models, disconnect and plug the clutch master cylinder supply hose from the side of the brake fluid reservoir **(see illustration)**.

8 Wipe clean the area around the brake pipe unions on the side of the master cylinder, and place absorbent rags beneath the pipe unions to catch any leaking fluid. Make a note of the correct fitted positions of the unions, then unscrew the union nuts and carefully withdraw the pipes. Plug or tape over the pipe ends and master cylinder orifices, to minimise the loss of brake fluid, and to prevent the entry of dirt into the system. Wash off any spilt fluid immediately with cold water.

9 On models fitted with a master cylinder mounted brake warning light switch, disconnect the wiring plug from the switch. Unbolt and then remove the switch.

10 Unscrew and remove the two nuts and washers securing the master cylinder to the vacuum servo unit, remove the heat shield (where fitted), then withdraw the unit from

the engine compartment **(see illustration)**. Remove the O-ring from the rear of the master cylinder, and check it for damage, renew if required.

Overhaul

11 If the master cylinder is faulty, it must be renewed. Repair kits are not available from VW dealer, so the cylinder must be treated as a sealed unit.

12 The only items that can be renewed are the mounting seals for the fluid reservoir; if these show signs of deterioration, prise them out with a screwdriver. Lubricate the new seals with clean brake fluid, and press them into the master cylinder ports.

Refitting

13 Remove all traces of dirt from the master cylinder and servo unit mating surfaces, and fit a new O-ring to the groove on the master cylinder body.

14 Fit the master cylinder to the servo unit, ensuring that the servo unit pushrod enters the master cylinder bore centrally. Refit the heat shield (where applicable), and the master cylinder mounting nuts, then tighten them to the specified torque.

15 Wipe clean the brake pipe unions, then refit them to the master cylinder ports and tighten them securely.

16 Refit the hydraulic fluid reservoir; making sure it is entered correctly in the rubber grommets.

17 On manual transmission models, reconnect the clutch master cylinder supply hose to the reservoir.

18 Refill the master cylinder reservoir with new fluid, and bleed the complete hydraulic system as described in Section 2.

19 Reconnect the wiring to the brake level sender unit and brake light switch as applicable.

20 Refit the engine cover and air trunking where necessary, and then reconnect the battery negative lead.

14 Handbrake – adjustment

1 To check the handbrake adjustment, first apply the footbrake firmly several times to establish correct pad-to-disc clearance, then apply and release the handbrake several times.

2 Applying normal moderate pressure, pull the handbrake lever to the fully applied position, counting the number of clicks from the handbrake ratchet mechanism. If adjustment is correct, there should be approximately 4 to 7 clicks before the handbrake is fully applied. If this is not the case, adjust as follows.

3 On most models the adjuster nut is accessible at the rear of the centre console. On some models the rear cover must be removed **(see illustration)**.

4 If adjustment is required slacken the rear wheel nuts. Chock the front wheels, then jack up the rear of the vehicle and support it on axle stands (see 'Jacking and support 13 '. Remove both rear wheels.

5 With the handbrake fully released, slacken the handbrake adjuster nut until both the rear caliper handbrake levers are back against their stops **(see illustration)**.

6 From this point, tighten the adjusting nuts until both handbrake levers just move off the caliper stops. Ensure that the gap between each caliper handbrake lever and its stop is between 1.0 and 1.5 mm, and ensure

14.3 The adjuster nut (shown with console removed)

14.5 Use a socket or deep off set ring spanner to slacken the adjuster nut

14.6a Turn the adjuster nut until a gap (A) of between 1.0 and 1.5 mm can be seen (C II 41 type caliper)

14.6b Turn the adjuster nut until a gap (A) of between 1.0 and 1.5 mm can be seen (Bosch caliper)

both the right- and left-hand gaps are equal **(see illustrations)**. Check that both wheels/ discs rotate freely, and then check the adjustment by applying the handbrake fully and counting the clicks from the handbrake ratchet (see paragraph 2). If necessary, re-adjust.

7 Once adjustment is correct refit the rear wheels and lower the vehicle to the ground. Where removed, refit the cover.

15 Handbrake lever – removal and refitting

Removal

1 Remove the centre console as described in Chapter 11, Section 25.

2 If desired, remove the handbrake lever cover sleeve by depressing the locating tag with a screwdriver, then sliding the sleeve from the lever.

3 Disconnect the wiring plug from the handbrake 'on' warning light switch **(see illustration)**.

4 Slacken the handbrake cable adjuster nut sufficiently to allow the ends of the cables to be disengaged from the equaliser plate **(see illustration)**.

5 Unclip the console support bracket, unscrew the retaining nuts, and withdraw the lever and bracket assembly from the floor **(see illustration)**.

Refitting

6 Refitting is a reversal of removal, bearing in mind the following points.

a) *Prior to refitting the centre console, adjust the handbrake as described in Section 14.*

b) *Check the operation of the handbrake 'on' warning switch prior to refitting the centre console.*

16 Handbrake cables – removal and refitting

Removal

Note: *There are minor differences in the removal and refitting of the cables between earlier (up to 2007) and later models. However removal and refitting is essentially the same for all models.*

1 Remove the cup holder form the rear of the centre console (as described in Chapter 11

15.3 Disconnect the wiring plug

15.5 Handbrake lever mounting nuts (rear hidden)

Section 25) to gain access to the handbrake lever. The handbrake cable consists of two sections, a right- and a left-hand section, which are linked to the lever by an equaliser plate. Each section can be removed individually.

2 Chock the front wheels, then jack up the rear of the car and support it on axle stands.

3 Slacken the handbrake cable adjuster nut sufficiently to allow the ends of the cables to be disengaged from the equaliser plate, see Section 15.

4 Working back along the length of the cable, note its correct routing, and free it from all

15.4 Slacken the cable

16.4 Unbolt the bracket

the relevant guides and retaining clips **(see illustration)**.

5 Disengage the inner cable from the caliper handbrake lever, then compress the outer cable locking tabs and remove the cable from the bracket **(see illustrations)**. Withdraw the cable from underneath the vehicle.

Refitting

6 Refitting is a reversal of removal, bearing in mind the following points.
a) When locating the handbrake cable sheath in the guide on the rear trailing arm, the cable clamping ring must lie in the middle of the clip.
b) Before refitting the centre console, adjust the handbrake as described in Section 14.

17 Handbrake warning light switch – removal and refitting

Removal

1 Remove the centre console, with reference to Chapter 11, Section 25 if necessary.
2 Disconnect the wiring plug from the switch.
3 Release the securing lugs, and remove the switch from the handbrake lever assembly **(see illustration)**.

Refitting

4 Refitting is a reversal of removal.

18 Brake light switch – removal and refitting

Note: Early models (up to 11/07 approximately) have the switch fitted to the brake pedal. Later models have the switch fitted to the master cylinder.

Brake pedal mounted switch

Removal

Note: The switch has been updated. Always replace the old style switch with the new

16.5a Release the cable inner from the lever

version. The new version can be identified by the brightly coloured tip of the plunger.
1 Remove the drivers side facia lower trim panel/storage compartment as described in Chapter 11 Section 26.
2 If required, remove the screw and pull out the air distribution duct.
3 Disconnect the wiring plug **(see illustration)** depress the brake pedal and then rotate the switch 45 degrees anti-clockwise to remove it.

Refitting

4 Refitting is a reversal of removal, but do not refit the old style switch – always fit the new style switch regardless of the condition of the old switch.

Master cylinder mounted switch

Removal

5 The brake light switch is located on the lower part of the master cylinder **(see illustration)**. Remove the engine top cover, and where applicable, remove the air inlet trunking to improve access. On models fitted with a particulate filter remove the heat shield and differential pressure sensor (complete with the sensor mounting bracket).
6 Disconnect the wiring from the switch.
7 Unscrew the mounting bolt, then pull the switch from the bottom of the master cylinder, and remove it from the locking lug at the top.

Refitting

8 Refitting is a reversal of removal, but tighten the mounting bolt to the specified torque.

16.5b Release the outer cable

19 Anti-lock braking system (ABS) – general information and precautions

1 The anti-lock braking system (ABS) fitted as standard to all models, prevents wheel lock-up under heavy braking, and not only optimises stopping distances, but also improves steering control. By electronically monitoring the speed of each roadwheel in relation to the other wheels, the system can detect when a wheel is about to lock-up, before control is actually lost. The brake fluid pressure applied to that wheel's brake caliper is then decreased and restored ('modulated') several times a second until control is regained. The system components are: four wheel-speed sensors, a hydraulic unit with integral Electronic Control Unit (ECU), brake lines and a dashboard-mounted warning light. The four wheel-speed sensors are mounted on the wheel hub carriers. Each wheel has a rotating toothed hub mounted on the driveshaft (front) or on the hub (rear). The wheel speed sensors are mounted in close proximity to these hubs. The teeth produce a voltage waveform whose frequency varies with the speed of the hubs. These waveforms are transmitted to the ECU, and used to calculate the rotational speed of each wheel. The ECU has a self-diagnostic facility, to inhibit the operation of the ABS if a fault is detected, lighting the dashboard-mounted warning light. The braking system

17.3 Unclip the handbrake warning light switch

18.3 Disconnect the wiring plug

18.5 Brake light switch

will then revert to conventional, non-ABS operation. If the nature of the fault is not immediately obvious upon inspection, the vehicle must be taken to a VW dealer, who will have the diagnostic equipment required to interrogate the ABS ECU electronically and pin-point the problem.

2 There are two ABS systems fitted to the models covered in this Manual.

3 The Mark 70 version includes a traction control system (TCS), which uses the basic ABS system, with an additional pump and valves fitted to the hydraulic actuator. If wheelspin is detected at a speed below 30 mph, one of the valves opens, to allow the pump to pressurise the relevant brake, until the spinning wheel slows to a rotational speed corresponding to the speed of the vehicle. This has the effect of transferring torque to the wheel with most traction. At the same time, the throttle plate is closed slightly, to reduce the torque from the engine.

4 The Mark 60 version includes electronic differential locking (EDL) and an electronic stability programme (ESP). The EDL system applies the brake of the spinning wheel in order to transfer torque to the wheel with the better grip. On models with ESP, the system recognises critical driving conditions and stabilises the vehicle by individual wheel braking and by intervention in the engine

20.3 Remove the battery tray

control, which occurs independently of the position of the brake and accelerator pedals.

5 The operation of the ABS system is entirely dependent on electrical signals. To prevent the system responding to any inaccurate signals, a built-in safety circuit monitors all signals received by the ECU. If an inaccurate signal or low battery voltage is detected, the ABS system is automatically shut down, and the warning light on the instrument panel is illuminated, to inform the driver that the ABS system is not operational. Normal braking will still be available, however.

6 If a fault does develop in the ABS system, the car must be taken to a VW dealer or suitably equipped garage for fault diagnosis and repair.

20 Anti-lock braking system (ABS) components – removal and refitting

Hydraulic unit and electronic control

Removal

1 The hydraulic unit (valve block) and electronic control (modulator) are combined in a single assembly. The unit is mounted on the left-hand side of the engine bay behind the battery.

2 Disconnect and then remove the battery as described in Chapter 5A Section 3.

3 Unclip and remove the battery shrouds and then remove the battery tray (see illustration).

4 A brake pedal depressor must now be installed. Jack up and support the front left-hand wheel and the rear left-hand wheel. Remove both wheels and connect a hose and collection bottle to both front and rear bleed nipples. Open the bleed nipples and depress the brake pedal a minimum of 60 mm. Hold the brake pedal in this position using the brake pedal depressing tool. Do not remove

the brake pedal depressor. Close the bleed nipples.

5 Identify and mark the position of the brake lines on the ABS hydraulic unit. Place shop towels below the unit and then disconnect the wiring plug from the ABS modulator. Seal the plug in a clean plastic bag if there is any chance it will be contaminated by brake fluid.

6 Remove the brake lines from the unit. Seal all the brake lines and the hydraulic unit openings with suitable plugs. Unbolt the complete assembly from the mounting bracket and remove it from the vehicle.

7 On the bench unbolt the electronic control modulator from the valve block. Recover the seals. Seal the modulator in a plastic bag and keep the hydraulic unit (valve block) upright at all times.

Refitting

8 Refitting is a reversal of removal noting the following points:

a) The electronic control unit (modulator) can only be removed and refitted a maximum of two times.

b) If a new control unit is fitted it must be programmed to the vehicle using suitable diagnostic equipment.

c) Bleed the brakes, using pressure bleeding equipment if possible.

Front wheel sensor

Removal

9 Chock the rear wheels, then firmly apply the handbrake, jack up the front of the car and support on axle stands (see Jacking and vehicle support). Remove the appropriate front roadwheel.

10 Disconnect the electrical connector from the sensor by carefully lifting up the retaining tag, and pulling the connector from the sensor (see illustration).

11 Slacken and remove the hexagon socket-head bolt securing the sensor to the hub carrier, and remove the sensor from the car (see illustration).

20.10 Disconnect the wiring connector...

20.11 ...and unbolt the front wheel sensor

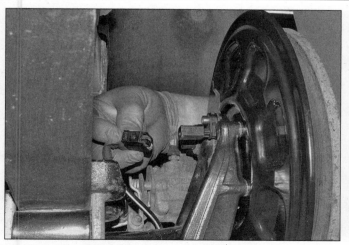

20.17a Disconnect the wiring plug

20.17b Remove the fixing bolt and...

Refitting

12 Ensure that the sensor and hub carrier sealing faces are clean.

13 Apply a thin coat of multi-purpose grease to the mounting hole inner surface, then fit the sensor to the hub carrier. Refit the retaining bolt and tighten it to the specified torque.

14 Ensure that the sensor wiring is correctly routed and retained by all the necessary clips, and reconnect the wiring connector.

15 Refit the roadwheel, then lower the car to the ground and tighten the roadwheel bolts to the specified torque.

Rear wheel sensor

Removal

16 Chock the front wheels, then jack up the rear of the car and support it on axle stands (see *Jacking and vehicle support*). Remove the appropriate roadwheel.

17 Disconnect the wiring plug, remove the bolt and pull out the sensor **(see illustrations)**.

Refitting

18 Refitting is a reversal of removal.

Reluctor rings

19 The reluctor rings are integral with the wheel bearings (front and rear), and can only be inspected after removal of the hub assembly. If faulty, the bearings must be renewed as described in Chapter 10 Section 3 (front) and Chapter 10, Section 9 (rear).

21 Vacuum pump – testing, removal and refitting

Testing

1 The basic test should be to first exhaust the vacuum by pressing the brake pedal repeatedly – the pedal will feel hard with little travel once the vacuum is exhausted. Start the engine whilst keeping your foot on the brake. The pedal should move down slightly as the vacuum builds up. Further comprehensive testing is described below.

2 A comprehensive test of the braking system vacuum pump requires a vacuum gauge. First, remove the engine top cover to access the vacuum hose.

3 Disconnect the vacuum hose from the pump, and connect the gauge to the pump union using a suitable length of hose.

4 Start the engine and allow it to idle, and then measure the vacuum created by the pump. As a guide, after one minute, a minimum of approximately 500 mm Hg should be recorded. If the vacuum registered is significantly less than this, it is likely that the pump is faulty. However, seek the advice of a VW dealer before condemning the pump.

5 Reconnect the vacuum hose. Overhaul of the vacuum pump is not possible, since no major components are available separately for it. If faulty, the complete pump assembly must be renewed.

Removal

Note: *There are several variants of the vacuum pumped fitted, depending on the engine type. All 'PD' engines have tandem pumps that act as lift pumps to supply the injectors with fuel. Removal and refitting of all variants is essentially the same.*

Note: *A new pump O-ring will be required on refitting.*

6 Remove the engine cover and then remove the air filter housing as described in Chapter Section.

7 On models fitted with a tandem pump, anticipate some fuel spillage as the pump is removed (Place rags or shop towels below the pump).

8 Disconnect the fuel lines and immediately seal them.

9 Disconnect the small vacuum pipe from the vacuum hose connector on the top of the vacuum pump **(see illustration)**.

10 Pull the vacuum hose from the top of the pump, noting the rubber seal may stay on the vacuum pump outlet pipe **(see illustration)**.

20.17c ...remove the sensor

21.9 Disconnect the small vacuum pipe (common rail engine)

21.10 Remove the vacuum hose and rubber seal (common rail)

21.11a Vacuum pump securing bolts (1.9 PD engine)

21.11b Vacuum pump securing bolts (1.6 CR engine)

11 Unscrew the mounting bolts and withdraw the vacuum pump from the cylinder head **(see illustrations)**. Recover the O-ring seal and discard, as a new one will be required for refitting.

Refitting

12 Fit the new O-ring seal to the vacuum pump, and apply a smear of oil to aid installation.

13 Manoeuvre the vacuum pump into position, making sure that the slot in the pump drive gear aligns with the slot on the pump driveshaft.

14 Refit the pump retaining bolts, and tighten to the specified torque.

15 Reconnect the vacuum hoses and secure with the retaining clip (where fitted). If the vacuum hose seal is still fitted to the outlet pipe on the vacuum pump, remove it and fit it inside the end of the vacuum hose before refitting.

16 Refit the air intake pipe and engine top cover.

Chapter 10
Suspension and steering systems

Contents

Degrees of difficulty

Easy, suitable for novice with little experience | **Fairly easy,** suitable for beginner with some experience | **Fairly difficult,** suitable for competent DIY mechanic | **Difficult,** suitable for experienced DIY mechanic | **Very difficult,** suitable for expert DIY or professional

Specifications

Front suspension
Type . . . . Independent, with MacPherson struts incorporating coil springs, telescopic shock absorbers and anti-roll bar

Rear suspension
Type . . . . Beam axle with leaf springs, separate telescopic shock absorbers. Models with a payload of over 1,100 Kg also have an anti-roll bar

Steering
Type . . . . Rack-and-pinion. Hydraulic or Electro-mechanical with power assistance as standard

Wheel alignment and steering angles*
Ride height:
  Front . . . . 420-440 mm
  Rear4 . . . . 27-457 mm
Front wheel:
  Camber. . . . . - 0°06' ± 30'
  Maximum difference between sides. . . . . 0°45'
  Castor . . . . 7° 11' ± 30'
  Maximum difference between sides. . . . . 0°30'
  Toe setting . . . . 0°00' ± 10'
  Toe-out on turns (20° left or right): . . . . 1° 23' ± 20'
Rear wheel:
  Camber angle. . . . . -1°15' ± 15'
  Maximum difference between sides. . . . . 0°30'
  Toe setting . . . . 0°+20' ± 15'
  Maximum difference between sides. . . . . 0°20'
Figures are for standard suspension. Refer to VW for alternative suspension and the latest figures.

Roadwheels
Type . . . . Steel or Aluminium alloy

Tyres

Size*	Front pressure (bar)	Rear pressure (bar)
195/65 R15 91T	2.1 – 2.4	2.5 – 2.8
205/55 R16 94H	2.6 – 2.7	2.6 – 3.2
205/50 R17 93H	2.6 – 2.7	2.6 – 3.2

Examples given are for common tyre sizes. Always check the tyre size fitted to the vehicle before checking pressure

Torque wrench settings

	Nm	lbf ft
Front suspension		
Anti-roll bar link nuts*	65	48
Anti-roll bar to subframe:		
Stage 1	20	15
Stage 2	Angle-tighten a further 90°	
Hub bolt*		
Heaxgon head bolt		
Stage 1	200	148
Stage 2	Angle-tighten a further 180°	
12 point bolt (with ribs under head)		
Stage 1	70	52
Stage 2	Angle-tighten a further 90°	
12 point bolt (with NO ribs under head)		
Stage 1	200	148
Stage 2	Angle-tighten a further 180°	
Hub to wheel bearing housing*		
Stage 1	70	52
Stage 2	Angle-tighten a further 90°	
Lower arm:		
To subframe (front): *		
Stage 1	70	52
Stage 2	Angle-tighten a further 180°	
To lower balljoint nuts: *		
Cast steel lower arm	60	44
Forged aluminium/sheet steel lower arm	100	74
Steel arm (with steel subframe)		
Stage 1	40	30
Stage 2	Angle-tighten a further 45°	
To subframe (rear, steel subframe)*		
Stage 1	70	52
Stage 2	Angle-tighten a further 180°	
Mounting bracket to body (rear): *		
Stage 1	70	52
Stage 2	Angle-tighten a further 180°	
Mounting bracket to bracket (subframe): *		
Stage 1	50	37
Stage 2	Angle-tighten a further 90°	
Mounting nut/bolt to subframe (rear steel subframe): *		
Stage 1	70	52
Stage 2	Angle-tighten a further 90°	
Rear engine (pendulum) mounting bolts: *		
To subframe:		
Stage 1	100	74
Stage 2	Angle-tighten a further 90°	
To transmission:		
Stage 1	50	37
Stage 2	Angle-tighten a further 90°	
Subframe-to-underbody/bracket bolts*:		
Stage 1	70	52
Stage 2	Angle-tighten a further 90°	
Splash plate to wheel bearing housing	10	7
Suspension strut:		
Bottom clamp*:		
Stage 1	70	52
Stage 2	Angle-tighten a further 90°	
Upper mounting*:		
Stage 1	15	11
Stage 2	Angle-tighten a further 90°	
Upper piston rod nut*	60	44

Always replace the nuts/bolts

Rear suspension

ABS speed sensor	8	6
Anti-roll bar bracket to axle	60	44
Anti-roll bar drop link nut *	65	48
Anti-roll bar drop link upper bolt: *		
Stage 1	60	44
Stage 2	Angle-tighten a further 90°	
Bump stop bolt	55	41
Hub to stub axle bolt: *		
Stage 1	180	133
Stage 2	Angle-tighten a further 180°	
Leaf spring:		
Rear shackle bolts*	60	44
Front pivot nut/bolt*	100	74
U bolt nuts: *		
Stage 1	60	44
Stage 2	Angle-tighten a further 90°	
Shock absorber:		
Upper nut/bolt*		
Stage 1	100	74
Stage 2	Angle-tighten a further 90°	
Lower nut/bolt*:		
Stage 1	75	37
Stage 2	Angle-tighten a further 90°	
Splash shield to wheel bearing housing	9	6
Stub axle (up to model year 2008 only)*		
Stage 1	75	37
Stage 2	Angle-tighten a further 90°	

Always replace the nuts/bolts

Steering

Crash bar (above brake/clutch pedal) bolt	20	15
Power steering pump to mounting bracket bolts	35	26
Power steering pump pressure hose bolts	9	6
Steering column:		
To mounting bracket bolts	20	15
Mounting bracket to body	20	15
Strut to mounting bracket/body	20	15
Universal joint to steering gear bolt*	30	22
Steering gear:		
To subframe*:		
Stage 1	50	37
Stage 2	Angle-tighten a further 90°	
Shield (Torx bolts)	6	4
Steering wheel to column*:		
Stage 1	30	22
Stage 2	Angle-tighten a further 90°	
Track rod end to track rod	70	66
Track rod end to wheel bearing housing nut: *		
Stage 1	20	15
Stage 2	Angle-tighten a further 90°	
Track rod to steering gear rack	100	74

Always replace the nuts/bolts

Roadwheels

Roadwheel bolts	120	89

1 General Information

1 The independent front suspension is of the MacPherson strut type, incorporating coil springs and integral telescopic shock absorbers. The struts are located by transverse lower suspension arms, which use rubber inner mounting bushes, and incorporate a balljoint at the outer ends. The front wheel bearing housings, which carry the wheel bearings, brake calipers and the hub/disc assemblies, are attached to the MacPherson struts by clamp bolts, and connected to the lower arms through the balljoints. A front anti-roll bar is fitted to all models. The anti-roll bar is rubber-mounted, and is connected to both lower suspension arms by short links.

2 The rear suspension is a very traditional leaf spring and rigid axle assembly, with telescopic shock absorbers. An anti-roll bar is fitted to all models except those with a 1100 Kg payload rating. Drop links connect the anti-roll bar to the chassi. On early models a stub axle is bolted to the axle, on later models (2008 on) the stub axle is part of the main axle.

3 The safety steering column incorporates an intermediate shaft at its lower end. The intermediate shaft is connected to both the steering column and steering gear by universal joints, although the shaft is supplied as part of the column assembly and cannot be separated. Both the inner steering column and intermediate shaft have splined sections that collapse during a major frontal impact. The outer column is also telescopic with two sections, to facilitate reach adjustment.

4 The steering gear is mounted onto the front subframe, and is connected by two track rods, with balljoints at their inner and outer ends, to the steering arms projecting rearwards from the wheel bearing housings. The track rod ends are threaded to the track rods in order to allow adjustment of the front wheel toe setting. The steering gear has either electro-mechanical assistance (with an integrated control circuit) or hydraulic power steering (with an accessory belt driven steering pump). Power steering is only functional when the engine is running.

5 All models are fitted with an Anti-lock Brake System (ABS), and can also be fitted with a Traction Control System (TCS), an Electronic Differential Lock (EDL) system and an Electronic Stability Program (ESP). The ABS may also be referred to as including EBD (Electronic Brake Distribution), which means it adjusts the front and rear braking forces according to the weight being carried. The TCS may also be referred to as ASR (Anti Slip Regulation).

6 The TCS system prevents the front wheels from losing traction during acceleration by reducing the engine output. The system is switched on automatically when the engine is started, and it utilises the ABS system sensors to monitor the rotational speeds of the front wheels.

7 The ESP system extends the ABS, TCS and EDL functions to reduce wheel spin in difficult driving conditions. It does this by using highly sensitive sensors that monitor the speed of the vehicle, lateral movement of the vehicle, the brake pressure, and the steering angle of the front wheels. If, for example, the vehicle is tending to oversteer, the brake will be applied to the front outer wheel to correct the situation. If the vehicle is tending to understeer, the brake will be applied to the rear inside wheel. The steering angle of the front wheels is monitored by an angle sensor on the top of the steering column.

8 The TCS/ESP systems should always be switched on, except when driving with snow chains, driving in snow or driving on loose surfaces, when some wheel spin may be advantageous. The ESP switch is located in the centre of the facia.

9 Some models are also fitted with an Electronic Differential Lock (EDL), which reduces unequal traction from the front wheels. If one front wheel spins 100 rpm or more faster than the other, the faster wheel is slowed down by applying the brake to that wheel. The system is not the same as the traditional differential lock, where the actual differential gears are locked. Because the system applies a front brake, in the event of a brake disc overheating the system will shut down until the disc has cooled. No warning light is displayed if the system shuts down. As is the case with the TCS system, the EDL system uses the ABS sensors to monitor front wheel speeds.

2 Front wheel bearing housing (swivel hub) – removal and refitting

Note: *Renewal of the hub bearings does not require removal of the wheel bearing housing (see Section 3). This Section describes removal of the wheel bearing housing leaving the suspension strut in situ, however, if necessary it can be removed together with the suspension strut, and then separated on the bench. All self-locking nuts and bolts disturbed on removal must be renewed as a matter of course.*

Removal

1 Remove the wheel trim/hub cap (as applicable) and loosen the driveshaft retaining bolt (hub bolt) by 90° with the vehicle resting on its wheels. Also loosen the wheel bolts. Note: Do not loosen the hub bolt more than 90° at this stage, or the wheel bearing may be damaged.

2 Apply the handbrake, then jack up the front of the vehicle and support it on axle stands (see *Jacking and vehicle support*). Remove the front roadwheel.

2.4 Removing the brake hose/wiring bracket

3 Unscrew and remove the driveshaft retaining bolt. Check that the driveshaft moves freely in the hub before proceeding.

4 Remove the ABS wheel sensor as described in Chapter 9, Section 20. Also, unbolt the brake hose/wiring bracket from the strut **(see illustration)**.

5 Remove the brake disc as described in Chapter 9, Section 6. This procedure includes removing the brake caliper; however do not disconnect the hydraulic brake hose from the caliper. Using a piece of wire or string, tie the caliper to the front suspension coil spring, to avoid placing any strain on the hydraulic brake hose **(see illustration)**.

6 Unbolt the splash plate from the wheel bearing housing.

7 Loosen the nut securing the steering track rod balljoint to the wheel bearing housing. To do this, fit a ring spanner to the nut, and then hold the balljoint pin stationary using an Allen key. With the nut removed, it may be possible to release the balljoint from the wheel bearing housing by turning the balljoint pin with an Allen key. If not, leave the nut on by a few turns to protect the threads, then use a universal balljoint separator to release the balljoint. Remove the nut completely once the taper has been released.

8 Unscrew the front suspension lower balljoint-to-lower arm retaining nuts **(see illustration)**, then lever the lower arm down to

2.5 Suspend the caliper from the front suspension spring

2.8 Lower ball joint securing nuts

release the balljoint studs from the arm. Now use a soft-faced mallet to tap the driveshaft from the hub splines while pulling out the bottom end of the wheel bearing housing. If the driveshaft is tight on the splines, it may be necessary to use a puller bolted to the hub to remove it. Tie the driveshaft to one side.

9 Note which way round it is fitted, then unscrew the nut and remove the clamp bolt securing the wheel bearing housing to the bottom of the strut.

10 The wheel bearing housing must now be released from the strut. To do this, VW technicians insert a special tool into the split wheel bearing housing, and turn it through 90° to open up the clamp. A similar tool can be made out of an old screwdriver or bolt. Alternatively a suitable cold chisel can be driven into the split as a wedge. Slightly press inwards the top of the wheel bearing housing, and then push it downwards from the bottom of the strut **(see illustrations)**.

Refitting

11 Ensure that the driveshaft outer joint and hub splines are clean and dry, and then lubricate the splines with fresh engine oil. Also lubricate the threads and contact surface of the hub nut/bolt with oil.

12 Lift the wheel bearing assembly into position, and engage the hub with the splines on the outer end of the driveshaft. Fit the new hub bolt, tightening it by hand only at this stage.

13 Engage the wheel bearing housing with the bottom of the suspension strut; making sure that the hole in the side plate aligns with the holes in the split housing. Remove the tool used to open the split.

14 Insert the strut-to-wheel bearing housing clamp bolt from the front, and fit the new retaining nut. Tighten the nut to the specified torque.

15 Refit the lower arm balljoint to the lower arm, and tighten the nuts to the specified torque.

16 Refit the track rod balljoint to the wheel bearing housing, then fit a new retaining nut and tighten it to the specified torque. If necessary, hold the balljoint pin with an Allen key while tightening the nut.

17 Refit the splash plate and tighten the bolts.

18 Refit the brake disc and caliper with reference to Chapter 9, Section 6.

19 Refit the ABS wheel sensor as described in Chapter 9, Section 20.

20 Ensure that the outer joint is drawn fully into the hub, and then refit the roadwheel.

21 Have an assistant depress the brake pedal, and then tighten the driveshaft retaining bolt in the stages given in the Specifications. It is recommended that an angle gauge be used to ensure the correct tightening angle. Note: The car must not be standing on its wheels when tightening the bolt, or the wheel bearing may be damaged.

22 Lower the vehicle to the ground, tighten the roadwheel bolts, and refit the wheel trim/hub cap.

2.10a Tool used by VW technicians to open up the split wheel bearing housing

2.10c Using a cold chisel to open up the wheel bearing housing and release the suspension strut

3 Front hub bearings – renewal

Note: *The bearing is a sealed, pre-adjusted and pre-lubricated, double-row roller type, and requires no maintenance. It is bolted to the wheel bearing housing.*

1 Remove the wheel trim/hub cap (as applicable) and loosen the driveshaft retaining bolt (hub bolt) with the vehicle resting on its wheels. Note: Do not loosen the hub bolt more than 90° at this stage, or the wheel bearing may be damaged. Also loosen the wheel bolts.

2 Apply the handbrake, then jack up the front of the vehicle and support it on axle stands (see *Jacking and vehicle support*). Remove the front roadwheel.

3.7a Removing the front hub/wheel bearing from the wheel bearing housing

2.10b A home made version of the factory tool can also be used

2.10d Withdrawing the wheel bearing housing from the bottom of the suspension strut

3 Unscrew and remove the driveshaft retaining bolt.

4 Remove the ABS wheel sensor as described in Chapter 9, Section 20.

5 Remove the brake disc as described in Chapter 9, Section 6. This procedure includes removing the brake caliper; however do not disconnect the hydraulic brake hose from the caliper. Using a piece of wire or string, tie the caliper to the front suspension coil spring, to avoid placing any strain on the hydraulic brake hose.

6 Press the driveshaft outer stub towards the transmission as far as possible, then unscrew and remove the wheel bearing retaining bolts from the rear of the housing.

7 Remove the hub/wheel bearing complete with hub from the outside of the housing while sliding it from the driveshaft splines **(see illustrations)**.

3.7b Front hub/wheel bearing

8 Fit the new wheel bearing to the housing and engage the hub splines with the driveshaft outer stub.

9 Refit the brake disc and caliper with reference to Chapter 9, Section 6.

10 Refit the ABS wheel sensor with reference to Chapter 9, Section 20.

11 Pull the driveshaft outer stub fully into the hub and fit a new hub bolt, hand-tight at this stage.

12 Ensure that the outer joint is drawn fully into the hub, and then refit the roadwheel.

13 Tighten the driveshaft retaining bolt in the stages given in the Specifications. It is recommended that an angle gauge be used to ensure the correct tightening angle. Note: The car must not be standing on its wheels when tightening the bolt, or the wheel bearing will be damaged.

14 Lower the vehicle to the ground and tighten the roadwheel bolts.

4 Front suspension strut – removal, overhaul and refitting

Note: *This section describes removal of the suspension strut leaving the wheel bearing housing in situ, however, if necessary it can be removed together with the wheel bearing housing, then separated on the bench. All self-locking nuts and bolts disturbed on removal must be renewed as a matter of course.*

4.3 Disconnect the anti-roll bar drop link from the strut

Removal

1 Remove the wheel trim/hub cap (as applicable) and loosen the driveshaft retaining bolt (hub bolt) with the vehicle resting on its wheels. Note: Do not loosen the hub bolt more than 90° at this stage, or the wheel bearing may be damaged. Also loosen the wheel bolts.

2 Apply the handbrake, then jack up the front of the vehicle and support it on axle stands (see *Jacking and vehicle support*). Remove the appropriate roadwheel.

3 Unscrew the nut and disconnect the anti-roll bar link from the strut **(see illustration)**.

4 Release the ABS sensor wiring from the strut.

5 Unscrew and remove the driveshaft retaining bolt **(see illustration)**.

4.5 Unscrew and remove the driveshaft retaining bolt

6 Unscrew the front suspension lower balljoint-to-lower arm retaining nuts, then lever the lower arm down to release the balljoint studs. Now use a soft-faced mallet to tap the driveshaft from the hub splines while pulling out the bottom end of the wheel bearing housing **(see illustrations)**. If the driveshaft is tight on the splines, it may be necessary to use a puller bolted to the hub to remove it. Tie the driveshaft to one side, then refit the lower balljoint to the lower arm and secure with the nuts, hand-tightened.

7 Note which way round it is fitted, then unscrew the nut and remove the clamp bolt securing the wheel bearing housing to the bottom of the strut **(see illustration)**.

8 The wheel bearing housing must now be released from the strut. To do this, VW technicians insert a special tool into the split wheel bearing housing, and turn it through 90° to open up the clamp. A similar tool such as an Allen key can be used, or alternatively a suitable cold chisel can be driven into the split as a wedge. Slightly press inwards the top of the wheel bearing housing, and then push it downwards from the bottom of the strut **(see illustration)**. Support the wheel bearing housing to one side without straining the hydraulic brake hose.

9 Remove the wiper arms, windscreen cowl, plenum chamber front panel and the windscreen wiper motor (or motors) as described in Chapter 12 Section 19.

4.6a Unscrew the securing nuts...

4.6b ...detach the lower arm from the balljoint studs...

4.6c ...and withdraw the driveshaft from the hub splines

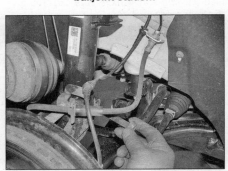
4.7 Remove the clamp bolt...

4.8 ...then use a suitable tool to expand the split, so that the strut can be pulled from the wheel bearinghousing

4.11a Unscrew the upper mounting bolts...

4.11b ...and lower the strut from under the wheel arch

4.13 Compress the coil spring with the compressor tool

10 To ensure correct refitting, mark the strut upper mounting in relation to the body. If the reason for removing the strut is overhaul, loosen the upper mounting centre nut one turn, while holding the piston rod with an Allen key.

11 Support the strut, then unscrew the upper mounting bolts and lower the strut from under the wheel arch **(see illustrations)**.

Overhaul

⚠️ *Warning: Before attempting to dismantle the suspension strut, a suitable tool to hold the coil spring in compression must be obtained. Adjustable coil spring compressors are readily available, and are recommended for this operation. Any attempt to dismantle the strut without such a tool is likely to result in damage or personal injury.*

12 With the strut removed from the car, clean away all external dirt. If necessary, mount it upright in a vice during the dismantling procedure.

13 Fit the spring compressor, and compress the coil spring until all tension is relieved from the upper spring seat **(see illustration)**.

14 Unscrew and remove the upper centre retaining nut, whilst retaining the strut piston with a suitable Allen key, then remove the mounting, thrust bearing, and coil spring **(see illustrations)**.

15 Remove the protective sleeve and upper bearing race, and then remove the bump

stop from the upper mounting **(see illustrations)**.

16 With the strut assembly now completely dismantled, examine all the components for wear, damage or deformation, and check the bearing for smoothness of operation. Renew any of the components as necessary.

17 Examine the strut for signs of fluid leakage. Check the strut piston for signs of pitting along its entire length, and check the strut body for signs of damage. While holding it in an upright position, test the operation of the strut by moving the piston through a full stroke, and then through short strokes of 50 to 100 mm. In both cases, the resistance felt should be smooth and continuous. If the resistance is jerky, or uneven, or if there is any visible sign of

wear or damage to the strut, renewal is necessary.

18 If any doubt exists about the condition of the coil spring, carefully remove the spring compressors, and check the spring for distortion and signs of cracking. Renew the spring if it is damaged or distorted, or if there is any doubt as to its condition.

19 Inspect all other components for signs of damage or deterioration, and renew as necessary.

20 Assemble the bump stop to the upper mounting, and then refit the upper bearing race and protective sleeve to the mounting. The larger diameter of the bump stop must be against the upper mounting.

21 Fit the coil spring (together with the compressor tool) onto the strut, making sure

4.14a Unscrew the upper centre nut...

4.14b ...then remove the mounting, thrust bearing and coil spring

4.15a Remove the protective sleeve...

4.15b ...and upper bearing race...

4.15c ...then remove the bump stop from the upper mounting

its lower (larger diameter) end is correctly located against the spring seat stop.

22 Refit the thrust bearing and upper mounting, then screw on a new retaining nut. Tighten the nut to the specified torque while holding the piston rod with an Allen key.

Refitting

23 Manoeuvre the strut into position under the wheel arch, and locate in the suspension strut turret in the previously noted position. If a new strut is being fitted, locate it so that one of the two arrows marked on the upper mounting point's forwards, and the bolt holes are aligned. Insert the bolts and tighten to the specified torque.

24 Refit the plenum chamber cover and wiper arms.

25 Engage the wheel bearing housing with the bottom of the suspension strut; making sure that the hole in the side plate aligns with the holes in the split housing. Raise the housing, while pressing it inwards to assist entry. Use a trolley jack if necessary. When fully entered, remove the tool used to open the split.

26 Insert the new strut-to-wheel bearing housing bolt from the front, and fit the new retaining nut. Tighten the nut to the specified torque.

27 Unscrew the nuts from the lower balljoint and lever down the lower arm to release it from the wheel bearing housing. Insert the outer end of the driveshaft through the hub and engage it with the splines. Fit the new hub bolt, tightening it by hand only at this stage.

28 Refit the lower arm balljoint to the lower arm, and tighten the nuts to the specified torque. Where applicable, refit the headlight range control sensor arm to the lower arm and tighten the nut.

29 Refit the ABS wheel sensor as described in Chapter 9 Section 20.

30 Ensure that the outer joint is drawn fully into the hub, and then refit the roadwheel.

31 Have an assistant depress the brake pedal, and then tighten the driveshaft retaining bolt in the stages given in the Specifications. It is recommended that an angle gauge be used to ensure the correct tightening angle. Note: The car must not be standing on its wheels when tightening the bolt, or the wheel bearing may be damaged.

32 Lower the vehicle to the ground and tighten the roadwheel bolts.

5 Front suspension lower arm – removal, overhaul and refitting

Note: *The lower arm is available in either cast steel, sheet steel or aluminum. There are also two versions of the arm. Early models (up to around 2010) have a separate rear bush; on later models the rear bush is part of the control arm. When renewing the arm, make sure the correct type is fitted according to model. VW subframe locating pins (T10096) or similar are required for the work on the early lower arms, to ensure correct front wheel alignment. All self-locking nuts and bolts disturbed on removal must be renewed as a matter of course.*

Removal

1 Apply the handbrake, then jack up the front of the vehicle and support it on axle stands (see *Jacking and vehicle support*). Remove the appropriate front roadwheel and the engine compartment undertray.

2 Unscrew the front suspension lower balljoint-to-lower arm retaining nuts, then lever down the lower arm to release the arm from the balljoint studs **(see illustrations)**.

3 At this stage when removing the arm on early models, VW technicians use locating pins T10096 in place of the rear outer subframe mounting bolts to ensure correct front wheel alignment. If these pins are not available, only remove and refit one lower arm at a time, and mark the position of the subframe accurately with dabs of paint.

4 Unscrew and remove the rear outer mounting bolt **(see illustrations)** and, where available, substitute it with a locating pin tightened to 20 Nm (early models).

5 Unscrew and remove the front mounting bolt, then support the lower arm and unscrew the two rear inner mounting bolts (early models). On later models remove the front

5.2a Remove the nuts and...

5.2b ...lower the arm away from the hub

5.4a Remove the outer mounting bolt (early models)

5.4b On later models remove the nut and bolt

5.5a Undo the inner front mounting bolt ...

5.5b ...and the inner rear mounting bolts

5.5c Remove the front bolt

bolt **(see illustrations)**. Remove the lower arm from beneath the car.

Overhaul

6 Thoroughly clean the lower arm, then check carefully for cracks or any other signs of wear or damage, paying particular attention to the rubber mounting bushes. A hydraulic press and suitable spacers is the easy way to install new bushes, however it is also possible using a length of threaded bar and suitable spacers/sockets to press the bushes out of the arm and to install the new ones. Dip the bushes in a mild solution of washing-up liquid and water.

7 When fitting a new front mounting bush, it must be initially tilted with one lip in the bore. As the bush is inserted, it will straighten up **(see illustrations)**. Make sure the bush is centred in its bore.

8 On early models, after pressing a new rear mounting bush into the rear mounting bracket, press the bracket and bush fully onto the lower arm rear pivot.

9 After pressing a new rear mounting bush into the rear mounting bracket, press the bracket and bush fully onto the lower arm rear pivot.

Refitting

10 Locate the lower arm on the subframe and insert the front mounting bolt loosely.

11 On early models, insert the two rear outer mounting bolts loosely, then position the inner bolt hole in the exact position noted during removal. If a VW location pin was used on removal, the bracket will be correctly positioned on the pin. Tighten the two outer bolts to the specified torque, then remove the pin and refit the inner bolt, and tighten to the specified torque.

12 Lightly tighten the front mounting bolt.

13 Lever down the lower arm and locate the balljoint studs in their holes. Fit the new nuts and tighten to the specified torque.

14 Raise the arm using a suitable jack until the suspension is in the unladen position. Measure the distance from the hub nut centre to the wheel arch and adjust the distance

5.5d Remove the arm (later models shown)

5.7a A suitable setup for bush removal

5.7b The new bush must enter the arm off centre

5.7c Two sockets are used to allow clearance for the lip of the bush

5.7d Adjust the position of the bush so that it protrudes equally on both side of the arm

5.7e If replacing the rear bush (later models) note the alignment marks

5.14 Raise the arm until the hub centre to wheel arch dimension meets the ride height specification

as required to meet the specifications **(see illustration)**.

Caution: Exercise extreme care as the vehicle may be lifted off the axle stand during this procedure. An alternative approach is to refit the wheel and tighten the arm bolts with the vehicle on the ground (or wheel ramps).

15 Tighten the front mounting bolt to the specified torque.

16 Refit the roadwheel and undertray, and lower the car to the ground.

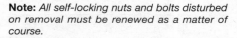

6 Front suspension lower arm balljoint – removal, inspection and refitting

Note: *All self-locking nuts and bolts disturbed on removal must be renewed as a matter of course.*

Removal

Method 1

1 Remove the wheel bearing housing as described in Section 2.

2 Unscrew and remove the balljoint retaining nut **(see illustration)**, then release the balljoint from the wheel bearing housing using a universal balljoint separator. Withdraw the balljoint.

Method 2

3 Remove the wheel trim/hub cap (as

6.2 Front suspension lower arm balljoint retaining nut

applicable) and loosen the driveshaft retaining bolt (hub bolt) with the vehicle resting on its wheels. Note: Do not loosen the hub bolt more than 90° at this stage, or the wheel bearing may be damaged. Also loosen the wheel bolts.

4 Apply the handbrake, then jack up the front of the vehicle and support it on axle stands (see *Jacking and vehicle support*). Remove the appropriate roadwheel.

5 Unscrew and remove the driveshaft retaining bolt.

6 Unscrew the front suspension lower balljoint-to-lower arm retaining nuts, then lever the lower arm down to release the balljoint studs. Now use a soft-faced mallet to tap the driveshaft from the hub splines while pulling out the bottom end of the wheel bearing housing. If the driveshaft is tight on the splines, it may be necessary to use a puller bolted to the hub to remove it. It is not necessary to remove the driveshaft completely from the hub. Retain the wheel bearing housing away from the lower arm by inserting a block of wood between the strut and the inner body panel.

7 Unscrew and remove the balljoint retaining nut, then release the balljoint from the wheel bearing housing using a universal balljoint separator. Withdraw the balljoint **(see illustrations)**.

Inspection

8 With the balljoint removed, check that it

moves freely, without any sign of roughness. Check also that the balljoint rubber gaiter shows no sign of deterioration, and is free from cracks and splits. Renew as necessary.

Refitting

Method 1

9 Fit the balljoint to the wheel bearing housing and fit the new retaining nut. Tighten the nut to the specified torque setting, noting that the balljoint shank can be retained with an Allen key if necessary to prevent it from rotating.

10 Refit the wheel bearing housing with reference to Section 2.

Method 2

11 Fit the balljoint to the wheel bearing housing and fit the new retaining nut. Tighten the nut to the specified torque setting, noting that the balljoint shank can be retained with an Allen key if necessary to prevent it from rotating.

12 Remove the wooden block and move the strut inwards, then refit the balljoint to the lower arm using new nuts, and tighten them to the specified torque.

13 Refit the driveshaft retaining bolt and tighten it sufficiently to draw the driveshaft fully into the hub, then refit the roadwheel.

14 Have an assistant depress the brake pedal, and then tighten the driveshaft retaining bolt in the stages given in the Specifications. It is recommended that an angle gauge be used to ensure the correct tightening angle. Note: The car must not be standing on its wheels when tightening the bolt, or the wheel bearing may be damaged.

15 Lower the vehicle to the ground and tighten the roadwheel bolts.

7 Front anti-roll bar – removal and refitting

Note: *As the subframe must be lowered during this procedure, VW subframe locating pins (T10096) or similar are required ensuring correct front wheel alignment. All self-locking nuts and bolts disturbed on removal must be renewed as a matter of course.*

6.7a Use a torx key to counterhold the balljoint shank

6.7b Install the balljoint separator. Note the nut positioned to protect the balljoint threads

6.7c Remove the balljoint

7.3 Disconnect the drop link from the anti-roll bar

7.5a Undo the two mounting bolts...

7.5b ...to release the anti-roll bar clamp on the subframe

Removal

1 Apply the handbrake, then jack up the front of the vehicle and support it on axle stands (see *Jacking and vehicle support*). Remove both front roadwheels and the engine compartment undertray.

2 Inside the car, undo the nuts and remove the trim beneath the foot pedals for access to the steering column universal joint. Unscrew the clamp bolt and pull the universal joint from the steering gear pinion.

3 The anti-roll bar may be removed with or without the side links. Unscrew the nuts securing the links to the struts or anti-roll bar as required **(see illustration)**.

4 Working on each side in turn, unscrew the front suspension lower balljoint-to-lower arm retaining nuts, then disconnect the track rod ends with reference to Section 23.

5 Unscrew the bolts securing the anti-roll bar clamps to the subframe **(see illustrations)**. Mark the anti-roll bar to indicate which way round it is fitted, and the position of the rubber mounting bushes; this will aid refitting.

6 Unscrew and remove the engine/ transmission rear mounting bolts from the transmission.

7 Support the subframe with a trolley jack and block of wood. If not using the special VW locating pins T10096, accurately mark the position of the subframe to ensure correct wheel alignment.

8 Unscrew the mounting bolts and slightly lower the subframe, taking care not to damage the electrical wiring. Where available, fit the VW locating pins to facilitate refitting.

9 Lift the anti-roll bar forwards over the bracket, and lower it to the floor.

10 Carefully examine the anti-roll bar components for signs of wear, damage or deterioration, paying particular attention to the rubber mounting bushes. Renew worn components as necessary.

Refitting

11 Refitting is a reversal of removal but tighten all nuts and bolts to the specified torque where given. When refitting the subframe, align it with the marks made on removal, or use the special VW location pins before tightening the mounting bolts. To assist entry of the steering gear gaiter through the bulkhead, apply a soapy solution to it. Have the front wheel alignment checked at the earliest opportunity.

8 Front anti-roll bar drop link – removal and refitting

Note: *All self-locking nuts and bolts disturbed on removal must be renewed as a matter of course.*

Removal

1 Apply the handbrake, then jack up the front of the vehicle and support it on axle stands (see *Jacking and vehicle support*). Remove the relevant front roadwheel.

2 Unscrew and remove the nuts securing the link to the strut and anti-roll bar **(see illustrations)**.

3 Inspect the link rubbers for signs of damage or deterioration. If evident, renew the link complete.

Refitting

4 Refitting is a reversal of removal, but tighten the nuts to the specified torque.

9 Rear hub/wheel bearings – checking and renewal

Note: *The rear wheel bearings cannot be renewed independently of the rear hub, because the outer races are formed in the hub itself. If excessive wear is evident, the rear hub must be renewed complete. The rear hub bolt must always be renewed after removal.*

Checking

1 Chock the front roadwheels, then jack up the rear of the vehicle and support on axle stands (see *Jacking and vehicle support*). Release the handbrake and grasp the wheel at the six 'o'clock position and check for any play in the bearing. Repeat the procedure holding

8.2a Counter hold the shank, unbolt and...

8.2b ...remove the link from the strut

8.2c Repeat the procedure at the anti-roll bar

9.1 Check the bearings for play

9.4 Remove the disc

9.5 Removing the dust cap

9.6 Slacken and then remove the hub nut

the wheel at the quarter to three position **(see illustration)**. Finally spin the wheel by hand whilst listening for the distinctive rumble sound of a worn wheel bearing.

Removal

2 Slacken the appropriate wheel nuts. Chock the front roadwheels, then jack up the rear of the vehicle and support on axle stands (see *Jacking and vehicle support*). Unbolt the relevant wheel and then release the handbrake.
3 Remove the rear brake caliper and mounting bracket with reference to Chapter 9, Section 9. Do not disconnect the hydraulic brake pipe. Move the caliper just clear of the brake disc, without bending the hydraulic pipe excessively, and support it with welding rod or on an axle stand.
4 Undo the crosshead screw then withdraw the brake disc from the hub **(see illustration)**.
5 Remove the dust cap from the centre of the

hub using a screwdriver or cold chisel **(see illustration)**.
6 Unscrew and remove the hub bolt, using a multi-spline tool or hex key **(see illustration)**. Note that it is tightened to a high torque and a socket extension bar may be required to loosen it. The bolt must be renewed whenever removed.
7 Pull the hub and bearing assembly off the hub **(see illustration)**. In some cases it may be necessary to use a suitable puller the free the hub from the stub axle.
8 Examine the hub and bearings for wear, pitting and damage. If any damage is evident, renew the hub complete.

Refitting

9 Wipe clean the stub axle, then check that the bearing races are adequately lubricated with suitable grease. Check that the inner bearing race is located correctly in the hub.
10 Locate the hub as far as possible on the stub axle.
11 Screw on the new bolt and tighten it to the specified torque **(see illustration)**.
12 Check the dust cap for damage and renew it if necessary. Use a hammer to carefully tap the cap into the hub. Note: A badly fitting dust cap will allow moisture to enter the bearing, reducing its service life.
13 Refit the brake disc and tighten the crosshead screw.
14 Refit the rear brake mounting bracket and caliper with reference to Chapter 9, Section 9.
15 Refit the roadwheel and lower the vehicle to the ground.

10 Rear stub axle

Note: *A removable stub axle is only fitted to early models. From 2008 on the stub axle is part of the main axle and any problem with the stub axle will require the replacement of the complete axle.*

Removal

1 Chock the front roadwheels, then jack up the rear of the vehicle and support on axle stands (see *Jacking and vehicle support*). Remove the relevant rear roadwheel.
2 Remove the hub and bearing as described in Section 9.
3 Unbolt the stub axle and remove it followed by the dust shield.

Refitting

4 Refitting is a reversal of removal, but use new bolts.

11 Rear leaf spring – removal and refitting

Removal

1 Chock the front roadwheels, then jack up the rear of the vehicle and support on axle stands (see *Jacking and vehicle support*). Remove the relevant rear wheel and place a jack under the rear axle **(see illustration)**.

9.7 Remove the hub

9.11 Tighten the new bolt to the specified torque

11.1 Support the axle with a jack

11.3a Remove the nuts…

11.3b …remove the U bolts and…

11.3c …recover the saddle plate

11.4a Remove the shackle plate bolt

11.4b Remove the pivot bolt

11.4c Remove the leaf spring

2 Unbolt the shock absorber lower mounting.
3 Unbolt the nuts from the saddle plate and then remove the plate and U bolts **(see illustrations)**.
4 Unbolt the leaf spring from the shackle plates and the front mounting. A blanking grommet must be removed to allow the lower shackle bolt to be removed. Lower the spring, rotate it and remove it from the rear of the vehicle **(see illustrations)**.
5 With the spring removed, check the condition of the bushes for damage. Obtain new ones if necessary. The bushes can be removed using a suitable arrangement of washers, sockets, spacers and threaded bar **(see illustration)**.

Refitting

6 Raise the rear axle until the rear suspension is set to the correct ride-height given in the

Specifications and then fully tighten the new mounting bolts. Note: To ensure even rear suspension, both springs should be renewed at the same time.

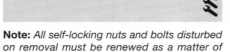

12 Rear shock absorber – removal and refitting

Note: *All self-locking nuts and bolts disturbed on removal must be renewed as a matter of course.*

Removal

1 Before removing the shock absorber, an idea of how effective it is can be gained by depressing the rear corner of the car. If the shock absorber is in good condition, the body should rise then settle in its normal position. If

the body oscillates more than this, the shock absorber is defective. Note: To ensure even rear suspension, both rear shock absorbers should be renewed at the same time.
2 Chock the front roadwheels, then jack up the rear of the vehicle and support on axle stands (see *Jacking and vehicle support*). Remove the relevant rear roadwheel.
3 Position a trolley jack and block of wood beneath the rear axle and raise the axle so that the shock absorber is slightly compressed.
4 Unscrew the lower mounting bolt, then unscrew the upper mounting bolts and withdraw the shock absorber **(see illustrations)**.
5 If necessary, the action of the shock absorber can be checked by mounting it upright in a vice. Fully depress the rod, and then pull it up fully. The piston rod must move smoothly over its complete length.

11.5 Removing the leaf spring bushes

12.4a Unscrew the rear shock absorber lower mounting bolt…

12.4b …and upper mounting bolt

13.4 Rear anti-roll bar mounting clamp bolts

14.3 Remove the lower nut

14.4 The upper mounting

Refitting

6 Locate the shock absorber in the rear wheel arch, then insert the upper mounting bolts and tighten to the specified torque.
7 Extend the shock absorber if necessary, and insert the lower mounting bolt loosely.
8 Raise the rear axle until the rear suspension is set to the correct ride-height given in the Section and then fully tighten the shock absorber lower mounting bolt.
9 Refit the roadwheel and lower the vehicle to the ground.

13 Rear anti-roll bar – removal and refitting

Removal

1 Chock the front roadwheels, then jack up the rear of the vehicle and support on axle stands (see *Jacking and vehicle support*). Remove both rear roadwheels.
2 Working on each side in turn, unscrew the nut and detach the connecting links from the anti-roll bar, see Section 14.
3 Mark the anti-roll bar to indicate which way round it is fitted, and the position of the rubber mounting bushes; this will aid refitting.
4 Unscrew the bolts securing the anti-roll bar clamps to the rear subframe, and recover the clamps (see illustration).

Refitting

5 Refitting is a reversal of removal but tighten all nuts and bolts to the specified torque.

14 Rear anti-roll bar drop link – removal and refitting

Removal

1 Chock the front roadwheels, then jack up the rear of the vehicle and support on axle stands (see *Jacking and vehicle support*). Remove the relevant rear roadwheel.
2 Note that upper part of the connecting link to the body has a bush and the lower part of the drop link has a balljoint.

3 Unscrew the nut securing the ball joint to the anti-roll bar (see illustration). Counterhold the shank with a torx key (or hex key depending on the model).
4 Reach up and remove the upper bolt (see illustration). Lower the drop link from the vehicle.
5 Inspect the link rubber/balljoint for signs of damage or deterioration. If evident, renew the link complete.

Refitting

6 Refitting is a reversal of removal, but renew the retaining nuts and tighten to the specified torque.

15 Rear axle – removal and refitting

Removal

Note: *The rear axle can be removed in several ways, but as the most likely reason for removal is either due to accident damage or (on models with an integrated stub axle) because the stub axle is damaged. Removal of the axle as a separate component is described below.*
1 Remove the wheel trim, prise out the disk cap and slacken the stub axle hub nut.
2 Chock the front roadwheels, then jack up the rear of the vehicle and support on axle stands (see *Jacking and vehicle support*). Remove both roadwheels.
3 Support the axle beam with a trolley jack (ideally two jacks should be used) and then

disconnect the wiring plugs from the ABS sensors (see illustration).
4 Remove the brake calipers as described in Chapter 9 Section 9 and then remove the rear brake disks (Chapter 9 Section 6).
5 Where possible, unbolt and remove the stub axle as described in Section 10.
6 Unbolt the anti-roll bar from the axle and then where fitted disconnect the ride height sensor (models with HID/Zenon headlights only).
7 Unbolt both lower shock absorber mounting bolts.
8 At both sides unbolt the U bolt clamps and remove the plates. With the aid of an assistant, slowly lower the axle beam on the trolley jack(s) and remove it from the vehicle.

Refitting

9 Refitting is a reversal of removal.

16 Rear bump stop – removal and refitting

Removal

1 Chock the front roadwheels, then jack up the rear of the vehicle and support on axle stands (see *Jacking and vehicle support*). Remove the relevant rear roadwheel.
2 Remove the mounting bolt and lower the bump stop out from the axle (see illustration).

Refitting

3 Refitting is a reversal of removal.

15.3 Support the axle

16.2 Remove the bump stop

17 Vehicle level sensor –
removal and refitting

Removal

1 The front senser for the headlight range control system is located on the left-hand side of the front subframe, and incorporates an arm and link attached to the left-hand front lower suspension arm. The rear senser is bolted to the left-hand side of the rear subframe, and an arm and link is attached to a bracket on the lower transverse link.

2 To remove the front senser, apply the handbrake then jack up the front of the vehicle and support it on axle stands (see *Jacking and vehicle support*). Remove the front roadwheel, and then note the position of the senser on the lower arm. Unscrew the nut and disconnect the link and bracket from the lower arm. Disconnect the wiring then unscrew the bolt and remove the senser from the front subframe.

3 To remove the rear sensor, chock the front roadwheels and then jack up the rear of the vehicle and support on axle stands (see *Jacking and vehicle support*). Disconnect the wiring from the sensor. Unscrew the nut securing the link to the shock absorber.

4 The sensor is fixed to the body with rivets. Using a drill, remove the rivets and withdraw the sensor.

Refitting

5 Refitting is a reversal of removal, but tighten the mounting bolts to the specified torque. If the rear sensor has been removed, it must be refitted with new rivets.

6 The operation of the sensor(s) should be checked by a VW dealer or garage equipped with the required diagnostic equipment.

18 Steering wheel –
removal and refitting

 Warning: During the airbag removal and refitting procedures, avoid sitting in the front seats.

Removal

1 Set the front wheels in the straight-ahead position, and release the steering lock by inserting the ignition key.

2 Disconnect the battery negative (earth) lead as described in Chapter 5A Section 3.

3 Adjust the steering column to its highest position, then extend it into the passenger compartment as far as possible, and lock it in this position.
Caution: To prevent any discharge of static electricity into the airbag circuit, temporarily touch the vehicle bodywork before disconnecting the wiring.

4 Remove the driver's airbag as described in Chapter 12, Section 27.

18.5a A splined socket will be required

18.6a The steering wheel should be marked for its central position

 Warning: Position the airbag in a safe and secure place, away from the work area.

5 Using a multi-spline socket, unscrew and remove the retaining bolt, while holding the steering wheel stationary **(see illustrations)**. Discard the retaining bolt – a new one must be fitted.

6 Check if the steering wheel is marked in relation to the column. If not, use a dab of paint to mark them, and then ease the steering wheel from the column splines by firmly rocking it side-to-side **(see illustrations)**.

Refitting

7 Locate the steering wheel on the column splines making sure that the previously made marks are correctly aligned.

8 Refit the retaining bolt and tighten to the specified torque while holding the steering wheel stationary.

9 Refit the driver's airbag with reference to Chapter 12, Section 27.

10 Reconnect the battery negative (earth) lead.

19 Steering column – removal,
inspection and refitting

Removal

1 Disconnect the battery negative lead as described in Chapter 5A Section 3.

2 Remove the steering wheel as described in Section 18.

18.5b ...unscrew and remove the bolt

18.6b Removing the steering wheel

3 Return the steering to the straight-ahead position. Adjust the steering column to its lowest position and extend it into the passenger compartment as far as possible, and then lock it in this position.

4 Unclip and remove the upper shroud from the steering column, then undo the two upper screws and single lower screw and remove the lower shroud from the steering column, as described in Chapter 11, Section 24.

5 Remove the lower facia storage/fuse box cover compartment as described in Chapter 11, Section 26.

6 Undo the retaining screw and remove the footwell heater ducting from above the pedals **(see illustration)**.

7 Remove the switch assembly from the top of the steering column as described in Chapter 12, Section 5.

8 Disconnect the wiring connector from the transponder around the ignition switch, and

19.6 Remove the footwell air ducting

19.8a Disconnect the wiring plug…

19.8b …and release the wiring loom securing clips

19.10a Remove the crash bar

19.10b Remove the cover

19.11 Remove the pinch bolt

then release the wiring retaining clips from the steering column **(see illustrations)**.

9 Follow the wiring loom down the length of the steering column, undo the earth cable retaining nut (where fitted), release the retaining clips and remove the wiring loom from under the steering column, noting its fitted position.

10 Working in the footwell, release the plastic fixings and remove the cover from the base of the column. On later models with manual transmission remove the crash bar (next to the clutch pedal) **(see illustrations)**.

11 Undo the clamp bolt from the steering column lower universal joint. Unscrew the clamp bolt and pull the universal joint from the steering gear pinion. Note that the pinion shaft

has a cut-out to enable fitting of the clamp bolt, and the splined pinion shaft incorporates a flat making it impossible to assemble the joint to the shaft in the wrong position **(see illustration)**. Discard the clamp bolt; a new one should be used on refitting.

12 Note that the inner and outer columns, and the intermediate shaft, are telescopic, to facilitate the reach adjustment. It is important to keep the splined sections of the inner steering column engaged with each other while the steering column is removed. If they become detached due to the outer column sections being separated, especially on a vehicle, which has completed a high mileage, it is possible that rattling noises may occur.

13 Support the steering column, then unscrew and remove the mounting bolts. Withdraw the steering column from inside the car **(see illustrations)**. Note that the mounting bracket on the bulkhead has locating lug, which aligns with a slot on the top of the steering column. *Caution: Do not carry the steering column by suspending it from the universal joint or intermediate shaft, as this will damage the universal joint and steering column bushes. Also, do not bend the joints by more than 90°.*

14 If necessary, remove the ignition switch/steering column lock with reference to Section 20.

Inspection

15 The steering column is designed to collapse in the event of a front-end crash, to prevent the steering wheel injuring the driver. Before refitting the steering column, examine the column and mountings for signs of damage and deformation.

16 Check the inner column sections for signs of free play in the column bushes. If any damage or wear is found on the steering column bushes, the column must be renewed as an assembly.

17 The intermediate shaft is permanently attached to the inner column and cannot be renewed separately. Inspect the universal

19.13a Undo the mounting bolts (two shown and two not visible) …

19.13b …and withdraw the steering column

20.4 Disconnect the wiring plug

20.5 Peel back the label

20.6a Insert two thin screwdrivers in the recesses...

joints for excessive wear. If evident, the complete steering column must be renewed.

Refitting

18 Where removed, refit the ignition switch/ steering column lock/switch carrier with reference to Section 20.
19 Refit the steering column to the bulkhead bracket, making sure it located on the locating lug. Insert the mounting bolts, and tighten to the specified torque, starting with the upper bolts first and then the lower bolts.
20 Attach the universal joint on the steering gear pinion splines, making sure the road wheels and steering wheel are in the correct position. Insert the new clamp bolt, and tighten to the specified torque.
21 Reconnect the earth cable and tighten the retaining nut, then refit the wiring harness under the steering column.
22 Reconnect the wiring to the ignition switch transponder and secure the wiring in its retaining clips.
23 Refit the footrest trim and footwell vent under the steering column.
24 Refit the light switch assembly with reference to Chapter 12, Section 5.
25 Refit the lower facia panels, as described in Chapter 11, Section 26.
26 Refit the lower and upper shrouds, as described in Chapter 11, Section 24.
27 Refit the steering wheel with reference to Section 18.
28 Reconnect the battery negative lead.
29 On models with ESP, the steering angle sensor basic settings must be set by a VW dealer or suitably equipped garage using specialist diagnostic equipment.

20 Ignition switch/lock cylinder – removal and refitting

Ignition switch

Note: *Early models have a slightly different switch fitted; however removal and refitting is similar in both cases.*

Removal

1 Disconnect the battery negative lead as described in Chapter 5A Section 3.
2 Remove the steering wheel as described in Section 18.
3 Unclip and remove the upper shroud from the steering column and then remove the lower shroud from the steering column, as described in Chapter 11, Section 24.
4 Insert the key and turn to the 'on' position. Release the retaining clip and disconnect the wiring plug from the rear of the ignition switch **(see illustration)**.
5 Where required, peel back the label **(see illustration)**.
6 Using two small screwdrivers in the slots in the outer housing release the two retaining clips, and then withdraw the ignition electrical switch **(see illustrations)**.

Refitting

7 Refit the switch to the steering lock housing and press in until the two retaining clips engage. Making sure the slot in the rear of the switch is aligned correctly.
8 Reconnect the wiring plug to the ignition switch.

20.6b ...and withdraw the electrical switch

9 Refit the upper and lower shrouds, and tighten the screws.
10 Refit the steering wheel with reference to Section 18.
11 Reconnect the battery negative lead.

Lock cylinder

Removal

12 Carry out the procedures as described in paragraphs 1 and 3.
13 Disconnect the wiring connector from the transponder around the ignition switch **(see illustration 20.8a)**.
14 Insert the ignition key and turn the lock cylinder to the drive/on position (which is 90° from off position).
15 Insert a piece of wire 1.2 mm in diameter in the drilling next to the ignition key, slide it in to release the locking lever, then withdraw the lock cylinder from the housing **(see illustrations)**. To make the piece of wire

20.15a Hole provided in the ignition switch

20.15b insert a thin rod through the hole ...

20.15c ...to release the locking lever

locate in the locking lever easier, file an angle on the end of the wire.

Refitting

16 Refit the lock cylinder with the ignition key in the Drive position, then remove the wire.
17 Reconnect the wiring connector to the transponder.
18 Refit the upper and lower shrouds, and tighten the screws.
19 Refit the steering wheel with reference to Section 18.
20 Reconnect the battery negative lead.

Ignition switch/lock cylinder housing

Removal

21 The ignition switch/lock housing is integral with the switch assembly carrier, which is secured to the steering column with shear-head bolts **(see illustration)**.
22 To remove the housing first remove the steering column as described in Section 19.
23 The switch/lock carrier is secured by shear-head bolts, and the heads are broken off in the tightening procedure. To remove the old bolts, either drill them out, or use a sharp cold chisel to cut off their heads or turn them anti-clockwise. Withdraw the carrier from the steering column.
24 When refitting locate the switch/lock carrier on the steering column, and insert the new shear-head bolts. Tighten the bolts until their heads break off.
25 The remaining procedure is a reversal of removal.

21 Steering rack assembly – removal, overhaul and refitting

1 Power steering is fitted to all models. Early models had either a Hydraulic Power Steering (HPS) system fitted or an Electrical Power Steering (EPS) system. Later models (circa 2011 on) are all fitted with EPS systems.
2 Early models have an aluminium subframe and later models (2011 on) have a steel subframe fitted. As the subframe must be lowered during this procedure, VW subframe locating pins (T10096 for aluminium subframes and T10096 plus T10452 for steel subframes) or similar are required to ensure correct front wheel alignment. New subframe mounting bolts, track rod balljoint nuts, steering gear retaining bolts, and an intermediate shaft universal joint clamp bolt will be required on refitting.
3 Regardless of which type of power steering is fitted, removal and refitting of the steering rack is essentially the same.
4 Several versions of the Electrical Power Steering (EPS) rack are fitted to the Caddy range. Where an earlier version is fitted replacement steering racks may be the later version. All the versions are compatible with all vehicles, but a modified wiring loom will be required where a later generation steering rack is fitted to an earlier vehicle.

Removal

5 Disconnect the battery negative lead (refer to Chapter 5A Section 3).

6 Apply the handbrake, then jack up the front of the vehicle and support it on axle stands positioned on the underbody, leaving the subframe free (see *Jacking and vehicle support*). Position the steering straight-ahead, and then remove both front roadwheels. Also remove the engine compartment undertray.
7 Inside the vehicle, undo the screws and remove the plastic cover for access to the universal joint connecting the steering inner column to the steering gear pinion (see Section 19). Unscrew and remove the clamp bolt, and pull the universal joint from the pinion splines. Note: The steering gear pinion incorporates a cut-out for the clamp bolt, and therefore the joint can only be fitted in one position. Discard the clamp bolt; a new one should be used on refitting.
8 Remove the battery and battery tray with reference to Chapter 5A Section 3.
9 On models with EPS, unclip the plastic cover from the wiring loom, which runs along the left-hand chassis leg under the battery tray. Trace the wiring loom from the steering rack, undo the retaining nuts and disconnect the wiring connections so that the wiring loom can be removed with the steering rack assembly **(see illustrations)**.
10 On models fitted with HPS to minimise the loss of hydraulic fluid clamp the return hose with a brake pipe clamp. Place a container below the steering rack and then remove the hydraulic pipes from the steering rack. Seal the pipes and the openings in the steering rack.
11 Disconnect the track rod ends from the

20.21 Steering lock housing shear bolts

21.9a Unclip the wiring cover …

21.9b …disconnect the wiring from the fusebox…

21.9c …disconnect the earth cable …

21.9d …disconnect the wiring plug connector …

21.9e …and lift the wiring loom out of position

21.14 Undo the lower rear mounting bracket bolts

21.15 Undo the exhaust mounting bracket bolts

steering arms on the front wheel bearing housings, as described in Section 23.

12 Working on each side in turn, disconnect the anti-roll bar links to the struts, as described in Section 8.

13 Working on each side in turn, unscrew the front suspension lower balljoint-to-lower arm retaining nuts, then lever the lower arms down to release the balljoint studs, as described in Section 6.

14 Unscrew and remove the engine/transmission rear mounting bolts from the transmission (see illustration).

15 Unbolt the exhaust system mounting from the subframe (see illustration). Where applicable unbolt the exhaust system heat shield from the subframe.

16 On models fitted with a fuel fired auxiliary heater disconnect the exhaust pipe from the subframe.

17 Support the subframe with a trolley jack and block of wood. If not using the special VW locating pins T10096, accurately mark

21.17a Mark the position of the front...

21.17b ...and rear subframe mounting positions (aluminium subframe)

the position of the subframe to ensure correct wheel alignment (see illustrations).

18 Unscrew the mounting bolts and slightly lower the subframe (see illustrations), taking care not to damage the electrical wiring, as it is being lowered. Where

available, fit the VW locating pins to facilitate refitting.

19 Lower the subframe together with the steering gear to the floor, then undo the retaining screws and remove the heat shield from over the steering gear.

21.18a Subframe front and rear mounting bolts (one side shown aluminium subframe)

21.18b Subframe mounting bolts (one side shown, steel subframe)

21.20a Disconnect the wiring connector on the rear ...

21.20b ...and the front of the steering electric motor ...

e) *On models with ESP, the steering angle sensor basic settings must be set by a VW dealer (or suitably equipped garage) using specialist diagnostic equipment.*
f) *If a new a EPS rack has been fitted, it must also be adapted to the vehicle by a VW dealer (or suitably equipped garage) using suitable diagnostic equipment.*
g) *On HPS systems refill the power steering reservoir and bleed the power steering system as described in Section 24.*

22 Steering rack gaiters and track rods – renewal

21.20c ...then undo the wiring loom securing bolt

Overhaul

22 Examine the steering gear assembly for signs of wear or damage, and check that the rack moves freely throughout the full length of its travel, with no signs of roughness or excessive free play between the steering gear pinion and rack.

23 It is not possible to overhaul the steering gear assembly housing components, and if it is faulty, the assembly must be renewed. The only components that can be renewed individually are the steering gear gaiters, the track rod end balljoints and the track rods, as described later in this Chapter.

Refitting

24 Refitting is a reversal of removal, noting the following points:

a) *Align the subframe with the marks made on removal, or use the special VW location pins before tightening the mounting bolts.*
b) *Make sure that all mounting bolts are tightened to the specified torque.*
c) *Make sure wiring connections are secure and that the wiring loom is routed correctly.*
d) *Have the front wheel alignment checked at the earliest opportunity.*

Steering gear rubber gaiters

1 Remove the track rod end balljoint as described in Section 23. Also, unscrew the locking nut from the track rod arm, after noting its position.

2 Wipe clean the rubber gaiter to prevent entry of dirt or moisture. Note the fitted position of the gaiter on the track rod, then release the retaining clips and slide the gaiter off the steering gear housing and track rod **(see illustration)**.

3 Wipe clean the track rod and the steering gear housing, and then apply a film of suitable grease to the surface of the rack. To do this, turn the steering wheel as necessary to fully extend the rack from the housing, then reposition it in its central position.

4 Carefully slide the new gaiter onto the track rod, and locate it on the steering gear housing. Position the gaiter as previously noted on removal, making sure that it is not twisted, then lift the outer sealing lip of the gaiter to equalise air pressure within the gaiter.

5 Secure the gaiter in position with new retaining clips. Where crimped-type clips are used, pull the clip as tight as possible, and locate the hooks in their slots. Remove any

20 On EPS models disconnect all wiring from the steering gear assembly **(see illustrations)**. Release the wiring loom from the clips along the steering rack and subframe, noting its fitted position.

Caution: Do not touch the wiring terminals on the electronic control unit, as a static electricity discharge may damage the internal components.

21 Unbolt the steering gear from the subframe **(see illustration)**, and carefully place it on the floor taking care not to damage the electronic control unit.

21.21 Steering rack mounting bolts

22.2 Steering rack gaiter securing clips

23.3 Slacken the lock nut

23.4a Using an Allen key to hold the ball joint shank while loosening the nut

23.4b Release the track rod ball joint

slack in the clip by carefully compressing the raised section. In the absence of the special crimping tool, a pair of side-cutters may be used, taking care not to cut the clip.

6 Screw on the locking nut, then refit the track rod end balljoint as described in Section 23.

Track rods

7 Remove the relevant steering gear rubber gaiter as described earlier. If there is insufficient working room with the steering gear mounted in the car, remove it as described in Section 21 and hold it in a vice while renewing the track rod.

8 Hold the steering rack stationary with one spanner on the flats provided, then loosen the balljoint nut with another spanner. Fully unscrew the nut and remove the track rod from the rack.

9 Locate the new track rod on the end of the steering rack and screw on the nut. Hold the rack stationary with one spanner and tighten the balljoint nut to the specified torque. A crow's foot adapter may be required since the track rod prevents access with a socket, and care must be taken to apply the correct torque in this situation.

10 Refit the steering gear or rubber gaiter with reference to the earlier paragraphs or Section 21. On completion check and, if necessary, adjust the front wheel alignment as described in Section 25.

23 Track rod end –
removal and refitting

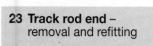

Note: *A new balljoint retaining nut will be required on refitting.*

Removal

1 Apply the handbrake, then jack up the front of the vehicle and support it on axle stands (see *Jacking and vehicle support*). Remove the relevant roadwheel.

2 If the track rod end is to be re-used, mark its position in relation to the track rod to facilitate refitting.

3 Unscrew the track rod end locknut by a quarter of a turn **(see illustration)**. Do not

23.4c Use a ball joint separator to release the track rod ball joint if it is a tight fit

move the locknut from this position, as it will serve as a handy reference mark on refitting.

4 Loosen and remove the nut securing the track rod end balljoint to the wheel bearing housing, and release the balljoint tapered shank using a universal balljoint separator. Note that the balljoint shank has a hexagon hole – hold the shank with an Allen key while loosening the nut **(see illustrations)**.

5 Counting the exact number of turns necessary to do so, unscrew the track rod end from the track rod **(see illustration)**.

6 Carefully clean the balljoint and the threads. Renew the balljoint if its movement is sloppy or too stiff, if excessively worn, or if damaged in any way; carefully check the stud taper and threads. If the balljoint gaiter is damaged, the complete balljoint assembly must be renewed; it is not possible to obtain the gaiter separately.

Refitting

7 Screw the track rod end onto the track rod by the number of turns noted on removal. This should bring the track rod end to within a quarter of a turn of the locknut, with the alignment marks that were made on removal (if applicable) lined up. Tighten the locknut.

8 Refit the balljoint shank to the steering arm on the wheel bearing housing, then fit a new retaining nut and tighten it to the specified torque. Hold the shank with an Allen key if necessary.

9 Refit the roadwheel, then lower the car to the ground and tighten the roadwheel bolts to the specified torque.

23.5 Unscrewing the track rod end from the track rod

10 Check and, if necessary, adjust the front wheel toe setting as described in Section 25.

24 Power steering pump
– removal and refitting and bleeding

Removal

1 Remove the auxiliary drivebelt as described in Chapter 1 Section 29.

2 Hold the power steering pump pulley with a pin tool or strap wrench and slacke the pulley mounting bolts.

3 Clamp the low pressure supply hose with a brake hose clamp. Place a shop towels beneath the pump and then remove the hose clip. Remove the hose and seal the opening in the pump.

4 Unbolt and then remove the pressure hose from the pump. Seal the hose and the opening in the pump.

5 Remove the mounting bolts and lift the pump out of the engine bay.

Refitting

6 Refitting is a reversal of removal. Bleed the pump as described below.

Bleeding

7 Apply the handbrake, then jack up the front of the vehicle and support it on axle stands (see *Jacking and vehicle support*).

8 Top up the fluid level in the reservoir and then run the engine at idle for a minimum of five minutes.

25.1 Front wheel geometry

9 Stop the engine and check the fluid level. Top up as required.

10 Restart the engine and turn the steering wheel from lock to lock three times without holding the steering wheel against the stop.

11 Stop the engine and check the fluid level. Top up the flid level if necessary.

12 Lower the vehicle to the ground, start the engine and turn the steering from lock to lock a minimum of five times – again without holding the steering wheel against the stop.

13 The steering bleeding procedure is complet when no air bubbles are present in the reservoir. Repeat the procedure if necessary. Top up the fluid level if necessary.

25 Wheel alignment and steering angles – general information

Definitions

1 A car's steering and suspension geometry is defined in three basic settings – all angles are expressed in degrees; the steering axis is defined as an imaginary line drawn through the axis of the suspension strut, extended where necessary to contact the ground **(see illustration)**.

2 Camber is the angle between each roadwheel and a vertical line drawn through its centre and tyre contact patch, when viewed from the front or rear of the car. Positive camber is when the roadwheels are tilted outwards from the vertical at the top; negative camber is when they are tilted inwards.

3 The front Camber angle is only adjustable by loosening the front suspension subframe mounting bolts and moving it slightly to one side. The camber angle can be checked using a camber checking gauge. This will also alter the Castor angle.

4 The rear Camber angle is only adjustable by loosening the upper transverse inner mounting nut, then turning the eccentric bolt (this can be turned left or right to a maximum range of 90°). The camber angle can be checked using a camber checking gauge. This will also alter the Castor angle.

5 Castor is the angle between the steering axis and a vertical line drawn through each roadwheel's centre and tyre contact patch, when viewed from the side of the car. Positive castor is when the steering axis is tilted so that it contacts the ground ahead of the vertical; negative castor is when it contacts the ground behind the vertical. Slight castor angle adjustment is possible by loosening the front suspension subframe bolts and moving it slightly to one side. This also alters the Camber angle.

6 Castor is not easily adjustable, and is given for reference only; while it can be checked using a castor checking gauge, if the figure obtained is significantly different from that specified, the car must be taken for careful checking by a professional, as the fault can only be caused by wear or damage to the body or suspension components.

7 Toe is the difference, viewed from above, between lines drawn through the roadwheel centres and the car's centre-line. Toe-in is when the roadwheels point inwards, towards each other at the front, while toe-out is when they splay outwards from each other at the front.

8 The front wheel toe setting is adjusted by screwing the track rod(s) in/out of the outer balljoint(s) to alter the effective length of the track rod assembly.

9 Rear wheel toe setting is adjusted by loosening the lower transverse inner mounting nut, and then turning the eccentric bolt (this can be turned left or right to a maximum range of 90°).

10 If the figures obtained are significantly different from that specified, the car must be taken for careful checking by a professional, as the fault can only be caused by wear or damage to the body or suspension components.

Checking and adjustment

11 Due to the special measuring equipment necessary to check the wheel alignment, and the skill required to use it properly, the checking and adjustment of these settings is best left to a VW dealer or similar expert. Note that most tyre-fitting centres now possess sophisticated checking equipment.

Chapter 11
Bodywork and fittings

Contents

Section number

Body exterior fittings – removal and refitting 20
Bonnet – removal, refitting and adjustment 8
Bonnet lock – removal and refitting 10
Bonnet release cable – removal and refitting 9
Central locking components – description, removal and refitting . . . 17
Centre console – removal and refitting. 25
Crossmember – removal and refitting 27
Door – removal, refitting and adjustment 11
Door handle and lock components – removal and refitting 13
Door inner trim panel – removal and refitting 12
Door window glass and regulator – removal and refitting 14
Facia panel assembly – removal and refitting 26
Front bumper cover – removal and refitting 6
Front seat belt tensioning mechanism – general information 22

Section number

General Information 1
Interior trim – removal and refitting 24
Maintenance – bodywork and underframe. 2
Maintenance – upholstery and carpets 3
Major body damage – repair 5
Minor body damage – repair 4
Mirrors and associated components – removal and refitting. 18
Rear bumper – removal and refitting 7
Seat belt components – removal and refitting 23
Seats – removal and refitting 21
Tailgate and support struts – removal and refitting 15
Tailgate lock components – removal and refitting 16
Windscreen, sliding door and rear window glass –
    general information. 19

Degrees of difficulty

Easy, suitable for novice with little experience | **Fairly easy,** suitable for beginner with some experience | **Fairly difficult,** suitable for competent DIY mechanic | **Difficult,** suitable for experienced DIY mechanic | **Very difficult,** suitable for expert DIY or professional

Specifications

Torque wrench settings	Nm	lbf ft
Bonnet hinge nuts	22	16
Door hinges (front):		
Stage 1*	20	15
Stage 2	Angle-tighten a further 90°	
Upper hinge nut	14	10
Door lock	20	15
Crossmember bolts/nuts	20	15
Front window glass clamp bolts	8	6
Front seat belt adjuster bolt	20	15
Front seat belt lower mounting bolt (microencapsulated)*	40	30
Front seat belt stalk to seat frame bolt (microencapsulated)*	20	15
Front seat mounting retaining bolts	40	30
Inertia reel mounting bolts	40	30
Rear door hinges	20	15
Third row seat bolts	55	41
Seat belt and stalk anchorage bolts	40	30
Sliding door:		
Upper guide bolts	18	13
Lower guide bolts	30	22
Hinge bolts	65	48
Striker plate bolts	20	15
Tailgate hinge bolts	10	7

*Renew the bolts

1 General Information

1 The body shell is made of pressed-steel sections of varying thickness, with many of the structural panels being made from high tensile steel. Most components are welded together, either by traditional spot welding or where increased rigidity is required by continuous laser welding. Structural adhesives are used to bond some body panels. The front wings are bonded to a deformable panel that is then bolted to the main bodyshell.

2 The bonnet, door, and some other vulnerable panels are made of zinc-coated metal, and are further protected by being coated with an anti-chip primer before being sprayed.

3 Extensive use is made of plastic materials, mainly in the interior, but also in exterior components. The front and rear bumpers, and front grille, are injection-moulded from a synthetic material that is very strong and yet light. Plastic components such as wheel arch liners are fitted to the underside of the vehicle, to improve the body's resistance to corrosion.

2 Maintenance –
bodywork and underframe

1 The general condition of a vehicle's bodywork is the one thing that significantly affects its value. Maintenance is easy, but needs to be regular. Neglect, particularly after minor damage, can lead quickly to further deterioration and costly repair bills. It is important also to keep watch on those parts of the vehicle not immediately visible, for instance the underside, inside all the wheel arches, and the lower part of the engine compartment.

2 The basic maintenance routine for the bodywork is washing – preferably with a lot of water, from a hose. This will remove all the loose solids, which may have stuck to the vehicle. It is important to flush these off in such a way as to prevent grit from scratching the finish. The wheel arches and underframe need washing in the same way, to remove any accumulated mud, which will retain moisture and tend to encourage rust. Paradoxically enough, the best time to clean the underframe and wheel arches is in wet weather, when the mud is thoroughly wet and soft. In very wet weather, the underframe is usually cleaned of large accumulations automatically, and this is a good time for inspection.

3 Periodically, except on vehicles with a wax-based underbody protective coating, it is a good idea to have the whole of the underframe of the vehicle steam-cleaned, engine compartment included, so that a thorough inspection can be carried out to see what minor repairs and renovations

are necessary. Steam cleaning is available at many garages, and is necessary for the removal of the accumulation of oily grime, which sometimes is allowed to become thick in certain areas. If steam-cleaning facilities are not available, there are some excellent grease solvents available which can be brush-applied; the dirt can then be simply hosed off. Note that these methods should not be used on vehicles with wax-based underbody protective coating, or the coating will be removed. Such vehicles should be inspected annually, preferably just prior to Winter, when the underbody should be washed down, and any damage to the wax coating repaired. Ideally, a completely fresh coat should be applied. It would also be worth considering the use of such wax-based protection for injection into door panels, sills, box sections, etc, as an additional safeguard against rust damage, where such protection is not provided by the vehicle manufacturer.

4 After washing paintwork, wipe off with a chamois leather to give an unspotted clear finish. A coat of clear protective wax polish will give added protection against chemical pollutants in the air. If the paintwork sheen has dulled or oxidised, use a cleaner/polisher combination to restore the brilliance of the shine. This requires a little effort, but such dulling is usually caused because regular washing has been neglected. Care needs to be taken with metallic paintwork, as special non-abrasive cleaner/polisher is required to avoid damage to the finish. Always check that the door and ventilator opening drain holes and pipes are completely clear, so that water can be drained out. Brightwork should be treated in the same way as paintwork. Windscreens and windows can be kept clear of the smeary film that often appears, by the use of proprietary glass cleaner. Never use any form of wax or other body or chromium polish on glass.

3 Maintenance –
upholstery and carpets

1 Mats and carpets should be brushed or vacuum-cleaned regularly, to keep them free of grit. If they are badly stained, remove them from the vehicle for scrubbing or sponging, and make quite sure they are dry before refitting. Seats and interior trim panels can be kept clean by wiping with a damp cloth. If they do become stained (which can be more apparent on light-coloured upholstery), use a little liquid detergent and a soft nail brush to scour the grime out of the grain of the material. Do not forget to keep the headlining clean in the same way as the upholstery. When using liquid cleaners inside the vehicle, do not over-wet the surfaces being cleaned. Excessive damp could get into the seams and padded interior, causing stains, offensive odours or even rot.

2 If the inside of the vehicle gets wet accidentally, it is worthwhile taking some trouble to dry it out properly, particularly where carpets are involved. Do not leave oil or electric heaters inside the vehicle for this purpose.

4 Minor body damage – repair

Scratches

1 If the scratch is very superficial, and does not penetrate to the metal of the bodywork, repair is very simple. Lightly rub the area of the scratch with a paintwork renovator, or a very fine cutting paste, to remove loose paint from the scratch, and to clear the surrounding bodywork of wax polish. Rinse the area with clean water.

2 Apply touch-up paint to the scratch using a fine paintbrush; continue to apply fine layers of paint until the surface of the paint in the scratch is level with the surrounding paintwork. Allow the new paint at least two weeks to harden, and then blend it into the surrounding paintwork by rubbing the scratch area with a paintwork renovator or a very fine cutting paste. Finally, apply wax polish.

3 Where the scratch has penetrated right through to the metal of the bodywork, causing the metal to rust, a different repair technique is required. Remove any loose rust from the bottom of the scratch with a penknife, and then apply rust-inhibiting paint to prevent the formation of rust in the future. Using a rubber or nylon applicator, fill the scratch with bodystopper paste. If required, this paste can be mixed with cellulose thinners to provide a very thin paste that is ideal for filling narrow scratches. Before the stopper-paste in the scratch hardens, wrap a piece of smooth cotton rag around the top of a finger. Dip the finger in cellulose thinners, and quickly sweep it across the surface of the stopper-paste in the scratch; this will ensure that the surface of the stopper-paste is slightly hollowed. The scratch can now be painted over as described earlier in this Section.

Dents

4 When deep denting of the vehicle's bodywork has taken place, the first task is to pull the dent out, until the affected bodywork almost attains its original shape. There is little point in trying to restore the original shape completely, as the metal in the damaged area will have stretched on impact, and cannot be reshaped fully to its original contour. It is better to bring the level of the dent up to a point, which is about 3 mm below the level of the surrounding bodywork. In cases where the dent is very shallow anyway, it is not worth trying to pull it out at all. If the underside of the dent is accessible, it can be hammered out gently from behind, using a mallet with

a wooden or plastic head. Whilst doing this, hold a suitable block of wood firmly against the outside of the panel, to absorb the impact from the hammer blows and thus prevent a large area of the bodywork from being 'belled-out'.

5 Should the dent be in a section of the bodywork that has a double skin, or some other factor making it inaccessible from behind, a different technique is called for. Drill several small holes through the metal inside the area – particularly in the deeper section. Then screw long self-tapping screws into the holes, just sufficiently for them to gain a good purchase in the metal. Now the dent can be pulled out by pulling on the protruding heads of the screws with a pair of pliers.

6 The next stage of the repair is the removal of the paint from the damaged area, and from an inch or so of the surrounding 'sound' bodywork. This is accomplished most easily by using a wire brush or abrasive pad on a power drill, although it can be done just as effectively by hand, using sheets of abrasive paper. To complete the preparation for filling, score the surface of the bare metal with a screwdriver or the tang of a file, or alternatively, drill small holes in the affected area. This will provide a really good 'key' for the filler paste.

7 To complete the repair, see the Section on filling and respraying.

Rust holes or gashes

8 Remove all paint from the affected area, and from an inch or so of the surrounding 'sound' bodywork, using an abrasive pad or a wire brush on a power drill. If these are not available, a few sheets of abrasive paper will do the job most effectively. With the paint removed, you will be able to judge the severity of the corrosion, and therefore decide whether to renew the whole panel (if this is possible) or to repair the affected area. New body panels are not as expensive as most people think, and it is often quicker and more satisfactory to fit a new panel than to attempt to repair large areas of corrosion.

9 Remove all fittings from the affected area, except those, which will act as a guide to the original shape of the damaged bodywork (e.g. headlight shells etc). Then, using tin snips or a hacksaw blade, remove all loose metal and any other metal badly affected by corrosion. Hammer the edges of the hole inwards, in order to create a slight depression for the filler paste.

10 Wire-brush the affected area to remove the powdery rust from the surface of the remaining metal. Paint the affected area with rust-inhibiting paint, if the back of the rusted area is accessible, treat this also.

11 Before filling can take place, it will be necessary to block the hole in some way. This can be achieved by the use of aluminium or plastic mesh, or aluminium tape.

12 Aluminium or plastic mesh, or glassfibre matting, is probably the best material to use for a large hole. Cut a piece to the approximate size and shape of the hole to be filled, then position it in the hole so that its edges are below the level of the surrounding bodywork. It can be retained in position by several blobs of filler paste around its periphery.

13 Aluminium tape should be used for small or very narrow holes. Pull a piece off the roll, trim it to the approximate size and shape required, then pull off the backing paper (if used) and stick the tape over the hole; it can be overlapped if the thickness of one piece is insufficient. Burnish down the edges of the tape with the handle of a screwdriver or similar, to ensure that the tape is securely attached to the metal underneath.

Filling and respraying

14 Before using this Section, see the Sections on dent, deep scratch, rust holes and gash repairs.

15 Many types of bodyfiller are available, but generally speaking, those proprietary kits, which contain a tin of filler paste and a tube of resin hardener, are best for this type of repair. A wide, flexible plastic or nylon applicator will be found invaluable for imparting a smooth and well-contoured finish to the surface of the filler.

16 Mix up a little filler on a clean piece of card or board – measure the hardener carefully (follow the maker's instructions on the pack), otherwise the filler will set too rapidly or too slowly. Using the applicator, apply the filler paste to the prepared area; draw the applicator across the surface of the filler to achieve the correct contour and to level the surface. As soon as a contour that approximates to the correct one is achieved, stop working the paste – if you carry on too long, the paste will become sticky and begin to 'pick-up' on the applicator. Continue to add thin layers of filler paste at 20-minute intervals, until the level of the filler is just proud of the surrounding bodywork.

17 Once the filler has hardened, the excess can be removed using a metal plane or file. From then on, progressively finer grades of abrasive paper should be used, starting with a 40-grade production paper, and finishing with a 400-grade wet-and-dry paper. Always wrap the abrasive paper around a flat rubber, cork, or wooden block – otherwise the surface of the filler will not be completely flat. During the smoothing of the filler surface, the wet-and-dry paper should be periodically rinsed in water. This will ensure that a very smooth finish is imparted to the filler at the final stage.

18 At this stage, the dent should be surrounded by a ring of bare metal, which in turn should be encircled by the finely 'feathered' edge of the good paintwork. Rinse the repair area with clean water, until all of the dust produced by the rubbing-down operation has gone.

19 Spray the whole area with a light coat of primer – this will show up any imperfections in the surface of the filler. Repair these imperfections with fresh filler paste or bodystopper, and once more smooth the surface with abrasive paper. Repeat this spray-and-repair procedure until you are satisfied that the surface of the filler, and the feathered edge of the paintwork, are perfect. Clean the repair area with clean water, and allow to dry fully.

20 The repair area is now ready for final spraying. Paint spraying must be carried out in a warm, dry, windless and dust-free atmosphere. This condition can be created artificially if you have access to a large indoor working area, but if you are forced to work in the open, you will have to pick your day very carefully. If you are working indoors, dousing the floor in the work area with water will help to settle the dust, which would otherwise be in the atmosphere. If the repair area is confined to one body panel, mask off the surrounding panels; this will help to minimise the effects of a slight mis-match in paint colours. Bodywork fittings (e.g. chrome strips, door handles etc) will also need to be masked off. Use genuine masking tape, and several thicknesses of newspaper, for the masking operations.

21 Before commencing to spray, agitate the aerosol can thoroughly, and then spray a test area (an old tin, or similar) until the technique is mastered. Cover the repair area with a thick coat of primer; the thickness should be built up using several thin layers of paint, rather than one thick one. Using 400-grade wet-and-dry paper, rub down the surface of the primer until it is really smooth. While doing this, the work area should be thoroughly doused with water, and the wet-and-dry paper periodically rinsed in water. Allow to dry before spraying on more paint.

22 Spray on the top coat, again building up the thickness by using several thin layers of paint. Start spraying at one edge of the repair area, and then, using a side-to-side motion, work until the whole repair area and about 2 inches of the surrounding original paintwork is covered. Remove all masking material 10 to 15 minutes after spraying on the final coat of paint.

23 Allow the new paint at least two weeks to harden, then, using a paintwork renovator, or a very fine cutting paste, blend the edges of the paint into the existing paintwork. Finally, apply wax polish.

Plastic components

24 With the use of more and more plastic body components by the vehicle manufacturers (e.g. bumpers. spoilers, and in some cases major body panels), rectification of more serious damage to such items has become a matter of either entrusting repair work to a specialist in this field, or renewing complete components. Repair of such damage by the DIY owner is not really feasible, owing to the cost of the equipment and materials required for effecting such repairs. The basic technique involves making a groove along the line of the crack in the plastic, using a rotary burr in a power drill. The damaged part is then welded back together, using a hot-air gun to heat up and fuse a plastic filler rod into the groove. Any excess plastic is then removed, and the area rubbed down to a smooth finish. It is important that a filler rod of the correct plastic is used, as body components can be made of a variety of different types (e.g. polycarbonate, ABS, polypropylene).

25 Damage of a less serious nature (abrasions, minor cracks etc) can be repaired by the DIY owner using a two-part epoxy filler repair material. Once mixed in equal proportions, this is used in similar fashion to the bodywork filler used on metal panels. The filler is usually cured in twenty to thirty minutes, ready for sanding and painting.

26 If the owner is renewing a complete component himself, or if he has repaired it with epoxy filler, he will be left with the problem of finding a suitable paint for finishing which is compatible with the type of plastic used. At one time, the use of a universal paint was not possible, owing to the complex range of plastics encountered in body component applications. Standard paints, generally speaking, will not bond to plastic or rubber satisfactorily. However, it is now possible to obtain a plastic body parts finishing kit, which consists of a pre-primer treatment, a primer and coloured top coat. Full instructions are normally supplied with a kit, but basically, the method of use is to first apply the pre-primer to the component concerned, and allow it to dry for up to 30 minutes. Then the primer

is applied, and left to dry for about an hour before finally applying the special-coloured top coat. The result is a correctly coloured component, where the paint will flex with the plastic or rubber, a property that standard paint does not normally possess.

5 Major body damage – repair

1 Where serious damage has occurred, or large areas need renewal due to neglect, it means that complete new panels will need welding-in, and this is best left to professionals. If the damage is due to impact, it will also be necessary to check completely the alignment of the body shell, and this can only be carried out accurately by a VW dealer using special jigs. If the body is left misaligned, it is primarily dangerous, as the car will not handle properly, and secondly, uneven stresses will be imposed on the steering, suspension and possibly transmission, causing abnormal wear, or complete failure, particularly to such items as the tyres.

6 Front bumper cover – removal and refitting

Note: *Depending on the year of production and the trim level slight changes to the removal and refitting procedures may be necessary. On early models with colour coordinated bumper covers the grille must be removed first. On all other models the grille is removed with the cover and then removed from the bumper cover on the bench (where the grille is removable).*

Removal

1 Apply the handbrake, then jack up the front of the vehicle and support it on axle stands (see *Jacking and vehicle support*). For ease of access, remove both front road wheels. Alternatively turn the wheels from lock to lock as required.

2 Either completely remove both front wing liners **(see illustration)** or remove the fixings from the front edge of the wing liner and carefully fold the wing liner into the wheel arch. Repeat the procedure on the opposite side.

3 At the front edge of the wheel arch, remove the 'scrivet' or screws from the trailing edge of the bumper. Unclip the bumper from the wings **(see illustrations)**.

4 Work along the base of the bumper cover and remove the lower fixings **(see illustration)**. On models built up to 2011 remove the horizontal screws (accessed through the lower air vent at either side of the number plate carrier).

5 Open the bonnet and (on early models up to 2011 with colour coordinated covers) undo the two screws securing the grille to the bonnet slam panel. Remove the grille and then remove the now exposed screws.

6 On models where the grille is part of the bumper cover, remove the upper screws and then release the central retaining clips using a small screwdriver. **(see illustrations)**.

6.2 Remove the wing liners

6.3a Remove the 'scrivet' or screw

6.3b Unclip the bumper from the front wing

6.4 Remove the lower screws

6.6a Remove the screws...

6.6b ...and release the clips

6.7 Remove the bumper

7.2 Remove the screws

7.3a The right-hand upper nut is hidden behind a blanking grommet

7 With the aid of an assistant pull the cover forward and (where fitted) disconnect the wiring loom and headlight washer hoses before fully removing the bumper cover **(see illustration)**.

8 On models with headlamp washers, remove the washer jets as described in Chapter 12, Section 21.

9 If required the air vents and blanking panels panels can now be removed from the bumper cover by unclipping them.

Refitting

10 Refitting is a reverse of the removal procedure, ensuring that the bumper ends engage correctly with the locating clips on the edge of the front wing panels. Make sure all wiring plugs are reconnected.

---

7   Rear bumper – removal and refitting

Note: *The bumper cover is removed with the bumper carrier (reinforcement) and then the cover is removed from the carrier on the bench. Alternatively it is possible to remove the cover separately. Depending on the model, it is possible that slight changes to the removal and refitting procedures may be necessary.*

Removal

1 To improve access, chock the front wheels,

7.3b Remove the nuts from the inside of the rear panel….

and then jack up the rear of the vehicle and support it on axle stands (see *Jacking and vehicle support*).

2 Remove the fixings (2 or 3 per side) from the rear wheel arch **(see illustration)**.

3 Working from below undo the nuts securing the bumper to the bodywork **(see illustrations)**.

4 With the help of an assistant, pull the bumper from the rear wheel arch panels at both sides. Withdraw the bumper from the rear of the vehicle and (where fitted) disconnect the wiring from the parking sensors **(see illustration)**.

5 With the bumper on the bench, remove the fixings **(see illustration)** and unclip the cover from the reinforcement panel.

7.3c …and from the outside (shown with cover removed)

Refitting

6 Refitting is a reverse of the removal procedure, ensuring that the bumper ends engage correctly with the rear wing/wheel arch panels, as the bumper is refitted.

---

8   Bonnet – removal, refitting and adjustment

Removal

1 Open the bonnet and using a pencil or felt tip pen, mark the outline of each bonnet hinge relative to the bonnet, to use as a guide on refitting **(see illustration)**.

2 Unclip the washer jets from under the rear

7.4 Release the bumper from the wheel arch

7.5 Remove the fixings

8.1 Precisely mark the position of the bonnet in relation to the hinge

8.2a Unclip the washer jet

8.2b …disconnect the washer hose…

8.2c …then release the grommet from the bonnet

8.3 Unclip the bonnet strut

8.5 Remove the trim piece to access the hinge

edge of the bonnet and disconnect the washer hoses **(see illustrations)**. Release the rubber grommet from the bonnet and withdraw the washer hose from inside the bonnet. Where necessary, disconnect the wiring from the jet heating elements.

3 Before disconnecting the gas support strut, get help from an assistant to support the bonnet. Using a small screwdriver release the retaining clip, and then disconnect the gas support strut from the bonnet **(see illustration)**.

4 Undo the bonnet retaining nuts **(see illustration 8.1)**, and then (with the aid of an assistant) carefully lift the bonnet clear. Store the bonnet out of the way in a safe place.

5 Inspect the bonnet hinges for signs of wear and free play at the pivots, and if necessary renew. Each hinge is secured to the body by bolts – 2 on some models, 3 on others. Mark the position of the hinge on the body then undo the retaining bolts and remove it from the vehicle **(see illustration)**. On refitting, align the new hinge with the marks and tighten the retaining bolts.

Refitting and adjustment

6 With the aid of an assistant, offer up the bonnet and loosely fit the retaining bolts. Align the hinges with the marks made on removal, and then tighten the retaining bolts/nuts securely.

7 Refit the washer hose, wiring and gas strut in the reverse order of removal.

8 Close the bonnet, and check for alignment with the adjacent panels. If necessary, unscrew the hinge bolts and re-align the bonnet. Once the bonnet is correctly aligned, tighten the hinge bolts. Check that the bonnet fastens and releases satisfactorily.

9 Bonnet release cable – removal and refitting

Removal

1 The bonnet release cable is in two sections, with a coupling located over the right-hand side of the bonnet slam panel. To remove the shorter front section cable, remove the bonnet lock as described in Section 10.

2 To remove the rear section, first release the coupling from over the slam panel, as described in Section 10, paragraph 4

3 Working inside the vehicle, locate the release lever and pull it out slightly, then insert a small screwdriver into the gap between the release lever and its securing clip. Let the lever return to its original position, then release the clip with a screwdriver (note that the clip may fall behind the trim) **(see illustrations)**.

9.3a Insert a screwdriver…

9.3b …to release the securing clip

9.4a Undo the plastic retaining nut...

9.4b ...and screw/clip ('scrivet')...

9.4c ...then remove the trim panel

9.5 Unscrew the release handle mounting bracket screws

9.6 Unclip the release cable from the lever

9.11 Slide the securing clip into the handle before refitting

4 Remove the plastic screw and then remove the 'scrivet'. Prise up the sill trim and remove it **(see illustrations)**.

5 Undo the two retaining screws and withdraw the bonnet release lever from the bottom of the A-pillar **(see illustration)**.

6 Release the outer cable from the mounting bracket, and then detach the inner cable from the lever **(see illustration)**.

7 Working along the length of the cable and noting its correct routing, free it from any retaining clips/ties and release the cable sealing grommet from the bulkhead.

8 Tie a length of string to the end of the cable inside the vehicle, and then withdraw the cable through into the engine compartment.

9 Once the cable is free, untie the string and leave it in position in the vehicle; the string can then be used to draw the new cable back into position.

Refitting

10 Tie the inner end of the string to the end of the cable, and then use the string to draw the bonnet release cable back from the engine compartment. Once the cable is through, untie the string.

11 Refitting is a reversal of removal. Note: Before refitting the bonnet release lever, fit the securing clip back into the lever first**(see illustration)** and then push the lever back into place.

12 Ensure the rubber grommet in the bulkhead is fitted correctly, and the cable is

correctly routed and secured to all the relevant retaining clips.

13 Before closing the bonnet, check the operation of the release lever and cable.

10 Bonnet lock –
removal and refitting

Removal

1 Open the bonnet and then on models built up to 2010 with a standard bumper cover, remove the cover as described in Section 6

2 On early models with a colour coordinated bumper cover remove the grille. On later models (2010 on) the lock can be accessed without removing any of the bumper components.

10.3 Disconnecting the bonnet lock wiring connector

3 Disconnect the wiring for the contact micro switch at the connector located by the right-hand headlight **(see illustration)**.

4 Disconnect the bonnet cable at the join adapter located by the right-hand headlight. Unclip the cover and release the two parts of the cable **(see illustration)**. This will allow the cable to be disconnected from the bonnet lock.

5 Note the location of the three mounting bolts (early models) or the two bolts (later models). Note also that on some models with a fixed grille the bumper cover must be removed first. Unscrew the bolts and remove them.

6 Prise the lock from the crossmember, and withdraw the cable and wiring from the front panel, release them from any retaining clips. If required lift the cover and unhook the release

10.4 Disconnect the two parts of the cable

10.6a Remove the lock

10.6b Unclip the micro switch

10.6c Unclip and then...

10.6d ...unhook the bowden cable

11.1 Make alignment marks and measure the door gaps

cable end fitting from the lock lever **(see illustrations)**.

Refitting

7 Refitting is a reversal of removal. Check the operation of the release cable before closing the bonnet. The best method is to close the lock with a screwdriver and then use the release handle to confirm correct operation. If adjustment is necessary, loosen the bonnet lock retaining bolts, and adjust the position of the lock to suit. Finally, tighten the bolts.

11 Door – removal, refitting and adjustment

Note: *The hinge bolts must always be renewed if loosened.*

Front doors

Removal

1 Before removing the door, measure the door gaps and mark them as required **(see illustration)**. Make alignment marks on both hinges.
2 Open the door then disconnect the wiring at the A- or B-pillar as applicable. To do this, first release the rubber bellows by pressing the small tab at the top. Pull down the locking lever and disconnect the wiring plug **(see illustrations)**.
3 Remove the nut from the upper hinge bolt **(see illustration)**.
4 Slacken the lower hinge bolts and then with an assistant supporting the door fully remove the bolts. Lift the door of the upper hinge bolt and with the aid of an assistant remove it **(see illustration)**.
5 Examine the hinges for signs of wear or damage. If renewal is necessary, the upper hinge can only be removed (or adjusted) after the facia panel is removed Section 26. The lower hinge can be removed after the kick panel is removed Section 24. Before removing the hinges, accurately mark their position to ensure correct refitting.

11.2a Release the rubber bellows

11.2b Release the locking lever

11.3 Upper door hinge nut

11.4 Remove the lower hinge bolts

11.11 Door lock striker mounted on the B-pillar

11.12 Measure the door gaps before removal

11.13a Removing the lower stop

Refitting

6 Where renewed, fit the hinges and tighten the bolts to the specified torque.

7 With the aid of an assistant, offer up the door to the vehicle and locate it on the guide bolt. Fit the new hinge bolts and tighten to the specified torque.

8 Reconnect the wiring plug and secure with the locking lever, then refit the rubber bellows.

Adjustment

9 Close the door and check the door alignment with the surrounding body panels. There must be an even gap all around, and the door must be level with the surrounding body panels.

10 Adjustment can only be made at the A-pillar. There is no adjustment possible at the door itself.

11 Check that the striker enters the door lock centrally as the door is closed, and if necessary adjust the position of the striker by loosening its mounting bolts **(see illustration)**.

Sliding door

Removal

12 Before removing the door, measure the door gaps and mark them as required **(see illustration)**. Make alignment marks on both hinges.

13 The door can be removed by either removing the roller brackets from the guide rails by removing the stops or by removing the brackets from the door. We opted to remove the upper and lower guide rail stops **(see illustrations)**.

14 An assistant and the support of a trolley jack will now be required. Protect the door by padding the head of the jack and then raise the jack to just take the weight of the door.

15 Working from the inside, unbolt and then remove the door check strap **(see illustration)**.

16 Again with the aid of an assistant, slide the door along and off the guide rails. Remove the hinges/guide rollers from door as required.

Refitting

17 Refitting is a reversal of removal. Check the operation of the door and adjust as required.

Adjustment

18 Where adjustment is required first slacken the upper and lower locking pegs at the front edge of the door. They should be just slackened enough to allow the pegs to move as the door slides home.

19 Vertical adjustment can be made at all of the hinges/roller guides and horizontal adjustment at the upper guide/roller. There should be a gap of approximately 4 mm all round the door frame.

20 In and out adjustment (to ensure that the door is flush with the surrounding body panels) can be made at the upper and lower guide rollers. Note however that the trailing edge of the sliding door must be slightly proud of the bodywork. This will minimise any wind noise. Adjustment of the latch/striker pin on the C-pillar in combination with adjustment of the roller guides will be necessary to

11.13b If the door is removed by removing the brackets, mark the position carefully as this is where the door alignment is adjusted

ensure the trailing edge is slightly proud of the bodywork.

21 When the alignment is correct fully tighten the locking pegs and refit the door trim panel.

Rear doors

Removal

22 Both rear doors are removed in a similar manner. Remove the door trim panel as described in Section 12.

23 Disconnect the wiring plugs from the high level brake light, door lock and number plate lamp. Where fitted disconnect the wiring plug from the washer and wiper system and feed the loom (and hose if fitted) out through the door frame **(see illustrations)**.

11.15 Remove the check strap

11.23a Disconnect the wiring plugs

11.23b Feed the loom through the door frame

11.24 Uhook the check strap and remove the bolts

11.25 Upper rear door hinge bolts

24 Unhook and the unbolt the check strap **(see illustration)** and then slacken the hinge bolts. Do not fully remove the bolts at this point.

25 With an assistant holding the door, fully remove the bolts **(see illustration)** and then remove the door.

Refitting

26 Refitting is a reversal of removal. Adjust the door if required as described below.

Adjustment

27 The adjustment method for both doors is the same, but always adjust the right-hand door first.

28 Partially remove the door seal in the hinge area and then slacken the upper and lower hinges (at the door). Slacken and move inward the upper and lower striker plates.

29 Adjust the door so that all the door gaps are even. Repeat the procedure for the left-hand door. Tighten the hinge bolts and then if in/out adjustment is required slacken the hinge bolts on the body. Adjust the doors so that they are flush. Finally adjust the position of the upper and lower striker plates so that the doors shut and lie flush when closed. Further adjustment can also be made at the striker plates catches if required.

12 Door inner trim panel – removal and refitting

Note: *As the trim panel is removed, the retaining trim clips may be damaged. It might be prudent to obtain new trim clips before proceeding.*

Removal

1 Switch off the ignition, before disconnecting any wiring connectors.

Front door

2 On vehicles fitted with manual windows release the winder handle by sliding the locking clip away from the handle. Release the handle from the shaft.

3 On vehicles fitted with power windows, prise up the switch panel and disconnect the wiring plug **(see illustration)**. Note that is also possible to disconnect the switch wiring plug as the trim panel is removed.

4 Remove the grab handle cover and then remove the now exposed fixings **(see illustrations)**.

5 Undo the retaining screws from the lower edge of the trim panel **(see illustration)**.

6 Release the door trim panel studs, carefully

12.3 Prise out the switch panel

12.4a Prise off...

12.4b ...and remove the cover

12.4c Remove the screws

12.5 Undo the door trim lower screws

12.6 Unclip the door trim panel

12.7a Unclip the door handle cable

12.7b Disconnect the wiring connector

12.10a Use a trim tool under the head of the rivet to help removal

12.10b There is no need to completely remove the centre pin to remove the 'scrivet'

12.11 Clip on the left shows how it should be, before refitting the trim panel

levering between the panel and door with a flat-bladed lever. Work around the outside of the panel, and when all the studs are released, lift the door trim panel upwards and off the window slot. Support the panel away from the door **(see illustration)**.

7 Unclip the release handle cable and disconnect the multiplug **(see illustrations)**.

8 If required the trim from the inside of the door mirror can now be unclipped from the door frame. Refer to Chapter 12, Section 23.

Sliding door and rear doors

9 The rear door panels are all secured with 'scrivet' type fasteners. Many vehicles will also have aftermarket plywood panels fitted over the factory door panels.

10 Remove the scrivet using a 3 mm hex key and pull it from the panel **(see illustrations)**.

Refitting

11 Before refitting, check whether any of

the trim panel retaining studs where broken on removal, and renew them as necessary. If the retaining clip part of the stud has been pressed down onto the stud, then it will need to be withdraw back into position to the end of the centre stud **(see illustration)**. The Refitting of the trim panel is then a reversal of removal. Check the operation of the door electrical equipment.

12 On models with manual windows refit the winder handle so that it is approximately 45 degrees below horizontal with the window fully closed.

13 Door handle and lock components – removal and refitting

Note: *The exterior handle and cylinder lock can be removed from the outside of the door.*

All other components (except the handle support bracket) are removed with the main component carrier as described below.

FRONT DOORS

Removal

Door lock cylinder/ door handle end cap

1 Open the door, then remove the blanking plug from the rear edge of the door to access the retaining screw **(see illustration)**.

2 Pull out the door release handle slightly and slacken the retaining screw whilst pushing on the screw and pulling on the lock cylinder **(see illustrations)**.

Note: *Do not remove the screw completely – it should be captive. Only slacken the bolt sufficiently to release the lock cylinder. If the bolt is slackened too far (or removed) the locking plate may well become detached from the support bracket.*

13.1 Remove the cover

13.2a Slacken the retaining screw...

13.2b ...and pull out the lock cylinder

13.5a Unclip the cable and...

13.5b ...then slide out the handle

13.5c Recover the gasket

13.7 Secure the glass in position

3 If required the cover can now be removed from the cylinder by unclipping it.

Exterior door handle

4 Depending on the door being worked on, either remove the door lock cylinder or door handle end cap, as described previously in this Section.

5 Pull out the handle and using a screwdriver unhook the release cable from the handle. Unhook and then slide out the handle (**see illustrations**). Recover the gasket.

Exterior door handle mounting plate and component carrier

6 Remove the exterior door handle as described in this Section and then remove the door inner trim panel as described in Section 12.

7 Release the window retaining clamp(s) and pull up the window glass as described in Section 14. Secure it in the closed position with adhesive tape (**see illustration**).

8 On the outside of the door, undo the retaining screw from the front of the door handle aperture (**see illustration**).

9 To access the mounting plate the door carrier panel must be removed. The loudspeaker, window regulator and door lock are all mounted to this panel.

10 Remove the cover, lower the latch and then disconnect the wiring multiplug at the A-pillar (**see illustrations**). Push the wiring loom into the door frame.

11 Disconnect the wiring plug from the door mirror and (where fitted) from the aerial and earth connection (**see illustrations**).

12 Remove the bolts from the lock (**see illustration**).

13.8 Undo the retaining screw

13.10a Open the cover and...

13.10b ...disconnect the wiring plug

13.11a Disconnect the aerial lead (models with a mirror mounted aerial only)

13.11b Unbolt the earth cable

13.12 Remove the bolts

13.13 Remove the bolts

13.14 Remove the component carrier panel

13.17a Disconnect the wiring plug

13.17b Drive out the pins

13.19 The spring loaded bracket locked into position

13.28 The spring correctly hooked over the release arm

13 Work around the panel and remove the outer mounting bolts **(see illustration)**.

14 Manoeuvre the panel from the door frame by pushing the panel up slightly and then pulling out the lower half. Remove the panel diagonally (towards the hinges), work the regulator and lock assembly free and then remove the panel **(see illustration)**.

15 Remove the additional mounting bolt from the door shut (just below the handle release screw). Reaching up inside the door, slide the exterior handle support to the rear edge of the door, and then disengage it from the outer panel. Remove the bracket from the door frame.

Door lock

16 Release the the window glass from the retaining clamp(s) and tape it up in the closed position **(see illustration 13.7)** as described in Section 14. Remove the component carrier panel as described above.

17 With the carrier panel on the bench remove the protective cover where fitted, disconnect the wiring plug and then remove the bracket fasteners by driving out the pins with a punch **(see illustrations)**. Alternatively unclip the lock from the support bracket.

18 Turn the lock assembly over and disconnect the bowden cable. If the lock is to be replaced drill out the rivet from the support bracket (the bracket is not supplied with a replacement lock) and remove it.

Refitting

Exterior door handle support plate

19 With the support bracket on the bench, check that the spring loaded arm is locked against the handle. If not compress the spring loaded lever into the frame and lock it flush with the support frame by by sliding the lock cylinder plate into the indents on the arm **(see illustration)**. The lock cylinder retaining plate will need to be adjusted to allow this. Refit the support bracket and then refit the exterior handle as described below.

Exterior handle lock cylinder

20 Pull out the door handle slightly and insert the lock cylinder housing/end cap into the door handle mounting-bracket.

21 Whilst keeping pressure on the lock cylinder/end cap, tighten the screw in the rear edge of the door to 4Nm.

22 Refit the blanking plug to cover the screw at the rear edge of the door.

23 Check the operation of the lock before closing the door, by sliding a screwdriver into the lock to operate the mechanism.

Exterior door handle

24 If removed, locate the gasket on the door handle aperture.

25 Insert the handle into the door at the front (hinge) end first, and then pivot the handle back into position. Reconnect the bowden cable. Slide the handle towards the front

of the door, to lock it back in position in the mounting bracket. Fit the lock cylinder (or end cap) and tighten the securing screw. As the screw is tightened the lock cylinder/end cap will be locked in place and the spring loaded arm will pull the exterior handle tightly against the door. (There should be a loud 'click' as the spring loaded arm snaps into position).

26 The remainder of refitting is a reversal of removal.

Door lock

27 The door lock and component support/carrier panel are fitted as a single assembly in the factory. However it is also possible to separate the lock from the component support panel and fit the lock first. The lock wiring plug must be reconnected before the component support panel is fully fitted.

28 Before refitting the lock and carrier panel the spring should be hooked over the bowden cable pivot arm **(see illustration)**.When the release handle is fitted and the cable hooked up this guarantees that the lock is in the neutral position. The first pull of the outer handle will release the spring from the arm. Note however that it is possible to refit the cable to the outer handle without hooking the spring over the arm. If this method is used it is essential that no tension is on the cable when clipping it into the outer handle.

29 The remainder of refitting is a reversal of removal. Refit the window regulator as described in Section 14.

13.31 Remove the bolts

13.32 Remove the drain

13.33 Remove the contact plate

SLIDING DOOR LOCK ASSEMBLY

Removal

Door lock and remote release mechanism

30 Remove the door trim panel as described in Section 12.

31 Remove the two screws at the trailing edge of the door and lower the lock into the door frame **(see illustration)**. Unclip the bowden cable from the lock.

32 At the release mechanism unclip the drain hose and then using a sharp knife cut through the adhesive and remove the drain **(see illustration)**.

33 Remove the contact switch from the door shut and disconnect the wiring plug and **(see illustration)**.

34 At the door shut unclip the cover from the child safety lock and then remove the two screws **(see illustrations)**.

35 Disconnect the wiring plug from the remote release mechanism **(see illustration)**and unclip the plug from the door panel.

36 Working inside the door frame remove the bolts from the lock and lower it from the door from **(see illustration)**.

37 With the lock on the bench remove the bowden cable if required. Note however that the bowden cable is supplied complete with the remote release mechanism.

External handle and support bracket

38 Remove the door trim panel as described in Section 12.

39 Remove the water drain and release mechanism as described above. Note that if only the external handle and lock barrel (where fitted) require attention the water drain and remote release mechanism can be left in place.

40 At the support bracket slacken the screw **(see illustration)**.

41 Lift the handle slightly and then pull out the lock cylinder. Unhook and remove the door handle **(see illustration)**.

42 If required the mounting bracket can now be removed from the door frame. Remove the screw from the door outer panel and then

13.34a Remove the cover and...

13.34b ...then remove the screws

13.35 Disconnect the wiring plug

13.36 Remove the bolts

13.40 Slacken the captive screw

13.41 Remove the cylinder

13.42a Remove the screw…

13.42b …and gasket

13.42c Unhook and lower the support bracket from the door

remove the bracket from the door frame (see illustrations).

Interior release handle

43 Using a plastic trim tool remove the trim cover (see illustration).
44 Remove the two screws and then remove the handle by pulling it up and out of the door frame (see illustration).

Refitting

45 Refitting is a reversal of removal, but note:
a) New sealant may be required to secure the lock drain in position.
b) When refitting the external handle check that it interlocks with the support bracket correctly.

c) The internal release handle cover is best fitted with the remote release mechanism removed – or at least lowered. The release handle link rod can then be guided into the remote release housing and the lock button can be guided up into the trim panel.

REAR DOOR LOCK ASSEMBLY

Removal

Locks

46 There are four locks (two per door) fitted to the rear doors. Remove the rear door trim as described in Section 12.
47 If working on the lower lock, disconnect

the link rod from the door handle, unbolt the lock from the door frame and lower it sufficiently to gain access to the wiring plug (where fitted). Disconnect the wiring plug and remove the lock from the door (see illustration).
48 The release handle and bowden cable must be removed before the upper lock can be removed – as described in the next section below (see illustrations).

Right-hand door release handle

49 Remove the rear door trim as described in Section 12.
50 Unclip the link rod from the handle, remove the bolt and then remove the handle from the door (see illustration).

13.43 Remove the cover

13.44 Remove the handle

13.47 Remove the lower lock

13.48a Remove the bolts

13.48b Disconnect the bowden cable

13.50 Remove the release handle

13.52 Unclip the link rod

13.53a Remove the bolts

13.53b Unclip the second link rod as the handle is removed

13.56 Remove the plate

13.57 Remove the link rod control

13.58 Remove the ring

13.59a Remove the spring clip

Left-hand door release handle

51 Remove the rear door trim as described in Section 12.
52 Unclip the shorter link rod **(see illustration)**.
53 Remove the mounting bolts and rotate the handle assembly to release the link rod **(see illustrations)**.
54 Remove the handle from the door frame and recover the sealing ring from either the key cylinder or the housing.

Lock cylinder

55 Remove the rear door trim as described in Section 12.
56 Remove the release handle as described above. Unbolt the security plate **(see illustration)**.
57 Depress the locking tabs and remove the link rod control ring **(see illustration)**.
58 Prise open the locking tabs and remove the interlock ring **(see illustration)**.
59 Prise up and remove the key cylinder retaining ring and then withdraw the key cylinder **(see illustrations)**.

Remote release unit

60 Remove the rear door trim as described in Section 12.
61 Disconnect the lower lock link rod ball joint and the unclip the upper lock bowden cable **(see illustrations)**.
62 Disconnect the link rods from the door release handle/lock as described above and then remove the link rods from the control unit.

13.59b Push out the key cylinder

13.61a Pop off the ball joint

13.61b Unhook the bowden cable

13.63a Disconnect the wiring plug

13.63b Remove the control unit

14.2 Prise out the access caps

63 Disconnect the wiring plug and then unbolt and remove the control unit **(see illustrations)**.

Refitting

64 Refitting is a reversal of removal.

14 Door window glass and regulator – removal and refitting

Removal

Window glass

1 Remove the door inner trim panel as described in Section 12.
2 Prise out the access caps from the inner door panel **(see illustration)**.
3 Temporarily connect the wiring to the switches, then switch on the ignition, and lower the window glass until the bolts attaching it to the regulator are visible through the access holes. If there is a fault with the electric motor, remove the motor in order to lower the glass.
4 Loosen the bolts on the regulator to release the window glass clamps **(see illustration)**. There is no need to remove the remove bolts completely.
5 Remove the inner weatherseal/trim from the door frame. Lift the rear of the window glass so that it is tilted. Lift it upwards and remove it from the outside of the door **(see illustration)**.

14.4 Loosen the window glass clamps

Window motor and regulator

Note: *If only the window motor is faulty, it can be removed without disturbing the glass or component carrier panel.*
6 Remove the door inner trim panel as described in Section 12.
7 Remove the door window glass as described earlier. If the only work required is to the regulator then disconnect the glass from the regulator and slide it to the top of the frame, securing it in place with strong tape **(see illustration 13.7)**.
8 Disconnect the wiring plug at the motor, remove the bolts and lift the motor from the component carrier frame **(see illustrations)**.
9 To acces the regulator the component carrier panel must be removed as described in Section 13. With the component carrier

removed from the vehicle, drill out the rivets and remove the regulator.

Refitting

Door window glass

10 Carefully lower the tilted window glass into the door and engage it with the regulator clamps. Apply light downwards pressure to the glass to make sure it is correctly located in the channels, then tighten the regulator clamp bolts.
11 If necessary, the window may be checked for correct operation at this stage by connecting the wiring to the switches.
12 Refit the access caps.
13 Refit the door inner trim panel with reference to Section 12.

14.8a Disconnect the wiring plugs

14.8b Remove the bolts...

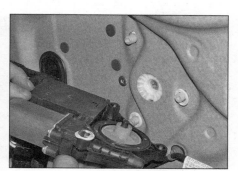

14.8c ...and lift off the motor

Window motor and regulator

14 Refitting is a reversal of removal, noting the following points:
a) *Fit new rivets to the regulator (if removed).*
b) *After refitting the component carrier panel check the operation of the door locking mechanism.*
c) *Refit the motor and temporarily refit the window switch to check the function before fitting the trim panel.*
d) *Refit the door inner trim panel with reference to Section 12.*

15 Tailgate and support struts – removal and refitting

Removal

Tailgate

1 Remove the screws from the pull handle and then remove the 'scrivets' from the trim. Remove the panel.
2 Disconnect the wiring plugs from the rear wiper, the high level brake light and the lock.
3 Disconnect the screen washer hose and then unclip the wiring loom and feed it, up and out of the tailgate. Repeat the procedure for the screen washer hose.
4 Using a suitable marker pen, draw around the outline of each hinge marking its correct position on the tailgate. Slacken, but DO NOT remove the hinge bolts.
5 With the help of an assistant to support the tailgate, remove the support struts as described below.
Caution: The tailgate is heavy. At least one assistant will be required to remove it.
6 Unscrew and remove the bolts securing the hinges to the tailgate.
7 Inspect the hinges for signs of wear or damage and renew if necessary.

Support struts

 Warning: The support struts are filled with a gas under pressure. They must not be opened and they and must be disposed of safely.

8 With the help of an assistant, support the tailgate in the open position.
9 Using a small flat-bladed screwdriver lift the locking clip, and pull the gas support strut off

17.10a Using a small screwdriver, release the clip...

its balljoint mounting on the tailgate. Repeat the procedure on the lower strut mounting and remove the strut from the vehicle body. Note: If the gas strut is to be re-used, the locking clip must not be taken all the way out, or the clip will be damaged.

Refitting

Tailgate

10 Refitting is the reverse of removal, aligning the hinges with the marks made before removal. Tighten retaining bolts to the specified torque.
11 On completion, close the tailgate and check its alignment with the surrounding panels. If necessary slight adjustment can be made by unscrewing the retaining bolts and repositioning the tailgate on its hinges.

Support struts

12 Refitting is a reverse of the removal procedure, ensuring that the strut is securely retained by its retaining clips.

16 Tailgate lock components – removal and refitting

Removal

Tailgate lock

1 Open up the tailgate and remove the trim panel as described in Section 15.
2 Disconnect the wiring plug from the lock and unhook the link rod.
3 Undo the retaining bolts and remove the lock from the lower edge of the tailgate.

Tailgate handle/release unit

Note: *There are slight variations in the design of the handle between the pre 2011 and post 2011 models. The removal procedure is essentially the same though.*

4 Open up the tailgate and remove the trim panel as described in Section 15.
5 Disconnect the wiring from the handle/release unit. On models fitted with a lock/key cylinder unclip the link rod.
6 On some models the latch carrier must now be removed, before the handle can be removed.
7 Undo the nuts holding the unit to the tailgate and then remove it.

17.10b ...and open the battery cover

8 The handle/release unit can now be withdrawn from the tailgate.

Refitting

9 Refitting is a reversal of removal, however, before refitting the trim panel, check the operation of the lock components.

17 Central locking components – description, removal and refitting

Description

1 The central locking system consists of the following main components. Note that the central locking and anti-theft alarm systems share some components (see Chapter 12):
a) *Convenience system onboard supply control unit located behind the driver's side facia panel.*
b) *Door control units integrated in the window regulator motors.*
c) *Electric door lock actuators integrated in the door locks.*
d) *Tailgate/Rear door lock actuator located in the tailgate/rear door, together with the release button.*
e) *Anti-theft alarm horn located in the plenum chamber.*
f) *Bonnet contact switch located on the bonnet lock.*
g) *Remote control transmitter on the ignition key fob.*

Removal

2 Before working on any electrical circuit, disconnect the battery negative lead (refer to Section 5A Section 3).

Convenience system control unit

3 Remove the lower right-hand section of the facia as described in Section 26. Unbolt and lower the fuse holder to access the control unit.
4 Disconnect the wiring plug and remove it.

Door control unit

5 Remove the window regulator motor as described in Section 14.

Electric door lock actuator

6 Remove the door lock (see Section 13).

Tailgate/boot lid lock activator

7 Remove the tailgate handle/release unit as described in Section 16.

Bonnet contact switch

8 Remove the bonnet lock as described in Section 10. If necessary, the operating cable may remain attached to the lock.
9 On the lock, release the tab and push the switch from the slotted holes.

Remote control transmitter battery

Note: *Two versions of the key and remote control are fitted. Battery replacement is similar for both versions.*
10 Using a screwdriver inserted in the slot, separate the transmitter unit cover from the key **(see illustrations)**.

17.11a Remove the battery...

17.11b ...noting which way it is fitted

17.12a Use a screwdriver at the point shown to...

17.12b ...separate the two halves

17.12c Unclip the switch section from the battery holder...

17.12d ...and remove the battery

11 Carefully prise out the battery, noting which way round it is fitted **(see illustrations)**.
12 Earlier versions are removed in a similar manner **(see illustrations)**.

Refitting

13 Refitting is a reversal of removal, except where a new fuel tank actuator is required on 07/2012 on vehicles. On these vehicles the mounting keyhole slots must be modified to accept the new actuator.This requires the cutting of two additional vertical slots at the end of the keyholes. These should be cut so that the distance from the centre line of the keyhole slot to the base of the new vertical slot is 6 mm. Corrosion protection and remedial paintwork will

be required after the slots are cut. On completion check the operation of the central locking system.

---

18 Mirrors and associated components – removal and refitting

Removal
Exterior mirror

1 Remove the door inner trim panel as described in Section 12.
2 If not already removed, unclip the small inner trim panel from the door frame **(see illustration)** and (where fitted) disconnect the speaker wiring connector.

3 Trace the wiring from the exterior mirror and disconnect the wiring plug at the window regulator motor/control unit. On models with the aerial integrated into the mirror frame, disconnect the coaxial cable and earth cable **(see illustration 13.11a)**.
4 Unscrew the mounting bolts while supporting the exterior mirror, then withdraw the exterior mirror from the door while guiding the wiring through the hole **(see illustrations)**.

Mirror glass

Note: *The mirror glass can be removed with the mirror in place or with the mirror on the bench. For clarity the procedure is shown with the mirror removed from the vehicle.*

18.2 Remove the trim panel

18.4a Undo the mirror retaining bolts...

18.4b ...and guide the loom through the door frame

18.5a Remove the base panel...

18.5b ...and then unclip the surround

18.6a Unclip the glass

18.6b The location of the locking tabs at
the rear of the mirror glass

18.7 Disconnect the wiring

19 Windscreen, sliding door and rear window glass – general information

1 These areas of glass are bonded in position with a special adhesive. Renewal of such fixed glass is a difficult, messy and time-consuming task, which is beyond the scope of the home mechanic. It is difficult, unless one has plenty of practice, to obtain a secure, waterproof fit. Furthermore, the task carries a high risk of breakage; this applies especially to the laminated glass windscreen. In view of this, owners are strongly advised to have this sort of work carried out by one of the many specialist windscreen fitters.

20 Body exterior fittings – removal and refitting

5 Remove the panel from the base of the mirror and then remove the glass surround **(see illustrations)**.
6 Using a trim tool unclip the glass from the motor **(see illustrations)**.
7 Disconnect the wiring connectors from the mirror heating element **(see illustration)**. Take care here as it is easy to pull the male section of the connect free form the glass. Remove the glass.

Mirror switch

8 Refer to Chapter 12, Section 5.

Refitting

9 Refitting is the reverse of the relevant removal procedure. When refitting the mirror glass, press firmly at the centre taking care

not to use excessive force, as the glass is easily broken.
Caution: Wear protective gloves and glasses to prevent personal injury.

Interior mirror

10 If rear view mirror is fitted with a rain sensor ensure the ignition is off (remove the key).
11 On models fitted with a simple anti-dazzle mirror, grasp the stalk and rotate the mirror 90 degrees anticlockwise to remove it.
12 On models fitted with a rain sensor unclip and separate the covers and then disconnect the wiring plug. Slide the mirror downwards to release it from the base **(see illustrations)**.
13 Refitting is a reversal of the removal procedure.

Wheel arch liners and body under-panels

1 The various plastic covers fitted to the underside of the vehicle are secured in position by a mixture of screws, nuts and retaining clips and removal will be fairly obvious on inspection. Work methodically around the panel removing its retaining screws and releasing its retaining clips until the panel is free and can be removed from the underside of the vehicle. Most clips used on

18.12a Unclip the sides of the mirror
housing...

18.12b ...disconnect the wiring
connector...

18.12c ...and slide the mirror from its
mounting bracket

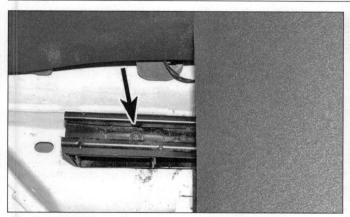

21.2 Seat rear mounting bolt (one side shown)

21.3 Seat front mounting bolt – spline type socket required

the vehicle are simply prised out of position. Remove the wheels to ease the removal of the wheel arch liners.

2 On refitting, renew any retaining clips that may have been broken on removal, and ensure that the panel is securely retained by all the relevant clips and screws.

Body trim strips and badges

3 The various body trim strips and badges are held in position with a special adhesive tape and locating lugs. Removal requires the trim/badge to be heated, to soften the adhesive, and then carefully lifted away from the surface. Due to the high risk of damage to the vehicle's paintwork during this operation, it is recommended that this task should be entrusted to a VW dealer.

21 Seats – removal and refitting

Note: *Refer to the warnings in Chapter 12, Section 26, on airbags.*

Removal

Front seats

Note: *Some vehicles have no electrical connections to the front seats. Where wiring connectors are present the number under the seat will vary depending on the vehicle specification.*

1 On models fitted with wiring to the front seats, disconnect the battery negative lead (refer to Chapter 5A Section 3).

2 Slide the seat forwards as far as possible and unscrew the rear mounting bolts (**see illustration**).

3 Slide the seat rearwards as far as possible and unscrew the front mounting bolts (**see illustration**).

 Warning: As a precaution against unintentional electrostatic discharge into the airbag, briefly touch part of the vehicle body before disconnecting the wiring.

4 Tilt the seat back slightly and unbolt the protective cover to access the wiring connectors. Disconnect the wiring connectors – where fitted. VW technicians fit an adapter to the airbag wiring connector as a safety precaution; however, wrap the wiring connectors with insulation tape or similar, to prevent any contact of the wiring.

5 Check that the wiring harness is released from any clips in the floor, and then remove the headrests from the seat backs; this will give more room when removing the seat from the vehicle.

6 When removing the seat from the vehicle, do not lift the seat by the seat belt stalk or by the seat adjustment levers. If necessary, have an assistant help to remove the seat, as it is heavy, and surrounding trim panels may be otherwise damaged. Make sure that the seat runners do not damage the paintwork as the seat is withdrawn.

7 If required the front seat subframes can now be removed. Remove the protective cover from the wiring plugs(where fitted). Unclip the connectors from the subframe and remove the mounting bolts.

8 Remove the mounting bolts and tuck the loom under the carpet to protect it from damage.

Refitting

9 Refitting is a reversal of removal, but tighten the mounting bolts to the specified torque where given.

22 Front seat belt tensioning mechanism – general information

1 All models covered in this manual are fitted with either a standard inertia reel seatbelts or a seat belt pre-tensioner system incorporated in each of the inertia reels.

2 Where fitted the pre-tensioner system is designed to instantaneously take up any slack in the seat belt in the case of a sudden frontal impact, therefore reducing the possibility of injury to the front seat occupants. The seat belt tensioner is triggered by a frontal impact

above a predetermined force. Lesser impacts, including impacts from behind, will not trigger the system.

3 When the system is triggered, the explosive gas in the tensioner mechanism retracts and locks the seat belt. This prevents the seat belt moving and keeps the occupant firmly in position in the seat. Once the tensioner has been triggered, the seat belt will be permanently locked and the assembly must be renewed.

4 There is a risk of personal injury if the system is triggered inadvertently when working on the vehicle, and it is therefore strongly recommended that any work involving the seat belt inertia reels be entrusted to a VW dealer. Note the following warnings before contemplating any work on the front seat belts.

 Warning: Do not expose the tensioner mechanism to temperatures in excess of 100°C.

 Warning: Before removing any components, disconnect the battery negative lead (refer to Disconnecting the battery in the Reference Chapter at the end of this manual.

 Warning: If the tensioner mechanism is dropped, it must be renewed, even it has suffered no apparent damage.

Warning: Do not allow any solvents to come into contact with the tensioner mechanism.

 Warning: Do not attempt to open the tensioner mechanism as it contains explosive gas.

 Warning: Tensioners must be discharged before they are disposed of, but this task should be entrusted to a VW dealer.

Warning: Some of the bolts securing the seat belts are microencapsulated and need to be heated with a hot air blower before they are slackened. Microencapsulated means that the threads of the bolts are coated with a locking compound from new. New bolts will be required for refitting.

23 Seat belt components – removal and refitting

Warning: Refer to Section 22 before proceeding.

Front seat belt removal

1 Disconnect the battery negative lead (as described in Chapter 5A Section 3).
2 Unclip the cover and then unbolt the upper mounting **(see illustrations)**.
3 Remove the upper and lower trim panels from the B-pillar with reference to Section 24.
4 Pull back the carpet, then unscrew and remove the seat belt lower anchor mounting bolt and remove the belt from the floor **(see illustration)**. Note that the bolt may be microencapsulated and must be heated with a hot air blower before being loosened. Protect the seat belt with a dampened cloth while heating the bolt. Discard the bolt and obtain a new one. Also, note that the threads of the corresponding nut must be cleaned with a tap before fitting the new bolt.
Warning: As a precaution against unintentional electrostatic discharge, briefly touch part of the vehicle body before disconnecting the wiring.
5 Where fitted, release the locking clip and disconnect the wiring connector from the inertia reel.
6 Unscrew the mounting bolt and remove the inertia reel from the bottom of the B-pillar.
7 Undo the screws and remove the belt guide from the B-pillar.
8 To remove the belt height adjustment (where fitted) remove the securing bolt from the top of the adjuster and lift upwards to release from the pillar.

Front seat belt stalk removal

9 Remove the front seat assembly as described in Section 21.

23.2a Unclip the cover…

23.2b …and unbolt the upper mounting

10 Slide the seat runners forward to access the seat belt stalk retaining bolt, under the seat frame. Unscrew and remove the bolt securing the stalk to the seat, and remove the stalk. The stalk must be turned through 90º in order to remove it. Note that the bolt is microencapsulated and must be heated with a hot air blower before being loosened. Protect the seat with a dampened cloth while heating the bolt. Discard the bolt and obtain a new one. Also, note that the threads of the corresponding nut must be cleaned with a tap before fitting the new bolt.

Refitting

11 Refitting is a reversal of the removal procedure, ensuring that all the seat belt units are located correctly and mounting bolts are securely tightened to their specified torque. Check all the trim panels are securely retained by all the relevant retaining clips.

24 Interior trim – removal and refitting

Interior trim panels

1 The interior trim panels are secured

using either screws or various types of trim fasteners, usually studs or clips.
2 Check that there are no other panels overlapping the one to be removed; usually there is a sequence that has to be followed, and this will only become obvious on close inspection.
3 Remove all obvious fasteners, such as screws. If the panel will not come free, it will be held by hidden clips or fasteners. These are usually situated around the edge of the panel and can be prised up to release them; note, however, that they can break quite easily so new ones should be available. The best way of releasing such clips, without the correct type of tool, is to use a large flat-bladed screwdriver. If a considerable amount of trim requires removal a wise investment will be a comprehensive set of plastic trim tools **(see illustration)**. Note in many cases that the adjacent sealing strip must be prised back to release a panel.
4 When removing a panel, never use excessive force or the panel may be damaged; always check carefully that all fasteners or other relevant components have been removed or released before attempting to withdraw a panel.
5 On models with side airbags, disconnect

23.4 Seat belt lower anchorage bolt

24.3 A useful selection of trim removal tools will avoid damage to the paintwork or trim panel

24.7a Remove the end panel and then...

24.7b ...the lower section of the A-pillar panel

24.8 Remove the small panel

the battery negative lead (refer to Section 5A Section 3).

6 Refitting is the reverse of the removal procedure; secure the fasteners by pressing them firmly into place and ensure that all disturbed components are correctly secured to prevent rattles.

A-pillar

7 Remove the facia end panel by unclipping it and then prise free the lower section of the A-pillar trim **(see illustrations)**.

8 Unclip the smaller panel from above the quarter light **(see illustration)**.

9 Work the panel free from the windscreen pillar and the A-pillar **(see illustration)**.

10 Refitting is a reversal of removal, but

refit any clips that have been left behind in the A-pillar to the panel. The main panel will require patience to fit – we fabricated a hooked tool from welding rod to guide the main panel clips into position.

B-pillar

11 Remove the cover and unbolt the upper seatbelt mount. Partially remove the door seal as required

12 Prise free the midsection of the B-pillar, noting how it locates into the bottom panel **(see illustrations)**.

13 Remove the bolts and grab handle from the overhead storage compartment – where fitted and then prise free the upper B-pillar trim panel.

14 If working on the sliding door side then the base panel also forms the sliding door step panel. Removal of the partition will also be required if fitted **(see illustrations)**.

15 Remove the trim clips and prise up the panel.

16 Refitting is a reversal of removal.

Sill trims

17 The removal of the right-hand door sill trim panel is described in Section 9.

18 On the left hand door, unclip the the A-pillar base panel **(see illustration)**.

19 Remove the screw and partially remove the door weather seal. The B-pillar base panel must now be partially (or completely)

24.9 Unclip the main panel

24.12a Remove the centre section...

24.12b ...noting the locating tabs at the base

24.14a Remove the partition

24.14b Remove the trim clips

24.18 Unclip the panel

24.19a Remove the screw

24.19b Remove the panel

24.22a Remove the blanking plugs

24.22b Pull up the panel to remove it

24.23 Unclip the panel

removed. Prise up and remove the doorstep panel (see illustrations).
20 Refitting is a reversal of removal.

Rear door/Tailgate panels

21 Remove the bolts from both load securing eyes.
22 Prise out the blanking plugs, remove the fixings and then pull up the panel (see illustrations).
23 The upper latch cover (models with rear doors only) is unclipped to remove it (see illustration).
24 Refitting is a reversal of removal.

Steering column shrouds

25 Remove the steering wheel as described in Chapter 10, Section 18.
26 Unclip the upper shroud from the bottom of the instrument panel and the top of the steering column, then remove it from the vehicle (see illustrations).
27 Undo the retaining screw from under the steering column lower shroud and the top of the steering column, then remove it from the vehicle (see illustrations).
28 Refitting is the reverse of removal.

Glovebox/storage compartment

29 On models fitted with a passenger airbag, disconnect the battery before proceeding.
30 Open the glovebox (where fitted) to

24.26a Unclip the upper shroud from the column...

24.26b ...and from the instrument panel

24.27a Undo the lower screw...

24.27b ...the two upper screws...

24.27c ...then lower the shroud from the steering column

24.30a Remove the lower screws...

24.30b ...and then the upper screws

24.32 Disconnect the wiring plugs as required

access the fixings. Remove the upper and lower screws **(see illustrations)**.

31 On models with a glovebox, remove the facia end panel by prising it off. Disconnect the glovebox lamp.

32 Pull the glovebox/storage compartment forward and where fitted disconnect the Passenger Airbag Disable (PAD) switch, the audio unit auxiliary connector and the glovebox cooling duct – all where fitted **(see illustration)**.

33 Refitting is the reverse of removal.

Carpets

34 The passenger compartment floor carpet

is in one piece and is secured at its edges by screws or clips, usually the same fasteners used to secure the various adjoining trim panels.

35 Carpet removal and refitting is reasonably straightforward but very time-consuming because all adjoining trim panels must be removed first, as must components such as the seats, the centre console and seat belt lower anchorages.

Headlining

36 The load area headlining is secured to the roof by standard scrivet type trim clips.

Where fitted the bulkhead and support strut will have to be removed before removing the headlining. In the passenger compartment the headlining can be removed after the removal of the overhead storage compartment (or cargo net storage) the grab handles and the sunvisors

37 To remove the sun visors and grab handles, the plastic covers have to be unclipped first, to gain access to the securing screws **(see illustrations)**

25 Centre console – removal and refitting

Removal

Note: *It is possible to remove the centre console with both front seats in position, however removal of the console is considerably easier if they are both removed first (as described in Section 21).*

1 Switch off the ignition.

2 On both sides, unclip the trim panels from the front of the console **(see illustration)**.

3 Lift out the covering, remove the single screw (if fitted) and withdraw the switch panel from the front of the console. Disconnect the

24.37a Carefully unclip the covers...

24.37b ...and undo the retaining screws

24.37c Unclip the cover to access the screw for the sunvisor

24.37d Unclip the cover to access the screw for the sunvisor locating mount

25.2 Remove the footwell trim panels

25.3a Remove the tray cover and...

25.3b ...then the compartment

25.3c Lift out the tray

25.4a Remove the screw

25.4b Remove the screws

wiring connectors, as the panel is removed **(see illustrations)**.

4 Remove the screw from behind the storage compartment/ashtray and then remove the screws from the front edge of the console **(see illustrations)**.

5 Prise up the gear lever gaiter and move the gear lever to access the screw **(see illustrations)**.

6 At the front outer edge of the console remove the screws from both sides **(see illustrations)**.

7 Remove the storage compartment housing and disconnect the wiring plug from the 12v power outlet **(see illustration)**.

8 The front section of the console can now be lifted out and over the gear lever **(see illustration)**.

25.5a Release the gaiter...

25.5b ...and remove the screw

25.6a Remove the left-hand front screws...

25.6b ...and open the fuse box cover to access the right-hand fixings

25.7 Remove the housing

25.8 Lift out the front section

25.9 Remove the screws

25.10 Remove the main section of the console

26.6 Unclip the covers from the sides of the facia

9 At the rear of the console, remove the cup holder cover (if fitted) and remove the screws **(see illustrations)**.

10 Check that all the fixings have been removed and then lift the main section of the console up and over the handbrake. Note that it may be necessary to slacken off the handbrake cables to do this **(see illustration)**.

Refitting

11 Refitting is a reversal of removal. Adjust the handbrake if required.

26.10a Prise up the compartment

26.10b Remove the screws

26 Facia panel assembly – removal and refitting

Note: *Refer to the warnings in Chapter 12 for airbags.*

Removal

1 Disconnect the battery negative lead (as described in Chapter 5A Section 3).
2 Remove the front section of the centre console as described in Section 25.
3 Remove the steering column shrouds as described in Section 24.
4 Remove the steering column control unit and switch assembly, as described in Chapter 12 Section 5.
5 Remove the instrument panel as described in Chapter 12 Section 11.
6 Prise out the trim panels from each end of the facia **(see illustration)**.
7 Remove the A-pillar upper trim panels, as described in Section 24.
8 Remove the storage compartment/glovebox as described in Section 24.
9 On models fitted with a passenger air bag remove the airbag as described in Chapter 12 Section 27.
10 Prise up the central storage compartment. Remove the now exposed screws **(see illustrations)**.
11 Working from the bottom of the panel and up the sides remove the facia centre panel using a plastic trim tool **(see illustrations)**.
12 Remove the radio/CD or navigation unit, as described in Chapter 12 Section 22.
13 Remove the Climatronic/heater controls, as described in Chapter 3 Section 9. On climatronic models remove the sunlight

26.11a Work the panel free from the bottom…

26.11b …and then the sides

sensor from the top of the facia. Disconnect the wiring plug as the sensor is removed.
14 Disconnect the wiring connector from the hazard switch and if fitted the PAD warning light. Access is restricted.

15 Remove the driver's storage compartment/fuse box cover. Disconnect the wiring plugs from the multifunction switch and the DLC (Data Link Connector) as the compartment is removed **(see illustrations)**.

26.15a Remove the panel…

26.15b …and disconnect the wiring plugs

26.16 Remove the grille

26.17a Removing the right-hand lower screws…

26.17b …and the left-hand screws

26.17c Screws at the centre of the facia

26.17d Screws are also located in the instrument panel binnacle

26.17e Remove the facia

27.5 Mark the position of the crossmember

16 Prise free and remove the facia sparker grill and (where fitted) remove the speaker **(see illustration)**.

17 Working logically from one side to the other, locate the facia cover screws. Unscrew the retaining screws from the facia assembly. These are mostly black self-tapping screws – not the silver coloured screws. With the help of an assistant, pull out the panel from the bulkhead clips and remove it from the vehicle **(see illustrations)**. As the facia is being removed, disconnect any loom retaining clips.

Refitting

18 Refitting is a reversal of the removal procedure, noting the following points:

a) Ensure the facia guides engage correctly with the clips on the bulkhead. As the facia is being fitted, check that all wiring is routed as noted during removal.

b) On completion, reconnect the battery and check that all the electrical components and switches function correctly.

27 Crossmember – removal and refitting

Note: The most likely reason to remove the crossmember is to gain access to the heater housing and in particular the air conditioning components. If this is the case then the AC system must be degassed by a garage equipped with an AC service station. Many garages and specialists will offer a mobile service at a reasonable cost.

Note: There are minor differences in the construction of the crossmember. Early models (up to 06/07) have a crossmember made of several components bolted together. On later models the main structure is a one piece welded component. Removal and refitting is essentially the same for both versions.

Removal

1 Remove the facia panel as described in Section 26.

2 Unbolt the steering column from the crossmember (as described in Chapter 10 Section 19). There is no need to remove it completely, but if it is left attached to the steering rack and laid on the floor then care must be taken not to damage the column switches etc.

3 Working inside remove the central air distribution ducts from the heater housing and then (on early models) remove the side support panels from the transmission tunnel.

4 Unbolt the crossmember from the left and right-hand support struts and then unbolt the crossmember from the heater housing.

5 Mark the position of the crossmember in relation to the A-pillars **(see illustration)** and then unbolt the crossmember. Check that all sections of the wiring loom are unclipped from the crossmember and then with the aid of an assistant remove the crossmember.

Refitting

6 Refitting is a reversal of removal.

Chapter 12
Body electrical system

Contents

Degrees of difficulty

Easy, suitable for novice with little experience | **Fairly easy,** suitable for beginner with some experience | **Fairly difficult,** suitable for competent DIY mechanic | **Difficult,** suitable for experienced DIY mechanic | **Very difficult,** suitable for expert DIY or professional

Specifications

System type . . . . 12 volt negative earth

Fuses . . . . See *Wiring diagrams*

Bulbs	Wattage	Type
Brake light	21W	P21W
Brake light – High level	LED	
Cornering light (models with bi-Zenon bulbs)	55W	H7
Door entry light (in door)	5W	Festoon
Footwell light	5W	W5W
Front direction indicators (to 09/06 and from 08/10)	21W	PY21W
Front direction indicators (10/06 to 07/10)	21W	H21W
Front direction indicator side repeater	5W	WY5W
Front foglight		
Front foglight (early models)	55W	H11
Front foglight	51W	HB4
Front sidelight	5W	W5W
Front sidelight (with daytime running bulb)	21/5W	P21/5W
Glovebox light	3W	Festoon

Bulbs (continued)

	Wattage	Type
Headlight:		
Halogen headlights (to 2010)		
Dipped beam	55W	H7U
Main beam	55W	H1
Halogen headlights (2011)		
Main/dipped beam	60/55W	H4
Halogen headlights (2011 on)		
Dipped beam	55W	H7
Main beam/daytime running lights	15/55W	H15
Gas discharge headlights (Zenon)		
Main/dipped beam (Bi-xenon)	42V/35W	D3S
Interior light (reading)	5W	W5W
Interior light (courtesy)	10W	Festoon
Interior light (vanity mirror)	5W	Festoon
Load area light	10W	Festoon
Number plate light	5W	C5W
Rear direction indicators	21W	PY21W
Rear sidelight/fog	21/4W	P21/4W
Reversing light	21W	P21W

Torque wrench settings

	Nm	lbf ft
Crash sensor mounting bolt	9	7
Passenger airbag and bracket retaining screws	9	7
Wiper arm securing nut:		
Front	20	15
Rear	12	9

---

1 General information and precautions

⚠ **Warning: Before carrying out any work on the electrical system, read through the precautions given in 'Safety First!' at the beginning of this manual, and in Chapter 5A.**

1 The electrical system is of 12-volt negative earth type. Power for the lights and all electrical accessories is supplied by a lead-acid type battery, which is charged by the alternator.

2 This Chapter covers repair and service procedures for the various electrical components not associated with the engine. Information on the battery, alternator and starter motor can be found in Chapter 5A.

3 It should be noted that prior to working on any component in the electrical system, the ignition and all electrical consumers must be switched off. Additionally, where stated, the battery negative lead must be disconnected, as described in Chapter 5A Section 3.

4 Some models are fitted with gas discharge headlight systems, which include automatic range control to reduce the possibility of dazzling oncoming drivers. Note the special precautions which apply to these systems as given in Section 6.

2 Electrical fault finding – general information

Note: *Refer to the precautions given in 'Safety First!' and in Chapter 5A before starting work. The following tests relate to testing of the main electrical circuits, and should not be used to test delicate electronic circuits (such as anti-lock braking systems), particularly where an electronic control module is used.*

General

1 A typical electrical circuit consists of an electrical component; any switches, relays, motors, fuses, fusible links or circuit breakers related to that component, and the wiring and connectors which link the component to both the battery and the chassis. To help to pin-point a problem in an electrical circuit, wiring diagrams are included at the end of this Chapter. Note: Many of the circuits are controlled by computerised systems (for instance, the windscreen wipers will only operate with the bonnet closed), so before assuming there are faults, it is worthwhile checking if specific conditions apply.

2 Before attempting to diagnose an electrical fault, first study the appropriate wiring diagram to obtain a complete understanding of the components included in the particular circuit concerned. The possible sources of a fault can be narrowed down by noting if other components related to the circuit are operating properly. If several components or circuits fail at one time, the problem is likely to be related to a shared fuse or earth connection.

3 Electrical problems usually stem from simple causes, such as loose or corroded connections, a faulty earth connection, a blown fuse, a melted fusible link, or a faulty relay (refer to Section 3 for details of testing relays). Visually inspect the condition of all fuses, wires and connections in a problem circuit before testing the components. Use the wiring diagrams to determine which terminal connections will need to be checked in order to pin-point the trouble spot.

4 The basic tools required for electrical fault finding include a circuit tester or voltmeter (a 12-volt bulb with a set of test leads can also be used for certain tests); a self-powered test light (sometimes known as a continuity tester); an ohmmeter (to measure resistance); a battery and set of test leads; and a jumper wire, preferably with a circuit breaker or fuse incorporated, which can be used to bypass suspect wires or electrical components. Before attempting to locate a problem with test instruments, use the wiring diagram to determine where to make the connections.

5 To find the source of an intermittent wiring

fault (usually due to a poor or dirty connection, or damaged wiring insulation), a wiggle test can be performed on the wiring. This involves wiggling the wiring by hand to see if the fault occurs as the wiring is moved. It should be possible to narrow down the source of the fault to a particular section of wiring. This method of testing can be used in conjunction with any of the tests described in the following sub-Sections.

6 Apart from problems due to poor connections, two basic types of fault can occur in an electrical circuit – open-circuit, or short-circuit.

7 Open-circuit faults are caused by a break somewhere in the circuit, which prevents current from flowing. An open-circuit fault will prevent a component from working, but will not cause the relevant circuit fuse to blow.

8 Short-circuit faults are caused by a short somewhere in the circuit, which allows the current flowing in the circuit to escape along an alternative route, usually to earth. Short-circuit faults are normally caused by a breakdown in wiring insulation, which allows a feed wire to touch either another wire, or an earthed component such as the bodyshell. A short-circuit fault will normally cause the relevant circuit fuse to blow.

Finding an open-circuit

9 To check for an open-circuit, connect one lead of a circuit tester or voltmeter to either the negative battery terminal or a known good earth.

10 Connect the other lead to a connector in the circuit being tested, preferably nearest to the battery or fuse.

11 Switch on the circuit, bearing in mind that some circuits are live only when the ignition switch is moved to a particular position.

12 If voltage is present (indicated either by the tester bulb lighting or a voltmeter reading, as applicable), this means that the section of the circuit between the relevant connector and the battery is problem-free.

13 Continue to check the remainder of the circuit in the same fashion.

14 When a point is reached at which no voltage is present, the problem must lie between that point and the previous test point with voltage. Most problems can be traced to a broken, corroded or loose connection.

Finding a short-circuit

15 To check for a short-circuit; first disconnect the load(s) from the circuit (loads are the components which draw current from a circuit, such as bulbs, motors, heating elements, etc).

16 Remove the relevant fuse from the circuit, and connect a circuit tester or voltmeter to the fuse connections.

17 Switch on the circuit, bearing in mind that some circuits are live only when the ignition switch is moved to a particular position.

18 If voltage is present (indicated either by the tester bulb lighting or a voltmeter reading,

as applicable), this means that there is a short circuit.

19 If no voltage is present, but the fuse still blows with the load(s) connected, this indicates an internal fault in the load(s).

Finding an earth fault

20 The battery negative terminal is connected to earth – the metal of the engine/transmission and the car body – and most systems are wired so that they only receive a positive feed, the current returning through the metal of the car body. This means that the component mounting and the body form part of that circuit. Loose or corroded mountings can therefore cause a range of electrical faults, ranging from total failure of a circuit, to a puzzling partial fault. In particular, lights may shine dimly (especially when another circuit sharing the same earth point is in operation), motors (e.g. wiper motors or the radiator cooling fan motor) may run slowly, and the operation of one circuit may have an apparently unrelated effect on another. Note that on many vehicles, earth straps are used between certain components, such as the engine/transmission and the body, usually where there is no metal-to-metal contact between components due to flexible rubber mountings, etc.

21 To check whether a component is properly earthed, disconnect the battery (refer to the warnings given in the Reference section at the rear of the manual) and connect one lead of an ohmmeter to a known good earth point. Connect the other lead to the wire or earth connection being tested. The resistance reading should be zero; if not, check the connection as follows.

22 If an earth connection is thought to be faulty, dismantle the connection and clean back to bare metal both the bodyshell and the wire terminal or the component earth connection mating surface. Be careful to remove all traces of dirt and corrosion, and then use a knife to trim away any paint, so that a clean metal-to-metal joint is made. On reassembly, tighten the joint fasteners securely; if a wire terminal is being refitted, use serrated washers between the terminal and the bodyshell to ensure a clean and secure connection. When the connection is

remade, prevent the onset of corrosion in the future by applying a coat of petroleum jelly or silicone-based grease or by spraying on (at regular intervals) a proprietary ignition sealer or a water dispersant lubricant.

3 Fuses and relays – general information

Fuses and fusible links

1 Fuses are designed to break a circuit when a predetermined current is reached, in order to protect the components and wiring, which could be damaged by excessive current flow. Any excessive current flow will be due to a fault in the circuit, usually a short-circuit (see Section 2).

2 The main fuses are located in the fusebox on the driver's side of the facia. Open the storage compartment cover and depress the catch to fully lower the cover **(see illustration)**. If required the compartment cover can be removed completely by pulling it free from the hinges.

3 To remove a fuse, first switch off the circuit concerned (or the ignition), and then pull the fuse out of its terminals **(see illustration)**.

4 The wire within the fuse should be visible; if the fuse has blown it will be broken or melted.

5 Always renew a fuse with one of the correct rating; never use a fuse with a different rating from that specified.

6 Refer to the wiring diagrams for details of the fuse ratings and the circuits protected. The fuse rating is stamped on the top of the fuse; the fuses are also colour-coded as follows.

Colour	Rating
Light brown	5A
Brown	7.5A
Red	10A
Blue	15A
Yellow	20A
White or clear	25A
Green	30A
Orange	40A

3.2 Interior fusebox

3.3 Removing a fuse from the facia fusebox

3.8a Slide the locking tabs in the direction of the arrows…

3.8b …to access the fuse and relay box in the engine compartment

7 Never renew a fuse more than once without tracing the source of the trouble. If the new fuse blows immediately, find the cause before renewing it again; a short to earth as a result of faulty insulation is most likely. Where a fuse protects more than one circuit, try to isolate the fault by switching on each circuit in turn (where possible) until the fuse blows again. Always carry a supply of spare fuses of each relevant rating on the vehicle.

8 Additional fuses and relays are located in the fusebox located on the left-hand side of the engine compartment. Release the two securing clips and withdraw the cover to gain access to the fuses and relays **(see illustrations)**.

9 To renew a fusible link, first disconnect the battery negative terminal. Unscrew the retaining nuts then remove the blown link from the front of the engine compartment fusebox **(see illustration)**. Fit the new link to its terminals and reconnect the leads. Ensure the link and leads are correctly seated then refit the retaining nuts and tighten securely. Clip the cover back into position then reconnect the battery.

Relays

10 A relay is an electrically operated switch, which is used for the following reasons:

a) A relay can switch a heavy current remotely from the circuit in which the current is flowing, allowing the use of lighter-gauge wiring and switch contacts.
b) A relay can receive more than one control input, unlike a mechanical switch.
c) A relay can have a timer function – for example, the intermittent wiper relay.

11 Most of the relays are located on the relay plate behind the driver's side facia, however, additional relays are located in the engine compartment fusebox **(see illustration 3.8)**.

12 Access to the relays can be obtained after removing the driver's side lower facia panel/ storage compartment as described in Chapter 11, Section 26 **(see illustration)**. Identification details of the relays are given at the start of the wiring diagrams.

13 If a circuit or system controlled by a relay develops a fault, and the relay is suspect, operate the system. If the relay is functioning, it should be possible to hear it click as it is energised. If this is the case, the fault lies with the components or wiring of the system. If the relay is not being energised, then either the relay is not receiving a main supply or a switching voltage, or the relay itself is faulty. Testing is by the substitution of a known good unit, but be careful – while some relays are identical in appearance and in operation, others look similar but perform different functions.

14 To remove a relay, first ensure that the relevant circuit is switched off. The relay can then simply be pulled out from the socket, and pushed back into position.

15 The direction indicator/hazard flasher relay is integral with the hazard warning switch. Refer to Section 5 for the switch removal procedure.

4 Electrical connectors

1 Most electrical connections on these vehicles are made with multiwire plastic connectors. The mating halves of many connectors are secured with locking clips molded into the plastic connector shells. The mating halves of some large connectors, such as some of those under the instrument panel, are held together by a bolt through the center of the connector.

2 To separate a connector with locking clips, use a small screwdriver to pry the clips apart carefully, then separate the connector halves. Pull only on the shell, never pull on the wiring harness, as you may damage the individual wires and terminals inside the connectors. Look at the connector closely before trying to separate the halves. Often the locking clips are engaged in a way that is not immediately clear. Additionally, many connectors have more than one set of clips.

3 Each pair of connector terminals has a male half and a female half. When you look at the end view of a connector in a diagram, be sure to understand whether the view shows the harness side or the component side of the connector. Connector halves are mirror images of each other, and a terminal shown on the right side end-view of one half will be on the left side end-view of the other half.

4 It is often necessary to take circuit voltage

3.9 Fusible link on the front of the fuse/relay box

3.12 Relays located behind the facia

measurements with a connector connected. Whenever possible, carefully insert a small straight pin (not your meter probe) into the rear of the connector shell to contact the terminal inside, then clip your meter lead to the pin. This kind of connection is called "backprobing." When inserting a test probe into a terminal, be careful not to distort the terminal opening. Doing so can lead to a poor connection and corrosion at that terminal later. Using the small straight pin instead of a meter probe results in less chance of deforming the terminal connector. "T" pins are a good choice as temporary meter connections. They allow for a larger surface area to attach the meter leads too.

5 Typical electrical connectors:

4.5a Most electrical connectors have a single release tab that you depress to release the connector

4.5b Some electrical connectors have a retaining tab which must be pried up to free the connector

4.5c Some connectors have two release tabs that you must squeeze to release the connector

4.5d Some connectors use wire retainers that you squeeze to release the connector

4.5e Critical connectors often employ a sliding lock (1) that you must pull out before you can depress the release tab (2)

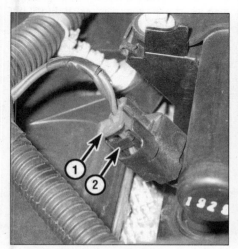
4.5f Here's another sliding-lock style connector, with the lock (1) and the release tab (2) on the side of the connector

4.5g On some connectors the lock (1) must be pulled out to the side and removed before you can lift the release tab (2)

4.5h Some critical connectors, like the multi-pin connectors at the Electronic Control Module employ pivoting locks that must be flipped open

5.4 Disconnect the wiring connector

5.5a Undo the retaining screw

5.5b Insert a 2.5mm pin to release the front securing clip

5.5c Release the rear clip and remove control unit

5.5d Two securing clips

5.6a Release the two securing clips...

5.6b ...and remove the airbag clock spring/ slip-ring unit

5.7a Slide a feeler blade down to release the securing clip...

5.7b ...then unclip and remove the switch

5 Switches – removal and refitting

Note: *Before working on any electrical systems switch off the ignition and all electrical consumers and remove the ignition key.*

Ignition switch

1 Refer to Chapter 10, Section 22 10.

Wiper and indicator/ cruise switches

2 Check that the front wheels are pointing straight-ahead and the steering wheel is in its centre position, then remove the steering wheel as described in Chapter 10 Section 18.
3 Remove the steering column shrouds, as described in Chapter 11 Section 24.

Models up to 2010

4 Disconnect the wiring connectors from the electronic control unit **(see illustration)**.
5 Remove the steering column electronics control unit, from below the steering column. To do this, undo the single retaining screw, then insert a 2.5 mm diameter rod (drill bit) through the hole provided (below the screw hole), and release the centre clip. Now use a screwdriver to release the rear clip. Pull down the control unit from the column switch carrier **(see illustrations)**.
6 The airbag clock spring/slip-ring must be held in its centre position while it is removed, to ensure correct refitting. Unclip the airbag clock spring/slip-ring from the combination switch carrier by lifting the retaining hooks **(see illustrations)**.
7 Remove the relevant switch by inserting a 1.0 mm feeler gauge through the slot provided to release the switch from the carrier. Release the securing clip at the rear of the switch and slide the switch forwards out from the housing **(see illustrations)**.
8 Refitting is a reversal of removal.

Models from 2010

Note: *On these models the lighting and wiper switch is one unit and cannot be renewed separately.*

9 Disconnect the wiring connectors from the airbag clock spring/electronic control unit. Note this is one unit and cannot be separated.
10 On switch assembly manufactured by VALEO, undo the three retaining screws and withdraw the airbag clock spring/electronic control unit from over the steering column **(see illustration)**. Release the locking tabs and remove the switch assembly **(see illustration)**.
11 On switch assembly manufactured by KOSTAL, undo the retaining screw at the lower part of the assembly, then release the two upper securing clips, then withdraw the airbag clock spring/electronic control unit from over the steering column. Undo the securing screw from the lower part of the assembly, and then remove the switch assembly.
12 Refitting is a reversal of removal. Note, as the switch assembly is being refitted, make sure the indicator switch is in the centre position; otherwise the reset lever if extended can break off as the switch is fitted.

Lighting switch

13 With the light switch in position O, press the switch centre inwards and turn it slightly to the right. Hold this position and pull the switch from the dash **(see illustration)**. Removing the facia end panel makes this task slightly easier.
14 As the switch is withdrawn from the dash, disconnect the wiring plug **(see illustration)**.
15 To refit the switch, first reconnect the wiring plug, then hold the switch and press the rotary part inwards and slightly to the right. Insert the switch into the dash, turn the rotary part to position O and release. Check the switch for correct operation.

Headlamp range control and instrument illumination switch

16 Remove the lighting switch as described in paragraphs 13 to 15.
17 Remove the driver's side facia lower panel/storage compartment **(see illustrations)**.
18 Lower the panel, disconnect the wiring plug and push out the switch **(see illustrations)**.
19 Refitting is a reversal of removal.

Air conditioning/rear window heating switches

20 The switches are integral with the heater control panel, and cannot be removed separately. Refer to Chapter Section for details of heater control panel removal and refitting.

Heater blower motor switch

21 The switch is integral with the heater control panel, and cannot be removed separately. Refer to Chapter Section for details of heater control panel removal and refitting.

Hazard warning

22 Remove the heater control panel as described in Chapter 3 Section 9.
23 Reach up through the opening and (with difficulty) release the switch. Pull the switch

5.10a Remove the screws

5.10b Release the catches

5.13 Press the switch centre inwards and turn it slightly to the right to remove

5.14 Disconnect the wiring plug

5.17a Remove the end panel...

5.17b ...and remove the screws

5.18a Disconnect the wiring plug

5.18b Depress the locking tabs to release the switch

5.23a Remove the switch

5.23b The switch removed, showing the location of the locking tabs

5.29 Unclip the switch from inside the glovebox

forward and disconnect the wiring plug **(see illustrations)**.

24 Refitting is a reversal of removal.

ESP/ASR(TCS)/Parking sensor switches etc.

25 Remove the tray from the front of the centre console as described in Chapter 11 Section 25.

26 Release the retaining clips and withdraw the switch from the top of the switch panel.

27 Refitting is a reversal of removal.

Passenger air bag on/off switch

28 Remove the glovebox or storage compartment (depending on the trim level) as described in Chapter 11 Section 24.

29 Release the retaining clips and withdraw the switch from inside the glovebox **(see illustration)**.

30 Refitting is a reversal of removal.

Driver's door locking switch and mirror control switch

31 Remove the door inner trim, as described in Chapter 11 Section 12.

32 Remove the screws, lift out the switch panel and disconnect the wiring plug(s) **(see illustrations)**.

33 Refitting is a reversal of removal.

Electric window switch assembly

34 The switch can be prised up from the door panel with a trim tool **(see illustration)** and the switch disconnected. In some cases where there is a risk of damage to the door panel, remove the door panel and push the switch out from the rear – as described in Chapter 11 Section 12.

35 Refitting is a reversal of removal.

Handbrake 'on' warning switch

36 Refer to Chapter 9 Section 17.

Brake light switch

37 Refer to Chapter 9 Section 18.

Reversing light switch

38 Refer to Chapter 7A Section 6.

Courtesy light switches

39 The courtesy light switches are integrated into the door lock mechanisms and cannot be renewed independently. If the courtesy light switch is faulty, renew the door lock mechanism as described in Chapter 11 Section 13.

Luggage area light switch

40 The luggage compartment light switch is integrated into the tailgate lock mechanism, and cannot be renewed independently. If the luggage compartment light switch is faulty, renew the tailgate lock mechanism as described in Chapter 11 Section 15, 16.

Interior monitoring deactivation switch

41 Carefully prise the switch from the B-pillar trim panel. Disconnect the wiring plug.

42 Refitting is a reversal of removal.

Rain and light sensor

43 The windscreen wipers/lights (depending on model) are automatically activated, when the sensor located in the interior mirror base detects droplets of water/darkness.

44 Remove the interior mirror, as described in Chapter 11 Section 18.

45 Remove the plastic trim/stay, and disconnect the wiring connector from the sensor **(see illustration)**.

5.32a Remove the screws and...

5.32b ...lift out the switch panel...

5.32c ...and separate the switch from the handle

5.34 Prise out the switch

5.45 Disconnect the wiring connector from the sensor

46 The mirror base/sensor is bonded to the windscreen (see illustration). Whilst it is possible to remove the base by means of a scraper, great care must be exercised to avoid damaging the windscreen.

47 Due to the hazardous chemicals involved, it is recommended that the bonding of the mirror base to the windscreen be entrusted to a VW dealer or suitably equipped specialist.

48 With the base/sensor in place, refit the mirror with reference to Chapter 11 Section 18.

6 Bulbs (exterior lights) – renewal

General

1 Whenever a bulb is renewed, note the following points:
a) *Switch off the ignition and all electrical consumers before commencing work.*
b) *Remember that if the light has just been in use the bulb may be extremely hot.*
c) *Always check the bulb contacts and holder, ensuring that there is clean metal-to-metal contact. Clean off any corrosion or dirt before fitting a new bulb.*
d) *Wherever bayonet-type bulbs are fitted ensure that the spring-tensioned arms bear firmly against the bulb contacts.*
e) *Always ensure that the new bulb is of the correct rating and that it is thoroughly clean before fitting it.*

5.46 Sensor and mirror base fitted to windscreen

Headlight mounted bulbs (Halogen)

Headlight main beam

Note: *Do not touch the glass envelope of the bulb if it is to be re-used.*

Note: *There are minor differences between the earlier headlights (up to 2010) and the later headlights. Early models all used a H1 type main beam bulb and later models a H4 type bulb. H4 type bulbs combine the main and dipped beam into a single bulb. Later higher specification models combine the main beam with the daytime running lights in a H15 type bulb. Regardless of the type of headlight fitted, the bulb replacement procedure is essentially the same.*

2 Working in the engine compartment, remove the cover from the rear of the headlight (see illustration).

6.2 Remove the cover

3 Remove the wiring plug by working from the bulb, release the spring clips and remove the bulb (see illustrations).

4 When handling the new bulb, use a tissue or clean cloth to avoid touching the glass with the fingers; moisture and grease from the skin can cause blackening and rapid failure of this type of bulb. If the glass is accidentally touched, wipe it clean using methylated spirit.

5 Install the new bulb; ensuring that it is located correctly in the headlight unit, turn it clockwise to secure it in position.

6 Refit the headlight cover, making sure that it is secure.

Headlight dip beam

Note: *Do not touch the glass envelope of the bulb if it is to be re-used.*

7 Working in the engine compartment,

6.3a Remove the wiring plug

6.3b Compress and...

6.3c ...release the spring retaining clip

6.3d Remove the bulb (H4 type bulb)

6.3e On early models remove the cover...

6.3f ...and remove the H1 type bulb

6.7a Release the spring and...

6.7b ...remove the cover

6.8 Remove the bulb complete with the bulb holder

release the spring clip and remove the cover **(see illustrations)**.

8 Reach into the headlight and turn the bulb holder anti-clockwise to remove it. **(see illustration)**. The bulb can then be pulled out from the bulb holder.

9 When handling the new bulb, use a tissue or clean cloth to avoid touching the glass with the fingers; moisture and grease from the skin can cause blackening and rapid failure of this type of bulb. If the glass is accidentally touched, wipe it clean using methylated spirit.

10 Fit the new bulb to the bulb holder, ensuring that the location lugs are aligned, then fit the bulb holder to the headlight and turn clockwise to secure.

11 Refit the headlight cover, making sure that it is secure.

Front sidelight

12 Working in the engine compartment

either remove the cover from the rear of the headlight or locate the bulb holder extension.

13 Carefully pull the sidelight bulb holder from the headlight unit. Note that access is restricted. On some models the bulb is a push-fit in the holder and can be removed by grasping the end of the bulb and pulling it out. On other versions the bulb is a bayonet fit **(see illustrations)**.

14 Refitting is a reversal of removal, making sure that the headlight cover is securely refitted.

Front direction indicator

15 On models fitted with H7 headlight bulbs, remove the cover from the rear of the headlight. Turn the bulb holder anticlockwise and remove the bulb holder complete with the bulb. Remove the bulb from the bulb holder.

16 On all other models remove the bulb holder **(see illustration)**.

17 Depress and then turn the bulb to release it from the bulb holder **(see illustration)**.

18 When handling the new bulb, use a tissue or clean cloth to avoid touching the glass with the fingers; moisture and grease from the skin can cause blackening and rapid failure of this type of bulb. If the glass is accidentally touched, wipe it clean using methylated spirit.

19 Fit the new bulb to the bulb holder, then fit the bulb holder to the headlight and turn clockwise to secure.

20 Where removed, refit the headlight cover.

Gas discharge headlights (Bi-zenon)

Warning: The headlight bulb contains gas at very high pressure, and it is recommended that gloves and eye protection be worn to prevent potential personal injury.

Note: *Do not touch the glass envelope of the bulb if it is to be re-used.*

Main beam/dipped beam

21 The main and dipped beams are the same 'bi-zenon' bulb. A mechanical shutter effects the change from main to dip beam and visa versa. This has the advantage that both headlight aims are automatically adjusted depending on the vehicle ride height.

22 Remove the cover from the rear of the headlight.

23 Disconnect the wiring plug and then rotate the starter unit in the 'open' direction to remove it.

24 When handling the new bulb, use a tissue or clean cloth to avoid touching the glass with

6.13a Pull the bulb from the bulb holder

6.13b Remove the bulb holder and...

6.13c ...push and turn the bulb to remove it

6.16 Remove the bulb and holder

6.17 Remove the bulb

6.32a Remove the lamp and then...

6.32b ...disconnect the bulb holder

6.35a Remove the screws...

the fingers; moisture and grease from the skin can cause blackening and rapid failure of this type of bulb. If the glass is accidentally touched, wipe it clean using methylated spirit.

25 Fit the new gas discharge bulb and locking ring to the headlight and turn clockwise to secure. Refit the starter unit and reconnect the wiring plug.

26 Refit the headlight cover, making sure that it is secure.

Caution: After refitting a gas discharge headlamp, the basic setting of the Automatic Range Control system should be checked.

Front foglight

27 If not already done so, turn off the ignition and remove the vehicle key. Unclip the cover from the front of the foglight. Note there is a slight variation to the design, depending on the year of production.

28 Remove the fixings and pull the lamp forward, disconnecting the wiring plug as the foglight is removed.

29 Turn the bulbholder anti-clockwise and remove it complete with bulb from the rear of the foglight. Note: The bulb is integral with the bulbholder.

30 Fit the new bulb using a reversal of the removal procedure.

Direction indicator side repeater

31 The side repeater is mounted in the front wing. Protect the paint work with masking tape if required.

32 Push the repeater against the spring tension and then lift the rear of the lamp out

6.35b ...lift off the bulb holder...

of the wing. Disconnect the wiring plug as the lamp is withdrawn **(see illustrations)**.

33 Pull the bulb straight out from the bulb holder to remove it.

Rear light cluster

Wing mounted lights

34 Remove the rear light cluster as described in Section 8.

35 Release the retaining clips and remove the bulb holder from the rear of the cluster **(see illustrations)**.

36 Fit the new bulb using a reversal of the removal procedure.

High-level brake light

Note: *The light is of LED design; therefore if faulty the complete unit must be renewed. Note that the LEDs are arranged in groups of four, and if just one group fails, the light still*

6.35c ...and replace the relevant bulb

meets legal requirement. Failure of more than one group renders the light illegal.

37 Remove the high-level light unit as described in Section 8.

Number plate light

38 The number plate lights are either screwed into place or clipped into place. Release the securing clip or screw and withdraw the light unit from the tailgate **(see illustrations)**.

39 Fit the new bulb using a reversal of the removal procedure.

| 7 | **Bulbs (interior lights) –** renewal | |

General

1 Whenever a bulb is renewed, note the following points:

a) *Switch off the ignition and all electrical consumers before commencing work.*

b) *Remember that if the light has just been in use the bulb may be extremely hot.*

c) *Always check the bulb contacts and holder, ensuring that there is clean metal-to-metal contact between them. Clean off any corrosion or dirt before fitting a new bulb.*

d) *Wherever bayonet-type bulbs are fitted ensure that the live contact(s) bear firmly against the bulb contact.*

e) *Always ensure that the new bulb is of the correct rating and that it is completely clean before fitting it.*

6.38a Unscrew the lamp...

6.38b ...and remove the festoon type bulb

7.2a Using a small screwdriver…

7.2b …unclip the lens

7.3 Remove the bulb

7.6 Remove the lamp

7.7a Remove the cover…

7.7b …and then remove the bulb

Front courtesy/reading light

2 Using a small screwdriver, release the lens **(see illustrations)**.

3 Either pull free the wedge type bulb (reading light) or push and unclip the festoon type bulb (courtesy light) **(see illustration)**. Note that some models only have a single festoon type bulb fitted.

4 Fit the new bulb(s) using a reversal of the removal procedure.

Rear load area lights

5 There are slight variation in the design of the rear light, depending on the year of production. Removal and refitting of the bulbs is essentially the same for all models.

6 Using a screwdriver, carefully release the locking lugs and remove the lamp from the roof **(see illustration)**. Disconnect the wiring plug.

7 Remove the cover. Push and unclip the festoon type bulb **(see illustrations)**.

8 Fit the new bulb and light unit using a reversal of the removal procedure.

Vanity mirror lights

9 Carefully prise the light unit from its location in the headlining **(see illustrations)**. The festoon-type bulb is a push-fit in the spring contacts

10 Refitting is a reverse of the removal procedure.

Heater/ventilation control panel illumination

11 The control panel is illuminated by LEDs built into the panel. Consequently, if a fault develops, renewal of the panel is necessary.

Switch illumination

12 The switch illumination bulbs are integral with the switches. If a bulb fails, the complete switch must be renewed.

7.9a Prise out the vanity mirror light…

7.9b …and remove the festoon-type bulb

8.4 Disconnect the wiring plug

8.5a Remove the front mounting bolt...

8.5b ...loosen, but do not remove the rear mounting

8.5c Remove the upper mounting bolts

8.6 Remove the headlight

8.14 Unclip the trim panel

8 Exterior light units – removal and refitting

1 Before removing any light units, switch off the ignition and all electrical consumers, and then remove the ignition key.

Headlight

2 On early models it is possible to remove the headlight by partially releasing the bumper cover at the relevant side. On later models (2011 on with H7 type bulbs) remove the front bumper cover as described in Chapter 11, Section 6.

3 Mark the position of the headlight mountings to ensure correct alignment on refitting

4 Disconnect the wiring plug **(see illustration)**.

5 Remove the front the lower mounting screw, loosen the rear and then remove the upper bolts **(see illustrations)**.

6 Pull the headlight forward to remove it **(see illustration)**.

7 Refitting is a reversal of removal, but on completion, check that the headlight is aligned flush with the surrounding bodywork. If not, turn the eccentric adjustment bushing on the inside of the headlight as required. Finally, have the headlight alignment checked at the earliest opportunity.

Gas discharge bulb control unit/ starter

Caution: After refitting a gas discharge headlamp, the basic setting of the Automatic Range Control system should be checked. Because of the requirement for specialised equipment, this can only be carried out by a VW dealer or suitably equipped specialist. The headlight bulb contains gas at very high pressure, and it is recommended that gloves and eye protection be worn to prevent potential personal injury.

8 Remove the headlight as described above.

9 Undo the retaining screws, and remove the control unit from the base of the headlight. Disconnect the wiring plugs.

10 Undo the screws and remove the output control unit from the side of the headlight.

Note that the electrical connections are automatically separated when the unit is removed. Check the condition of the seal.

11 Refitting is a reversal of removal.

Wing mounted side repeater

12 Removal of the lamp is described in Section 6.

Front foglight

13 The foglight is removed for bulb replacement as described in Section 6.

Rear light cluster

14 Open the rear doors or tailgate and (where fitted) unclip the trim panel **(see illustration)**.

15 Remove the upper and lower fixings and then unhook the lamp from the ball headed sockets to remove it **(see illustrations)**.

8.15a Remove the fixings (lower shown)

8.15b Remove the lamp – note the position of the mounting points

8.16 Disconnect the wiring plug

8.18a Remove the screws...

8.18b ...lift out the brake light and disconnect the wiring plug

16 Disconnect the wiring plug and remove the light cluster (see illustration).
17 Refitting is a reversal of removal, making sure that the alignment lugs locate on refitting.

High level brake light

Note: *The light is of LED design; therefore if faulty the complete unit must be renewed. Note that the LEDs are arranged in groups of four, and if just one group fails, the light still meets legal requirement. Failure of more than one group renders the light illegal.*
18 Remove the fixings and lift out the brake light. Disconnect the wiring plug (see illustrations).
19 Fit the new light unit using a reversal of the removal procedure.

Rear number plate light

20 The procedure is described as part of the rear number plate light bulb renewal procedure in Section 6.

9 Headlight beam adjustment components – removal and refitting

Headlight adjustment switch

1 The switch is integral with the instrument illumination switch.

2 Removal and refitting of the switch assembly is covered in Section 5.

Headlight range adjustment motor

Note: *Only models fitted with H7 type bulbs and manufactured before 2010 have a replaceable range control motor. On all other models the headlight must be replaced if the motor is faulty.*
3 Remove the headlight (see Section 8).
4 Release the securing clip and remove the plastic cover from the rear of the headlight unit.
5 Remove the mounting screws and then release the motor by pulling it up (off the socket) and then down.
6 Working inside the rear of the light unit, disconnect the wiring connector from the range control motor and remove it.
7 Refitting is a reversal of removal, making sure the ball joint mounting is correctly located in the headlight reflector.

Gas discharge headlights

8 The range control motor cannot be removed from the headlight unit. If faulty renew the headlight unit as described in Section 8.

Automatic range control ECU

Note: *Although it is possible to remove and refit the ECU, the new unit will need to be coded before it will function correctly. This task can only be carried out by a VW dealer or suitably equipped specialist.*
9 The ECU is located behind the drivers

10.2 Headlight adjustment screws

side storage compartment. Open the compartment, pull off the lid and remove the compartment as described in Chapter 11 Section 24.
10 Release the locking lever and open the wiring connector so that it can be disconnected.
11 Undo the mounting screw and withdraw the ECU from the side of the glovebox.
12 Refitting is a reversal of removal, but make sure the ECU is correctly located in the bracket before reconnecting the wiring.

Vehicle level sender

13 Refer to Chapter 10, Section 17.

10 Headlight beam alignment – general information

1 Accurate adjustment of the headlight beam is only possible using optical beam setting equipment and this work should be carried out by a VW dealer. All MOT test centres will have this equipment.
2 For reference, the headlights can be manually adjusted using the adjuster assemblies fitted to the top of each light unit (see illustration). Note that the illustrations shows the early type headlight, but later models are similar.

11 Instrument panel – removal and refitting

Removal

1 Switch off the ignition and all electrical consumers and remove the ignition key. Release the steering wheel adjustment handle, pull the wheel out as far as possible, and set it in the lowest position.
2 Carefully prise out the steering column upper gap cover, and then undo the two

11.2a Unclip the upper shroud from the instrument panel (steering wheel removed for clarity)…

11.2b …and undo the retaining screws

11.3a Pull out the instrument panel and withdraw it from the facia…

screws at the lower part of the instrument panel **(see illustrations)**.

3 Release the upper retaining clips and carefully pull the instrument panel from the facia. On early models (up to 2010) the panel will automatically disconnect from the wiring plug. On later models release the locking lever and disconnect the wiring plug from the rear of the instrument panel **(see illustrations)**.

Refitting

4 Refitting is a reversal of removal.

12 Instrument panel components – removal and refitting

1 It is not possible to dismantle the instrument panel. If any of the gauges are faulty, the complete instrument panel must be renewed.

13 Service interval indicator – general information and resetting

1 All models are equipped with a service interval indicator. This is displayed on the information panel in the centre of the instrument panel.
2 Vehicles may be set to fixed or variable service intervals depending on the production number. Suitable diagnostic equipment is the only way to alter the service interval from fixed to variable service.

3 The display is reset using reset button in the instrument panel. Resetting is described in the relevant part of Chapter 1 Section 8.

14 Clock – removal and refitting

1 The clock is integral with the instrument panel, and cannot be removed separately. The instrument panel is a sealed unit, and if the clock, or any other components, are faulty, the complete instrument panel must be renewed. Refer to Section 11 to remove it.

15 12v Power outlets – removal and refitting

1 All models have a central power outlet. Other models may have one at the rear of the centre console.

Removal

Note: *A special tool is available that will allow the retaining sleeve of the power outlet to be easily removed on models that have an illuminated socket (T40148).*
2 Disconnect the battery negative lead (refer to Chapter 5A Section 3).
3 Remove the panel **(see illustration)** as described in Chapter 11, Section 25.
4 Where fitted, remove the bulb holder.
5 Release the retaining clips and push the centre element of the lighter out of the outer plastic mounting.

11.3b …then release locking clip to disconnect the wiring connector

Refitting

6 Refitting is a reversal of removal.

16 Horn – removal and refitting

Removal

1 Switch off the ignition and all electrical consumers and remove the ignition key.
2 Jack up and support the front of the vehicle (see *Jacking and support*) Remove the engine undershield. Note on some models there are two horns, one at each side of the vehicle.
3 Reach up and disconnect the wiring plug and then unscrew the mounting bolt. Remove the horn together with the mounting bracket **(see illustrations)**.

15.3 Remove the panel

16.3a Disconnect the wiring plug…

16.3b …and undo the bolt (shown with bumper removed for clarity)

4 If required, unscrew the nut on the top of the horn to remove the bracket.

Refitting

5 Refitting is a reversal of removal.

17 Speedometer sensor – general information

1 No electronic speedometer sensor is fitted to the models covered in this manual. Vehicle speed is determined from the ABS wheel sensor signals, and processed by the engine management ECU.

18 Wiper arm – removal and refitting

Removal

1 Operate the wiper motor, then switch off so that the wiper arms return to the at-rest position. Alternatively, set the wiper blades to the Winter/Service (vertical) position by operating the wipers within 10 seconds of switching off the ignition. Note: The wiper motor will only operate with the bonnet closed.

2 Stick a piece of masking tape to the glass along the edge of the wiper blade to use as an alignment aid on refitting (see illustration).

3 On front wiper arms, prise off the wiper arm spindle nut cover (where fitted) and then slacken but do not completely remove the spindle nut. Lift the blade off the glass and carefully rock the wiper arm from side to side, until it releases from the spindle. Remove the spindle nut and the wiper arm (see illustrations). Note: If both windscreen wiper arms are to be removed at the same time mark them for identification; the arms are not interchangeable.

4 On rear wiper arms, unclip the spindle nut cover, then slacken but do not completely remove the spindle nut. Lift the blade off the glass and carefully rock the wiper arm from side to side, until it releases from the spindle. Remove the spindle nut and wiper arm (see illustrations).

18.2 Make alignment marks with a piece of tape

5 If any of the arms are a tight fit on the spindle, the arm can be removed from the spindle using a small puller (see illustration).

Refitting

6 Ensure that the wiper arm and spindle splines are clean and dry, and then refit the arm to the spindle, aligning the wiper blade with the tape fitted on removal. Refit the spindle nut, tightening it securely, and clip the nut cover back in position.

Note: Where the wipers were set to the service position in paragraph 1, they will only resume their normal position after actuating the wipers twice, or after starting a journey when the speed of the car is greater than 1 mph.

18.3a Remove the cover

18.3b Unscrew the spindle nut...

18.3c ...and remove the wiper arm

18.4a Prise up the cover and...

18.4b ...remove the nut...

18.4c ...then remove the tailgate wiper arm

18.5 Use a small puller to remove wiper arm, if required

19.4a Remove the rubber seal...

19.4b ...and then the cover

19.5a Remove the hinge covers and insulation

19 Windscreen wiper motor and linkage – removal and refitting

Removal

1 The windscreen wiper system has an APP (alternating park position) function. Every second time the wipers are switched off, the wiper arm is moved up slightly from its lowest position in order to maintain the efficiency of the wiper blades. If the motor crank is disconnected, it must be reset by first deactivating the APP function, however, this requires the use of diagnostic equipment not available to the home mechanic. It is therefore important to accurately mark the crank in relation to the motor spindle before removing it. Reactivation of the function occurs automatically after 100 cycles of the wiper movement, and this also applies to new motors.

2 Remove the wiper arms as described in Section 18.

3 Disconnect the battery negative lead (as described in Chapter 5A Section 3).

4 Pull off the rubber sealing strip from the top of the bulkhead and then remove the plenum chamber cover/windscreen cowl **(see illustrations)**. Note that the panel is a tight fit in the gutter at the base of

19.5b Work along the panel, remove the bolts...

19.5c ...and lift out the panel

the windscreen. Apply plenty of lubricant and slowly ease the panel free from the gutter.

Caution: Do not use a screwdriver to lever between the cowling and windscreen, as this is likely to result in the windscreen cracking.

5 Remove the hinge cover panels and then remove the plenum chamber front panel insulation followed by the panel itself **(see illustrations)**.

6 Disconnect the wiring plug from the wiper motor **(see illustration)**.

7 Unscrew the mounting bolts and manoeuvre the windscreen wiper motor and linkage out from the plenum chamber **(see illustrations)**.

8 Where required, recover the washers and spacers from the motor mounting rubbers, noting their locations, then inspect the rubbers for signs of damage or deterioration, and renew if necessary.

9 The motor can be separated from the linkage. To separate the motor from the linkage, proceed as follows:

a) *Make alignment marks between the motor spindle and the linkage to ensure correct alignment on refitting, and note the orientation of the linkage.*

b) *Unscrew the nut securing the linkage crank to the motor spindle.*

c) *Unscrew the three bolts securing*

19.6 Disconnecting the wiring plug

19.7a Remove the bolts...

19.7b ...and lift out the motor

19.9 Wiper motor retaining screws

19.10 Align the locating peg with the grommet

20.4 Disconnect the wiring plug…

20.5 …and washer fluid hose from the tailgate wiper motor

20.6a Tailgate wiper motor securing nuts

20.6b Removing the tailgate wiper motor

the motor to the mounting plate **(see illustration)**, and then remove the motor.

Refitting

10 Refitting is a reversal of removal, bearing in mind the following points.
a) If the motor has been separated from the linkage, ensure that the marks made on the motor spindle and linkage before removal are aligned, and ensure that the linkage is orientated as noted before removal.
b) Ensure that the washers and spacers are fitted to the motor mounting rubbers as noted before removal.
c) Make sure the locating peg aligns with the grommet in the bulkhead, when refitting **(see illustration)**.
d) Refit the wiper arms as described in Section 18.

---

20 Rear wiper motor – removal and refitting

Removal

1 Remove the wiper arm as described in Section 18.
2 Recover the wiper motor shaft sealing ring – note the orientation.

Models with a tailgate

3 Open the tailgate, then unclip the cover from the wiper motor.
4 Release the locking clip and unplug the wiring connector from the motor **(see illustration)**.

5 Disconnect the washer fluid hose from the washer nozzle connector on the motor assembly **(see illustration)**.
6 Unscrew the three nuts securing the motor, and then withdraw the assembly. Note the position of the rubber sealing ring, renew if necessary **(see illustrations)**.

Models with rear doors

7 Remove the door trim panel as described in Chapter 11 Section 12.
8 Remove the lock carrier and lock cylinder as described in Chapter 11 Section 13.
9 Release the locking clip and unplug the wiring connector from the motor.
10 Disconnect the washer fluid hose from the washer nozzle connector on the motor assembly.
11 Remove the mounting bolts and then withdraw the motor from the door frame.

Refitting

12 Refitting is a reversal of removal, but

21.2a Undo the retaining bolt…

ensure that the motor shaft rubber sealing ring/grommet is correctly refitted to prevent water leaks, and refit the wiper arm with reference to Section 18.

---

21 Washer system components – removal and refitting

Washer fluid reservoir and pumps

Note: *Models fitted with Xenon headlights have an additional washer pump fitted above the windscreen washer pump. Where fitted this is removed after the windscreen washer pump has been removed.*
1 Switch off the ignition and all electrical consumers and remove the ignition key.
2 In the engine compartment, unscrew the mounting bolt and remove the top from the reservoir filler neck **(see illustrations)**.

21.2b …and remove the filler neck

21.4 Disconnect the wiring connector

21.5 Disconnect the washer fluid hose(s)

21.6 Remove the pump

3 Remove the front bumper cover as described in Chapter 11, Section 6.
4 Disconnect the wiring connector from the top of the washer pump **(see illustration)**.
5 Note the position of the hose(s), and then disconnect them from the washer pump **(see illustration)**. Position a suitable container beneath the reservoir to catch spilt fluid.
6 To remove the washer pump, pull it upwards from the reservoir and out from its rubber grommet **(see illustration)**.
7 Where fitted, disconnect the wiring plug from the fluid level sender unit.
8 Release the retaining clips and disconnect the wiring loom from the side of the washer reservoir.
9 Unclip the wiring loom and washer hose. Remove the fixings then remove the reservoir from the vehicle. Note that models fitted with a fuel fired auxiliary heater have a different reservoir fitted **(see illustration)**.
10 Refitting is a reversal of removal.

Windscreen washer jets

11 Open the bonnet, and pull the washer jet towards the front of the bonnet, and down to remove. Release the securing clip and disconnect the washer tube (and wiring where applicable), then remove the washer jet, See Chapter 11, Section 8.

12 Refitting is a reversal of removal. Note that the aim of the jet can be adjusted using a screwdriver and turning the eccentric shaft at the base of the washer jet.

Tailgate washer jet

13 Switch off the ignition and all electrical consumers and remove the ignition key.
14 Unclip the cover from the wiper arm spindle for access to the washer jet **(see illustration)**, and pull the jet from the centre of the spindle.
15 On refitting, ensure that the jet is securely pushed into position. Check the operation of the jet. If necessary, adjust the nozzle, aiming the spray at a point slightly above the area of glass swept by the wiper blade.

Headlight pop-up washer jets

16 Switch off the ignition and all electrical consumers and remove the ignition key.
17 Carefully pull the washer jet out from the front bumper to its full extent, and hold it. Carefully prise the end cap from the washer jet.
18 Still holding the washer jet, lift the securing clip slightly, and pull the jet from the lift cylinder.
19 Refitting is a reversal of removal. Operate the washers several times to bleed any trapped air.

Headlight pop-up washer jet lift cylinder

20 Remove the washer jet end cap as described in paragraphs 19 and 20.
21 Remove the front bumper as described in Chapter 11, Section 6.
22 Undo the two retaining screws, and withdraw the cylinder.
23 Clamp the hose, squeeze the retaining clip, and disconnect the hose.
24 Refitting is a reversal of removal. Operate the washers several times to bleed any trapped air.

22 Audio unit – removal and refitting

Note: *A variety of audio systems are fitted to the Caddy range of vehicles. These range from a simple Radio through to an integrated navigation system (SatNav). Removal and refitting is similar for all systems apart from models fitted with the DX-R4 model navigation system and the basic radio (R110). This Section only applies to standard-fit audio equipment.*

21.9 The reservoir fixings

21.14 Remove the washer jet

22.3a Release the surround at the base…

22.3b …work it free at the sides and remove it

22.4a Undo the screws…

22.4b …withdraw the unit and…

22.4c …disconnect the wiring plug(s) and aerial leads

22.12 Radio keys are used to withdraw the unit

Radio/CD player

1 All audio units are equipped with an electronic anti-theft system, linked to the instrument panel. If the voltage supply to the radio is temporarily disconnected, the radio will function again when the supply is reconnected, without entering the safety code number, provided the radio is located in the original vehicle. Should the radio operation be blocked, normal operation can be restored by entering the correct anti-theft code.

Removal

2 Where fitted, remove any CDs which may be in the unit. Switch off the ignition and all electrical consumers, and remove the ignition key.

3 Carefully unclip the trim panel from around the audio unit (see illustrations).

4 Undo the mounting screws, and pull out the unit until the wiring plugs can be disconnected (see illustrations). Release the locking clips and disconnect the wiring connectors from the rear of the unit.

5 Withdraw the radio/CD player unit from the facia.

6 On models fitted with the R110 radio insert the removal tools (T10057 or commercially available equivalent) into the slots provided to remove the unit. Pull out the unit and disconnect the wiring plugs.

7 On models fitted with the DX-R4 radio standard 'U' shaped pins are used to release the unit.

Refitting

8 Refitting is a reversal of removal.

CD changer

Removal

9 The CD changer (where fitted) is located the storage compartment beneath the armrest located between the driver and passenger front seats. It is fitted with special mounting clips, requiring the use of special removal tools (Volkswagon release key set 3316), which should be supplied with the vehicle. The keys can also be obtained from an in-car entertainment specialist.

10 Switch off the ignition and all electrical consumers, and remove the ignition key.

11 Open the armrest and remove any CDs which may be in the unit.

12 Insert the tools into the slots on each side of the unit and push them until they snap into place (see illustration). The CD changer/media storage compartment can then be pulled out of the armrest using the tools, and any wiring connectors disconnected.

Refitting

13 Refitting is a reversal of removal.

MP3/Media player connector

14 Where fitted the connectors for the media player are located in the glovebox or storage compartment on models built up to 2010. On later models the the connectors are fitted under the centre console armrest.

15 Remove the glovebox or storage compartment as described in Chapter 11 Section 24. Disconnect the wiring plugs and then release the connectors.

16 Where the connectors are fitted to the centre console storage compartment a set of release keys will be required (T10057 or commercially available equivalent). Insert the keys and release the housing. Pull up the housing and disconnect the wiring plug at the rear.

17 Refitting is a reversal of removal.

23 Loudspeakers – removal and refitting

Front treble/mid range speaker

1 Switch off the ignition and all electrical consumers, and remove the ignition key.

2 Prise up the speaker cover – protect the facia if necessary (see illustration).

3 The speaker is either a simple clip fit or is held in place with screws. Remove the speaker from the housing and disconnect the speaker wiring plug.

4 Refitting is a reversal of removal.

23.2 Remove the grille

Front speakers

5 Switch off the ignition and all electrical consumers, and remove the ignition key.
6 Remove the door inner trim, as described in Chapter 11, Section 12.
7 Disconnect the wiring plug from the loudspeaker **(see illustration)**.
8 Drill out the retaining rivets, and withdraw the speaker from the door **(see illustration)**. Recover the rubber sealing ring between the speaker and door trim.
9 Refitting is a reversal of removal, but new rivets will be required.

24 Radio aerials, filters and modules – removal and refitting

Aerials

1 On models built up to 2010 the radio aerial is either integrated into the front windscreen or mounted on the cab roof. The windscreen is bonded in position with a special adhesive. If the aerial is faulty, a new windscreen must be fitted. On later models the aerial is incorporated into the door mirror. Models fitted with a basic audio system have the aerial fitted to the left-hand door mirror only. Models fitted with a DAB radio and/or SatNav have aerials fitted to both door mirrors.

Roof mounted aerial

2 The roof lining must be removed to access the aerial base. This requires removal of:
a) Cabin light
b) Grab handles
c) Sun visors
d) Storage compartment
e) Cargo net
f) A-pillar trims
g) B-pillar trims
3 The removal procedure is described in Chapter 11 Section 24 (interior trim) and Section 7 of this Chapter (interior bulbs).
4 Partially remove the door weather seal and then remove any remaining trim clips. Lower the roof lining and remove it from the vehicle.
5 Carefully lower the rear of the headlining, taking care not to damage it. Disconnect the wiring; note the fitted position of the wiring,

23.7 Disconnect the wiring plug

as there may be more than one connector, depending on model.
6 Unscrew the securing nut and withdraw the aerial base from the roof. Hold the aerial base as the nut is being unscrewed to prevent the base from rotating and scratching the roof panel. Recover the rubber spacer.
7 Refitting is a reversal of removal, but make sure that the two guide lugs on the rubber spacer are correctly located in the aerial base.

Door mirror mounted aerial

8 Remove the mirror and then remove the mirror glass as described in Chapter 11 Section 18.
9 Unscrew the cable clamp and amplifier **(see illustrations)**.
10 Unclip the flexible aerial circuit board **(see illustration)**. Separate the aerial cable from the mirror motor cable and feed it through the mirror housing.

Amplifiers

11 The aerials that are integrated into the windscreen have amplifiers. These are hidden behind the front right-hand edge of the roof lining. To access them the roof lining must be partially lowered.
12 Remove the A-pillar and B-pillar trims as described in Chapter 11 Section 24. Remove the grab handle (where fitted) and sun visor. Carefully lower the roof lining sufficiently to gain access..
Caution: Any damage to the wiring or connector will require the replacement of the rear window. Exercise extreme caution

23.8 The door mounted loudspeaker is secured with rivets

when removing the wiring plug and tape the wire out of harms way once removed.
13 Disconnect the wiring plug, remove the bolt and lower the amplifier from the roof.
14 Refitting is a reversal of removal.

25 Anti-theft alarm system and engine immobiliser – general information

Note: *This information is applicable only to the anti-theft alarm system fitted by VW as standard equipment.*
1 Many models in the range are fitted with an anti-theft alarm system as standard equipment. The alarm has switches on all the doors (including the tailgate/boot lid), the bonnet and the ignition switch. If the tailgate, bonnet or any of the doors are opened whilst the alarm is set, the alarm horn will sound and the hazard warning lights will flash. Some models are equipped with an internal monitoring system, which will activate the alarm system if any movement in the cabin is detected.
2 The alarm is set using the key in the driver's or passenger's front door lock or with the central locking remote control transmitter. The alarm system will then start to monitor its various switches approximately 30 seconds later.
3 All models are fitted with an immobiliser system, which is activated by the ignition switch. A transponder reading coil on the ignition switch reads a code contained within the ignition key. The system sends a signal

24.9a Remove the clamp and...

24.9b ...unscrew the amplifier

24.10 Unclip the aerial

to the engine management electronic control unit (ECU), which allows the engine to start if the code is correct. If an incorrect ignition key is used, the engine will not start.

4 If a fault is suspected with the alarm or immobiliser systems, the vehicle should be taken to a VW dealer for examination. They will have access to a special diagnostic tester that will quickly trace any fault present in the system.

26 Airbag system – general information and precautions

 Warning: Before carrying out any operations on the airbag system, disconnect the battery negative terminal (refer to 'Disconnecting the battery' in the Reference section at the rear of this manual). When operations are complete, make sure no one is inside the vehicle when the battery is reconnected.

Warning: Note that the airbags must not be subjected to temperatures in excess of 90°C. When the airbag is removed, ensure that it is stored with the pad upwards to prevent possible inflation.

Warning: Do not allow any solvents or cleaning agents to contact the airbag assemblies. They must be cleaned using only a damp cloth.

27.4a Insert a screwdriver...

 Warning: The airbags and control unit are both sensitive to impact. If either is dropped or damaged they should be renewed.

1 A driver's airbag is fitted as standard equipment to the Caddy range. Most models also have a passenger airbag. Side airbags are fitted to some models. The airbag system consists of the airbag unit (complete with gas generator), which is fitted to the steering wheel (driver's side), facia (passenger's side) and front seats, an impact sensor, the control unit and a warning light in the instrument panel.

2 The airbag system is triggered in the event of a heavy frontal or side impact above a predetermined force, depending on the point of impact. The airbag is inflated within milliseconds and forms a safety cushion between the driver and the steering wheel, the passenger and the facia, and in the case of side impact, between front seat occupants and the sides of the cabin. This prevents contact between the upper body and cabin interior, and therefore greatly reduces the risk of injury. The airbag then deflates almost immediately.

3 Every time the ignition is switched on, the airbag control unit performs a self-test. The self-test takes approximately 3 seconds and during this time the airbag warning light on the facia is illuminated. After the self-test has been completed the warning light should go out. If the warning light fails to come on,

27.4b ...to release the airbag clips (early models – shown with the airbag removed)

remains illuminated after the initial 3-second period or comes on at any time when the vehicle is being driven, there is a fault in the airbag system. The vehicle should then be taken to a VW dealer for examination at the earliest possible opportunity.

27 Airbag system components – removal and refitting

Note: *Refer to the warnings in Section 26 before carrying out the following operations.*
1 Disconnect the battery negative lead (refer to Chapter 5A Section 3) then continue as described under the relevant heading.
Caution: To prevent any discharge of static electricity into the airbag circuit, temporarily touch the vehicle bodywork before disconnecting the wiring from any airbag unit.

Driver's airbag

Note: *There are minor differences in the mounting of the airbag. Removing and refitting is essentially the same for all models.*
2 Set the front wheels to the straight-ahead position, and release the steering lock by inserting the ignition key.
3 Adjust the steering column to its highest position by releasing the adjustment handle, then extend the steering wheel as far as possible. Lock the column in this position.
4 With the spokes in the vertical position, insert a screwdriver approximately 8 mm into the hole in the upper rear of the steering wheel hub, then move it up to release the clip and free the airbag locking lug **(see illustrations)**. Now turn the steering wheel through 180° and release the remaining airbag locking lug.
5 Carefully withdraw the airbag module from the steering wheel, release the locking clip and disconnect the wiring connector **(see illustration)**. On later models the airbag is disconnected at the steering wheel, not the airbag.
6 Turn the steering wheel to its central, straight-ahead position.

27.4c On later models the spring clips are part of the airbag

27.5 Disconnect the wiring as it is removed

27.9 Disconnect the wiring plug

27.15a Remove the panel

27.15b Disconnect the wiring plug

 Warning: Position the airbag in a safe and secure place, away from the work area.

7 When refitting make sure the steering wheel is in the straight-ahead position, then locate the airbag module in position and reconnect the wiring. Carefully press in the module until both locking lugs are heard to engage. Reconnect the battery negative lead, ensuring that nobody is inside the vehicle as the lead is connected.

Passenger's airbag

8 Remove the passenger side glovebox (or storage compartment on some models) with reference to Chapter 11 Section 24.
9 Release the locking clip and disconnect the wiring from the passenger's airbag **(see illustration)**.
10 Undo the mounting screws, then remove the airbag and side brackets from under the facia.

 Warning: Position the airbag in a safe and secure place, away from the work area.

Caution: Before fitting a new airbag, it will need to be checked to see if an additional earth cable will be required. At the rear of the airbag unit, check to see if there is an earth wire going from the wiring block connector to one of the securing nuts on the airbag unit. If there is no earth cable, an earth wire will need to be connected to one of the mounting bracket retaining bolts and to the earth on the lower sill, behind the kick trim panel. The earth cable needs to have a cross section of 1mm and be 600mm in length.

11 Refitting is a reversal of removal, but tighten the mounting screws to the specified torque. If the airbag housing is made of plastic, use locking fluid on the screws before refitting. Reconnect the battery negative lead, ensuring that nobody is inside the vehicle as the lead is connected. If an additional earth cable needs to be fitted (see caution above), attach it to the earth point behind the sill trim panel.

Front seat side impact airbags

12 The side impact air bags are integral with the seats. As seat upholstery removal

27.20a Airbag wiring contact unit centre setting – type 1

requires considerable skill and experience, if it is to be carried out without damage, it is best entrusted to an expert.

Airbag control unit

13 The airbag control unit is located beneath the centre of the facia, under the heater housing.
14 Remove the trim from the passenger's side of the centre console with reference to Chapter 11 Section 25.
15 Remove the support panel, release the locking lever and disconnect the wiring from the control unit **(see illustrations)**.
16 Unscrew the nuts and remove the control unit from the vehicle.
17 Refitting is the reverse of removal making sure the wiring connector is securely reconnected. Reconnect the battery negative lead, ensuring that nobody is inside the vehicle as the lead is connected.

Airbag wiring contact unit

18 The airbag contact unit/clock spring is part of the steering column switch assembly, remove the contact unit as described in Section 5.
19 On early models (up to 07/2010) the airbag clock spring/slip-ring must be held in its central position while it is removed, to ensure correct refitting. Unclip the airbag

27.20b Airbag wiring contact unit centre setting – type 2

clock spring/slip-ring from the combination switch carrier by lifting the retaining hooks.
20 Before refitting the airbag clock spring/slip-ring, check that it is in its central position as follows. There are two types fitted according to manufacturer as shown **(see illustrations)**. With the first type, the black rectangles must be visible in the window. With the second type, the yellow strip must be visible as shown.
21 The remaining procedure is a reversal of removal. Reconnect the battery negative lead, ensuring that nobody is inside the vehicle as the lead is connected.

Passenger airbag on/ off switch

22 The switch is located inside the glovebox or storage compartment. Remove the switch with reference to Section 5.

Crash sensors

23 Crash sensors are fitted at the base of the B-pillar. Remove the seat and the seat frame as described in Chapter 11 Section 21 to access the sensor.
24 Disconnect the wiring plug from the crash sensor and then remove the fixings.
25 Refitting is a reversal of removal. Make sure that nobody is inside the vehicle when first switching on the ignition.

28.9 Unclip the sensor…

28.10 …and disconnect the wiring plug

28 Parking aid components
– general information, removal and refitting

General information

1 The parking aid system is available as a standard fitment on higher specification models, and optional on other models. Four ultrasound sensors are located in the rear bumper. These measure the distance to the closest object behind or in front of the car, and inform the driver using acoustic signals from a warning buzzer. The nearer the object, the more frequent the acoustic signals.
2 The system includes a control unit and self-diagnosis program, and therefore, in the event of a fault, the vehicle should be taken to a VW dealer.

3 Switch off the ignition and all electrical consumers and remove the ignition key, before removing any electrical components.

Control unit

4 The parking aid control unit for the rear sensors is located behind the right-hand load area side panel on models built up to 2012. On later models the control unit is fitted behind the relay plate. Remove the panel as described in Chapter 11 Section 24 to access the control unit on early models. On later models access is possible after removal of the relay plate/fuse box – refer to Chapter 11, Section 17.
5 Depress the locking lugs and disconnect the wiring plugs from the control unit.
6 Unclip the unit from the mounting bracket above the relays.

7 Refitting is a reversal of removal.

Range/distance sensor

8 Remove the bumper cover as described in Chapter 11 Section 7.
9 Remove the sensor **(see illustration)**.
10 Disconnect the wiring plug **(see illustration)**.
11 Refitting is a reversal of removal. Press the sensor firmly into position until the retaining clips engage.

Warning buzzer

12 The warning buzzer is located behind the relay plate. Remove the drivers side lower panel (as described in Chapter 11 Section 26) and lower the fuse box and relay plate to access the buzzer.
13 Refitting is a reversal of removal.

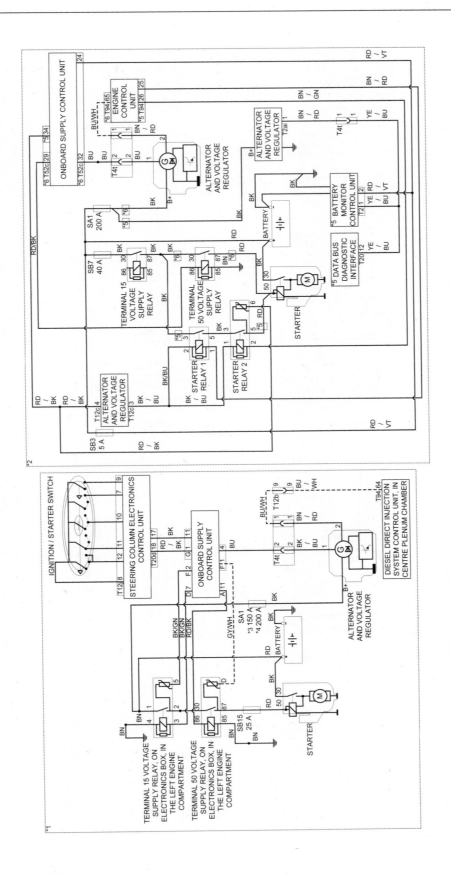

Starting and charging

*1 Up to July 2010
*2 From August 2010
*3 Models with 90 A / 110 A alternator
*4 Models with 140 A alternator
*5 Only models with start / stop
*6 Only models without start / stop

Heating and cooling – Climatic (from August 2010)

*1 LHD models
*2 RHD models

Heating and cooling – Climatic (up to July 2010)

*1 Up to April 2005
*2 From May 2005
*3 Up to April 2007
*4 From May 2007
*5 Only models with electromechanical power steering
*6 Only models with hydraulic power steering

Heating and cooling – Climatronic (from August 2010)

*1 RHD models

Heating and cooling – Climatronic (up to July 2010)

*1 Only models with electromechanical power steering
*2 Only models with hydraulic power steering
*3 Only models with auxiliary coolant heater
*4 Up to April 2008
*5 From May 2008
*6 Up to April 2009
*7 From May 2009

Seat heating – from August 2010

*1 LHD models
*2 RHD models
*3 Only models with climatic
*3 Only models with climatronic
*4 Only models with climatronic
*5 Only models with no air conditioning system

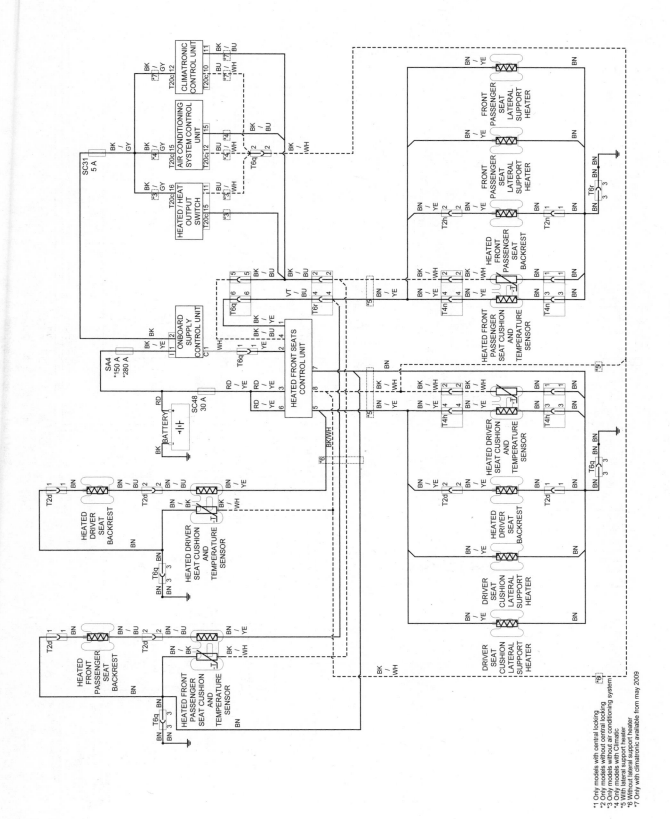

Seat heating – from June 2006 to July 2010

*1 Only models with central locking
*2 Only models without central locking
*3 Only models without air conditioning system
*4 Only models with Climatic
*5 With lateral support heater
*6 Without lateral support heater
*7 Only with climatronic available from may 2009

Seat heating – up to May 2006

*1 Models with heated driver seat only
*2 Models with heated driver and front passenger seats only
*3 Only models without air conditioning system
*4 Only models with Climatic
*5 With lateral support heater
*6 Up to April 2005
*7 From May 2005
*8 With lateral support heater
*9 Without lateral support heater

Power windows

*1 Up to May 2006
*2 From June 2006 April 2008
*3 From November 2007 up to April 2008
*4 From November 2008 to July 2010
*5 From May 2010 to July 2010
*5 From August 2010 to April 2011
*6 From May 2011
*7 Left hand drive
*8 Right hand drive

Central locking – from August 2010

Central locking – May 2008 to July 2010

*1 Only models with remote control
*2 Only models with anti-theft alarm system
*3 Only models with interior monitor sensor
*4 Only models with left sliding door
*5 Only models with right sliding door
*6 Only models with rear lid
*7 Only models with 2ⁿᵈ seat row
*8 Only Caddy Maxi
*9 Only models with left and right sliding doors
*10 Only models with wing doors

Central locking – up to April 2008

Washers and wipers – from August 2010

*1 Only models with rain and light sensor
*2 Only models without rain and light sensor
*3 Up to April 2011
*4 From May 2011
*5 Only models with rear window wiper
*6 Only models without rear window wiper
*7 Only models with wing doors
*8 Only models with rear lid

Washers and wipers – up to July 2010

*1 Only models with no rear window wiper
*2 Only models with rear window wiper
*3 Only models with rear lid
*4 Only models with wing doors
*5 From May 2004 to September 2006
*6 Up to April 2004
*7 Headlight washer
*8 Up to October 2006
*9 From November 2006 to July 2010
*10 RHD models
*12 Up to October 2008
*13 From November 2008
*14 Up to April 2008
*15 From May 2008 to October 2008

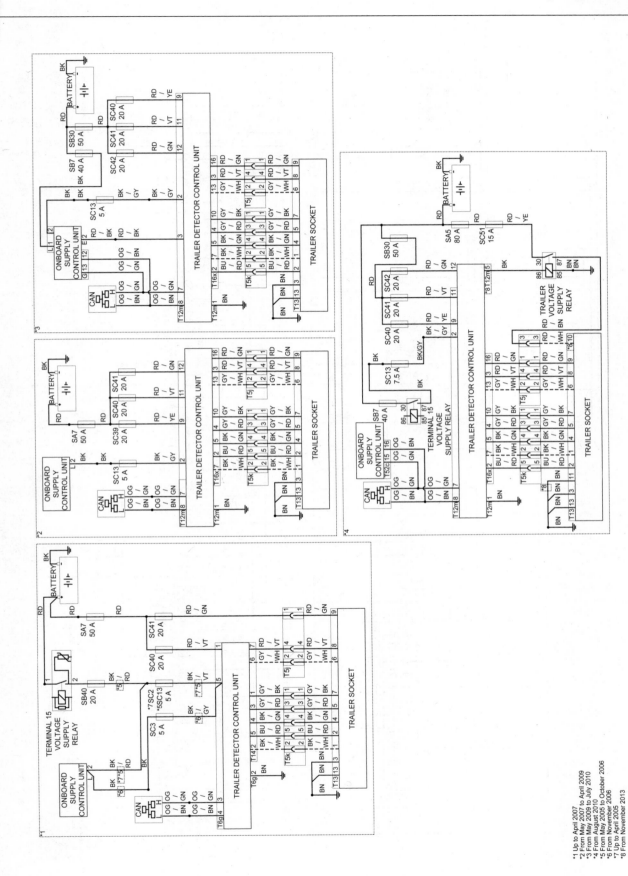

Exterior lights – Trailer coupling

*1 Up to April 2007
*2 From May 2007 to April 2009
*3 From May 2009 to July 2010
*4 From August 2010
*5 From May 2005 to October 2006
*6 From November 2006
*7 Up to April 2005
*8 From November 2013

Exterior lights – from August 2010 (Part 1)

*1 H4 headlights
*2 H7 headlights
*3 Only models with daytime running lights
*4 Only models with rear lid
*5 Only models with wing doors
*6 Bi-xenon headlights
*7 Up to April 2011
*8 From May 2011

Exterior lights – from August 2010 (Part 2)

Exterior lights – from June 2006 up to July 2010

*1 Only models with fog lights
*2 Only panel van
*3 Only Kombi models
*4 With Navigation system
*5 Without Navigation system
*6 Only models with wing doors
*7 Only models with rear lid
*8 Up to April 2008
*9 From May 2008
*10 Up to October 2008
*11 From November 2008
*12 With rain and light sensor
*13 From May 2007
*14 Up to April 2007

Exterior lights – up to May 2006

*1 Only models with fog lights
*2 Only panel van
*3 For models with convenience system
*4 Only Kombi models
*5 With Navigation system
*6 Without Navigation system
*7 From May 2004
*8 Only models with wing doors
*9 Only models with rear lid
*10 Up to April 2004

Interior lights – from May 2008

*1 Up to July 2010
*2 From August 2010
*3 Up to October 2008
*4 From November 2008
*5 Only models with wing doors
*6 Only models with rear lid
*7 Only Camper
*8 Not for Camper
*9 Only models with luggage compartment light
*10 Only models without luggage compartment light

Interior lights – up to April 2008

*1 Only models with illuminated vanity mirror
*2 Only for front interior light with reading lights
*3 Only for front interior light without reading lights
*4 Only models with wing doors
*5 Only models with rear lid
*6 Form November 2006
*7 Up to October 2007

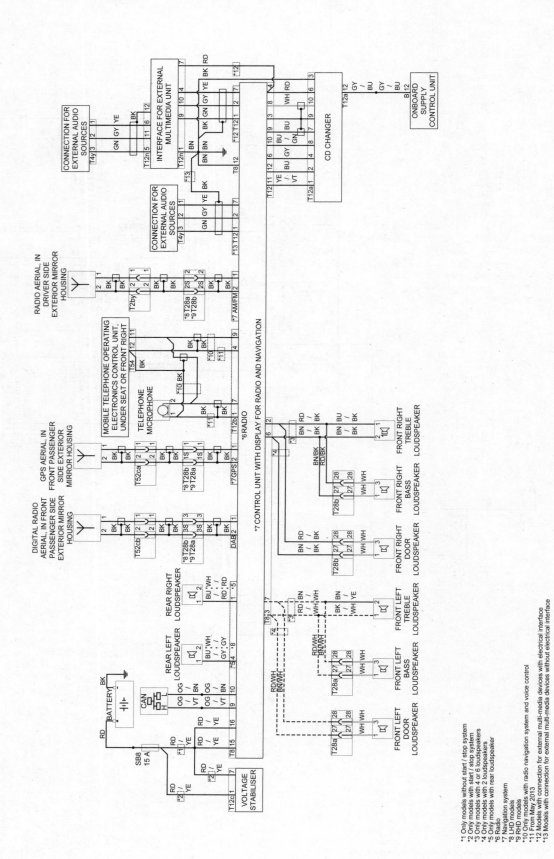

Sound system – from August 2010

*1 Only models without start / stop system
*2 Only models with start / stop system
*3 Only models with 4 or 6 loudspeakers
*4 Only models with 2 loudspeakers
*5 Only models with rear loudspeaker
*6 Radio
*7 Navigation system
*8 LHD models
*9 RHD models
*10 Only models with radio navigation system and voice control
*11 From May 2013
*12 Models with connection for external multi-media devices with electrical interface
*13 Models with connection for external multi-media devices without electrical interface

Sound system – up to July 2010

*1 Only models with rear loudspeaker
*2 With CD changer / CD player
*3 Without CD changer / CD player
*4 From May 2007 to October 2008
*5 From November 2008
*6 Up to April 2009
*7 From May 2009
*8 Radio
*9 Navigation system
*10 Up to April 2005
*11 From May 2005
*12 With mobile telephone / preparation for mobile telephone
*13 With connection for external audio source

Fuel pump

*1 Up to April 2008
*2 From May 2008
*3 Only models with auxiliary coolant heater
*4 Only models without auxiliary coolant heater

MAIN FUSE BOX IN ENGINE COMPARTMENT (UP TO APRIL 2005)

FUSE/RELAY	VALUE	DESCRIPTION
FL1	200 A	Alternator 140 A, 150 A also used for alternator 90 A / 110 A
FL2	80 A	Power steering control module
FL3	80 A	Radiator fan
FL4	70 A	Onboard supply control unit
FL5	-	Not used
FL6	100 A	Fuses on fuse holder C
FL7	50 A	Fuses on fuse holder C

MAIN FUSE BOX IN ENGINE COMPARTMENT

FROM MAY 2005 TO OCTOBER 2006

FUSE/RELAY	VALUE	DESCRIPTION
FL1	200 A	Alternator 140 A, also used 150 A for alternator 90 A / 110 A
FL2	80 A	Power steering control module
FL3	80 A	Radiator fan, 50 A also used
FL4	80 A	Onboard supply control unit, 50 A also used
FL5	-	Not used
FL6	100 A	Fuses on fuse holder C
FL7	50 A	Fuses on fuse holder C

FROM NOVEMBER 2006 TO AUGUST 2007

FUSE/RELAY	VALUE	DESCRIPTION
FL1	200 A	Alternator 140 A, also used 150 A for alternator 90 A / 110 A
FL2	80 A	Power steering control module
FL3	80 A	Radiator fan, 50 A also used
FL4	80 A	Onboard supply control unit, 50 A also used
FL5	100 A	Fuses on fuse holder C
FL6	-	Not used
FL7	50 A	Fuses on fuse holder C

Fuses and relays

FROM SEPTEMBER 2007 TO APRIL 2008

FUSE/RELAY	VALUE	DESCRIPTION
FL1	200 A	Alternator 140 A, also used 150 A for alternator 90 A / 110 A
FL2	80 A	Power steering control module
FL3	80 A	Radiator fan, 50 A also used
FL4	80 A	Onboard supply control unit, 50 A also used
FL5	100 A	Fuses on fuse holder C
FL6	100 A	High heat output relay
FL7	50 A	Fuses on fuse holder C

MAIN FUSE BOX IN ENGINE COMPARTMENT FROM MAY 2008

FUSE/RELAY	VALUE	DESCRIPTION
FL1	200 A	Alternator 140 A, also used 150 A for alternator 90 A / 110 A
FL2	80 A	Power steering control module
FL3	50 A	Radiator fan
FL4	80 A	Onboard supply control unit, 50 A also used
FL5	100 A	Fuses on fuse holder C
FL6	50 A	Low heat output relay
FL7	100 A	High heat output relay

Fuses and relays (continued)

FUSE AND RELAY BOX IN ENGINE COMPARTMENT UP TO APRIL 2005

FUSE/RELAY	VALUE	DESCRIPTION
F1	30 A	ABS control module
F2	30 A	ABS control module
F3	-	Not used
F4	5 A	Onboard supply control unit
F5	-	Not used
F6	-	Not used
F7	5 A	Brake pedal switch, Engine control modules, Clutch position sender
F8	10 A	Exhaust gas recirculation valve, Activated charcoal filter solenoid valve 1, Variable intake manifold changeover valve, Protective resistor, Radiator fan control unit, Intake manifold flap motor
F9	10 A	Fuel pump relay, Glow plug relay, Automatic glow period control module
F10	10 A	Exhaust gas recirculation valve, Charge pressure control solenoid valve, Exhaust gas recirculation fan switch-over valve
F11	30 A	Diesel direct injection system control module
F12	-	Not used
F13	-	Not used
F14	-	Not used
F15	25 A	Starter
F16	15 A	Steering column electronics panel insert
F17	10 A	Control unit in dash panel insert
F18	-	Not used
F19	15 A	Control module with display for radio and navigation system or Radio
F20	10 A	Mobile telephone operating electronics control module
F21	-	Not used
F22	-	Not used
F23	-	Not used
F24	10 A	Data bus diagnostic interface
F25	-	Not used

Fuses and relays (continued)

F26	5 A	Terminal 30 voltage supply relay
F27	10 A	Heater element for crankcase breather
F28	-	Not used
F29	-	Not used
F30	20 A	Auxiliary heater control unit
F31	30 A	Windscreen wiper motor
F32	40 A	Glow plug 1, Glow plug 2
F33	40 A	Glow plug 3, Glow plug 4
F34	-	Not used
F35	-	Not used
F36	-	Not used
F37	-	Not used
F38	10 A	Headlight range control regulator, Left and right headlamp levelling actuator
F39	5 A	Oil level and oil temperature sensor, Control unit in dash panel insert
F40	20 A	Fuses on fuse holder C, Fuses 1 to 6, 9 to 16 and 25 to 27
F41	-	Not used
F42	10 A	Air mass meter
F43	-	Not used
F44	-	Not used
F45	-	Not used
F46	-	Not used
F47	40 A	Onboard supply control unit, left headlight
F48	40 A	Onboard supply control unit, right headlight
F49	-	Not used
F50	-	Not used
F51	50 A	Glow plugs
F52	-	Not used
F53	25 A	Driver door control unit, Front passenger door control unit
F54	50 A	Radiator fan control unit
R1	-	Terminal 15 voltage supply relay
R2	-	Terminal 15 voltage supply relay
R3	-	Glow plug relay
R4	-	Terminal 30 voltage supply relay

Fuses and relays (continued)

FUSE AND RELAY BOX IN ENGINE COMPARTMENT

FROM MAY 2005 TO APRIL 2008

FUSE/RELAY	VALUE	DESCRIPTION
F1	-	Not used
F2	15 A	Steering column electronics control module
F3	5 A	Onboard supply control unit
F4	30 A	ABS control module
F5	15 A	Mechatronics unit for dual clutch gearbox
F6	5 A	Control unit in dash panel insert
F7	-	Not used
F8	15 A	Control module with display for radio and navigation system or Radio
F9	10 A	Mobile telephone operating electronics control module
F10	10 A	Terminal 30 voltage supply relay
F11	20 A	Auxiliary heater control unit
F12	5 A	Data bus diagnostic interface
F13	30 A	Diesel direct injection system control module
F14	-	Not used
F15	5 A	Fuel pump relay
F16	30 A	ABS control module
F17	20 A	Onboard supply control unit
F18	30 A	Special vehicle control unit
F19	30 A	Windscreen wiper motor
F20	40 A	Glow plug 3, Glow plug 4
F21	10 A	Lambda probe heater
F22	5 A	Clutch positon sender
F23	10 A	Exhaust gas recirculation valve, Exhaust gas recirculation valve, Charge pressure control solenoid valve, Exhaust gas recirculation cooler changeover valve, 5 A also used
F24	10 A	Intake manifold flap motor, Radiator fan control unit, Protective resistor
F25	40 A	Onboard supply control unit, right headlight
F26	40 A	Onboard supply control unit, left headlight
F27	50 A	Glow plugs, 40 A also used for Glow plug 1, Glow plug 2

Fuses and relays (continued)

F28	40 A	Terminal 15 voltage supply relay 2
F29	30 A	Driver door control unit, Front passenger door control unit
F30	30 A	Fuses on fuse holder C, fuses 18, 19, 36, 53 to 56
R1	-	Terminal 15 voltage supply relay
R2	-	Glow plug relay

FROM MAY 2008 TO JULY 2010

FUSE/RELAY	VALUE	DESCRIPTION
F1	-	Not used
F2	-	Not used
F3	5 A	Onboard supply control unit
F4	30 A	ABS control module
F5	15 A	Mechatronics unit for dual clutch gearbox
F6	5 A	Control unit in dash panel insert, Steering column electronics control module
F7	40 A	Terminal 15 voltage supply relay 2
F8	15 A	Control module with display for radio and navigation system or Radio
F9	5 A	Mobile telephone operating electronics control module
F10	10 A	Terminal 30 voltage supply relay
F11	20 A	Auxiliary heater control unit
F12	5 A	Data bus diagnostic interface
F13	30 A	Diesel direct injection system control module
F14	-	Not used
F15	5 A	Fuel pump relay
F16	30 A	Onboard supply control unit, right headlight
F17	20 A	Onboard supply control unit
F18	30 A	Special vehicle control unit
F19	30 A	Windscreen wiper motor
F20	40 A	Glow plug 3, Glow plug 4
F21	10 A	Lambda probe heater
F22	5 A	Clutch positon sender
F23	10 A	Exhaust gas recirculation valve, Exhaust gas recirculation valve, Charge pressure control solenoid valve, Exhaust gas recirculation cooler changeover valve, 5 A also used
F24	10 A	Intake manifold flap motor, Radiator fan control unit, Protective resistor
F25	40 A	ABS control module
F26	40 A	Onboard supply control unit
F27	50 A	Glow plugs, 40 A also used for Glow plug 1, Glow plug 2
F28	-	Not used
F29	30 A	Fuses on fuse holder C, fuses 18, 19, 36 to 39, 57 to 58
F30	30 A	Fuses on fuse holder C, fuses 39 to 41
R1	-	Terminal 15 voltage supply relay
R2	-	Glow plug relay

Fuses and relays (continued)

FROM AUGUST 2010

FUSE/RELAY	VALUE	DESCRIPTION
F1	-	Not used
F2	30 A	Mechatronics unit for dual clutch gearbox
F3	5 A	Battery monitoring control unit, Onboard supply control unit
F4	20 A	ABS control unit, ABS hydraulic unit
F5	15 A	Mechatronics unit for dual clutch gearbox
F6	5 A	Control unit in dash panel insert, Steering column electronics control unit
F7	40 A	Terminal 15 voltage supply relay
F8	15 A	Control module with display for radio and navigation system or Radio
F9	5 A	Mobile telephone operating electronics control module
F10	5 A	Main relay, Engine control unit, Engine compartment current supply relay
F11	30 A	Auxiliary heater control unit
F12	5 A	Data bus diagnostic interface
F13	30 A	Engine control unit
F14	15 A	Fuel pressure regulation valve, Fuel metering valve
F15	5 A	Low heat output relay, High heat output relay, Fuel pump relay, Electric fuel pump 2 relay, Automatic glow period control unit
F16	30 A	Onboard supply control unit
F17	15 A	Horn relay
F18	30 A	Special vehicle control unit
F19	30 A	Wiper motor control unit
F20	-	Not used
F21	10 A	Lambda probe heater
F22	5 A	Clutch position sender, Brake light switch
F23	10 A	Air mass meter, Charge pressure control solenoid valve, Exhaust gas recirculation cooler changeover valve
F24	10 A	Radiator fan control unit, Secondary air pump relay, Additional coolant pump relay, Coolant regulating valve
F25	40 A	ABS hydraulic pump, ABS control unit
F26	30 A	Onboard supply control unit
F27	50 A	Glow plug control unit
F28	-	Not used
F29	50 A	Fuses on fuse holder C, fuses 35, 39, 54, 55, 59, 60
F30	50 A	Fuses on fuse holder C, fuses 40 to 42
R1	-	Main relay
R2	-	Secondary air pump relay, Additional coolant pump relay, Relay for gas shut-off valves

Fuses and relays (continued)

FUSE BOX IN PASSENGER COMPARTMENT

UP TO APRIL 2005

FUSE/RELAY	VALUE	DESCRIPTION
F1	-	Not used
F2	5 A	Trailer detector control unit
F3	5 A	Heater / heat output switch, High pressure sender
F4	-	Not used
F5	-	Not used
F6	-	Not used
F7	5 A	Heated front seats
F8	5 A	Washer jets
F9	5 A	Airbag control unit
F10	5 A	Mobile telephone operating electronics control unit
F11	10 A	Power control unit
F12	-	Not used
F13	-	Not used
F14	5 A	Traction control system switch, TCS and ESP button, ABS control unit
F15	10 A	Reversing light switch, Auxiliary heater operating relay (From May 2004)
F16	5 A	Data bus diagnostic interface
F17	-	Not used
F18	-	Not used
F19	-	Not used
F20	-	Not used
F21	-	Not used
F22	5 A	Remote control receiver for auxiliary coolant heater
F23	10 A	Brake light switch, Brake lights, High level brake light bulb, ABS control unit
F24	10 A	Light switch, Air conditioning system control unit
F25	30 A	Heated driver seat control unit
F26	10 A	Engine control units
F27	15 A	Rear window wiper motor (From May 2004)
F28	20 A	Light switch, 5 A also used
F29	15 A	Rear window wiper motor (up to April 2004)
F30	-	Not used
F31	15 A	Auxiliary heater operating relay
F32	15 A	Washer pump
F33	-	Not used
F34	-	Not used
F35	40 A	Fresh air blower, Auxiliary heater operating relay

Fuses and relays (continued)

F36	-	Not used
F37	15 A	Right dipped beam bulb (models without central locking)
F38	15 A	Left dipped beam bulb (models without central locking)
F39	-	Not used
F40	20 A	Trailer detector control unit
F41	20 A	Trailer socket
F42	30 A	12 V socket
F43	15 A	Fuel pump relay, Fuel system pressurisation pump
F44	5 A	Interior monitoring sensor, Vehicle inclination sender, Alarm horn
F45	5 A	Aerial selection control unit
F46	7.5 A	Onboard supply control unit
F47	30 A	Cigarette lighter, rear cigarette lighter, 25 A also used
F48	20 A	Headlight washer system relay, Headlight washer system pump
F49	10 A	Driver door control unit, Front passenger door control unit
F50	-	Not used
F51	-	Not used
F52	25 A	Fresh air blower, Onboard supply control unit
F53	25 A	Convenience system central control unit
F54	-	Not used
F55	-	Not used
F56	-	Not used
F57	-	Not used
F58	-	Not used

FROM MAY 2005 UP TO APRIL 2007

FUSE/RELAY	VALUE	DESCRIPTION
F1	-	Not used
F2	5 A	Data bus diagnostic interface, Engine control unit
F3	5 A	Headlight range control regulator, Left headlight range control motor, Right headlight range control motor
F4	5 A	Mobile telephone operating electronics control unit (Only models with telephone)
F5	15 A	Air mass meter
F6	5 A	Airbag control unit, Front passenger side airbag deactivated warning lamp
F7	5 A	Air conditioning system control unit
F8	5 A	Washer jets
F9	10 A	Power steering control unit
F10	10 A	Reversing light switch, Auxiliary heater operation relay
F11	-	Not used
F12	-	Not used
F13	5 A	Trailer detector control unit
F14	5 A	TCS and ESP button, ABS control unit, Brake light switch
F15	5 A	Selector lever, Selector lever control unit, Mechatronic unit for dual clutch gearbox (Only for DSG)
F16	5 A	High pressure sender, Oil level and oil temperature sender, Control unit in dash panel insert
F17	7.5 A	Left tail light and rear fog light bulb (without central locking), Rear fog light cut-out contact switch (with trailer operating and without central locking)
F18	-	Not used

Fuses and relays (continued)

F19	-	Not used
F20	5 A	Automatic gearbox control unit
F21	5 A	Selector lever, Selector lever sensors control unit (Only for DSG)
F22	5 A	Remote control receiver for auxiliary coolant heater (Only with remote control)
F23	-	Not used
F24	10 A	Light switch, Heater / heat output switch, Air conditioning system control unit
F25	-	Not used
F26	-	Not used
F27	-	Not used
F28	5 A	Light switch
F29	15 A	Rear window wiper motor
F30	5 A	Heater / heat output switch, Air conditioning system control unit
F31	15 A	Onboard supply control unit
F32	5 A	Washer jets
F33	40 A	Heater / heat output switch, Air conditioning system control unit
F34	-	Not used
F35	-	Not used
F36	-	Not used
F37	15 A	Right dipped beam bulb (without central locking)
F38	15 A	Left dipped beam bulb (without central locking)
F39	-	Not used
F40	20 A	Trailer detector control unit
F41	20 A	Trailer socket
F42	30 A	12 V socket, 15 A also used
F43	15 A	Fuel pump relay
F44	5 A	Interior monitoring sensor, Vehicle inclination sender, Alarm horn
F45	5 A	Aerial selection control unit
F46	7.5 A	Onboard supply control unit
F47	25 A	Cigarette lighter
F48	20 A	Headlight washer system relay, Headlight washer system pump
F49	10 A	Driver and passenger door control unit
F50	25 A	Convenience system central control unit
F51	30 A	Heated front seats control unit
F52	25 A	Fresh air blower, Onboard supply control unit, Heated rear window
F53	-	Not used
F54	-	Not used
F55	-	Not used
F56	-	Not used
F57	5 A	Accident data memory (From June 2006) or not used
F58	10 A	No information available or not used

Fuses and relays (continued)

FROM MAY 2007 TO APRIL 2009

FUSE/RELAY	VALUE	DESCRIPTION
F1	-	Not used
F2	-	Not used
F3	-	Not used
F4	-	Not used
F5	-	Not used
F6	-	Not used
F7	-	Not used
F8	-	Not used
F9	10 A	No information available or not used
F10	5 A	Data bus diagnostic interface, Engine control unit
F11	5 A	Parking aid control unit
F12	10 A	No information available or not used
F13	5 A	Headlight range control regulator, Left and right headlight range control motor, TCS and ESP button, Selector lever(for DSG), Brake light switch, Brake light relay, ABS control unit, Trailer detector control unit, Power steering control unit
F14	5 A	Air mass meter, Reversing light switch, Auxiliary heater operating relay
F15	5 A	Airbag control unit
F16	5 A	High pressure sender, Oil level and oil temperature sender, Control unit in dash panel insert
F17	7.5 A	Left tail light and rear fog light bulb (without central locking), Rear fog light cut-out contact switch (with trailer operating and without central locking)
F18	-	Not used
F19	-	Not used
F20	10 A	No information available or not used
F21	10 A	Selector lever, Selector lever sensors control unit (Only for DSG)
F22	-	Not used
F23	-	Not used
F24	5 A	Interior monitoring sensor, Vehicle inclination sender, Alarm horn
F25	-	Not used
F26	-	Not used
F27	20 A	Automatic gearbox control unit
F28	5 A	Light switch (without central locking)
F29	15 A	Rear window wiper motor
F30	25 A	Light switch (with central locking)
F31	5 A	Heater / heat output switch, air conditioning system control unit, Washer jets
F32	15 A	Onboard supply control unit
F33	40 A	Heater / heat output switch, air conditioning system control unit
F34	-	Not used
F35	-	Not used
F36	20 A	No information available or not used
F37	15 A	Right dipped beam (without central locking)
F38	15 A	Left dipped beam (without central locking)
F39	20 A	Trailer detector control unit
F40	20 A	Trailer detector control unit

Fuses and relays (continued)

F41	20 A	Trailer detector control unit
F42	30 A	12 V socket
F43	15 A	Fuel pump relay
F44	-	Not used
F45	20 A	Headlight washer system relay, Headlight washer system pump
F46	7.5 A	Onboard supply control unit
F47	25 A	Cigarette lighter
F48	30 A	Heated front seats control unit
F49	10 A	Driver and passenger door control units
F50	25 A	Convenience system control unit
F51	30 A	No information available or not used
F52	25 A	Fresh air blower relay, Onboard supply control unit, Heated rear window
F53	-	Not used
F54	-	Not used
F55	-	Not used
F56	-	Not used
F57	5 A	No information available or not used
F58	-	Not used

FUSE BOX IN PASSENGER COMPARTMENT FROM MAY 2009

FUSE/RELAY	VALUE	DESCRIPTION
F1	-	Not used
F2	-	Not used
F3	-	Not used
F4	-	Not used
F5	-	Not used
F6	-	Not used
F7	-	Not used
F8	-	Not used
F9	10 A	No information available or not used
F10	5 A	Data bus diagnostic interface, Engine control unit
F11	5 A	Parking aid control unit
F12	10 A	No information available or not used
F13	5 A	Headlight range control regulator, Left and right headlight range control motor, TCS and ESP button, Selector lever(for DSG), Brake light switch, Brake light relay, ABS control unit, Trailer detector control unit, Power steering control unit
F14	5 A	Air mass meter, Reversing light switch, Auxiliary heater operating relay
F15	5 A	Airbag control unit, Front passenger side airbag deactivated warning lamp

Fuses and relays (continued)

F16	5 A	High pressure sender, Oil level and oil temperature sender, Control unit in dash panel insert
F17	7.5 A	Left tail light and rear fog light bulb (without central locking), Rear fog light cut-out contact switch (with trailer operating and without central locking)
F18	5 A	No information available or not used
F19	10 A	No information available or not used
F20	7.5 A	Onboard supply control unit
F21	10 A	Selector lever, Selector lever sensors control unit (Only for DSG)
F22	10 A	Driver and passenger control unit
F23	10 A	No information available or not used
F24	5 A	Interior monitoring sensor, Vehicle incliantion sender, Alarm horn
F25	-	Not used
F26	10 A	No information available or not used
F27	15 A	Cut - out relay for air conditioning system magnetic coupling
F28	5 A	Light switch (without central locking)
F29	15 A	Rear window wiper motor
F30	25 A	Light switch (without central locking)
F31	5 A	Heater / heat output switch, air conditioning system control unit, Washer jets
F32	15 A	Windscreen and rear window washer pump
F33	40 A	Heater / heat output switch, air conditioning system control unit, Auxiliary heater operation relay
F34	-	Not used
F35	10 A	Fluorescent light in rear of high roof
F36	-	Not used
F37	15 A	Right dipped beam (without central locking)
F38	15 A	Left dipped beam (without central locking)
F39	20 A	No information available or not used
F40	20 A	Trailer detector control unit
F41	20 A	Trailer detector control unit
F42	20 A	Trailer detector control unit
F43	15 A	Fuel pump relay
F44	40 A	Fresh air blower
F45	20 A	Headlight washer system relay, Headlight washer system pump
F46	15 A	Treble tone horn, Bass tone horn, Horn relay
F47	25 A	Cigarette lighter
F48	30 A	Heated front seats control unit
F49	30 A	Driver and passenger control unit
F50	25 A	Convenience system control unit
F51	30 A	No information available or not used
F52	25 A	Fresh air blower relay, Onboard supply control unit, Heated rear window
F53	15 A	12 V socket
F54	-	Not used
F55	-	Not used
F56	-	Not used
F57	5 A	No information available or not used
F58	10 A	No information available or not used
F59	-	Not used
F60	-	Not used

Fuses and relays (continued)

RELAY BOX IN PASSENGER COMPARTMENT

UP TO APRIL 2005

FUSE/RELAY	VALUE	DESCRIPTION
R1	-	Not used
R2	-	Headlight washer system relay
R3	-	Fuel pump relay
R4	-	Not used
R5	-	Not used
R6	-	Not used
R7	-	Auxiliary heater operation relay
R8	-	Not used
R9	-	Not used

FROM MAY 2005 TO APRIL 2007

FUSE/RELAY	VALUE	DESCRIPTION
R1	-	Not used
R2	-	Headlight washer system relay
R3	-	Not used
R4	-	Fresh air blower relay
R5	-	Not used
R6	-	Not used
R7	-	Auxiliary heater operation relay
R8	-	Terminal 50 voltage supply relay
R9	-	Not used

Fuses and relays (continued)

FROM MAY 2007 TO JULY 2010

FUSE/RELAY	VALUE	DESCRIPTION
R1	-	Brake light relay
R2	-	Headlight washer system relay
R3	-	Fuel pump relay
R4	-	Fresh air blower relay
R5	-	Low heat output relay or not used
R6	-	Cut - out relay for air conditioning system magnetic coupling
R7	-	Auxiliary heater operation relay
R8	-	Terminal 50 voltage supply relay
R9	-	Not used

RELAY BOX IN PASSENGER COMPARTMENT FROM MAY 2010

FUSE/RELAY	VALUE	DESCRIPTION
R1	-	Horn relay, Headlight washer system relay
R2	-	Fuel pump relay
R3	-	Terminal 50 voltage supply relay
R4	-	Auxiliary heater operation relay or X-contact relief relay
R5	-	Fuel supply relay
R6	-	Starter relay 2 or not used
R7	-	Terminal 15 voltage supply relay or high heat output relay
R8	-	Electric fuel pump 2 relay
R9	-	Heated rear window relay or low heat output relay
R10	-	Auxiliary heater operation relay or X-contact relief relay
R11	-	High heat output relay or terminal 15 voltage supply relay
R12	-	Low heat output relay or heated rear window relay
R13	-	Fresh air blower relay
R14	-	Starter relay 2 or flashing lights relay

Fuses and relays (continued)

Dimensions and weights

Note: *All figures and dimensions are approximate and may vary according to model. Refer to manufacturer's data for exact figures.*

Dimensions
Overall length . . . . 4405 mm
Overall width (including mirrors). . . . . 2062 mm
Overall height . . . . 1652 mm
Wheelbase . . . . 2682 mm

Weights
Kerb weight . . . . 1400 to 1481 kg
Maximum gross vehicle weight . . . . 2150 to 2235 kg
Maximum payload (without driver). . . . . 750 Kg
Maximum towing capacity (braked trailer) . . . . 1200 to 1500 Kg
Maximum roof load . . . . 100 Kg

Fuel economy

Although depreciation is still the biggest part of the cost of motoring for most car owners, the cost of fuel is more immediately noticeable. These pages give some tips on how to get the best fuel economy.

Working it out

Manufacturer's figures

Car manufacturers are required by law to provide fuel consumption information on all new vehicles sold. These 'official' figures are obtained by simulating various driving conditions on a rolling road or a test track. Real life conditions are different, so the fuel consumption actually achieved may not bear much resemblance to the quoted figures.

How to calculate it

Many cars now have trip computers which will

display fuel consumption, both instantaneous and average. Refer to the owner's handbook for details of how to use these.

To calculate consumption yourself (and maybe to check that the trip computer is accurate), proceed as follows.

1. Fill up with fuel and note the mileage, or zero the trip recorder.
2. Drive as usual until you need to fill up again.
3. Note the amount of fuel required to refill the tank, and the mileage covered since the previous fill-up.
4. Divide the mileage by the amount of fuel used to obtain the consumption figure.

For example:

Mileage at first fill-up (a) = 27,903
Mileage at second fill-up (b) = 28,346
Mileage covered (b - a) = 443
Fuel required at second fill-up = 48.6 litres

The half-completed changeover to metric units in the UK means that we buy our fuel

in litres, measure distances in miles and talk about fuel consumption in miles per gallon. There are two ways round this: the first is to convert the litres to gallons before doing the calculation (by dividing by 4.546, or see Table 1). So in the example:

48.6 litres ÷ 4.546 = 10.69 gallons
443 miles ÷ 10.69 gallons = 41.4 mpg

The second way is to calculate the consumption in miles per litre, then multiply that figure by 4.546 (or see Table 2).

So in the example, fuel consumption is:

443 miles ÷ 48.6 litres = 9.1 mpl
9.1 mpl x 4.546 = 41.4 mpg

The rest of Europe expresses fuel consumption in litres of fuel required to travel 100 km (l/100 km). For interest, the conversions are given in Table 3. In practice it doesn't matter what units you use, provided you know what your normal consumption is and can spot if it's getting better or worse.

Table 1: conversion of litres to Imperial gallons

litres	1	2	3	4	5	10	20	30	40	50	60	70
gallons	0.22	0.44	0.66	0.88	1.10	2.24	4.49	6.73	8.98	11.22	13.47	15.71

Table 2: conversion of miles per litre to miles per gallon

miles per litre	5	6	7	8	9	10	11	12	13	14
miles per gallon	23	27	32	36	41	46	50	55	59	64

Table 3: conversion of litres per 100 km to miles per gallon

litres per 100 km	4	4.5	5	5.5	6	6.5	7	8	9	10
miles per gallon	71	63	56	51	47	43	40	35	31	28

Maintenance

A well-maintained car uses less fuel and creates less pollution. In particular:

Filters

Change air and fuel filters at the specified intervals.

Oil

Use a good quality oil of the lowest viscosity specified by the vehicle manufacturer (see *Lubricants and fluids*). Check the level often and be careful not to overfill.

Spark plugs

When applicable, renew at the specified intervals.

Tyres

Check tyre pressures regularly. Under-inflated tyres have an increased rolling resistance. It is generally safe to use the higher pressures specified for full load conditions even when not fully laden, but keep an eye on the centre band of tread for signs of wear due to over-inflation.

When buying new tyres, consider the 'fuel saving' models which most manufacturers include in their ranges.

Driving style

Acceleration

Acceleration uses more fuel than driving at a steady speed. The best technique with modern cars is to accelerate reasonably briskly to the desired speed, changing up through the gears as soon as possible without making the engine labour.

Air conditioning

Air conditioning absorbs quite a bit of energy from the engine – typically 3 kW (4 hp) or so. The effect on fuel consumption is at its worst in slow traffic. Switch it off when not required.

Anticipation

Drive smoothly and try to read the traffic flow so as to avoid unnecessary acceleration and braking.

Automatic transmission

When accelerating in an automatic, avoid depressing the throttle so far as to make the transmission hold onto lower gears at higher speeds. Don't use the 'Sport' setting, if applicable.

When stationary with the engine running, select 'N' or 'P'. When moving, keep your left foot away from the brake.

Braking

Braking converts the car's energy of motion into heat – essentially, it is wasted. Obviously some braking is always going to be necessary, but with good anticipation it is surprising how much can be avoided, especially on routes that you know well.

Carshare

Consider sharing lifts to work or to the shops. Even once a week will make a difference.

Electrical loads

Electricity is 'fuel' too; the alternator which charges the battery does so by converting some of the engine's energy of motion into electrical energy. The more electrical accessories are in use, the greater the load on the alternator. Switch off big consumers like the heated rear window when not required.

Freewheeling

Freewheeling (coasting) in neutral with the engine switched off is dangerous. The effort required to operate power-assisted brakes and steering increases when the engine is not running, with a potential lack of control in emergency situations.

In any case, modern fuel injection systems automatically cut off the engine's fuel supply on the overrun (moving and in gear, but with the accelerator pedal released).

Gadgets

Bolt-on devices claiming to save fuel have been around for nearly as long as the motor car itself. Those which worked were rapidly adopted as standard equipment by the vehicle manufacturers. Others worked only in certain situations, or saved fuel only at the expense of unacceptable effects on performance, driveability or the life of engine components.

The most effective fuel saving gadget is the driver's right foot.

Journey planning

Combine (eg) a trip to the supermarket with a visit to the recycling centre and the DIY store, rather than making separate journeys.

When possible choose a travelling time outside rush hours.

Load

The more heavily a car is laden, the greater the energy required to accelerate it to a given speed. Remove heavy items which you don't need to carry.

One load which is often overlooked is the contents of the fuel tank. A tankful of fuel (55 litres / 12 gallons) weighs 45 kg (100 lb) or so. Just half filling it may be worthwhile.

Lost?

At the risk of stating the obvious, if you're going somewhere new, have details of the route to hand. There's not much point in achieving record mpg if you also go miles out of your way.

Parking

If possible, carry out any reversing or turning manoeuvres when you arrive at a parking space so that you can drive straight out when you leave. Manoeuvering when the engine is cold uses a lot more fuel.

Driving around looking for free on-street parking may cost more in fuel than buying a car park ticket.

Premium fuel

Most major oil companies (and some supermarkets) have premium grades of fuel which are several pence a litre dearer than the standard grades. Reports vary, but the consensus seems to be that if these fuels improve economy at all, they do not do so by enough to justify their extra cost.

Roof rack

When loading a roof rack, try to produce a wedge shape with the narrow end at the front. Any cover should be securely fastened – if it flaps it's creating turbulence and absorbing energy.

Remove roof racks and boxes when not in use – they increase air resistance and can create a surprising amount of noise.

Short journeys

The engine is at its least efficient, and wear is highest, during the first few miles after a cold start. Consider walking, cycling or using public transport.

Speed

The engine is at its most efficient when running at a steady speed and load at the rpm where it develops maximum torque. (You can find this figure in the car's handbook.) For most cars this corresponds to between 55 and 65 mph in top gear.

Above the optimum cruising speed, fuel consumption starts to rise quite sharply. A car travelling at 80 mph will typically be using 30% more fuel than at 60 mph.

Supermarket fuel

It may be cheap but is it any good? In the UK all supermarket fuel must meet the relevant British Standard. The major oil companies will say that their branded fuels have better additive packages which may stop carbon and other deposits building up. A reasonable compromise might be to use one tank of branded fuel to three or four from the supermarket.

Switch off when stationary

Switch off the engine if you look like being stationary for more than 30 seconds or so. This is good for the environment as well as for your pocket. Be aware though that frequent restarts are hard on the battery and the starter motor.

Windows

Driving with the windows open increases air turbulence around the vehicle. Closing the windows promotes smooth airflow and

reduced resistance. The faster you go, the more significant this is.

And finally . . .

Driving techniques associated with good fuel economy tend to involve moderate acceleration and low top speeds. Be considerate to the needs of other road users who may need to make brisker progress; even if you do not agree with them this is not an excuse to be obstructive.

Safety must always take precedence over economy, whether it is a question of accelerating hard to complete an overtaking manoeuvre, killing your speed when confronted with a potential hazard or switching the lights on when it starts to get dark.

Conversion factors

Length (distance)

Inches (in)	x 25.4	= Millimetres (mm)	x 0.0394	= Inches (in)
Feet (ft)	x 0.305	= Metres (m)	x 3.281	= Feet (ft)
Miles	x 1.609	= Kilometres (km)	x 0.621	= Miles

Volume (capacity)

Cubic inches (cu in; in^3)	x 16.387	= Cubic centimetres (cc; cm^3)	x 0.061	= Cubic inches (cu in; in^3)
Imperial pints (Imp pt)	x 0.568	= Litres (l)	x 1.76	= Imperial pints (Imp pt)
Imperial quarts (Imp qt)	x 1.137	= Litres (l)	x 0.88	= Imperial quarts (Imp qt)
Imperial quarts (Imp qt)	x 1.201	= US quarts (US qt)	x 0.833	= Imperial quarts (Imp qt)
US quarts (US qt)	x 0.946	= Litres (l)	x 1.057	= US quarts (US qt)
Imperial gallons (Imp gal)	x 4.546	= Litres (l)	x 0.22	= Imperial gallons (Imp gal)
Imperial gallons (Imp gal)	x 1.201	= US gallons (US gal)	x 0.833	= Imperial gallons (Imp gal)
US gallons (US gal)	x 3.785	= Litres (l)	x 0.264	= US gallons (US gal)

Mass (weight)

Ounces (oz)	x 28.35	= Grams (g)	x 0.035	= Ounces (oz)
Pounds (lb)	x 0.454	= Kilograms (kg)	x 2.205	= Pounds (lb)

Force

Ounces-force (ozf; oz)	x 0.278	= Newtons (N)	x 3.6	= Ounces-force (ozf; oz)
Pounds-force (lbf; lb)	x 4.448	= Newtons (N)	x 0.225	= Pounds-force (lbf; lb)
Newtons (N)	x 0.1	= Kilograms-force (kgf; kg)	x 9.81	= Newtons (N)

Pressure

Pounds-force per square inch (psi; lbf/in^2; lb/in^2)	x 0.070	= Kilograms-force per square centimetre (kgf/cm^2; kg/cm^2)	x 14.223	= Pounds-force per square inch (psi; lbf/in^2; lb/in^2)
Pounds-force per square inch (psi; lbf/in^2; lb/in^2)	x 0.068	= Atmospheres (atm)	x 14.696	= Pounds-force per square inch (psi; lbf/in^2; lb/in^2)
Pounds-force per square inch (psi; lbf/in^2; lb/in^2)	x 0.069	= Bars	x 14.5	= Pounds-force per square inch (psi; lbf/in^2; lb/in^2)
Pounds-force per square inch (psi; lbf/in^2; lb/in^2)	x 6.895	= Kilopascals (kPa)	x 0.145	= Pounds-force per square inch (psi; lbf/in^2; lb/in^2)
Kilopascals (kPa)	x 0.01	= Kilograms-force per square centimetre (kgf/cm^2; kg/cm^2)	x 98.1	= Kilopascals (kPa)
Millibar (mbar)	x 100	= Pascals (Pa)	x 0.01	= Millibar (mbar)
Millibar (mbar)	x 0.0145	= Pounds-force per square inch (psi; lbf/in^2; lb/in^2)	x 68.947	= Millibar (mbar)
Millibar (mbar)	x 0.75	= Millimetres of mercury (mmHg)	x 1.333	= Millibar (mbar)
Millibar (mbar)	x 0.401	= Inches of water (inH$_2$O)	x 2.491	= Millibar (mbar)
Millimetres of mercury (mmHg)	x 0.535	= Inches of water (inH$_2$O)	x 1.868	= Millimetres of mercury (mmHg)
Inches of water (inH$_2$O)	x 0.036	= Pounds-force per square inch (psi; lbf/in^2; lb/in^2)	x 27.68	= Inches of water (inH$_2$O)

Torque (moment of force)

Pounds-force inches (lbf in; lb in)	x 1.152	= Kilograms-force centimetre (kgf cm; kg cm)	x 0.868	= Pounds-force inches (lbf in; lb in)
Pounds-force inches (lbf in; lb in)	x 0.113	= Newton metres (Nm)	x 8.85	= Pounds-force inches (lbf in; lb in)
Pounds-force inches (lbf in; lb in)	x 0.083	= Pounds-force feet (lbf ft; lb ft)	x 12	= Pounds-force inches (lbf in; lb in)
Pounds-force feet (lbf ft; lb ft)	x 0.138	= Kilograms-force metres (kgf m; kg m)	x 7.233	= Pounds-force feet (lbf ft; lb ft)
Pounds-force feet (lbf ft; lb ft)	x 1.356	= Newton metres (Nm)	x 0.738	= Pounds-force feet (lbf ft; lb ft)
Newton metres (Nm)	x 0.102	= Kilograms-force metres (kgf m; kg m)	x 9.804	= Newton metres (Nm)

Power

Horsepower (hp)	x 745.7	= Watts (W)	x 0.0013	= Horsepower (hp)

Velocity (speed)

Miles per hour (miles/hr; mph)	x 1.609	= Kilometres per hour (km/hr; kph)	x 0.621	= Miles per hour (miles/hr; mph)

Fuel consumption*

Miles per gallon, Imperial (mpg)	x 0.354	= Kilometres per litre (km/l)	x 2.825	= Miles per gallon, Imperial (mpg)
Miles per gallon, US (mpg)	x 0.425	= Kilometres per litre (km/l)	x 2.352	= Miles per gallon, US (mpg)

Temperature

Degrees Fahrenheit = (°C x 1.8) + 32   Degrees Celsius (Degrees Centigrade; °C) = (°F - 32) x 0.56

It is common practice to convert from miles per gallon (mpg) to litres/100 kilometres (l/100km), where mpg x l/100 km = 282

Spare parts are available from many sources, including maker's appointed garages, accessory shops, and motor factors. To be sure of obtaining the correct parts, it will sometimes be necessary to quote the vehicle identification number. If possible, it can also be useful to take the old parts along for positive identification. Items such as starter motors and alternators may be available under a service exchange scheme – any parts returned should be clean.

Our advice regarding spare parts is as follows.

Officially appointed garages

This is the best source of parts which are peculiar to your car, and which are not otherwise generally available (eg, badges, interior trim, certain body panels, etc). It is also the only place at which you should buy parts if the car is still under warranty.

Accessory shops

These are very good places to buy materials and components needed for the maintenance of your car (oil, air and fuel filters, light bulbs, drivebelts, greases, brake pads, touch-up paint, etc). Components of this nature

sold by a reputable shop are usually of the same standard as those used by the car manufacturer.

Besides components, these shops also sell tools and general accessories, usually have convenient opening hours, charge lower prices, and can often be found close to home. Some accessory shops have parts counters where components needed for almost any repair job can be purchased or ordered.

Motor factors

Good factors will stock all the more important components which wear out comparatively quickly, and can sometimes supply individual components needed for the overhaul of a larger assembly (eg, brake seals and hydraulic parts, bearing shells, pistons, valves). They may also handle work such as cylinder block reboring, crankshaft regrinding, etc.

Engine reconditioners

These specialise in engine overhaul and can also supply components. It is recommended that the establishment is a member of the Federation of Engine Re-Manufacturers, or a similar society.

Tyre and exhaust specialists

These outlets may be independent, or members of a local or national chain. They frequently offer competitive prices when compared with a main dealer or local garage, but it will pay to obtain several quotes before making a decision. When researching prices, also ask what extras may be added – for instance fitting a new valve, balancing the wheel and tyre disposal all both commonly charged on top of the price of a new tyre.

Other sources

Beware of parts or materials obtained from market stalls, car boot sales, on-line auctions or similar outlets. Such items are not invariably sub-standard, but there is little chance of compensation if they do prove unsatisfactory. In the case of safety-critical components such as brake pads, there is the risk not only of financial loss, but also of an accident causing injury or death.

Second-hand components or assemblies obtained from a car breaker can be a good buy in some circumstances, but this sort of purchase is best made by the experienced DIY mechanic.

Vehicle identification numbers

Modifications are a continuing and unpublicised process in vehicle manufacture, quite apart from major model changes. Spare parts manuals and lists are compiled upon a numerical basis, the individual vehicle identification numbers being essential to correct identification of the component concerned.

When ordering spare parts, always give as much information as possible. Quote the car model, year of manufacture and registration, chassis and engine numbers as appropriate.

The Vehicle Identification Number (VIN) plate is visible from the outside of the vehicle, through the left-hand lower corner of the windscreen. It is stamped into the right-hand suspension strut. A further plate is also attached to the base of the left-hand B-pillar **(see illustrations)**.

A Vehicle Data Sticker is fitted to the interior fuse box cover. It contains the VIN, vehicle type, engine power, transmission type, engine and transmission codes, paint number, interior equipment, optional extras, and PR numbers (for maintenance schedule) **(see illustration)**.

On diesel engines the engine number is stamped into the front of the cylinder block, next to the engine to transmission joint. A barcode identification sticker is located on the top of the timing cover or on the right-hand end of the cylinder head **(see illustration)**.

Vehicle Identification Number (VIN) located on the left-hand front edge of the windscreen

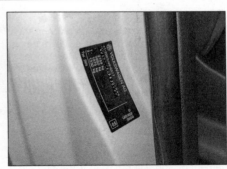

Vehicle Identification Number (VIN) at the base of the B-pillar

The vehicle data sticker

Engine code sticker on the top of the timing cover on diesel engines

Whenever servicing, repair or overhaul work is carried out on the car or its components, observe the following procedures and instructions. This will assist in carrying out the operation efficiently and to a professional standard of workmanship.

Joint mating faces and gaskets

When separating components at their mating faces, never insert screwdrivers or similar implements into the joint between the faces in order to prise them apart. This can cause severe damage which results in oil leaks, coolant leaks, etc upon reassembly. Separation is usually achieved by tapping along the joint with a soft-faced hammer in order to break the seal. However, note that this method may not be suitable where dowels are used for component location.

Where a gasket is used between the mating faces of two components, a new one must be fitted on reassembly; fit it dry unless otherwise stated in the repair procedure. Make sure that the mating faces are clean and dry, with all traces of old gasket removed. When cleaning a joint face, use a tool which is unlikely to score or damage the face, and remove any burrs or nicks with an oilstone or fine file.

Make sure that tapped holes are cleaned with a pipe cleaner, and keep them free of jointing compound, if this is being used, unless specifically instructed otherwise.

Ensure that all orifices, channels or pipes are clear, and blow through them, preferably using compressed air.

Oil seals

Oil seals can be removed by levering them out with a wide flat-bladed screwdriver or similar implement. Alternatively, a number of self-tapping screws may be screwed into the seal, and these used as a purchase for pliers or some similar device in order to pull the seal free.

Whenever an oil seal is removed from its working location, either individually or as part of an assembly, it should be renewed.

The very fine sealing lip of the seal is easily damaged, and will not seal if the surface it contacts is not completely clean and free from scratches, nicks or grooves. If the original sealing surface of the component cannot be restored, and the manufacturer has not made provision for slight relocation of the seal relative to the sealing surface, the component should be renewed.

Protect the lips of the seal from any surface which may damage them in the course of fitting. Use tape or a conical sleeve where possible. Where indicated, lubricate the seal lips with oil before fitting and, on dual-lipped seals, fill the space between the lips with grease.

Unless otherwise stated, oil seals must be fitted with their sealing lips toward the lubricant to be sealed.

Use a tubular drift or block of wood of the appropriate size to install the seal and, if the seal housing is shouldered, drive the seal down to the shoulder. If the seal housing is unshouldered, the seal should be fitted with its face flush with the housing top face (unless otherwise instructed).

Screw threads and fastenings

Seized nuts, bolts and screws are quite a common occurrence where corrosion has set in, and the use of penetrating oil or releasing fluid will often overcome this problem if the offending item is soaked for a while before attempting to release it. The use of an impact driver may also provide a means of releasing such stubborn fastening devices, when used in conjunction with the appropriate screwdriver bit or socket. If none of these methods works, it may be necessary to resort to the careful application of heat, or the use of a hacksaw or nut splitter device. Before resorting to extreme methods, check that you are not dealing with a left-hand thread!

Studs are usually removed by locking two nuts together on the threaded part, and then using a spanner on the lower nut to unscrew the stud. Studs or bolts which have broken off below the surface of the component in which they are mounted can sometimes be removed using a stud extractor.

Always ensure that a blind tapped hole is completely free from oil, grease, water or other fluid before installing the bolt or stud. Failure to do this could cause the housing to crack due to the hydraulic action of the bolt or stud as it is screwed in.

For some screw fastenings, notably cylinder head bolts or nuts, torque wrench settings are no longer specified for the latter stages of tightening, "angle-tightening" being called up instead. Typically, a fairly low torque wrench setting will be applied to the bolts/nuts in the correct sequence, followed by one or more stages of tightening through specified angles.

When checking or retightening a nut or bolt to a specified torque setting, slacken the nut or bolt by a quarter of a turn, and then retighten to the specified setting. However, this should not be attempted where angular tightening has been used.

Locknuts, locktabs and washers

Any fastening which will rotate against a component or housing during tightening should always have a washer between it and the relevant component or housing.

Spring or split washers should always be renewed when they are used to lock a critical component such as a big-end bearing retaining bolt or nut. Locktabs which are folded over to retain a nut or bolt should always be renewed.

Self-locking nuts can be re-used in non-critical areas, providing resistance can be felt when the locking portion passes over the bolt or stud thread. However, it should be noted that self-locking stiffnuts tend to lose their effectiveness after long periods of use, and should then be renewed as a matter of course.

Split pins must always be replaced with new ones of the correct size for the hole.

When thread-locking compound is found on the threads of a fastener which is to be re-used, it should be cleaned off with a wire brush and solvent, and fresh compound applied on reassembly.

Special tools

Some repair procedures in this manual entail the use of special tools such as a press, two or three-legged pullers, spring compressors, etc. Wherever possible, suitable readily-available alternatives to the manufacturer's special tools are described, and are shown in use. In some instances, where no alternative is possible, it has been necessary to resort to the use of a manufacturer's tool, and this has been done for reasons of safety as well as the efficient completion of the repair operation. Unless you are highly-skilled and have a thorough understanding of the procedures described, never attempt to bypass the use of any special tool when the procedure described specifies its use. Not only is there a very great risk of personal injury, but expensive damage could be caused to the components involved.

Environmental considerations

When disposing of used engine oil, brake fluid, antifreeze, etc, give due consideration to any detrimental environmental effects. Do not, for instance, pour any of the above liquids down drains into the general sewage system, or onto the ground to soak away, as this is likely to pollute your local environment. Many local council refuse tips provide a facility for waste oil disposal, as do some garages. You can find your nearest disposal point by calling the Environment Agency on 03708 506 506 or by visiting www.oilbankline.org.uk.

Note: It is illegal and anti-social to dump oil down the drain. To find the location of your local oil recycling bank, call 03708 506 506 or visit www.oilbankline.org.uk.

The jack supplied with the vehicle tool kit should only be used for changing the roadwheels – see Wheel changing at the front of this book. When carrying out any other kind of work, raise the vehicle using a hydraulic (or 'trolley') jack, and always supplement the jack with axle stands positioned under the vehicle jacking points.

When using a hydraulic jack or axle stands, always position the jack head or axle stand head under one of the relevant jacking points.

To raise the front and/or rear of the vehicle, use the jacking/support points at the front and rear ends of the door sills, indicated by the triangular depressions in the sill panel **(see illustration)**. Position a block of wood with a groove cut in it on the jack head to prevent the vehicle weight resting on the sill edge; align the sill edge with the groove in the wood so that the vehicle weight is spread evenly over the surface of the block. Supplement the jack with axle stands (also with slotted blocks of wood) positioned as close as possible to the jacking points **(see illustrations)**.

Do not jack the vehicle under any other part of the sill, sump, floor pan, or any of the steering or suspension components. With the vehicle raised, an axle stand should be positioned beneath the vehicle jack location point on the sill.

 Warning: Never work under, around, or near a raised car, unless it is supported in at least two places.

Front and rear jacking points

The jacking points are indicated by an arrow on the sill

Use an axle stand with a suitable block of wood

Introduction

A selection of good tools is a fundamental requirement for anyone contemplating the maintenance and repair of a motor vehicle. For the owner who does not possess any, their purchase will prove a considerable expense, offsetting some of the savings made by doing-it-yourself. However, provided that the tools purchased meet the relevant national safety standards and are of good quality, they will last for many years and prove an extremely worthwhile investment.

To help the average owner to decide which tools are needed to carry out the various tasks detailed in this manual, we have compiled three lists of tools under the following headings: *Maintenance and minor repair*, *Repair and overhaul*, and *Special*. Newcomers to practical mechanics should start off with the *Maintenance and minor repair* tool kit, and confine themselves to the simpler jobs around the vehicle. Then, as confidence and experience grow, more difficult tasks can be undertaken, with extra tools being purchased as, and when, they are needed. In this way, a *Maintenance and minor repair* tool kit can be built up into a *Repair and overhaul* tool kit over a considerable period of time, without any major cash outlays. The experienced do-it-yourselfer will have a tool kit good enough for most repair and overhaul procedures, and will add tools from the *Special* category when it is felt that the expense is justified by the amount of use to which these tools will be put.

Maintenance and minor repair tool kit

The tools given in this list should be considered as a minimum requirement if routine maintenance, servicing and minor repair operations are to be undertaken. We recommend the purchase of combination spanners (ring one end, open-ended the other); although more expensive than open-ended ones, they do give the advantages of both types of spanner.

☐ *Combination spanners:*
   Metric - 8 to 19 mm inclusive
☐ *Adjustable spanner - 35 mm jaw (approx.)*
☐ *Spark plug spanner (with rubber insert) - petrol models*
☐ *Spark plug gap adjustment tool - petrol models*
☐ *Set of feeler gauges*
☐ *Brake bleed nipple spanner*
☐ *Screwdrivers:*
   Flat blade - 100 mm long x 6 mm dia
   Cross blade - 100 mm long x 6 mm dia
   Torx - various sizes (not all vehicles)
☐ *Combination pliers*
☐ *Hacksaw (junior)*
☐ *Tyre pump*
☐ *Tyre pressure gauge*
☐ *Oil can*
☐ *Oil filter removal tool (if applicable)*
☐ *Fine emery cloth*
☐ *Wire brush (small)*
☐ *Funnel (medium size)*
☐ *Sump drain plug key (not all vehicles)*

Repair and overhaul tool kit

These tools are virtually essential for anyone undertaking any major repairs to a motor vehicle, and are additional to those given in the *Maintenance and minor repair* list. Included in this list is a comprehensive set of sockets. Although these are expensive, they will be found invaluable as they are so versatile - particularly if various drives are included in the set. We recommend the half-inch square-drive type, as this can be used with most proprietary torque wrenches.

The tools in this list will sometimes need to be supplemented by tools from the *Special* list:

☐ *Sockets to cover range in previous list (including Torx sockets)*
☐ *Reversible ratchet drive (for use with sockets)*
☐ *Extension piece, 250 mm (for use with sockets)*
☐ *Universal joint (for use with sockets)*
☐ *Flexible handle or sliding T "breaker bar" (for use with sockets)*
☐ *Torque wrench (for use with sockets)*
☐ *Self-locking grips*
☐ *Ball pein hammer*
☐ *Soft-faced mallet (plastic or rubber)*
☐ *Screwdrivers:*
   Flat blade - long & sturdy, short (chubby), and narrow (electrician's) types
   Cross blade – long & sturdy, and short (chubby) types
☐ *Pliers:*
   Long-nosed
   Side cutters (electrician's)
   Circlip (internal and external)
☐ *Cold chisel - 25 mm*
☐ *Scriber*
☐ *Scraper*
☐ *Centre-punch*
☐ *Pin punch*
☐ *Hacksaw*
☐ *Brake hose clamp*
☐ *Brake/clutch bleeding kit*
☐ *Selection of twist drills*
☐ *Steel rule/straight-edge*
☐ *Allen keys (inc. splined/Torx type)*
☐ *Selection of files*
☐ *Wire brush*
☐ *Axle stands*
☐ *Jack (strong trolley or hydraulic type)*
☐ *Light with extension lead*
☐ *Universal electrical multi-meter*

Sockets and reversible ratchet drive

Brake bleeding kit

Torx key, socket and bit

Hose clamp

Angular-tightening gauge

Special tools

The tools in this list are those which are not used regularly, are expensive to buy, or which need to be used in accordance with their manufacturers' instructions. Unless relatively difficult mechanical jobs are undertaken frequently, it will not be economic to buy many of these tools. Where this is the case, you could consider clubbing together with friends (or joining a motorists' club) to make a joint purchase, or borrowing the tools against a deposit from a local garage or tool hire specialist.

The following list contains only those tools and instruments freely available to the public, and not those special tools produced by the vehicle manufacturer specifically for its dealer network. You will find occasional references to these manufacturers' special tools in the text of this manual. Generally, an alternative method of doing the job without the vehicle manufacturers' special tool is given. However, sometimes there is no alternative to using them. Where this is the case and the relevant tool cannot be bought or borrowed, you will have to entrust the work to a dealer.

- [ ] Angular-tightening gauge
- [ ] Valve spring compressor
- [ ] Valve grinding tool
- [ ] Piston ring compressor
- [ ] Piston ring removal/installation tool
- [ ] Cylinder bore hone
- [ ] Balljoint separator
- [ ] Coil spring compressors (where applicable)
- [ ] Two/three-legged hub and bearing puller
- [ ] Impact screwdriver
- [ ] Micrometer and/or vernier calipers
- [ ] Dial gauge
- [ ] Tachometer
- [ ] Fault code reader
- [ ] Cylinder compression gauge
- [ ] Hand-operated vacuum pump and gauge
- [ ] Clutch plate alignment set
- [ ] Brake shoe steady spring cup removal tool
- [ ] Bush and bearing removal/installation set
- [ ] Stud extractors
- [ ] Tap and die set
- [ ] Lifting tackle

Buying tools

Reputable motor accessory shops and superstores often offer excellent quality tools at discount prices, so it pays to shop around.

Remember, you don't have to buy the most expensive items on the shelf, but it is always advisable to steer clear of the very cheap tools. Beware of 'bargains' offered on market stalls, on-line or at car boot sales. There are plenty of good tools around at reasonable prices, but always aim to purchase items which meet the relevant national safety standards. If in doubt, ask the proprietor or manager of the shop for advice before making a purchase.

Care and maintenance of tools

Having purchased a reasonable tool kit, it is necessary to keep the tools in a clean and serviceable condition. After use, always wipe off any dirt, grease and metal particles using a clean, dry cloth, before putting the tools away. Never leave them lying around after they have been used. A simple tool rack on the garage or workshop wall for items such as screwdrivers and pliers is a good idea. Store all normal spanners and sockets in a metal box. Any measuring instruments, gauges, meters, etc, must be carefully stored where they cannot be damaged or become rusty.

Take a little care when tools are used. Hammer heads inevitably become marked, and screwdrivers lose the keen edge on their blades from time to time. A little timely attention with emery cloth or a file will soon restore items like this to a good finish.

Working facilities

Not to be forgotten when discussing tools is the workshop itself. If anything more than routine maintenance is to be carried out, a suitable working area becomes essential.

It is appreciated that many an owner-mechanic is forced by circumstances to remove an engine or similar item without the benefit of a garage or workshop. Having done this, any repairs should always be done under the cover of a roof.

Wherever possible, any dismantling should be done on a clean, flat workbench or table at a suitable working height.

Any workbench needs a vice; one with a jaw opening of 100 mm is suitable for most jobs. As mentioned previously, some clean dry storage space is also required for tools, as well as for any lubricants, cleaning fluids, touch-up paints etc, which become necessary.

Another item which may be required, and which has a much more general usage, is an electric drill with a chuck capacity of at least 8 mm. This, together with a good range of twist drills, is virtually essential for fitting accessories.

Last, but not least, always keep a supply of old newspapers and clean, lint-free rags available, and try to keep any working area as clean as possible.

Micrometers

Dial test indicator ("dial gauge")

Oil filter removal tool (strap wrench type)

Compression tester

Bearing puller

This is a guide to getting your vehicle through the MOT test. Obviously it will not be possible to examine the vehicle to the same standard as the professional MOT tester. However, working through the following checks will enable you to identify any problem areas before submitting the vehicle for the test.

It has only been possible to summarise the test requirements here, based on the regulations in force at the time of printing. Test standards are becoming increasingly stringent, although there are some exemptions for older vehicles.

An assistant will be needed to help carry out some of these checks.

The checks have been sub-divided into four categories, as follows:

1 Checks carried out **FROM THE DRIVER'S SEAT**

2 Checks carried out **WITH THE VEHICLE ON THE GROUND**

3 Checks carried out **WITH THE VEHICLE RAISED AND THE WHEELS FREE TO TURN**

4 Checks carried out on **YOUR VEHICLE'S EXHAUST EMISSION SYSTEM**

---

1 Checks carried out **FROM THE DRIVER'S SEAT**

Handbrake (parking brake)

☐ Test the operation of the handbrake. Excessive travel (too many clicks) indicates incorrect brake or cable adjustment.
☐ Check that the handbrake cannot be released by tapping the lever sideways. Check the security of the lever mountings.

☐ If the parking brake is foot-operated, check that the pedal is secure and without excessive travel, and that the release mechanism operates correctly.
☐ Where applicable, test the operation of the electronic handbrake. The brake should engage and disengage without excessive delay. If the warning light does not extinguish when the brake is disengaged, this could indicate a fault which will need further investigation.

Footbrake

☐ Depress the brake pedal and check that it does not creep down to the floor, indicating a master cylinder fault. Release the pedal,

wait a few seconds, then depress it again. If the pedal travels nearly to the floor before firm resistance is felt, brake adjustment or repair is necessary. If the pedal feels spongy, there is air in the hydraulic system which must be removed by bleeding.

☐ Check that the brake pedal is secure and in good condition. Check also for signs of fluid leaks on the pedal, floor or carpets, which would indicate failed seals in the brake master cylinder.
☐ Check the servo unit (when applicable) by operating the brake pedal several times, then keeping the pedal depressed and starting the engine. As the engine starts, the pedal will move down slightly. If not, the vacuum hose or the servo itself may be faulty.

Steering wheel and column

☐ Examine the steering wheel for fractures or looseness of the hub, spokes or rim.
☐ Move the steering wheel from side to side and then up and down. Check that the steering wheel is not loose on the column, indicating wear or a loose retaining nut. Continue moving the steering wheel as before, but also turn it slightly from left to right.

☐ Check that the steering wheel is not loose on the column, and that there is no abnormal movement of the steering wheel, indicating wear in the column support bearings or couplings.
☐ Check that the ignition lock (where fitted) engages and disengages correctly.
☐ Steering column adjustment mechanisms (where fitted) must be able to lock the column securely in place with no play evident.

Windscreen, mirrors and sunvisor

☐ The windscreen must be free of cracks or other significant damage within the driver's field of view. (Small stone chips are acceptable.) Rear view mirrors must be secure, intact, and capable of being adjusted.

☐ The driver's sunvisor must be capable of being stored in the "up" position.

Seat belts and seats

Note: *The following checks are applicable to all seat belts, front and rear.*

☐ Examine the webbing of all the belts (including rear belts if fitted) for cuts, serious fraying or deterioration. Fasten and unfasten each belt to check the buckles. If applicable, check the retracting mechanism. Check the security of all seat belt mountings accessible from inside the vehicle, ensuring any height adjustable mountings lock securely in place.
☐ Seat belts with pre-tensioners, once activated, have a "flag" or similar showing on the seat belt stalk. This, in itself, is not a reason for test failure.
☐ The front seats themselves must be securely attached and the backrests must lock in the upright position.

Doors

☐ Both front doors must be able to be opened and closed from outside and inside, and must latch securely when closed.

Bonnet and boot/tailgate

☐ The bonnet and boot/tailgate must latch securely when closed.

2 Checks carried out WITH THE VEHICLE ON THE GROUND

Vehicle identification

☐ Number plates must be in good condition, secure and legible, with letters and numbers correctly spaced – spacing at (A) should be 33 mm and at (B) 11 mm. At the front, digits must be black on a white background and at the rear black on a yellow background. Other background designs (such as honeycomb) are not permitted.

☐ The VIN plate and/or homologation plate must be permanently displayed and legible.

Electrical equipment

☐ Switch on the ignition and check the operation of the horn.
☐ Check the windscreen washers and wipers, examining the wiper blades; renew damaged or perished blades. Also check the operation of the stop-lights.

☐ Check the operation of the sidelights and number plate lights. The lenses and reflectors must be secure, clean and undamaged.
☐ Check the operation and alignment of the headlights. The headlight reflectors must not be tarnished and the lenses must be undamaged.
☐ Switch on the ignition and check the operation of the direction indicators (including the instrument panel tell-tale) and the hazard warning lights. Operation of the sidelights and stop-lights must not affect the indicators - if it does, the cause is usually a bad earth at the rear light cluster. Indicators should flash at a rate of between 60 and 120 times per minute – faster or slower than this could indicate a fault with the flasher unit or a bad earth at one of the light units.
☐ Check the operation of the rear foglight(s), including the warning light on the instrument panel or in the switch.
☐ The warning lights must illuminate in accordance with the manufacturer's design. For most vehicles, the ABS and other warning lights should illuminate when the ignition is switched on, and (if the system is operating properly) extinguish after a few seconds. Refer to the owner's handbook.

Footbrake

☐ Examine the master cylinder, brake pipes and servo unit for leaks, loose mountings, corrosion or other damage. If ABS is fitted, this unit should also be examined for signs of leaks or corrosion.

☐ The fluid reservoir must be secure and the fluid level must be between the upper (**A**) and lower (**B**) markings.

☐ Inspect both front brake flexible hoses for cracks or deterioration of the rubber. Turn the steering from lock to lock, and ensure that the hoses do not contact the wheel, tyre, or any part of the steering or suspension mechanism. With the brake pedal firmly depressed, check the hoses for bulges or leaks under pressure.

Steering and suspension

☐ Have your assistant turn the steering wheel from side to side slightly, up to the point where the steering gear just begins to transmit this movement to the roadwheels. Check for excessive free play between the steering wheel and the steering gear, indicating wear or insecurity of the steering column joints, the column-to-steering gear coupling, or the steering gear itself.
☐ Have your assistant turn the steering wheel more vigorously in each direction, so that the roadwheels just begin to turn. As this is done, examine all the steering joints, linkages, fittings and attachments. Renew any component that shows signs of wear or damage. On vehicles with power steering, check the security and condition of the steering pump, drivebelt and hoses.
☐ Check that the vehicle is standing level, and at approximately the correct ride height.

Shock absorbers

☐ Depress each corner of the vehicle in turn, then release it. The vehicle should rise and then settle in its normal position. If the vehicle continues to rise and fall, the shock absorber is defective. A shock absorber which has seized will also cause the vehicle to fail.

Exhaust system

☐ Start the engine. With your assistant holding a rag over the tailpipe, check the entire system for leaks. Repair or renew leaking sections.

3 Checks carried out WITH THE VEHICLE RAISED AND THE WHEELS FREE TO TURN

Jack up the front and rear of the vehicle, and securely support it on axle stands. Position the stands clear of the suspension assemblies. Ensure that the wheels are clear of the ground and that the steering can be turned from lock to lock.

Steering mechanism

☐ Have your assistant turn the steering from lock to lock. Check that the steering turns smoothly, and that no part of the steering mechanism, including a wheel or tyre, fouls any brake hose or pipe or any part of the body structure.
☐ Examine the steering rack rubber gaiters for damage or insecurity of the retaining clips. If power steering is fitted, check for signs of damage or leakage of the fluid hoses, pipes or connections. Also check for excessive stiffness or binding of the steering, a missing split pin or locking device, or severe corrosion of the body structure within 30 cm of any steering component attachment point.

Front and rear suspension and wheel bearings

☐ Starting at the front right-hand side, grasp the roadwheel at the 3 o'clock and 9 o'clock positions and rock gently but firmly. Check for free play or insecurity at the wheel bearings, suspension balljoints, or suspension mount-ings, pivots and attachments.
☐ Now grasp the wheel at the 12 o'clock and 6 o'clock positions and repeat the previous inspection. Spin the wheel, and check for roughness or tightness of the front wheel bearing.

☐ If excess free play is suspected at a component pivot point, this can be confirmed by using a large screwdriver or similar tool and levering between the mounting and the component attachment. This will confirm whether the wear is in the pivot bush, its retaining bolt, or in the mounting itself (the bolt holes can often become elongated).

☐ Carry out all the above checks at the other front wheel, and then at both rear wheels.

Springs and shock absorbers

☐ Examine the suspension struts (when applicable) for serious fluid leakage, corrosion, or damage to the casing. Also check the security of the mounting points.
☐ If coil springs are fitted, check that the spring ends locate in their seats, and that the spring is not corroded, cracked or broken.
☐ If leaf springs are fitted, check that all leaves are intact, that the axle is securely attached to each spring, and that there is no deterioration of the spring eye mountings, bushes, and shackles.

☐ The same general checks apply to vehicles fitted with other suspension types, such as torsion bars, hydraulic displacer units, etc. Ensure that all mountings and attachments are secure, that there are no signs of excessive wear, corrosion or damage, and (on hydraulic types) that there are no fluid leaks or damaged pipes.
☐ Inspect the shock absorbers for signs of serious fluid leakage. Check for wear of the mounting bushes or attachments, or damage to the body of the unit.

Driveshafts (fwd vehicles only)

☐ Rotate each front wheel in turn and inspect the constant velocity joint gaiters for splits or damage. Also check that each driveshaft is straight and undamaged.

Braking system

☐ If possible without dismantling, check brake pad wear and disc condition. Ensure that the friction lining material has not worn excessively, (A) and that the discs are not fractured, pitted, scored or badly worn (B).

☐ Examine all the rigid brake pipes underneath the vehicle, and the flexible hose(s) at the rear. Look for corrosion, chafing or insecurity of the pipes, and for signs of bulging under pressure, chafing, splits or deterioration of the flexible hoses.
☐ Look for signs of fluid leaks at the brake calipers or on the brake backplates. Repair or renew leaking components.
☐ Slowly spin each wheel, while your assistant depresses and releases the footbrake. Ensure that each brake is operating and does not bind when the pedal is released.

☐ Examine the handbrake mechanism, checking for frayed or broken cables, excessive corrosion, or wear or insecurity of the linkage. Check that the mechanism works on each relevant wheel, and releases fully, without binding.

☐ It is not possible to test brake efficiency without special equipment, but a road test can be carried out later to check that the vehicle pulls up in a straight line.

Fuel and exhaust systems

☐ Inspect the fuel tank (including the filler cap), fuel pipes, hoses and unions. All components must be secure and free from leaks. Locking fuel caps must lock securely and the key must be provided for the MOT test.

☐ Examine the exhaust system over its entire length, checking for any damaged, broken or missing mountings, security of the retaining clamps and rust or corrosion.

Wheels and tyres

☐ Examine the sidewalls and tread area of each tyre in turn. Check for cuts, tears, lumps, bulges, separation of the tread, and exposure of the ply or cord due to wear or damage. Check that the tyre bead is correctly seated on the wheel rim, that the valve is sound and properly seated, and that the wheel is not distorted or damaged.

☐ Check that the tyres are of the correct size for the vehicle, that they are of the same size and type on each axle, and that the pressures are correct.

☐ Check the tyre tread depth. The legal minimum at the time of writing is 1.6 mm over the central three-quarters of the tread width. Abnormal tread wear may indicate incorrect front wheel alignment or wear in steering or suspension components.

☐ If the spare wheel is fitted externally or in a separate carrier beneath the vehicle, check that mountings are secure and free of excessive corrosion.

Body corrosion

☐ Check the condition of the entire vehicle structure for signs of corrosion in load-bearing areas. (These include chassis box sections, side sills, cross-members, pillars, and all suspension, steering, braking system and seat belt mountings and anchorages.) Any corrosion which has seriously reduced the thickness of a load-bearing area (or is within 30 cm of safety-related components such as steering or suspension) is likely to cause the vehicle to fail. In this case professional repairs are likely to be needed.

☐ Damage or corrosion which causes sharp or otherwise dangerous edges to be exposed will also cause the vehicle to fail.

Towbars

☐ Check the condition of mounting points (both beneath the vehicle and within boot/hatchback areas) for signs of corrosion, ensuring that all fixings are secure and not worn or damaged. There must be no excessive play in detachable tow ball arms or quick-release mechanisms.

4 Checks carried out on **YOUR VEHICLE'S EXHAUST EMISSION SYSTEM**

Petrol models

☐ The engine should be warmed up, and running well (ignition system in good order, air filter element clean, etc.).

☐ Before testing, run the engine at around 2500 rpm for 20 seconds. Let the engine drop to idle, and watch for smoke from the exhaust. If the idle speed is too high, or if dense blue or black smoke emerges for more than 5 seconds, the vehicle will fail. Typically, blue smoke signifies oil burning (engine wear); black smoke means unburnt fuel (dirty air cleaner element, or other fuel system fault).

☐ An exhaust gas analyser for measuring carbon monoxide (CO) and hydrocarbons (HC) is now needed. If one cannot be hired or borrowed, have a local garage perform the check.

CO emissions (mixture)

☐ The MOT tester has access to the CO limits for all vehicles. The CO level is measured at idle speed, and at 'fast idle' (2500 to 3000 rpm). The following limits are given as a general guide:

At idle speed – Less than 0.5% CO
At 'fast idle' – Less than 0.3% CO
Lambda reading – 0.97 to 1.03

☐ If the CO level is too high, this may point to poor maintenance, a fuel injection system problem, faulty lambda (oxygen) sensor or catalytic converter. Try an injector cleaning treatment, and check the vehicle's ECU for fault codes.

HC emissions

☐ The MOT tester has access to HC limits for all vehicles. The HC level is measured at 'fast idle' (2500 to 3000 rpm). The following limits are given as a general guide:

At 'fast idle' – Less then 200 ppm

☐ Excessive HC emissions are typically caused by oil being burnt (worn engine), or by a blocked crankcase ventilation system ('breather'). If the engine oil is old and thin, an oil change may help. If the engine is running badly, check the vehicle's ECU for fault codes.

Diesel models

☐ The only emission test for diesel engines is measuring exhaust smoke density, using a calibrated smoke meter. The test involves accelerating the engine at least 3 times to its maximum unloaded speed.

Note: *On engines with a timing belt, it is VITAL that the belt is in good condition before the test is carried out.*

☐ With the engine warmed up, it is first purged by running at around 2500 rpm for 20 seconds. A governor check is then carried out, by slowly accelerating the engine to its maximum speed. After this, the smoke meter is connected, and the engine is accelerated quickly to maximum speed three times. If the smoke density is less than the limits given below, the vehicle will pass:

Non-turbo vehicles: 2.5m-1
Turbocharged vehicles: 3.0m-1

☐ If excess smoke is produced, try fitting a new air cleaner element, or using an injector cleaning treatment. If the engine is running badly, where applicable, check the vehicle's ECU for fault codes. Also check the vehicle's EGR system, where applicable. At high mileages, the injectors may require professional attention.

Engine

- [ ] Engine fails to rotate when attempting to start
- [ ] Engine rotates, but will not start
- [ ] Engine difficult to start when cold
- [ ] Engine difficult to start when hot
- [ ] Starter motor noisy or excessively rough in engagement
- [ ] Engine starts, but stops immediately
- [ ] Engine idles erratically
- [ ] Engine misfires at idle speed
- [ ] Engine misfires throughout the driving speed range
- [ ] Engine hesitates on acceleration
- [ ] Engine stalls
- [ ] Engine lacks power
- [ ] Engine backfires
- [ ] Oil pressure warning light illuminated with engine running
- [ ] Engine runs-on after switching off
- [ ] Engine noises

Cooling system

- [ ] Overheating
- [ ] Overcooling
- [ ] External coolant leakage
- [ ] Internal coolant leakage
- [ ] Corrosion

Fuel and exhaust systems

- [ ] Excessive fuel consumption
- [ ] Fuel leakage and/or fuel odour

Clutch

- [ ] Pedal travels to floor – no pressure or very little resistance
- [ ] Clutch fails to disengage (unable to select gears)
- [ ] Clutch slips (engine speed increases, with no increase in vehicle speed)
- [ ] Judder as clutch is engaged
- [ ] Noise when depressing or releasing clutch pedal

Manual transmission

- [ ] Noisy in neutral with engine running
- [ ] Noisy in one particular gear
- [ ] Difficulty engaging gears
- [ ] Vibration
- [ ] Jumps out of gear
- [ ] Lubricant leaks

DSG transmission

- [ ] Fluid leakage
- [ ] General gear selection problems
- [ ] Transmission fluid brown, or has burned smell
- [ ] Engine will not start in any gear, or starts in gears other than Park or Neutral
- [ ] Transmission slips, shifts roughly, is noisy, or has no drive in forward or reverse gears

Driveshafts

- [ ] Clicking or knocking noise on turns (at slow speed on full-lock)

Braking system

- [ ] Vehicle pulls to one side under braking
- [ ] Noise (grinding or high-pitched squeal) when brakes applied)
- [ ] Brakes binding
- [ ] Excessive brake pedal travel
- [ ] Brake pedal feels spongy when depressed
- [ ] Excessive brake pedal effort required to stop vehicle
- [ ] Judder felt through brake pedal or steering wheel when braking

Suspension and steering

- [ ] Vehicle pulls to one side
- [ ] Excessive pitching and/or rolling around corners, or during braking
- [ ] Lack of power assistance
- [ ] Wandering or general instability
- [ ] Excessively stiff steering
- [ ] Excessive play in steering
- [ ] Wheel wobble and vibration
- [ ] Tyre wear excessive

Electrical system

- [ ] Battery will not hold a charge for more than a few days
- [ ] Ignition/no-charge warning light remains illuminated with engine running
- [ ] Ignition/no-charge warning light fails to come on
- [ ] Lights inoperative
- [ ] Instrument readings inaccurate or erratic
- [ ] Horn inoperative, or unsatisfactory in operation
- [ ] Windscreen/tailgate wipers inoperative, or unsatisfactory in operation
- [ ] Windscreen/tailgate washers inoperative, or unsatisfactory in operation
- [ ] Electric windows inoperative, or unsatisfactory in operation
- [ ] Central locking system inoperative, or unsatisfactory in operation

Introduction

The vehicle owner who does his or her own maintenance according to the recommended service schedules should not have to use this section of the manual very often. Modern component reliability is such that, provided those items subject to wear or deterioration are inspected or renewed at the specified intervals, sudden failure is comparatively rare. Faults do not usually just happen as a result of sudden failure, but develop over a period of time. Major mechanical failures in particular are usually preceded by characteristic symptoms over hundreds or even thousands of miles. Those components that do occasionally fail without warning are often small and easily carried in the vehicle.

With any fault-finding, the first step is to decide where to begin investigations. Sometimes this is obvious, but on other occasions, a little detective work will be necessary. The owner who makes half a dozen haphazard adjustments or component renewals may be successful in curing a fault (or its symptoms). However, will be none the wiser if the fault recurs, and ultimately may have spent more time and money than was necessary. A calm and logical approach will be found to be more satisfactory in the long run. Always take into account any warning signs or abnormalities that may have been noticed in the period preceding the fault – power loss, high or low gauge readings, unusual smells, etc. – and remember that failure of components such as fuses or spark plugs may only be pointers to some underlying fault.

The pages which follow provide an easy-reference guide to the more common problems which may occur during the operation of the vehicle. These problems and their possible causes are grouped under headings denoting various components or systems, such as Engine, Cooling system, etc. The general Chapter which deals with the problem is also shown in brackets; refer to the relevant part of that Chapter for system-specific information. Whatever the fault, certain basic principles apply. These are as follows:

Verify the fault. This is simply a matter of being sure that you know what the symptoms are before starting work. This is particularly important if you are investigating a fault for someone else, who may not have described it very accurately.

Do not overlook the obvious. For example, if the vehicle will not start, is there petrol in the tank? (Do not take anyone else's word on this particular point, and do not trust the fuel gauge either!) If an electrical fault is indicated, look for loose or broken wires before digging out the test gear.

Cure the disease, not the symptom. Substituting a flat battery with a fully-charged one will get you off the hard shoulder, but if the underlying cause is not attended to, the new battery will go the same way. Similarly, changing oil-fouled spark plugs for a new set will get you moving again, but remember that the reason for the fouling (if it was not simply an incorrect grade of plug) will have to be established and corrected.

Do not take anything for granted. Particularly, do not forget that a new component may itself be defective (especially if it's been rattling around in the boot for months). Also do not leave components out of a fault diagnosis sequence just because they are new or recently fitted. When you do finally diagnose a difficult fault, you will probably realise that all the evidence was there from the start.

Diesel fault diagnosis

The majority of starting problems on small diesel engines are electrical in origin. The mechanic who is familiar with petrol engines but less so with diesel may be inclined to view the diesel's injectors and pump in the same light as the spark plugs and distributor, but this is generally a mistake.

When investigating complaints of difficult starting for someone else, make sure that the correct starting procedure is understood and is being followed. Some drivers are unaware of the significance of the preheating warning light – many modern engines are sufficiently forgiving for this not to matter in mild weather, but with the onset of winter, problems begin.

As a rule of thumb, if the engine is difficult to start but runs well when it has finally got going, the problem is electrical (battery, starter motor or preheating system). If poor performance is combined with difficult starting, the problem is likely to be in the fuel system. The low-pressure (supply) side of the fuel system should be checked before suspecting the injectors and high-pressure pump. The most common fuel supply problem is air getting into the system, and any pipe from the fuel tank forwards must be scrutinised if air leakage is suspected. Normally the pump is the last item to suspect, since unless it has been tampered with, there is no reason for it to be at fault.

Engine

Engine fails to rotate when attempting to start

- [ ] Battery terminal connections loose or corroded (*Weekly checks*).
- [ ] Battery discharged or faulty (Chapter 5A).
- [ ] Broken, loose or disconnected wiring in the starting circuit (Chapter 5A).
- [ ] Defective starter solenoid or switch (Chapter 5A).
- [ ] Defective starter motor (Chapter 5A).
- [ ] Starter pinion or flywheel ring gear teeth loose or broken (Chapter 2A, 2B or 2C).
- [ ] Engine earth strap broken or disconnected (Chapter 5A).

Engine rotates, but will not start

- [ ] Fuel tank empty.
- [ ] Battery discharged (engine rotates slowly) (Chapter 5A).
- [ ] Battery terminal connections loose or corroded (*Weekly checks*).
- [ ] Fuel injection system fault (Chapter 4A).
- [ ] Air in fuel system (Chapter 4A).
- [ ] Major mechanical failure (e.g. timing belt) (Chapter 2A, 2B or 2C).

Engine difficult to start when cold

- [ ] Battery discharged (Chapter 5A).
- [ ] Battery terminal connections loose or corroded (*Weekly checks*).
- [ ] Fuel injection system fault (Chapter 4A).
- [ ] Preheating system fault (Chapter 5B).
- [ ] Low cylinder compressions (Chapter 2A, 2B or 2C).

Engine (continued)

Engine difficult to start when hot

- [ ] Air filter element dirty or clogged (Chapter 1).
- [ ] Fuel injection system fault (Chapter 4A).
- [ ] Low cylinder compressions (Chapter 2A, 2B or 2C).

Starter motor noisy or excessively rough in engagement

- [ ] Starter pinion or flywheel ring gear teeth loose or broken (Chapter 2A, 2B or 2C).
- [ ] Starter motor mounting bolts loose or missing (Chapter 5A).
- [ ] Starter motor internal components worn or damaged (Chapter 5A).

Engine starts, but stops immediately

- [ ] Blocked injector/fuel injection system fault (Chapter 4A).
- [ ] Faulty injector(s) (Chapter 4A).
- [ ] Air in fuel system (Chapter 4A).

Engine idles erratically

- [ ] Air filter element clogged (Chapter 1).
- [ ] Uneven or low cylinder compressions (Chapter 2A, 2B or 2C).
- [ ] Camshaft lobes worn (Chapter 2A, 2B or 2C).
- [ ] Timing belt incorrectly tensioned (Chapter 2A, 2B or 2C).
- [ ] Blocked injector/fuel injection system fault (Chapter 4A).
- [ ] Faulty injector(s) (Chapter 4A).

Engine misfires at idle speed

- [ ] Vacuum leak at the inlet manifold or associated hoses (Chapter 4A or Chapter 9).
- [ ] Blocked injector/fuel injection system fault (Chapter 4A).
- [ ] Faulty injector(s) (Chapter 4A).
- [ ] Uneven or low cylinder compressions (Chapter 2A, 2B or 2C).
- [ ] Disconnected, leaking, or perished crankcase ventilation hoses (Chapter 4B).

Engine misfires throughout the driving speed range

- [ ] Fuel filter choked (Chapter 1).
- [ ] Fuel pump faulty, or delivery pressure low (Chapter 4A).
- [ ] Fuel tank vent blocked, or fuel pipes restricted (Chapter 4A).
- [ ] Faulty injector(s) (Chapter 4A).
- [ ] Uneven or low cylinder compressions (Chapter 2A, 2B or 2C).
- [ ] Blocked injector/fuel injection system fault (Chapter 4A).

Engine hesitates on acceleration

- [ ] Blocked injector/fuel injection system fault (Chapter 4A).
- [ ] Faulty injector(s) (Chapter 4A).

Engine stalls

- [ ] Fuel filter choked (Chapter 1).
- [ ] Fuel tank vent blocked, or fuel pipes restricted (Chapter 4A).
- [ ] Blocked injector/fuel injection system fault (Chapter 4A).
- [ ] Faulty injector(s) (Chapter 4A).
- [ ] Air in fuel system (Chapter 4A).

Engine lacks power

- [ ] Timing belt incorrectly fitted or tensioned (Chapter 2A, 2B or 2C).
- [ ] Fuel filter choked (Chapter 1).
- [ ] Uneven or low cylinder compressions (Chapter 2A, 2B or 2C).
- [ ] Blocked injector/fuel injection system fault (Chapter 4A).
- [ ] Brakes binding (Chapter 9).
- [ ] Clutch slipping (Chapter 6).

Engine backfires

- [ ] Timing belt incorrectly fitted or tensioned (Chapter 2A, 2B or 2C).
- [ ] Blocked injector/fuel injection system fault (Chapter 4A).

Oil pressure warning light illuminated with engine running

- [ ] Low oil level, or incorrect oil grade (*Weekly checks*).
- [ ] Faulty oil pressure warning light switch (Chapter 2A, 2B or 2C).
- [ ] Worn engine bearings and/or oil pump (Chapter 2A, 2B or 2D).
- [ ] High engine operating temperature (Chapter 3).
- [ ] Oil pressure relief valve defective (Chapter 2A, 2B or 2C).
- [ ] Oil pick-up strainer clogged (Chapter 2A, 2B or 2C).

Engine runs-on after switching off

- [ ] Excessive carbon build-up in engine (Chapter 2A, 2B or 2C).
- [ ] High engine operating temperature (Chapter 3).

Engine noises

Pre-ignition (pinking) or knocking during acceleration or under load

- [ ] Incorrect grade of fuel.Excessive carbon build-up in engine (Chapter 2A, 2B or 2C).

Whistling or wheezing noises

- [ ] Leaking exhaust manifold gasket or pipe-to-manifold joint (Chapter 4B).
- [ ] Leaking vacuum hose (Chapter 4A or Chapter 9).
- [ ] Blowing cylinder head gasket (Chapter 2A, 2B or 2C).

Tapping or rattling noises

- [ ] Worn valve gear or camshaft (Chapter 2A, 2B or 2C).
- [ ] Ancillary component fault (coolant pump, alternator, etc.) (Chapter 3 or Chapter 5A).

Knocking or thumping noises

- [ ] Worn big-end bearings (regular heavy knocking, perhaps worsening under load) (Chapter 2D).
- [ ] Worn main bearings (rumbling and knocking, perhaps less under load) (Chapter 2D).
- [ ] Piston slap (most noticeable when cold) (Chapter 2D).
- [ ] Ancillary component fault (coolant pump, alternator, etc.) (Chapter 3 or Chapter 5A).

Cooling system

Overheating

- ☐ Insufficient coolant in system (*Weekly checks*).
- ☐ Thermostat faulty (Chapter 3).
- ☐ Radiator core blocked, or grille restricted (Chapter 3).
- ☐ Electric cooling fan or thermoswitch faulty (Chapter 3).
- ☐ Pressure cap faulty (Chapter 3).
- ☐ Inaccurate temperature gauge sender unit (Chapter 3).
- ☐ Airlock in cooling system.

Overcooling

- ☐ Thermostat faulty (Chapter 3).
- ☐ Inaccurate temperature gauge sender unit (Chapter 3).

External coolant leakage

- ☐ Deteriorated or damaged hoses or hose clips (Chapter 3).
- ☐ Radiator core or heater matrix leaking (Chapter 3).
- ☐ Pressure cap faulty (Chapter 3).
- ☐ Coolant pump seal leaking (Chapter 3).
- ☐ Boiling due to overheating (Chapter 3).
- ☐ Core plug leaking (Chapter 2D).

Internal coolant leakage

- ☐ Leaking cylinder head gasket (Chapter 2A, 2B or 2C).
- ☐ Cracked cylinder head or cylinder bore (Chapter 2D).

Corrosion

- ☐ Infrequent draining and flushing (Chapter 1).
- ☐ Incorrect coolant mixture or inappropriate coolant type (Chapter 1).

Fuel and exhaust systems

Excessive fuel consumption

- ☐ Air filter element dirty or clogged (Chapter 1).
- ☐ Fuel injection system fault (Chapter 4A).
- ☐ Faulty injector(s) (Chapter 4A).
- ☐ Tyres under-inflated (*Weekly checks*).

Fuel leakage and/or fuel odour

- ☐ Damaged fuel tank, pipes or connections (Chapter 4A).
- ☐ Excessive noise or fumes from exhaust system (Chapter 4B).
- ☐ Leaking exhaust system or manifold joints (Chapter 4B).
- ☐ Leaking, corroded or damaged silencers or pipe (Chapter 4B).
- ☐ Broken mountings causing body or suspension contact (Chapter 2A, 2B or 2C).

Clutch

Pedal travels to floor – no pressure or very little resistance

- ☐ Hydraulic fluid level low/air in hydraulic system (Chapter 6).
- ☐ Broken clutch release bearing or fork (Chapter 6).
- ☐ Broken diaphragm spring in clutch pressure plate (Chapter 6).

Clutch fails to disengage (unable to select gears)

- ☐ Clutch disc sticking on transmission input shaft splines (Chapter 6).
- ☐ Clutch disc sticking to flywheel or pressure plate (Chapter 6).
- ☐ Faulty pressure plate assembly (Chapter 6).
- ☐ Clutch release mechanism worn or incorrectly assembled (Chapter 6).

Clutch slips (engine speed increases, with no increase in vehicle speed)

- ☐ Clutch disc linings excessively worn (Chapter 6).
- ☐ Clutch disc linings contaminated with oil or grease (Chapter 6).
- ☐ Faulty pressure plate or weak diaphragm spring (Chapter 6).

Judder as clutch is engaged

- ☐ Clutch disc linings contaminated with oil or grease (Chapter 6).
- ☐ Clutch disc linings excessively worn (Chapter 6).
- ☐ Faulty or distorted pressure plate or diaphragm spring (Chapter 6).
- ☐ Dual mass flywheel worn (Chapter 2A, 2B or Chapter 2C).
- ☐ Worn or loose engine or transmission mountings (Chapter 2A, 2B or 2C).
- ☐ Clutch disc hub or transmission input shaft splines worn (Chapter 6, 7A or 7B).

Noise when depressing or releasing clutch pedal

- ☐ Worn clutch release bearing (Chapter 6).
- ☐ Worn or dry clutch pedal bushes (Chapter 6).
- ☐ Faulty pressure plate assembly (Chapter 6).
- ☐ Pressure plate diaphragm spring broken (Chapter 6).
- ☐ Broken clutch disc cushioning springs (Chapter 6).
- ☐ Dual mass flywheel worn (Chapter 2A, 2B or 2C).

Manual transmission

Noisy in neutral with engine running

☐ Input shaft bearings worn (noise apparent with clutch pedal released, but not when depressed) (Chapter 7A).*
☐ Clutch release bearing worn (noise apparent with clutch pedal depressed, possibly less when released) (Chapter 6).

Noisy in one particular gear

☐ Worn, damaged or chipped gear teeth (Chapter 7A).*

Difficulty engaging gears

☐ Clutch fault (Chapter 6).
☐ Worn or damaged gear linkage (Chapter 7A).
☐ Incorrectly adjusted gear linkage (Chapter 7A).
☐ Worn synchroniser units (Chapter 7A).*

Vibration

☐ Lack of oil (Chapter 7A).
☐ Worn bearings (Chapter 7A).*

Jumps out of gear

☐ Worn or damaged gear linkage (Chapter 7A).
☐ Incorrectly adjusted gear linkage (Chapter 7A).
☐ Worn synchroniser units (Chapter 7A).*
☐ Worn selector forks (Chapter 7A).*

Lubricant leaks

☐ Leaking differential output oil seal (Chapter 7A).
☐ Leaking housing joint (Chapter 7A).*
☐ Leaking input shaft oil seal (Chapter 7A).

Although the corrective action necessary to remedy the symptoms described is beyond the scope of the home mechanic, the above information should be helpful in isolating the cause of the condition. This should enable the owner can communicate clearly with a professional mechanic.

DSG transmission

Fluid leakage

Note: *Due to the complexity of the automatic transmission, it is difficult for the home mechanic to properly diagnose and service this unit. For problems other than the following, the vehicle should be taken to a dealer service department or automatic transmission specialist. Do not be too hasty in removing the transmission if a fault is suspected, as most of the testing is carried out with the unit still fitted.*
Automatic transmission fluid is usually dark in colour. Fluid leaks should not be confused with engine oil, which can easily be blown onto the transmission by airflow. To determine the source of a leak, first remove all built-up dirt and grime from the transmission housing and surrounding areas using a degreasing agent, or by steam-cleaning. Drive the vehicle at low speed, so airflow will not blow the leak far from its source. Raise and support the vehicle, and determine where the leak is coming from.
☐ General gear selection problems
Chapter 7B, Section 4 deals with checking and adjusting the selector cable on automatic/DSG transmissions. The following are common problems which may be caused by a poorly-adjusted cable:
☐ Engine starting in gears other than Park or Neutral.
☐ Indicator panel indicating a gear other than the one actually being used.

☐ Vehicle moves when in Park or Neutral.
☐ Poor gear shift quality or erratic gearchanges.

Transmission fluid brown, or has burned smell

☐ Transmission fluid level low (Chapter 7B).
☐ If the fluid appears to have deteriorated badly it is recommended that it is renewed.
☐ Engine will not start in any gear, or starts in gears other than Park or Neutral
☐ Incorrect selector cable adjustment (Chapter 7B).

Transmission slips, shifts roughly, is noisy, or has no drive in forward or reverse gears

There are many probable causes for the above problems, but unless there is a very obvious reason (such as a loose or corroded wiring plug connection on or near the transmission), the car should be taken to a franchise dealer for the fault to be diagnosed. The transmission control unit incorporates a self-diagnosis facility, and any fault codes can quickly be read and interpreted by a dealer with the proper diagnostic equipment.

Driveshafts

Clicking or knocking noise on turns (at slow speed on full-lock)

☐ Lack of constant velocity joint lubricant, possibly due to damaged gaiter (Chapter 8).

☐ Worn outer constant velocity joint (Chapter 8).
☐ Vibration when accelerating or decelerating
☐ Worn inner constant velocity joint (Chapter 8).
☐ Bent or distorted driveshaft (Chapter 8).

Braking system

Vehicle pulls to one side under braking

Note: *Before assuming that a brake problem exists, make sure that the tyres are in good condition and correctly inflated, that the front wheel alignment is correct, and that the vehicle is not loaded with weight in an unequal manner. Apart from checking the condition of all pipe and hose connections, any faults occurring on the anti-lock braking system should be referred to a VW dealer for diagnosis.*

☐ Worn, defective, damaged or contaminated brake pads on one side (Chapter 9).
☐ Seized or partially seized brake caliper piston (Chapter 9).
☐ A mixture of brake pad lining materials fitted between sides (Chapter 9).
☐ Brake caliper mounting bolts loose (Chapter 9).
☐ Worn or damaged steering or suspension components (Chapter 10).

Noise (grinding or high-pitched squeal) when brakes applied)

☐ Brake pad friction lining material worn down to metal backing (Chapter 9).
☐ Excessive corrosion of brake disc. This may be apparent after the vehicle has been standing for some time (Chapter 9).
☐ Foreign object (stone chipping, etc.) trapped between brake disc and shield (Chapter 9).

Brakes binding

☐ Seized brake caliper piston(s) (Chapter 9).
☐ Incorrectly adjusted handbrake mechanism (Chapter 9).
☐ Faulty master cylinder (Chapter 9).

Excessive brake pedal travel

☐ Faulty master cylinder (Chapter 9).
☐ Air in hydraulic system (Chapter 9).
☐ Faulty vacuum servo unit (Chapter 9).

Brake pedal feels spongy when depressed

☐ Air in hydraulic system (Chapter 9).
☐ Deteriorated flexible rubber brake hoses (Chapter 1).
☐ Master cylinder mounting nuts loose (Chapter 9).
☐ Faulty master cylinder (Chapter 9).

Excessive brake pedal effort required to stop vehicle

☐ Faulty vacuum servo unit (Chapter 9).
☐ Faulty brake vacuum pump (Chapter 9).
☐ Disconnected, damaged or insecure brake servo vacuum hose (Chapter 9).
☐ Primary or secondary hydraulic circuit failure (Chapter 9).
☐ Seized brake caliper piston(s) (Chapter 9).
☐ Brake pads incorrectly fitted (Chapter 9).
☐ Brake pads contaminated (Chapter 9).

Judder felt through brake pedal or steering wheel when braking

☐ Excessive run-out or distortion of discs (Chapter 9).
☐ Brake pad worn (Chapter 1).
☐ Brake caliper mounting bolts loose (Chapter 9).
☐ Wear in suspension or steering components or mountings (Chapter 10).

Rear wheels locking under normal braking

☐ Rear brake pads contaminated (Chapter 9).
☐ ABS system fault (Chapter 9).

Suspension and steering

Vehicle pulls to one side

Note: *Before diagnosing suspension or steering faults, be sure that the trouble is not due to incorrect tyre pressures, mixtures of tyre types, or binding brakes.*

☐ Defective tyre (*Weekly checks*).
☐ Excessive wear in suspension or steering components (Chapter 10).
☐ Incorrect front wheel alignment (Chapter 10).
☐ Accident damage to steering or suspension components (Chapter 10).

Excessive pitching and/or rolling around corners, or during braking

☐ Defective shock absorbers (Chapter 10).
☐ Broken or weak spring and/or suspension component (Chapter 10).
☐ Worn or damaged anti-roll bar or mountings – where applicable (Chapter 10).

Lack of power assistance

☐ Faulty rack-and-pinion steering gear (Chapter 10).
☐ Faulty electric power steering motor (Chapter 10).

Wandering or general instability

☐ Incorrect front wheel alignment (Chapter 10).
☐ Worn steering or suspension joints, bushes or components (Chapter 10).
☐ Roadwheels out of balance (Chapter 10).
☐ Faulty or damaged tyre (*Weekly checks*).
☐ Wheel bolts loose (Chapter 10).
☐ Defective shock absorbers (Chapter 10).

Excessively stiff steering

☐ Lack of steering gear lubricant (Chapter 10).
☐ Seized track rod end balljoint or suspension balljoint (Chapter 10).
☐ Incorrect front wheel alignment (Chapter 10).
☐ Steering rack or column bent or damaged (Chapter 10).

Excessive play in steering

☐ Worn steering column intermediate shaft universal joint (Chapter 10).
☐ Worn steering track rod end balljoints (Chapter 10).
☐ Worn rack-and-pinion steering gear (Chapter 10).
☐ Worn steering or suspension joints, bushes or components (Chapter 10).

Wheel wobble and vibration

☐ Front roadwheels out of balance (vibration felt mainly through the steering wheel) (Chapter 10).
☐ Rear roadwheels out of balance (vibration felt throughout the vehicle) (Chapter 10).
☐ Roadwheels damaged or distorted (Chapter 1).
☐ Faulty or damaged tyre (*Weekly checks*).
☐ Worn steering or suspension joints, bushes or components (Chapter 10).
☐ Wheel bolts loose (Chapter 1).

Tyre wear excessive

Tyres worn on inside or outside edges

☐ Tyres under-inflated (wear on both edges) (*Weekly checks*).
☐ Incorrect camber or castor angles (wear on one edge only) (Chapter 10).
☐ Worn steering or suspension joints, bushes or components (Chapter 10).
☐ Excessively hard cornering.
☐ Accident damage.

Tyre treads exhibit feathered edges

☐ Incorrect toe setting (Chapter 10).

Tyres worn in centre of tread

☐ Tyres over-inflated (*Weekly checks*).

Tyres worn on inside and outside edges

☐ Tyres under-inflated (*Weekly checks*).

Tyres worn unevenly

☐ Tyres/wheels out of balance (Chapter 1).
☐ Excessive wheel or tyre run-out (Chapter 10).
☐ Worn shock absorbers (Chapter 10).
☐ Faulty tyre (*Weekly checks*).

Electrical system

Battery will not hold a charge for more than a few days

Note: *For problems associated with the starting system, refer to the faults listed under 'Engine' earlier in this Section.*

☐ Battery defective internally (Chapter 5A).
☐ Battery terminal connections loose or corroded (*Weekly checks*).
☐ Auxiliary drivebelt worn or incorrectly adjusted (Chapter 1).
☐ Alternator not charging at correct output (Chapter 5A).
☐ Alternator or voltage regulator faulty (Chapter 5A).
☐ Short-circuit causing continual battery drain (Chapter 5A).

Ignition/no-charge warning light remains illuminated with engine running

☐ Auxiliary drivebelt broken, worn, or incorrectly adjusted (Chapter 1).
☐ Alternator brushes worn, sticking, or dirty (Chapter 5A).
☐ Alternator brush springs weak or broken (Chapter 5A).
☐ Internal fault in alternator or voltage regulator (Chapter 5A).
☐ Broken, disconnected, or loose wiring in charging circuit (Chapter 5A).

Ignition/no-charge warning light fails to come on

☐ Warning light LED defective (Chapter 12).
☐ Broken, disconnected, or loose wiring in warning light circuit (Chapter 12).
☐ Alternator faulty (Chapter 5A).

Lights inoperative

☐ Bulb blown or LED unit faulty (Chapter 12).
☐ Corrosion of bulb or bulbholder contacts (Chapter 12).
☐ Blown fuse (Chapter 12).
☐ Faulty relay (Chapter 12).
☐ Broken, loose, or disconnected wiring (Chapter 12).
☐ Faulty switch (Chapter 12).

Instrument readings inaccurate or erratic

Fuel or temperature gauges give no reading

☐ Faulty gauge sender unit (Chapter 4A).
☐ Wiring open-circuit (Chapter 12).
☐ Faulty gauge (Chapter 12).

Fuel or temperature gauges give continuous maximum reading

☐ Faulty gauge sender unit (Chapter 4A).
☐ Wiring short-circuit (Chapter 12).
☐ Faulty gauge (Chapter 12).

Horn inoperative, or unsatisfactory in operation

Horn operates all the time

☐ Horn push either earthed or stuck down (Chapter 12).
☐ Horn cable-to-horn push earthed (Chapter 12).

Horn fails to operate

☐ Blown fuse (Chapter 12).
☐ Cable or cable connections loose, broken or disconnected (Chapter 12).
☐ Faulty horn (Chapter 12).

Horn emits intermittent or unsatisfactory sound

☐ Cable connections loose (Chapter 12).
☐ Horn mountings loose (Chapter 12).
☐ Faulty horn (Chapter 12).

Windscreen/tailgate wipers inoperative, or unsatisfactory in operation

Wipers fail to operate, or operate very slowly

☐ Bonnet not closed (built-into the electronic control system) (Chapter 11).
☐ Wiper blades stuck to screen, or linkage seized or binding (*Weekly checks* and Chapter 12).
☐ Blown fuse (Chapter 12).
☐ Cable or cable connections loose, broken or disconnected (Chapter 12).
☐ Faulty relay (Chapter 12).
☐ Faulty wiper motor (Chapter 12).

Wiper blades sweep over too large or too small an area of the glass

☐ Wiper arms incorrectly positioned on spindles (Chapter 12).
☐ Excessive wear of wiper linkage (Chapter 12).
☐ Wiper motor or linkage mountings loose or insecure (Chapter 12).

Wiper blades fail to clean the glass effectively

☐ Wiper blade rubbers worn or perished (*Weekly checks*).
☐ Wiper arm tension springs broken, or arm pivots seized (Chapter 12).
☐ Insufficient windscreen washer additive to adequately remove road film (*Weekly checks*).

Electrical system (continued

Windscreen/tailgate washers inoperative, or unsatisfactory in operation

One or more washer jets inoperative

- [ ] Blocked washer jet (Chapter 12).
- [ ] Disconnected, kinked or restricted fluid hose (Chapter 12).
- [ ] Insufficient fluid in washer reservoir (*Weekly checks*).

Washer pump fails to operate

- [ ] Broken or disconnected wiring or connections (Chapter 12).
- [ ] Blown fuse (Chapter 12).
- [ ] Faulty washer switch (Chapter 12).
- [ ] Faulty washer pump (Chapter 12).

Electric windows inoperative, or unsatisfactory in operation

Window glass will only move in one direction

- [ ] Faulty switch (Chapter 12).

Window glass slow to move

- [ ] Regulator seized or damaged, or in need of lubrication (Chapter 11).
- [ ] Door internal components or trim fouling regulator (Chapter 11).
- [ ] Faulty motor (Chapter 11).

Window glass fails to move

- [ ] Blown fuse (Chapter 12).
- [ ] Faulty relay (Chapter 12).
- [ ] Broken or disconnected wiring or connections (Chapter 12).
- [ ] Faulty motor (Chapter 11).

Central locking system inoperative, or unsatisfactory in operation

Complete system failure

- [ ] Blown fuse (Chapter 12).
- [ ] Faulty relay (Chapter 12).
- [ ] Broken or disconnected wiring or connections (Chapter 12).
- [ ] Faulty control unit (Chapter 11).

Latch locks but will not unlock, or unlocks but will not lock

- [ ] Faulty control unit (Chapter 11).
- [ ] Broken or disconnected latch operating rods or levers (Chapter 11).
- [ ] Faulty relay (Chapter 12).

One actuator fails to operate

- [ ] Broken or disconnected wiring or connections (Chapter 12).
- [ ] Faulty actuator (Chapter 11).
- [ ] Broken, binding or disconnected latch operating rods or levers (Chapter 11).
- [ ] Fault in door lock (Chapter 11).

A

ABS (Anti-lock brake system) A system, usually electronically controlled, that senses incipient wheel lockup during braking and relieves hydraulic pressure at wheels that are about to skid.

Air bag An inflatable bag hidden in the steering wheel (driver's side) or the dash or glovebox (passenger side). In a head-on collision, the bags inflate, preventing the driver and front passenger from being thrown forward into the steering wheel or windscreen.

Air cleaner A metal or plastic housing, containing a filter element, which removes dust and dirt from the air being drawn into the engine.

Air filter element The actual filter in an air cleaner system, usually manufactured from pleated paper and requiring renewal at regular intervals.

Air filter

Allen key A hexagonal wrench which fits into a recessed hexagonal hole.

Alligator clip A long-nosed spring-loaded metal clip with meshing teeth. Used to make temporary electrical connections.

Alternator A component in the electrical system which converts mechanical energy from a drivebelt into electrical energy to charge the battery and to operate the starting system, ignition system and electrical accessories.

Alternator (exploded view)

Ampere (amp) A unit of measurement for the flow of electric current. One amp is the amount of current produced by one volt acting through a resistance of one ohm.

Anaerobic sealer A substance used to prevent bolts and screws from loosening. Anaerobic means that it does not require oxygen for activation. The Loctite brand is widely used.

Antifreeze A substance (usually ethylene glycol) mixed with water, and added to a vehicle's cooling system, to prevent freezing of the coolant in winter. Antifreeze also contains chemicals to inhibit corrosion and the formation of rust and other deposits that

would tend to clog the radiator and coolant passages and reduce cooling efficiency.

Anti-seize compound A coating that reduces the risk of seizing on fasteners that are subjected to high temperatures, such as exhaust manifold bolts and nuts.

Anti-seize compound

Asbestos A natural fibrous mineral with great heat resistance, commonly used in the composition of brake friction materials. Asbestos is a health hazard and the dust created by brake systems should never be inhaled or ingested.

Axle A shaft on which a wheel revolves, or which revolves with a wheel. Also, a solid beam that connects the two wheels at one end of the vehicle. An axle which also transmits power to the wheels is known as a live axle.

Axle assembly

Axleshaft A single rotating shaft, on either side of the differential, which delivers power from the final drive assembly to the drive wheels. Also called a driveshaft or a halfshaft.

B

Ball bearing An anti-friction bearing consisting of a hardened inner and outer race with hardened steel balls between two races.

Bearing

Bearing The curved surface on a shaft or in a bore, or the part assembled into either, that permits relative motion between them with minimum wear and friction.

Big-end bearing The bearing in the end of the connecting rod that's attached to the crankshaft.

Bleed nipple A valve on a brake wheel cylinder, caliper or other hydraulic component that is opened to purge the hydraulic system of air. Also called a bleed screw.

Brake bleeding

Brake bleeding Procedure for removing air from lines of a hydraulic brake system.

Brake disc The component of a disc brake that rotates with the wheels.

Brake drum The component of a drum brake that rotates with the wheels.

Brake linings The friction material which contacts the brake disc or drum to retard the vehicle's speed. The linings are bonded or riveted to the brake pads or shoes.

Brake pads The replaceable friction pads that pinch the brake disc when the brakes are applied. Brake pads consist of a friction material bonded or riveted to a rigid backing plate.

Brake shoe The crescent-shaped carrier to which the brake linings are mounted and which forces the lining against the rotating drum during braking.

Braking systems For more information on braking systems, consult the *Haynes Automotive Brake Manual*.

Breaker bar A long socket wrench handle providing greater leverage.

Bulkhead The insulated partition between the engine and the passenger compartment.

C

Caliper The non-rotating part of a disc-brake assembly that straddles the disc and carries the brake pads. The caliper also contains the hydraulic components that cause the pads to pinch the disc when the brakes are applied. A caliper is also a measuring tool that can be set to measure inside or outside dimensions of an object.

Camshaft A rotating shaft on which a series of cam lobes operate the valve mechanisms. The camshaft may be driven by gears, by sprockets and chain or by sprockets and a belt.

Canister A container in an evaporative emission control system; contains activated charcoal granules to trap vapours from the fuel system.

Canister

Carburettor A device which mixes fuel with air in the proper proportions to provide a desired power output from a spark ignition internal combustion engine.

Carburettor

Castellated Resembling the parapets along the top of a castle wall. For example, a castellated balljoint stud nut.

Castellated nut

Castor In wheel alignment, the backward or forward tilt of the steering axis. Castor is positive when the steering axis is inclined rearward at the top.

Catalytic converter A silencer-like device in the exhaust system which converts certain pollutants in the exhaust gases into less harmful substances.

Catalytic converter

Circlip A ring-shaped clip used to prevent endwise movement of cylindrical parts and shafts. An internal circlip is installed in a groove in a housing; an external circlip fits into a groove on the outside of a cylindrical piece such as a shaft.

Clearance The amount of space between two parts. For example, between a piston and a cylinder, between a bearing and a journal, etc.

Coil spring A spiral of elastic steel found in various sizes throughout a vehicle, for example as a springing medium in the suspension and in the valve train.

Compression Reduction in volume, and increase in pressure and temperature, of a gas, caused by squeezing it into a smaller space.

Compression ratio The relationship between cylinder volume when the piston is at top dead centre and cylinder volume when the piston is at bottom dead centre.

Constant velocity (CV) joint A type of universal joint that cancels out vibrations caused by driving power being transmitted through an angle.

Core plug A disc or cup-shaped metal device inserted in a hole in a casting through which core was removed when the casting was formed. Also known as a freeze plug or expansion plug.

Crankcase The lower part of the engine block in which the crankshaft rotates.

Crankshaft The main rotating member, or shaft, running the length of the crankcase, with offset "throws" to which the connecting rods are attached.

Crankshaft assembly

Crocodile clip See Alligator clip

D

Diagnostic code Code numbers obtained by accessing the diagnostic mode of an engine management computer. This code can be used to determine the area in the system where a malfunction may be located.

Disc brake A brake design incorporating a rotating disc onto which brake pads are squeezed. The resulting friction converts the energy of a moving vehicle into heat.

Double-overhead cam (DOHC) An engine that uses two overhead camshafts, usually one for the intake valves and one for the exhaust valves.

Drivebelt(s) The belt(s) used to drive accessories such as the alternator, water pump, power steering pump, air conditioning compressor, etc. off the crankshaft pulley.

Accessory drivebelts

Driveshaft Any shaft used to transmit motion. Commonly used when referring to the axleshafts on a front wheel drive vehicle.

Driveshaft

Drum brake A type of brake using a drum-shaped metal cylinder attached to the inner surface of the wheel. When the brake pedal is pressed, curved brake shoes with friction linings press against the inside of the drum to slow or stop the vehicle.

Drum brake assembly

E

EGR valve A valve used to introduce exhaust gases into the intake air stream.

EGR valve

Electronic control unit (ECU) A computer which controls (for instance) ignition and fuel injection systems, or an anti-lock braking system. For more information refer to the *Haynes Automotive Electrical and Electronic Systems Manual.*

Electronic Fuel Injection (EFI) A computer controlled fuel system that distributes fuel through an injector located in each intake port of the engine.

Emergency brake A braking system, independent of the main hydraulic system, that can be used to slow or stop the vehicle if the primary brakes fail, or to hold the vehicle stationary even though the brake pedal isn't depressed. It usually consists of a hand lever that actuates either front or rear brakes mechanically through a series of cables and linkages. Also known as a handbrake or parking brake.

Endfloat The amount of lengthwise movement between two parts. As applied to a crankshaft, the distance that the crankshaft can move forward and back in the cylinder block.

Engine management system (EMS) A computer controlled system which manages the fuel injection and the ignition systems in an integrated fashion.

Exhaust manifold A part with several passages through which exhaust gases leave the engine combustion chambers and enter the exhaust pipe.

Exhaust manifold

F

Fan clutch A viscous (fluid) drive coupling device which permits variable engine fan speeds in relation to engine speeds.

Feeler blade A thin strip or blade of hardened steel, ground to an exact thickness, used to check or measure clearances between parts.

Feeler blade

Firing order The order in which the engine cylinders fire, or deliver their power strokes, beginning with the number one cylinder.

Flywheel A heavy spinning wheel in which energy is absorbed and stored by means of momentum. On cars, the flywheel is attached to the crankshaft to smooth out firing impulses.

Free play The amount of travel before any action takes place. The "looseness" in a linkage, or an assembly of parts, between the initial application of force and actual movement. For example, the distance the brake pedal moves before the pistons in the master cylinder are actuated.

Fuse An electrical device which protects a circuit against accidental overload. The typical fuse contains a soft piece of metal which is calibrated to melt at a predetermined current flow (expressed as amps) and break the circuit.

Fusible link A circuit protection device consisting of a conductor surrounded by heat-resistant insulation. The conductor is smaller than the wire it protects, so it acts as the weakest link in the circuit. Unlike a blown fuse, a failed fusible link must frequently be cut from the wire for replacement.

G

Gap The distance the spark must travel in jumping from the centre electrode to the side

Adjusting spark plug gap

electrode in a spark plug. Also refers to the spacing between the points in a contact breaker assembly in a conventional points-type ignition, or to the distance between the reluctor or rotor and the pickup coil in an electronic ignition.

Gasket Any thin, soft material - usually cork, cardboard, asbestos or soft metal - installed between two metal surfaces to ensure a good seal. For instance, the cylinder head gasket seals the joint between the block and the cylinder head.

Gasket

Gauge An instrument panel display used to monitor engine conditions. A gauge with a movable pointer on a dial or a fixed scale is an analogue gauge. A gauge with a numerical readout is called a digital gauge.

H

Halfshaft A rotating shaft that transmits power from the final drive unit to a drive wheel, usually when referring to a live rear axle.

Harmonic balancer A device designed to reduce torsion or twisting vibration in the crankshaft. May be incorporated in the crankshaft pulley. Also known as a vibration damper.

Hone An abrasive tool for correcting small irregularities or differences in diameter in an engine cylinder, brake cylinder, etc.

Hydraulic tappet A tappet that utilises hydraulic pressure from the engine's lubrication system to maintain zero clearance (constant contact with both camshaft and valve stem). Automatically adjusts to variation in valve stem length. Hydraulic tappets also reduce valve noise.

I

Ignition timing The moment at which the spark plug fires, usually expressed in the number of crankshaft degrees before the piston reaches the top of its stroke.

Inlet manifold A tube or housing with passages through which flows the air-fuel mixture (carburettor vehicles and vehicles with throttle body injection) or air only (port fuel-injected vehicles) to the port openings in the cylinder head.

J

Jump start Starting the engine of a vehicle with a discharged or weak battery by attaching jump leads from the weak battery to a charged or helper battery.

L

Load Sensing Proportioning Valve (LSPV) A brake hydraulic system control valve that works like a proportioning valve, but also takes into consideration the amount of weight carried by the rear axle.

Locknut A nut used to lock an adjustment nut, or other threaded component, in place. For example, a locknut is employed to keep the adjusting nut on the rocker arm in position.

Lockwasher A form of washer designed to prevent an attaching nut from working loose.

M

MacPherson strut A type of front suspension system devised by Earle MacPherson at Ford of England. In its original form, a simple lateral link with the anti-roll bar creates the lower control arm. A long strut - an integral coil spring and shock absorber - is mounted between the body and the steering knuckle. Many modern so-called MacPherson strut systems use a conventional lower A-arm and don't rely on the anti-roll bar for location.

Multimeter An electrical test instrument with the capability to measure voltage, current and resistance.

N

NOx Oxides of Nitrogen. A common toxic pollutant emitted by petrol and diesel engines at higher temperatures.

O

Ohm The unit of electrical resistance. One volt applied to a resistance of one ohm will produce a current of one amp.

Ohmmeter An instrument for measuring electrical resistance.

O-ring A type of sealing ring made of a special rubber-like material; in use, the O-ring is compressed into a groove to provide the sealing action.

O-ring

Overhead cam (ohc) engine An engine with the camshaft(s) located on top of the cylinder head(s).

Overhead valve (ohv) engine An engine with the valves located in the cylinder head, but with the camshaft located in the engine block.

Oxygen sensor A device installed in the engine exhaust manifold, which senses the oxygen content in the exhaust and converts this information into an electric current. Also called a Lambda sensor.

P

Phillips screw A type of screw head having a cross instead of a slot for a corresponding type of screwdriver.

Plastigage A thin strip of plastic thread, available in different sizes, used for measuring clearances. For example, a strip of Plastigage is laid across a bearing journal. The parts are assembled and dismantled; the width of the crushed strip indicates the clearance between journal and bearing.

Plastigage

Propeller shaft The long hollow tube with universal joints at both ends that carries power from the transmission to the differential on front-engined rear wheel drive vehicles.

Proportioning valve A hydraulic control valve which limits the amount of pressure to the rear brakes during panic stops to prevent wheel lock-up.

R

Rack-and-pinion steering A steering system with a pinion gear on the end of the steering shaft that mates with a rack (think of a geared wheel opened up and laid flat). When the steering wheel is turned, the pinion turns, moving the rack to the left or right. This movement is transmitted through the track rods to the steering arms at the wheels.

Radiator A liquid-to-air heat transfer device designed to reduce the temperature of the coolant in an internal combustion engine cooling system.

Refrigerant Any substance used as a heat transfer agent in an air-conditioning system. R-12 has been the principle refrigerant for many years; recently, however, manufacturers have begun using R-134a, a non-CFC substance that is considered less harmful to the ozone in the upper atmosphere.

Rocker arm A lever arm that rocks on a shaft or pivots on a stud. In an overhead valve engine, the rocker arm converts the upward movement of the pushrod into a downward movement to open a valve.

Rotor In a distributor, the rotating device inside the cap that connects the centre electrode and the outer terminals as it turns, distributing the high voltage from the coil secondary winding to the proper spark plug. Also, that part of an alternator which rotates inside the stator. Also, the rotating assembly of a turbocharger, including the compressor wheel, shaft and turbine wheel.

Runout The amount of wobble (in-and-out movement) of a gear or wheel as it's rotated. The amount a shaft rotates "out-of-true." The out-of-round condition of a rotating part.

S

Sealant A liquid or paste used to prevent leakage at a joint. Sometimes used in conjunction with a gasket.

Sealed beam lamp An older headlight design which integrates the reflector, lens and filaments into a hermetically-sealed one-piece unit. When a filament burns out or the lens cracks, the entire unit is simply replaced.

Serpentine drivebelt A single, long, wide accessory drivebelt that's used on some newer vehicles to drive all the accessories, instead of a series of smaller, shorter belts. Serpentine drivebelts are usually tensioned by an automatic tensioner.

Serpentine drivebelt

Shim Thin spacer, commonly used to adjust the clearance or relative positions between two parts. For example, shims inserted into or under bucket tappets control valve clearances. Clearance is adjusted by changing the thickness of the shim.

Slide hammer A special puller that screws into or hooks onto a component such as a shaft or bearing; a heavy sliding handle on the shaft bottoms against the end of the shaft to knock the component free.

Sprocket A tooth or projection on the periphery of a wheel, shaped to engage with a chain or drivebelt. Commonly used to refer to the sprocket wheel itself.

Starter inhibitor switch On vehicles with an automatic transmission, a switch that prevents starting if the vehicle is not in Neutral or Park.

Strut See MacPherson strut.

T

Tappet A cylindrical component which transmits motion from the cam to the valve stem, either directly or via a pushrod and rocker arm. Also called a cam follower.

Thermostat A heat-controlled valve that regulates the flow of coolant between the cylinder block and the radiator, so maintaining optimum engine operating temperature. A thermostat is also used in some air cleaners in which the temperature is regulated.

Thrust bearing The bearing in the clutch assembly that is moved in to the release levers by clutch pedal action to disengage the clutch. Also referred to as a release bearing.

Timing belt A toothed belt which drives the camshaft. Serious engine damage may result if it breaks in service.

Timing chain A chain which drives the camshaft.

Toe-in The amount the front wheels are closer together at the front than at the rear. On rear wheel drive vehicles, a slight amount of toe-in is usually specified to keep the front wheels running parallel on the road by offsetting other forces that tend to spread the wheels apart.

Toe-out The amount the front wheels are closer together at the rear than at the front. On front wheel drive vehicles, a slight amount of toe-out is usually specified.

Tools For full information on choosing and using tools, refer to the *Haynes Automotive Tools Manual.*

Tracer A stripe of a second colour applied to a wire insulator to distinguish that wire from another one with the same colour insulator.

Tune-up A process of accurate and careful adjustments and parts replacement to obtain the best possible engine performance.

Turbocharger A centrifugal device, driven by exhaust gases, that pressurises the intake air. Normally used to increase the power output from a given engine displacement, but can also be used primarily to reduce exhaust emissions (as on VW's "Umwelt" Diesel engine).

U

Universal joint or U-joint A double-pivoted connection for transmitting power from a driving to a driven shaft through an angle. A U-joint consists of two Y-shaped yokes and a cross-shaped member called the spider.

V

Valve A device through which the flow of liquid, gas, vacuum, or loose material in bulk may be started, stopped, or regulated by a movable part that opens, shuts, or partially obstructs one or more ports or passageways. A valve is also the movable part of such a device.

Valve clearance The clearance between the valve tip (the end of the valve stem) and the rocker arm or tappet. The valve clearance is measured when the valve is closed.

Vernier caliper A precision measuring instrument that measures inside and outside dimensions. Not quite as accurate as a micrometer, but more convenient.

Viscosity The thickness of a liquid or its resistance to flow.

Volt A unit for expressing electrical "pressure" in a circuit. One volt that will produce a current of one ampere through a resistance of one ohm.

W

Welding Various processes used to join metal items by heating the areas to be joined to a molten state and fusing them together. For more information refer to the *Haynes Automotive Welding Manual.*

Wiring diagram A drawing portraying the components and wires in a vehicle's electrical system, using standardised symbols. For more information refer to the *Haynes Automotive Electrical and Electronic Systems Manual.*

Note: *References throughout this index are in the form* **"Chapter number"** • **"Page number"**. *So, for example, 2C•15 refers to page 15 of Chapter 2C.*

Note: *References throughout this index are in the form "Chapter number" • "Page number". So, for example, 2C•15 refers to page 15 of Chapter 2C.*

Note: *References throughout this index are in the form* **"Chapter number"** • **"Page number"**. *So, for example, 2C•15 refers to page 15 of Chapter 2C.*

Preserving Our Motoring Heritage

The Model J Duesenberg Derham Tourster. Only eight of these magnificent cars were ever built – this is the only example to be found outside the United States of America

Almost every car you've ever loved, loathed or desired is gathered under one roof at the Haynes Motor Museum. Over 300 immaculately presented cars and motorbikes represent every aspect of our motoring heritage, from elegant reminders of bygone days, such as the superb Model J Duesenberg to curiosities like the bug-eyed BMW Isetta. There are also many old friends and flames. Perhaps you remember the 1959 Ford Popular that you did your courting in? The magnificent 'Red Collection' is a spectacle of classic sports cars including AC, Alfa Romeo, Austin Healey, Ferrari, Lamborghini, Maserati, MG, Riley, Porsche and Triumph.

A Perfect Day Out

Each and every vehicle at the Haynes Motor Museum has played its part in the history and culture of Motoring. Today, they make a wonderful spectacle and a great day out for all the family. Bring the kids, bring Mum and Dad, but above all bring your camera to capture those golden memories for ever. You will also find an impressive array of motoring memorabilia, a comfortable 70 seat video cinema and one of the most extensive transport book shops in Britain. The Pit Stop Cafe serves everything from a cup of tea to wholesome, home-made meals or, if you prefer, you can enjoy the large picnic area nestled in the beautiful rural surroundings of Somerset.

John Haynes O.B.E., Founder and Chairman of the museum at the wheel of a Haynes Light 12.

Graham Hill's Lola Cosworth Formula 1 car next to a 1934 Riley Sports.

The Museum is situated on the A359 Yeovil to Frome road at Sparkford, just off the A303 in Somerset. It is about 40 miles south of Bristol, and 25 minutes drive from the M5 intersection at Taunton.
Open 9.30am - 5.30pm (10.00am - 4.00pm Winter) 7 days a week, *except Christmas Day, Boxing Day and New Years Day*
Special rates available for schools, coach parties and outings Charitable Trust No. 292048